DRIVE LINE ENGINEERING—Book I

The Institution of Mechanical Engineers

Proceedings 1969–70 · Volume 184 · Part 3 I

Conference on

DRIVE LINE ENGINEERING

Book I

1 BIRDCAGE WALK · WESTMINSTER · LONDON

© The Institution of Mechanical Engineers 1972

Book I ISBN 0 85298 076 0 √
Book II ISBN 0 85298 077 9
Library of Congress Catalog Card Number 70-184580

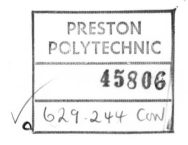

CONTENTS—Book I

           Sessions 4 and 5 are published in Book II

Drive Line Engineering

A CONFERENCE was held at the Hotel de France, Jersey, Channel Islands, from 13th to 17th April 1970. The conference was sponsored by the Automobile Division of the Institution of Mechanical Engineers, and 223 delegates registered to attend.

OPENING OF CONFERENCE

The conference was formally opened on the morning of Monday, 13th April by D. Downs, Chairman of the Automobile Division.

CONFERENCE CHAIRMAN'S COMMENTS

F. Shaw—The drive line can be defined as the sum of the components from the surface of the engine flywheel to the contact between tyres and road surfaces. Many problems are the result of designers' work when they understood only the units and not the whole complicated system.

The purpose of this conference was to bring together all the knowledge which could be gathered, to be discussed by as many leading drive-line engineers from Europe and elsewhere as could be assembled. The contents will demonstrate how successfully this was achieved.

There was some consideration of the past when designers were doubtful about the correctness of a scaled down American torque converter type of automatic transmission as being the best for Europe. Attempts were made to invent systems simple enough for any single car company to make economically.

Certain definite facts emerged as guide lines to the future:

(1) Fluid couplings of any sort cannot be used satisfactorily with dog couplings in a gear train.

(2) Magnetic powder clutches are ideal on paper but are not readily adapted to automotive use in cars.

(3) It must be possible to over-ride the transmission selection.

(4) The driver should always retain control of the engine. Throttle blippers and ignition-cut devices should be avoided.

(5) Stepless transmissions cannot be over-ridden in a practical manner.

(6) Hydrostatic systems are stepless if they are to be successful and therefore do not meet condition 3.

(7) Basically the best system is the hydrokinetic one with a stepped epicyclic unit hydraulically operated by friction elements following a torque converter coupling.

(8) One motor company alone cannot be competitive.

(9) Large production is essential, and widespread acceptance of automatic transmission depends on its price being reduced to not more than 10 per cent of the car cost. A big cost reduction depends on high volume production. A plant capacity of 500–1000 units per day is roughly the volume necessary for low cost production.

Hydrokinetic systems such as the Borg Warner, General Motors, Chrysler, and Z.F. systems seem very acceptable for 2 litre and over and the Automotive Products unit fills a need in the 1 to 2 litre range.

It does not appear likely that we will ever achieve the simple solution of a hydrokinetic torque converter as the sole means of power transmission since the requirements of high starting torque, a wide range of torque multiplication, and a high average operating efficiency cannot all be satisfactorily met.

For cars under 2 litre, and for heavy duty 'stop–start' service, a new concept is required such as hydrostatic units, ranging from simple variable displacement pumps and motor units using swash-plates and slipper pads to more complex shunt drive systems to eliminate swash-plate wear.

There are also rolling friction type drives such as the Perbury gear where power is transmitted through the oil film between a set of rollers and toroidal discs, the gear ratio changes being effected by changes in roller angle.

One can see the production type design of hydrokinetic units having a torque converter of either $9\frac{1}{4}$ in or 11 in with various vane configurations to produce torque characteristics. Production design stall speed would be between 1600 and 2200 rev/min and a torque ratio of 1·9 to 2·4 which must be tailored to suit the application. Given the torque curve, the torque converter characteristics, the gear ratios and the vehicle rolling resistance, the complete tractive effort and performance curves can be quickly plotted by use of the digital computer. By this method it is also possible to select part throttle changes under all driving conditions.

The main problem with automatic transmission design is to produce optimum shift quality consistent with good friction element durability. Many engineers lay more emphasis on the development of fluids to improve this area but, though the fluid is important, the friction material is more so.

There is no reason why the torque converter and gear set cannot operate at engine speeds up to 8000 rev/min. Torque converters should be selected large enough to do the job or an early decision be made to fit oil coolers.

With a good knowledge of materials, treatments and processes it is possible to increase the capacity of gearboxes and axles by up to 100 per cent without increasing the size, and with consequent economies.

Smaller and more compact cars mean that the transmission units must also be kept compact.

Higher sustained speeds, due to the increased use of motorways, and particularly immediately after the take-over of a new car, create problems of friction wear and overheating. The type of lubricant helps, but the stage has been reached where forced lubrication is required in both manual gearboxes and axles.

The higher speeds have also introduced vibration problems which cannot be cured completely by balancing the rotating parts.

Phasing of universal joints in propeller and drive shafts can eliminate part of the problem, as will constant velocity joints.

Greater care should be taken over mounting design and tooth numbers in both gearboxes and axles to avoid unwanted frequencies.

The tremendously improved tyre to road adhesion means that much of the torque of the powerful new engines can be utilized and the transmission receives more load instead of it being dissipated at the wheels.

Modern manufacturing techniques such as friction and high-frequency welding, flow machining, powder metallurgy, investment casting, and cold forming can be called upon to reduce cost and, by the elimination of heavy sections, we can put the strength where it is required. Plastics (with due concern for their thermal characteristics) can be ideally used. The proper application of shot peening and cold rolling can achieve a standard of fatigue resistance to a truly amazing degree. Let us then concern ourselves with using modern knowledge in designing small new units of high capacities, to suit modern cars. Let us use the new production techniques to manufacture these units to a standard of quality and perfection seldom seen today.

The conference indicates that for the future friction clutches for manual gearboxes will of necessity be smaller in diameter and yet capable of dealing with high speeds and torques.

The modern diaphragm spring clutch is advantageous in that the pressure load is evenly distributed and not a series of high load areas as in the coil spring clutches. Modern congested traffic conditions will cause owners to ask for lighter operating pedal loads, with particular reference to the load to hold the clutch disengaged. As the facing materials are improved to allow for higher unit loads without deterioration, and with freedom from judder, advantage will be taken to reduce the clutch diameter with a corresponding increase in release load. This will inevitably result in the adoption of power assisted clutch operation as a matter of course.

It is also conceivable that the use of ceramic plates together with improved fabric ones may permit the use of multi-plate small diameter clutches which do not suffer from drag characteristics.

There will be a call for manual gearboxes for a good many years, both for conventional in-line use and for trans-axle types. The general trend will be to four-speed boxes, fully synchronized, with very light and smooth gear selection, possibly even power assisted or pneumatic. Better manufacturing techniques will reduce the rotating mass and result in quieter, more seemly, units. There will be nothing revolutionary or startling in the development except for possibly the adoption of manual versions of an automatic gearbox to reduce production costs. The tendency towards five-speed gearboxes will phase out, and will be satisfied by four-speed boxes, or will turn again to the semi-automaticity of an overdrive of the de Normanville pattern. There will be short-lived attempts to bring to life the face dog or synchromesh type of twin-ratio boxes with so-called power changes which in reality depend on ignition cuts and throttle blips. It has always been wrong for a gearbox control system to 'mess about with the engine' and in these days of emission control, refrigeration etc. it cannot be tolerated at all.

Most of the basic principles mentioned earlier for automatic transmissions are applicable and the need for compactness is equally true of automatics as of manual gearboxes.

Improvements in facing materials and a realization that deflection of bands and friction plates is wasteful in energy absorption, will go a long way to keeping down the size of automatic transmission units.

There will be a call for an automatic transmission unit utilizing one or two basic sets of running gear. Probably to suit 1 or $2\frac{1}{2}$ litre in one case, and 3 to say 6 litre in the other.

There will be case-forms to suit individual customer requirements and these will probably be moulded from carbon fibre plastics by a simple easily adapted process. The brain will be computerized and, by changing a key card, one will be able to select a programme to suit road and driving conditions. Importantly one programme will take out all the inhibitions of automaticity and give a straightforward fast manual shift. A thorough study of the fluid behaviour pattern at shift times is an essential part of this development.

It is certain that steps will be taken to improve the efficiency of automatic units and for this reason the favoured design will remain basically mechanical and epicyclic, coupled with a hydraulic torque converter. For good shift qualities friction elements will be used and these will probably continue to be hydraulically actuated with the signals from engine and road (or driver) being electronically computerized.

High efficiency and fast smooth shifts, with a feeling of being kicked in the back on down shifts when required, will be the general pattern.

The type of small car unit popularized by D.A.F. will very likely have a minor but important place in the future but in all probability it will be adapted to use the the very fine high velocity chains which have been developed over recent years.

Heavy vehicles and public transport will tend to follow a hydrostatic pattern because this is better when size is not so important.

Propeller shafts and drive shafts will all be of the constant velocity type. Improved friction welding skills and the use of carbon fibre plastics should bring the cost so low that their application will be universal. Balance will be better controlled and weights will be kept much lower than at present.

The knowledge of hypoid spiral bevel gears has reached such a pitch that one cannot see anything else supplanting them for some time. Differential units will in all probability become purely frictional and combine the advantages of a true differential with those of a limited spin unit.

The real need will be for tolerance to much higher operating temperatures due to high torques and small units, and compact tunnels with close proximity exhaust systems.

We will more and more rely on lubricant additives until there will be really very little other than additive, but this is an attractively inexpensive way to keep down the size and cost of the assemblies.

Lubricants will probably be synthetic anyway. The hydraulic system of four-wheel drive will find a natural place in the utility services such as police and ambulances, but will not, I think, supplant the mechanical system in general.

Four-wheel-drive cars will lose out in efficiency, but will have a place for special applications. True off-road vehicles will always require four-wheel drive. Chain drives will be used increasingly for four-wheel drive systems.

The problem of dependable sealing of units has been with us for fifty years or more. It is certainly better today that it was three years ago and the oil seal manufacturers are spending a good deal of time and money in tackling the problem more scientifically. Better control of raw materials and properly effective vulcanizing, coupled with accurate manufacturing processes and correct assembly can do much to alleviate the problem. Perhaps dry lubricant is the final answer, or perhaps a deliberate large clearance between shaft and housing and a coating of lubricant repellent is really the only solution.

The conventional front-engined, gearbox, prop-shaft, axle, in line configuration is here for the foreseeable future, and will very likely become once more the most favoured one.

Front-wheel drive packages are perhaps to remain popular for small cars and amongst the rally cross fraternity. This style lends itself well to low floor shooting brakes, small ambulances, etc. The electrically-propelled car can be dismissed or accepted with equal ease dependent upon the answer to a simple question. Has anyone yet invented a battery or fuel cell which is viable, and can give 250 miles of sustained power with no gradual fall off and with easy replacement? I think not! The electrically propelled vehicle is better confined to large vehicles with plenty of battery storage space and for local steady-speed use rather than long distance high-speed journeys.

When we reach the field of diesel generator, electrically-propelled city buses these can be of immense value and far superior to old fashioned trolley cars.

A lot of work is necessary in the development of synchromesh mechanisms for heavy commercial vehicles. The type of unit used in motor cars is not up to the job for the heavy inertias involved and when they are satisfactory it is more by luck than judgement. A system of multiple cones or self-energizing on the Porsche principle is required. It is becoming increasingly clear that a close look at bearing calculation parameters is necessary because experience indicates a tendency to use larger bearings than necessary. Plain bearings should always be considered with care to select the right material for the application.

A lot of advantage can be taken of careful design of shafting and the elimination of stress concentration factors.

A study of the relationship of proof tests and theoretical prediction is very rewarding and many authors and delegates have underlined this clearly.

There is much information on all aspects of drive line engineering in the following pages and every effort has been made to present it in a readable fashion. Those who were present in Jersey will enjoy re-living it, and those who were not will gain by the experience.

SOCIAL EVENTS

The conference Gala Dance and Ball was held in the Empire Room of the Hotel de France on the evening of Friday, 17th April.

ORGANIZING COMMITTEE

The committee responsible for organizing the conference comprised F. Shaw (Chairman), R. J. Love, E. J. Davies, T. H. Millward and J. F. B. Harper.

SESSION 1

Paper 1. Friction Clutches and Clutch Control Mechanisms

D. A. DAVIES, BSc

Chief Engineer, Borg & Beck Co. Ltd, Automotive Products Group, Leamington Spa, Warwickshire.

Part 1 of this paper states the basic requirements of clutches and then discusses the various factors which must be considered in the initial stages of clutch design and specification for particular applications. The differing types of clutches used over a wide range of operating conditions are described and changes likely to be seen in future designs are mentioned. A small section is devoted to facing friction materials which are one of the most important components of the clutch. Finally the steps taken to ensure satisfactory performance in a specific vehicle model are explained.

Part 2 first considers the basic requirement and characteristics and then the ergonomic factors involved. There are three common methods of control, two being mechanical, namely lever and rod system and cable system, and the third hydraulic, all of which are discussed in some detail. With each of these methods some form of power assistance may be necessary to ensure a satisfactory pedal load and the various methods by which this can be achieved are considered.

PART 1—FRICTION CLUTCHES

INTRODUCTION

The main function of a clutch is to transmit drive from a power source to a driven unit, or conversely to break the drive from a power source to a driven unit. Both functions are equally important and for automotive use there are several other factors which are essential to a satisfactory installation.

Operation must be possible when the engine is rotating at any speed, with control remote from the clutch unit. The take-up of drive has to be smooth, gradual, and under the operator's control throughout to provide acceleration of the driven member as required. In addition release must be immediate, with no residual drag, for ease of gear change. These requirements are most suitably obtained with the friction clutch.

The first requirement of any friction device is to establish its torque transmitting capabilities. A survey of published literature reveals only two methods of calculating clutch torque: one based on the assumption of uniform pressure and the other on the uniform rate of wear over the clutch plate. As the results of wear tests show that, except for initial wear-in on the outer radius, the clutch facing wears fairly uniformly, the assumption of uniform wear would appear reasonable.

Moreover, for the ratio of inside diameter to outside diameter normally encountered on clutch driven plate facings, it is immaterial which method of calculation is used since the values obtained are within 3 per cent of each other, with the uniform wear assumption giving the lower results. Whichever formula is used, the accuracy of the results depends on knowing the correct values of the coefficient of friction (μ) and clamping load, both of these parameters varying with operating conditions.

The variation of clamping load is purely mechanical, being basically related to speed, and these effects can be calculated. However, the value of μ—being dependent on speed, pressure and temperature, with temperature varying over a considerable range—is more complex. To determine the value of μ for any particular application one must consider the gradeability of the vehicle concerned; that is, the work done by the clutch during one start from rest on a gradient. During any such engagement, clutch slip occurs until the power source and the driven member are rotating at the same speed. During the slip period, part of the kinetic energy is dissipated as heat and the clutch must be capable of absorbing this heat and still be able to drive full torque from the power source, after repeated operation. To ensure this, due consideration must be given to engine performance, vehicle weight, overall gear ratios, tyre sizes, etc. The significance of this was noticed by variation in performance and life of the same clutch and engine combination in different vehicles doing the same type of work.

The formulae used for these calculations are given in Appendix 1.1.

A gradeability curve for a typical application is given in Fig. 1.1. Examination of this curve shows that the maximum gradient on which the vehicle is expected to start should not be too far around the curve, as slight variations in tractive effort can then make large differences in the work done by the clutch. While these variations are unlikely to result in clutch slip (except in extreme cases) they can have a very detrimental effect upon the life expectancy of the clutch unit.

From service experience on passenger car and commercial applications, values which give satisfactory performance can be established. With commercial vehicles, because of the many possible combinations, the details of each individual vehicle and type of duty must be known. Typical results from various vehicles are given in Table 1.1.

Table 1.1. Examples of heat generated per unit of pressure plate weight and heating factor for starts on a 1:8 gradient of various vehicles in the fully laden condition

Class of vehicle	Heat generated per unit of pressure plate weight	Heating factor
Small saloon .	7600	870
Medium saloon	9920	1100
Large saloon .	9040	1220
5 ton commercial vehicle	1666	330
13 ton commercial vehicle	2370	360
22 ton commercial vehicle	910	340
28 ton commercial vehicle	1640	350

Car evaluations have been made with maximum torque at 3000 rev/min and commercial vehicles with maximum torque at appropriate speeds.

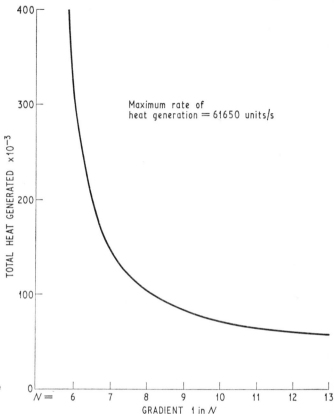

Fig. 1.1. Typical gradeability curve for 16-ton 'on highway' truck

By suitable substitution it can be seen to be possible to consider the variation of all aspects of the installation and study their effect on the overall performance of the clutch. An alternative method of assessing clutch life is by the prediction of the clutch facing surface temperatures for specific usage conditions. Theoretical solutions of surface temperatures are based on the one-dimensional equation of heat flow, and considerable work has been done by Newcombe, in particular, on obtaining solutions to this equation based on the assumption of a uniform thermal flux at the surface.

The surface temperature will be affected by some of the following components:

(*a*) Surface temperature rise during a period of continuous slipping.
(*b*) Surface temperature rise during a single engagement.
(*c*) Bulk temperature.
(*d*) Localized surface temperatures.

Continuous slipping

This is by far the most damaging of all clutch applications and can occur in practice when a vehicle is held stationary on a hill by slipping the clutch.

4

D. A. DAVIESD. A. DAVIES

Initially the pressure plate can be considered as an infinite solid and the temperature rise is dependent only upon the rate of heat generation per unit area and the slip time. Thereafter the temperature rises at a rate which is inversely proportional to the thickness of the pressure plate.

Single engagement

In a single clutch engagement slip time will not normally exceed a few seconds and the pressure plate can be considered as infinitely thick since only the immediate vicinity of the plate surface will be heated during the slip time.

Although cooling is an important factor in long-term losses, for single engagements and continuous slips up to 30 s, typical cooling losses are 2 per cent for a 10 s slip and 5 per cent for a 30 s slip, and can usually be ignored.

Bulk temperature

The surface temperatures generated from a single engagement will be of a transient nature and thereafter the heat will be conducted to the remainder of the pressure plate which will assume a uniform temperature. Between engagements cooling of the clutch will take place by convection, and under these conditions Newton's law of cooling can be used to predict the bulk temperature at any time. For repeated engagements the bulk temperature will tend towards a limiting value when the heat input per engagement is equal to the heat lost during cooling between engagements. By applying Newton's law of cooling to clutch applications, made at equal intervals of time, the limiting temperature rise can be obtained. The rate of heat transfer depends on how well the clutch is ventilated. With inertia limitations restricting the thermal capacity of the pressure plate, clutch ventilation is important in reducing the temperatures obtained.

Localized temperatures

The usual equations quoted for the surface temperatures assume the heat factor to be evenly distributed over the surface of the lining. This will only be so in the case of a well-bedded driven plate. In practice the bedding pattern of a clutch driven plate will vary throughout the life of a clutch and in addition some lining materials cause localized temperatures known as heat spotting.

Considering the mechanics of localized temperatures, it would be reasonable to assume in the case of the pressure plate that the local temperatures occur as a ripple on the average surface temperature caused by the alternate wiping by the contact area of the driven plate. This is further complicated by any distortions which occur in the pressure plate because of the heat effect. However, on the driven plate the same area would be in contact with the pressure plate continuously and could cause higher localized temperatures on the lining.

CORRELATION OF PREDICTED AND EXPERIMENTAL RESULTS

Investigations carried out to measure surface temperatures for continuous slip conditions gave reasonable agreement of predicted and experimental results for the lower rates of energy dissipation but considerable variations at the higher rates of energy dissipation. At first this was thought to be due to uneven work sharing

Proc Instn Mech Engrs 1969–70   Vol 184 Pt 3IProc Instn Mech Engrs 1969–70   Vol 184 Pt 3I between the pressure plate and flywheel sides at the higher rates of energy dissipation. However, further testing gave no clear indication of uneven work sharing between the pressure plate and flywheel side. Analysis of the results showed that at the higher rate of heat generation, high temperatures with rapid changes of gradient were present on both the flywheel and pressure plate side. This is indicative of uneven heat generation caused by non-uniform contact between the lining and mating surface, although an attempt was made to eliminate this feature by light duty operation of the clutch prior to the start of any test. Further evidence of uneven heat generation was shown on examination of the flywheel which revealed local heat spotting. Thus it appears that the discrepancy betwen predicted and experimental results may be due to the assumption of a uniform heat flux generation on theoretical analysis which is not so in practice.

CONSIDERATION OF WORK AND TEMPERATURE CALCULATIONS FOR PREDICTING CLUTCH LIFE

Any system used in assessing clutch life will be arbitrary in some way. The 'work done' method results in arbitrary values for specific conditions, and the temperature prediction would give a physical value, but only for an arbitrary chosen work duty. The work done calculation would give tabulated results for taking up from rest on an incline for a range of gradients, engine speeds, and gears.

Work done per pound is closely related to bulk temperature reached when no temperature gradients remain. From Newcombe's work it can be shown that the heating factor per square inch is related to the maximum temperature during one application. It would appear that pressure plate weight should be designed on the basis of work done per pound and the facing area on the basis of heating factor per square inch. Heating factor per square inch and work done per square inch are both related by different functions of engine speed and a gradient factor to brake horsepower per square inch.

The difficulty with temperature prediction for life assessment is the choice of duty to be used as a basis for the calculation. Something purely arbitrary offers no advantage over the work calculation methods previously discussed.

The inclusion of cooling in the consideration of clutch design would be most easily accommodated by using temperature prediction methods, but cooling by means of ventilation is so varied for each different application that cooling at the moment must be ignored on basic clutch calculations. Work now being carried out on recirculatory air ventilating systems could, in the near future, allow a common cooling factor to be used in clutch life calculations.

COMMERCIAL CLUTCHES

Coil spring clutches

These have been the standard form of clutch for a number of years and have gradually evolved into a form indicated by Fig. 1.2. This type of clutch is fitted to most current commercial vehicles. It consists of a single driven member clamped between the flywheel and the pressure plate by a ring of helical coil springs which are retained in the compressed state by a cover pressing.

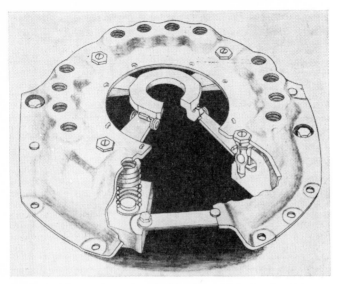

Fig. 1.2. Illustration of typical 'coil spring' clutch with strap drive

The pressure plate was originally driven by means of lugs which fitted into a cover, but this method has been replaced by spring steel straps, arranged tangentially. Normal drive torque places the straps in tension and the straps are stiff enough to absorb overdrive torques in compression without failure. The straps are also flexible to allow axial movement of the pressure plate for release and wear.

Release of the driven member is effected by the inwards movement of four equally spaced levers, which pivot about a pin held stationary in relation to the cover, causing the pressure plate to move back against the load of the thrust springs.

As wear on the driven plate facings occurs, the pressure plate follows up under the action of the thrust springs, thus clamping load is a maximum in the new position and reduces with wear to a minimum in the fully worn condition. Consideration must be given to this reduction in clamping load when specifying for any particular application.

Typical curves for clamp load and release load are shown in Fig. 1.3 which illustrates the above points.

To ensure satisfactory operation during service life, the load and travel efficiency in the clutch assembly must be kept to a maximum. As the clutch is virtually inaccessible for lubrication purposes, the efficiencies which can be achieved in the new condition must, as far as possible, be maintained during the life of the clutch. In addition, oil, grease, etc. must be kept from the friction material on the driven member, since the coefficient of friction of the normal organic material can be drastically reduced by such contamination and give rise to clutch slip.

Centrifugal effects must also be considered, particularly with the growing use of high-speed diesel engines. The dynamic centre of gravity of the release lever

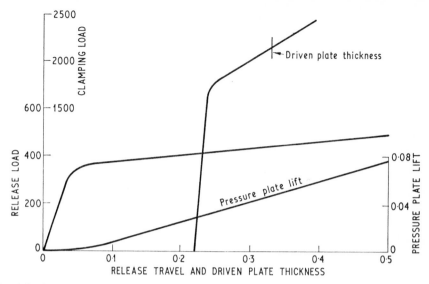

Fig. 1.3. Clamping load, release load, and pressure plate lift characteristics of coil spring clutch

should be as near as possible to the pivot point to minimize effects on clutch clamping and release loads. Thrust springs are also affected by speed and bow considerably, giving rise to reduced clamping loads. They can also cause unexpected foul conditions.

To avoid large variations in release loads between the new and the worn conditions, the overall spring rate should be kept to a minimum. While straps for pressure plate drive are desirable to reduce friction and maintain balance, they have an adverse effect in this respect by increasing the overall spring rate.

Diaphragm spring clutches

Recently the application of this type of clutch, as illustrated in Fig. 1.4, has spread from cars and light commercial vehicles to vehicles up to 22 ton gross vehicle weight. While they have the same basic advantages as those used on automotive applications there are, at present, limitations to their use on the heavier commercial applications for the following reasons:

(1) It is sometimes difficult to obtain the same amount of driven plate wear as is available on the heavier commercial coil spring clutches.

(2) On the more arduous, off-highway applications, it is possible that the spring loads can be affected by high temperatures.

Lever Belleville clutches

It is possible, by suitable design, to overcome the disadvantages of the two previous forms of clutch—i.e. the coil spring clutch and the diaphragm spring clutch—by combining the benefits of each and avoiding the disadvantages. The

Fig. 1.4. Illustration of typical 'diaphragm spring' clutch with strap drive

clamp load is obtained by means of a plain Belleville spring, which is less affected by centrifugal force than the diaphragm spring and is not so limited in design. The clutch release is obtained by means of a normal lever system which has a much higher travel efficiency than the diaphragm spring fingers. Care must be taken in lever design to ensure the benefits of the Belleville are not lost in the centrifugal effects of the lever system.

A typical lever Belleville clutch is illustrated in Fig. 1.5.

Wet clutches

The use of these clutches is growing rapidly, particularly for arduous duty. The clutches can be any of the three types discussed previously. They have the advantage that friction material wear is negligible and, because all movements are less, the release loads remain almost constant and centrifugal effects are greatly reduced. Friction in the assembly is also kept to a minimum.

There are some requirements peculiar to this type of clutch. The bell housing must be sealed and a pump and filter are normally required to ensure oil flow. Tests have shown that a positive flow of directed oil is preferable for satisfactory clutch operation. As the friction materials used on wet clutch applications are normally paper based, an oil flow indicator is desirable because the clutch will rapidly burn out if the flow is interrupted.

With the lower coefficients of friction on wet clutch applications ($0.08–0.1$ for organic materials, $0.1–0.12$ for paper based facing materials) a much larger clutch or a multi-plate clutch is usually necessary as compared with the normal dry type.

Recent developments carried out on twin plate clutches have shown that the system illustrated in Fig. 1.6 gives a satisfactory oil supply to both plates and has the advantage of requiring less pressure for operation.

Finally, for satisfactory performance of the clutch system it is necessary to ensure that the temperature of the oil does not exceed a certain maximum, by providing some method of oil cooling. In cold weather the engine should be run

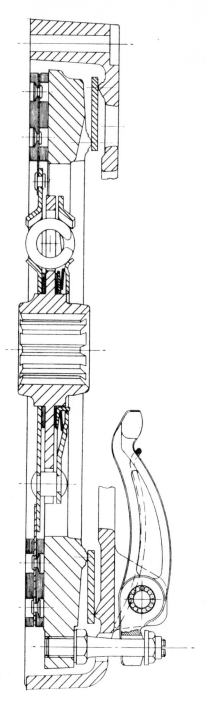

Fig. 1.5. Section through lever Belleville clutch

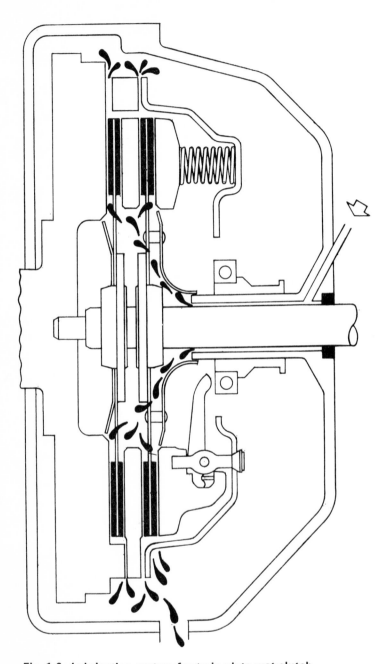

Fig. 1.6. Lubrication system for twin plate wet clutch

for some time to give the oil a reasonable degree of viscosity to ensure sufficient oil flow.

Driven plates

In their simplest form these consist of an annulus of friction material either side of a disc, which is fixed to a hub having a spline which is a sliding fit on the gearbox first motion shaft.

Over the years various improvements have been incorporated, both for better clutch performance and for general driveline quality. By far the most common improvement is the introduction of axial cushioning between the friction faces. This has the advantage of ensuring satisfactory bedding of the facing material and a more even distribution of the work load. It also provides progressive take-up over a greater pedal travel (permitting a greater degree of vehicle control) and prevents snatch. Both these items have a considerable effect on clutch facing life: the first because the more even distribution of the work load over the whole area minimizes the tendency of high point loading with consequent high temperatures, resulting in lower μ values and subsequent clutch slip; the second, by providing greater controllability, allows lower engine speeds to be used at take-up, resulting in much longer clutch life.

To transmit torque more smoothly during take-up and normal driving, springing is often included which allows angular rotation between the hub and the outer part of the driven plate. This is usually achieved by a ring of compression springs arranged circumferentially, which reduce shock torques and torsional oscillations produced at the flywheel. Besides giving more comfort, this arrangement obviously benefits other components in the driveline. A damping arrangement is also included and this amounts to a miniature clutch in the centre of the driven plate. An illustration of a driven plate incorporating all these developments is shown in Fig. 1.7.

Unlike cars there have not been many instances in the U.K. where the standard springing and damping arrangements have had to be varied to control a transmission rattle or noise. Those that have occurred have been resolved to a level which has been acceptable to the vehicle operators.

The standard friction materials for many years have been organic, with a small number of arduous applications using either sintered iron or sintered bronze. As used at present these sintered materials have the disadvantage of high inertia; however, these disadvantages can be reduced by the use of cerametallic materials. The main use of these materials is, at present, for off-highway applications, but is being rapidly extended to normal on-highway duties. Some development work is still required on the effect of the design parameters of brake horsepower per square inch and pounds per square inch as these are currently somewhat restrictive. Once resolved, however, the use of such materials should increase enormously.

Design trends

Coil spring

Here the immediate aim is to increase efficiencies, mainly by reducing friction and centrifugal effects.

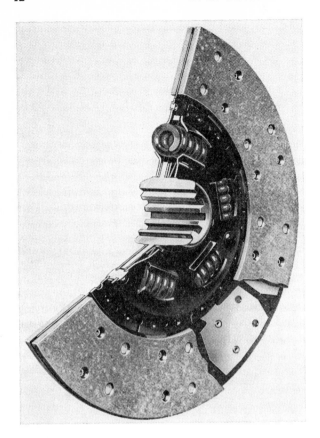

Fig. 1.7. Typical spring
centre driven plate
with damping device

In the long term the question to be answered is 'Have these clutches any place in the world of the high-speed diesel?' Vehicle manufacturers are seeking lower pedal loads, and because of economics this must be achieved wherever possible without recourse to servo assistance. To this end the advantage of a constant clamping load clutch is obvious. It can be shown that a clutch with pull type release has a better inherent efficiency than the normal push type. The future trend will probably be towards a clutch incorporating both these features, and a reduction in release load in the order of 20–25 per cent should be achieved.

Diaphragm spring

Recent developments have improved the efficiency of these clutches by supporting the bottom fulcrum ring with an additional pressing, as illustrated in Fig. 1.8. The advantages obtained with this type of clutch are discussed under automotive clutches.

Future developments could be, as with the coil spring clutch, the use of pull type release to take advantage of increased travel efficiencies.

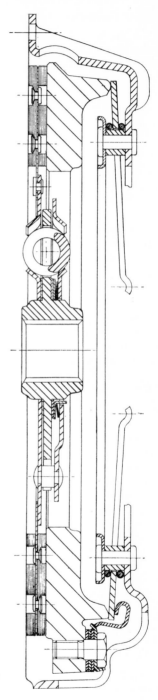

Fig. 1.8. Section through clutch with continuously supported fulcrum ring

Lever Belleville

Some of the developments previously mentioned for the coil spring and diaphragm spring could also be applied to the lever Belleville clutch. In addition, the pure Belleville will probably be replaced by the scalloped bore Belleville, operating on a large radius fulcrum, by means of which it will be possible to reduce the large differential between peak and valley clamping loads and, in addition, permit a larger degree of wear on the friction facings.

Driven plates

In line with increasing cover assembly efficiencies, one of the aims of driven plate development will be the reduction in the axial cushioning while still retaining desirable take-up characteristics. Any such reduction, together with a smaller free run-out condition, will mean a smaller release travel and consequent lighter operating conditions.

A higher coefficient of friction of the facing material, coupled with an ability to perform at higher temperatures, would allow the use of a smaller clutch. Such materials are the cerametallics mentioned previously. To enable their successful use on the smaller clutches the torque capacities of the present spring centre driven plates must be correspondingly increased.

Investigations are proceeding into alternative methods of driven plate centre springing to replace the normal coil spring with its linear load–deflection curve. A more suitable load–deflection curve would have a parabolic characteristic with low initial rate which gradually increases. Such an arrangement should permit complete rationalization in a given range of sizes.

Ventilation

As previously mentioned, a considerable amount of investigation has been carried out on a suitable form of air cooling which will suit all applications. The main objection to clutch ventilation is that any holes opened in the bell housing allow the ingress of dirt which seriously affects the operating efficiency of the clutch unit. The system proposed is a fully sealed self-circulating system which uses the clutch as the central pump. The air is guided into the centre of the clutch and it is then possible, with suitable bell housing design, to re-route the air back in a completely closed loop. If necessary a cooler can be placed with advantage in the air line.

The proposed system is shown in Fig. 1.9. Test results have indicated that a temperature reduction in the order of 15 per cent can be achieved.

INDUSTRIAL CLUTCHES

This type of application can be separated into two categories: (1) vehicles such as agricultural and industrial tractors, and (2) stationary engines.

Agricultural and industrial tractors

Clutches as previously described for commercial vehicles are usually used on these applications. Because the work duty is often more arduous, the safety

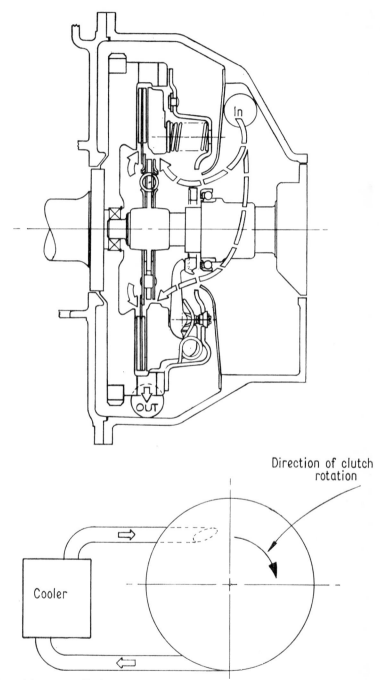

Fig. 1.9. Closed-loop ventilation system

factors are improved by an increase in clutch size and torque capacity. The problems associated with high rotational speeds have, as yet, placed no restrictions on present designs, though consideration must be given to ensure satisfactory clutch pedal operating loads.

The friction materials used are either heavy duty organic, sintered, or cera-metallic, the latter becoming increasingly popular.

For agricultural tractors, there is often the necessity for a power take-off (p.t.o.) to drive ancillary equipment and this is usually provided in one of three forms. The first is a fixed drive from the cover assembly direct to a coupling or to a p.t.o. gearbox which is separate from the main transmission box. The second is a form of twin clutch where one driven plate is for the main drive and the other for the p.t.o. Each drive can be operated independently by means of its own release mechanism, by two pedals on the tractor. The third is a variation of the second, but only one pedal is required on the vehicle. In this system one driven plate is released with partial travel of the release mechanism while the other still drives, further release travel then frees the second driven plate, still holding the first driven plate in the disengaged position. Either the p.t.o. or the main drive clutch can be released first, depending on the arrangement required. All systems have co-axial shafts for transmission of drive.

The operation of these three clutches is illustrated in Fig. 1.10.

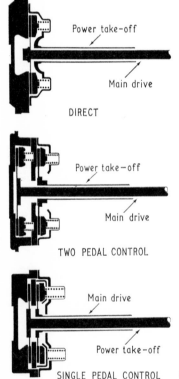

DIRECT

TWO PEDAL CONTROL

SINGLE PEDAL CONTROL   **Fig. 1.10. Alternative forms of power take-off**

Stationary engines

Clutches on these engines are often required to run for long periods in both the engaged and disengaged position. This is unlike the requirements for automotive type clutches which are normally held released for short periods by the operator. Although the clutch needs to be engaged and disengaged while the engine is running, quality of take-up is not as critical as that demanded for automotive applications.

For these reasons, over-centre type clutches are frequently used. The basic friction drive is the same with the clamping load usually applied by means of a link or cam mechanism instead of spring. The system multiplies the effort applied by the operator and retains the majority of the load by the mechanism going slightly over-centre, the residual strain in the distorted mechanism being converted into a clamping force. The degree of over-centre is fixed and the clamping load controlled by adjustment of the load needed by the operator to pass through the over-centre position. Care must be taken in design to ensure that a minimum differential exists between the peak load and the effective clamping load, in the driving condition, as, when adjusted to give a satisfactory clamping load, it is possible that the effort required by the operator would be too high. When released the mechanism will hold the pressure plate in the retracted position without attention from the operator.

Over-centre clutches are available in single, twin, and triple plate form with a maximum capacity of 4000 lb/ft which is factored in relation to the engine torque according to the type of duty required.

Friction materials for these clutches can be either of the organic or sintered type, depending on the type of duty envisaged. Drive is either by internal splined hub or by external gear teeth cut into the friction materials.

Both types of clutch are illustrated in Figs 1.11 and 1.12.

Design trends

Development will, in the main, concentrate on improving the high-speed suitability of this type of clutch. This is currently in hand and it may be found that modifications are required to ensure correct operation. Besides actual failure due to speed, the link mechanism in particular must be studied as speed may affect the clamp or release position and produce slip or drag, respectively.

AUTOMOTIVE CLUTCHES

Diaphragm spring clutches

The introduction of the diaphragm spring clutch, which is now almost universally employed on automotive applications, entailed a considerable development programme to establish its characteristics, production feasibility, and satisfactory installation on vehicles. This development continues with regard to improving durability, clutch capacity, and clutch operating loads.

The diaphragm spring clutch, when used on automotive applications, has many advantages over the coil spring type clutch which was previously fitted. These advantages can be classified as follows:

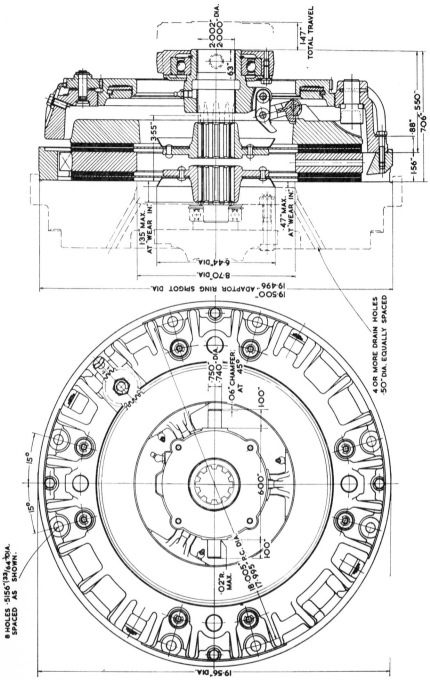

Fig. 1.11. Power take-off with spline drive and cam over-centre mechanism

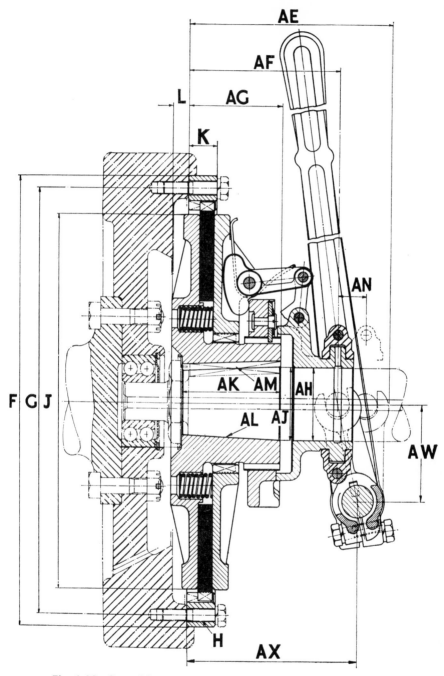

Fig. 1.12. Gear driven power take-off with link over-centre mechanism

(1) It is a more compact means of storing energy, in terms of actual length, leading to a smaller clutch envelope.

(2) It is more suitable for higher rotational speeds, since the spring load is not so affected by centrifugal force. Care, however, must be taken in the design to ensure optimum results.

(3) The load–deflection curve is not linear and hence, by suitable design and selection of operating positions, lower release loads can be obtained. To avoid excessive over-centre effects on applications, due regard must be given to the relationship of peak and valley loads. Typical clamp and release load characteristics are given in Fig. 1.13.

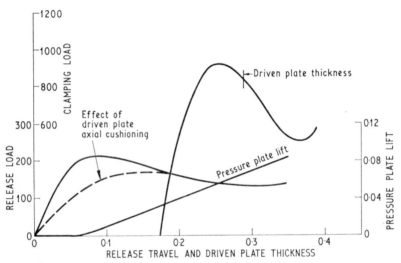

Fig. 1.13. Clamping load, release load, and pressure plate lift characteristics of diaphragm spring clutch

(4) As the facings wear, the clamp load does not fall, but in fact increases. In practice, with a suitable selection of stress ranges, this increase in clamp load can be partially offset by a fall of up to 5 per cent in the overall spring load, thus maintaining clutch release loads at a more constant level.

(5) The design is such that it lends itself to strap drive location of the pressure plate and the elimination of struts, eye bolts, levers, etc. all with their associated wear points, friction build-up, and changes of characteristics such as occur in coil spring clutches.

Two basic types of clutch are in common use—'ratio release' and 'direct release'. The 'ratio release' type of clutch employs as its energy source a Belleville spring having integral fingers extending towards the centre. The clamping load is obtained by compressing the Belleville portion of the spring between fulcrums on the pressure plate and cover, the clutch being released by applying a load at the finger tips. The reaction to the release load is taken at another fulcrum ring attached to the cover, and the load on the pressure plate is removed allowing the pressure plate to lift to free the driven plate.

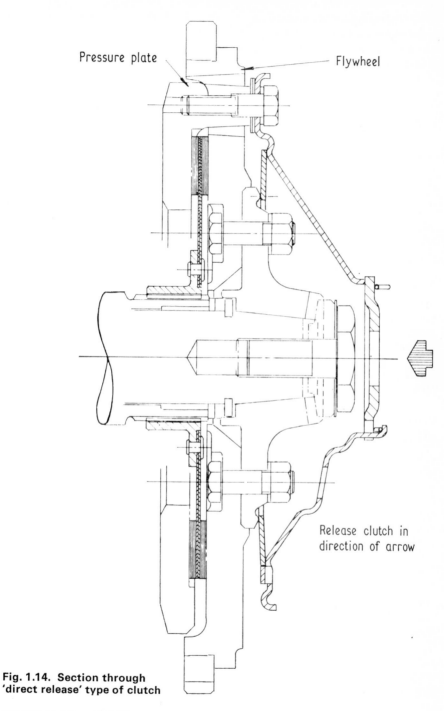

Pressure plate

Flywheel

Release clutch in
direction of arrow

**Fig. 1.14. Section through
'direct release' type of clutch**

The 'direct release' type of clutch employs a simple Belleville spring compressed between flywheel and cover and is released by applying a direct load to the cover, which in turn moves the pressure plate away from the driven member. In this type of clutch the release load is the same as the clamping load and no lever ratio effect is obtained.

Both types of clutch are illustrated in Figs 1.4 and 1.14.

Lever Belleville clutches

Although the load efficiency of the diaphragm spring clutch is high, it has the disadvantage of a low travel efficiency. This is caused by deflection of the spring fingers when the release load is applied to the tips, in order to withdraw the pressure plate. The lever Belleville clutch was designed to overcome the disadvantage of low travel efficiency obtained with the diaphragm clutch, while still retaining the load efficiency. Later designs of diaphragm clutches have considerably improved travel efficiency and, therefore, the possible advantages of a lever Belleville clutch, when applied to automotive applications, are now not as great as they were.

'S' type clutches

In the 'S' type clutch the clamping force is obtained from a load spring mounted away from the clutch cover. The load is transmitted from the spring by means of a linkage, which includes an automatic wear adjuster, to the cover assembly. Because the linkage multiplies the effort, only a low load spring is required and since there are no space limitations a very low rate can be achieved. The release bearing is thus under load in the clutch engaged position and under no load in the released condition. The clutch is illustrated in Fig. 1.15.

CLUTCH DESIGN TRENDS

Cover assembly

On cover assemblies, the aim has been to improve durability and travel efficiencies. These improvements have been obtained on the latest design of clutches by the addition of a support ring under the lower fulcrum wires and the additional use of hardened rivets or sleeves. This support ring gives rigidity to the assembly, which minimizes the effect of eccentricities in the release mechanism on clutch durability. Also, a greater travel efficiency is given to the system by a reduction in rivet tipping (see Fig. 1.9).

Further improvements in durability can be obtained by curving the ends of the diaphragm spring fingers allowing the use of a flat-faced release bearing. The present radiused type of bearing assembly must necessarily wear the diaphragm spring fingers, and, if the release mechanism is eccentric to the centre-line of rotation of the clutch assembly, can give rise to excessive side loadings of the diaphragm spring with consequent heavy wear problems.

Driven plates

The development of driven plates with greater angular movements and variable rates is necessary to meet the more sophisticated requirements of the motoring

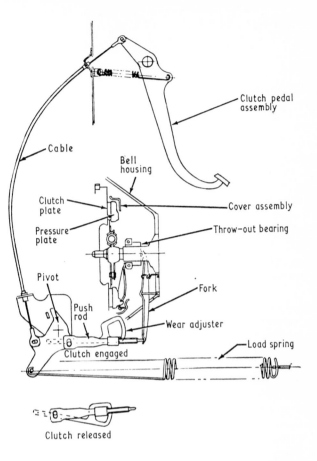

Fig. 1.15. Arrangement of 'S' type clutch

public. It is envisaged that driven plates with 10° movement on drive and 10° movement on overdrive will soon be standard equipment on many vehicles. These plates will vary from a three-stage load characteristic for the more normal applications, to a multi-stage load characteristic for those applications which have idler gear rattle problems. Curves showing the various required characteristics are given in Fig. 1.16.

These many stages are necessary because of the straight load–deflection characteristics of the coil springs at present used to transmit the engine torque. The use of this type of spring to obtain the required characteristics must, of necessity, greatly add to the complexities of design and give rise to greatly increased production and quality control problems. The obvious need is a characteristic which approaches that of a parabolic function, with a spring rate gradually increasing with angular deflection. Recent development has shown that this characteristic is possible to obtain, with the further advantage of increased hysteresis with increasing torque. It is hoped that this form of characteristic will allow one driven plate centre to be used for many applications.

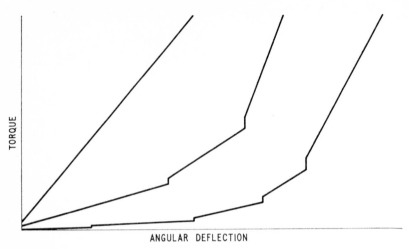

TORQUE

ANGULAR DEFLECTION

Fig. 1.16. Line diagram of single-, three-, and five-stage spring centre characteristics. Note: no hysteresis shown

COMPETITION CLUTCHES

The majority of racing clutches produced are now of the diaphragm spring type.
These clutches are produced in three basic forms, single, twin, and triple driven
plate, with each clutch assembly having a choice of different diaphragm springs
and pressure plates of differing ratios, giving a range of torque capacities from
60 to 850 lb/ft.

All the above clutches have gear drive, i.e. drive to the pressure plates is by
means of an internally gear cut adaptor ring forged in aluminium alloy and hard
anodized to prevent wear. The height of the adaptor ring varies to accept single,
twin, or triple driven plate. The cover is also in cast alloy with a fulcrum ring
formed in the casting and hard anodized to prevent wear at this point. The driven
plates are solid, comprising a disc with a 1 in band of sintered material on each side
and a splined hub to suit the gearbox first motion shaft spigoted and riveted to it.
The pressure plates and intermediate pressure plates are of steel. On the triple
plate version organic facings bonded to the disc are sometimes used in place of the
sintered materials previously mentioned. The gear drive is illustrated in Fig. 1.17.

Clutch design trends

The emphasis is on easier production, cost and weight reduction without
affecting the performance or strength of the clutch.

Gear drive to the pressure plates has been replaced by a lug drive arrangement
which allows the cover and lug to be cast in one piece, thus dispensing with the
adaptor ring. The bolts which secure the cover assembly to the flywheel pass
through each of six equally spaced lugs which are approximately 0·75 in wide, and
the pressure plates are machined with small protrusions which locate on either
side of the lugs to provide drive. This method exposes 90 per cent of the peripheral area of the clutch's internal components to the air. The clutch runs cooler

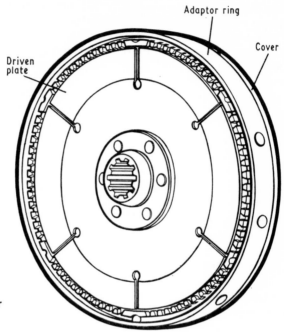

Fig. 1.17. Illustration of gear driven pressure plate and splined driven plate

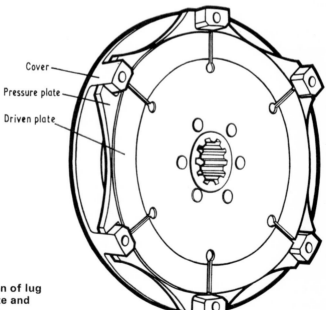

Fig. 1.18. Illustration of lug driven pressure plate and splined driven plate

and lining dust is thrown off centrifugally to prevent jamming of the pressure plates on release, which has occurred in the past with a gear drive arrangement. This arrangement is shown in Fig. 1.18.

Alloy pressure plates sprayed with suitable hard wearing surfaces of steel, etc., have proved satisfactory under racing conditions, but owing to the high cost and the time taken to produce them it is impractical to make them a production item.

With 7-litre racing engines torque figures of 550–600 lb ft are quite normal, and in order to have a reserve of torque capacity the clutch must be capable of coping with 800 lb ft. For torques above this figure, four-plate clutch assemblies will be needed because of the unit loading on the driven plate facings.

Friction materials

Continual development testing is taking place on both sintered and organic materials with regard to wear and μ values. However, little improvement has been found on those facings which have already become established on racing applications.

FRICTION MATERIALS

Many types of facing materials are used on automotive, commercial, and industrial applications, and can usually be classified under the following main headings:

    (1) Millboard
    (2) Moulded
    (3) Woven
    (4) Sintered
    (5) Cerametallic

The facing material specified will depend upon the severity of the application and will range from millboard for the lighter duties to cerametallics for the most arduous.

For the clutch manufacturer the testing of friction materials is a continuous process with two aims: (a) ensuring that the quality of existing production materials is maintained; and (b) establishing performance levels for new materials.

Production quality control

A basic specification is agreed with the supplier for all facings accepted for production. At present this is limited to basic physical properties of a material, such as density, burst strength, etc. but will shortly be extended to include other properties which will affect performance on the vehicle. For example, the F.A.S.T. machine, or to give it its proper name, the friction assessment screening test, has been developed for the sample testing of friction materials under constant torque conditions. μ values, temperatures, and wear characteristics are recorded, the μ value being obtained by measuring the pressure necessary to maintain the constant torque. This specification will in no way supersede the rigorous tests to which facings are at present subjected, but will serve as a guarantee of continued quality during production runs. By this means it is hoped to avoid cases, such as have occurred in the past, where variations in facing quality have given rise to serious service problems.

Testing of new materials

All new materials submitted for approval are subjected to a rigorous test programme. Thorough rig testing gives comparative values for burst, wear, and μ values, and importance is placed at this stage on the anti-stiction properties of the material.

Burst tests are carried out under controlled conditions, at various temperatures, to obtain a burst characteristic curve for the material up to the maximum anticipated operating temperature. The maximum duty level of the friction material is established by wear tests representing various degrees of operating conditions. These tests also establish the values of μ for these duty levels.

On the satisfactory completion of the rig testing, vehicle tests are instituted at all levels up to the maximum duty previously decided. Also included are special tests to assess the anti-judder characteristics of the facing materials.

It is now possible, by examining overall characteristics of any particular application, to select an appropriate facing to ensure satisfactory values and wear life. However, vehicle prototype testing is still necessary, as individual model peculiarities can give rise to judder and other phenomena.

ENGINEERING SPECIFICATIONS

The concept of engineering specification or design certification demands that various parameters of product performance are defined and specified. In broad terms these parameters are:

(a) the load- and torque-carrying capacity of the product;
(b) the fatigue life;
(c) the wear life; and
(d) the consistency of performance.

The definition and detailed test specification, together with the required frequency with which these tests are to be carried out, will vary with each product and must be the joint responsibility of supplier and customer.

For clutches the tests will of necessity be divided between the cover assembly and driven plate. For the cover assembly, in this example coil spring, they could consist of the following:

(1) A minimum pressure plate lift and a maximum release load for a specified release travel.

(2) A minimum cover assembly clamping load for specified driven plate thicknesses.

(3) A stated cover assembly balance condition.

(4) A stated speed at which the clutch must be capable of being run for 5 s in the disengaged position.

(5) A stated number of cycles which the clutch must be capable of performing while rotating at a specified speed and is being actuated through the clutch release mechanism to a given travel.

(6) The final test would probably be a torque capacity test which would be done in conjunction with the driven plate. Here it must be proved that the clutch is capable of driving engine torque under various operating conditions.

For the driven plate assembly, the tests would probably consist of the following:

(1) When clamped under a load equivalent to that of the cover assembly clamping load, the driven plate should freely rotate when the load is removed a distance equivalent to the minimum lift specified for the cover assembly.

(2) A stated minimum number of cycles which the damper springs must be capable of performing without failure when the hub is oscillated through an angle greater than that obtained with maximum engine torque.

(3) A stated number of cycles which the driven plate cushion segments must be capable of performing without failure, when a specified static pressure plate load is applied and released.

(4) Driven plate facings should not stick to mating surfaces and must conform to the S.M.M.T. 130 approval test.

(5) The driven plate balance to be within a stated amount.

It is also possible that a separate specification will be raised for facing materials, as previously discussed, to ensure the maintenance of quality of a material which is the most important part of any clutch application.

In all the preceding it is not only necessary that the tests themselves be specified in complete detail, but also the method of testing be equally explicit, in order that the whole can become a quality control function.

To comply with any safety regulations which might be considered in the future, it is essential that careful consideration be given to all aspects of burst when compiling engineering specifications.

CLUTCH INSTALLATION AND VEHICLE TEST PROCEDURES

Here the main objective is to ensure that the proposed clutch is installed satisfactorily in the vehicle. These checks should be carried out at experimental, prototype, pre-production, and production stages of manufacture. It is then possible to establish any variations that might occur in clutch operating conditions over the full development programme on the vehicle. These changes could be brought about by necessary changes to the vehicle, clutch, or the clutch release mechanism.

For each stage of development, all clutches are checked to specification prior to despatch to customer. When installed on the vehicle the customer's release system is thoroughly checked in accordance with an established procedure. These vehicle checks would include:

(1) Flywheel and gearbox alignment.

(2) Clutch release system, including details of (a) release fork deflection at maximum release load, (b) ensuring that mechanical links do not foul and that clevis pins and fulcrum pins are free and offer minimum frictional resistance, (c) ensuring the best possible bleed condition of the hydraulic system,

(*d*) checking for foul condition of release fork and linkage for maximum pedal travel, and (*e*) checking available wear-in at release lever and slave cylinder, etc.

Figures are also taken of the following: (*a*) pedal effort, (*b*) pedal travel, (*c*) master cylinder push rod travel, (*d*) slave cylinder push rod travel, and (*e*) release bearing travel. All readings are taken on the engagement and disengagement stroke of the clutch pedal.

These tests are carried out with the engine stationary and with the engine at idling speed. On certain applications further tests might be necessary at higher engine speeds. From these figures not only can it be established that the appropriate travels are being obtained with a satisfactory pedal load characteristic, but also the travel and load efficiencies of the overall system can be determined.

PART 2—CLUTCH CONTROL MECHANISMS

CHARACTERISTICS AND REQUIREMENTS

The main object of the mechanism is to transmit linear movement and input loads from the driver, as efficiently as possible, to the clutch release bearing. The mechanism should be durable, requiring minimum maintenance during the life of the vehicle, and will have been achieved at minimum cost.

The output travel required to effect release of the driven plate is dependent on the type of clutch being used and is usually specified as a minimum. Also, to obviate any possible clutch damage, a certain maximum travel must not be exceeded. Typical requirements for car type and commercial vehicle clutches, together with loads, are given in Table 1.2.

The amount of travel available at the clutch pedal is usually of the order of 5 in for a car and 8 in for a large commercial vehicle. This travel is limited by human

Table 1.2. Typical release travels and release loads for automotive and commercial vehicle clutches

AUTOMOTIVE DIAPHRAGM SPRING CLUTCHES

Application	Release travel		Release load	
	in	mm	lb	kg
Small saloon . .	0·24	6·1	200	91
Medium saloon . .	0·28	7·1	250	113
Large saloon . .	0·42	10·7	280	127

COMMERCIAL COIL SPRING CLUTCHES

Application	Release travel		Release load	
5 ton . . .	0·5	12·7	380	172
13 ton . . .	0·5	12·7	500	226
22 ton . . .	0·45	11·4	600	272
28 ton . . .	0·45	11·4	700	317
32 ton . . .	0·45	11·4	750	340

skeleton dimensions and space availability in the driving compartment. Therefore, the overall travel ratio of the system is determined primarily by a travel requirement and hence directly specifies the pedal load. Generally acceptable pedal loads are of the order of 25 to 35 lb for cars and 60 to 90 lb for commercial vehicles. Some countries legislate for clutch pedal loads, travels, and positions.

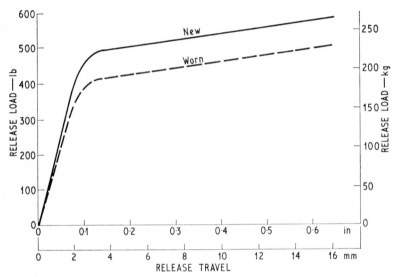

Fig. 1.19. Typical release load curve for coil spring clutch on non-cushioned driven plate

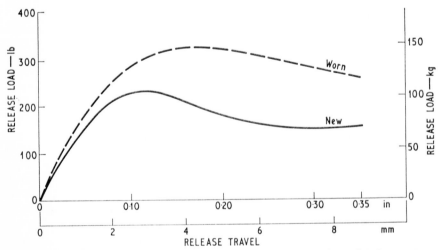

Fig. 1.20. Typical release load curve for diaphragm spring clutch on non-cushioned driven plate

The two types of clutch in common usage today—i.e. coil spring and diaphragm spring—give completely different load characteristics and consideration must be given to these differing characteristics in the design of any release system. Typical release load curves are shown in Figs 1.19 and 1.20 for the two types of clutch mentioned. The traditional coil spring clutch gives a heavier release load in the new condition than the worn. This characteristic is, however, reversed with the diaphragm clutch. This increase in load in the worn condition with a diaphragm clutch is also accompanied by a greater tendency to over-centre.

This over-centre feel can be controlled by careful design considerations of clutch and driven plate characteristics.

The problem of judder which affects many vehicles can, in several instances, be referred directly back to a poor release installation system. Care must therefore be taken to ensure correct alignment of the system and to ensure that it is not affected by power plant or chassis movement or by chassis or body deflection.

The required durability of the mechanism depends upon the type of vehicle usage envisaged. The average number of clutch operations is approximately 5 per mile with upper and lower limits of 0·5 and 30 for motorway and heavy traffic conditions, respectively. A combination of the vehicle total life requirements and the above values will give a target life of a release mechanism.

ERGONOMIC CONSIDERATIONS OF CLUTCH RELEASE SYSTEMS

The introduction of the diaphragm clutch to the majority of car applications, with its relatively low release loads, has been of great benefit in reducing the problem of driver fatigue consequent upon our increasing traffic density. This lesser work load content has also allowed the designer of the clutch release system to consider a greater variation in driver size and strength for correct pedal and seating arrangements.

The response of feel of the engagement process of the clutch is an important factor in the controllability of any vehicle. Ideally it should be possible to disengage by an unimpeded single pedal stroke, the pedal environment being able to cater for a most heavy-footed type of driver. The clutch should be capable of being engaged by keeping the heel of the left foot on the floor to act as a hinge and reaction point and articulating the foot about this point. This ideal engagement condition is totally dependent upon clutch pedal loads; should the pedal load be too high then this form of re-enagement control can be extremely tiring to the driver.

The characteristics of the diaphragm spring clutch, however, lend themselves to this form of re-engagement. The start of engagement of a clutch should be about one-third pedal travel and full engagement at about two-thirds travel. Also the engagement section of the pedal travel should be characterized by a linear movement and some compensation will have to be made to allow for the sometimes non-linear characteristics of the clutch.

Although it was mentioned in the previous paragraph that the diaphragm spring clutch lends itself to the ideal re-engagement control, it can, if not correctly designed, have the completely opposite effect.

To obtain the optimum condition with a diaphragm clutch, the driven plate cushion characteristic must be correctly aligned with the diaphragm spring

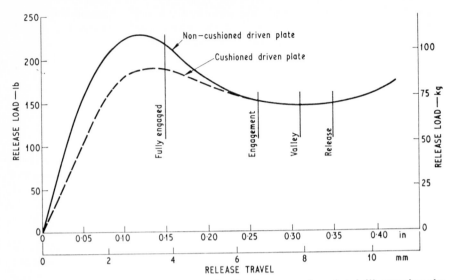

Fig. 1.21. Typical release load curve of a diaphragm spring clutch illustrating the effects of non-cushioned and cushioned driven plates

characteristic. Fig. 1.21 shows the complete release load curve of a diaphragm clutch on a non-cushioned and cushioned driven plate. It can be seen that the driven plate cushion reduces the effect of over-centre and gives a satisfactory release characteristic.

Should the clutch release load curve tend towards over-centre and clutch engagement occur near the valley of this release curve, then clutch controllability will be minimized. Examination of the curve in Fig. 1.21 shows that if the engagement is in the valley of the spring then the release must be able to go through the valley. Engagement will then occur at the point of change from positive to negative rate and all sense of feel will be lost. The design should be such that the full release travel just reaches the valley of the curve and then the re-engagement will occur on the constant negative rate section of the release load curve.

Return springs, which are usually an essential part of any release system, should be light and located as near to the pedal end of the release system as possible, remembering that they increase the pedal load directly and introduce greater frictional losses through this higher load.

MECHANICAL SYSTEMS

Two forms of mechanical system are in common use: (1) lever and rods, and (2) cable. Both systems are about equal in cost and are often used in cars and light commercial vehicles. With the first system it is common to use an equalizer bar relay lever which enables clutch control to be performed without resultant load on the power unit. This method, with the advent of high-efficiency p.t.f.e.-lined cables, is tending to become superseded by method (2). Here it is still necessary to use as large a movement as possible to overcome the effects of stiction or lack of response in the cable.

In the initial design stage it is essential that sufficient pedal travel be specified to compensate for the inherent deflections in any such system. It is also essential that proper regard be given, if a cable be used, to the sealing to keep out water and dirt.

With mechanical systems, some form of adjustment is required at certain specified intervals. This adjustment can be done at the release fork or the clutch pedal. The most usual form of system, which is applicable to the majority of commercial applications, allows a clearance between the clutch release bearing and clutch release lever. This clearance varies from 0·04 in with smaller diaphragm clutches to 0·25 in for the heavier commercial and industrial applications. As the clutch wears in service the release levers move backwards towards the release bearing. Should the clutch not be adjusted, then partial release of the clutch will occur with consequent disastrous effects upon clutch life.

Another system which is becoming increasingly popular on automotive applications has the bearing continuously in contact with the clutch and allows the clutch pedal inside the vehicle to move backwards. This form of system tends to show the driver the need for clutch readjustment. Should this system be considered, and if a diaphragm clutch is being used, regard must be given to the effect of over stroke upon fatigue life of the spring, and linkage friction should be kept to a minimum to prevent overloading of the bearing.

It is worth noting that the overall mechanical efficiency of mechanical or hydraulic systems is of the order of 60–70 per cent. This efficiency, however, can be further reduced by an inefficient release fork within the bell housing. To ensure optimum efficiency, consideration must be given to all parts of the system, as each is equally important.

HYDRAULIC SYSTEMS

Hydraulic systems fall into two categories: (a) where a nominal clearance of 0·04–0·25 in is arranged between the clutch fingers and the release bearing to cater for wear of the clutch disc and facings; and (b) where the clutch release bearing is in constant contact with the clutch fingers and the system is arranged to be self-adjusting to compensate for clutch wear.

This second method, commonly called hydrostatic, relies on having a slave cylinder piston which floats between wide limits along the bore of the slave cylinder, thus following the state of wear of the clutch facings, through the load of a spring situated in the base of the slave cylinder. Any change in volume of hydraulic fluid trapped in the system is allowed through the feed port of the master cylinder when the clutch pedal is in the up position.

Great care should be exercised during the design stage to ensure suitable location of the bleed tappings of the slave cylinder, as trapped air in the system has a considerable effect on release efficiency.

The main advantages of hydraulic systems are that they can be applied to most installations and cater easily for power unit movement. Also, if used on commercial vehicles, they allow tilting of the cab without major problems. Criticisms that have been made of hydraulically operated clutch systems can be generally divided into three kinds, associated with three different types of losses:

(1) Excessive pedal effort required to disengage the clutch. This involves the question of friction losses in the units and hydraulic deflection losses in the system, which limits the leverage that can be applied.

(2) Hysteresis effects—that is, the differences between loads and efforts are given points in the pedal stroke depending on whether the clutch is being engaged or disengaged. This is, of course, associated with the internal friction mentioned in (1) and gives rise to uncertain feel and control of the return stroke leading to the possibility of clutch slip and hence low clutch lining life.

(3) The effect of restriction and dynamic conditions, i.e. the efficiency of the system to return and allow engagement. Sluggishness gives rise to clutch slip during engagement and reduces lining life.

These criticisms have been the subject of various investigations and the results and conclusions are reviewed below.

Load transmission

The two hydraulic units concerned in the system (master and slave cylinder) can have their friction slightly reduced by special seal design. However, the characteristic hydraulic efficiency curve is only altered very slightly, and indeed it is necessary, in the case of the slave cylinder, to preserve a certain amount of friction to prevent the piston being drawn back by the depressions that can exist in the pipeline. It has been established that a short slave cylinder stroke, which of course requires a large piston, should be more efficient in transmitting loads than the smaller long stroke piston. However, it has also been shown that, above a certain size, the displacement losses become a greater percentage of the total stroke and reduce the overall efficiency. This limits the maximum size of the slave cylinder that can be practically employed, apart from the obvious limitations of space to accommodate the unit. Recent developments for car applications have used slave cylinders to $1\frac{1}{8}$ in diameter with $\frac{5}{8}$ in diameter master cylinders, and it is felt that this is about the practical limit that can be utilized without a serious drop in overall efficiency.

There is further evidence in this connection that the general effect of increasing the hydraulic operating pressure of the system does improve the load transmission efficiency of the system, especially at the lower end of the pressure range, presumably shifting the working range towards the higher efficiency part of the curve.

Hysteresis

Considerable improvements with regard to the reduction of the overall hysteresis on hydraulic operation of clutches has been established with the introduction of the diaphragm spring type of clutch on automotive applications. The inherently low friction content of this type of clutch is ideally suited to hydraulic operation.

Coil spring clutches, with their inherently greater friction, are less suited to hydraulic operation. The reduction of these losses in the coil spring type of clutch, which is now used mainly on commercial applications, is being achieved with certain design changes to the components. This has been made even more necessary with the introduction of a high-speed diesel engine on commercial applications.

Dynamic effect

Comprehensive tests carried out on a variety of units under dynamic conditions have shown that the instantaneous transmission efficiency can be considerably improved by increasing the bore of the pipeline. This is more marked with hydraulic units of larger capacity, and, of course, by speeding up the re-engagement of the clutch, reduces clutch slip and improves lining life.

From the foregoing it can be seen that the most benefit is obtained by:

(a) reducing the size of the master cylinder and increasing the slave cylinder up to a certain size and also, within practical limits, raising the general operating pressure;

(b) increasing the pipe size;

(c) reducing clutch hysteresis.

POWERED SYSTEMS

With some clutches of a high torque capacity, for large commercial vehicles, release loads are often high and acceptable pedal loads cannot be achieved within the normal ergonomic relationships.

Examples of the maximum release loads that can be encountered on clutches from 12 to 17 in, together with their required release travels, are given in Table 1.3.

Table 1.3

Clutch size and type		Maximum travel		Maximum release load	
in	mm	in	mm	lb	kg
12 A.S.	305	0·54	13·7	700	317
12 A.S. twin	305	0·65	16·5	750	340
13 A.S.	330	0·54	13·7	700	317
13 A.S. twin	330	0·65	16·5	750	340
14 A.S.	356	0·50	12·7	765	347
14 A.S. twin	356	0·65	16·5	810	367
15 A.S.	381	0·50	12·7	765	347
15 A.S. twin	381	0·65	16·5	1000	453
16 A.S.	406	0·50	12·7	1000	453
16 A.S. twin	406	0·70	17·8	1080	490
17 A.S.	432	0·50	12·7	1000	453
17 A.S. twin	432	0·70	17·8	1080	490

A method of reducing the pedal loads encountered with these high release loads is to make use of air pressure, which is normally available on these vehicles, to operate a servo. The controls on the system must be sensitive and the amount of assistance should be proportional to the effort applied.

Hydraulic line pressure boosters, similar to those used on braking systems, seem attractive but suffer from the disadvantage of lack of response. The system most normally considered employs an air ram which can be used, depending on the design, with or without the normal hydraulic slave cylinder. The necessary response and feel with such a system is obtained by providing a servo-controlled air supply which has a feedback loop to the hydraulic line.

There is no limit to the reduction that can be achieved in pedal loads using such systems, but it has been found that too low a pedal load on commercial vehicles can lead to insensitivity and abuse in clutch control. Since the control stroke is on

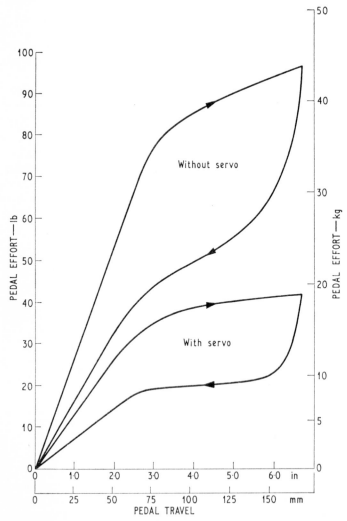

Fig. 1.22. Typical pedal effort curve illustrating the advantages of fitting a servo

clutch engagement, it is the minimum load which is the criterion, and the maximum load will be the minimum plus the hysteresis in the system. Thus it can be seen that the system hysteresis has to be kept to a minimum to avoid excessive pedal loads on initial release.

As the air supply system is used for other essential services, such as brakes, there must be automatic isolation of the clutch system if failure occurs within it.

The advantages that can be obtained on a particular application with the use of servo assistance are illustrated in Fig. 1.22.

One probable development of clutch operation will be the adoption of powered hydraulic systems, which are currently being installed on some new commercial vehicles for brake actuation.

Powered hydraulic systems basically comprise a reservoir of pressurized fluid, and pressures up to 2000 lb/in^2 are anticipated. This higher pressure, compared with the air pressure at present available, will enable much smaller diameter units to be employed and give greater freedom on positioning the servo within the clutch release system. The positioning in the system, however, may be dictated by the degree of feel which can be achieved.

The higher pressure supply, for clutch actuation, will almost certainly be a separate circuit for applying a boost to the operating circuit—the degree of boost being controlled by the input operating pressure. A separate circuit is also needed to ensure that clutch release can be effected, although at a much higher pedal load, if the engine is not running or if there is a failure in the high-pressure supply.

It is also considered that such a system will give a greater control of clutch operation than a valve which bleeds off from the high-pressure source to operate the clutch directly.

CONCLUSIONS

The more critical approach of the whole of the automotive industry to the quality and durability of its products has increased the need for more specialized knowledge with regard to clutch design. Any improvements found necessary to meet these requirements have had to be economically viable and capable of manufacture by mass production methods. The trend towards improved design and increased technical knowledge continues, but it has only been found possible in this paper to discuss briefly a few of the parameters involved.

ACKNOWLEDGEMENTS

The author wishes to thank his colleagues in the industry for their assistance and the Directors of the Company for permission to publish this paper.

APPENDIX 1.1. WORK DONE AND LIFE PREDICTION CALCULATIONS

Because of the many variables which are effective during clutch engagement, it was decided that a sophisticated method of calculation was still prone to considerable error. A simplified form of calculation was therefore developed and service experience used to establish satisfactory parameters.

The method used considers a single start on a gradient and makes the following assumptions:

 (1) The engine delivers constant torque at constant speed during the take-up.
 (2) The clutch is instantaneously engaged to transmit engine torque.

Notation

A Total facing area.
G Overall gear ratio.
g Gravitational constant.
H Heating factor.
N Engine speed
n Transmission efficiency.
P Pressure plate weight.
Q Total heat generated.
q Maximum rate of heat generation.
R Rolling radius of tyre.
r Rolling resistance.
T Engine and clutch torque.
W Gross vehicle weight.
θ Gradient resistance.

Road speed equivalent to engine speed: $\dfrac{NR}{G}$ . . . . . . (1.1)

Tractive effort: $\dfrac{TGn}{R}$ . . . . . . (1.2)

Accelerating force: $\dfrac{TGn}{R}-(r+\theta)$ . . . . . (1.3)

Accleration: $\left[\dfrac{TGn}{R}-(r+\theta)\right]\dfrac{q}{W}$ . . (1.4)

Slip time to reach balance speed: $t=\dfrac{NR}{G(4)}$ . . . . . . (1.5)

Rate of engine work: $TN=q$ . . . . . (1.6)
Total work done by engine during take-up: TNt . . . . . . (1.7)

Total heat generated: $Q=\dfrac{TNt}{2}$ . . . . . (1.8)

Heat generated per unit of pressure
   plate weight: $\dfrac{Q}{P}$ . . . . (1.9)

From these results, in conjunction with Newcombe's work on temperature calculations, a heating factor can be derived. By comparison with known service results the heating factor, together with the heat generated per unit of pressure plate weight and the gradeability (illustrated in Fig. 1.1), can be used to predict clutch performance and life.

The MS. of this paper was received at the Institution on 23rd February 1970 and accepted for publication on 2nd March 1970.

Paper 2. Friction Facings for Clutches

A. Jenkins, B Sc
Manager, Research and Development Division, Ferodo Ltd

T. P. Newcomb, B Sc, D Sc, C Eng, M I Mech E
Principal Research Officer, Research and Development Division, Ferodo Ltd

R. C. Parker, Ph D, C Eng, F I Mech E
Director, Research and Development Division, Ferodo Ltd, Chapel-en-le-Frith, Stockport, Cheshire

This paper describes the various types of clutch facing materials in current use, and discusses both their frictional characteristics and applications in dry clutches and oil-immersed transmissions. During development, experimental materials must undergo exhaustive testing, and in order to establish meaningful tests clutch usage in service has been investigated, and equations are presented which enable the energy dissipation during a single clutch engagement to be determined. Comment is made on the engagement characteristics of the various materials and attempts to assess clutch judder are described. Special tests, made to show that the material satisfies other requirements, are also mentioned.

INTRODUCTION

A friction clutch must be capable of transmitting its design torque at all times. It has to operate over a wide range of duties and should not lose efficiency at high temperatures. The friction facing material must therefore have an adequate and stable coefficient of friction, μ, and an acceptable wear rate and should not cause thermal or mechanical damage to the opposing plate. It should give a smooth take-up and be free from noise during engagements. It should not be permanently affected by contaminants, unduly shrink, swell, or distort and so affect the engagement characteristics during service, and must have adequate mechanical strength. When not in use the facing should not adhere to the opposing surfaces.

Clutch facing materials must therefore undergo exhaustive testing during development and these tests include the measurement of their friction and wear characteristics and physical properties at the temperatures reached in service.

Operating temperatures in clutches depend on the rate of working of the friction surfaces and the thermal capacity and cooling rate of the opposing metal members. The rates of working can be determined from measurements made on vehicles, and using data from such measurements dynamometer tests can be devised to measure μ and wear over the appropriate range of temperatures and duties. Physical tests and tests of a special nature have also to be made to ensure that all the other requirements mentioned above are satisfied.

This paper describes the types of friction material available, their friction and wear characteristics, and the test procedures used in their evaluation.

Notation

E Energy dissipated per engagement.
F Rolling resistance.

I_e	Inertia of all parts rotating at engine speed on input part of clutch.
I_s	Inertia of sun gear.
I_v	Equivalent moment of inertia of vehicle on output side of clutch.
m	Final drive ratio.
P	$(= 1/I_e + 1/I_v)$.
Q	$(= T_e/I_e + T_v/I_v)$.
R	Overall drive ratio, gearbox ratio.
r	Rolling radius.
T_b	Torque exerted by band brake.
T_c	Torque capacity of clutch.
T_d	Drag torque.
T_e	Torque exerted by engine.
T_g	Torque due to gradient resistance.
T_r	Torque due to rolling resistance.
T_v	Resistive torque on output side of clutch.
t_s	Slipping time.
W	Weight of vehicle.
η	Mechanical efficiency.
μ	Coefficient of friction.
Ω_1, Ω_2	Initial angular velocity of I_e and I_v respectively.
1 in y	Gradient of hill.

FRICTION MATERIALS AND THEIR CHARACTERISTICS

Friction materials are complex, multiphase composites which may contain as many as 15 components.

In organic-based materials the components can be classified into three groups: reinforcing fibres, which confer strength on the composite; particulate fillers (both organic and inorganic), which are selected for their effect on performance and processing; and bonding agents, which are usually resins, rubbers, or a combination of the two, and which bind the fibres and fillers together and confer on the composite the required physical properties.

Sintered metal and cermet types of friction material are also complex mixtures of metallic and non-metallic powders in which the inter-particle bond is developed by the sintering process. In view of the number of bond systems used in friction materials and the processes available for their manufacture, it is not surprising that many forms of facing which have a wide range of physical properties have been developed and are currently available.

Physical properties typical of resin–asbestos and sintered materials are shown in Table 2.1.

The choice of mating material is, in principle, as important as that of the friction facing (1)–(3)*. In practice, however, the selection of the opposing material is largely decided on economic grounds and for ease of fabrication, and for dry applications a fine-grained cast iron having a Brinell hardness above 200 is almost universally used. In oil-immersed applications, medium-high carbon steel discs that preferably have a pearlite structure are used. Surface finish should be

* References are given in Appendix 2.1.

Table 2.1. Physical properties of friction materials

Physical property	Resin based materials	Sintered metals
Thermal conductivity	0·000 13 Btu/ft s °F (0·80 W/m °C)	0·0026 Btu/ft s °F (16 W/m °C)
Specific heat capacity	0·3 Btu/lb °F (1·25 kJ/kg °C)	0·1 Btu/lb °F (0·42 kJ/kg °C)
Specific gravity	1·6 for woven to 2·8 for moulded facings	5·0
Modulus of elasticity	$0·5 \times 10^6$ lb/in^2 ($3·45 \times 10^6$ kN/m^2)	$2·1 \times 10^6$ lb/in^2 ($14·5 \times 10^6$ kN/m^2)
Ultimate tensile strength. . . .	4000 lb/in^2 (27 500 kN/m^2)	6500 lb/in^2 (44 800 kN/m^2)
Ultimate shear strength	1700 lb/in^2 (11 700 kN/m^2)	5100 lb/in^2 (35 200 kN/m^2)
Ultimate compressive strength . . .	18 000 lb/in^2 (124 000 kN/m^2)	22 250 lb/in^2 (153 000 kN/m^2)
Rivet holding capacity	10 000 lb/in^2 (68 950 kN/m^2)	—
Brinell hardness number	6 to 15	13
Thermal expansion	$0·3 \times 10^{-4}$/°F ($0·5 \times 10^{-4}$/°C)	$0·07 \times 10^{-4}$/°F ($0·13 \times 10^{-4}$/°C)

better than 60 μin and is obtained by surface grinding or by employing cold rolled steel having the requisite finish.

Materials used for dry applications

Early materials were based on utilizing the fibrous nature of asbestos in the form of a textile cloth in which the yarns were frequently reinforced by metal wire. Facings are made by impregnating rings of 'grey' woven asbestos cloth with solutions of cashew or oil-modified cresol resins, following which the rings are dried to remove solvent, densified by die moulding, and heated to polymerize the resin.

Facings of this type have the disadvantages that the orientation of warp is constant over the disc and that they are expensive because of the high wastage of cloth involved in manufacture. A modified form of facing was therefore developed in which rings were produced by weaving the asbestos yarn into a helical form, and impregnating and curing the resin in the manner described previously. Woven facings have a μ between 0·35 and 0·4 below 150°C, as shown in Fig. 2.1; at higher temperatures μ falls progressively with increasing temperature and is approximately 0·2 at 300°C.

In order to further reduce raw material costs, asbestos millboard facings were developed and are manufactured by forming a slurry of asbestos fibre in water

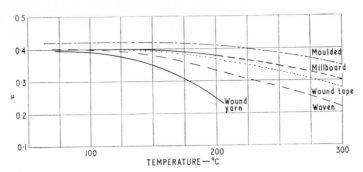

Fig. 2.1. Variation of μ with temperature for different types of facing materials

using starch as binder. A porous asbestos sheet, from which the clutch rings are blanked, is made from the slurry on a modified papermaking machine, waste material being reconstituted. The rings are vacuum impregnated with resin solutions similar to those used for woven types, press-flattened, and baked. Millboard facings have a μ of about 0·4 at temperatures below 150°C. At higher temperatures the μ falls appreciably and becomes erratic, giving rise to inconsistent performance and harsh engagement. Furthermore, wear rate at these temperatures becomes extremely high (Fig. 2.2).

The development of both woven and millboard facings is restricted because formulation changes involving filler additions can only be made via the resin binder. Both types of facing, however, have enjoyed wide popularity in automotive and commercial vehicle clutches.

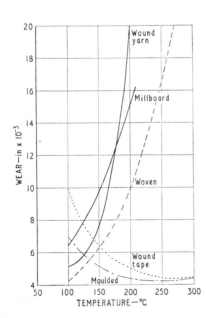

Fig. 2.2. Variation of wear with temperature for different types of facing materials

To increase the range of formulation, and thereby improve performance characteristics, fibres are used either in the form of yarn or as tape or braid which can be coated with a complex dope of resins, rubbers, and drying oils containing substantial amounts of friction modifying agents.

Wound yarn facings have a simple structure and are made by impregnating a filament (frequently containing approximately 30%wt zinc wire) with 'dope', drying to promote 'tack', and winding on a mandrel between pressure plates in either a random or a regular manner to produce a flat, preformed disc. Preforms are press-cured to the appropriate density and heated to further polymerize the complex bond system.

Facings of this type have a stable μ of 0·38 at temperatures below 150°C and have an extremely low wear rate. At temperatures above 150°C the friction falls progressively with temperature and the wear rate is increased several fold. At higher operating temperatures, however, this type of facing does not show the erratic behaviour of millboard types and its engagement characteristics remain very good. Consequently, it has been extensively used in automotive clutches operating at 0·25–0·5 hp/in^2 (289–578 kW/m^2).

Asbestos tape or braid facings, which are usually reinforced with copper or brass wire, are made in a similar way, multi-impregnation with dope being necessary to obtain the required pick-up of impregnant. After drying to obtain the required tack, the tape or braid is wound in a manner similar to that used for wound yarn facings except that the mandrel used produces a V-form cross-section in the disc which effects mechanical interlocking of the tape to give greater strength. The V-form is accentuated during press-curing of the disc and further improves the strength.

These materials have a μ of approximately 0·4 at 100°C which falls progressively to about 0·28 at 300°C. Wear rate, although higher than that of other materials when operating at light duty (100°C), decreases with increasing temperature, and in the range 200–300°C is much lower than that of any material described so far. As a result of this decrease in wear rate with increasing duty, and the inbuilt flexibility due to their construction, wound tape facings have been used extensively in commercial vehicle and industrial tractor clutches over the past 20 years. However, the facings, operating at horsepower ratings between 0·5 and 1·0, are expensive in both raw materials and processing, and for this reason, plus the limitations of formulation and mechanical strength associated with impregnated products, moulded materials have been developed in which long asbestos fibre is intimately mixed with a wide range of organic powders and inorganic fillers such as metal oxide and mineral powders.

Moulded materials usually contain approximately 40%wt asbestos fibre, 30–40%wt of fillers of various types, and 20–30%wt binder phase (resin or resin–rubber combination). The powders are dry-mixed in a conventional blending machine and compacted at room temperature in steel dies. In certain cases, semi-cured organic fillers or cured self-scrap are added to increase the organic content without causing exudation of the bond during the subsequent press-curing operation, which further consolidates the disc and partially cures the resin. Polymerization of the resin is completed by baking. Where a simple groove pattern is required in the working face of the disc it may be possible to die mould to size, in which case the disc is 'finished' by a simple deburring operation. In the majority of cases, however, clutch facings are machined on outside diameter and bore, and ground to thickness.

Present-day moulded facing materials have a μ of about 0·4 at temperatures up to 200°C which falls slightly to 0·35 at 300°C. Their wear rate is higher than that of wound yarn facings at low duties but becomes much lower at temperatures above 150°C where it is comparable with that of the wound tape facing. In heavy duty clutches operating in the temperature range 200–300°C, the overall performance and wear rate of moulded and wound tape facings are superior to those of all other resin-based materials, with the moulded material having the advantage of lower cost.

Resin–asbestos materials operate satisfactorily in the majority of clutch applications. However, where extremely high temperatures are developed, either by the arduous nature of the duty or by operator abuse, the organic resins and rubbers used to bond both textile and non-textile facings begin to denature and may cause fade. Bonds having a higher temperature resistance were therefore investigated and this work led to the development of sintered metal and cermet materials in which the various constituents are bound by the sintering together of metallic powder particles. When the composition has a relatively minor proportion of non-metallic fillers, the type of material is termed 'sintered'; if the mineral loading is heavy, the term 'cermet' is applied.

Both types of material consist of complex mixtures of metallic and non-metallic powders and are made by powder metallurgy techniques (4). Materials of this type, which are usually based on copper and iron powders, have a specific gravity of about 5 and low strength, approximately 9000 lb/in² (62 050 kN/m²). For this reason it is necessary to support the friction material on some form of steel reinforcing member through which the clutch torque is transmitted.

Sintered metal materials have a μ of approximately 0·3 up to 300°C and work at normal pressures similar to those used with organic facings (25–75 lb/in²; 147–441 kN/m²). Cermet facing materials work best at normal pressures of approximately 100 lb/in² (689 kN/m²) and have a μ equal to 0·4.

Sintered materials do not necessarily have better wear properties than organic based materials at light duties. This can be seen from some comparative tests made on facings of the same size; tests were also made on a cermet material in pad form, riveted back to back on each arm of a four-paddle clutch. In these tests, the organic and sintered metal facings worked at maximum rates of 0·7 hp/in² (809 kW/m²) of friction face, whereas the cermet button, having a surface area of about one-fifth that of the full annulus, worked at approximately 3·5 hp/in² (4046 kW/m²). The wear rates are plotted in Fig. 2.3a, b, and c respectively and it can be seen that at temperatures below 150°C the wear rate of the organic material is better than that of the sintered facing, although inferior to that of the cermet button arrangement. As the temperature increases to 300°C the sintered metal and cermet materials both show superior life although wear of the opposing plate is only substantially improved with the paddle clutch.

The high specific gravity of sintered metals can give rise to undesirable inertia effects and this, together with their high cost, has so far limited their use to industrial applications. Cermet buttons, although having high densities, do not

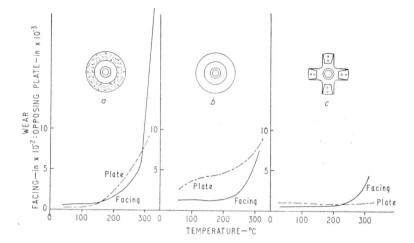

a Organic facing. *b* Sintered facing. *c* Cermet button.

Fig. 2.3. Facing and opposing plate wear versus temperature

suffer from the first disadvantage because of their relatively small rubbing area, and show some economic advantage over sintered materials.

Materials for oil-immersed applications

Many resin–asbestos and sintered materials, although originally developed for dry applications, have been used successfully in oil in the form of clutch facings or band linings. However, as automatic transmissions became increasingly popular, special materials such as resin-impregnated paper, 'semi-metallic', and resin-graphite types were developed and are described below.

For use as facings, materials are frequently required in the form of annuli approximately 0·010 in thick which may be grooved on the working surface. It is therefore necessary to bond the facing on to a supporting core plate to transmit the drive. Materials used as band linings must be sufficiently flexible to bond to the inside radius of the band and must have adequate compressive and shear strengths to withstand the normal loads and shear forces developed at the band-end during use. Consequently, whilst paper-based, woven, and moulded asbestos-based types are widely used, sintered and resin–graphite materials are rarely employed in band lining form.

Resin-impregnated materials for oil-immersed applications are manufactured in a manner similar to that used for millboard facings with the exception that multi-impregnation with several different resins (with intermediate bakes) may be necessary to obtain the required performance. Paper-based materials have a high μ (0·11) and are low in cost. They are capable of working at some 2 hp/in^2 (2312 kW/m^2) of friction face and of dissipating kinetic energies approaching 1500 ft lb/in^2 (3150 kJ/m^2). Their wear rate is relatively high and their resistance to thermal degradation—that is, to 'burning'—is low. Surface grooving of the

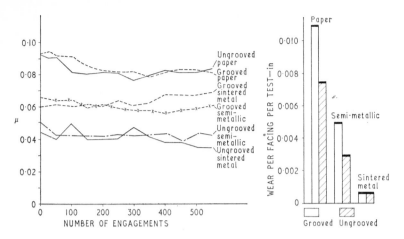

Fig. 2.4. Comparison of μ and wear of grooved facings with plain facings for different types of friction materials operating in oil

facing gives no increase in μ and significantly increases wear rate (Fig. 2.4). Consequently they have been used primarily as plain facings in car automatic gearboxes.

Woven materials are virtually identical to those used for dry applications, brass wire frequently being woven into the fabric. They have great flexibility and conform well to opposing surfaces and these features, together with their high μ (0·08) and low wear rate, have led to their wide application as band linings. They are capable of working at 1·6 hp/in² (1850 kW/m²) and of dissipating kinetic energies approaching 750 ft lb/in² (1575 kJ/m²). Woven materials have the ability to operate satisfactorily where oil starvation occurs, and are therefore widely used in band form.

Moulded materials are made by methods similar to those used to make facings which operate dry. There are two types: those which do not contain metal particles, and those in which the metal content may be as high as 40% wt and which are usually referred to as 'semi-metallic' materials. In the form of plain (i.e. ungrooved) discs, both have a low μ ($\sim$ 0·04–0·05). A higher and more stable friction can be obtained by grooving the friction facing—the grooves presumably interfering with the establishment of hydrodynamic lubrication between the surfaces and thereby increasing μ. The grooves also permit the heat developed at the friction interface to be removed more rapidly by the oil.

It can be seen from Fig. 2.4 that the μ of 'semi-metallic' materials is raised to 0·06–0·08 by grooving, but there is some increase in the wear rate over that of plain facings.

The energy dissipation (1500 ft lb/in²; 3150 kJ/m²) of materials of this type is no higher than that of resin-impregnated paper and the advantage lies in their greater durability and their superior ability to withstand high facing pressures. Furthermore, they give satisfactory performance at medium duties without incurring the extra cost associated with the use of sintered metal.

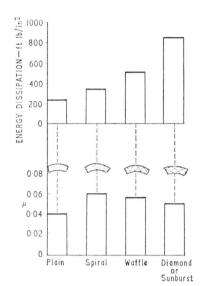

Fig. 2.5. Comparison of μ and energy dissipation of various grooved facings with a plain facing of a typical sintered metal material operating in oil

Sintered friction materials for operation in oil are produced as described previously and vary only slightly in composition from those used in dry applications. Like the moulded materials, they have a low μ (0·04) which is effectively increased to 0·06, without any increase in the wear rate, by machining a number of grooves in the working surfaces. The type of groove pattern used depends to some extent on individual preference, but three types are widely used—namely, spiral, waffle (in which square lands of friction material are produced by the groove pattern) and the 'sun-burst' design (in which the lands are diamond-shaped). The increase in μ and the energy absorption capacity between a typical sintered metal friction material having groove patterns and that of a plain facing is shown in Fig. 2.5.

The principal advantages of sintered metals lie in their extreme durability under normal service conditions and their ability to perform satisfactorily under marginal conditions (such as may be produced by oil starvation) when operating temperatures become extremely high.

Consequently, they are used in power shift transmissions working at up to 2 hp/in² (2312 kW/m²) of facing area under operating pressures as high as 1000 lb/in² (6890 kN/m²). In such applications the higher initial expenditure can be recovered by reduced maintenance costs.

The most recently developed materials for use in oil-immersed transmissions are of the resin–graphite type. These materials are produced by dry-mixing powdered resin, graphite, and friction modifiers and cold-compacting the mix in steel dies in a manner similar to the production of metal powder compacts. The required physical properties and mechanical strength are developed by a press-curing operation after which the facings are bonded to a steel core. Resin–graphite materials have a μ of 0·1 and are capable of working at 3 hp/in² (3468 kW/m²) of friction facing, when their wear rate is slightly less than that of resin impregnated paper types but considerably greater than that of sintered materials. They are intermediate in cost between asbestos paper-based and sintered materials and may be expected to displace the latter in many types of transmission. They have three further major advantages over sintered types in that transfer of material from the friction face to the steel opposing plate is eliminated, coning is much reduced, and they are not affected by the presence of e.p. additives in the transmission fluid, whereas sintered friction materials show a gradual fall off in friction owing to the formation of metal sulphides and metallic soaps, etc.

CLUTCH USAGE AND ENERGY DISSIPATION

To develop realistic tests which simulate service operation it is necessary to know the various conditions under which clutch engagements are made. Measurements have therefore been made during clutch engagements of road speed, vehicle acceleration and deceleration, slipping time, and change in engine speed, when a vehicle is driven over various terrains. These data have been used to calculate the energy dissipated during an engagement, as shown below.

During normal operation the bulk pressure plate temperature rarely exceeds 110°C. When a car is driven hard in hilly regions and applications made from initial engine speeds around 3000 rev/min, the pressure plate temperature increases to about 150–175°C. Considerably more work is done when the clutch is slipped on a steep gradient, and pressure plate temperatures between 250 and 275°C are frequently experienced under these conditions.

Manual gearbox—normal usage

The energy dissipated during a single clutch engagement is determined by considering the engine and transmission to be a two-inertia system (**5**)–(**11**). If it is assumed that the torque capacity of the clutch is maintained constant during the engagement, the slipping t_s and energy dissipated E can be determined from

$$t_s = \left(\frac{\Omega_1 - \Omega_2}{PT_c - Q}\right) \quad \cdot \quad \cdot \quad \cdot \quad \cdot \quad \cdot \quad (2.1)$$

and

$$E = \frac{T_c t_s}{2}(\Omega_1 - \Omega_2) \quad \cdot \quad \cdot \quad \cdot \quad \cdot \quad \cdot \quad (2.2)$$

where

$$P = \frac{1}{I_e} + \frac{1}{I_v}, \qquad Q = \frac{T_e}{I_e} + \frac{T_v}{I_v}$$

in which T_e is the torque output of the power unit and T_c is the torque which the clutch is capable of transmitting. The resistive torque T_v on the output side of the clutch is $\eta T_d/R$, where R is the overall drive ratio, T_d (the drag torque) is the sum of the torque T_r due to rolling resistance and the torque T_g due to gradient resistance, and η is the mechanical efficiency of the transmission and may be taken as 0·95. T_r is the product of the rolling resistance F, which can be determined from road tests, and the rolling radius r of the wheels. T_g is given by $T_g = Wr/y$, where W is the weight of the vehicle (including road wheels) and 1 in y is the gradient. I_e is the moment of inertia of all the parts running at the engine speed on the input side of the clutch and Ω_1 is their initial angular velocity. I_v is the moment of inertia of the output side of the clutch and consists of the sum of the inertia-equivalent of the mass of the vehicle and inertia of the four wheels and brake discs or drums when all are referred to the primary shaft.

Other contributions to the secondary inertia come from the gearbox mainshaft plus driven plate and the layshaft, and are neglected in these calculations. Ω_2 is the initial angular velocity of I_v.

For a small saloon car, $W = 2240$ lb (1016 kg), $r = 10\cdot25$ in (0·26 m), making the inertia-equivalent of the vehicle $I_v = 0\cdot23$ lb ft/s^2 (0·312 N m/s^2) in first gear position when R is 14·99. I_e for the vehicle is 0·11 lb ft/s^2 (0·149 N m/s^2). The maximum torque, T_e, developed by the engine is 60 lb ft (81·35 N m) and road tests show that the free deceleration at low speed is $0\cdot02g$, making $T_v = 2\cdot4$ lb ft (3·25 N m). The clutch torque capacity is 75 lb ft (101·7 N m).

From measurements made on the actual car the value of Ω_1 was found to be 314 rad/s (3000 rev/min) in hard-driven engagements when first gear was engaged from rest. From equations (2.1) and (2.2) the slipping time during take-up is 0·7 s and E is 8185 ft lb (11·1 kJ). If a similar application is made on a 1 in 6 gradient where the resistive torque now becomes 23·6 lb ft (32·0 N m), the slipping time is increased to 0·87 s and the work done is increased to 10 300 ft lb (13·96 kJ) with a mean rate of working of 0·6 hp/in^2 (694 kW/m^2) of friction material.

For a commercial vehicle, $W = 16$ tons (16 260 kg), $r = 19\cdot4$ in (0·49 m), $I_v = 1\cdot93$ lb ft/s^2 (2·62 N m/s^2), $I_e = 2\cdot0$ lb ft/s^2 (2·71 N m/s^2), $T_e = 380$ lb ft (515 N m), and $T_c = 450$ lb ft (610 N m). If a clutch engagement is made in first gear $(R = 39)$ on the level at an initial engine speed of 209 rad/s, the slipping time is 0·8 s and the energy dissipated by the clutch is 37 600 ft lb (51·0 kJ).

Equations (2.1) and (2.2) enable the slipping time and energy dissipated in an application to be calculated with a resonable degree of accuracy. The results can then be used to devise an inertia test for a dynamometer to simulate the energies and rates of working during a normal engagement. The examples shown are typical of applications made at lower duties. Higher energies are involved when the clutch is deliberately slipped during take-up.

Severe usage (slipping clutch)

Most work is done by the clutch if the driver presses the accelerator pedal to maintain a constant high engine speed while making an engagement on a steep gradient. For a comfortable ride for the occupants of the vehicle the torque build-up should increase at an approximately linear rate with time, and if the engine speed is maintained constant, the total slipping time t_s, including the time taken to release the handbrake, is given by

$$t_s = \frac{2\Omega_1 I_v T_c}{(T_c - T_v)^2} \qquad \cdot \quad \cdot \quad \cdot \quad \cdot \quad \cdot \quad \cdot \quad (2.3)$$

and the energy dissipated during slipping is given by

$$E = \frac{\Omega_1{}^2 I_v}{6(T_c - T_v)^2}(T_v{}^2 + 2T_c T_v + 3T_c{}^2) \qquad \cdot \quad \cdot \quad \cdot \quad \cdot \quad (2.4)$$

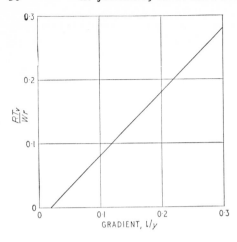

Fig. 2.6. Variation of RT_v/Wr with gradient

The use of graphs enables the work to be determined for any vehicle of known W, r, R, I_v, and Ω_1. Fig. 2.6 shows the variation of RT_v/Wr with the gradient of the hill assuming, as is the case for most vehicles, that the free deceleration is $0.02g$. This graph enables the value of T_v to be calculated for any slope. Knowing T_v and the other parameters, E can now be calculated from Fig. 2.7 which shows the variation of $6E/I_v\Omega_1^2$ with the ratio T_v/T_c. As an example, when an engagement is made on the car considered previously on a 1 in 8 gradient, Fig. 2.6 shows that $T_v = 18.4$ lb ft (24.9 N m) and $T_v/T_c = 0.244$, making $6E/I_v\Omega_1^2 = 6.3$ and hence $E = 32\,500$ ft lb (44.1 kJ) for a constant engine speed of 3500 rev/min. This is

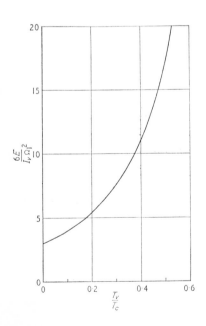

Fig. 2.7. Variation of $6E/I_v\Omega_1^2$ with T_v/T_c for a slipping clutch on a hill

equivalent to an energy dissipation of 890 ft lb/in² (1870 kJ/m²) of facing material and a mean rate of working of 0·41 hp/in² (474 kW/m²) of friction material.

For the commercial vehicle mentioned previously the corresponding energy dissipated is 213 000 ft lb (288·8 kJ) during a slipping time of 6·5 s if the engine speed is held constant at 2000 rev/min. This is equivalent to an energy dissipation of 898 ft lb/in² (1890 kJ/m²) of facing material and a mean rate of working of 0·25 hp/in² (289 kW/m²) of friction material.

These duties are typical of those required to be simulated in a slip test made on a dynamometer.

Automatic gearbox

In an automatic gearbox, one friction element is applied progressively while another is gradually released until the gear change is completed. Frequently, a multi-disc clutch and a band brake are used to control a compound planetary-gear set. The clutch during a power-on upshift must absorb the kinetic energy lost by the change in engine speed as well as a percentage of the work done by the engine during the engagement period.

If it is assumed that the engine torque is constant, that the clutch and brake torque are independent of slip speed during a ratio change, and that there is no change in vehicle speed during take-up so that $\Omega_2 = \Omega_1/R$, then the slipping time t_s and energy dissipated during an engagement can be determined from the equations

$$t_s = \frac{I_T(\Omega_1 - \Omega_2)}{[R/(R-1)]T_c - T_a} \quad \cdots \quad \cdots \quad (2.5)$$

$$E = \frac{I_T}{2}(\Omega_1 - \Omega_2)^2 + \tfrac{1}{2}T_a t_s(\Omega_1 - \Omega_2) \quad \cdots \quad (2.6)$$

where

$$I_T = \frac{I_e\left[1 + \dfrac{I_s}{I_e}\left\{\dfrac{I_e}{I_v}\left(\dfrac{R}{R-1}\right)^2 + \dfrac{1}{(R-1)^2}\right\}\right]}{1 + \dfrac{I_e}{I_v} + \dfrac{I_s}{I_v}} \quad \cdots \quad (2.7)$$

and

$$T_a = \frac{T_e\left[1 + \left(\dfrac{R}{R-1}\right)\dfrac{I_s}{I_v}\right] + T_b\left[\dfrac{I_e}{I_v}\left(\dfrac{R}{R-1}\right) + \left(\dfrac{1}{R-1}\right)\right] + T_v\left[\dfrac{I_e}{I_v} - \dfrac{I_s}{(R-1)I_v}\right]}{1 + \dfrac{I_e}{I_v} + \dfrac{I_s}{I_v}} \quad (2.8)$$

In these equations R is the gear ratio, T_c the torque capacity of the multi-disc clutch, T_b the torque exerted by a band brake, T_v the resistive torque (given by T_d/m, where m is the final drive ratio), I_e the engine inertia, I_s the inertia of the sun gear, and I_v the equivalent moment of inertia of the vehicle (given by Wr^2/gm^2).

As an example, if a gear change is made from third to top gear, where $R = 1·45$ and $\Omega_1 = 576$ rad/s, then $\Omega_2 = 576/1·45 = 397$ rad/s and, for the vehicle considered, $I_s = 0·0248$ lb ft/s² (0·0336 N m/s²), $I_e = 0·149$ lb ft/s² (0·202 N m/s²), $W = 3000$ lb (1360 kg), $m = 4·2$, $I_v = 5·28$ lb ft/s² (7·16 N m/s²), $T_c = 150$ lb ft

(203·4 N m), $T_e = 90$ lb ft (122 N m), $T_b = 90$ lb ft (122 N m), and $T_v = 50$ lb ft (67·8 N m). From equations (2.5) and (2.6), $t_s = 0·31$ s and $E = 13\,350$ ft lb (18·1 kJ), which is equivalent to an energy absorption of 343 ft lb/in² (721 kJ/m²) of facing material and a mean rate of working of 2·0 hp/in² (2312 kW/m²) of friction material.

This energy rating value is typical of what a friction material must withstand under severe usage in an automatic transmission.

PERFORMANCE TESTING—DYNAMOMETERS AND CARS

The performance of a clutch assembly is influenced by its mechanical design and by the characteristics of the friction material. Consequently, prior to making tests on the complete unit, the friction material manufacturer must be able to assess separately the μ and wear behaviour of a facing. This is done by making dynamometer tests on a single facing over the temperature range which may be experienced in service.

Friction tests on a single facing

In a clutch assembly the temperature of the pressure plate is higher than that of the flywheel because of its lower thermal capacity, so that if μ varies with temperature pressure plate and flywheel facings work at different rates. Distortion of the facing can also introduce a non-uniform pressure distribution over its surface and cause fluctuation in the radius at which the load on the facing acts. Furthermore, high temperatures may also affect the springs and significantly reduce the clamping force. Precise measurements of μ and wear of the facings cannot thus readily be made on the complete assembly.

To minimize these effects tests are made on a single facing assembly with the flange width of the facing reduced as far as possible. The facing is riveted to a solid spinner plate which, in turn, is fixed to the flywheel of the machine. The opposing member is a clutch pressure plate which is attached to the torque arm shaft. Temperature is measured by two thermocouples embedded in the stationary pressure plate.

The load on the facing is varied by means of a hydraulic system to maintain the required constant torque and, knowing the load, μ can be calculated.

In these tests, groups of applications are made at such a frequency of application that the pressure plate is maintained at constant temperatures of 100, 150, 200, and 250°C respectively throughout each group. Each engagement is made at a constant speed of 1500 rev/min for a 2-s duration. For the 100 and 150°C groups the energy dissipation is 288 ft lb/in² (300 kW/m²) of facing area with the torque at half the maximum capacity of the clutch. At temperatures of 200 and 250°C, the rate of working is twice that at lower temperatures and the torque level corresponds to maximum capacity of the clutch. After the heavy duty applications a further low-temperature group is made to examine the recovery characteristics of the friction material. A typical test result is shown in Fig. 2.8.

Energy rating tests using a clutch assembly

While single facing tests of the type described previously are of interest to the friction material manufacturer, the primary concern of the clutch designer is that

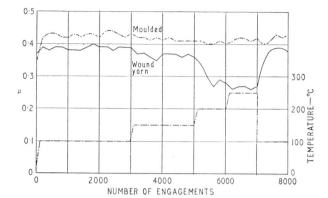

Fig. 2.8. Variation of μ with temperature during single facing tests using typical moulded and wound yarn facings

the unit as a whole will meet the design requirements, and consequently it is necessary to make tests on the full clutch assembly—that is, flywheel, spinner plate, and pressure plate.

Similar tests to those made on single facings, but at a slightly higher rate of working, are used to determine torque output and the effect of temperature on the wear of both friction facing and opposing plate. Friction measurements are made at intervals of 250 engagements, by making a stop to rest under the full spring load of the clutch, the velocity of the flywheel being adjusted so that the energy absorbed is the same as that absorbed during each slip. The spring load–deflection curve for the clutch is measured before and after each group of applications to minimize errors due to variation in clamping load. Wear is determined by measuring, at ambient temperature, the distance between the pressure plate securing rivets and the back of the flywheel with the clutch in the fully clamped position.

A similar approach has been used in the development of an energy rating for tractor clutches, in which the energy input to the clutch is 66 000 ft lb (89·5 kJ) and the mean rates of working during light and medium duty testing are 0·29 and 0·57 hp/in² (335 and 659 kW/m²) of facing area, whereas the mean rate at heavy duty (that is, at full spring load) varies between 0·7 and 0·9 hp/in² (809 and 1040 kW/m²), depending on the μ of the facing material.

The testing of materials for oil immersed applications

In wet clutch tests overload conditions are used to establish the failure point of a material and its wear rate. A third test is used to measure its μ and friction–velocity characteristics.

The energy rating test is made on an assembly consisting of one friction disc and two opposing plates as used in the Borg-Warner 35 automatic transmission, the inertia of the dynamometer flywheel used being some 10 times that of an average passenger car engine. The schedule consists of groups of three applications at energy dissipations, increasing in regular steps to a value of 3500 ft lb/in² (7350 kJ/m²) of facing area using a maximum pressure of 250 lb/in² (1724 kN/m²). The slip times vary between 1 and 20 s depending on the μ of the material under test. To ensure that the operating temperature (measured by a thermocouple welded to the rear side of the opposing plate) is typical of those obtained in service, cooling oil thermostatically controlled at 65°C is pumped through the clutch pack at the rate of 0·6 gal/min.

The test is terminated when the failure point of the material is reached, as evidenced by the erratic form of the torque curve. The mean torque output and μ during an engagement are calculated from the stopping time, while the variation in torque output throughout an engagement is derived by electrically differentiating the tachometer output.

The schedule for assessing wear consists of one group of 550 engagements from 2500 rev/min to rest at a one-minute cycle using an application pressure of 119 lb/in² (820 kN/m²) of facing area. The total energy dissipation per engagement is 7620 ft lb (10·33 kJ), equivalent to 584 ft lb/in² (1227 kJ/m²) of facing area. Torque output and μ are calculated as before, the mean rate of working for a μ of 0·1 being 0·44 hp/in² (508·6 kW/m²).

The engagement characteristics are determined from friction measurements (12) made at steady speeds within the important speed range 1–100 rev/min and at various pressures and oil temperatures. The effect of base oils and oil additives is also investigated and an ungrooved paper-based friction material MP2 is used as a control.

Car testing

Since the performance of a facing cannot easily be measured on a vehicle, subjective assessments of the behaviour of the clutch are made on three types of vehicle tests. Facing wear and the condition of opposing members after test are also assessed. The three categories of vehicle tests are given below.

(a) Normal service

Facings are fitted to the clutches of the Works Fleet cars which are used by many different drivers under normal service conditions. Reports from drivers are restricted to the comments expected for Works Fleet operators, so that a nil report is taken as evidence that the clutch is satisfactory. It is not generally known by the drivers that clutch facings are on test. Wear of the facings is measured at 20 000 mile (32 187 km) intervals.

(b) Brake test vehicles

These vehicles are driven by experienced test drivers and subjective comments about the clutch are obtained after each day's running. The clutch usage is more severe on these vehicles which are generally driven hard, and snatched gear changes are required during brake fade testing. At 3000 mile (4828 km) intervals a quite severe clutch assessment test is performed. Any tendency for the clutch to judder or slip is determined on starts from rest at very low (1000 rev/min) and high (4000 rev/min) engine speeds on flat ground and on various slopes using first, second, and reverse gears. These tests are made with the clutch cold, with the engine and clutch at normal operating temperature, and with the clutch hot after a hill ascent test, when 15 starts from rest are made during a 1·5 mile (2·41 km) ascent of a hill having an average gradient of 1 in 7. Wear measurements and examinations of the facings are made every 12 000 miles (19 312 km). The rates of wear on these cars are about three times that on the Works Fleet vehicles.

(c) Clutch test vehicle

To examine quickly the behaviour of a particular facing on a vehicle the clutch is subjected to a repeated bedding procedure on a 2·0 mile (3·22 km) circuit with 21 gear changes and four starts from rest being made on each lap. Ten miles normal driving is made immediately before and after each day's work on this circuit. The clutch judder assessment described above is performed on this schedule after each 250 miles (402·3 km) bedding. Wear is measured after four groups of 250 miles, the total distance for the test being about 1500 miles (2414 km). This schedule is obviously much more severe than normal service and the rate of wear of materials is approximately nine times that on the Works Fleet vehicles.

The car tests on clutch facings are confirmatory tests following considerable development testing on the dynamometers, and by using these tests a new facing material may be compared with standard materials under a wide range of clutch usage conditions.

ENGAGEMENT CHARACTERISTICS

A gear shift mechanism, whether dry or oil-immersed, should give a smooth and progressive engagement. Under certain circumstances vibrations may be induced within the system during engagement and may be amplified by the drive-line. In dry clutches, vibration of this type is of low frequency, and is known as transmission judder. In oil-immersed transmissions the vibration is of much higher frequency and is colloquially referred to as 'squawk'.

Judder depends not only on the clutch and its facing but also on the stiffness, inertia, and other properties of the driveline. If these various factors could all be isolated and their magnitudes determined, a complete analysis of the driveline could then be made. The conditions under which instability occurs could then be established and a system free from judder could be designed accordingly.

However, many factors, amongst them the friction–velocity characteristics of a facing, are difficult to measure under the conditions in which judder is experienced and consequently work has been limited to empirical investigations. In one such series of investigations wound tape, wound yarn, moulded, and mill-board facings, respectively, were tested in a clutch mounted on an inertia dynamometer, in a driveline on a laboratory rig, and in a number of cars.

Dynamometer tests have been made using a full clutch assembly with the shaft directly connected to a torsion bar of low inertia with a permitted rotation of about 30° at a torque output of approximately one-quarter the torque capacity of the clutch. Torsional oscillations during clutch engagements were detected by strain gauges fixed to the torsion bar and recorded on a high-speed instrument. Although the elasticity of the assembly was typical of that of a driveline of a car to which the particular assembly might be fitted, results showed virtually no difference in behaviour between the four types of facing and the method could not be used as a discriminatory test.

Further laboratory tests were made using the chassis of a car selected for its known tendency to judder. In these tests, second gear was selected and, with the engine running at 1000 rev/min, the clutch was partially engaged thereby moving the car forward a distance of approximately 10 ft (3·0 m). When the engine speed had fallen to 350 rev/min the clutch was disengaged and the vehicle returned to its original position. Vibration characteristics of the driveline were determined during the forward acceleration of the vehicle by a recording accelerometer. Measurements were made at every 200th application during a series of 10 000 applications. The recorded vibration depended in a critical manner upon the position of the accelerometer, the clutch release speed, the precise manner in which the clutch was assembled after relining, and the tyre pressures. As in the dynamometer tests no significant difference in behaviour between the various types of material could be detected.

Tests made on a number of cars concurrently with those in the laboratory and using a similar recording system were equally uninformative. In consequence, recent testing has been made on a subjective basis by skilled drivers specifically responsible for making clutch tests.

With regard to the engagement characteristics of oil-immersed clutches the type of oil used and the additives incorporated in it are important. The variation of μ with velocity at the friction surface affects the smoothness of a gear change and tests on resin-impregnated paper and sintered metal facings in oils typical of those used in automobile automatic transmissions and power shift units have been made at speeds from 1 to 100 rev/min at facings pressures of 80 and 200 lb/in^2

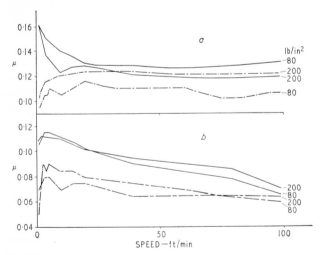

——— Industrial transmission oil.
— – — Automotive transmission oil.
a Resin impregnated paper. b Sintered metal (spiral grooved).

Fig. 2.9. Variation of μ with speed for two materials operating at different pressures in two oils

(552 and 1379 kN/m²) (Fig. 2.9). It can be seen that although the variation in friction with pressure for any one oil is small, the μ and friction–velocity relationship vary with the type of oil used. However, the maximum energy dissipation rate of the clutch is not substantially affected by the type of oil but is determined by the friction material.

SPECIAL TESTS
Adhesion tests

A clutch facing is said to 'stick' when the clutch assembly will not disengage after being left in a clamped position for long periods in a humid atmosphere, as may occur in storage. Sticking is due to corrosion at the interface of the friction material and the opposing member, and is more apparent in smaller clutches. Clutch facing adhesion is measured by placing a clutch assembly in a humidity chamber at 40°C for 72 h and then exposing it to atmosphere for a similar period. The bolts attaching the body of the clutch unit to the flywheel are removed and the axial load at which the surfaces separate is measured, the maximum permissible load being equivalent to 0·75 lb/in² (5·17 kN/m²) of facing area.

The degree of sticking is related to the type of bond used. All families of facings are subject to this phenomenon and are treated in sodium nitrite solution of varying concentrations until the acceptable limit of adhesion is obtained.

Distortion tests

Erratic clutch engagement can be caused by misalignment of the clutch mechanism or distortion of the facing. Facing distortion is caused by differential thermal expansion and shrinkage at the temperatures developed in service, whilst the flexural modulus determines the ease with which the facing will deflect under load. Because of interaction of these factors, clutch facing distortion measurements are made on clutch assemblies mounted on a dynamometer. The distortion is determined by measuring the distance between pressure plate and flywheel faces when the clutch is in the 'free' and clamped positions at temperatures up to 300°C.

Woven and wound yarn facings are less prone to distort than are moulded and millboard types, largely because of their smaller flexural modulus, but there are marked differences between members of each class of facings.

Burst tests

One of the more important physical properties of a facing is its ability to withstand the stresses developed during rotation at high speed which is related to its size, density, etc. This is assessed by measuring the rotational speed at which the clutch facing ruptures or 'bursts'. Burst tests are made on a machine consisting of a steel chamber in which single clutch facings are clamped at their internal diameter by means of four spring clips to an adaptor plate of suitable size to accommodate the bore of the facing. The facing is then rotated at an acceleration of 200 rev/s² until failure occurs. The burst speed is measured at room temperature, 100°C, 200°C, and in certain cases at 300°C. In tests at elevated temperature the facing is heated by radiation while rotating at 170–200 rev/min. It is usual to

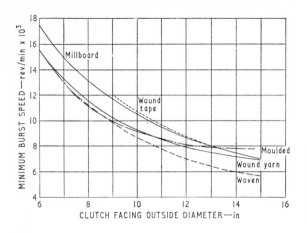

Fig. 2.10. Minimum burst speeds of various sized undrilled facings of different types of materials at ambient temperature

test at least six facings from the same batch of material to obtain a representative value of the bursting speed. Fig. 2.10 shows the minimum acceptable burst speeds at room temperature of various sizes of undrilled facings of different types of material. At 200°C the burst speeds are 30–35 per cent below room temperature values, and at 300°C about 50 per cent below the room temperature values.

CONCLUSIONS

This paper describes the manufacture, testing, and performance characteristics of friction facing materials in current use. Such materials are continually being improved to meet the increased energy dissipations brought about by greater engine speeds and torques in the more sophisticated types of clutches and automatic transmissions now becoming widely used.

ACKNOWLEDGEMENTS

The authors wish to thank Dr R. T. Spurr, Mr M. W. Moore, Mr B. Watton, Mr N. Millner, Mr K. Baker, and Mr R. H. Gibbon of the Research and Development Division of Ferodo Ltd for their assistance and criticism; they also express their gratitude to the Directors of the Company for permission to publish this paper.

APPENDIX 2.1

REFERENCES

(1) NEWCOMB, T. P. and SPURR, R. T.   *Braking of road vehicles* 1967, 179 (Chapman & Hall Ltd, London).

(2) ANGUS, H. T., LAMB, A. D. and SCHOLES, J. P. 'Conditions leading to failure of cast iron brakes', *B.C.I.R.A. External Rept No. 515* 1966.

(3) LAMB, A. D. 'Material and technique factors in the machining of iron castings', *B.C.I.R.A. External Rept No. 520* 1966.

(4) JENKINS, A. 'Powder-metal-based friction material', *Powder Metallurgy* 1969 **12** (No. 24), 503.

(5) M'EWEN, E. 'The theory of gear-changing', *Proc. Auto. Div., Instn mech. Engrs* 1949–50, 30.

(6) HASSELGRUBER, H. 'Die Berechnungen der Temperaturen an Reibungskupplungen', Dissertation, Technische Hochschule, Aachen, 1953; see also *Temperaturberechnungen für mechanische Reibkupplungen* 1959 (Vieweg und Sohn, Braunschweig).

(7) JANIA, Z. J. 'Friction-clutch transmissions', *Machine Design* 1958 **30** (Nos 23–26).

(8) ODIER, J. 'Contributon aux bases mécaniques et thermiques fondamentales des opérations d'embrayage', *Mach.-outil fr.* 1959 (No. 149), 63; (No. 150), 51; (No. 151), 49.

(9) NEWCOMB, T. P. 'Temperatures reached in friction clutch transmissions', *J. mech. Engng Sci.* 1960 **2**, 273.

(10) NEWCOMB, T. P. 'Calculation of surface temperature reached in clutches when the torque varies with time', *J. mech. Engng Sci.* 1961 **3**, 340.

(11) NEWCOMB, T. P. 'Clutch temperatures', *Auto. Engr* 1964 **54**, 145.

(12) EVANS, E. M. and WHITTLE, J. 'Friction in wet clutches', *Tribology Conv., Proc. Instn mech. Engrs* 1967–68 **182** (Pt 3N), 132.

The MS. of this paper was received at the Institution on 14th October 1969 and accepted for publication on 12th November 1969.

Paper 3. Centrifugal Clutches for Automotive Use

C. W. TRIDGELL, C Eng, M I Mech E
British Leyland Power Jacks Ltd, Acton, London, W.3.

This paper describes two distinct types of centrifugal clutch used for automotive transmission. Pivoted or expanding shoe clutches, although more commonly used in industrial applications, have been successfully applied in road vehicles. Two designs are described, one of which is used in conjunction with a hydrokinetic coupling to prevent slip and increase efficiency once the drive has been taken up. Dry plate clutches have been most favoured because they can combine the function of automatic take-up with the ability to be disengaged when required to change gear, independent of the speed of rotation. Calculations are given in Appendix 3.1 for one of five different designs considered. Design features are discussed and a typical clutch performance is shown related to the associated engine torque curve. The advantages and disadvantages of centrifugal clutches are outlined.

INTRODUCTION

Since the inception of the internal combustion engine as the driving force in motor vehicles, designers have been faced with the problem of disconnecting the driveline from the engine to prevent stall when the speed drops below the point at which the engine is self-sustaining, and of reconnecting it gradually to accelerate the vehicle from rest. It was evidently desirable that these functions should be automatic and not depend on the ability of the driver. To achieve this, designers naturally turned to the centrifugal principle, being no doubt well familiar with the centrifugal governors as used on steam engines. Centrifugal force, being directly related to speed, is particularly useful when applied to clutches because it can be utilized to sense the speed of rotation and to provide the force to transmit torque, thus combining governor and actuator in one unit.

In the last 70 years many hundreds of patents have been filed on centrifugal clutches. They are widely and successfully used for industrial applications, particularly in connection with electric motors to reduce starting current by allowing the motor to accelerate under reduced load, but they have had a rather chequered career in internal combustion engined vehicles where operating conditions are less predictable.

Development of the fluid flywheel and torque converter has tended to subdue the use of the centrifugal clutch, but some of the more recent developments in friction materials may initiate a renewed interest as they seem to reduce wear rates, judder, and other undesirable features associated with friction clutches.

SHOE CLUTCHES

In the earliest forms of centrifugal clutch—the shoe type clutch—two or more weights fitted with friction facings on their outer peripheries are driven by the engine within a drum connected either direct or by way of a gearbox to the road wheels (Fig. 3.1). Restraining springs control the movement of the weights or shoes until the desired engagement speed is reached, at which point the weights move outwards until they contact the drum. A further increase in speed, and hence in centrifugal force, presses the shoes into contact with the drum and thus transmits torque to the driving wheels.

Clutches of this type have continued to attract designers because of their basic simplicity, and variations of the design have been applied with differing degrees of success. The simple design shown in Fig. 3.1, although still employed in industrial applications, was soon abandoned for automotive use in favour of a swinging arrangement giving reduced friction between the shoe and driving member (Fig. 3.2).

Pivoting the shoe from one end provides a simple design but suffers from the disadvantage of unequal lining wear, and a swinging link design, as shown in Fig. 3.3, is considered to be more satisfactory. Links can be arranged to give both positive and negative servo action, but in automotive use negative servo is employed on take-up to reduce snatch and, as a result, positive servo force arises on overrun, helping to keep the shoes in contact with the drum below the engagement speed, thus transmitting the braking torque of the engine for a longer period than occurs with the simple pivoted design.

Detailed construction varies considerably in complexity with the degree of servo action the designer tries to incorporate, and in some clutches toggle mechanisms have been built into the link arrangement to accentuate the servo

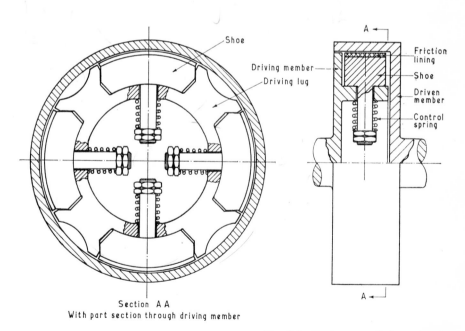

Section A A
With part section through driving member

Fig. 3.1. Early type of shoe clutch

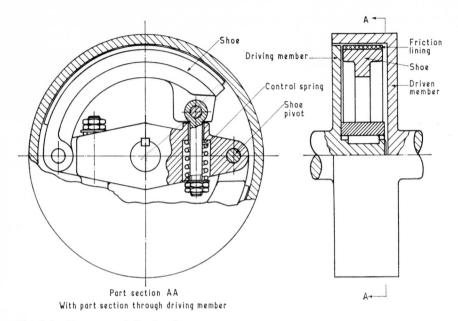

Part section AA
With part section through driving member

Fig. 3.2. Shoe type C.F. clutch

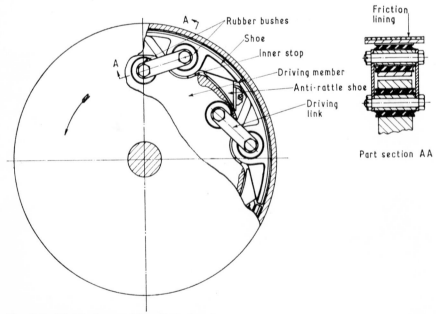

Part section AA

Fig. 3.3. Multi-shoe trailing link clutch

forces on overrun and reduce the slip period. However, these complications have had limited success, mainly because of the number of pivots required and the wear and frictional inconsistency which occurs at these points in a substantially unlubricated assembly. Another method of achieving the same result is to reduce the weight of the shoe and supplement the centrifugal force with a separate bob weight acting on a cam face formed on the inside of the shoe, thus augmenting the force derived from the shoe itself. Difficulties appear to arise in any design using a multiplying leverage due to the change in geometry which occurs as the shoes wear, and if this is not kept within reasonable limits the performance characteristics may be very different with new and worn linings.

It is obvious that in a change from drive to overrun the forces in the attachment pivots are reversed, and any existing play will cause rattle which can be a source of annoyance, particularly on passenger vehicles. To overcome this, and to reduce the lubrication problem, the clutch shown in Fig. 3.3 uses rubber bushes. The rubber is also used as the restraining force to control initial take-up speed by torsionally pretensioning the inner bushes to bias the shoes away from the drum. To ensure an even approach of the shoes to the drum in this design, and to avoid noise under idling conditions, a sliding pad arrangement is incorporated on the trailing end of each shoe to control its angle of approach to the drum.

So far mention has only been made of shoe clutches used as the prime connection between engine and transmission, but they have achieved greater success in less critical applications such as the so-called 'fluid clutch' (Fig. 3.4), in which the shoes are attached to the output member of a fluid flywheel and operate within a drum carrying the drive member of the coupling, the drum in its turn being connected to the engine crankshaft. The shoes have radial slots which fit over the reaction member to provide lateral guidance and are driven by a pin passing through lugs on the shoes and sliding blocks located by slots in the reaction member. A garter spring let into a groove on the side of the shoes determines the speed of engagement.

The purpose of the centrifugal clutch in this case is to eliminate the slip which always occurs with a fluid flywheel and so achieve maximum efficiency and fuel economy. In practice the fluid flywheel takes up the drive, and as the output speed rises the centrifugal force on the shoes overcomes the tension of the garter spring and there is a gradual transfer of transmission forces until full torque is finally being transmitted by the shoes. Wear on the linings is low because much of the take-up slip has already been overcome before the clutch starts to engage, and the clutch shoes are running in oil. An interesting feature of the design is the grooving of the inside face of the drum to provide a greater effective surface area; this shows some advantage in the effective coefficient of friction due to a wedge action as the lining material is forced into the grooves. It also imparts longitudinal stability to the assembly under active conditions. Mounting the shoes on the output member ensures full engine braking down to idling speed and permits a dead engine to be started by towing.

The main drawback of the shoe-type centrifugal clutch has been that it cannot be disengaged for gear changing and, consequently, considerably more design and development effort has been concentrated on automated versions of the dry plate clutch.

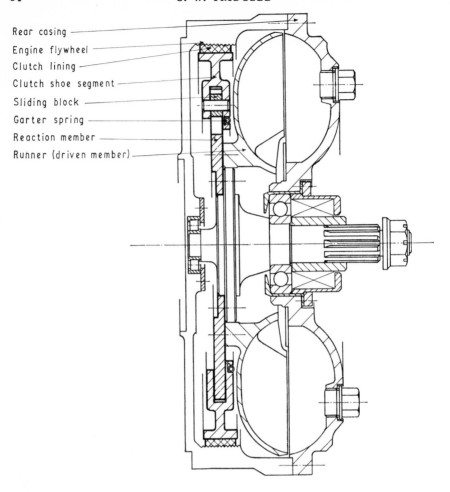

Rear casing
Engine flywheel
Clutch lining
Clutch shoe segment
Sliding block
Garter spring
Reaction member
Runner (driven member)

Fig. 3.4. Fluid clutch

DRY PLATE CLUTCHES

The essential feature of a centrifugal clutch designed for disengagement at speed is that the force transmitted by the bob weights to the friction faces is limited and there is usually a resilient connection in the linkage to allow the pressure member to be withdrawn. Fig. 3.5 shows a typical dry plate centrifugal clutch with conventional disengagement by means of a thrust pad. This clutch is housed partly in a hollowed out flywheel with pockets in the rim to accommodate the three bob weights. A substantial steel pressing, dished at the centre for strength, takes the place of the conventional clutch housing and provides means for attaching the clutch to the flywheel. The bob weights are in the form of bell crank levers with the main mass concentrated at the end of one of the arms. These levers are pivoted on forks attached to the main pressing and to reduce friction they are fitted with small needle roller bearings. Inboard of the pivot the levers are notched to carry links which have mating knife edges and transmit the force generated by the bob weights to a second pressing, generally known as a spring plate. Between the spring plate and the main pressing are six small springs which serve to hold them apart until the centrifugal force produced by the weights is

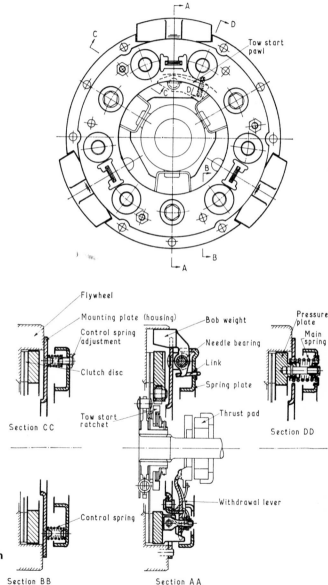

Fig. 3.5. C.F. clutch with separate control springs

sufficient to overcome their preload. Engagement speed of the clutch is determined by the preload on these springs, three of which are fitted with adjustment screws. The main clutch springs are situated between the back of the presser plate and the underside of the spring plate and are trapped to a predetermined length by a stud and nut; when the spring plate is urged towards the flywheel by the bob weights, the presser plate moves with it until the clutch disc is contacted. As the speed gradually increases, load is applied to the clutch disc directly proportional to the centrifugal force generated by the weights, during which period they remain at a substantially constant radius. When the load on the clutch disc equals the preload in the main clutch springs the weights once more begin to move outwards against the combined loads of both control and clutch springs until they finally reach their stops.

With an unworn clutch disc and the weights fully out the main springs are compressed to a condition where the load they apply to the pressure plate is approximately 135–150 per cent more than that required to transmit full engine torque. This includes allowance for the reduction in spring force as the clutch disc wears.

Manual withdrawal is achieved in exactly the same way as with a conventional clutch, through levers pivoted from the housing reacting on studs attached to the pressure plate. The main clutch springs are always designed to have the minimum possible rate to keep withdrawal load low and maintain the torque transmitting load as near constant as practicable between a new and worn clutch disc.

Provision is made for tow starting by incorporating pawls spring biased into engagement with a ratchet when the clutch is stationary and capable of transmitting drive from the road wheels to the engine. As soon as the engine starts the pawls are centrifugally flung out of engagement and remain in that condition during normal functioning of the clutch.

The use of two separate sets of springs—one for control, the other for wear—makes for ease of adjustment of the take-up speed but incorporates a large number of small parts. The clutch illustrated in Fig. 3.6 reduces the number of components by utilizing the main clutch springs to provide the control function. In this case the clutch is self-contained and designed to bolt straight on to the face of the flywheel, the weight pockets being formed in the clutch housing. Bob weights on the end of bell crank levers pivoted from the housing react on to a spring plate. Studs attached to the pressure plate pass through holes in the levers approximately half-way between the pivot and the spring plate reaction point, and carry stepped washers which engage the levers on the opposite side to the spring plate. The clutch springs situated between the pressure plate and the spring plate tend to force them apart, and apply equal and opposite forces to the lever. However, as the load from the pressure plate is taken at a point closer to the lever pivot, a couple is produced which tends to rotate the bell cranks and hold the weights against the edge of the pressure plate which forms the inner stop. There is no separate adjustment for engagement speed, which is determined by the lever ratios, size of weights, and pre-load of the main springs.

Another interesting feature of this design is the arrangement for tow starting by manually engaging the clutch with the engine at rest. This is achieved by pivoting the studs which pass through the weight levers and spring, biasing them

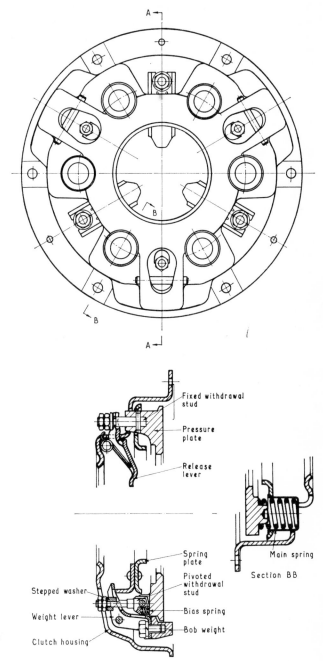

Fig. 3.6. C.F. clutch with combined main and control springs

to a position where the stepped washer no longer locates on the lever. In normal circumstances centrifugal force maintains the studs in position for automatic withdrawal, but if the manual withdrawal levers are depressed with the clutch stationary, then the load is taken off the studs and the bias springs pivot them out of engagement so that when the levers are released the pressure plate can move forward and engage the clutch disc. In these circumstances the spring load on the pressure plate is reduced but is still sufficient to overcome engine compression and permit starting by towing. Once the engine has started and the clutch spins above engagement speed the bob weights pivot the levers in and centrifugal force replaces the studs in their normal position.

Fig. 3.7 is a typical torque–speed curve showing the effect of transferring loads from the withdrawal studs to the main springs steepening the engagement curve, thus reducing the slip band and at the same time permitting low rate main springs to be used. Low rate springs are desirable because they limit normal withdrawal loads and reduce preload error arising from variations in the static fitted spring length which is non-adjustable. The small slip band has the disadvantage of reducing vehicle manoeuvrability because of the rapid increase in torque transmitted for relatively small changes in engine speed. In development of vehicles fitted with this type of clutch several attempts were made to improve manoeuvrability by making the throttle controls more sensitive to initial pedal movement, and some degree of success was achieved.

Another design using the same principle of a swinging weight, but this time on a

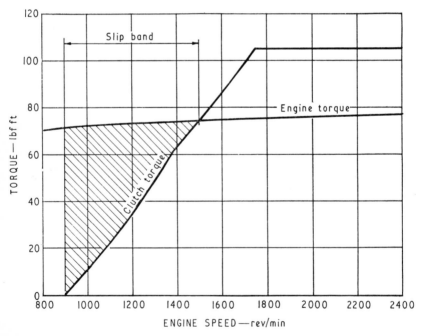

Fig. 3.7. Torque–speed curve for clutch shown in Fig. 3.6

commercial vehicle, is shown in Fig. 3.8. The weights are pivoted from the spring plate and are in the shape of a T; the longest of the three arms carries the weight while the other two react, respectively, on to the pressure plate and on to a spring which controls the engagement speed. As the engine increases speed the control spring is compressed and the pressure plate advances until it touches the clutch disc when further rotation of the weight takes place about the pressure plate stud so that the spring plate is pulled back, increasing the load on the main clutch springs until the weight contacts its stop. Because of the slower speeds and higher torques involved, six bob weights and a total of 18 springs are used. This clutch was claimed to operate quite satisfactorily but suffered from rattle—perhaps not unexpectedly in view of the large masses attached to the spring plate which is

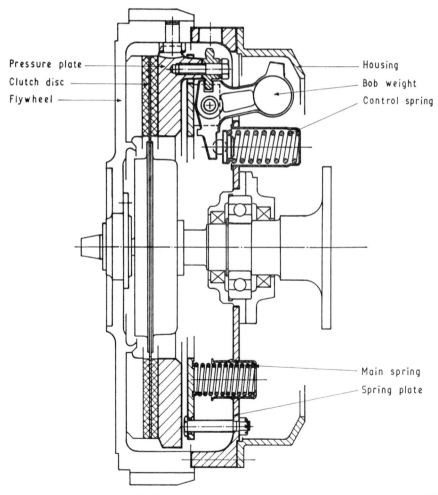

Fig. 3.8. Commercial vehicle C.F. single dry plate clutch

free to move longitudinally and, in consequence, radially by virtue of the working clearances.

The clutch shown diagrammatically in Fig. 3.9 uses a different approach to the problem. It consists of the same basic elements (pressure plate, spring plate, and pivoted weights), but the weights are carried in a separate cage mounted on a bearing within the housing. The weights, in the form of rollers, react on to a cam plate mounted on a bearing attached to the spring plate. Separate control and clutch springs are used, the control springs being situated between the flywheel and pressure plate. For automatic engagement the weight carrier is driven from the clutch housing by a second small friction clutch disc, spring-loaded against the housing. With an increase in engine speed the weights are centrifuged

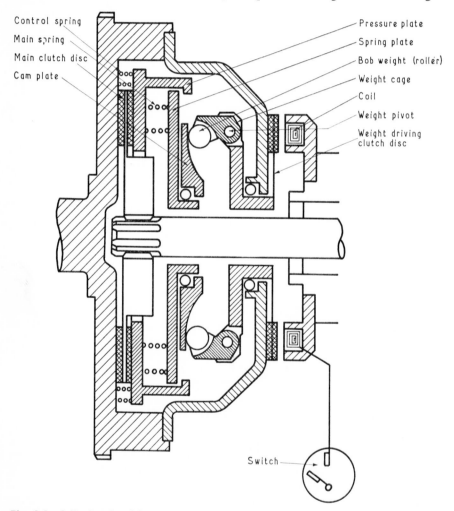

Fig. 3.9. C.F. clutch with separate weight control clutch

outwards, but at the start they have a low moment about the pivot and consequently the clutch control springs are of quite a light nature. As the weights now move outwards this moment increases until, towards the end of the movement, they achieve maximum leverage. At the same time the reaction from the cam track is reducing, and the combination of the increasing centrifugal moment and decreasing spring moment permits the use of relatively small weights situated closer to the centre of the clutch than in the more conventional designs and thus helps to maintain a low inertia. A further advantage of this cam arrangement is that the clutch disengages at a speed lower than engagement speed and with a snap action which assists in reducing wear on the clutch disc. It also improves manoeuvrability by increasing slip at low speed without increasing the overall slip band.

Disengagement for gear changing is achieved electrically by a coil attached to the face of the gearbox which, when energized, withdraws the small clutch disc from its contact with the clutch housing and brings it into contact with the coil housing where it acts as a brake and brings the weight carrier to a standstill, disengaging the main clutch. To re-engage, current is cut off in the coil allowing the small clutch plate to recontact the housing and accelerate the weights at a controlled rate which is determined by the degree of slip on the small clutch plate.

The latest developments in centrifugal clutch design have tended to depart from the integral arrangement where one clutch disc serves for both centrifugal and manual engagement and instead favours a conventional manually operated clutch combined with a separate centrifugal clutch. Fig. 3.10 shows a typical example in which the bob weights each comprise three rollers rotating about a common axis which act between the pressure plate and a cone formed in an outer clutch housing. The pressure plate is held back by control springs (not shown) and as the speed of rotation increases, the weights wedge between the pressure plate and the housing, overcoming the control springs and applying a torque-generating load to a clutch disc flexibly attached by strap springs to the casing of the gear change clutch which is free to rotate concentrically with the flywheel. A freewheel device is fitted between the casing and the flywheel which ensures that the braking action of the engine is available under all conditions of running and when the vehicle is parked. It also enables the engine to be started by towing. Use of two clutch plates lengthens the life of the clutch and enables facing materials to be selected appropriate to their individual functions. For instance, sintered materials might be used on the centrifugal clutch because high loads will be produced by the bob weights and movement can be kept to a minimum, whereas softer asbestos-based materials can still be employed in the gear changing clutch. Better dimensional control of sintered materials and their more rigid nature implies smaller clearance movements which assist in obtaining a better balance by virtue of the smaller bob weight movement required.

With rollers acting against a simple inclined face and unsprung reaction plate, the torque-transmitting load is directly proportional to the increase in centrifugal force on the weights; this is not necessarily ideal for controllable take-up.

A clutch intended for use with an automatic gearbox is shown in Fig. 3.11. On the back of the pressure plate this clutch uses a profiled cam track which is designed to give a rapidly reducing mechanical advantage for approximately the initial 33 per cent of the weight movement, partially offsetting the increasing

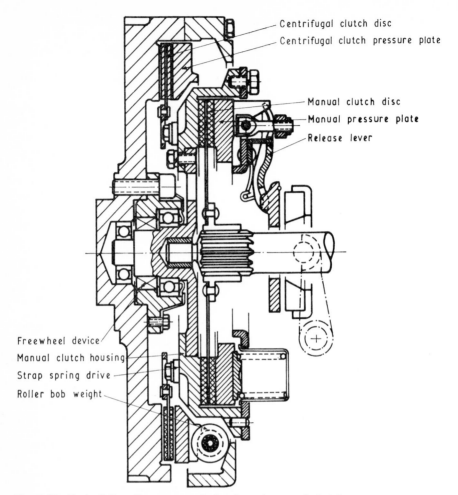

Fig. 3.10. Twin C.F. roller operated clutch and manual clutch

centrifugal force and providing a speed band with relatively constant torque for manoeuvring. The remaining weight movement has an increasing mechanical advantage, which keeps the total slip band reasonable. Although the clutch has only been tried experimentally it is reported to give good results and makes handling much easier for the inexperienced driver.

ADVANTAGES

Centrifugal clutches have the main advantage of being cheap to produce and are capable of being made to suit a range of individual power units by simple changes within a basic design. When properly installed, correctly designed, and sensibly used, they require no more maintenance than conventional dry plate clutches and are just as readily serviced.

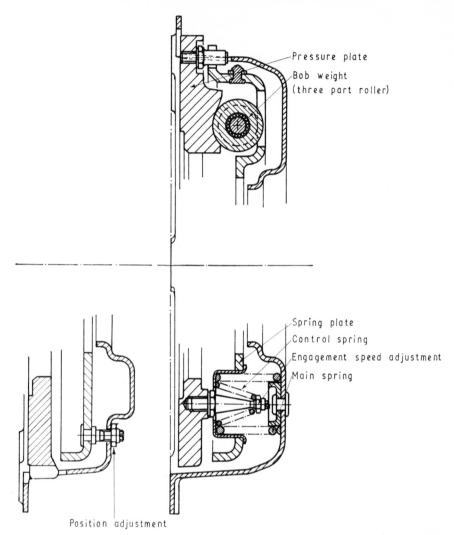

Pressure plate

Bob weight
(three part roller)

Spring plate

Control spring

Engagement speed adjustment

Main spring

Position adjustment

Fig. 3.11. C.F. roller clutch with profiled cam track

Engagement characteristics could be developed to provide a high degree of manoeuvrability, although it appears that this feature has not been fully exploited, possibly because almost all centrifugal clutch development, at least in the U.K., has been centred around clutches for use with manual gearboxes already in existence and to fit into bell housings designed for conventional clutches.

DISADVANTAGES

Main transmission clutches on automotive vehicles used with manual gearboxes all suffer at the hands (or feet) of the driver, and the centrifugal clutch is no exception. In fact, due to its built-in slip at low engine speeds, it is more open to abuse. This arises obviously because the slip prevents the engine from labouring and the driver does not get much indication of when to change gear. This results in overheating of the clutch disc and causes rapid wear in exactly the same way as occurs with a manual clutch that is deliberately slipped.

Most disadvantages generally associated with centrifugal clutches are due to their employment with manual gearboxes. A typical example is free-wheeling which occurs following a gear change due to the clutch centrifugally disengaging during the change and the resulting jerk when the accelerator pedal is depressed, causing the clutch to re-engage almost instantaneously as road and engine speeds synchronize. A device sometimes incorporated to overcome this comprises a free-wheel combined with a limited torque drive to control acceleration of the engine from the road wheels. Many external devices have also been tried, the most common being a mechanism to adjust the throttle stop and so maintain engine speed above minimum clutch engagement speed during the change.

Perhaps the most legitimate complaint against centrifugal dry plate clutches and shoe clutches can also be levelled at manual clutches—i.e. judder. There is, however, one main difference: on a manual clutch judder, when it occurs, can frequently be controlled by changing the relationship between clutch load and engine speed, thus making the take-up acceptable, but with an automatic clutch this relationship is fixed and when judder occurs it becomes a major problem, involving component changes to eliminate it.

CONCLUSIONS

Many informed people are of the opinion that automotive centrifugal clutches belong to a past era, and the evidence certainly points to this with the steady increase in the use of hydrokinetic couplings in conjunction with automatic and, to a smaller degree, manual gearboxes. Nevertheless, several types are still produced and they have a place on the cheap automatic transmission for which there may well be an increasing demand.

The illustrated example of a shoe clutch in conjunction with a fluid flywheel is of particular interest, and it is possible that this type of application may increase. Little, if any, development work appears to have been carried out in the past few years and it is interesting to speculate on the performance that might be achieved using more recently developed friction materials and possibly oil-immersed mechanisms.

Dry plate clutches with roller mechanisms of the type illustrated in Fig. 3.11 seem to have development potential beyond that so far achieved. Speculating on the possibilities it would appear practical to obtain a performance curve of the type shown in Fig. 3.12 based on a variation of mechanical advantage through the weight movement starting at 8:1, reducing to 4:1, and then rapidly increasing to 16:1. Introducing a high mechanical advantage at the end of the weight movement would 'lock' the clutch into engagement and give rise to rapid disengagement at a predetermined speed, similar to the more complicated design shown in Fig. 3.9.

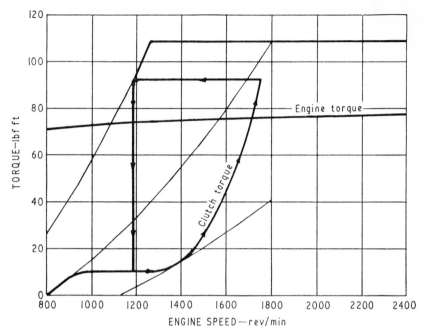

Fig. 3.12

Evidently, the advantages to be expected from such a clutch could be:

(*a*) Less critical engagement due to relatively constant low torque over much of the engagement speed range.

(*b*) Reduction of judder problems for the same reason.

(*c*) Reduced wear by rapid disengagement to low torque condition and reduction of speed range over which high torque and slip can occur together.

ACKNOWLEDGEMENTS

The author wishes to thank Newton & Bennett Ltd for permission to publish this paper, and also extends his gratitude to the following companies for providing data from which the illustrations have been prepared: Alford & Alder (Engineers) Ltd, Borg & Beck Co. Ltd, Ferodo S.A. (Paris), Fichtel & Sachs A.G., Leyland Motors Ltd, Self Changing Gears Ltd, and Twiflex Couplings Ltd.

APPENDIX 3.1. CALCULATIONS FOR CLUTCH SHOWN IN FIG. 3.6

In the following formulae leverages are assumed to remain constant as small changes due to rotation of the weight lever are negligible. The clutch disc is assumed solid, i.e. without 'cushion' or 'crimp'. In practice most clutch discs are not solid and the theoretical torque curve will be modified by an amount dependent on the rate and extent of the 'cushion' which can be considered as reducing the clearance x. (See Fig. 3.13.)

The transition period is the period between the pressure plate contacting the clutch disc and the centrifugal force overcoming the spring preload.

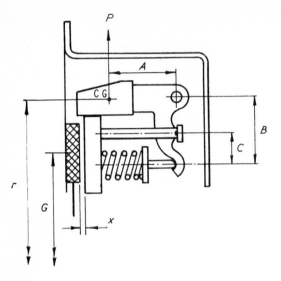

Fig. 3.13. Mechanical diagram

Notation (SI units given in parentheses).

G Mean plate radius, ft (m).
g Gravitational acceleration, ft/s^2 (m/s^2).
m Mass ($= W/g$), lb (kg).
P Centrifugal force acting on weights, lbf (N).
R Total spring rate, lbf/in (N/m).
r Radius of centre of gravity of weights, ft (m).
T Torque transmitted by clutch, lbf ft (N m).
W Total weight of bob weights, lbf (N).
Y Load exerted by pressure plate on disc, lbf (N).
μ Coefficient of friction of clutch disc.
ω Angular velocity of weights, rad/s.

Suffixes

1   Conditions at initial engagement speed.
2   Conditions at end of transition period.

$$T = Y \times 2\mu G \qquad \dots \dots \quad (3.1)$$

During the transition stage,

$$Y = \frac{A}{B}(P - P_1)\left(1 + \frac{P_1}{P_2 - P_1}\right) \quad \dots \dots \quad (3.2)$$

Following the transition stage,

$$Y = \frac{A}{B}P \qquad \dots \dots \dots \quad (3.3)$$

$$P = m\omega^2 r \qquad \dots \dots \dots \quad (3.4)$$

During the transition stage r is assumed to be constant, and following the transition stage

$$r = r_2 + \left(\frac{P-P_2}{R}\right)\left(\frac{A}{B}\right)^2 \quad \cdots \quad (3.5)$$

Hence, during transition:

$$T = 2\mu G \frac{A}{B}(m\omega^2 r - m\omega_1{}^2 r_1)\left(1 + \frac{m\omega_1{}^2 r_1}{m\omega_2{}^2 r_2 - m\omega_1{}^2 r_1}\right)$$

Substituting r_2 for r and r_1:

$$T = 2\mu G \frac{A}{B}(mr_2)^2(\omega^2 - \omega_1{}^2)\left(\frac{1}{mr_2} + \frac{\omega^2}{\omega_2{}^2 - \omega_1{}^2}\right) \quad \cdots \quad (3.6)$$

Following the transition stage:

$$T = 2\mu G \frac{A}{B}m\omega^2\left[r_2 + \left(\frac{P-P_2}{R}\right)\left(\frac{A}{B}\right)^2\right]$$

$$T = 2\mu G \frac{A}{B}m\omega^2\left[r_2 + \left(\frac{m\omega^2 r - m\omega_2{}^2 r_2}{R}\right)\left(\frac{A}{B}\right)^2\right] \quad \cdots \quad (3.7)$$

It can be shown that $\omega_2{}^2 = \omega_1{}^2(B/C)$, hence the ratio B/C determines the length of the transition period.

APPENDIX 3.2

BIBLIOGRAPHY

BEACH, K. 'Manual of mechanical power transmission', *Power transmission* 1953, 3rd edition, 285.

BEACH, K. 'Centrifugal clutch design', *Product Engng* 1962 **33** (Pt 2, July), 56.

GILES, J. G. *Automatic and fluid transmissions* 1961.

HELDT, P. M. *Torque converters or transmissions* 1955, 5th edition.

SPOTTS, M. F. 'The Bochory automatic clutch', *The Motor* 1957 (9th October).

SPOTTS, M. F. 'S.C.G. fluid clutch', *Auto. Engr* 1961 **51**, 208.

SPOTTS, M. F. 'Design formula for expanding shoe centrifugal clutch', *Product Engng* 1962 (July).

SPOTTS, M. F. 'New design formulas for long-shoe centrifugal clutches', *Product Engng* 1964 (February), 89.

WARDLE, E. T. 'Design and application of clutches', *Engng Mater. Des.* 1963 **6** (November), 796.

The MS. of this paper was received at the Institution on 5th November 1969 and accepted for publication on 24th December 1969.

Paper 4. Fluid Couplings for Road Vehicle Transmissions

J. ELDERTON, BSc, CEng, MIMechE

The paper describes those couplings which are two-element hydrodynamic transmissions in themselves and a practical approach to formulating a comprehensive prediction of fluid coupling performance is suggested. It deals with a selection of a coupling for a specific application with direct reference to the special design restrictions imposed by automatic gearbox applications. Mass production needs and testbed work on a prototype are also described.

INTRODUCTION

Fluid couplings are two-element hydrodynamic transmissions transmitting torque through a circulating vortex of fluid, usually thin mineral oil, there being no mechanical driving connection between the vaned primary (impeller) and secondary (runner) members. A particularly smooth power flow is achieved, and fluid couplings have long been used with internal combustion engines for completely isolating from each other the torsional vibrations in driving and driven shafts.

The fluid coupling was invented by Dr Föttinger around 1905, and in the years following the 1914–18 War it became widely used for marine propulsion, following an intensive development programme by the Vulcan Company at Hamburg, when optimum circuit shape, numbers of vanes for different coupling sizes, and basic characteristics were experimentally determined.

In 1926 H. Sinclair noted the shortcomings of the friction clutches used on the London omnibus 'K' type chassis, and realized that scope existed for employing fluid couplings, especially on congested city routes. He further appreciated that when the centrifugal characteristics of a fluid coupling were combined with the very wide speed range of a petrol engine, then a particularly flexible transmission resulted. Additionally, the fluid coupling in its existing form was simplified, the impeller and runner being enclosed within a single casing containing a constant oil filling, and the external filling pump, oil coolers and piping as used for the marine version eliminated.

The first trials were made in 1927 at the Associated Equipment Company Limited works in Walthamstow using a cone-type friction clutch and sliding gearbox. The tests were encouraging, and further developments led to the adoption by the Daimler Company in 1930 of the fluid coupling with an epicyclic gearbox which is the standard transmission employed on London buses to the present day.

From these initial developments have stemmed the designs reviewed in this paper, all of which, with the exception of the prototype described at the conclusion, have been manufactured in very large numbers indeed for automobile and heavy road vehicle purposes.

BASIC PRINCIPLES

A fluid coupling can be considered as two hollow bowls having radial vanes within as shown in Fig. 4.1, with the lower bowl connected to the prime-mover, and the upper bowl to the load. When the lower bowl is filled with liquid and rotated by the prime-mover, the liquid is flung outwards and upwards under centrifugal force, constrained by the vanes and the bowl periphery. It passes across the gap between the two elements at the outer periphery, and in circulating radially inwards through the vanes of the upper bowl produces a torque at the output shaft, and so drives the load. The liquid then returns to the lower element at its inner periphery and the process will be repeated.

A speed difference between input and output is essential in order to circulate fluid and thereby transmit torque. The fluid therefore flows continuously in a helical path between impeller and runner, as shown in Fig. 4.1*b*. This speed difference is normally expressed in the form of percentage slip, i.e.

$$\text{Percentage slip} = \left(\frac{\text{Input speed} - \text{Output speed}}{\text{Input speed}} \right) \times 100$$

the speeds being given in rev/min.

A coupling operating with its runner stationary, i.e. at 100 per cent slip, is said to be 'stalled'.

The impeller acts as a centrifugal pump and hence the horsepower input to the fluid coupling is equal to the product of the quantity of fluid discharged into the runner in unit time and the change in moment of momentum of this fluid as it passes through the impeller vanes. As the fluid coupling consists of only two elements, this same fluid must pass also through the runner, suffering a corresponding decrease in moment of momentum; the torque input from the prime-mover is therefore always equal to the torque output to the driven machine. For

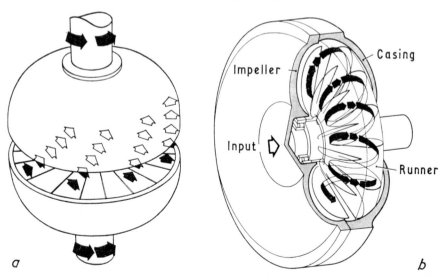

a   *b*

Fig. 4.1. Simple presentation of fluid coupling

a given value of transmitted torque, the slip corresponds to the requisite difference in centrifugal heads between impeller and runner, to circulate the mass of fluid against the friction and shock losses in the vane passages.

With input and output torques equal, it follows that

$$\text{Percentage efficiency} = \left(\frac{\text{Output speed}}{\text{Input speed}}\right) \times 100 = (100 - \text{Percentage slip})$$

The fluid coupling obeys the same fundamental laws as all centrifugal machines for the same slip, the horsepower transmitted is proportional to

(a) the fifth power of the profile diameter of the working circuit,
(b) the cube of the input speed,
(c) the density of the working fluid.

Many efforts have been made to formulate a theoretical prediction of fluid coupling performance. Unfortunately, these treatments do not produce results wholly supported by tests, since neither the resultant mass of fluid in circulation nor its effective radii of entry and exit from the impeller can be accurately predicted or measured. This is particularly true of fluid couplings operating with reduced oil fillings. It is therefore usual to adopt a practical approach, in which test results are obtained for one size of fluid coupling at a convenient speed, such results then being applied to other sizes and other speeds using the principle of geometric similarity. The predictions so obtained apply with good accuracy over a fairly wide range of sizes and speeds.

Accordingly, the laws can be expressed as

$$\text{Horsepower} \propto D^5 \times N^3 \times \rho$$

Conventionally, this equation is expressed as

$$\text{Horsepower} = K \times \frac{N^3}{100} \times D^5$$

The profile diameter is expressed in metres, and the speed in rev/min, to give convenient numerical values to the resultant K factor.

This K factor therefore includes the density of the fluid since it is additionally found in practice that the differences in performance with different fluids are not wholly explained by the variation in density. Clearly, other factors, such as the viscosity at the operating temperatures, also have an important effect.

From the foregoing,

$$\text{Torque (kg m)} = \frac{K \times D^5 \times N^2}{1396}$$

Figs 4.2a and c show typical relationships between the factor K and slip for modern designs of fluid coupling operating with various oil fillings.

Figs 4.2b and d illustrate the application of such couplings to a petrol and a diesel engine, respectively. Fig. 4.2b shows a typical petrol engine full torque characteristic, having a top speed of 4500 rev/min and an idling speed of 300 rev/min. Using the equations above, and taking the experimental K/slip curve designated 'Filling A', for each point on the engine characteristic a K value can be calculated and from the test curve the slip determined. Appropriate

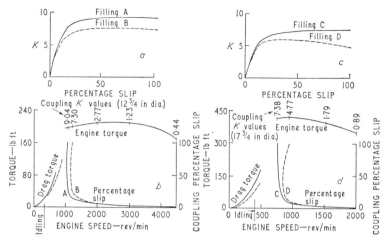

Fig. 4.2. Combination of prime-mover and fluid coupling characteristics

K values have been noted along the engine curve, whilst the fluid coupling slip is plotted beneath.

With falling engine speed, the slip across the fluid coupling will progressively increase to a point at which the slip increases very sharply and the fluid coupling stalls. If the engine is operating under full torque conditions, its speed cannot be pulled below this point, which is the 'full torque stalling speed'. With further reduction of engine speed, the transmitted torque decreases according to a square law relationship (since the slip across the coupling remains unchanged at 100 per cent) until the idling speed of the engine is reached. The magnitude of this torque at idling speed determines the tendency of the vehicle to creep when stationary with a gear engaged.

In combining engine and fluid coupling characteristics to select a suitable coupling size, the acceptable full torque stalling speed is usually the dominant factor. If this speed is raised, the idling drag torque will be reduced, but the effective working range of the engine is also reduced, and the heat generated in the fluid coupling at stall is increased. On the other hand, if this speed is reduced it has the effect of increasing the idling drag torque, and thus a compromise has to be struck. In practice, it is found that for an automobile petrol engine, a fairly low stalling speed is desirable, to give a good sensation of initial acceleration from rest. Furthermore, if this speed is too high, the increased noise level gives an impression of 'fussiness' to the transmission.

A second coupling characteristic is shown corresponding to a different oil filling 'B' together with its effect on the stalling speed.

For vehicle traction work, there should be a good range of adjustment to the stalled torque, whilst producing little change in the required low value of slip over the working range. It is of no avail increasing the fluid coupling size to reduce the slip over the working range, unless the circuit characteristics are such that the reduced value of stalled K and hence of oil filling could still yield good running slip figures.

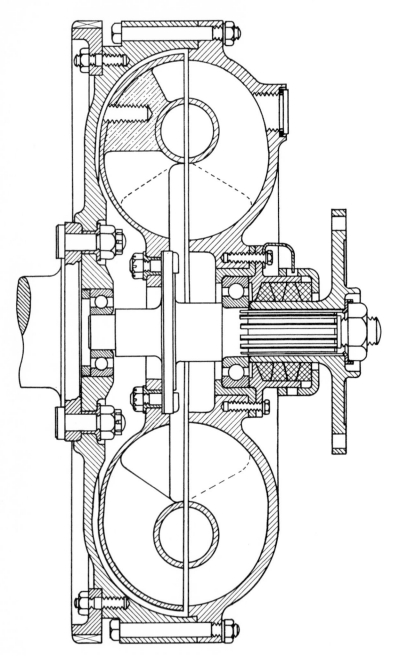

Fig. 4.3. Section of 1930 fluid flywheel

It is usual to employ flat radial vanes, set at right angles to the plane of rotation, to give equal performance for either sense of rotation, and also good engine braking when overrunning.

Figs 4.2c and d give a similar presentation for applying a fluid coupling to a diesel engine for a heavy road vehicle. It is found that the maximum stalled K should be rather lower than for a petrol engine, in view of the reduced speed range of the diesel and its different idling performance.

Preference is sometimes shown for the use of an undersized fluid coupling in conjunction with a lock-out friction clutch in parallel with the hydraulic circuit. One such design has a centrifugally actuated clutch mounted on the output shaft and thus responsive to running speed. When this speed has risen sufficiently, the clutch engages and cuts out the hydraulic circuit. An alternative arrangement employs an oil servo piston operated multi-plate clutch in conjunction with a sophisticated governor control.

When considering these features, it is important to remember that the fluid coupling confers a vital element of flexibility by virtue of its slip, and the installation must be carefully investigated to ensure that there is no possibility of torsional vibration interaction with the clutch engaged.

The foregoing underlines the essential need for a sharp transition in the fluid coupling characteristics between the high slip starting condition and the low slip running regions, to extend the latter over the widest possible engine speed range.

FLUID FLYWHEEL (1930)

Fig. 4.3 shows the section of the fluid coupling fitted by the Daimler Company to the Double 6 '30' chassis and named a 'fluid flywheel'. The working circuit was of 344 mm (13·54 in) profile, and its contour based on that employed by the Vulcan marine couplings mentioned earlier. The impeller had 28 equally spaced vanes, alternately long and short, and the runner 30 such vanes, since it had been found that if equal numbers of vanes on impeller and runner were employed, noise and torque oscillations were generated, as all vanes intercepted simultaneously. A core ring was fitted to both impeller and runner to give consistent performance during starting and initial acceleration of the vehicle. The elements were of heat-treated aluminium alloy, and the oil was contained by a packed gland.

Initially the couplings were operated completely filled with oil, but it was quickly found that an air space was required to cater for thermal expansion effects. The filling plug was therefore re-sited to limit the maximum quantity to about 85 per cent of the total circuit volume. Fig. 4.4a shows K/slip curves, based on the circuit space completely filled, and with the reduced filling actually employed. The bad effect of reduced filling on the working slip range is particularly noticeable.

Fig. 4.4b shows the combined characteristics of engine and coupling, and illustrates the important point that only during periods of hard acceleration or maximum vehicle speed is full engine torque normally employed. The torque requirement is normally of a much lower order, and the coupling slip correspondingly reduced.

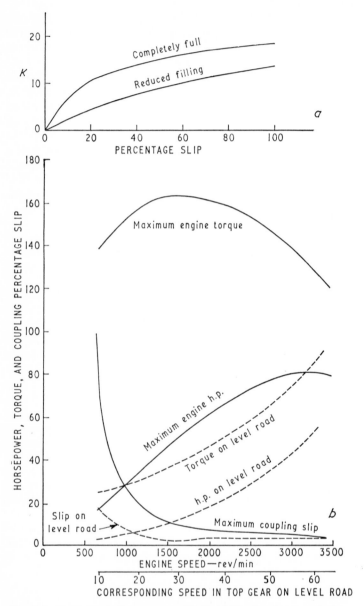

Fig. 4.4. Vehicle performance with fluid flywheel transmission

VULCAN SINCLAIR TRACTION COUPLINGS
Reservoir and baffle

It was realized that if the stalled K could be reduced whilst at the same time maintaining a high circuit filling, then an improved slip over the operating range would be achieved. Alternatively, a larger fluid coupling could be used, operating at a reduced stalled K value, and although the working slip might be unchanged, a greater capacity for hard working would be realized, due to the increased heat dissipation ability.

To this end a reservoir chamber was fitted on the back of the runner, with transfer ports arranged so that when the driven shaft was stationary, and the engine idling, the reservoir chamber was filled with fluid from the working circuit. On accelerating, this oil was transferred back to the working circuit to give an effectively higher filling and thus lower slip. The reservoir also acted as an expansion and air separation chamber to counter the effect of prolonged working at high temperature in bad traffic conditions.

The optimum volume of the reservoir was found to be 20–30 per cent of the circuit capacity, and by suitable adjustment of the oil quantity, a stalled K range of about 10–14, with good slip values, was obtained.

A later development was to fit a small annular baffle plate at the inner circuit profile some 20–30 per cent in diameter greater than this profile. With the runner stationary, or turning at low speeds, the counter-head developed in this member is zero, or of low order; the vortex therefore tends to cling to the circuit walls, and is interrupted by the baffle. In the working slip range, the greatly increased runner counter head compresses the vortex into the radially outer regions of the circuit, and the baffle then has little effect.

The addition of this baffle permitted the same results to be obtained with a reduced reservoir volume, giving a saving in axial length requirements, and also permitted further adjustment to the stalled K values. The improvement in performance compared with the 1930 fluid flywheel is shown in Fig. 4.6.

Multi-vane baffle coreless circuit with reservoir

In comparing the transient torque/slip characteristics of the fluid coupling during acceleration periods with those obtained from steady brake tests, there was a region where the slip under transient conditions was appreciably higher than that obtained for steady loads at the same speeds.

This indicated an interference between the core ring and the circulating vortex of fluid, but it was known that for a circuit with relatively few vanes, a core ring was essential to obtain consistent starting and acceleration results, together with the lowest possible working slip.

It was further known that by using an increased number of vanes, the stalled K could be raised, although the slip over the working range was increased, due to the lower oil filling necessary to achieve the same full torque stalling speed.

Prolonged experimentation evolved the combination of an increased number of vanes, a no-core guide ring, a small baffle, and a reservoir having a volume of about 15–20 per cent of that of the working circuit. With the elimination of the core ring, the separate reservoir chamber was abolished, communication with the working circuit being around the periphery of the runner. The section of such a

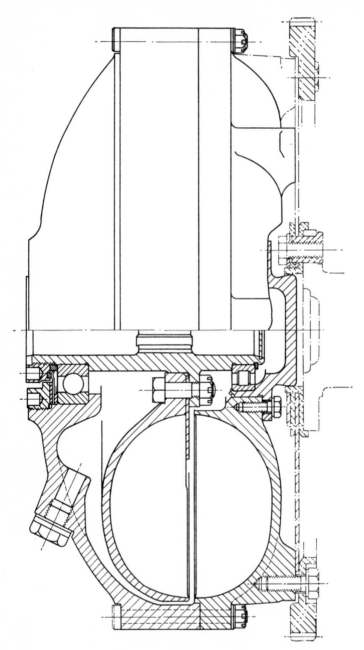

Fig. 4.5. Section of coupling with coreless multi-vane baffle circuit and reservoir

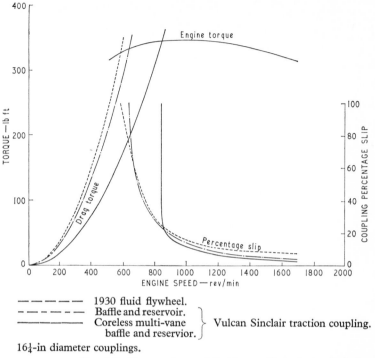

1930 fluid flywheel.
Baffle and reservoir.
Coreless multi-vane
baffle and reservoir.

Vulcan Sinclair traction coupling.

16¼-in diameter couplings.

Fig. 4.6. Comparison of fluid coupling characteristics

coupling is shown in Fig. 4.5, the circuit members and reservoir casing being gravity die castings in high tensile aluminium alloy. An all metal gland is employed, consisting of a tensioned spring steel diaphragm clamped at its outer periphery, and its beaded inner edge bearing on a lead bronze insert in the shaft nut.

The basic characteristics are those shown in Fig. 4.2, and Fig. 4.6 summarizes the improvement in performance with each successive design.

In the early versions, where sand castings were employed, the impeller and runner had differing numbers of vanes. With the much more expensive equipment required for die casting, the same number of vanes were used for each member but the individual vanes were pitched in three repeating sequences of progressively increasing interval. Thus a common corebox could be used for impeller and runner, whilst only a few vanes in each member intercepted simultaneously and rotational balance was not impaired. Fig. 4.8 shows such a vane arrangement in four repeating sequences as applied to fabricated members, where the expensive production machinery makes it equally desirable to have identical impeller and runner.

Furthermore, the increased number of vanes made it necessary to cut back two out of every three vanes in the region of the inner profile diameter, to avoid choking the vortex flow. Hence taking a 12¾-in (324-mm) diameter profile coupling as example, runner and impeller are provided with 45 vanes, 15 long and 30 short.

Subsequently, the fluid flywheel was redesigned to its present-day form, employing a multi-vane coreless circuit baffle but no appreciable reservoir volume.

AMERICAN AUTOMOBILE DEVELOPMENTS

After exhaustive tests, the Chrysler Corporation introduced fluid couplings on their 1938 Custom Imperial. These 14-in (356-mm) units were fabricated from

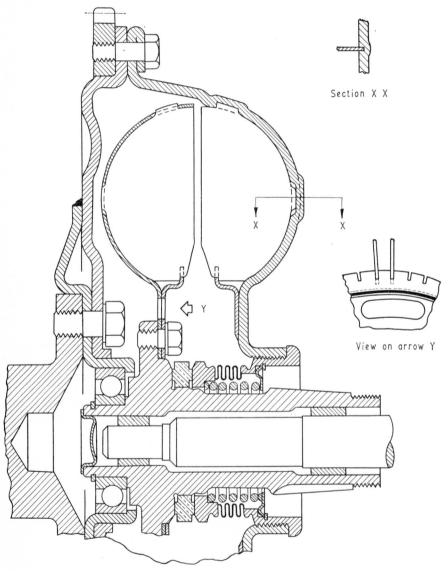

Section X X

View on arrow Y

Fig. 4.7. Section of mass-production type coupling

Fig. 4.8. Photograph of Hydramatic coupling elements

cold-rolled steel sheet, the casings and shells being pressings, and the 22 impeller vanes and 24 runner vanes stamped each with three tabs, by which they were spot welded to the toroidal shells.

The success of this initial venture led to the general adoption of multi-vane baffle coreless couplings by the Chrysler and General Motors groups. Improved mass production methods of fabrication were evolved, one example being illustrated in Fig. 4.7. Lugs on the vanes engage in slots in the shells, and a central slotted crown member, formed initially so that when welded in place it bears on the notched vane ends, applies spring pressure, and pushes the lugs against the ends of the slots.

This annular member therefore holds the vanes tightly in place, locates their inner ends, and can also constitute the baffle plate.

The spring-loaded gland incorporates a carbon and graphite ring floating between hardened steel faces. The bellows connection allows the gland to absorb small relative axial movements and manufacturing tolerances.

A further example of mass-production technology is the fluid coupling developed by General Motors for their Hydramatic transmission as shown in Fig. 4.8.

The impeller and runner are identical, the circuit having a large core ring and no baffle. The characteristics will be very similar to those illustrated in Fig. 4.4 for a completely full coupling, since the working circuit is fed by an external pump and is therefore maintained full at all times. The illustrations show clearly the method of construction in which the individual vanes are held in place by a system of slits and channels in the core ring and casing and tabs on the vanes. At the centre the vanes are retained by a riveted annular plate in a very similar manner to that illustrated in Fig. 4.7.

Engine torque is transmitted through the enclosing casing to a torque splitting epicyclic train, one member of which drives the impeller. It is therefore advantageous to have a working circuit with a progressively rising characteristic to achieve good load sharing, whilst the coupling slip in the working range will be acceptably low, since only a fraction of the total power is then crossing the fluid circuit.

In a method recently proposed for manufacturing fabricated elements, each stamped out blade has protuberances on its periphery, whilst the toroidal shells are simple pressings. The vanes are assembled within the shell and resistance welded under pressure. The protuberances then fuse into the shell, and the vanes sit snugly against its inner surface.

STEPPED RESERVOIR WORKING CIRCUIT

Although the Spicer Manufacturing Corporation had initiated the developments using an asymmetrical circuit, later research by J. M. Voith produced an improved construction, wherein the impeller was provided with a rim at its inner profile, to form a container within the impeller as shown in Fig. 4.9. Under working slip conditions the vortex flows between impeller and runner in the outer radial zones of the stepped circuit, the step having no effect. When, however, the runner is under near-stalled conditions, as when idling in gear or starting, the absence of runner counter centrifugal head allows the fluid to be driven into the reservoir chamber. The effective mass of liquid in circulation is thereby reduced and

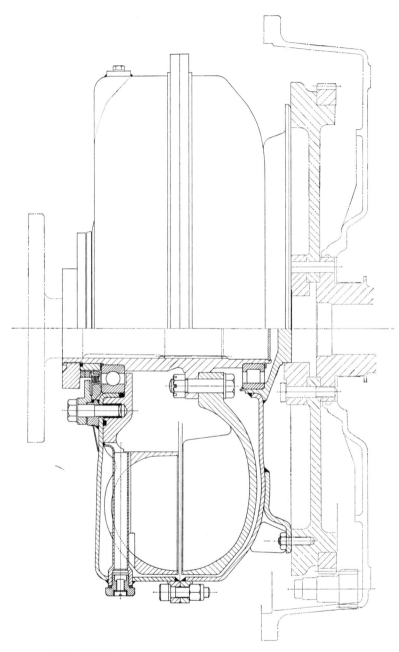

Fig. 4.9. Section of stepped reservoir working circuit coupling

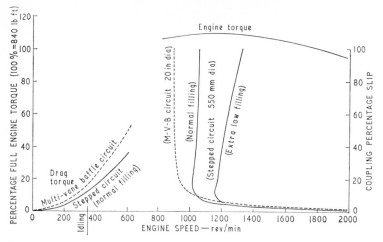

Fig. 4.10. Comparison of multi-vane baffle and stepped circuit coupling characteristics

results in a diminished stalled drag torque. With increasing engine speed, and consequent acceleration of the runner shaft, the oil is returned from the reservoir under centrifugal force to complete the filling of the working circuit. A wide range of stalled K values of low order are thereby obtained, in conjunction with good working slips.

For this construction, aluminium alloy circuit elements are employed within a fabricated steel casing, with an improved design of shaft gland. A floating ring of sintered graphite bronze runs between hardened steel faces, one on the shaft nut and the other on a ring carried by a spring-loaded steel diaphragm.

Fig. 4.10 illustrates the difference in characteristics between a 20-in (508-mm) multi-vane baffle circuit coupling and a 21·65-in (550-mm) stepped circuit coupling as applied to a diesel engine. The latter is some 10 per cent larger in diameter, but of the same overall length, yet both the drag torque and working slip figures are substantially reduced.

This circuit, therefore, not only gives minimum idling drag, but also extends the range of powers for which fluid couplings having no external oil circulation and cooling equipment can be used. The low values of stalled K attainable permit a large coupling, which gives increased self-dissipation capacity and reduced working slip.

Also presented in Fig. 4.10 is the performance with a very low circuit filling. This aspect of the stepped circuit is particularly valuable with the introduction of highly supercharged diesel engines having a comparatively narrow working range. These engines were initially developed to run at a constant maximum speed, or for operation with torque converters, but it is frequently desired to combine them with transmissions having fluid couplings and multi-ratio gearboxes. The stepped circuit characteristic can allow a sufficiently high full-torque stalling speed, and at the same time return a good working slip value.

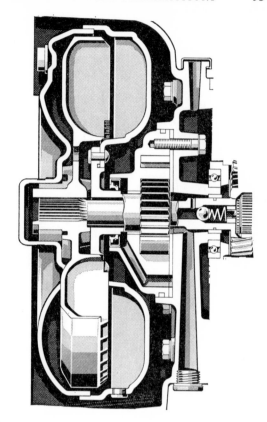

Fig. 4.11. Section of Daimler-Benz coupling

DAIMLER-BENZ FLUID COUPLING

Fig. 4.11 shows a cross-section of this design, which is maintained completely full in operation by an external pump and, furthermore, the coupling fluid is circulated through a heat exchanger formed integrally with the normal coolant radiator.

The available space was extremely limited in axial and radial directions, and a special circuit was evolved, having no baffle, the toroid being of cylindrical section at the outer profile, and essentially circular at the inner profile. This is claimed to have a reduced slip over the working range for the same full torque stalling speed as compared with a circuit of conventional profile.

PROTOTYPE FLUID COUPLING FOR AUTOMATIC TRANSMISSION

Nominally rated at 200 lb ft (27·6 kg m) torque, the unit was to be self-contained, and of a design that would allow ready modification to accommodate mass-production requirements. Maximum input speed was about 5000 rev/min and a full torque stalling speed of 1500 rev/min was specified. A range of adjustment on this figure was needed, since with a 'fast idling' speed of 600 rev/min, this would mean a drag of 16 per cent full torque with the vehicle stationary and gear engaged, and thus some modification might be required during road trials.

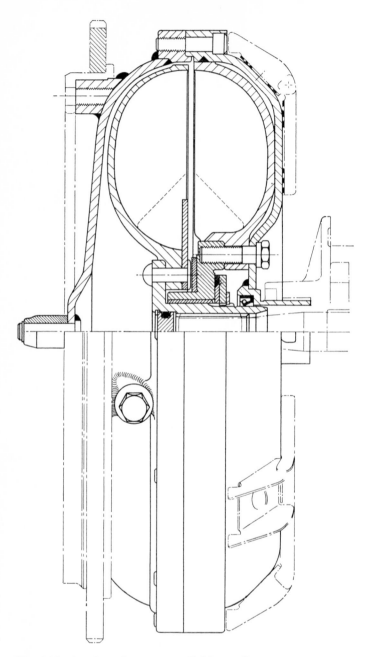

Fig. 4.12. Section of prototype fluid coupling

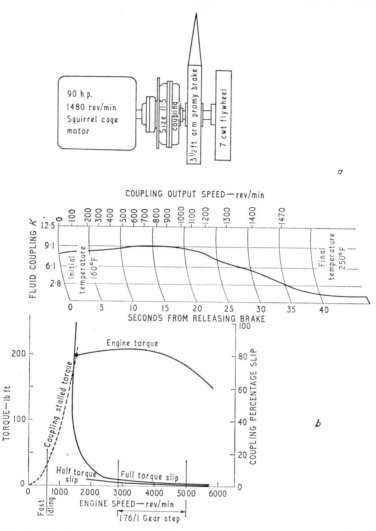

Fig. 4.13. Testbed arrangement and characteristics of prototype coupling

With the very tight time scale involved, an existing circuit type had to be used, and with the very stringent limits on axial and radial dimensions, the multivane baffle circuit was chosen, with a very small reservoir. Fig. 4.12 depicts the coupling section, for which aluminium alloy elements were utilized in a fabricated 7 s.w.g., 0·176-in (4·47-mm) steel casing. In view of the high rating of the unit, provision was made for inclusion of cooling blades at a later stage if found necessary during vehicle trials, and suitable air ducts were incorporated in the stationary housing. Whilst such blades, in conjunction with properly designed ducting, may be expected to raise the heat dissipation by some 30 per cent, they represent a source of noise and power wastage and are to be avoided if possible.

Although a thin mineral oil especially intended for hydraulic systems is normally employed, the initial tests were carried out using 10W/40 engine oil since, if found suitable, use of this universally obtainable fluid could be an important commercial advantage.

The first tests determined the baffle diameter required, with a filling of 120 fl. oz. (3·4 litres) of engine oil, to obtain a stalled torque of 200 lb ft (27·6 kg m) at 1500 rev/min. An identical result was achieved with 110 fl. oz. (3·12 litres) of hydraulic system oil. The coupling was then set up on an inertia acceleration rig as illustrated in Fig. 4.13. With the output shaft held stationary by the brake, the motor was switched on, thereafter the brake tripped and the fluid coupling accelerated the flywheel and brake from rest to full speed in about 30 seconds. A recording 3-phase unbalanced load wattmeter in the motor leads traced the coupling characteristic during the acceleration cycle. Subsequently, using the brake, a chart kW/motor brake horsepower calibration was obtained, and from this the coupling K determined. The output speed was recorded at 100 rev/min increments up to full speed and thus the accelerating transient K/slip curve could be derived. One such trace is illustrated in Fig. 4.13. Finally, with the flywheel removed, a series of slip readings over the working range were taken, with progressively increasing brake load. For these readings the actual slip revolutions over a 10-second period were measured, from which the percentage slip was accurately determined. The foregoing procedure was then repeated for a range of fillings.

Fig. 4.13b shows the combination of engine and coupling characteristics. The maximum transmission ratio step was 1·76:1, and the resultant coupling operating range, assuming a normal maximum of 5000 rev/min, is shown.

After evaluating the torque transmitting characteristics the fluid coupling was subjected to an overspeed and oil tightness test at 6500 rev/min. For this test, the coupling was overhung from a slender jackshaft carried in two bearings, to exaggerate any unbalance effect had it been present. During manufacture, the fluid coupling assembly filled with oil had been balanced to within $\frac{1}{4}$ in oz. (180 mm g).

ACKNOWLEDGEMENTS

The author wishes to thank the directors of Fluidrive Engineering Company Limited for permission to publish this paper, and all those who gave valuable assistance and advice in its preparation.

The MS. of this paper was received at the Institution on 19th August 1969 and accepted for publication on 14th October 1969.

Paper 5. Industrial Vehicle Torque Converter Transmissions

D. J. K. STUART
Brockhouse Engineering Ltd, Victoria Works, Hilltop, West Bromwich

The highway vehicle is concerned with transporting persons or freight over substantial distances, usually at as high an average speed as the conditions will permit. The high-performance private car and the door-to-door delivery vehicle represent opposite ends of the scale of the duty cycle. In the latter case, the very cycle itself—stop–start characteristics, the high percentage of standing time resulting in relatively small mileage, and the small penalty of limited maximum speed—represents cumulative factors in respect of which the basic economics of the battery-operated electric vehicle dominates other considerations.

Thus, in order to arrive at design specifications it is essential to consider the duty cycle which, in the case of all types of industrial vehicle, is characterized by the need to execute a high proportion of forward/reverse manoeuvres, long periods of low-speed operation, and the provision of an increasing complexity of powered auxiliary equipment.

INTRODUCTION

Industrial or off-highway vehicles can be broadly grouped into: agricultural tractors; agricultural tractor derivatives—(a) haulage, (b) earth-moving; special-purpose haulage; special-purpose earth-moving vehicles—dozers, graders, tractor shovels, etc.; lift trucks—front end, side loaders, straddle carriers; reach trucks; excavators; and cranes.

As this paper is principally concerned with the traction driveline, and the gearbox or equivalent in particular, cranes and excavators in which the special-duty cycle is normally accomplished when the vehicle is stationary will not be considered in detail. It follows that in circumstances where manoeuvring operations are required for these types of vehicle, the transmission equipment will, in these circumstances, correspond to those of lift trucks or earth-moving vehicles.

AGRICULTURAL TRACTORS

The sales of conventional forms of agricultural tractors have now reached a total value similar to that of medium and heavy commercial vehicles. In mass-production terms the standard versions of agricultural tractor outweigh the standard forms of all but the lightest commercial vehicles. It follows that the more popular range of agricultural tractor is very competitive in price, and manufacture is now dominated by very large companies, including a number of the major automobile makers (Ford, Fiat, British Leyland) and a small number of companies specializing in agricultural and earth-moving machinery (John Deer, Massey Ferguson, etc.)

It is against this background that the capital cost, to the customer, of sophistication must be weighed. Although the farm tractor is now used for an increasingly wide range of duties, constant-speed operation for all aspects of cultivation is still the prevalent activity, with relatively light haulage duty taking up the bulk of other use.

Not merely to maintain a high 'cruising' speed (using aircraft parlance), but because a number of the more specialized implements, especially those which are power driven, have a relatively narrow band of effective operational speed, it is desirable to maintain a constant-speed condition both for engine and vehicle. Under these circumstances, control by engine governor, with an adequate reserve of power, is most effective, and neither the torque-boosting characteristics of the torque converter nor the more sophisticated variable ratio control offered by the hydrostatic achieve the same basic result.

It is indeed significant that the present demand in respect of improved overall performance in agricultural tractors has centred almost entirely on increased power output, largely to give this back-up feature under variable resistance conditions.

It is true that both the torque converter and hydrostatic can be regulated or even bypassed to meet these circumstances, their proper use then being confined to other than traditionally agricultural operations (e.g. loading, haulage, etc.). However, these do not normally represent a sufficient part of the work cycle to justify a significant increase in vehicle cost.

From the point of view of vehicle geometry, some forms of hydrostatic could offer a distinct advantage, as the mechanical driveline as such could be eliminated. In practice, it is difficult to see how this advantage can be realized, as the conventional driveline arrangement engine–gearbox–axle also serves as the vehicle structure, and therefore represents a highly economic use of material that could not readily be met by a separate driveline.

AGRICULTURAL TRACTOR DERIVATIVES

Whereas, particularly in the higher horsepower range, there is a tendency towards increasingly specialized design for particular functions (e.g. shovel loaders), converted forms of the agricultural tractor are meeting the growing market for low-cost, off-road haulage and multi-purpose earth-moving vehicles. In either field, the main virtues of the tractor as a base are its low cost, resulting from the large scale of production, and the potential use of the driveline as the backbone of the vehicle structure. The conventional tractor gearbox has, however, some serious limitations, and these must be considered in relation to the two main types of application.

(a) Haulage

Converted tractors are used in many off-road haulage applications (sugar cane, forestry, etc.), and in most of these cases the conventional friction clutch requires skilful operation and necessitates considerable slippage to achieve satisfactory take-up from rest.

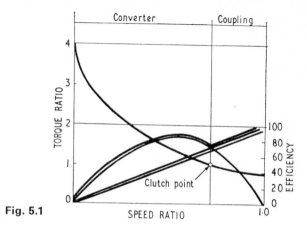

Fig. 5.1

Whereas the simple fluid coupling could overcome these drawbacks, the hydro-kinetic torque converter offers further advantage in providing a substantial build-up of torque with reducing speed (Fig. 5.1). This feature can be of considerable importance as, in cross-country work, the friction drag of the load can be high and will slow the tractor down very quickly during gear changes. It is customary to select a suitable gear ratio and to avoid shifting on the move. With a torque converter correctly matched to the engine, it is possible to select a substantially closer ratio, thereby enabling a much higher average speed to be achieved.

Although the torque converter replaces the function of a conventional clutch in taking up the drive, it is not readily disengaged to permit selection of gears, even forward and reverse in a conventional change-speed box. To overcome this problem a separate clutch is required, and this adds considerable cost to the simple torque converter installation.

In many cases where considerable manoeuvring is required and must be coupled with speed and smoothness of operation, a power shift forward/reversing unit is combined with the torque converter. The gearing as such is equivalent to the conventional forward/reverse gearing, and the extra cost of two hydraulic clutches (often wet multi-plate) is reduced by the elimination of a conventional clutch, as with the power shift arrangement it is easy to provide a neutral condition thereby permitting use of a range-change box. The suitability of this arrangement, i.e. torque converter, power shift forward/reverse package, is clearly dependent on the ability to design this into the conventional transmission structure. In most tractors, the length of the gearbox proper is determined by considerations of wheelbase, and there is length to spare to include a torque converter and power shift package. However, a good deal of ingenuity of design is necessary to fit this in without requiring major modification to the gearbox casing (Fig. 5.2).

On higher powered tractors there is sometimes need for power shift two, three, or four speed, but these types of transmission will be considered more fully in relation to special-purpose vehicles.

Fig. 5.2

(b) Earth-moving

Most significant of these vehicles is the backhoe/front loader combination, the familiar yellow-painted maid of all work seen in action on building sites and minor civil engineering works all over the world (Fig. 5.3). It is the operation of the shovel that performs the dual functions of dozer and shovel loader which makes the major demands on transmission. This contraption, rather like the schoolboy's penknife/screwdriver/bottle-opener device, can be criticized as representing a compromise in each role, but it is so adequate and adaptable that it has become the work-horse of building contractors and the backbone of the plant hirer's stable. It is alongside this concept that the torque converting–reversing unit sandwich package has acquired new recognition and, indeed, the new name of a 'shuttle' unit.

Driving hard into earth with the bucket lowered is normal practice, and since the vehicle is invariably brought to rest, this type of power stall gives rise to a

Fig. 5.3

Fig. 5.4

high mortality rate of conventional friction clutches. The torque converter, with its rising torque curve, is ideal for this application and has, not surprisingly, become an increasingly common feature.

SPECIAL-PURPOSE TOWING AND HAULAGE VEHICLES

The general requirements are similar to those relating to tractor-based haulage units. However, this category includes some low-speed applications on highway-type surfaces (e.g. aircraft-towing tractors (Fig. 5.4), small diesel locomotives) where there are particular conditions to be met in starting from rest. In the aircraft-towing situation, very high inertia load is coupled with the need for complete freedom from snatch in take-up, which feature is well provided by the torque converter. In this context it is worth while noting that increasing use is now being made in Europe of torque converters in normal highway trucks.

In specially designed towing vehicles, mass-produced engine/transmission/axle units cannot readily be incorporated, and it is much more common for the torque converter to be integrated with a power-shift forward/reverse unit, often including a reduction gear train (Fig. 5.5). At higher powers, and where a high, light load, transit speed is required, a range-change box is also incorporated.

The approach to the special-purpose cross-country haulage vehicle is similar, but for these purposes the range change is more likely to take the form of a power-shifted box in order to avoid loss of speed during shifts (Figs 5.6 and 5.7). These units often include a drop-box feature with double take-off to facilitate four-wheel drive arrangements (Fig. 5.8).

SPECIAL-PURPOSE EARTH-MOVING VEHICLES

Included in this category are the larger types of tracked and wheeled shovel loaders. There are many geometrical configurations, but the transmission

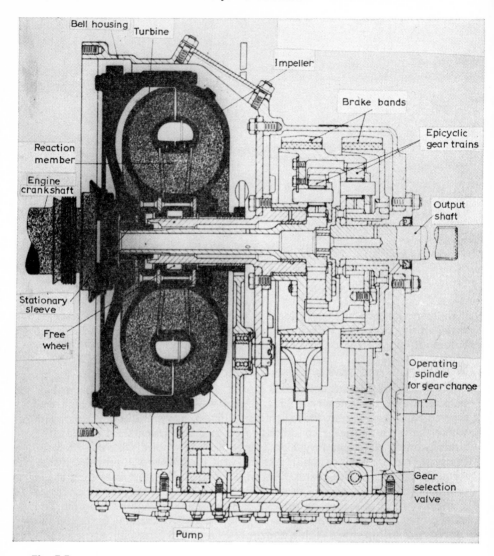

Fig. 5.5

requirements are characterized by high-vehicle stall torque, good forward/reverse
manoeuvrability, and, in many cases, four-wheel drive. Torque converter transmissions with power shift of up to 4 ratio are now virtually standard on the larger
shovel loaders (upwards of 150 hp) and are rapidly gaining ground in the smaller
sizes.

The driveline layout itself can present considerable problems, e.g. in the case of
pivot steer or tracked vehicles, and a form of fully hydraulic driveline has attrac-
tions. Other than in very simple forms (e.g. fixed displacement units), however,

Fig. 5.6

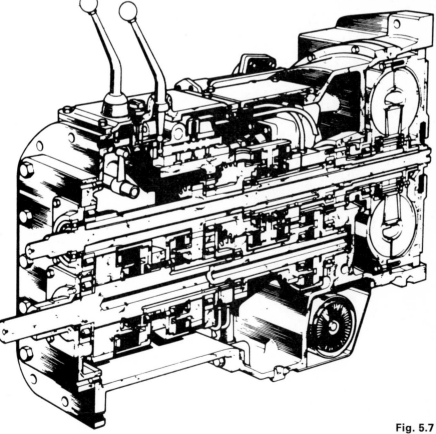

Fig. 5.7

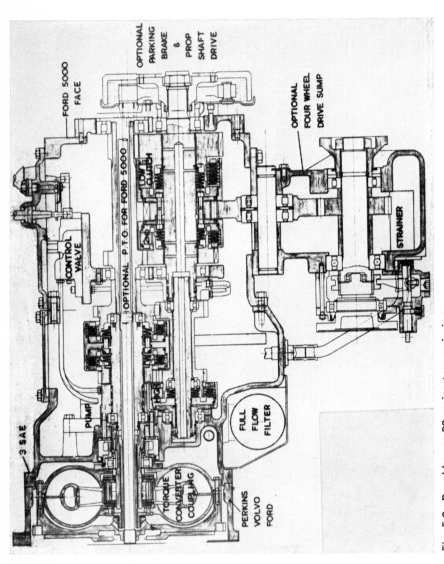

Fig. 5.8. Brockhouse 33 series transmission

Fig. 5.9. Brockhouse F.L.T. transmission fitted to conveyancer fork-lift truck

the cost of hydrostatic pumps and motors rises very sharply with size (power) and cannot seriously compete with the equivalent torque converter unit.

MECHANICAL-HANDLING VEHICLES

The fork-lift truck (Figs 5.9 and 5.10) has long been with us, but the continuing revolution in handling methods and the rapid rise of containerization can only stimulate the further extension of its use and the elaboration of its form (side loaders (Fig. 5.11), straddle carriers, etc.).

In each of these cases, excellent manoeuvrability is the 'keyword' and can virtually dictate the economics of a particular choice. The electric truck with the latest forms of control has substantial horsepower hour capacity and will increasingly dominate the lighter load, short-haul application, particularly in confined areas. However, the need for increased payload and longer hauls is creating new emphasis on the larger truck with increased performance, and this ensures the future of i.c.-engined versions.

Fig. 5.10

Fig. 5.11

The torque converter is eminently suitable for the continual stop–start condition and is steadily replacing dry-plate clutches and even the oil-immersed types which have been used on some trucks to alleviate the heat problems associated with prolonged slipping. In virtually all types of lift truck it is essential to design the driveline layout to suit the counterbalance requirements and to maintain traction on the loaded wheels (adjacent to the forks). In order to achieve counterbalance, the engine is often placed above and extending beyond the remote axle, thus necessitating a large drop in transmission line to the drive axle. Torque

Fig. 5.12

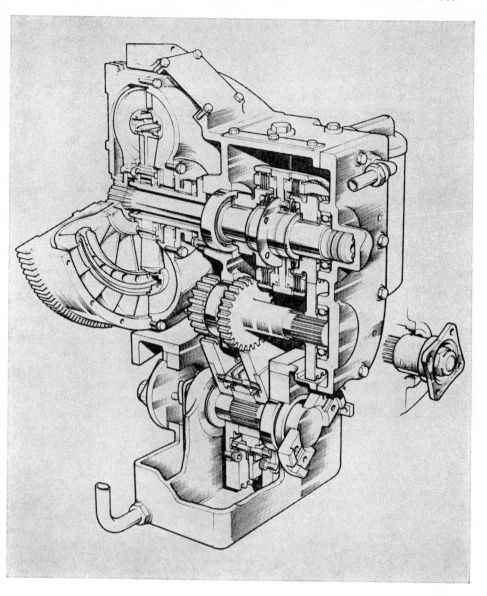

Fig. 5.13

converters have long been used in this application, usually with integral forward/ reverse shuttles, and in many cases the drop-box feature is built in the transmission casing layout. More recently, purpose-built torque converter transmission designs have become available with an axle unit (Fig. 5.12); this concept offering the truck designer a complete driveline package equivalent to the tractor skid.

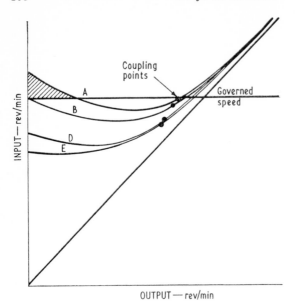

Fig. 5.14. Capacity variation of various converters (constant-input torque)

A two-speed change becomes desirable above a point in the power–weight range, and this normally occurs above about 8000/10 000 lb payload. Trucks are now required to travel appreciable distances between lifts, and a transit range is required to achieve satisfactory vehicle speeds. This can be achieved by a simple form of shift having the disadvantage, however, of requiring the vehicle to be stopped to select the higher range. Power-shifted, multi-speed units are available, but in this application, in which the vehicle is normally travelling on good surfaces with relatively low rolling resistance, it is possible to utilize synchromesh change (Fig. 5.13), thus achieving a relatively low-cost form of multi-speed unit. A particular characteristic of the lift truck is the necessity to subdivide, in varying proportions, the engine power between traction and auxiliaries (mainly the lift mechanism). Particularly, it is common to require very accurate control of forward or reverse movement (inching) whilst applying maximum power to the lift mechanism. Inching can readily be achieved with a torque converter by setting off control of the engine throttle against the brake; but this has the disadvantage of absorbing substantial engine power. Otherwise, there has been a good deal of rethinking in respect of torque converter matching to raise the engine speed at stall and to permit relatively high engine revolutions without full power absorption in the converter, thus making power available for auxiliaries (Figs 5.14 and 5.15).

Another, even more effective solution is the use of inching controls regulating the oil pressure on the drive clutches to permit controlled slipping (Fig. 5.16).

The hydrostatic transmission shows to particular advantage in this respect in that very high overall ratios can be obtained which can produce adequate traction force at very low speeds with minimal absorption of engine torque. This condition

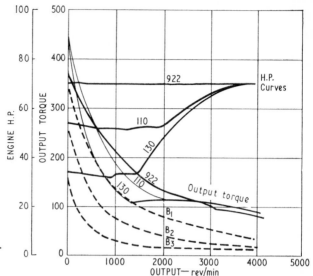

Fig. 5.15. Output torque curves comparing three transmitters on one engine

is achieved without the same danger of local heat generation as occurs with slipping clutches. The practical significance of the more elegant solution offered by the hydrostatic transmission is yet to be established, as this form of drive has only been used on a relatively small scale to date.

TORQUE CONVERTER TYPES AND CHARACTERISTICS

Thus far, the main range of applications for torque converters in industrial vehicles has been examined, and it has been seen that this form of fluid drive is particularly suitable for a number of conditions prevalent in the duty cycles. Unlike the highway vehicle, be it passenger car or freight-carrying truck, there is rarely any steady-speed cruise condition. Indeed, the fuel consumption as such is a much less significant factor than vehicle utilization in determining overall economics.

Even when multi-speed power shift is included in the transmission, it is desirable to utilize the torque converter characteristic to the full to minimize the frequency of ratio shift. Whereas in a road vehicle fully automatic selection (with a degree of overriding control) is possible, this would not be feasible in an industrial vehicle because it is essential to anticipate sudden changes in traction requirement.

Some of these changes, e.g. due to a sudden rise in resistance, may not be detectable visually by the driver. Furthermore, a smooth and instantaneous adjustment which can include a limited reduction of speed must be made. A jerk-free change to a lower ratio is a complicated process even when this is a power shift, particularly if the engine is operating at full torque prior to the down shift. There must be a temporary reduction of transmission torque to release a portion of the engine torque to allow the engine to accelerate. This will be followed by a

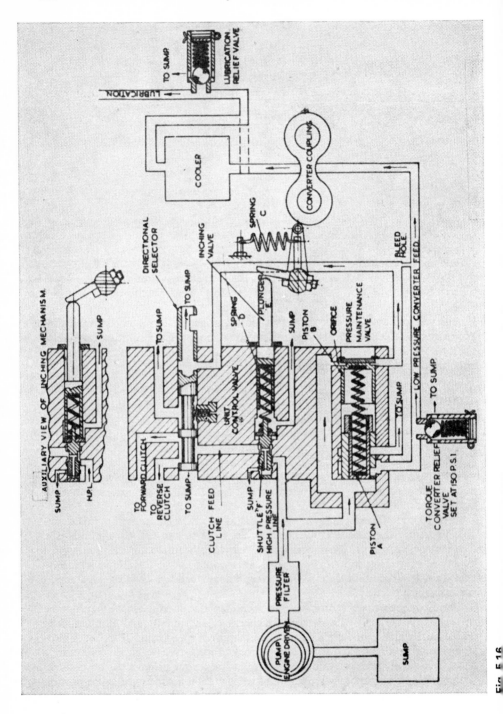

Fig. 5.16

fairly sudden build-up of torque as the engine reaches its speed corresponding to the lower ratio. In the road vehicle this problem is minimized by the use of the vehicle inertia, but this is far less significant in the industrial type of vehicle.

The torque converter with a relatively flat engine-speed characteristic provides a very high and well-matched ratio of response under these conditions. It can be thus appreciated that whereas in passenger vehicle automatic transmissions the torque conversion range must be restricted to starting from rest and accelerating at relatively low speeds for reasons of fuel economy, in many industrial vehicles the torque conversion range must extend over the greater part of the loaded operating-speed range of the vehicle.

It is also desirable to have high engine revolutions available at very low speeds to enable the auxiliary hydraulic pumps to operate near to maximum flow capacity.

It will readily be appreciated that relatively high overall efficiency over a wide output–speed range, coupled with high stall torque ratios, is essential with industrial vehicle torque converters. In this respect, the low cost, mass-produced automobile torque converters using pressed-steel blades and fabricated members are at a disadvantage, as inherent fluid entry losses with sharp leading edges of the blades at varying angles of incidence necessitate limited stall ratios and result in rapid fall-off in efficiency away from the design condition (at a specific torque ratio).

Furthermore, very careful matching of engine and vehicle characteristics is necessary, and many industrial torque converter manufacturers offer alternative blade shapes within the same basic size of converter. The production of the basic converter members invariably involves complicated casting techniques using a large number of sand cores, and manufacturing costs are considerable. Nevertheless, the torque converter itself is a very rugged mechanism, and wear is confined to associated thrust and journal bearings.

One of the more successful torque converter industrial transmissions employs a two-stage arrangement utilizing twin turbines, thereby achieving a stall ratio of 6:1. Coupled with a two-speed power shift this combination is generally accepted as equivalent to a four-speed unit, even though there is inevitably some additional efficiency loss in parts of the range.

The free-wheeling reaction member, which is an essential feature in the automobile application, still offers advantage in many applications, particularly when a high-speed cruising condition is an essential part of the duty cycle. However, there are a number of applications in which it offers little real advantage and is omitted from cost considerations.

COOLING

Some years ago the cooling of industrial vehicle transmissions was regarded as a problem when the advantages of continuous running in the conversion range were realized. It is now appreciated that adequate cooler design and circulation are essential features of the basic installation, and proper co-ordination between engine transmission and vehicle manufacturers at the design and application levels invariably deals with this problem in a radical and comprehensive manner.

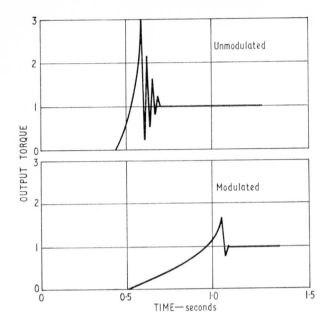

Fig. 5.17. Clutch engagement torque–time

It is not uncommon to utilize the engine radiator as the primary source of heat dissipation with a transmission oil–water heat exchanger as the secondary means of heat exchange. This arrangement can greatly assist in the stabilization of transmission oil temperature.

Virtually all torque converter installations incorporate boost pumps, maintaining pressure in the converter (to avoid cavitation) and creating a relatively high

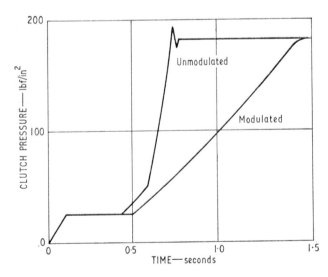

Fig. 5.18

rate of circulation for cooling purposes. These boost pumps, running at 100–250 lb/in², also provide hydraulic power to operate multi-plate clutches or brake-bands (where epicyclic reduction gears are used).

POWER-SHIFT BOXES

These take many forms, as is implied in the description of the various forms of torque converter application. It is sufficient to comment that increasing degrees of refinement and sophistication are developing, with increasing attention being paid to achieving the optimum balance between rate of response and smoothness of operation, particularly in respect of power shifting. Servo valves permitting accurate and sensitive control of clutch engagement to allow inching of the vehicle movement have now reached a high stage of development. In addition, clutch modulation during normal changes is now offered as an optional or standard feature on many units (Figs 5.17 and 5.18).

Great ingenuity is also being exercised in the basic design layout of many torque converter/transmission packages to provide, at a reasonable cost, a wide range of optional engine and output hook-ups. This, despite the fact that until relatively recently the industrial gearbox manufacturer was often expected to bridge an existing and arbitrary gap in the driveline in respect of both geometry and performance.

FUTURE DEVELOPMENTS

The industrial vehicle torque converter has now broken away from its successful and better known relation in the automobile transmission and could well benefit from further basic development. New applications will be found, and the combination with multi-speed boxes will certainly appear in a number of new arrangements.

The long-awaited battle with hydrostatic drive arrangements appears once again imminent in certain applications. In the ultimate, it is probable that each will find its own best field of application and that the two systems will be complementary. Indeed, a combination of both hydrostatic and hydrokinetic appears to have merit in some cases.

Reliability remains the keynote above all other considerations, and the torque converter designer must gain quiet satisfaction from contemplating the subtle swirling of lovely oil between elegant aerofoil shapes, which are spaced more than far enough apart for considerable comfort.

The MS. of this paper was received at the Institution on 28th October 1971 and accepted for publication on 28th October 1971.

Paper 6. Semi-automatic Transmissions Incorporating Hydrokinetic Torque Converters

R. FILDERMAN
Ferodo SA, Paris, France

This paper describes the well-known Ferodo semi-automatic transmission system in which the clutch operation is controlled automatically by the operation of the gear-change lever.

INTRODUCTION

In this paper semi-automatic transmissions incorporating hydrokinetic torque converters are discussed. Although the meaning of hydrokinetic torque converters will be perfectly clear, it is perhaps necessary to clarify what is meant by semi-automatic transmission.

These are transmissions which have a conventional synchromesh gearbox situated behind the torque converter. An additional clutch between these two items disconnects the gearbox input shaft from the converter output shaft, thus permitting synchronization to be achieved. These transmissions have a certain degree of automaticity, which eliminates the hand and foot controls for both the starting process and part of the transmission ratio changing process. It is left to the driver to manually change the mechanical gear ratios, as torque converter characteristics are such that this system of additional torque converting cannot entirely be replaced.

In the past, a certain number of semi-automatic transmissions have been designed, e.g. the Renault Transfluide and the Roverdrive, in which the disconnecting clutch was a reinforced conventional lever clutch. It has since been determined that although the clutch has to transmit a higher torque, owing to the converter torque multiplication, the energy dissipated during engagement is much lower than in a conventional clutch. This is because the converter absorbs all the energy dissipated during starting, and a part of it during gear shifting. Consideration was given to the possibility of designing a clutch which would be better suited to the particular operating conditions and which would occupy much less space, particularly in the axial direction. This is very important, because the torque converter usually occupies at least as much space as a conventional clutch.

Two recent designs have used very different methods to accommodate these particular requirements. Both designs have gained the acceptance of European motor manufacturers and the motoring public. They give promise of an interesting industrial future in spite of, or possibly because of, the gradually increasing acceptance of the fully automatic transmission. One of them will be discussed in more detail; but first, the advantages of semi-automatic transmissions will be considered.

THE ADVANTAGES OF SEMI-AUTOMATIC TRANSMISSIONS

The reason for the increasing acceptance of these transmissions is probably because semi-automatic transmissions give the customer a more satisfactory price ratio than do the fully automatic transmissions. They will therefore be more attractive to the most price-conscious buyers, i.e. those mainly in the small or medium car sections of the market.

Price

Obviously, a semi-automatic transmission will be cheaper than a fully automatic one, since it has fewer components. The hydraulic circuit is very simple, and the mechanical part of the transmission is a conventional gearbox produced at a very low price. This may be confirmed by comparing the price for either semi-automatic or fully automatic transmissions in the price lists of two manufacturers, one German and one French, who are offering both types of transmission on their different car models. In the first case the price is 460 DM for the semi-automatic compared to 795 DM for the fully automatic; in the second case it is 706 F for the semi-automatic compared to 1300 F for the fully automatic.

Driving conditions

Practice will soon demonstrate the improved driving conditions derived from a semi-automatic transmission when compared with a conventional clutch. Not only does the semi-automatic eliminate the operation of the clutch pedal and of one gear ratio, since the current practice is to fit three ratios where four are fitted with a conventional clutch, but the torque converter also allows quite acceptable starting performance. This applies even in intermediate gear and in all cases where the very highest performance of the car is not required. By this means, most city driving can be dealt with in intermediate gear without shifting gears.

This might seem a rather surprising statement. However, it will be better understood if the effect of the engine and flywheel inertias during acceleration are taken into consideration.

In Fig. 6.1 the transmission output torque is plotted against the speed of revolution, i.e. vehicle pulling force against vehicle speed, in steady-state conditions, for a four-speed conventional transmission and a three-speed with converter transmission. It might be concluded that performance on the converter intermediate gear will be rather low compared with the performance on the first with clutch. In Fig. 6.2 the same parameters have been plotted during acceleration, i.e. taking into account the engine and flywheel inertias. These inertias must be multiplied by the square power of the gear ratio to permit comparison with the vehicle inertia when considered from the gearbox output shaft. This means that the fraction of the engine torque which is absorbed by the engine for its own acceleration is very important on the lowest ratios, up to 20 per cent in first. This explains why the curves on Fig. 6.2 are closer to each other than on Fig. 6.1. It could be said that torque multiplication produced by a torque converter is more efficient during acceleration than torque multiplication produced by a mechanical gear ratio.

This is best illustrated by Fig. 6.3 which is a performance chart of a semi-

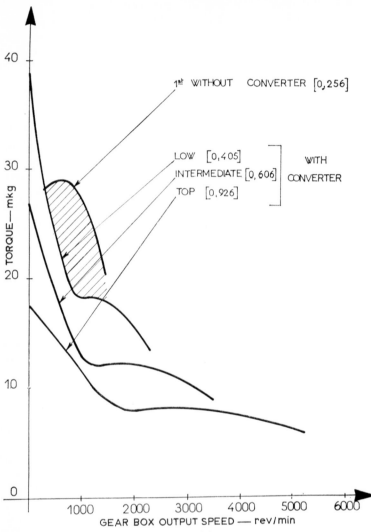

Fig. 6.1. Torque in steady-state condition

automatic transmission; here, distance is plotted against time when starting in each of the three gear ratios. It can be seen that the intermediate gear curve is closer to the low curve than to the top one. This accounts for the satisfactory performance in intermediate gear, mentioned above.

It will be clear that with a semi-automatic transmission, although the driver retains at all times complete control over the gearbox, he can dispense with most of the gear shifting necessary with a conventional transmission, and much more than would at first be thought possible. As is well known, fully automatic

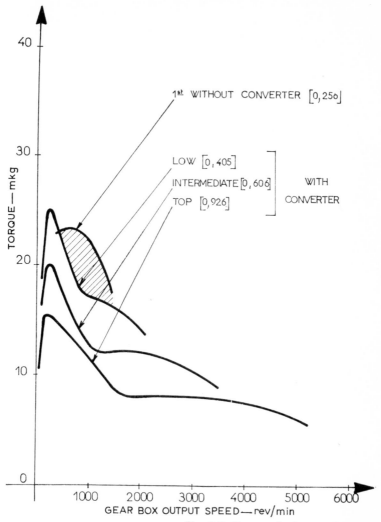

Fig. 6.2. Torque during acceleration

transmissions require occasional gear shifting, according to the prevailing driving conditions.

This can be summarized by stating that, generally speaking, semi-automatics give for a little more than half the price much more than half the satisfaction obtained from fully automatics.

DESCRIPTION OF THE VERTO TRANSMISSION

A particular highly developed semi-automatic design will now be discussed.

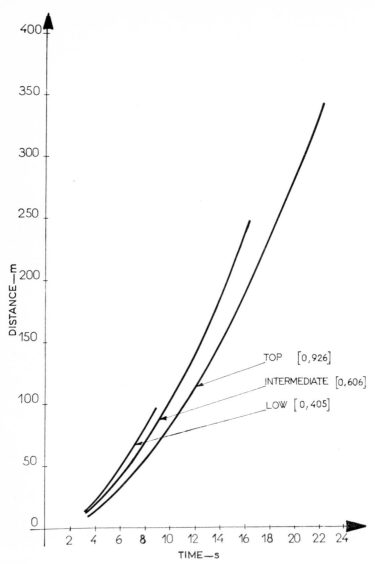

Fig. 6.3. Vehicle performance with converter

General layout

In the Verto design (Fig. 6.4), it was decided to incorporate the disconnecting clutch in the torque converter and operate it hydraulically. The two main reasons were (a) because it was less bulky than a dry clutch, and (b) because it was easier to modulate the clutch engagement characteristics in a simple manner.

The general layout and the hydraulic and electrical circuits of the Verto

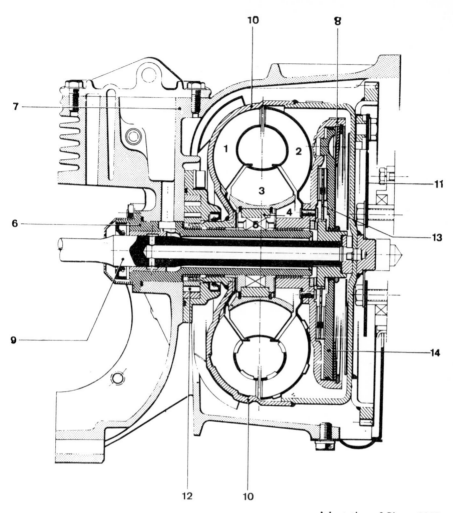

Adaptation of Simca 1000.

Fig. 6.4. Verto transmission

transmission are shown in Fig. 6.5. The converter is of the conventional sheet-metal bi-phased type, with an engine-driven impeller, turbine, free-wheeling stator, and housing. Torque ratio at stall is approximately 2:1. The turbine is riveted to the driving member of an oil-immersed clutch, which will be described in more detail later. The friction plate is splined to the converter output shaft, which is, at the same time, the gearbox input shaft or is connected to it. The whole assembly is a self-contained unit; it is closed by welding the impeller to the housing and cannot be stripped for repair. The gearbox is of the conventional layshaft synchromesh type, manufactured by the car manufacturer.

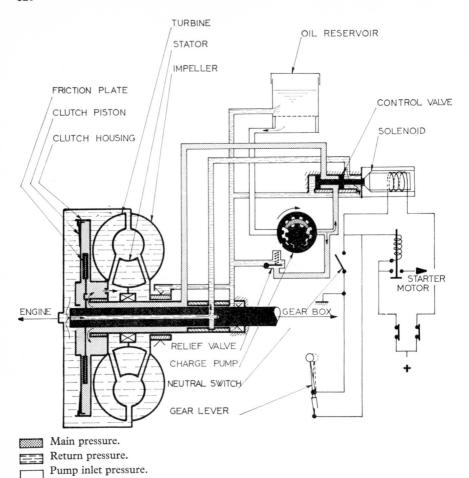

Main pressure.
Return pressure.
Pump inlet pressure.

Fig. 6.5. Hydraulic and electrical circuits (disengaged clutch)

The hydraulic circuit in the main comprises a gear pump driven by the engine through the converter, a relief valve which maintains the operating pressure at a constant level, a solenoid-operated control valve, and an oil sump or reservoir. There are only two passages leading to the converter. The first leads the working fluid between the stator tube and the shaft to the sealed clutch chamber. The other leads through a hole drilled in the shaft to the converter chamber proper. A pre-loaded check valve allows fluid to flow from the converter chamber to the clutch chamber for cooling, but not in the reverse direction. The control valve directs the oil under pressure to either one of these passages, and enables the other to discharge the fluid to the sump, i.e. to reverse the direction of oil flow. Thus it can be seen that in clutch-engaged condition the converter cavity which surrounds the clutch is pressurized, whereas the inside of the clutch is connected to the sump. In the disengaged condition the inside of the clutch is pressurized,

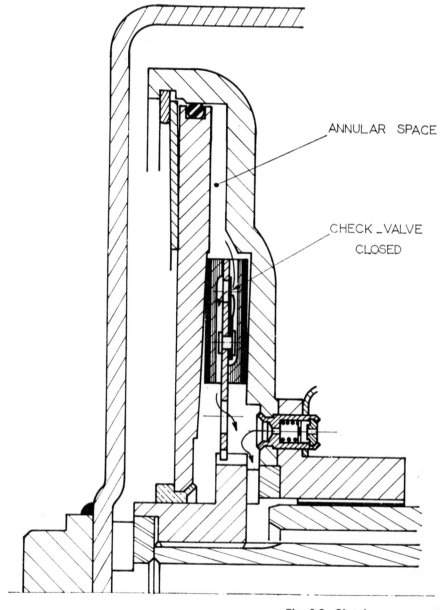

Fig. 6.6. Clutch engagement

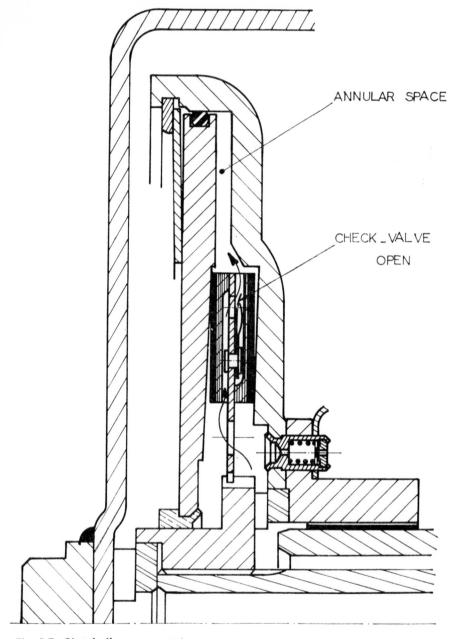

ANNULAR SPACE

CHECK _ VALVE
OPEN

Fig. 6.7. Clutch disengagement

whereas the converter cavity is without pressure. When direct air-cooling of the converter is insufficient, the circuit is completed with a cooling circuit.

The oil circuit is entirely sealed off from the ambient air, except for an open surface in the expansion reservoir. This surface is small, quiet, and relatively cool, which ensures that there is no oil oxidation taking place and therefore no need for frequent oil changes.

The main part of the electrical circuit comprises a solenoid which actuates the control valve, and a switch incorporated in the gear lever. This switch energizes the solenoid whenever the gear lever is grasped by the driver to shift gears, thus disengaging the clutch. An additional 'neutral' switch on the gearbox prevents the starter motor from being actuated when a gear ratio is engaged. It also disengages the clutch when the gearbox is in neutral to facilitate the engagement of a ratio from neutral.

Clutch

The clutch will now be described in more detail (see Figs 6.6 and 6.7). The clutch is a very compact unit, its overall thickness being hardly more than an inch. The two main parts of the driving member are the piston and cylinder of a very flat hydraulic ram which act simultaneously with the clutch pressure plates. This accounts for the extreme compactness of this clutch, there being no other mechanical parts, the hydraulic pressure acting directly on the pressure plates. The clutch is completed by a Belleville washer, the purpose of which is not to help the hydraulic pressure clamping the friction plate but only to counter-

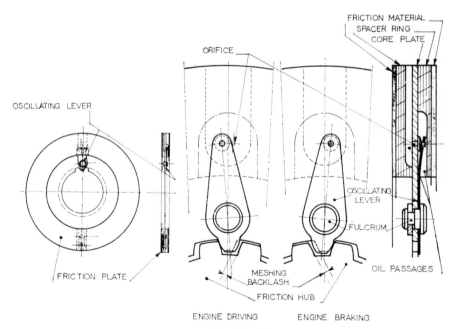

Fig. 6.8. Oscillating lever modulation valve

balance the centrifugal pressure head which builds up inside the clutch when changing down. Without the washer the clutch would have a tendency to remain disengaged when the friction plate velocity was high and the engine velocity low.

The friction plate is constructed from an internally toothed steel core plate driving a hub which is splined on the output shaft. On each side of the core plate there is bonded a moulded asbestos spacer ring on to which, in turn, the actual friction lining is bonded. This lining is of an automatic transmission paper material. The spacer rings house the engagement modulating devices. The principle of operation of these devices is that the engaging faces of the clutch piston and housing are slightly tapered, so that when the friction plate just engages the mating surfaces it seals a certain volume of fluid in the annular space between piston and housing on its outside diameter. Part of this volume must be evacuated to enable the piston to complete its travel. When disengaging the clutch, the same volume of oil must be fed to the same space. The fluid is evacuated through passages which are arranged in the spacer rings and controlled by two different valves.

One is a check-valve which is closed during engagement to confine the oil flow to the annular space (Fig. 6.7). It opens to let the fluid flow rapidly in the reverse

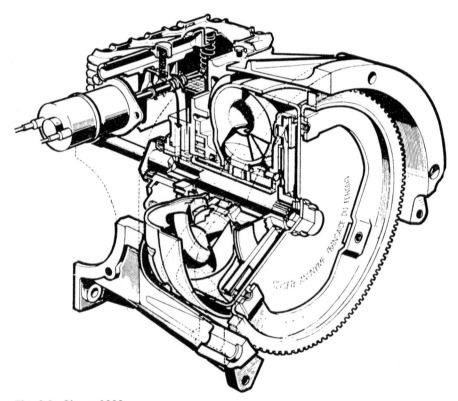

Fig. 6.9. Simca 1000

direction, thus providing for smooth engagement and quick disengagement of the clutch.

The other valve (Fig. 6.8) is a small oscillating lever with a geartooth-shaped extension meshing with the friction plate hub. As the core-plate teeth mesh with the hub—involving a certain amount of backlash—the plate can rotate through a small angle relative to the hub. Thus the valve may slightly oscillate relative to the core plate, according to whether the drive is from the engine through the converter, clutch, and gearbox to the wheels, or from the wheels in the engine-braking condition. When the valve oscillates, it can cover or uncover a hole drilled in the core plate. This hole bypasses the check-valve, so that the engagement characteristic is quicker when the engine drives the vehicle than when it brakes it. It is apparent that by these very simple devices it has been possible to obtain the proper clutch engagement and disengagement characteristics. Owing to the fact that they work only when the friction plate begins engagement with the mating surfaces, this is accomplished without any influence on the piston initial travel time.

It will be noted that the friction plate diameter is very small, being in a typical application 130 mm for a 8 m.daN engine torque. This is because the energy

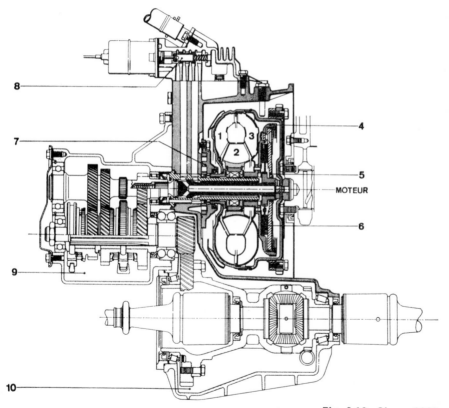

Fig. 6.10. Simca 1100

dissipation during engagement is very small owing to the presence of the torque converter, and that small amount of energy is easily disposed of by oil cooling. Further, it is advisable to have a small friction plate to limit the small viscosity drag to which any oil-immersed clutch is subject.

TWO VERTO ADAPTATIONS

The particulars of the remaining components of the transmission will not be discussed, other than to say that they are designed under current practice requirements for automatic transmissions. Two typical adaptations to production cars will now be considered.

The first one (Fig. 6.9) is a 1000-cm^3 rear-engine trans-axle. The converter is of 8 in diameter. All the auxiliary components—feed pump, filter, relief valve, control valve, and solenoid—are accommodated in the converter housing so that the transmission is a self-contained unit which can be fitted between engine and gearbox. The increase in length relative to the conventional dry clutch is only 30 mm. The only outside components are an additional oil reservoir to accommodate the oil thermal expansion, and the electrical circuit, including the gear-lever switch.

The second adaptation (Fig. 6.10) is a 1100-cm^3 transverse front engine. In this design the gearbox input shaft is co-axial with the crankshaft. This meant that the total length of the engine plus torque converter and housing plus gearbox had to be accommodated between the front wheels. It has therefore been necessary

Fig. 6.11. Transmission final inspection equipment

to design a torque converter which is quite different from the current practice, the torus section being flat and not circular. It has been possible to reduce the converter thickness by 13 mm, or $\frac{1}{2}$ in, which is a considerable amount. The various components are accommodated in the converter housing in much the same manner as in the previous design. The main difference is that, owing to the lack of space, direct converter cooling is insufficient and it has been necessary to provide an additional radiator to cool the transmission oil.

VERTO TRANSMISSION ASSEMBLY

Fig. 6.11 shows the transmission final inspection. All the transmissions are carefully checked for leakage and a 100 per cent test is carried out on a specially designed test-bed. On this test-bed the following values are checked: converter stall speed; clutch engagement and disengagement characteristics, displayed on a cathode tube; clutch drag torque; and working pressures.

CONCLUSION

Other adaptations of the Verto transmission are soon to appear. It is considered that this type of transmission has a promising future as an alternative to the fully automatic transmission, especially in the small and medium car ranges. In this field it offers many of the amenities of the fully automatic transmission at a lower price, in less space and with improved efficiency.

APPENDIX 6.1

Main operating characteristics of a typical adaptation of the Verto transmission.

Engine

Front transverse 1100-cm^3 engine.

Max. torque: 8·5 m.daN at 3000 rev/min.

Max. speed: 6500 rev/min.

Vehicle

Weight: 910 kg (empty).

Max. speed: 135 km/h.

Gear ratios:

Low (1st): 0·405.

Intermediate (2nd): 0·606.

Top (3rd): 0·926.

Reverse 0·265.

Axle 0·254.

Converter

Diameter: 216 mm ($8\frac{1}{2}$ in).

Stall speed: 2000 rev/min.

Torque ratio: 1·9.

Max. efficiency: 0·96.

Working pressure:

0·3 N/mm^2 min. at idle.

0·6 N/mm^2 max. at max. speed.

Oil capacity: 4 litres.

Charging pump capacity: 8·6 cm^3/rev.

Transmission fluid: ATF type A, suffix A.

The MS. of this paper was received at the Institution on 6th February 1970 and accepted for publication on 17th February 1970.

Paper 7. Automatic Gearboxes with Variable Drive—Mechanical

P. GROETSCH
Consultant, 6361 Rodheim, Waldstrasse 30, Germany.

This paper briefly mentions methods of obtaining changes of gear ratio between engine and driving wheels and defines 'infinitely variable' drives as 'stepless', indicating that although the number of ratios may be defined as 'infinite' there may be some restrictions in the ratio range of the gearbox. The latest developments of the PIV type of variable chain converter are described in detail with comments on production and cost.

INTRODUCTION

The internal combustion engine is not able to deliver power unless it reaches a minimum speed—the idling speed—necessary for proper breathing. This feature requires means for gradually connecting the running engine to the stationary vehicle without shock and overload. A clutch is needed capable of allowing speed difference while transmitting a limited torque to prevent the engine from being stalled.

The engine has a poor horsepower–torque–speed relation. The maximum torque with full throttle is reached near the middle of the speed range and drops off towards the high-speed end. The horsepower increases with speed and peaks near the maximum engine speed. Thus, in addition to having a limited speed range, the engine can only supply low horsepower at low rotating speed.

For good performance, high average ground speed, and satisfactory climbability, it is necessary to have high horsepower available even at low vehicle speeds. The optimum would be to have constant and maximum horsepower available at all ground speeds.

TRANSMISSIONS

Transmissions commonly allow utilization of full engine output at several ground speeds by changing the ratio between engine and rear wheels. Three or four steps are available which are shifted after disconnecting the engine and rear wheels by means of the clutch. Interruption of the power flow is undesirable because of the power loss involved during declutching, and can even become dangerous with heavy vehicles.

INFINITELY VARIABLE DRIVES

Constant horsepower gives a hyperbola of the output torque when plotted for different speeds. Stepped transmissions approach this curve in one point only for every ratio. Thus, the maximum horsepower is only available in one ground speed for every gear. Only infinitely variable drives would perform as desired and follow the speed–torque curve ideally as shown in curve A, Fig. 7.1. The torque

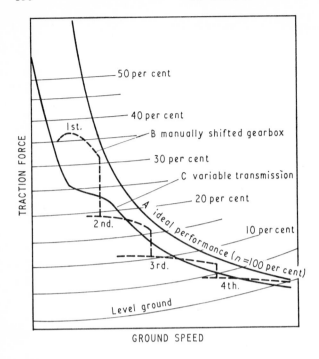

Fig. 7.1. Road performance of a car with variable transmission

on the rear wheels has been calculated for constant horsepower as a function of the ground speed, assuming 100 per cent efficiency. The steps of curve 'B' show the output torque or traction force for a car with a four-speed shift gearbox. The distance between the peaks of the steps and the ideal curve is due to the losses in the power path. Curve 'C' represents the function of a variable drive, in this case the combination of a hydraulic torque converter and a mechanical variable drive. Since the losses of a variable drive are larger than those of a shift gearbox, curve 'C' is lower than the peaks of the shift gear transmission but is parallel to the ideal hyperbola. The deviation at low speeds results from the torque converter.

There are three types of variable drive: hydraulic, electric, and mechanical. A variable drive has the following advantages over the shift gear transmission:

(a) the power flow is not interrupted when the ratio is changed;

(b) ratio change is accomplished smoothly since there are no steps, avoiding jerks which are uncomfortable to passengers and dangerous on slippery roads;

(c) there is no unexpected shifting, as occurs with automatic transmissions; and

(d) the engine speed does not vary unless the accelerator pedal position is altered, therefore a ratio change due to road load has no effect on engine speed.

The hydrodynamic torque converter is an infinitely variable drive which adjusts the torque ratio automatically according to the load. It is used in automobiles together with automatic shift gear transmissions. For use in cars this drive has a ratio range of only 2:1 with an efficiency of zero at the maximum torque conversion point. It is therefore only used as a torque amplifier and a clutch for the initial acceleration of the car.

Variable hydrostatic torque converters are used in special vehicles such as fork lift trucks, self-propelled threshers, and a few types of tractor. The range of torque multiplication is limited to approximately 4:1. This drive, however, gives problems in efficiency, noise, maximum possible input speed, and wear during the life of the drive which reduces efficiency owing to increased blow-by.

Electric variable transmissions, consisting of a generator on the prime mover and electric motors on the drive wheels, have been investigated and installed in large military equipment. They have also been tried in off-highway vehicles, but have been found to be costly, heavy, and not too efficient.

Mechanical variable drives have been used in automobiles from the first days of the combustion engine driven vehicle, but disappeared probably because of the increasing horsepower of the motors. An American patent from 1897 covers a variable V-belt drive, claiming advantages over the 'numerous friction drives of known design'.

Mechanical variable drives are usually friction or traction drives which have uniform output rotation if the input is uniform. There are basically two kinds of friction drives:

(1) Torque is transmitted by friction between one or several rollers running against a flat or curved disc. The rolling radius on that disc is adjustable, giving speeds according to the ratio of the running radii.

(2) A belt is wrapped through the V-groove of pulleys which are axially adjustable. The running radii are altered by axially displacing the conical sheaves, adjusting the speed ratio accordingly.

Both transmission types are possible with radius changes on either the input or the output member only, as well as with radius changes on input and output, thus increasing the total range with given overall dimensions. Roller type transmissions have the advantage that they can be built co-axially. The tangential force that can be transmitted by traction depends on the normal force and the coefficient of friction. The contact area has to be small because the direction of motion of the mated parts does not coincide, resulting in skidding and wear (see Fig. 7.2). The small contact area, on the other hand, limits the size of the normal force because unit pressure is limited as is the torque and horsepower that can be transmitted through one traction contact. Contacts can be multiple by arranging several rollers in parallel. All these contacts have to run with exactly identical ratios or recirculation of power will occur, resulting in possible overload and reduced overall efficiency.

Belt type variable drives use a wide rubber V-belt or a chain, or a chain-like belt, contacting the sheaves in the V-groove on the flanks of the belt or on contacts provided on the chain. The load is transmitted by friction between belt and sheaves. All load-carrying contact spots (a line when using a belt) run at identical ratio radii. 'Ratio fighting' cannot occur, as between the rollers of the roller type transmission, because of differences in the diameters of the parts or inaccuracies of the ratio setting device. The centre-line distance between input and output

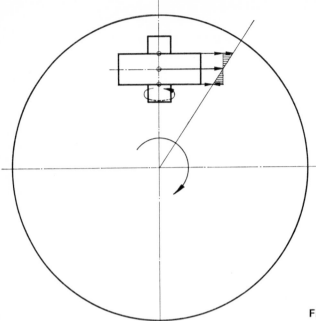

Fig. 7.2. Roller type
variable drive

shaft is sometimes a disadvantage, and also the fact that the ratio can only be changed as long as the transmission is rotating.

A car with a successful belt type drive has been on the market for over 10 years. The DAF car has two variable rubber V-belt drives installed in parallel arrangement. A reasonable life of the belts is achieved since each has to transmit only one-half of the engine horsepower. Belt replacement costs are low enough to allow an exchange several times during the life of the car.

Other variable mechanical transmissions are the Baier disc drive in Germany or the torus drive in the U.S.A.

THE VARIABLE CHAIN CONVERTER

Variable chain converters, which are an all-steel drive, have been developed and manufactured by P.I.V. Antrieb Werner Reimers KG and Reimers-Getriebe KG, Bad Homburg, Germany. A friction transmission with hardened steel running against hardened steel allows for loads that are much higher than those from drives using organic material on the contacts. The high permissible contact pressure between steel parts and oil cooling offset the disadvantage of a coefficient of friction as low as 6 per cent. Based on experience with industrial drives, P.I.V. developed chain converters for use in automotive vehicles where the transmission has to be compact and allow high rotational speeds and horsepower coupled with durability.

The chain converter consists of two pairs of conical sheaves located on shafts (Fig. 7.3). The sheaves of each pair are connected by splines allowing axial

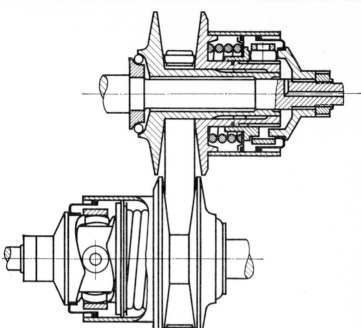

Fig. 7.3. Variable chain drive

movement while transmitting torque. A 'steel belt', a chain with links as short as possible, is wrapped through the V-grooves contacting the sheave surfaces on its sides. The contacts are on the ends of the chain pins, which are case hardened to allow the high contact pressure (Hertz) of more than 100 kp/mm² (140 000 lb/in²) (see Fig. 7.4). The chain is assembled from simple parts of stamped sheet steel

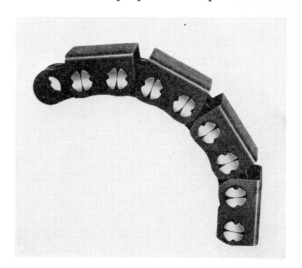

Fig. 7.4. Chain of variable drive

for economy. The pins carry the squeeze load and connect the links. Two pins per joint are designed for rolling motion to reduce wear and losses. Using these pins, tests show an improvement of efficiency of 1–4 per cent over cylindrical pins, the 4 per cent improvement occurring at high chain speed in overdrive position of the transmission.

The axial thrust which provides the normal force or contact pressure between chain and sheaves has to be high enough to transmit the chain pull by friction. The chain pull F_c depends on torque T and effective radius:

$$F_c = T/r$$

A circular cam arranged in the output sheave assembly provides the axial load necessary in proportion to the torque. The cam is designed with varying angle to bring the squeeze force necessary for each ratio because the chain pull to be transmitted to the sheave flanks depends on the radius on which the chain is running.

Proper design of this cam prevents overload of the transmitting contacts by providing only the normal force necessary to transmit the chain pull by friction. This in turn reduces wear, lowers the danger of brinelling, and boosts the efficiency even at partial loads. Theoretically no slip can occur if the cam has the correct angle. A limit is given by plastic deformation of the load-carrying contacts and excessive elastic deformation of the parts.

Another design feature improves the efficiency considerably. Fig. 7.3 shows that the axial load from both V-groove flanks are supported through the shaft. Losses resulting from highly loaded rotating thrust bearings, as they are used in many roller type transmissions, are avoided. Providing only the normal force, avoidance of highly loaded support bearings, use of rocking pins in the chain, plus the fact that no 'ratio fighting' occurs between the load-carrying contacts, results in the high efficiency of the chain converter shown in Fig. 7.5. An efficiency of 96 per cent was achieved with large drives in middle and low ratio settings. The efficiency is lower at high chain speeds but above about one-third of rated torque load the efficiency is 90 per cent or more at all speed settings.

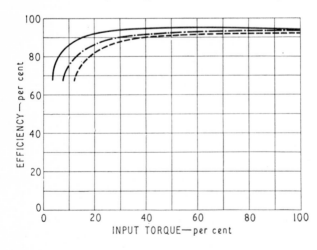

Fig. 7.5. Efficiency of a chain converter

A similar balancing force must be provided in the input sheave assembly. This force tries to squeeze the chain outwards, thus pulling it into the V-groove of the input sheaves, changing the drive to the low output speed position.

A cam provides part of the necessary force, the difference being supplied by hydraulic pressure acting on the sliding sheave. By increasing or lowering the hydraulic pressure the ratio setting of the drive can be altered. With a maximum of 20–30 kg/cm^2 (300–450 lb/in^2) the hydraulic pressure is not excessively high because the cam carries the main share.

The cams of the chain converter for automotive vehicles are designed for one direction of rotation and both directions of torque because torque reversals occur in vehicles. The ratio of the chain converter is controlled with the aid of hydraulic pressure and requires a pump with enough capacity to enable fast ratio changes at low engine and pump speed. An open centre valve, as shown in Fig. 7.6, provides

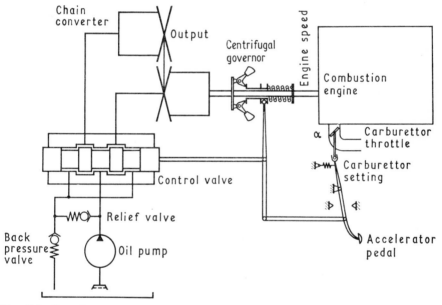

Fig. 7.6. Speed control system connected to the accelerator linkage of a combustion engine

the oil pressure by orificing the flow of hydraulic fluid. Like all hydraulic circuits an intake strainer and relief valves are required. Return oil cools and lubricates the chain converter and is piped wherever lubrication is needed. Minimum volume and pressure at low engine speed results in excessive flow at high engine speeds, reducing the overall efficiency. This problem is common with the automatic shift transmissions. A by-pass valve can be useful, with the hydraulic system designed for constant flow.

Thin oils are used, suited as hydraulic fluid and lubricant at the same time so they can be pumped at low ambient temperatures. They should have the anti-foam features common to hydraulic fluids and should be usable for lubrication of highly stressed gears. Exotic 'high traction' fluids are available or are in development which increase the coefficient of friction considerably. Mineral oils are less costly and more available. Artificial fluids bring problems with corrosion, wear, stability, and non-compatibility with seals.

Ratio control of the chain converter is easily achieved. One end of the lever that moves the valve spool is connected to the sliding sheave of one sheave assembly, the other end is operated by hand. A desired position of the sliding sheave can be selected; the valve spool feeds oil pressure into one of the cylinders of the sheave assemblies until the desired sheave position is reached. The sheave position and ratio will be stable until the free end of the ratio control lever is moved to another position. This simple type of ratio control was used for the first tests of a chain converter in a car in 1955, and later for agricultural tractors and other vehicles.

For cars the control system has to be fully automatic. Fig. 7.6 shows a simple automatic control system for a variable drive. A centrifugal governor relates the engine speed to the position of the accelerator pedal. This speed is maintained by the variable drive which changes to lower output speeds when the road load increases, and vice versa. The position of the accelerator pedal is equivalent to engine horsepower. The relation between carburettor setting and speed can be selected in design to achieve either maximum acceleration or optimum fuel economy (see Fig. 7.7). If the pedal is pushed to the floor, asking for maximum engine speed and horsepower, the chain converter changes to a low position as an automatic transmission shifts back at 'kick down'. The engine speeds up to the required level and the car accelerates with full horsepower. Taking the foot off the pedal causes the transmission to go to the overdrive position. Using the speed range of the engine and the ratio range of the chain converter, car speeds can be controlled with the accelerator pedal only, without any shifting of steps and without interrupting the power flow.

An additional lever can be provided or coupled to the shift lever which enables

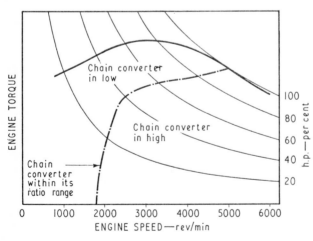

Fig. 7.7. Butterfly angle engine speed relation of an automatic control system with variable drive

the driver to select high engine speed without opening the carburettor throat; the engine is now working as a brake with *adjustable* braking action. The maximum engine speed is limited by the speed governor and it is not possible to overspeed and damage the engine. This feature is important in trucks and buses for downhill braking. The operator can shift the drive without interrupting the power flow, and the effect of the exhaust brake can be controlled and increased considerably.

This is only an example of a simple control system. Other systems can use mechanical, hydraulic, electrical, or pneumatic means. The engine speed could be maintained constant by a speed governor operating the throttle (as with tractor engines), and another speed governor on the drive shaft or output sheave assembly measures the ground speed of the vehicle. The desired vehicle speed is selected with the accelerator pedal.

The ratio of a variable belt drive cannot be changed without rotation. The faster the drive the faster are the ratio changes. Above 2500 rev/min input speed the idling chain converter can be cycled through the total speed range in about 0·5 s. Torque load increases the shifting time towards high output speeds and reduces the ratio changing time when changing to lower output speeds. It might be necessary to provide means in the control system that make the drive change ratio to the lowest position fast to ensure that low is selected for the next take off. This device could be triggered by an inertia valve at a high rate of deceleration and/or by low speeds.

Any shift gearbox with a straight through top gear runs quietly in that speed. Drive packs, as installed in cars with front engine and front wheel drive, always have the power going through at least one set of gears. These gears have to be of high quality. A chain drive makes noise from the radially loaded bearings and from the chain pins contacting the friction sheave surface. The volume of this noise is about equal to that of a gear transmission with ground gears. The frequency is in a lower part of the audible spectrum.

Running a short time without lubrication causes no damage to the chain converter and it can idle even at high speeds, as long as the antifriction bearings hold. Towing will not damage the chain converter, but installation of other components, such as clutches, may forbid it.

The 1955 car was in service until 1961. In 1957 two new cars were fitted with an improved version. One car had a 95 hp engine, the other over 70 hp. The latter car was taken out of service because of an accident after 160 000 km (100 000 miles) on car and transmission. The transmission was in working condition and showed surprisingly little wear. The other car has run 80 000 km (50 000 miles).

A modern chain converter was designed for high input speeds, small size, and low cost and was tested in the laboratory in 1967. The drive ran 1000 h, half of which with 55 hp, the other half with 62 hp and 5500 rev/min on the input. In the lowest output speed setting—equivalent to first gear—the transmission was tested for 10 h or 1 per cent of total test time. In a higher ratio—about the equivalent of second gear—test time was 40 h. A speed in approximately the third gear range was tested for 250 h, or 25 per cent of total test time, with the remainder of the test at high output speed settings. The speed ratio was changed every 24 h, with the test rig running day and night without an operator and protected by an overload shut-off. An electric motor was used as prime mover.

The chain converter was in working condition when the test was discontinued after the objective of 1000 h was achieved. The sheave flanks of the input showed wear on the small running radii, which are the areas that are most heavily loaded because of highest chain pull coinciding with the smallest running radius. Only a few chain links are in contact with the input V-groove. These links have to transmit the high chain pull, making high normal load and high contact stress necessary, which explains the occurrence of greatest wear in that location. It was probably not realistic to run the chain converter with full horsepower and highest engine speed at 'first gear' setting, but 1000 h with full load and other laboratory tests show good prospects for the use of the chain converter in an automotive gearbox.

TRANSMISSION UNITS FOR PASSENGER CARS

A variable drive alone is not yet a gearbox that can be fitted into a car. The chain converter replaces the three or four forward gears and brings other advantages. As with other transmissions, means for reverse rotation have to be provided as well as equipment to connect the stationary car with the running engine.

The simplest arrangement is a dry clutch, a forward–neutral–reverse shifter, and the chain converter. The dry clutch allows shifting of the gears and gets the car rolling. This is no fully automatic system, but might be a low cost compromise. The dry clutch is only needed for shifting when the car is stopped and for the initial acceleration of the vehicle inertia. Once the car is rolling, the speed can be regulated with the accelerator pedal and the clutch is no longer required. A

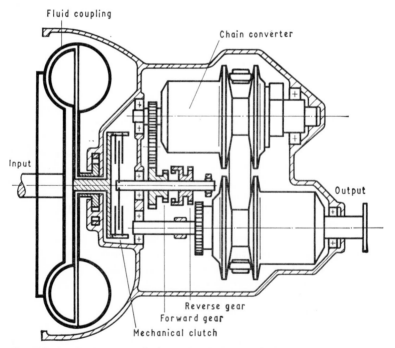

Fig. 7.8. Variable transmission with Reimers chain converter

centrifugal friction clutch would make such an arrangement fully automatic. Such clutches were tried in the late 1950s, but did not work satisfactorily.

Another possibility is the use of a hydrodynamic coupling. This fluid flywheel performs satisfactorily, but it never completely disengages. A small disconnect clutch can be installed to enable shifting of the forward–reverse gears, and a possible arrangement is shown in Fig. 7.8. This auxiliary clutch can be small because it is not used to accelerate the vehicle. It can be vacuum operated and automatically energized by a touch-contact in the shift lever button. Fig. 7.8 shows one of several possible designs for a car with standard driveline.

Another solution would be an arrangement similar to that shown in Fig. 7.9. A planetary gear set is used as reverser transmission. The power-shifted clutch locks sun gear and ring gear together for forward, and a brake band locks the carrier to the housing for reverse. A fluid flywheel completes the gearbox, which is equal in operator comfort to the automatic shift gear transmissions, but is truly infinitely variable. Pressure from the control system of the chain converter is used to operate clutch and brake as well as to lubricate the epicyclic gear train and to fill the hydrodynamic coupling.

Fig. 7.9 shows a hydrodynamic torque converter instead of a fluid clutch. The output torque is about doubled at the low end of the speed range. The ratio range of the chain converter can be cut to, for instance, 1:2·8, getting a maximum torque amplification of 1:5·6 overall. With a fluid coupling the chain converter has to provide a larger ratio range. Fig. 7.1 shows the road performance of an

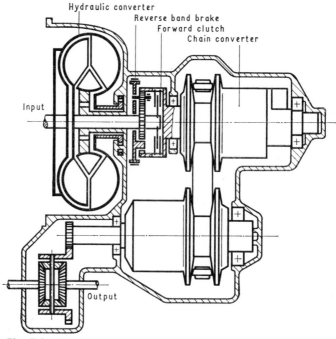

Fig. 7.9. Variable transmission with Reimers chain converter

arrangement of chain converter with fluid torque converter. A maximum torque is achieved which is considerably higher than with the first gear of a standard shift gearbox.

Passenger cars are built either with standard driveline, front engine, gearbox flanged to the engine, universal shaft, differential and final reduction in the rear axle, or with power pack in the front or rear. Fig. 7.8 shows a possible arrangement for cars with standard driveline. The variable belt drive has a natural centre-line distance of at least the sum of the half diameters of input and output pulley plus a small clearance for tolerances and shaft deflection. In the arrangement shown in the figure, the gear set reduces the distance between gearbox input and output. An additional gear set on the output could reduce the centre-line distance to zero. Gears are costly and should be avoided. The centre-line displacement could, of course, also be arranged sideways. It is possible to fit the transmission into standard cars.

Various arrangements are possible, but so far it has never been seriously considered to mount the drive on the differential and it may be worthwhile having a closer look at this possibility.

The offset between input and output of the chain converter, which looks like a disadvantage for cars with standard driveline, can be a real asset for cars with power pack. Cars with front engine and front wheel drive or rear engine and rear wheel drive have a U-shaped power path. The step from crankshaft centre-line to final drive centre-line is usually made with gears, and sometimes with a chain drive. It would be ideal if this chain drive is variable, accommodates the power transmission between the two shafts, and replaces the shift gears. Fig. 7.9 shows a possible arrangement. From a minimum centre-line distance—given by the pulley diameters—the distance between the shafts can be increased by using a longer chain.

COST

It is difficult to make a new part for a passenger car better and cheaper at the same time. For that reason several modern items in the car of today did not establish themselves quickly. It will not be possible to arrive at a reasonable cost calculation of a gearbox with chain converter for a small production. Components of the chain drive are new and unusual to the cost calculators of the automotive industry. Steels are ordinary with normal machining or heat treatment. Most of the machining is turning and grinding. Milling, hobbing, or broaching is used for the splines and cams only. The latter could be precision forged or cold pressed if quantities warrant it. Some parts, such as seals, balls, and snap rings, are shelf items. The chain contains a lot of experience but is reasonably inexpensive. Production on a large scale, using the manufacturing methods well known in the automotive industry, will make it possible to produce the automatic gearbox with the variable chain converter competitive in cost with the automatic shift gearboxes that are on the market today for the market of tomorrow.

This gearbox has the advantage that it is perfectly stepless, shifts without jerks and does not shift unexpectedly. Because of the relatively good efficiency, it is well suited for cars in the lower horsepower range where it is difficult to fit automatic shift gearboxes.

SUMMARY

Gearboxes with a mechanical variable chain converter are competitive in cost with the automatic shift gearbox, but the losses are smaller. The noise is similar to the drive system of a car with power pack. The centre-line offset can cause some difficulty in cars with standard driveline, but is an advantage for cars with power pack. Various arrangements are possible. The controls leave plenty of room to fulfil all kinds of wishes and could be a development engineer's dream.

The MS. of this paper was received at the Institution on 15th October 1969 and accepted for publication on 24th October 1969.

Paper 8. Manual Gearboxes for Trucks

E. RIDDLE

Chief Designer, Scammell Lorries Limited

INTRODUCTION

Taking a broad view of the world's transport, it is apparent that most goods are carried by road on trucks fitted with conventional stepped gearboxes, not far removed from the original Panhard et Levaseur invention. The strong position currently held by stepped transmissions in the truck industry is due less to startling mechanical innovations than it is to the lack of success by the manufacturers of torque converters, epicyclics, and hydrostatic devices to win over the truck operators who tend to regard these products as being complicated, expensive, and often less efficient.

With comparatively modest engineering resources, the manufacturers of stepped transmissions successfully hold a very large share of the market. It is therefore appropriate to take a quick glance at current trends and future possibilities and to wonder if a little more development initiative would not put them in an almost invulnerable position.

The range gearbox in 10 or 15 speed form is gaining ground, partly because of its surprisingly large input torque acceptance in comparison with similar wide ratio types. A 10-speed gearbox can be relied upon to take 50 per cent more torque than the five-speed gearbox from which it would have been developed; this is attributable to the very small ratio demands required of the main assembly. Splitter gearboxes do not share this advantage, and suffer from the great number of power operated shifts that are necessary in a full sequence of gear changes. Range gearboxes require only one automatic shift in a sequence and this is interlocked with neutral in the main gearbox to separate the inertia of the rotating parts from the clutch disc. A future development might be to further interlock the main gear lever, thereby inhibiting re-engagement prior to completion of the automatic shift.

Fuller (Fig. 8.1) have achieved an engineering and commercial success by combining the range idea with a twin layshaft layout, employing epicyclic principles to balance mainshaft loads and virtually eliminate the difficult mainshaft free running bearings. Fig. 8.2 shows a Leyland Thornycroft 10-speed range gearbox of conventional design and Fig. 8.3 shows a twin layshaft arrangement differing from the Fuller principle in that only one layshaft is employed at a time. It is noteworthy that first–second and third–fourth gear trains are identical, which occurs naturally if the difference in speed of the two layshaft primary drives corresponds to the square of the ratio step.

In retrospect, one of the most satisfactory multi-speed gearboxes developed by a firm in the Leyland group during a series of transmission experiments was the eight-speed 'straight' gearbox shown in Fig. 8.4. This avoided the complications of splitting and ranging, yet offered an overall ratio spread of 13:1 without sacrificing the close ratio step feature at the top end, these being uniformly

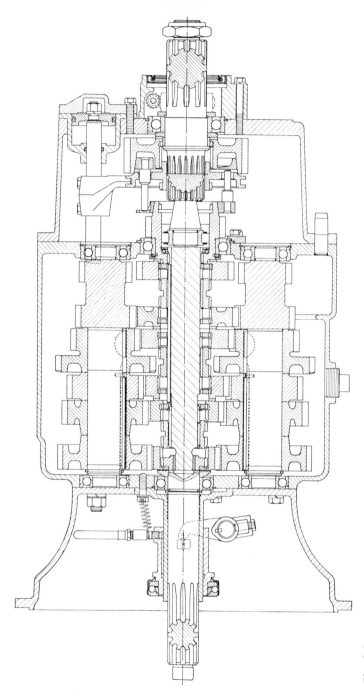

Fig. 8.1

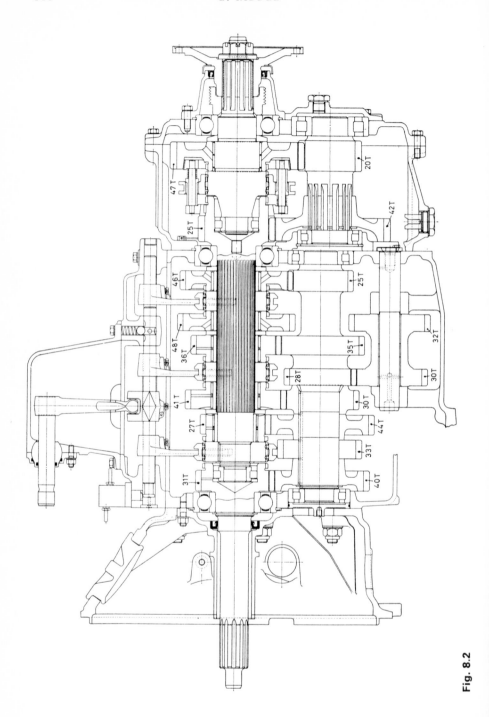

Fig. 8.2

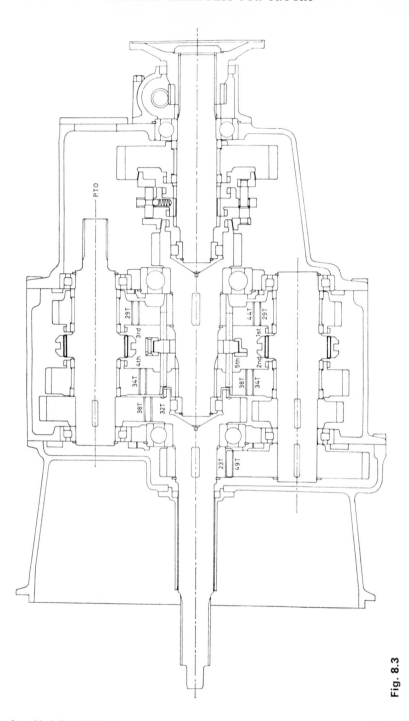

Fig. 8.3

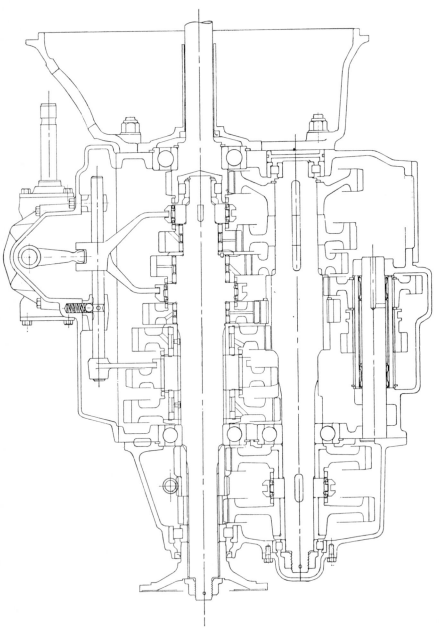

Fig. 8.4

increased in the lower gears on the assumption that close ratios are only justified for the more frequently used ratios. Another look at this philosophy for today's higher powered motorway trucks might possibly be worth while.

Recent advances in electronic control and sensing justifies further attention to the possibilities of adding automaticity to specially designed stepped gearboxes. The combination of a five-speed main gearbox and four-speed range assembly forming a 20-speed close ratio whole, might be a good subject for this. There is nothing daunting about the mechanical aspects of a 20-speed arrangement as it would differ little from the 15-speed types in general use. A set of ratios can be visualized with roughly 15 per cent steps, as follows:

Main gearbox	Range gearbox	Fouth range	Third range	Second range	First range
1·51	0·5	0·76	1·51	3·0	6·1
1·74	1·0	0·87	1·74	3·5	7·0
2·0	2·0	1·0	2·0	4·0	8·0
2·3	4·0	1·15	2·3	4·6	9·2
2·64		1·32	2·64	5·25	10·6

Success of such a project would, of course, depend on the speed at which gears could be power shifted in and out of engagement over the 15 per cent step without special aids other than brief automatic clutch disengagement and similar closing of the accelerator during upchanges—the clutch pedal being retained only for starting. The practicability of this idea could be easily assessed over a narrow range by altering one set of ratios in a standard gearbox to provide a 15 per cent step against one of its neighbours. An alternative type of stepped gearbox for which automaticity might be considered is the five-speed synchromesh based 10-speed range transmission.

Z.F. in Germany are apparently reviving the idea of a torque converter and five-speed synchromesh gearbox separated by an ordinary disc clutch used for gear changing only. This would undoubtedly reduce driver fatigue and also provide good starting characteristics.

Speculation apart, the body of this paper is devoted to a discussion of the more basic aspects of truck gearbox design for the benefit of automotive engineers who are not permanently engaged on transmission work, but occasionally become deeply involved, and for this reason it may not have anything new to say to the specialist gearbox designer.

RATING

The writer has used a variety of formulae for rating purposes during the last 30 years, and has finally come out in favour of 'Lloyd's rating' as a general purpose measure of gear capacity, depending on surface durability only. This formula will be found to give quick and easy comparisons between one design and another without the often inconclusive array of figures resulting from strength and wear calculations for wheels and pinions on both designs.

Justification for omission of strength calculations is based on the well-known principle that tooth strength is proportional to pitch, while wear is independent of it; thus strength is under the control of the designer, and by employing an adequate pitch he is able to ensure that wear is the limiting factor. So far as commercial vehicle gearboxes are concerned, the conventional total tooth numbers per gear train of 50–70 teeth covers this requirement quite easily, provided the gears are shot peened and not subjected to grinding in the tooth fillets. There is no objection to a quick check on strength by means of a formula of the type:

$$S_b = \frac{\text{Load/in} \times \text{d.p.}}{Y_{\text{fac.}}}$$

if limiting figures for the application are known. However, for general rating purposes Lloyd's rating will be found very serviceable. Further support for this view is derived from the fact that wear life varies as the cube of the safety factor, while strength life is more nearly related to the seventh power. It is therefore reasonable to assume that gears of adequate pitch will wear out before they break. When breakages occur, they are usually attributable to end loading, fillet grinding, metallurgical faults, failure to shot peen, or to the use of excessively fine pitches.

Lloyd's rating

Spur gears:

$$S_c = \frac{\text{Load/in}}{d} \times \frac{R+1}{R} \times 6\cdot 22$$

Helical gears:

$$S_c = \frac{\text{Load/in}}{d} \times \frac{R+1}{R} \times 5\cdot 0$$

Straight bevels:

$$S_c = \frac{\text{Load/in}}{d \sec a} \times \frac{R^2+1}{R^2} \times 6\cdot 22$$

Helical bevels:

$$S_c = \frac{\text{Load/in}}{d \sec a} \times \frac{R^2+1}{R^2} \times 5\cdot 0$$

where S_c is the surface stress criterion, d the pitch circle diameter of the pinion (for bevels this is measured at the centre of the effective face width), R the ratio of the pair (always greater than unity), and a the pitch cone angle of the pinion (angle between pitch line and pinion centre-line).

S_c is a stress criterion rather than a stress. Before leaving the subject it is worth pausing for a moment to see what the various factors in the expression for stress actually mean. The first is load/in of face divided by tooth flank radius (or, to be precise, a direct function of it), all gears of the same p.c.d. having the same tooth flank radius regardless of pitch. The second factor can only vary between 1 and 2, and takes into account the radius of the mating tooth flank relative to that of the pinion. Clearly, a pinion in mesh with a rack would be counted by the formula as having a stress corresponding to half that which would apply were it in mesh with another pinion of its own size. The last factor is merely a constant distinguishing helical gears from spur gears. For bevels the formula has to be modified to include the virtual pinion diameter and the virtual ratio.

This simple principle is applicable to single tooth contact conditions on the pitch line, and is supported by experience in so far as pitting usually occurs on the pitch line, which is not surprising in view of the change of sliding direction and consequent precarious lubrication conditions.

Third power relationships

There are three important mathematical relationships connected with rating which are essential to the transmission designer:

(1) *The torque capacities of geometrically similar gear assemblies are proportional to the cube of their leading dimensions.* This statement is true for wear and strength and is applicable to spurs, helicals, bevels, epicyclics, ball and roller bearings and, in a general way, to complete gearboxes. It is very convenient for comparing the torque capacities of differentials, or bevels of a particular ratio, as these assemblies are often naturally geometrically similar.

(2) *A gear subjected to occasional use can be stressed higher than one in permanent use, by the cube root of the inverse of its utilization.* For example, the second gear pinion of a six-speed gearbox might be in use for only one-twenty-seventh of the number of cycles required of the constant mesh pinion over a particular milage. It can therefore be stressed higher by the cube root of the inverse of $\frac{1}{27}$; that is, three times higher.

The converse of relationship (2) is equally important, namely: *At reduced load, life increases in proportion to the inverse cube of the load reduction.* In other words, if the load falls to half, life will be increased by eight times. This relationship is also true of ball bearings, and a variation of it is applicable to roller bearings.

(3) *If a gear assembly is subjected to a maximum torque M_1 for n_1 cycles and then lesser torques M_2 for n_2 cycles, etc., then the equivalent number of cycles at the higher load is:*

$$n_1 + n_2 \left(\frac{M_2}{M_1}\right)^3 + n_3 \left(\frac{M_3}{M_1}\right)^3 + \cdots$$

This principle can be usefully applied to rear axles, auxiliary gearboxes, etc., following main gearboxes, where very high stresses occur in first gear for short periods, with diminishing stresses predominating in the higher gears for longer periods.

The mixed load and running time conditions can consequently be condensed into an equivalent number of cycles in first gear at maximum torque, in which form torque capacity can be assessed and comparisons made with other vehicles or for other conditions.

DESIGN STRESSES

At the design stage it is possible to draw up a running time rota such as: first gear 3 per cent, second gear 5 per cent, third gear 10 per cent, fourth gear 15 per cent, fifth gear 25 per cent and overdrive 42 per cent, and convert it to utilization in terms of cycles, compared with the primary pinion, then by inverting and taking the cube root the permissible stress increase above that allocated to the primary pinion may be established. It is, in fact, advisable to draw up two such rotas, one for motorway conditions and another for something nearer to earth-moving so that the longer utilizations can be employed in each case, calling for more moderate stresses in the final result. This precaution is necessary as gearboxes are usually matched to a particular engine torque figure and expected to function satisfactorily regardless of conditions.

By making a summation of the duty rota in terms of output cycles at different torques on the principle of

$$n_1 + \left(\frac{M_2}{M_1}\right)^3 + n_2 \left(\frac{M_3}{M_1}\right)^3 + \cdots$$

it is possible to calculate the equivalent cycles relative to the primary pinion of any transmission assembly following the main gearbox, whence appropriate stresses can be established for these gear assemblies on the principle that their stresses may be higher than that set for the primary pinion by the cube root of the inverse of their utilization relative to that of the primary pinion. This procedure is, of course, applicable to range boxes, auxiliary boxes, transfer drives, and rear axles.

The idea of designing strictly to stresses established by the foregoing method is not entirely satisfactory due to doubts about duty rotas and also to the probability that maximum input torque is seldom called for in gears like first, owing to the risk of wheel spin, etc., while maximum torque can be applied indefinitely in, for example, overdrive on motorway conditions.

There is therefore a good case for retention of the conventional procedures of working to an arbitrary set of stress figures established by experience for particular conditions, as Table 8.1.

Table 8.1

Six-speed general purpose gearbox		Five-speed gearbox for use with range auxiliary	
Primary drive	$6\ 000S_c$	Primary drive . . .	$6\ 000S_c$
Overdrive	$6\ 800S_c$	Overdrive	$6\ 800S_c$
Top gear	—	Top gear	—
Fourth gear	$6\ 800S_c$	Third gear . . .	$6\ 800S_c$
Third gear	$8\ 500S_c$	Second gear . . .	$7\ 500S_c$
Second gear . . .	$15\ 000S_c$	First gear . . .	$9\ 500S_c$
First gear	$22\ 000S_c$	Reverse gear. . .	$25\ 000S_c$
Reverse gear . . .	$25\ 000S_c$		

These figures are, of course, maxima, and would apply to regular road-going trucks of the heavier type. In any new transmission project where uprating has to be taken into account, the designer would naturally opt for stresses no more than 75 per cent of the figures proposed.

Stresses in gearboxes for range use are very moderate as each gear has to be used twice; for example, first gear high range is not a particularly low ratio, is frequently used, and in consequence may be only moderately stressed. Corresponding maximum stresses for the actual range gears would be of the order of $16\ 500S_c$ for the first stage and $20\ 000S_c$ for the second stage.

Multiple tooth contact should always be approached warily; for example, a simple reverse idler subject to bi-directional flank loading naturally suffers a reduction in strength fatigue life, but its wear life is unaffected as the additional surface contact is applied to the opposite side of the tooth. In the case of an epicyclic sun wheel the situation is again different, the number of cycles being counted in terms of tooth contacts rather than revolutions, and the effect on wear and strength is therefore the same.

The general automotive engineer in the truck industry has a very large range of gear stresses to deal with, perhaps as low as $3000 S_c$ for an industrial engine to gearbox transfer drive, right up to $30\,000 S_c$ for a crawler gear intended for occasional use. This wide range of stresses can be confusing, but it is necessary for economic design, and the attention given to rating here is intended to throw a little light on this rather difficult subject.

BALL AND ROLLER BEARINGS

The life of a ball or roller bearing at its I.S.O. rated load is 10^6 cycles, B.10; that is to say, 90 per cent of the bearing will survive 10^6 cycles and 10 per cent will fall short of this figure. At reduced loads life extends in accordance with relationship (2). The generally accepted index for roller bearings is, however, 3·3. Bearing calculations are usually based on maximum engine torque and corresponding speed, but the position is complicated by the fact that each gear applies quite different speed and load conditions to the various bearings.

One way of assessing the life expentancy of bearings under mixed load and speed conditions is to calculate the life of each bearing in each gear separately, as though they were being worn out six times over. The result for a particular bearing is shown in Table 8.2.

Table 8.2. Bearing 'C' rating = 12 400 lb

Gear	Load, lb	$\dfrac{\text{'C' rating}}{\text{Load}}$ = Life factor	$(\text{Life factor})^3 \times 10^6$ = Life in cycles	Speed, rev/min	Speed, rev/h	$\dfrac{\text{Life in cycles}}{\text{rev/h}}$ = Life in hours
First	7000	1·78	$5·7 \times 10^6$	182	10 900	520
Second	3140	3·95	62×10^6	272	16 300	3 800
Third	1435	8·65	645×10^6	475	28 500	22 700
Fourth	797	15·6	3800×10^6	790	47 300	80 000
Fifth	0	—	—	—	—	∞
Sixth	2870	4·32	80×10^6	1615	97 000	830

A duty rota is then assumed for running time in each gear; for example, sixth 42 per cent, fifth 25 per cent, fourth 15 per cent, third 10 per cent, second 5 per cent, first 3 per cent.

The life of the bearing at maximum torque for this duty rota can then be taken as:

$$100 \div \frac{42}{830} + \frac{25}{\infty} + \frac{15}{80\,000} + \frac{10}{22\,700} + \frac{5}{3800} + \frac{3}{520} = 1710 \text{ h}$$

It is obvious that the average load will be less than the maximum by assuming a figure such as $\frac{2}{3}$ for this factor, and by applying relationship (2) it can be shown that the normal running life of the bearing will increase to $(\frac{3}{2})^3 \times 1710 = 5800$ h, corresponding roughly to 173 000 miles at 30 mile/h. This life milage is, incidentally, not nearly enough as the gearbox could easily operate 80 per cent of its life in overdrive and bearing trouble would then show at less than 100 000 miles in some cases.

A complete assessment of bearing life—starting with the computation of bearing loads and covering two duty rotas to ensure that the finished product will be suitable for all conditions—can be quite a lengthy business. Fortunately the bearing manufacturers have well-organized technical departments dealing with most aspects of this work. It is interesting to observe that the bearing industry at least attempts to predict the life of its products—the accuracy of the result depending on the applicability of the duty rota chosen—whereas gear manufacturers have only reached the stage where they can say that if certain stresses are not exceeded, the gears should last the life of the vehicle, given a measure of luck.

GEAR DESIGN

Gearboxes in the 300–800 lb ft class are likely to employ tooth pitches in the 4–7 d.p. range and total tooth numbers per train between 50 and 70. It is well understood that either the standard number of teeth, or one less than standard, can be employed, this facility being necessary to assist in accurately adjusting the ratios to the specification.

Where standard tooth numbers are employed, correction is usually apportioned in accordance with B.S. 436. However, K_p and K_w are often approximated to the nearest 0·1. For conditions where one tooth less than standard applies, and the ratio is greater than 3:1, it is advisable to make $K_p = 0.5$ and $K_w = 0$. For more moderate ratios, correction can be apportioned by judgement, giving the larger part to the smaller gear.

The one tooth less condition is an instance of centre distance extension, essential for extreme ratios such as first gear and overdrive; it results in a generally improved tooth, broader based for strength, and flatter involuted for surface durability as well as eliminating undercutting. In terms of rating it is probably worth something of the order of 10 or 15 per cent for both wear and strength and it might even be considered inadvisable to go to the limit of the stress figures proposed in Table 8.1 unless this precaution has been taken, so far as the more extreme ratios are concerned. A minor problem in design is the utilization of this facility in the choice of tooth numbers and yet ensuring the retention of the centre distance extension condition on first gear and overdrive.

Extended centre distances always result in slightly increased backlash. In the case of a commercial gearbox of 6 d.p., corrected so that $K_p = 0.5$ and $K_w = 0$ and having 60 or 70 teeth in the train, the increase in backlash would be about 0·003 in. For finer pitches or smaller extension the amount of extra backlash will be even less.

Therefore, a designer should never be apprehensive about extending centres and omitting a tooth on grounds of some doubt he may have in regard to the effect it will have on backlash, especially in the obviously important case of extreme ratio and coarse pitch.

Helical gears in British designed transmissions often have excessive helix angles to provide full overlap, such that $\pi/(\text{n.d.p. } \sin \sigma)$ is less than the face width, where σ is the helix angle. However, it seems that most of the advantages of improved durability and quietness can be obtained by employing helix angles of $10°$ or $15°$, as is frequently done in Continental and American transmissions. Adoption of this idea by British manufacturers would undoubtedly reduce the number of rather crude, straight-cut spur gears that we tend to specify where practical bearing arrangements preclude the use of full overlap helicals.

GEAR TOOTH LAYOUTS

A tooth layout of 1 d.p. scale is often helpful, provided it can be done quickly. The most satisfactory way of generating a tooth in a matter of minutes rather than hours is, briefly: fix the 1 d.p. standard rack on the drawing board, rounded edge upwards, and mark in the new pitch line representing the required correction, for example $K_p = 0.5$ would be 0.5 in higher than the nominal pitch line. Next, overlay a tracing sheet above the rack containing the standard pitch circle but with an enlarged outside diameter, the increased radial dimension of the outside diameter being 0.5 in, then roll it tangent fashion about a pencil point along the new pitch line of the rack, marking in the $20°$ rack flanks progressively on the overlay from a square set at $20°$. The overlay can be held down by means of weights during this process (the stages need not be equal). Anyone who has doubts about the accuracy of this procedure should try rolling it back to the starting position to show that there is no slip, even when the tangent condition is less than perfect. The resulting layout can be most useful, especially if the mating gear is also drawn in which case the pair can be rotated together in engagement about pins to show the lowest point of active face relative to a grinding step or protuberance hob run-out, etc. The effect of topping on contact ratio can also be seen (this should be done if crest width falls below 0.5 in on the 1 d.p. scale). Layouts of this type are of assistance in the design of dog clutch teeth which normally have no accepted standard.

Other purposes for which layouts can be of service are in the study of root fillet forms and in the design of gears requiring a high root circle for use with a topped mating gear. This is sometimes necessary in the accommodation of large internal bores.

Helical gears are generated and inspected in a normal plane; consequently in layout work the pitch diameter, outside diameter, and base circle diameters of helical gears have to be converted to virtual diameters by multiplying by $\sec^3 \sigma$.

GENERAL CONFIGURATION

The present generation of gearboxes employs cast iron cases and separate bell housings, the ends of which are machined over a broad area for attachment of alternative equipment. Shafts are built up on the bench and tilt-assembled into the casings—split casings and centre bearing arrangements being currently out of favour. Provision has to be made for right-hand, central and left-hand control, two

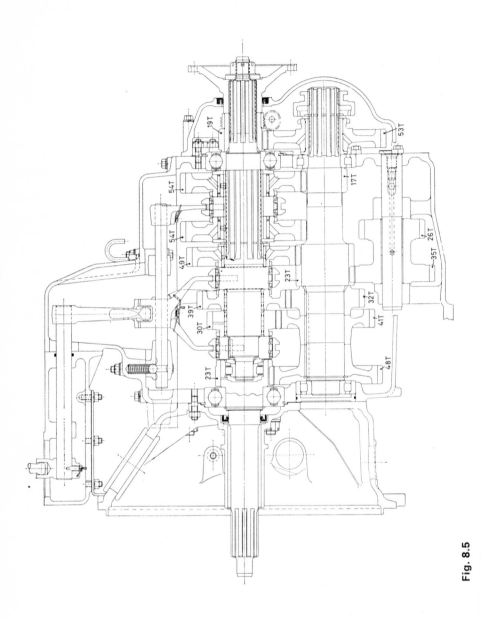

Fig. 8.5

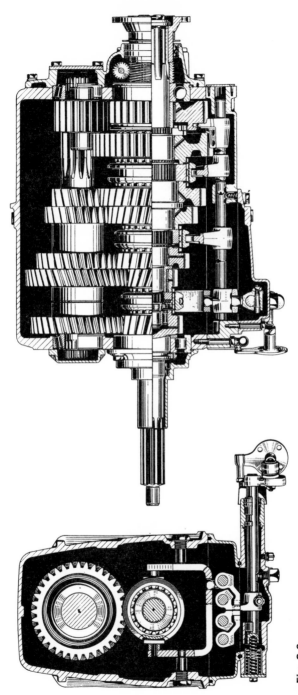

Fig. 8.6

p.t.os and options in clutch lever positions. Unless production is high it is usual to market a range version of the basic gearbox, manufactured from the same tooling.

The natural configuration is a five-speed and reverse unit with three double-ended dogs; this arrangement is justifiably popular as a basis for range and splitter types. However, today's diesel engines require even the simpler gearboxes to have at least six speeds, and it is the inclusion of the last gear, often an overdrive, that poses some of the more difficult problems. This is partly because seven gears (including reverse), unlike the five-speed arrangement, cannot easily be accommodated on a single span, and also because the odd number of gears results in the use of an uneconomic single ended dog for reverse or overdrive.

Fig. 8.5 shows an overhung overdrive, which frees internal space but tends to be hard on bearings. It is a feature of conventional gearboxes that bearing loads will largely cancel out if the gears are disposed in descending ratio order towards the rear. A tail mounted overdrive conflicts with this requirement. However, the difficulty can be overcome by making use of exceptionally large bearings.

Z.F. accommodate their sixth gear within the confines of the main casing by careful attention to the need for compact length dimensions and also by the use of a neat sliding reverse gear, Fig. 8.6. Another possibility is that of combining the first and second gear dog with the reverse wheel, as in Fig. 8.4.

When developing a particular configuration, a designer should give prime consideration to short length between shaft supports in realization of the fact that deflection varies as the cube of this dimension. Examination of the illustration will show that in all instances some attention has been paid to the need for minimum shaft length dimensions; shortness has also obviously had an important influence on the introduction of twin layshaft types.

DESIGN PROCEDURE

At the start of a new design of conventional gearbox it is reasonable to assume that the centre distance to face width ratio will be in the range 4:1 to 5:1 and that face widths will be approximately constant throughout. A fairly deep primary reduction is obviously desirable but ratios above 2:1 are usually impracticable owing to space requirements for the spigot bearing assembly. First gear pinion is likely to be of spur form and coarse pitch, hobbed deep into the shaft to provide the greatest possible ratio, often dictating the need for a high-capacity small bore tail bearing for the layshaft.

With these parameters in mind and a choice of centre distance that gives a primary pinion surface stress of about $5000S_c$, it is possible to sketch in the gear and shaft assembly to scale, roughly estimating the ratios, overall range, and gear stresses. At this stage a designer need not, in fact should not, think in terms of exact tooth numbers, d.ps, helix angles, corrections, etc., but should devote his attention to altering ratios: making first gear lower, overdrive higher, adjusting face widths to give required stresses, and finally asking himself, 'Is the scale right for the job it has to do?' It is a simple matter to redraw the layout 10 per cent larger or smaller to give 30 per cent more or less torque capacity, in accordance with relationship (1). Certainly it is easy, but it may also be the designer's last chance of matching the gearbox to a particular engine, and establishing the commercial viability of the project.

The preliminary layout can now be expanded by means of overlays to include shafts, dogs, casing, bearings, etc. The constant use of overlays will improve even the best initial layouts and are almost essential in achieving a compact overall length.

Shaft design

Layshafts should be designed, like any other gearbox shaft, on a basis of rigidity rather than strength. They usually include integral gears at the rear and pressed-on ones at the front. An idea of the force required to make a pressed fit can be useful in estimating the torque capacity of the assembled parts; for instance, a 10 000 lb fit on a $2\frac{1}{2}$-in diameter shaft implies a torque capacity of 12 500 lb in, enough for most conditions without the usual key. However, this is just how keys should be used, as a means of assisting a force fit.

The deflection of a layshaft can be calculated from $\delta = wl^3/48EI$ at the centre, assuming an equivalent cylindrical shaft diameter and taking second gear tangential load as acting at the centre of the shaft. This is very approximate, but one might be concerned if the deflection of a shaft in the 400–600 lb ft class exceeded 0·010 in.

Stresses would normally be calculated at the critical points from the end reactions in second gear; taking tangential loads only into consideration, a normal figure for layshaft stresses in these circumstances would be 5–7 turns/in².

Mainshafts should be stepped in lands towards a central abutment with the free running gears assembled from both ends, and to reduce the build-up of tolerances should be mounted on double rows of rollers seated directly on the shaft without intermediate sleeves. The use of sleeves is, however, justified occasionally to isolate free running wheels against thrust from another gear. Fig. 8.6 is an example of minimum use of inner sleeves; note also how circlips are employed effectively to contain thrust. Fig. 8.4 shows examples of large-diameter double row direct mounted rollers; double rows will be found to provide good stability and rotate better than single ones under the tilting action of the peripheral thrust.

LUBRICATION

Most modern gearboxes use splash lubrication, as pressure systems require radial outlet holes which seriously detract from the mainshaft's fatigue strength. Splash also avoids recirculation of impurities. Spigot bearings lubricate well through small holes at the tooth fillet, the direction of flow being inwards as the teeth mesh and outwards during the rest of the cycle. Owing to this action it is necessary to feed direct to the track, or to an internal ridge. The feeding of oil by this method to a groove will prove to be quite ineffective.

The two free running gears next to top can be usefully lubricated by the same method, two small-diameter holes in each being sufficient. However, the system is not effective for first, second, and third gears which are usually of large diameter and clearly subject to centrifugal force. The older system of splash through large-diameter holes, angle drilled into the boss is, therefore, commonly employed. It is often possible to get some sort of circulation from the rapid expulsion of oil at the ends of the face in the area of the meshing point, which can then be fed to the bearings. For obvious reasons gearbox oil levels are established well above the danger height for effective splash lubrication. It is, however, important to remember that churning losses at the higher speeds account for more than half the total friction losses, manual transmission being generally of high mechanical efficiency.

MANUFACTURE

The best general purpose truck gears are made from normalized blanks, carefully hobbed, crown shaved, gas carburized, direct quenched, tempered from a moderate temperature, and shot peened. Tooth fillets should never be ground and the grinding of flanks should be avoided unless the required noise level cannot be obtained by any other method. In this context it is as well to remember that pitch errors are a principal source of noise and that improvements in surface finish often contribute little or nothing to quietness.

Case hardness should not be less than 700 V.p.n. for gears and about 650 V.p.n. for dog teeth. Case depth is usually of the order of 0·06 in for 5 d.p. gears and 0·05 in for 6 d.p., the limit of case being defined as the depth at which hardness falls to 500 V.p.n.

Shot peening must become an accepted part of gear manufacture, as it already is in the manufacture of springs. The effect is to endow the surface with residual compressive stress, usually improving fatigue strength by as much as 30 per cent. The poorer gears are brought up to the level of the best, which are generally less affected. It is also useful in the removal of scale.

DISTORTION

Common types of distortion during heat treatment are changes in pressure angle, changes in helix angle, conical distortion of primary pinions, and the bending of shafts. Proper involute action depends on pressure angles being equal, for example, a 19·75° pressure angle pinion will run well with a wheel of the same angle, but not with one of 20·25°. Allowances may be made in manufacture for predicted distortions, but provided helix angles and pressure angles are equal within reasonable limits there is no need to hob them to peculiar angles merely to comply exactly with the drawing specification after heat treatment.

The trouble with allowing for distortion in manufacture is that the next batch of material may behave quite differently, in which case double errors would result. The Americans appear to look after themselves rather well in this respect, buying in larger quantities, insisting on close chemical composition, and studying hardenability curves against a previously established standard. They also manufacture from samples of a cast before accepting it, to establish that distortion is following a predicted pattern.

Paper 9. Manual Gearboxes in Cars

DR-ING. JOHANNES LOOMAN
Zahnradfabrik Friedrichshafen AG, Friedrichshafen, Germany.

The paper describes the type of gear, produced in millions every year, which can be found in most modern cars. Manual gears having now reached a high stage of development, improvements can be made only in construction details, in fitting the gears into the cars, and in the technique of finishing. Five manual gears are discussed and ten details of construction are explained. Finally, two examples of semi-automatic gears are given.

FOUR-SPEED LAY-SHAFT GEARS

In general, most cars are equipped with manual four-speed lay-shaft gears. This type of gear train has 11 gear wheels, is moderate in price, and the four speeds offer a sufficient utilization of the pull–velocity curve. From many examples, two standard gear types have developed.

With front engines and rear-wheel drive, the gearbox, clutch, and engine form a unit (Fig. 9.1). The flow of force is in two ratio stages: from the primary gear shaft through the constant in the lay shaft; and from there over the wheels of the individual speed to the co-axial driven shaft. The changes of the four forward speeds are made mainly through two synchronization assemblies, which are situated on the driven shaft near the wheels of the second and third gears; the fourth gear is clutched direct. The reverse gear is operated by a sliding wheel or jaw-tooth system.

The section shown in perspective illustrates the construction of a four-speed gear for light utility cars and for medium to heavy cars, e.g. BMW 2500 and 2800, with an output of 80–200 metric hp, inlet torque of 14–25 mkp, and ratio of $1:1–3·85:1$ for the larger and $1:1–5·61:1$ for the smaller torque.

The same wheel assembly is used in the Rover 2000 (Fig. 9.2) excepting the teeth of the reverse gear, which are placed directly on to the right gear-shift sleeve between the first and second gear wheels.

It is possible to combine the gear with axle drive and the differential driving gear in one closed casing for cars with front-wheel drive, and for those with rear-engine drive (Fig. 9.3). The gear is a single-stage lay-shaft gear without a direct gear-engaging system. The two synchronization assemblies for the four forward speeds are placed either on the driven shaft or on the lay shaft; alternatively, both are distributed in the two shafts. The reverse gear is operated by sliding.

The three-quarter section shows the ZF-Synchroma gearbox 4 DS-10, which is installed in cars and light utility cars weighing up to 1·7 Mp, output 60 metric hp, inlet torque 12 mkp, and ratio, according to version, of $0·87:1–4·10:1$. The distributed order of the synchronization assembly on the driven shaft and on the lay shaft gives a favourable construction of the shaft, compact design, and small overall length.

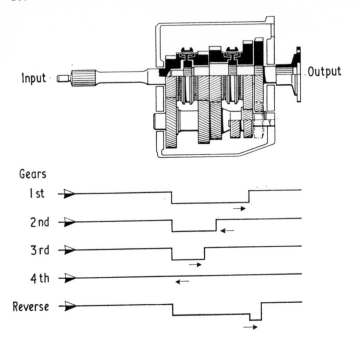

Input   Output

Gears

1 st

2 nd

3 rd

4 th

Reverse

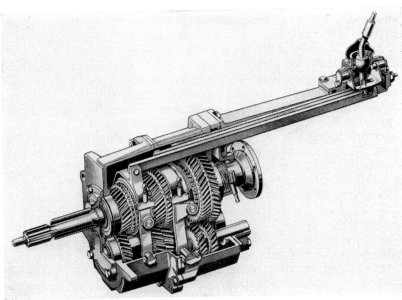

Fig. 9.1. Two-stage, four-speed lay-shaft gear without axle drive (ZF-Synchroma gearbox S4–18/3)

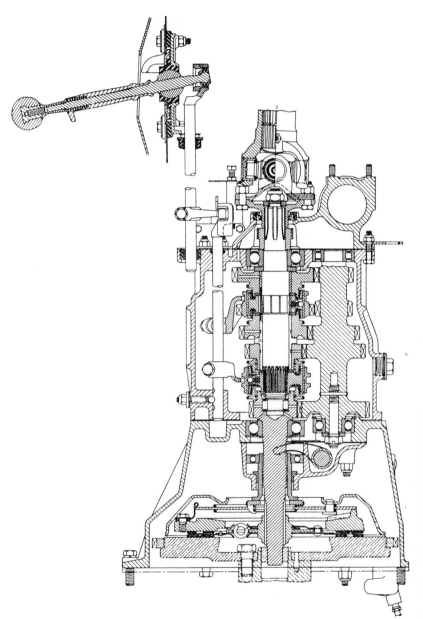

Fig. 9.2. Two-stage, four-speed gearbox (Rover 2000)

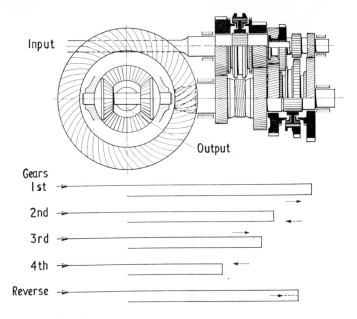

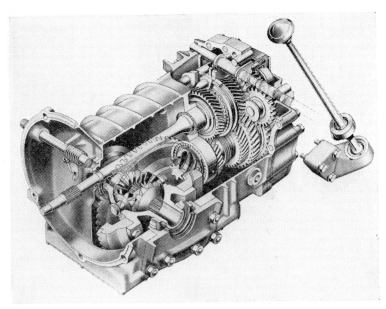

Fig. 9.3. Single-stage, four-speed lay-shaft gear with axle drive (ZF-Synchroma gearbox 4 DS–10)

FIVE-SPEED LAY-SHAFT GEARS

For sports and racing cars, five- or six-speed gears are necessary for the complete utilization of the pull–velocity curve. In addition, the varied applications of light utility cars—with slow speeds for transporting loads, and fast speeds for returning empty—demand from the engine a broad zone of speed and power, which can only be achieved with a five- or six-speed gear.

Fig. 9.4 shows the two-stage, five-speed gear of the Fiat 130, Fiat 135, and other cars. The output range is 80–200 metric hp, torque zone 15–50 mkp, with a ratio band of 1:1–6:1 for the load version and 0·85:1–3·85:1 for the high-speed version. The construction and flow of force can be seen in the wheel arrangement plan. A locking synchronization system is incorporated in the first to fifth gears. The reverse and first gears are shifted by clutching.

The single-stage, five-speed gears with axle drive (Fig. 9.5) are installed in sports and racing cars with an output up to 400 metric hp and a torque range of 30–45 mkp, e.g. cars from Alpine, Ford GT40, Mirage, and Matra. The gear

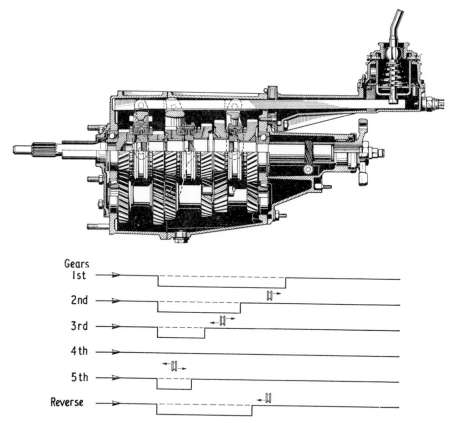

Fig. 9.4. Two-stage, five-speed lay-shaft gear without axle drive (ZF-Synchroma gearbox S5–18/3)

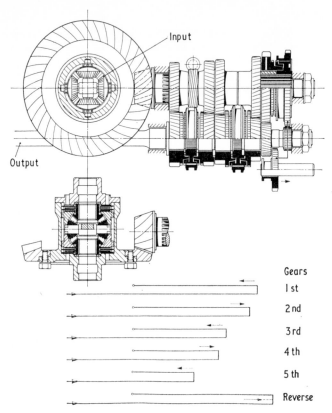

Input

Output

| Gears | |
| | |
Gears
1st
2nd
3rd
4th
5th
Reverse

Fig. 9.5. Single-stage, five-speed gearbox with axle drive (ZF-Synchroma gearbox 5 DS–25/1)

can be installed as shown in Fig. 9.2, or reversed, so that the driven shaft lies below and goes through underneath the wheel axle. So placed, the centre of gravity is low, which is preferable in racing cars.

CONSTRUCTIVE PARTICULARS

As stated in the introduction, the development of manual gears is now concentrated upon functional improvement and lower finishing costs. A few examples follow.

Finishing and cost requirements determine that only one gear-shift bar can be used in the gear of the Ford Escort. By lateral movement of the shift lever the gear-shift lever is turned and connected with the shift-fork.

The gears shown in Figs 9.1 and 9.4 illustrate a new gear-changing system. The ordinary connecting-rods and shift-forks were replaced by three flat belts, which are connected to their respective rocking arm by a swivel joint. The rocking arms are designed as framework and are pivoted in the middle or at the lower end with the casing. They are made of light metal pressure casting with integrally cast bushing and adjustment plates. Each flat belt, in combination with the rocking arm, is a sliding crank gear. This construction gives a simple but

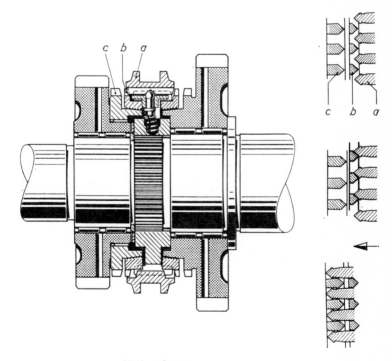

a Sliding sleeve.
b Synchronizer ring, e.g. 1500 rev/min.
c Clutch body with jaw-tooth system, e.g. 1000 rev/min.

Fig. 9.6. Lock synchronization

rigid shifting mechanism. Depending upon whether the rocking arm is pivoted at the middle or at the lower end of the casing, the shifting direction can be reversed and each type of connection can be achieved with the help of the shifting lever.

The shifter rod casing can be lengthened, as required, so that the gear handle can be placed near the driver at the correct position.

The casing is divided across the middle and composed of two parts. This is advantageous when casting and erecting.

The cage of the impeller pin-bearing is made of synthetic plastics. The low cost of this material was the deciding factor in making this change-over. In addition, it was shown that synthetic plastics cages have a greater capacity for resistance at higher revolutions than metal cages.

The running gear-tooth and the coupling gear-tooth systems of some gear-wheels are made in two parts, soldered or welded together (Figs 9.1 and 9.4). The advantages are the abolition of a gear-wheel–shaft connection, lower finishing costs, and small overall length; and, despite an adjoining bigger coupling gear wheel, the running gear wheel can be ground.

The lock synchronizations illustrated in Figs 9.1, 9.3, 9.4, and 9.5 are shown clearly in Fig. 9.6. If the sliding sleeve a is pushed a little towards the left, the synchronizer ring b presses upon the friction-cone of the left clutch body c. This turns the synchronizer ring to a buffer opposing, by the action of locking teeth, the forward pushing of the sliding sleeve. By constant pressure of the sliding sleeve, and by uniform revolution, the synchronizer ring is turned back

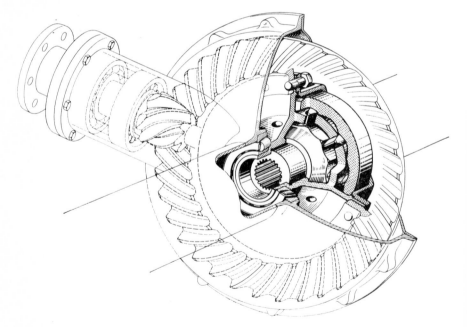

Fig. 9.7. ZF self-locking differential for curves with slide ring and radial cam-plate

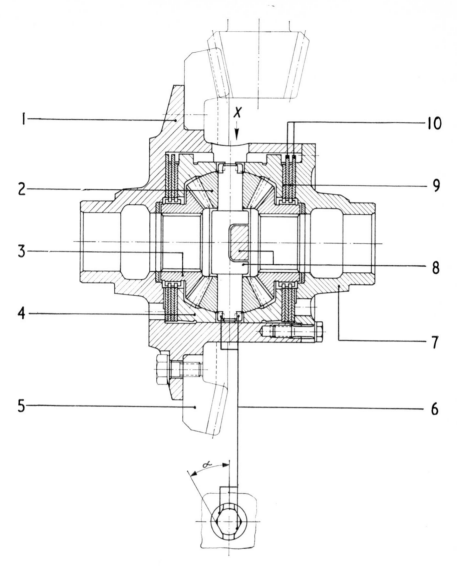

View of the differential axle seen in direction X

1 Differential cage.
2 Compensation bevel gear wheel.
3 Axle bevel gear wheel.
4 Pressure ring.
5 Axle drive bevel wheel.

6 Slanting plane on the live axle and pressure ring.
7 Lid.
8 Live axle.
9 Inner lamina.
10 Outer lamina.

Fig. 9.8. ZF lamellar self-locking differential (Lok-O-Matic)

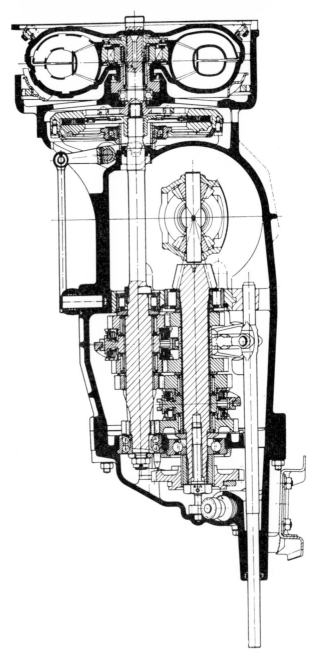

Fig. 9.9. Semi-automatic gear (Porsche Sportomatic)

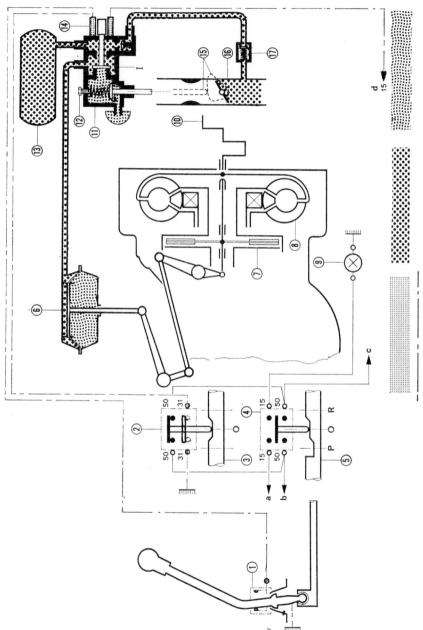

Fig. 9.10. The disengaging process

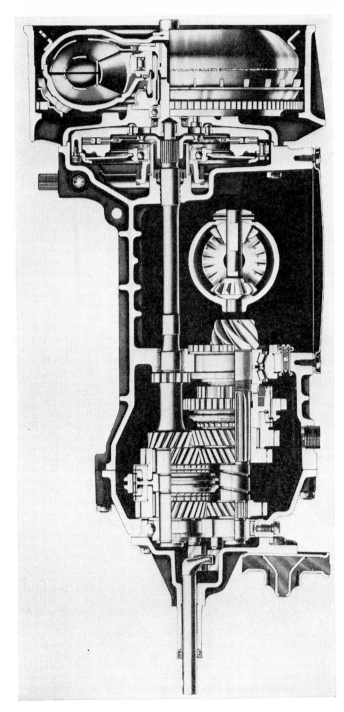

Fig. 9.11. Selector-automatic (VW 1300 and VW 1500 Beetle form)

over the pointed tooth area when the frictional force ceases. The sliding sleeve can now be pushed fully to the left and engaged with the jaw-tooth system of the left clutch body.

The racing car gear of Fig. 9.5 is operated through a remote control device,

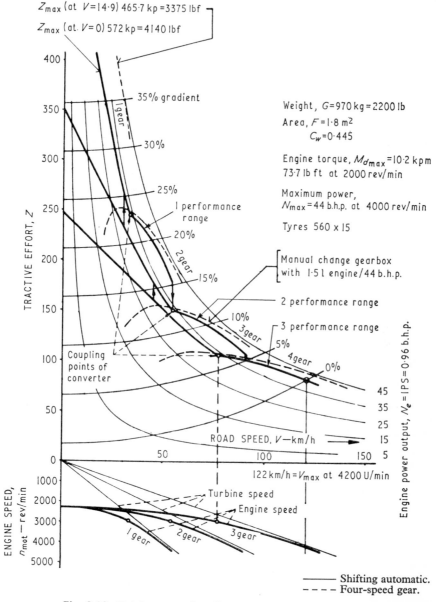

Fig. 9.12. Driving capacity diagram with traction curves (VW 1500)

————— Shifting automatic.
– – – – Four-speed gear.

which is secured by means of a link. It can only engage or disengage at one speed, avoiding the misengaging of gear which could over-accelerate the motor.

To cool these gears a lateral-channel pump could be attached at the rear end of the main shaft. It would run independently of the engine revolutions, sucking the lubrication oil from the gearbox and directing it to an oil-cooler. The oil would be conveyed directly through channels, borings, and pipelines to the tooth system of spur-bevel gear wheels and to the main and loose bearings.

In many cases, the axle drive contains a self-locking differential drive. For racing cars, a self-locking differential for curves is preferred, when hard working conditions prevail (Fig. 9.7). A lamellar self-locking differential would appear to be the most suitable arrangement for sports cars and ordinary cars (Fig. 9.8). With both types of construction the compensating movement is purposely complicated, so that with one wheel skidding, e.g. due to insufficient road traction, the other wheel gets an increased torque. The lamellar self-locking differential, which is dependent upon load and has been provided with the initial stress of a spring, has proved useful.

SEMI-AUTOMATIC GEARS

Finally, semi-automatic gears will be discussed. They are formally manual gears and belong to the thema of this paper. The semi-automatic gears (Fig. 9.9) which Porsche introduced at the international automobile exhibition held in Frankfurt in 1967 are composed of a Föttinger–Trilok converter, one single-disc dry coupling in a casing, and a conventional manual four-speed fully synchronized lay-shaft gear with a pair of bevel gear wheels and a compensating gear. The shift-coupling is necessary only to break the flow of force during change of speed. It does not have to perform the functions of a starting clutch, therefore it can be of small dimensions.

'Semi-automatic' refers to the automated controlled shifting coupling, therefore the term 'coupling-automatic' may be used (Fig. 9.10). By operating the manual shifting lever, an electrical connection is made and a pneumatic control valve with an electromagnet is brought into action. This actuates a low-pressure servomotor which opens the coupling. By further operation of the manual shift lever the desired gear changing can be performed with ease.

The semi- or selector automatic of the VW 1300 and 1500 (Fig. 9.11) also comprises one circulating converter, a single-disc dry coupling, and one three-speed manual gear, which is a common VW four-speed gear without the first gear.

In Fig. 9.12 the driving capacity diagram of this transformer–coupling gear combination is compared with an ordinary VW four-speed gear. The curves are known from the discussion on automated gears. The introduction of an automatic system in the coupling process is limited only by the cost factor. Such a system would give an essential improvement in the changing of gears, and would reduce the time taken perceptibly. Therefore the use of automatic gears instead of manual gears should be encouraged, thus hastening the day when fully automated automobile gears will be standard equipment throughout Europe.

The MS. of this paper was received at the Institution on 30th October 1969 and accepted for publication on 10th November 1969.

Paper 10. Manual Gearboxes—Cross-Country Vehicles

H. ADSHEAD, B Sc, C Eng, M I Mech E
The Rover Co. Ltd, Solihull, Warwickshire

The aspects of design peculiar to the transmission unit of the cross-country vehicle are dealt with in this paper. General problems associated with four-wheel-drive vehicles, inasmuch as they affect the transmission unit, are considered together with the effect of gear ratio range and controls on clutch life, related to operator usage. Consideration is also given to requirements of casings, transmission brakes, lubrication, sealing, and breathing. The provision for power take-off drives together with their power requirements are covered and the basic design of the transmission unit is considered in relation to service experience.

INTRODUCTION

The object of this paper is to present the points which are peculiar to manual transmissions of the cross-country vehicle. Papers presented elsewhere at this conference will have dealt with gearboxes for the conventional passenger car and the commercial vehicle. With regard to capacity, it will be obvious that the cross-country vehicle lies somewhere between these two.

Although I shall refer to the 'cross-country vehicle' throughout this paper the term is, perhaps, a misnomer, for in reality it is a multi-purpose vehicle having vast overall duties. It has been described as a complicated transmission machine, held together with girders and powered by an engine; the gearbox being the heart of the complex.

The specification for such a vehicle today is sophisticated to say the least; it is expected to traverse the highway 'doing the ton' (161 km/h) with the passenger comfort of a private car, and to be equally capable of performing off-highway duties of a very wide nature, including winching, towing, general power take-off (P.T.O.) work, military duties, etc. We know these vehicles by such names as Jeep, Landrover, Landcruiser, Laplander, etc., and their transmission units usually comprise either a three- or four-speed main gearbox, coupled directly or remotely to a two-speed transfer gearbox, giving an overall range of six or eight forward gear ratios and two reverse ratios. The transfer gearbox has two output shafts to enable the drive to be taken to all wheels. A cross-section of such a unit is shown in Fig. 10.1, whilst Fig. 10.2 shows the installation in a vehicle.

GENERAL CONSIDERATIONS

It is now usual to incorporate within the main gearbox some form of synchronizing mechanism on all forward gears. This is necessary because the type of vehicle under consideration is increasingly becoming an everyday type of conveyance for the general public, and therefore demands the facilities of a private car. These vehicles are reaching under-developed countries in ever-increasing

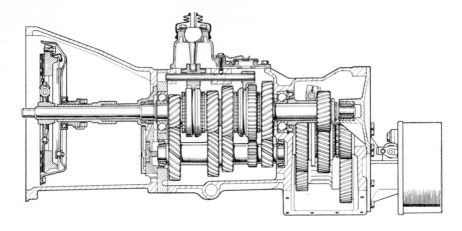

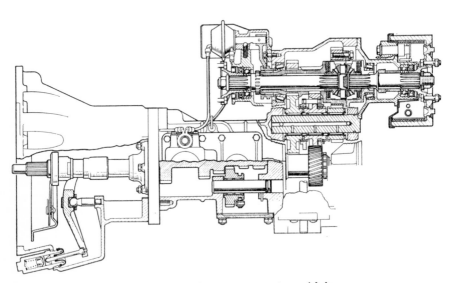

Fig. 10.1. Cross-section—gearbox for cross-country vehicle

numbers, but unfortunately the general standard of driving in some of these areas is very poor, and if a gear has no synchronizer it is most likely that it will not be used, as the driver will stay in too high a gear and slip the clutch, resulting in a shortened life for this component. Staying in too high a gear may also cause shunting with possible transmission damage due to torque reversals.

The wide ratio range of the transmission unit is also important with regard to operator usage. Lack of driver education in the use of the full range of gears

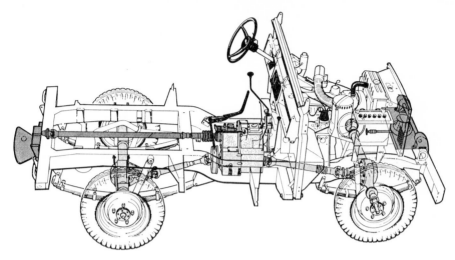

Fig. 10.2. Transmission layout—cross-country vehicle

can lead to the vehicles being held in the 'high' range of transfer gear in too many conditions. It is believed that as many as 80 per cent of drivers never get into the 'low' range of transfer gear; these drivers are reluctant to operate anything other than the main gearbox gear lever. To ensure that the driver fully utilizes this type of transmission, the designer should make the controls as simple as possible.

Because of the extremely wide range of operating conditions and the consequent wide range of ratios to cope with them, the resultant design of most manufacturers today is an 'all can do' transmission unit, which may well mean of course that some customers are purchasing units that have capabilities beyond their normal requirements. Possibly the ideal way of satisfying true demands would be to supply a basic unit of, say, five forward speeds, with an 'optional extra' reduction unit for those operators requiring ultra-low ratios. However, this is really a question of the economics of production; it is not an engineering problem. To date, manufacturers have not found this proposal to be viable, but the situation in the future could well change, depending upon increased production quantities and ever-increasing economic pressures.

Easy engagement of the transfer gears is desirable in order that the driver may change from 'high' to 'low' range without stopping the vehicle. This can be effected by relieving the leading edge of every other female dog tooth about 0·1 in (2·5 mm) and by completely removing every other male dog tooth. This allows the engaging teeth to drop into a large gap before finally being driven home (see Fig. 10.3). Normally the ratio range of the transfer gearbox can be around 3:1, and with such a large reduction conventional synchromesh mechanisms cannot withstand the enormous inertia that has to be absorbed.

Theoretically, it is desirable to have a true progression throughout the overall range of gears within the transmission unit, but this is not always easily obtained when the object of the manufacturers is to supply a standard set of ratios that will satisfy a wide range of customer requirements. In fact, overlapping of ratios

Fig. 10.3. Dog tooth relief for initial easy engagement

takes place on a number of manufacturers' units, but in actual practice this works out better than one would normally expect, because there are very few situations where a driver would expect to change right through the entire range of eight gears in the theoretically correct sequence. Provided that his training has made him fully aware of the capabilities of the unit, observation of the prevailing conditions enables him to select the appropriate gear well in advance of possible difficulties during off-highway operations.

Because of the extremely severe conditions that these vehicles may encounter, it is essential that some forms of anti-jumpout device be applied to the gears in both gearboxes. A great deal of reliance is placed on the availability of engine braking—for instance, when descending a steep muddy slope—as the use of the wheel brakes under these conditions may well transform the vehicle into an unstoppable sledge. Generally, the forms of anti-jumpout devices are the conventional stepped splines, angled flank dog teeth, etc., although more positive forms have been applied to the transfer selectors by some manufacturers.

The purpose of the transfer gearbox is to increase the useful range of gear ratios, and at the same time provide the output drives to the propeller shafts for front- and rear-wheel drive. The power flow should be arranged in such a manner that when 'high' range is selected, only rear-wheel drive is engaged, but with the option of engaging an all-wheel drive if required. When 'low' range is selected, the drive should be arranged so that it is automatically taken to all the wheels, thus sharing the available increased output torque.

It should be pointed out that when all-wheel drive is engaged on the majority of vehicles, the result is a positive drive between the front and rear propeller shafts, and therefore a return to normal two-wheel drive should be made as soon as the hazard has been cleared, thus eliminating tyre scrub and consequent harsh steering.

Some vehicles have permanent all-wheel drive, in which case a differential unit should be incorporated between the front and rear output of the transmission unit to prevent wind-up within the system. Provision must be made to lock out the differential unit in adverse tractive conditions, as loss of traction on one wheel will result in loss to all wheels. The use of a limiting-spin differential in this position has the advantage of coping with quite a lot of adverse tractive conditions without the driver effort that may otherwise be required with a simple type of differential. As with the non-differential type of drive, the 'diff-lock' should always be disengaged as soon as driving conditions permit.

A free-wheeling device may be used in the drive to the front wheels on all-wheel-drive vehicles. The inclusion of the unit means that all road wheels are driving, providing the engine is pulling and the vehicle is moving forward. When the vehicle is reversing or the engine is coasting, the drive is to the rear wheels only. If all-wheel drive is required in reverse, or engine braking is required in forward gears, use must be made of a locking device to eliminate the free-wheeling effect.

The engagement of the drive connecting front and rear output shafts can be made with a simple dog clutch. Obviously, there is only slight relative motion between the two shafts during normal running, and the engagement of the dogs may be delayed if they do not line up when selection is made. In order that the driver's selection may be followed by the earliest possible engagement, the sliding dog clutch should be spring loaded so that engagement takes place under end load as soon as the dog teeth line up. Alternatively, the sliding dog clutch may be actuated by a vacuum servo, which results in a similar action to the spring loaded type by allowing the dogs, when ready, to drop in under pressure although the operating lever may have been preselected several seconds before. A typical unit is shown in Fig. 10.4. Because of the relatively slow speed (if any) of the front to rear drive shafts, selection of all-wheel drive may be made whilst the vehicle is in motion, and no special lead-in is normally required on the dog teeth.

TRANSMISSION BRAKE

Cross-country vehicles normally have a transmission brake as an alternative to the usual hand brake arrangement of a conventional vehicle. It can sometimes be positioned higher in the vehicle than a wheel brake, and is therefore less likely to collect mud and water during wading operations. Any foreign matter that may be collected is quickly thrown off due to the high speed of the brake drum. As the torque reaction is less than a wheel brake, owing to the final drive reduction ratio, a comparatively small brake may normally be used. Internally expanding shoe brakes and external band brakes are both in common use.

The brake drum is usually carried on the rear output flange of the transmission unit, whilst the backplate is anchored to the transfer gearbox casing or speedometer drive housing. If vehicle layout permits, it is advantageous to mount the driver's hand brake lever and linkage entirely on the transmission unit, thus reducing motion to a minimum. A chassis mounted lever has to contend with the transmission unit mounting rubbers before doing any useful work.

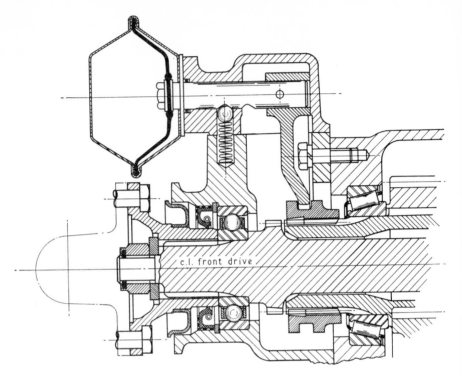

Fig. 10.4. Vacuum actuated front-wheel-drive engagement

REVERSE IDLER GEAR

The reverse idler gear within the cross-country transmission unit may well have to operate under load for prolonged periods. Early failure of the idler bearings has been encountered by operators when using their vehicles under such conditions as crop spraying between avenues of trees on plantations, when,

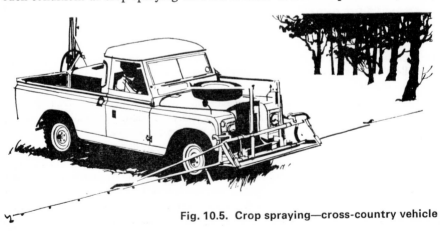

Fig. 10.5. Crop spraying—cross-country vehicle

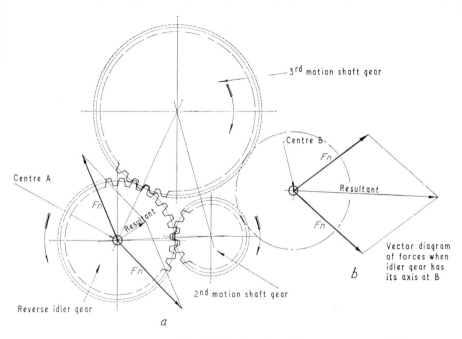

3rd motion shaft gear

Centre B

Fn

Resultant

Fn

Vector diagram
of forces when
idler gear has
b its axis at B

Centre A

Fn

Resultant

Fn

2nd motion shaft gear

Reverse idler gear

a

Fig. 10.6. Resultant forces on reverse idler gears

having reached the end of the line, they have been unable to proceed forward due to the layout of the trees and have been forced to return in reverse gear for the full length of the avenue. This is unusual, but it does happen and must be borne in mind (see Fig. 10.5).

The resultant radial load due to tangential and separating forces can best be reduced by locating the gears in the position shown in Fig. 10.6a. The disadvantage of this layout is that the reverse position on the main gear lever gate pattern is on the same side as third and fourth gear, whereas some operators prefer it to be alongside first and second gear, in order that the vehicle may more readily be rocked back and forth if it becomes bogged down in soft ground.

CASINGS

It is desirable to make the gearbox casings in aluminium alloy in order to keep the overall unit weight to a minimum. Even so, the total weight of the assembled unit may well be in the region of 250 lb (114 kg). The main and transfer gearbox casings can be either separate units bolted together or cast as an integral casing—this being usually dependent upon production machining capacity. One advantage of the integral construction is that the bearings are held in closer alignment than with separate casings, but although it is lighter overall, it makes a rather bulky individual casting (see Fig. 10.7).

In order that the gears may run as theoretically designed, careful attention must be made to ensure rigidity of the casings. Apertures for P.T.O. units and

Fig. 10.7. Gearbox casings—cross-country vehicles

for assembly purposes should be made as small as possible, and the flanges around them should be stiffened up to counteract the ill-effect of the openings on the rigidity of the casings. For the same reason, the covers for these apertures must also be of rigid construction. Cooling fins, whilst primarily beneficial during high-speed vehicle running and for stationary P.T.O. work, also give the casing increased beam strength. In order to reduce noise, flat surfaces should be avoided wherever possible.

LUBRICATION, SEALING, AND BREATHING

Oil lubrication of the gears is normally by dip, with splash lubrication to the remainder of the components. Where bearing lubrication is critical, a pressure feed should be used. A pump can often be easily accommodated on the second motion shaft of the main gearbox, and some form of filtration is desirable.

The main and transfer gearboxes usually have independent lubrication systems because the layout of the gears often results in different levels of oil. Different grades of oil may also influence this point; for instance, a unit having a limited-spin differential unit will most likely require an anti-squawk additive, which may not be tolerated within the main gearbox, mainly because of the stick–slip effect on the synchronizer cones.

Sealing of the units is very important on cross-country vehicles. The vehicle may very well be required to halt on steep slopes during surveying operations for instance, and lubricating oil must be prevented from escaping on to the clutch and the transmission brake. The exclusion of foreign matter is obviously just as important; the cross-country vehicle operates in every corner of the world, and sealing can be quite a problem in some desert areas where the dust is as fine as flour.

The sole use of labyrinths and oil return scrolls is not sufficient for complete sealing, but should be used in conjunction with lip or face type oil seals. It is usual to make use of a labyrinth or sheet steel shield to prevent the ingress of mud, dust, grit, grass, etc., and the shape of these deterrents is most important. For instance, when a vehicle has been wading, liquid mud runs down the gearbox casings and it must be deflected away from the oil seals as shown in Fig. 10.8b and c.

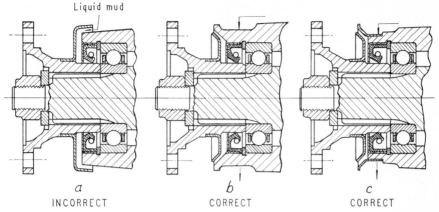

Fig. 10.8. Mud shields—output shafts

Any mud or other foreign matter that fails to be initially deflected will be thrown off by the rotating shields.

Breathing of the transmission unit may be carried out by the use of conventional baffled passages or a ball valve. Some liquid mud sets like concrete and it is wise to use a ball valve breather which incorporates a wobble top, the slight movement of which will ensure an air passage. Special precautions may be required on vehicles carrying out prolonged spells of wading, and some form of breathing tube may be required to allow the unit to breathe above floor level.

The flywheel housing should be ventilated to prevent overheating of the clutch, but provision must be made to seal the ventilator aperture when the vehicle is wading, in order to exclude foreign matter. This can be carried out by the use of plugs which can be fitted prior to wading and stowed during normal running.

PROVISION OF OUTLETS FOR POWER TAKE-OFF DRIVE UNITS

The P.T.O. unit is an essential feature of the cross-country vehicle, and the drive to these units is normally taken from the transmission unit. Operators expect every conceivable type of agricultural and industrial piece of equipment to be capable of being driven from these P.T.O. units, some whilst the vehicle is stationary, some on the move, and sometimes both.

When the vehicle is stationary the transfer gearbox is put into neutral gear and the drive to the P.T.O. can be varied in speed and power by the selection of the main gearbox gears in conjunction with an engine governor. When considering equipment which is being powered whilst the vehicle is on the move, the relationship of P.T.O. speed and vehicle speed is of some importance. In the case of powered trailers it is essential, of course, to match all the wheel speeds.

Rather than drive the equipment directly, it is sometimes more convenient to drive a hydraulic pump or generator from the transmission unit and then use the power of these to operate the equipment.

The most convenient point on the transmission to drive a P.T.O. unit is on the rear face of the transfer gearbox, co-axial with the main gearbox third motion shaft. The shaft has dog teeth which enable the P.T.O. to be engaged, and variation in speed is obtained by selection of any of the main gearbox gears in conjunction with an engine governor. A unit thus positioned is usually termed 'centre' power take-off and it can usually be further connected by way of a propeller shaft to a P.T.O. unit fixed to the rear of the vehicle.

In addition to the centre P.T.O. unit, the transfer gearbox can usually accommodate a P.T.O. unit fixed on the bottom of the casing. This unit engages one of the intermediate transfer gears. It is useful for obtaining a drive to the front of the vehicle for operating winches, etc., but it does limit the ground clearance of the vehicle.

The main gearbox is usually restricted to one facing on the side of the casing which can take a P.T.O. drive connected to one of the second motion shaft gears. This side fitting unit is not so versatile as the other positions because its speed is directly related to the engine and the constant gears only.

For vehicles which require power drive to a trailer, provision is made by replacing the centre P.T.O. unit with a similar unit which is driven within the transfer gearbox in a manner that enables the entire range of the transmission unit gears to be used, as the output shaft speeds obviously have to be matched to the transmission unit output speeds to the propshafts.

Table 10.1 shows the horsepower and speed requirements of various types of equipment to be driven by P.T.O. units. The absorption of power for most of the equipment is not normally great enough to have to take special measures within the running gear of the transmission unit, but for equipment that is to have prolonged use it is wise to check the transmission unit's capacity as an industrial unit.

Restrictions of power may have to be made under certain conditions, depending on how the drive is taken from the P.T.O. unit. For instance, on a centre P.T.O. where the drive is taken through a pulley or sheave to some belt- or rope-driven equipment, the power may well have to be restricted to prevent damage to the transmission unit mountings, but even so, up to 25 hp may be usually accommodated.

Normally there is no restriction of power to a trailer drive, for although this may well have the greatest power requirement of all the equipment, provision is easily made within the transfer gearbox. The available engine torque under normal conditions is, of course, being shared with one or both axles and any momentary overloading due to adverse conditions can be easily accommodated.

Table 10.1. Horsepower and speed requirements—gearbox-driven equipment

Type of equipment	Horse-power	Speed, rev/min	Location of drive
Agricultural field sprayer	10	540	Centre P.T.O.
Rotary grass cutter	15	540	Rear via centre P.T.O.
Electric generator (14 kVA) . . .	20	2400	Centre P.T.O.
Hydraulic platform and aircraft baggage loader	22	2500	Centre P.T.O.
Sewer and drain cleaner (water pressure at 900 lb/in²)	30	2000	Rear via centre P.T.O.
Air compressor (100 ft³/min at 100 lb/in²) .	35	2300	Centre P.T.O.
Winch (4000 lb pull at 5 ft/s) . . .	40	2300	Centre P.T.O.

BASIC DESIGN CONSIDERATIONS OF THE TRANSMISSION UNIT

Because of the extremely wide range of operator usage, it is virtually impossible to give clear-cut guidance on permissible working stresses in relation to the capacity of the transmission unit of the cross-country vehicle. However, this section will provide information which can be regarded as a starting point in the design of such a unit. It has often been stated that design is a compromise, and never was this more true than when applied in respect of the units under consideration.

As with all products, previous experience of service in the field is of prime importance and the following comments are based on many years of varied operator usage.

Gear centre distance

The initial determination of the gearbox gear centre distance is very important since this dimension largely influences the ultimate size of the unit. It has been determined that initially a modification of the formula proposed by Heldt (1)[*] may be used. Whereas Heldt proposes $C = 0.8\sqrt[3]{T}$ for commercial vehicle gearboxes, the formula may be modified to $0.6\sqrt[3]{T}$ for the cross-country transmission unit main gearbox, where C is the centre distance (in) and T the engine torque (lb ft).

The final centre distance may have to be modified, of course, after consideration of gear rating, maximum gear ratio, and the boundary dimensions of the shaft bearings.

Gears

It has been determined that the capacity of the gears may be based on B.S. 436, but with the basic bending stress factor modified to 0.8 of the quoted figures. Generally, the use of helical gears is made for the forward gears with straight spurs for reverse.

Satisfactory results have been obtained whilst using a nickel–molybdenum case-hardening steel, such as En 35A, the proportions being based on a bending stress factor of 40 000 and a surface stress factor of 11 000, the teeth having been crown shaved.

A normal pitch of 2·50 metric module with a helix angle of around 35° may be used for the constant gears and the third gear sets, whilst 2·75 metric module for second and first gear sets may be used with approximately 30° and 25° helix angles respectively. The transfer gears may also be around 2·75 metric module, but with a helix angle of about 20°. These steps in pitch and helix angle will give a sufficiently increased tooth size for the higher loaded gears and layshaft end thrust will be reasonably balanced.

Shafts

Like the remainder of the components within the transmission unit, the shafts are subject to momentary overloading due to adverse operating conditions. As an

[*] *The reference is given in Appendix 10.1.*

initial guide, however, experience has taught us that if the torsional stress at the root of the splines does not exceed half the tensile yield stress of the material, for gross laden highway conditions, then this factor will take care of overloading due to any adverse conditions that may be encountered during off-highway operations.

Bearings

The final selection of bearings will be the task of the bearing manufacturers' specialist applications engineer. However, a start must be made before he enters the picture and Table 10.2 shows the percentage usage, in miles, in each gear, that may be used.

Table 10.2. Percentage usage, in miles, in each gear

Transfer gear range	Gear				
	Fourth	Third	Second	First	Reverse
High . . .	69·0	12·0	7·0	2·5	0·5
Low . . .	4·0	2·5	1·5	0·75	0·25

A B10 life of 75 000 miles should be the target, using an equivalent constant input torque of 65–70 per cent.

CONCLUSIONS

It will be obvious that this is essentially a very practical type of vehicle, and as such it must be similarly treated from the point of view of gearbox design. Every endeavour has been made to emphasize the extremely wide variation of customer usage encountered, but even so, it is felt that this is an almost impossible task to convey without actual observation of the physical conditions involved.

Although this type of vehicle is usually described as 'go anywhere, do everything', a limitation must be made in the size of the unit, in order to safeguard the majority of customers from paying a cost penalty for some requirement that only a few may wish to have. For instance, it is known that in one part of the world a customer has found it more economical to grossly overload one of these vehicles and frequently pay the penalty of changing a broken axle shaft, rather than purchase initially a competitor's more robust vehicle costing twice the price. Whilst this type of customer's loyalty is appreciated, we must not neglect our 'bread and butter' customers.

It is the duty of management to define the limits of vehicle specification based on the economics of the world's markets; the challenge is then open to the engineer to satisfy these requirements.

APPENDIX 10.1

REFERENCE
(1) HELDT, P. M. *Torque convertors or transmissions* (Chilton Company).

The MS. of this paper was received at the Institution on 2nd December 1969 and accepted for publication on 19th January 1970.

Discussion during Session 1

It is acknowledged that all delegates attending the Conference took part in the discussion to some extent and in some form.

However, the whole discussion has been condensed and edited into a form more suitable for publication.

Papers 1 and 2

Following the presentation of the first two papers, Dr Newcomb (*Ferodo Ltd*) opened the discussion.

The manually operated clutch would, in time, disappear, he thought, but many aspects of it still required a great deal of study. The most important factor in the performance of friction materials was surface temperature.

Uniform heating over the whole of the surface area might be assumed in dealing generally with the problem of heat. But frequently, heating was not uniform. The size of contact areas could be estimated and localized spot temperatures calculated, but the distribution of these contact areas could not be predicted, so that this method was not particularly useful. With a forced cooling system a 15–20 per cent reduction in temperature could be expected.

However, the manufacturers of frictional materials preferred to meet requirements by the continuous development of products to withstand higher temperatures.

Mr Lucas (*Loughborough University*) was interested in the acceleration of vehicles with both manual and automatic transmissions. The period before complete clutch engagement was critical. Torque transmitted was obviously much influenced by the lining, contact surfaces and the driver's behaviour. Detailed knowledge of the torque/time characteristics was essential for the design of more sophisticated equipment.

Mr Nisbet (*Hoffman Pollard*) asked whether acceptable limits of misalignment and eccentricity between clutch housings and gearbox could be determined. Inaccuracies could drastically reduce the life of clutch bearings.

Mr Bissett (*Massey Ferguson*) reported how the diameter of a clutch, satisfactory in service, had been increased from 11 to 12 in, with no other change. The larger clutch had suffered from very severe clutch drag. An explanation would be much appreciated.

Mr Fuller (*Massey Ferguson*) asked for a recommended relationship between clutch torque, without slip, and the maximum engine torque to be transmitted. One specification gave maximum and minimum ratios of 3·3 and 1·7, respectively, but he felt the higher figure was excessive.

Dr Newcomb, in reply, thought it difficult to give figures on vehicle acceleration. The torque that the clutch must transmit without slip was easily determined. Other factors were the type of vehicle, its duty and the conditions of work, the all-up weight, the gear ratios, etc.

The performance of each facing material must be investigated for each application.

Whatever the characteristics of a material, performance in service was much affected by the way it was used. For example, the same material behaved very differently on rigidly mounted, than on cushion-driven, plates.

Misalignment could cause very rapid wear, particularly with diaphragm spring clutches, and side loading could lead to bearing failures. A TIR reading of 0·020 in should not be exceeded.

In some conditions and with some materials a drive torque could be transmitted without clamping. Some heavy-duty materials, particularly after light loading, developed 'glaze' and, operating against a smooth driven member, could transmit torque without clamping, possibly because the surfaces had not separated completely after previous clamping.

With tractor clutches it had been the practice to use a clutch/engine torque ratio as high as 3:1. Too high a figure gave problems in service and meant unduly large components. The tendency now was to reduce this ratio to between 2·5 and 3:1. However, abrupt clutch engagement could give rise to very high torque factors with organic friction materials, and grab conditions could occur with the sintered or ceramic type.

Mr Smailes (*Mintex Ltd*) said that to assess the properties of a friction material, tests should first ignore the detail of the clutch. Temperature was important but information was also required on the effects of pressure on material properties.

The use of embedded thermocouples had been mentioned. However, interface temperature was of much greater significance as a guide to performance though 'soak' temperatures could be useful. Information on how to measure interface temperatures and transient temperature rises during take-up was urgently needed.

Mr Lowe (*British Twin Disc*) wanted information on the effects of extended slip times on graphite materials, the permissible maximum operating face pressure and the conditions in which friction materials became interchangeable.

Mr Soul (*Lubrizol*) said the functioning of oil-immersed clutches was directly affected not only by the friction material but also by the oil in which they operated. Fig. 41.12 of Paper 41 showed the variations of the coefficient of friction with rubbing speeds for two automatic transmission fluids: there was a great difference in the respective coefficients of friction. Fig. 41.13 of the same paper showed the effects of additives (viscosity index improvers) on friction characteristics of a mineral oil.

One combination could show a decrease in friction as rubbing speed increased and another an actual increase at low rubbing speeds.

Mr Williams (*Laycock*) said the inertia testing of facing materials involved the engagement of a clutch against a static reaction member. But the energy dissipation rate for the same rate of engagement was very different with a driven plate of semi-metallic segments from that of an axial-cushion plate with organic facings. How could the results of such tests be compared?

Dr Newcombe (*Ferodo*) replied that sample tests were made on segments of a circle and the results gave a qualitative comparison. The test referred to in the paper concerned a full facing, extending through 360°. Ideally this should be an annulus of infinitesimal width so that the radius of torque was constant.

Many clutches had to operate under low clamping loads and, on a dynamometer, pressures, temperatures and velocities could be measured over a large range of loads.

Embedded thermocouples measured the temperature under the surface and surface temperatures could be extrapolated but the accuracy of the results was suspect. A rubbing thermocouple presented difficulties in practice. Transient temperatures could be measured with an infra-red cell but again there were many difficulties. The embedded thermocouple was preferred for clutch linings.

With moulded friction materials compatibility was important. If the opposing surfaces did not readily bed-in, high 'spot' temperatures could harden parts of the driven plate which further impeded the bedding-in process and lining surfaces could be damaged. With the new types of moulded materials, however, very little difficulty had been experienced.

Much had been published on sintered materials, particularly in America, where 1000 lbf/in^2 had been mentioned as permissible. Ferodo had tested them up to 250 lbf/in^2.

Graphitic materials were interchangeable with synthetic products but the coefficients of friction of the former were approximately double those of the latter.

Manufacturers appreciated the effects of various transmission fluids but these had little effect on the energy absorption capacity of a lining material. Further investigation was required: Figs 41.12 and 41.13 showed effects at low rubbing velocities, but there was an urgent need for more information under dynamic conditions at higher rubbing speeds, varying loads and other service conditions. Energy rating tests were particularly important: organic facings were insulators which prevented most of the heat generated from reaching the driven plate. The high conductivity of sintered facings permitted more rapid heat transfer.

Work done on railway brake blocks had provided some useful information, particularly on compatibility. Wheel locking had to be avoided and tread surfaces must not be damaged. An infra-red device had been developed which showed temperatures exceeding 1000°F, particularly where a 'fire streak' was visible on the trailing edge of the block.

A good bedding pattern, distributed evenly over the whole of both surfaces, was very important for all clutches and brakes; another significant factor was the friction-pad mounting. With a cushion-driven plate a better bedding pattern resulted than with rigid plates; and a pedal clutch incorporating this was also easier to operate. The mechanism of a pedal clutch affected the 'feel' of 'take-up'. The hysteresis of earlier types with coil springs (Fig. 1.2) gave the impression of delayed engagement and the conventional hydraulic system, with an efficiency of some 70 per cent, increased this impression. Diaphragm spring clutches (Fig. 1.4), due to their low hysteresis, gave a 'springy feel'. The addition of a hydraulic system damped this down, improving the feel of 'take-up'.

Though much research was in progress on clutch judder, basic parameters had not yet been established. Such an investigation was expensive and clutch judder was very rare indeed.

Mr Jenkins (*Ferodo*), in a written contribution, said judder was generally considered a self-sustaining 5–10 Hz vibration, caused by the coefficient of friction increasing with decrease in slip speed. As reported in Paper 2, however, it had not been possible to relate judder to the frictional velocity variation of the facing, or indeed to any of its frictional properties. Further work indicated a frequent increase in friction, during bedding, of up to about 10 per cent. But there was no correlation with judder.

To provide realistic conditions a further series of tests had been done on a Borg and Beck clutch rig, modified to include a spring mass system with a natural frequency about 10 Hz. The variation in torque had been measured but despite a great deal of effort, classical judder could not be reproduced. Thus, it was tempting to conclude that in the majority of cases, judder was due to the rotational speed of a drive shaft with some misalignment matching the natural frequency.

Dr Forster (*Daimler-Benz*) commented in writing on Fig. 2.4 and on the statement in Paper 2, 'The surface grooving of the facing gives no increase in μ and significantly increases wear rate'. His company had had similar experiences with too many grooves on the facing but with a normal grooving they had found considerable reduction of mean temperature and no increase in wear.

In SAE paper No. 6800852, p. 4, the author gave μ for modulated clutches as low as 0·02: was there any suitable material with friction as low as this?

He also asked for details of resin–graphitic material. The μ given in Fig. 2.4 seemed rather small. Daimler used values as high as 0·12. Under what test conditions had these values been found?

Finally, were the figures of energy dissipation of different materials given in the paper valid for continuous slipping? What were the temperatures, ranges, number of shifts, and so on?

Mr Jenkins (*Ferodo*) replied that a simple spiral groove had been used which reduced the normal area of contact by about 50 per cent. This was not considered the optimum but had been used to compare the organic-based with sintered plates which were conventionally grooved in this manner. The use of grooves in paper-based facings was not recommended: which grooves did Dr Forster refer to as 'normal'?

The information in SAE paper No. 6800852 was interesting. His firm had recently developed a resin–graphite friction material with $\mu = 0·08$–$0·12$, dependent on energy rating, and the ability to handle up to 3 hp/in². Its wear rate was comparable to sintered materials.

The test referred to in Fig. 2.4 consisted of 550 engagements of 0·5 s each from 2500 rev/min to rest on a 1 min cycle at a pressure of 118 lbf/in². The inertia of the dynamometer was 7·1 lbf/in² and the total energy dissipated per engagement was 7620 ft lb. For $\mu = 0·1$, the mean rate of work was 0·44 hp/in². They had purposely chosen a somewhat low result for friction to avoid under-design of transmission units.

Papers 3 and 4

Mr Elderton (*Fluidrive Engineering*) said the reasons for using light mineral oil in fluid couplings were (*a*) no cavitation damage due to the low speed of sound in oil; (*b*) little erosion or corrosion trouble; (*c*) excellent lubricating qualities;

(d) low cost; and (e) universal availability. The lower the viscosity of the oil chosen the less the intervane friction and hence the power loss and the heat generated; but too low a viscosity could cause bearing troubles.

A significant characteristic of special fluids for automobile applications, as compared with hydrocarbon oil, is the higher specific gravity. Whilst for a given filling, this produces an increase in torque, i.e. a reduction in slip, it does also mean that the stalled torque of the fluid coupling is increased, leading to a lower full-torque stalling speed. The desired full-torque stalling speed can be re-attained by reducing the quantity of fluid in the coupling, but such reduction is sometimes of sufficient magnitude to actually increase the minimum slip, relative to mineral oil. Overall, the disadvantages of the heavy special fluids outweighed the advantages.

Dr Stuart (*Brockhouse*) said that modern traffic conditions caused very high fluid temperatures in automatic transmissions and the fluids used must not deteriorate over long periods. Thus a very high viscosity index was most important.

Mr Avnir (*Ford*) discussed the efficiency of hydraulic couplings and torque converters. The general impression was that, with slow heavy machinery for industrial purposes, efficiencies were low and he sought opinions on possible future improvements.

He received the reply that some improvement was obtained from control mechanisms which permitted the filling of chambers in timed cycles. But this cost more, which many users were not prepared to accept. The trend at the moment was to investigate the development of new fluid circuits. But reliable service was the prime objective; a few gallons of fuel was a small price to pay for freedom from breakdown.

Mr Soul (*Lubrizol*) commented that fluids of widely different characteristics were used in torque converters, transmissions and fluid couplings. Information on the real requirements was urgently required.

Papers 6 and 7

The discussion of Paper 6 centred on the coefficients of friction of lining materials in various fluids. Why, for instance, was ATF Type A, Suffix A, specified for use with the Verto transmission?

Mr Filderman (*Verto*) explained that with other fluids in common use, some 'squawk' problems had been encountered. With the Verto (Fig. 6.6, Paper 6) it was difficult, if not impossible, to measure the actual coefficient during the engagement, for increased speed caused a centrifugal pressure-head both inside and outside the clutch cavity which varied throughout the engagement. Also, the pressure in the annular space outside the friction plate was unknown and pressure plates distorted slightly during engagement.

Dr Giles (*Consultant*) said that Paper 7 claimed that in the gearbox described there was no 'ratio fighting' but difficulties might be expected from the manner in which the link pins must engage with the pulley surfaces. As a pin approached the point of disengagement, it was transmitting torque through the frictional contact of its end right up to the point of disengagement. Thereafter there must be a small inward radial force to engage the pin with the other pulley surfaces. These conditions appeared conducive to wear and noise. They might be alleviated if the sheave surfaces were inclined at a small angle. It would, of course, be necessary to introduce some flexibility in the pins and links.

Mr Groetsch (*Consultant*) replied that some slip, up to 2 per cent, did occur. There was also some elasticity in the links and pins and in the side members of the pulleys. However likely noise and wear might appear, these transmissions were satisfactory in industrial applications, with a usual life of 10 000 h. An automotive drive had run without difficulty for 1000 h, while transmitting some 55–62 bhp at 5500 rev/min.

Papers 8, 9 and 10

Mr Avnir (*Ford*) referring to truck transmissions, said that synchronizers gave cause for concern. Sensing devices had been suggested to allow automatic change. No doubt this would impose additional loads on the synchronizers: how could their life be increased?

Mr Riddle replied that a molybdenum spray could increase synchro life. However, he was proposing ratios very close together, 15 or 20 steps with no synchronizers at all.

Mr Harper (*Eaton Yale and Town*) said that current gearboxes were cheap and reliable due to their simplicity. He very much doubted that 20-speed automatic gearboxes, not designed as such, would succeed.

In their own 13-speed box they had a splitter (used only in the high range) as well as a range shift and this gave about 35 per cent steps in the low range and 15 per cent steps at the top end. This combined the virtues of Mr Riddle's 8-speed box with those of the range shift.

He agreed that gear teeth should be designed for wear, except in first gear, where strength was paramount. Helical overlap gave quieter running and, since more than one tooth made contact all the time, loads could be increased.

Lastly, negative correction factors should be avoided: to get a good tooth form on the pinion, it was best either to adjust the tooth numbers or the centre distance or, possibly, the helix angle.

Mr Riddle replied that, regarding automation, they should remember that ordinary truck gearboxes cost well under £200 but specially-built automatics cost about £700 and were not always perfect. There was room in between. Apart from this he agreed with Mr Harper.

Mr Radcliffe, in a written contribution, felt that economy in weight and length would be achieved by using a 9-speed change gearbox (using first gear once only), with an overdrive splitter on the top four gears. This would have eight closely spaced ratios in the high range and five more widely spaced in the low range, an ideal combination for both motorway and general trucking operations.

He thought it better to design gears for adequate fatigue strength without shot peening, to leave a margin of increase from shot peening to suit increased engine capacity.

Considerable improvements in gear life had been obtained with positive correction to both wheel and pinion. Using one tooth less than the standard number to suit the established centre distance and helix angle, a quick 'rule of thumb' for apportioning the amount of correction was to make it proportional to the number of teeth on gear and pinion, respectively.

Mr Riddle's comment on excessive helix angles was not strictly true, as many British heavy trucks had gears with helix angles of 24°–16° which gave overlap ratios between 0·75 and 0·6. These showed both satisfactory life and quietness. The effect of overlap bearing loads could be considerably reduced if the number of teeth in each successive train of gears was increased by one and the helix angle reduced to suit. This provided a much better balance between the opposing thrust loads on the layshaft, thereby reducing the resultant load on the bearings.

Mr Jacobson (*A.A.*) said a helix angle of more than about 30°–33° caused a number of problems. In theory it gave much better contact but in gear-cutting, particularly in the shaving of harder steels, the lack of guidance of the cutter and the deflection of the teeth could produce a 'ripply' surface. There was a tendency to tear and gouge the steel, which meant a much longer period for bedding-in. Moreover, hard contact might extend to the very end of the gear teeth, which was undesirable; some tooth spacing accuracy was often lost.

The larger the helix angle and, hence, the larger the overlap, the more significant any slight deviation in both profile and spacing accuracy. Very large helix angles often resulted in a noisy gearbox. Was it not better to stick to a helix angle of under 25°, even if this meant sacrificing some overlap ratio? This would also limit the end-load on the bearings.

On the other hand (contrary to B.S. 436), there was much to be gained by some overlap. This might mean limiting the helix angle to 10°–12°. The B.S. 436 rating was based on ideal conditions; in practice there was a significant reduction of noise even with low helix angles. It was best either to adjust the tooth numbers or the centre distance or, possibly, the helix angle.

Mr Riddle thought that Mr Jacobson might have misunderstood him. There should certainly be overlap with helical gears when possible; if not, then half overlap, an overlap factor of 0·75 or 0·6.

Dr Looman (*Z.F.*) said that they used helix angles between 20° and 25°. There was a great difference between spur gears and helical gears in noise which was a minimum at 20 to 21° helix. At 30° there was an increase of noise and the forces on the bearing increased.

Mr Riddle thought he might have been wrong in saying that Z.F. used helical gears without overlap but he thought some of the Swedish and American makers did this when they could not handle the thrust. He thought it should be tried in Britain sometime.

SESSION 2

Paper 11. The Development of a Roller Chain Power Transmission System for the Automobile

D. N. C. DAVIES, C Eng, F I Mech E
Renold Ltd, Wythenshawe, Manchester

P. J. OWEN, C Eng, M I Mech E
Renold Ltd, Wythenshawe, Manchester

The paper describes the development of primary chain drives, especially for those cars which have transverse engines driving the front wheels. Particular attention is paid to the development of satisfactory means of adjustment and the achievement of high standards of silence in operation under all conditions, coupled with satisfactory life in service. Intensive rig and road tests, and the means of measuring results are described. The conclusions reached thus far are summarized.

INTRODUCTION

We should like to introduce this paper with a brief historical note concerning the assistance given by Renold at the time of the invention of the horseless carriage. The founder of our company, Hans Renold, was an ingenious Swiss inventor born in the year 1852. In 1879 he bought the Slater textile chain-making business in Salford; in 1880 he invented and patented the bush roller chain; in 1895 he invented and patented the inverted tooth chain. Renold provided the transmission drives for the first bicycle and for many of the first horseless carriages. A few years ago the wheel turned full circle, and we are able to present what we hope will be an interesting paper on motor vehicle chain transmission.

Vehicle transmission systems have undergone considerable development in the last few years. Even the manually controlled systems have not escaped a certain 'wind of change', for they have had to be adapted for new front wheel drive layouts.

Looking back now, it is strange to think that front wheel drive only became respectable a few years ago—about 1959, in fact, when a now popular small car appeared.

Since 1960 to our knowledge, and probably much earlier, a transverse engine car of some sort has lurked in the experimental department of almost every large manufacturer, and most chief engineers and technical directors have been thinking about 'integrated power packages', meaning a single assembly comprising engine, gearbox, and final drive, and sometimes, in addition, suspension and steering.

Invariably in engine/transmission layouts of this nature it is necessary to transfer the drive either laterally or vertically downwards from the crankshaft to the main shaft of the gearbox. Therefore, it is not surprising that chain drives are once more a feature of vehicle transmission.

We have, of course, been fully aware of these trends in vehicle transmission, and there have been recent examples in the U.K. (Jensen FF, Wolseley 1800 automatic) and the U.S.A. (Oldsmobile Toronado and Cadillac Eldorado).

Over many years we have built up a wide experience on all roller chain applications, including engine camshaft drives. In developing this experience our company has progressively built up at its Manchester works one of the best equipped engine test laboratories in the world for this class of work. During 1968, facilities were enlarged and transferred to a new site adjacent to the Renold H.Q. at Renold House.

Using this specialized facility, we undertook as early as 1962 to investigate, and subsequently successfully develop, a roller chain power transmission system linking the crankshaft and gearbox for integrated engine/transmission units. This work, a private venture by the company, but with the interest and co-operation of several automobile companies, has been carried out using engine/transmission units from 848 to 7000 cm^3.

The development story, with the technical detail, of this particular project is

Fig. 11.1. 850-cm^3 gear drive transmission

the subject of this paper, which is arranged and discussed under the following headings:

(1) Durability
(2) Audibility
(3) Adjustment for wear
(4) Road test experience
(5) Inertia
(6) Conclusions

DURABILITY

The initial work on this project was carried out using an 848-cm^3 engine transmission unit. This power pack comprises a four-cylinder, in-line, water-cooled petrol engine, with a manual four-speed gearbox and final drive assembly set 5·25 in below the crankshaft.

In this layout the clutch centre is mounted on the end of the crankshaft, and the driven member carries a spur gear at its inboard end. This 24-tooth gear meshes with a 31-tooth idler gear which in turn drives another 24-tooth gear on the input shaft of the gearbox, thereby bringing the main shaft clear of the crankshaft assembly, as shown in Fig. 11.1. The gears and selector mechanism are carried in the engine sump, not in a separate casing.

This primary train of three gears was replaced by a 1:1 ratio roller chain drive. In the first conversion from gears to chain, a 22/22-tooth drive using 0·375-in pitch (p.) triplex roller chain to B.S. 228:1962 was chosen to establish an initial assessment of chain durability.

These wear tests were carried out on a test bed with the engine/transmission in top gear and the final drive output shaft coupled to a hydraulic dynamometer, as shown in Fig. 11.2.

Chain wear tests of 100 h duration were commenced using a cyclic speed programme starting at 1000 crankshaft rev/min accelerating up to 3000 rev/min at full load and returning to 1000 rev/min every 15 min.

Initial tests under these conditions showed a fairly satisfactory chain wear pattern of 0·29 per cent increase in length in 100 h. It was realized, of course, that at critical speeds the characteristics of rotation of the crankshaft and gearbox shaft, etc., were reflected in the roller chain drive. Whilst these cyclic irregularities may occur at only two or three speeds in the operating range, it was considered necessary to ensure chain control in manual chain drives by fitting fixed vibration damper strips against both the slack and tight chain strands.

Because of the straight edges of the chain plates the damper facings, made in a medium nitrile rubber, need only be flat without any formed profile.

This modification, normal practice on camshaft drives, to control the chain run was made and resulted in a wear reduction of approximately 30 per cent, i.e. 0·2 per cent increase in length in 100 h.

Further repeat tests followed with the speed range increased to 5000 rev/min at full load. Again, wear results were of a satisfactory nature, 0·22 per cent after 100 h.

A final endurance test of 700 h, bringing the total run with chains to 1400 h,

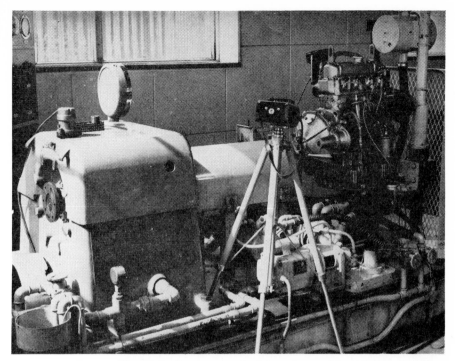

Fig. 11.2. Arrangement of test rig used for chain wear tests

resulted in a chain wear figure of only 0·5 per cent. This completed the work on this particular engine.

The wear test programme now proceeded on an 1100-cm³ version of the engine/transmission unit first used. Excepting the increased engine capacity, the transmission system is basically identical to the 848-cm³ unit.

The conversion to roller chain drive was again a 1:1 ratio of 22/22-tooth 0·375-in p. chain, 50 p. in length, but now increased to quadruplex width, as shown in Fig. 11.3.

Two fixed damper strips were again fitted to control the slack and tight chain strands.

Once more, wear tests gave good results, the total test time completed was approximately 1000 h, and wear figures in the order of 0·46 per cent were achieved following 450 h endurance runs.

AUDIBILITY

During the latter part of the roller chain wear tests on the 848- and 1100-cm³ engines, a parallel investigation was considered necessary to establish the effect of various parameters, such as wheel size, chain pitch, and centre distance on drive audibility.

For this purpose a special rig was designed consisting of two shafts mounted in bearings fitted in two housings; these housings, complete with shafts, were

Fig. 11.3. Quadruplex width roller chain

eccentrically located between two end plates. Rotation of the housings enabled quick setting and adjustment of the centre distance between the two shafts.

This rig, when mounted on an engine test bed, was coupled between a 1600-cm^3 four-cylinder petrol engine at one end driving the uppermost shaft, the transmission test chain connecting this to the lower shaft, which in turn was coupled to a DPX1 hydraulic dynamometer. This rig is shown in Fig. 11.4.

A thorough investigation now followed, aimed at assessing audibility levels of two sizes of chain, 0·375- and 0·50-in p., using wheel sizes ranging from 17 to 42 teeth. As might be expected, findings proved that the larger the chain wheel the quieter the drive. A chain of 0·375-in p. was entirely acceptable from an audibility aspect when using wheel sizes of 20 teeth (2·6 in diameter) and upwards. The larger and heavier 0·50-in p. chain running on 17 teeth (2·9 in diameter) wheels was considered too noisy for this application.

On considering the above findings—and bearing in mind that although the durability factor with 0·375-in p. chain was previously shown to be satisfactory there were limits to the application of chain of this pitch—further audibility work

Fig. 11.4. Drive audibility on test rig

was continued on an intermediate size specially manufactured roller chain of 0·4375-in p.

This roller chain, when run on sprockets of not less than 22 teeth (3·2 in diameter), had a satisfactory audibility level combined with a 38 per cent increase in bearing area on the 0·375-in p. chain.

It was now decided that 0·4375-in p. roller chain was to be the basis of a transmission drive which, up to this stage, appeared to satisfy both durability and audibility aspects when run on wheels even as small as 22 teeth. However, this roller chain is specially designed with new materials and new heat treatments to minimize wear and to maximize fatigue life with a tensile strength capable of dealing with high stresses in limited space.

ADJUSTMENT FOR WEAR

A vital problem now to be solved was chain adjustment to cater for wear and speed and torque changes. Thus far, all test work had been directed at establishing chain wear and noise level data; the next stage was to consider the application when fitted to the manual gearbox in the vehicle. In this situation the transmission drive would have to tackle rapid intermittent torque reversals, brought about by the action of the engine/transmission and vehicle inertia.

Test rig details

To deal with this problem the test rig described under 'Audibility' was modified to incorporate a flywheel fitted after the transmission drive roller chain, but before the dynamometer. The flywheel mass simulated the inertia of the vehicle, in which the 1600-cm^3 test engine was originally fitted.

This system enabled the engine to impart energy to the flywheel via the test chain, and on throttle shutdown the torque would reverse—energy would now flow from the flywheel to the engine through the transmission chain drive.

Of course, this test sequence gave abrupt chain changes from tight to slack strands, a condition which occurs in a vehicle transmission, and a condition which would have to be catered for in the final design of a chain drive. A further addition to this test rig was an electronic relay, actuated by the electric generator driving the engine tachometer. When coupled to a solenoid at the engine carburettor, this instrument enabled snap opening and shutting of the throttle to be executed on an automated cycle controlled by engine speed.

Method of adjustment

The variety of designs of adjusters for chains is considerable. Some are purely manual, i.e. they comprise jockey wheels or adjusting slippers which have to be reset periodically by hand, with the possibilities of neglect or maladjustment that this can involve. Others are automatic, having spring-loaded jockeys or spring blades which are only partially effective, as they do not control their vibrations. In addition, there are types with hydraulic damping, sometimes combined with a mechanical restraint mechanism, which are capable of satisfactory performance on arduous applications.

For this vehicle transmission drive a number of systems were tried, ranging from fixed rubber-covered damper strips to pivoted swinging arm automatic type adjusters having a positive non-return mechanism.

Our considerable experience of camshaft driving has proved that positive non-return mechanisms for adjusters are essential in the camshaft drive field. However, it was determined by considerable test work that automatic chain adjusters for transmissions needed quite a different approach. In fact, positive non-return adjusters proved to be completely unsatisfactory and resulted in a number of drive failures on the test bed. Nevertheless, an outstanding performance was achieved with a compact adjuster fitting inside the chain drive (fortunately roller chain can accept adjusters on either side) between the sprockets. This adjuster combined the ideal requirements of both spring and hydraulic damping behind the slipper heads without any mechanical restraint mechanism.

This design constituted two nitrile rubber slipper heads mounted on plates carried on plungers that were set to work one against each chain strand. Both these slipper head assemblies are carried in one cast-iron body, as stated, inside the drive between the two sprockets.

The slipper heads were kept in continuous contact with the chain strands by the pressure of a spring in each plunger. The overall width of the adjuster, i.e. minimum dimension over slipper heads, was designed so that the chain strands were not positively restrained during a slack/tight changeover when the drive was subjected to reversals of torque.

In addition to spring loading this adjuster, a hydraulic damping action was incorporated, with an interaction between each slipper head plunger. An oil reservoir, maintained full by the normal splash lubrication to the chain, was built into the top half of the cast-iron body. Oil is allowed into each of the plunger bores through drillings in the body and plunger, but it is prevented from returning to the reservoir by one-way valves. Both plungers will therefore fill with a non-returnable oil supply under the action of the springs forcing the slipper heads outwards.

To control and assist slipper head movement during torque reversals, an oil transfer port fitted with a restrictor hole connects both plunger chambers in the adjuster body. This feature, apart from the control on hydraulic damping, allows an interaction between the slipper heads; during a tight to slack changeover in the chain, oil would transfer from one chamber through the restrictor to the other. Therefore, hydraulic assistance is automatically given by the plunger assembly adjusting to the tight strand, transferring oil to the other plunger assembly, moving outwards, adjusting to the slack strand.

This adjuster, shown in Fig. 11.5, was subjected to intensive endurance

Fig. 11.5. Slipper head movement adjuster

testing on the engine/flywheel inertia test rig. One particular test, running under automatic cyclic control involving 400 test hours, subjected this adjuster design to 150 000 torque reversals. No snatch was observed in the drive, and all adjuster parts, including the nitrile slipper facings, performed satisfactorily and were considered well up to this application. The adjuster has been patented throughout the world.

ROAD TEST EXPERIENCE

Test rigs play an essentially useful part in development work, especially in the early evaluation of particular drive features. Comparative tests and controlled endurance testing, for example, can more often than not be better executed by rig testing where automatic repeatable cycling controls can be used.

There is no substitute for final development work on the actual application as a means of ascertaining all the data on chain drive performance. Therefore the next obvious step was to assess this transmission drive running in a vehicle.

Drive audibility in vehicles

A new 1100-cm^3 car was therefore purchased, and experience over 2500 miles was obtained with the original gear drive. Prior to converting to chain drive, audibility tests were carried out and recorded on tape. These recordings were taken inside the vehicle on road test with the equipment previously used in conjunction with the engine rig test programme.

Power to drive the recorder was obtained from a 24/230-V rotary converter housed in the vehicle luggage compartment. The recorder was carried on the rear seat of the car, and a unidirectional microphone positioned centrally on shock absorbers ahead of the front seats, pointing at the engine/transmission bulkhead. This situation gave what was considered to be the most lifelike reproduction of transmission noise in this vehicle.

Audibility records were taken at engine tickover, at various road speeds in all forward gears, and when accelerating and retarding. Additional runs were also made at speeds and loads which were critical, i.e. where in the light of road test experience it was considered that transmission noise levels were most prominent. These records were spaced out on tape, enabling the comparative noise recordings of the transmission when converted to chain drive to be inserted on tape next to the corresponding gear record.

On completing a set of comparative audibility tests, it was possible to replay the tape. This enabled a listener to compare immediately each test as it ran through into the next.

Drive durability in vehicles

Road testing the 1100-cm^3 car commenced with the transmission converted, first, to 0·375-in p. quadruplex on 24-tooth wheels and, finally, 0·4375-in p. duplex roller chain 46 p. long on 22/22-tooth chain wheels, all drives using the double-acting adjuster. A typical conversion is shown in Fig. 11.6.

Roller chain durability was assessed by chain length measurement at 0, 2500, 5000, 10 000, and 20 000 miles, the vehicle being driven on public roads over a 150-mile circuit, including a section of high-speed motorway.

From wear and audibility aspects, 0·4375-in p. duplex roller chain proved to be very satisfactory—the drive was particularly smooth, free from snatch, and with a marked reduction in the level of transmission noise throughout the speed range. In addition, this chain transmission does not suffer the distinctive gear chatter at engine tickover associated with so many of the standard drive arrangements.

Meanwhile, an 1800-cm^3 car was purchased, the design of which was basically similar but larger than the 1100-cm^3 model. This vehicle, when converted from gears to 0·4375-in p. duplex chain running on 30/30-tooth wheels (Fig. 11.7), proved entirely satisfactory from chain wear and audibility aspects. Road test work on transmission loading again showed chain safety factors of a high order; milage in excess of 30 000 has already been completed on this particular chain drive.

A further two cars, again 1100-cm^3 models, were now converted to this 0·4375-in p. duplex roller chain transmission, running on 22/22-tooth wheels.

Fig. 11.6. Typical conversion to duplex chain drive using the double-acting adjuster

These vehicles, operating from the company's branch sales offices, again show the smooth, low audibility characteristics of this type of drive combined with trouble-free running.

Whilst carrying out our test programme we became aware that General Motors had introduced a large 7-litre high-powered saloon with front wheel drive and an inverted tooth 0·375-in p. chain transmission—the Oldsmobile Toronado. It was decided to purchase a Toronado. On completion of 10 000 miles in the U.S.A. the car was shipped to the U.K. During this running time a rig was designed and run at Manchester to compare the wear properties of inverted tooth and roller chain. The chains were run for 1200 h, each under full engine torque conditions; our results are shown on Fig. 11.8. This result was a great encouragement, and we subsequently converted the Toronado to roller chain drive after completing and recording audibility of the inverted tooth drive.

The first drive fitted used 0·4375-in p. roller chain, approximately the same diameter wheels as originally fitted, and a special version of our hydraulic transmission adjuster. During our earlier running and load measurement we wondered

Fig. 11.7. Duplex chain drive as used on 1800-cm³ model car after conversion from gear drive

whether an adjuster was necessary with an automatic gearbox; comparative testing proved it to be unnecessary. A run of 10 000 miles was then completed using this drive, as seen in Fig. 11.9, performance being in every way satisfactory, and the drive gave a life indication of 200 000 miles. For the next stage of the tests we decided to reduce the chain wheel diameter by about 13 per cent, and a further 10 000-mile run was completed. Once again performance was good and a drive life of 200 000 miles indicated. Our final tests on the Toronado were to run a further 1000 miles on this drive, as seen in Fig. 11.10, at an average speed of over 98 mile/h on the M.I.R.A. circuit. On both these test drives, loads on the Toronado transmission were measured under various road/load conditions.

Subsequent work on two British cars—an Austin 1100 and a Wolseley 18/85—with automatic gearboxes converted to roller chain transmission has confirmed that provision of chain drive adjustment is unnecessary on cars fitted with automatic gearboxes.

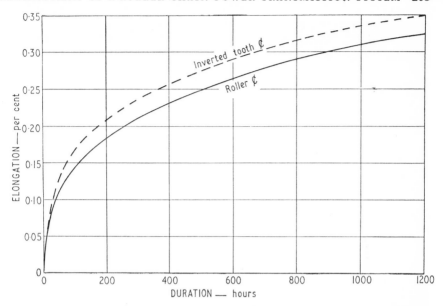

Fig. 11.8. Transmission wear tests, roller versus inverted tooth

Fig. 11.9. Oldsmobile Toronado drive, first conversion

Fig. 11.10. Oldsmobile Toronado drive, second conversion

Adjuster performance in the vehicle

Encouraged by these findings, another 1100-cm³ vehicle was obtained to speed up the development road test programme. Tests with a chain transmission fitted to this car were now aimed at assessing the capability of the chain adjuster to cater for extremely worn chains. Roller chains of 0·4375-in p. were worn artificially on a rig using an abrasive compound in place of a lubricant. A roller chain worn 1 per cent was then fitted in the transmission drive; observations on road test showed the vehicle to behave as if fitted with a new chain. The adjuster proved capable of controlling the roller chain without affecting drive smoothness or audibility.

Transmission loading in the vehicle

It was realized, of course, that high impact stresses could be imparted by the driver into the transmission system of a vehicle having a manual gearbox. Mismatching of gears, rapid starts, and misuse of the clutch pedal could all impose high impact loads on the chain. Therefore the development programme was now taken a step further by measuring the transmission loading under conditions of normal and abnormal use on the road.

Fig. 11.11. Right-hand side transmission shaft showing resistance strain-gauge wires

The vehicle right-hand side transmission shaft, shown in Fig. 11.11, was fitted with wire resistance strain gauges connected in a closed bridge circuit to measure torque. Wires from the gauges were taken out round the constant velocity joint, through the centre of the stub shaft to a slipring assembly mounted outside the road wheel on extended wheel nuts (see Fig. 11.12).

A bridge panel and decade resistance box, together with a pen recorder, powered by a 12-V battery, were used to record signals from the strain gauges. Prior to fitting in the vehicle, the shaft was calibrated statically in a torsion rig, care being taken not to apply any bending loads.

An intensive series of road testing was programmed to include acceleration, deceleration, impulsive loadings, mismatching of gears, hill starts, high speed, and braking tests. Work of this nature could not be carried out on public roads and so the facilities offered by the Motor Industry Research Association were used.

Results proved the factors of safety to be entirely adequate for the 0·4375-in p. duplex roller chain. Indeed, under normal driving, safety factors in excess of 17 were obtained and considered more than satisfactory for this transmission application.

Fig. 11.12. Slipring assembly mounted outside the road wheel

The test programme was made up as follows:

(1) *Acceleration and deceleration.* Maximum acceleration up to a given speed and then deceleration to rest, changing gears at the highest possible speeds up and down. For automatic gearboxes two tests were carried out: one under full normal automatic control, and one with manual selection and holding gears, where possible.

(2) *Impulsive loadings.* This involved applying a shock load to the transmission system by savage clutch engagement at high engine speed. With automatic boxes the selector was moved: neutral, reverse, neutral, drive, neutral, reverse, etc.

(3) *Hill start.* Starts were made or attempted on gradients of 1 in 3 and 1 in 4.

(4) *Maximum speed.*

(5) *Ride and handling.* Transmission load readings taken on circuits of the M.I.R.A. ride and handling course.

(6) *Braking.*

Summary of results

From our tests it was found that the lowest factors generally occurred during periods of maximum acceleration when the gears are changed up. This we considered due to high centrifugal force and mismatching of gear speeds in the gearbox. Fig. 11.13 shows extracts of the transmission torque on vehicles fitted with different gearboxes as gear changes take place.

(a) is a trace from a vehicle fitted with a manual gearbox and shows the characteristic oscillation set up in a manual transmission system after a gear change has been made or a snatch load applied; (b), (c), and (d) show automatic gearbox traces, and the significant change is the elimination of oscillation seen on (a).

(b) is an automatic box which causes high impulsive loading.

(c) is an automatic box which produced much lower peak loads at the gear change point.

Traces (a), (b), and (c) were recorded under high acceleration. Trace (d) is taken under normal driving conditions and shows much lower peak load.

Fig. 11.14 shows the safety factors derived from traces shown in Fig. 11.13.

The values of safety factor before a gear change takes place are greatly influenced by centrifugal chain loads. These are, of course, dependent on the diameter and speed of the chain wheel, and consequently upon the vehicle speed at which the gear change takes place. This causes the apparent lack of smoothness in Fig. 11.14(d), which is misleading, as can be seen by examining the actual factors.

The safety factors imposed under average conditions are at least 100 per cent better than those recorded under conditions of high acceleration.

An interesting detailed study was made of the load changes after substitution of the 55/56-tooth wheels on the Oldsmobile Toronado for the 45/46 tooth wheels.

INERTIA

Having reached this stage with our 1100- and 1800-cm^3 vehicles converted to roller chain drive we were satisfied with drive performance. The manufacturers

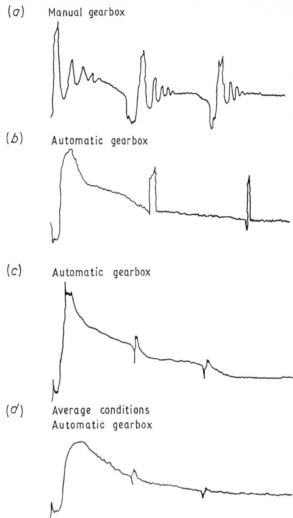

(a)   Manual gearbox

(b)   Automatic gearbox

(c)   Automatic gearbox

(d)   Average conditions
Automatic gearbox

Fig. 11.13. Transmission torques

were informed of those items which caused some disappointment from an unexpected direction, as is usual with most development work. We were informed that one of the transmission acceptance conditions with regard to their manual transmissions was the ability to drop immediately into first gear from about 40 mile/h. The inertia of the chain drive arrangement proposed proved too high to achieve this, so therefore a study of the inertia problem was initiated.

Inertia of gear primary drive system: 228·3 lb in².

Inertia of chain drive, 0·4375-in p. × 62 p. 30/30-tooth wheel: 365·3 lb in².

Inertia studies of various drive combinations eventually brought us to:

    54 pitches of 0·4375-in p. chain with
    22/22-tooth wheels designed for low inertia.

The moment of inertia on this drive was calculated to be 244·94 lb in² at 7·25 per cent increase over the gear drive. At this stage this drive was fitted to the 1800-cm³ car; changing down rapidly into first gear at over 40 mile/h was achieved, and we were back in business again.

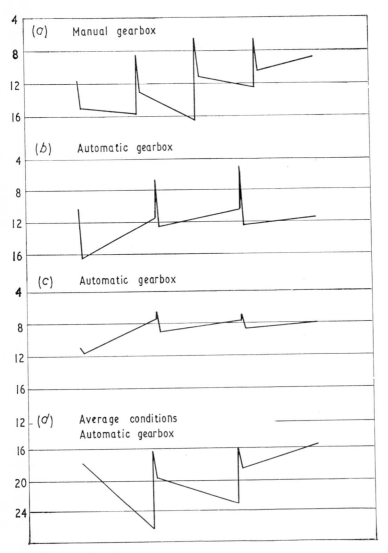

Fig. 11.14. Safety factors

CONCLUSIONS

(1) Roller chain has been proved an ideal solution to the problem of transmitting power from engine to gearbox on integral power/transmission drives for motor vehicles of any size, power, and speed.

(2) Roller chain drives correctly engineered run silently, and the problem of precise centre-to-centre tolerances, an essential feature of gear drives, does not exist on this product.

(3) On manual gearboxes an efficient form of chain adjuster, as described in the paper, is essential, and given the correct chain width and wheel selection for the application a life expectancy beyond that of associated components can be achieved without any sacrifice in smoothness or audibility.

(4) On automatic gearboxes a chain adjuster is not necessary, the torque converter providing the required shock-absorbing feature.

(5) A roller chain drive has the advantages of smooth pick-up at low speeds, easy change of ratio for special applications, low cost, and higher power transmission efficiency than gears with some consequent improvement in milage per gallon.

COMMENT

Although the roller chain transmission drives are not yet in standard use (it was not expected that existing drives would be converted), new models are using them in prototype form and design engineers are expressing approval and enthusiasm.

The MS. of this paper was received at the Institution on 7th October 1969 and accepted for publication on 28th October 1969.

Paper 12. The Inverted Tooth Chain as an Automotive Transmission Medium

M. S. HOAR
Morse Chain Division of Borg-Warner Ltd, Letchworth

Throughout the world's automotive industry, a great deal of thought is currently being directed towards achieving power transmission layouts which are both compact and weight-saving and which achieve the desired distribution of vehicle weight. This trend is particularly noticeable in Europe, where success in the market place depends to a large extent on giving greatest passenger space for the customer's money.

However, it was on a very non-European passenger car that a product was introduced which is now helping designers obtain maximum transmission compactness at minimum cost. The car was the Oldsmobile Toronado, and the product the Morse Hy-Vo® inverted tooth chain.

INTRODUCTION

The front wheel drive configuration of the 7-litre Toronado demanded a means of power transmission from the 'north–south' engine centre-line to the transmission centre-line lying parallel and some 11 in away. The drive was required to maintain the same direction of rotation as the crankshaft. Since there had been no previous investigations concerning this basic and vital link, considerable time and effort was spent in determining the best configuration. Two power transfer methods were considered. One method used a gear drive which required several precision mounted bearings for frictionless operation and to control the high thrust forces. An idler gear provided the proper direction of rotation on the driven gear. Since the three-gear transfer drive train from the engine to the transmission was the newest area in this design, an extensive test programme was initiated well before the design was finalized. Several types of gearing were proposed, including herringbone types for balanced thrust, experimental tooth profile gears with balanced loading, helical types of various pitch and helix angle, and straight spur gear combinations, all with various damping media to control noise. The alternative choice was a simple Hy-Vo chain and sprocket arrangement. After considering the features of each system, it was decided that the Hy-Vo chain and sprocket offered the most advantages, and the front wheel drive development programme began with this arrangement.

Hy-Vo had been widely used in heavy industrial applications for many years before the introduction of the Toronado, but intensive co-operation between the engineers of General Motors and Morse 'refined' the chain to provide an automatic transmission medium providing the following qualities:

(1) Silent operation up to its maximum speed of 14 000 ft/min.

(2) Minimum space and weight requirement to transmit power output.

(3) Fewer shafts and bearings than would be required with gears.

(4) Less load on remaining bearings.

(5) Longer service life than a gear set.

(6) Considerable degree of elasticity which helps to 'cushion' the drive.

(7) Cases can be lighter than with gears.

(8) Centre distance tolerance greater than with gears.

(9) No need during life for service or adjustment.

(10) More efficient power usage than gears or roller chain (99·7 per cent).

The validity of the decision to use this chain is proved by the service record of the Toronado. To date, more than 175 000 units have been built and no chain failures have been experienced. During the production life of this transmission unit, the Cadillac Eldorado has also been introduced, utilizing the same chain, and although engine capacity has risen from an initial 7 litres to 8·2 litres (the largest production car engine in the world), and power output from 350 to 410 b.h.p., no chain failures or complaints of chain noise have been experienced.

The chain used in this vehicle is 0·375 in pitch, 2 in wide × 124 pitches long. Sprocket size is 65 teeth (1:1 ratio) and centre distance between the two sprockets is 11·062 in. Ultimate tensile strength is 15 000 lb. At 5000 rev/min the chain is moving at a linear rate of 10 000 ft/min.

DETAILS OF OPERATION

Many of the above-mentioned properties of Hy-Vo can also be claimed for roller chain, but Hy-Vo has three factors in its favour which are of immense advantage:

(1) Pin-and-rocker joint, which eliminates the joint seizure problem associated with the conventional pin-and-bush chain joint when running at high speed.

(2) Action of pin-and-rocker joint under chain articulation provides pitch elongation, resulting in relative freedom from 'chordal action'.

(3) At no time are chain tensioners necessary. This applies equally to automatic and manual transmissions.

To elaborate on the above points, Fig. 12.1 shows the construction of the chain joint. It will be seen that the convex-faced pins provide the load-carrying contact and the pin faces only roll against one another, no rubbing motion being induced. Therefore, Hy-Vo can safely be run up to speeds as high as 14 000 ft/min.

The geometry of the pin-and-rocker joint is such that pitch elongation occurs when the chain is articulated (i.e. at the time of engagement with the sprocket). This 'pitch compensation' greatly reduces chordal effect, as shown in Fig. 12.2. This reduction in chordal effect enables the chain to run in a silent and vibration-free manner at the high linear speeds of which it is capable.

It can now be seen how the first part of the name Hy-Vo came to be chosen. 'Hy' stands for 'high velocity' and indicates the high-speed potential of the chain. 'Vo' is derived from the word 'involute' and refers to the form of the sprocket teeth. The involute tooth form used for the sprockets assists greatly in enabling the chain to run without tensioners. Fig. 12.3 illustrates the change in

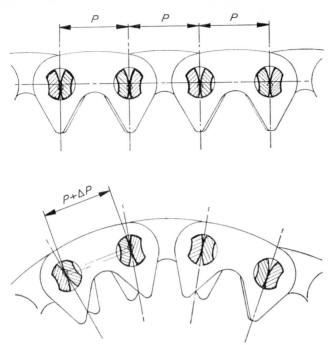

Fig. 12.1. Detail of Hy-Vo chain joint construction showing pitch elongation as chain is articulated

engagement between sprocket teeth and chain teeth as the chain wears. Chain wear will take the form of pitch elongation, and as the pitch increases, so the chain will move out to find its 'new' pitch circle. In doing so, it will engage further up the involute flank of the sprocket teeth, thus utilizing a different part of the involute and eliminating localized tooth wear.

Although an involute tooth form is used, this does not entail excessive production costs. The involute form is hobbed only, no subsequent shaving or further finishing operations being necessary. Since the chain normally wraps 180° of the sprocket, many teeth are sharing the transmission load and therefore the sprocket material can be of a much less expensive grade than would be necessary for the equivalent gear wheel, with only one or two teeth carrying the load. Heat treatment is aimed only at toughening the involute flanks to resist tearing on chain tooth engagement.

USE WITH AUTOMATIC TRANSMISSIONS

Closely following the introduction of the chain in the U.S.A. on the Toronado, two British cars were introduced utilizing this transmission medium.

The first application was in the Jensen fitted with the Ferguson four-wheel-drive system. This vehicle is powered by a 6·2 litre Chrysler engine and Torque-Flite automatic transmission. Morse Hy-Vo is used to transmit the required percentage of power to the front wheels. It will be seen that in this application

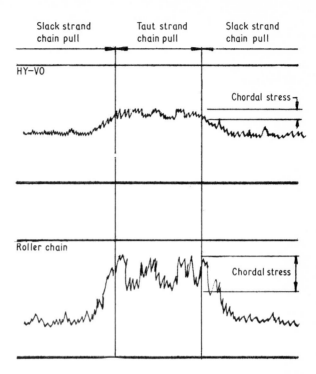

Fig. 12.2. Oscillograph recordings of stress levels in Hy-Vo and roller chains

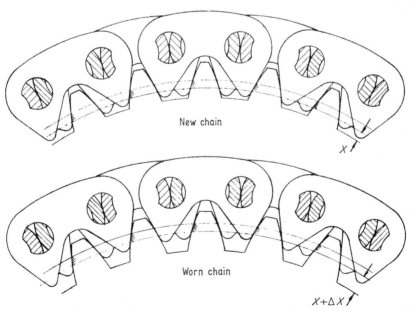

Fig. 12.3. Showing effect of chain wear on tooth engagement

the chain is required to transmit not only the output from the torque converter, but also the torque multiplication through the complete automatic transmission. This vehicle is currently using two chains, each $\frac{3}{8}$ in pitch × $1\frac{1}{8}$ in wide × 84 pitches long and each having a u.t.s. of 8400 lb. Sprocket sizes are 39T/41T on a centre distance of 8·250 in. At the approximate maximum speed for this car of 130 mile/h the chain speed is 6300 ft/min.

The second application in Britain was on the automatic transmission version of the British Leyland 1800. As with the Toronado, the chain transmits torque converter output to the epicyclic gear set. A single chain is used, $\frac{3}{8}$ in pitch × $1\frac{1}{8}$ in wide × 78 pitches, running on 38T/39T sprockets at 7·406 centres. Maximum chain speed is 7300 ft/min.

This British Leyland vehicle makes possible an interesting comparison of the bearing arrangements necessary for Morse chain and gears. Fig. 12.4 shows the bearing layout on the gear-driven manual version and also the Hy-Vo equipped automatic. The reduction in the number and size of bearings resulting from the use of the chain is self-evident. It should also be borne in mind that the bearings in the automatic box are required to carry the multiplication of engine torque brought about by the torque converter. The lack of any thrust bearings will also be observed.

In mid-1969 the use of Hy-Vo spread to Japan when Honda announced their new 1300 cm^3 passenger car. The automatic transmission version of this vehicle uses a chain $\frac{3}{8}$ in pitch × 1 in wide × 64 pitches long to drive between torque converter and epicyclic gear set. Sprocket sizes are 25 teeth driver and 31 teeth driven at 6·740 centres.

It is interesting to note that on all the aforementioned vehicles, the chain is lubricated with the automatic transmission and, indeed, it has been proved that automatic transmission fluid is one of the best possible lubricants. The main requirement of the lubricant is to provide a 'wash' of thin oil through the links of the chain, and transmission fluid, having an approximate SAE 5 viscosity classification, fulfils this function admirably.

It will be seen from the foregoing that the use of Morse Hy-Vo in conjunction with automatic transmission in production passenger vehicles is established. Further development work is progressing with various companies on new automatic transmission layouts, and it is hoped that future releases will show that chain widths have been reduced still further relative to the horsepower they are required to transmit. The foregoing examples quoted may be assumed to be the 'pioneers' in this transmission medium and consequently the chains are conservatively rated to ensure an adequate safety factor should any adverse service conditions have been overlooked. However, all production applications show a tendency to over-design with wear life well in excess of target figures.

USE WITH MANUAL TRANSMISSIONS

Equal success has been achieved in the use of Hy-Vo with manual transmissions. Morse has recently completed an intensive development programme with Honda which has resulted in the release of Hy-Vo chain on two Honda passenger vehicles.

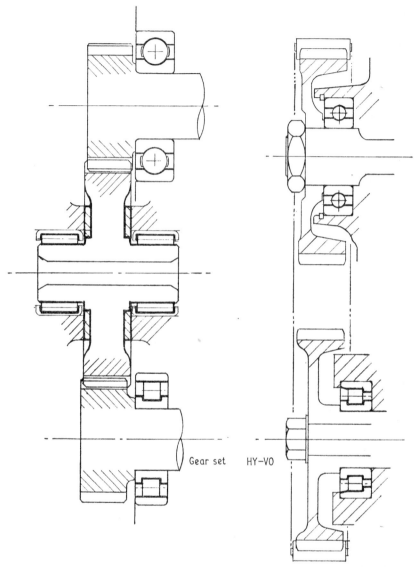

Gear set   HY–VO

Fig. 12.4. Illustrating simpler bearing arrangement with Hy-Vo

On the manual version of the Model 1300, the chain is used to transmit the drive direct from engine crankshaft to the flywheel and clutch, which are carried on the gearbox input shaft. One chain 0·375 in pitch × 1·250 in wide × 64 pitches long is used, having a u.t.s. of 9375 lb. This is sufficient to transmit drive for both the standard-engined model (producing 100 hp at 7200 rev/min and 79 lb ft at 4500 rev/min) and also the tuned version which has an output of 115 hp at 7500 rev/min and 86 lb ft at 5500 rev/min. Sprocket sizes and centre distance are the same as on the automatic transmission version. The chain lubricant supply is common with the engine, and no form of torsional oscillation damper is fitted between crankshaft and chain.

The successful application in quantity production of Hy-Vo in these manual transmission vehicles has been followed by development studies on the manual transmissions of several other companies, but at this stage the results achieved must remain confidential. However, it is betraying no confidences to indicate that the results have been very encouraging to Morse.

GAS TURBINES

One of the most interesting and arduous tasks yet performed has been to provide the transmission link between the gas turbine power unit and the Ferguson four-wheel-drive box on the Lotus Indianapolis racing cars in 1968. In this instance 3 in wide, 0·375 in pitch Hy-Vo 110 pitches long was used, running on 49-teeth sprockets at approximately 11-in centres. During the course of the 500 mile race, the Hy-Vo chains were required to transmit in excess of 550 hp at a linear speed of 11 500 ft/min. Not only did the chains successfully withstand this test, but also many hundreds of practice miles previously, and at the conclusion of the race no measurable wear was found.

CONCLUSIONS

The preceding details of the uses of Hy-Vo in established production vehicles (and more exotic media) show that this type of chain may now be considered as an automotive transmission medium in its own right. Not only does the inverted tooth chain provide a more economical means of transmission than the more complicated and weightier gear set, but advantages accrue by reason of its usage in terms of quietness and driveline resilience. This latter point cannot be too highly stressed in these days of ultra-short and compact drivelines. Hy-Vo can be a valuable means of restoring some of the resilience which is lost when designing away from the conventional front-engine/rear-wheel drive layout to either front-engine/front-wheel drive or rear-engine/rear-wheel drive.

Its speed capability and extremely high transmission efficiency are also very much in keeping with modern demands. It will be seen from the examples quoted that the full speed potential of the chain has hardly yet been utilized.

It should not be thought, since no examples of its usage on commercial vehicles have been given in this paper, that Hy-Vo is not applicable in a heavy duty role. Unfortunately, reasons of confidence must again prevail at this time, but Morse are working with several producers of heavy vehicles on some extremely interesting projects.

It is perhaps beyond the confines of the driveline paper, but passing mention must be made of the use of Hy-Vo as an ancillary drive medium. Vehicles are now running where this chain is used to drive compressors, alternators, and oil pumps, thus obviating the previous disadvantages associated with gears, roller chains, or belts.

Finally, it is hoped that these foregoing glimpses of the existing usages of this versatile transmission medium will help to show ways in which tomorrow's designs may be brought a little closer to fruition. The mid-engined car is perhaps a typical pointer to the way of progress in the 1970s, and even here Morse Hy-Vo has already been seen—on the Rover/Alvis sports car.

The MS. of this paper was received at the Institution on 16th January 1970 and accepted for publication on 19th January 1970.

Paper 13. Automatic Gearboxes, Hydrokinetic (Cars)

J. S. IVEY
Transmission Division, Borg-Warner Ltd, Letchworth, Herts.

E. J. DAVIS
Transmission Division, Borg-Warner Ltd, Letchworth, Herts.

This paper reviews the installation of automatic transmissions into vehicles, and the matching calibration of the transmission and converters to various types of engines and vehicles. Bench and field acceptance testing, with some reference to transmission manufacturers' approval of fluid and materials, are also discussed, and unorthodox automatic transmissions such as transaxle in-line and transverse, are reviewed. The paper finally examines volume production techniques of today's automatic transmissions and presents some remarks on future trends and requirements.

INSTALLATION

A specification form is forwarded to the manufacturer of the vehicle and, from these data, design of converter housing, extension housing and associated special parts, converter, and provisional transmission calibration can be determined. On receipt of the vehicle, a complete evaluation of performance, fuel consumption, and driveline resonance is carried out. The automatic transmission is then installed and a repeat of performance evaluation, followed by a durability check and final calibration, is completed before presenting the vehicle to the manufacturer.

CALIBRATION

Each engine variant requires a specific transmission calibration. After choosing a suitable converter, clutch packs, and servo sizes, a governor and control system are selected to produce the optimum shift speeds and quality whilst still maintaining good durability.

Numbers of clutch plates, basic servo diameters, and governors can be reasonably accurately predicted from engine performance curves; optimum shift quality can only be achieved by practical functional evaluation in the complete vehicle. 'Seat of the pants' shift quality and timing is still practised extensively but can only be successfully carried out by experienced automatic transmission engineers.

Modern techniques, particularly with new multi-speed transmissions, include the use of UV recorders, producing traces of shift application time, spacing, etc., together with accelerometers fitted to the vehicle to measure shift reaction.

In the current Borg-Warner transmissions, basic calibration is achieved by changing variables such as the shape of the governor curve, as illustrated in Fig. 13.1. Fig. 13.2 shows the effect of governor pressure, together with throttle pressure, on shift pattern.

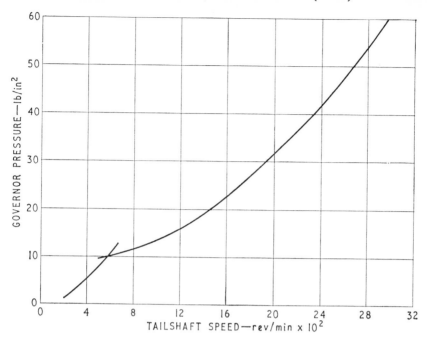

Fig. 13.1. Governor pressure

Throttle and line pressure curves (Fig. 13.3) can be varied by changing valve diameters, spring loads, and throttle valve cam forms, then by varying second speed servo diameters and springs and by the use of selected clutch and band friction elements, in conjunction with 3–2 circuit orifice sizes and control valve springs, a complete calibration is achieved. Fine tuning is achieved by some 300 permutations of control system variations being available which, with 60 combinations of governors, 40 servo/spring permutations, together with a total of 50 converter variants, cover all currently available engine types and applications ranging from 4-cylinder diesels to 12-cylinder petrol engines, rotary and gas turbines, and vehicles from sports cars and commercials to taxis, fork lift trucks, and 1- to 6-litre passenger cars.

An essential of the calibration is the correct relationship of the carburettor linkage to the throttle cable/cam linkage within the transmission which determines both shift point positions and shift quality. Figs 13.4 and 13.5 show the effect of maladjusted throttle linkages on throttle pressure and, in turn, line pressure and shift pattern.

A recent swing to manifold vacuum for pressure modulation has been halted by the introduction of automatics to diesel and petrol injection and rotary engines, not to mention certain multi-carburettored engines which suffer from poor manifold depression. Some exhaust emission systems alter the manifold vacuum characteristics to the extent that they are unusable as transmission signals.

Vehicle and engine design features can affect both shift quality and transmission durability. High engine inertia can adversely affect both shift quality and

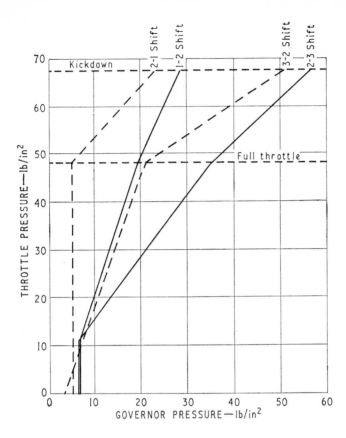

Fig. 13.2. Shift pattern relative to governor/throttle pressure

friction element durability. Engine and transmission mounts can affect shift quality. Close proximity of exhaust systems can affect transmission running temperatures. Split propeller shafts may promote judder on take-off whilst one-piece shafts, dependent on length, may introduce driveline vibrations. Four-cylinder engine applications are more prone to converter drive plate fatigue failures.

In cases where the driveline vibration level with a manual transmission is borderline, the introduction of an automatic transmission with an open torque converter may result in an unacceptable vibration level being introduced for reasons outlined below:

(*a*) An automatic transmission has an inherently weaker structure from the point of view of bending than a manual transmission. This is due to the concentric design, increased bulk, and the necessity to adapt one unit design to many vehicle configurations.

(*b*) The use of an open converter allows the critical vibration frequencies of the engine and driveline to phase in and out, with resultant airborne noise, known commonly as 'heterodyne'.

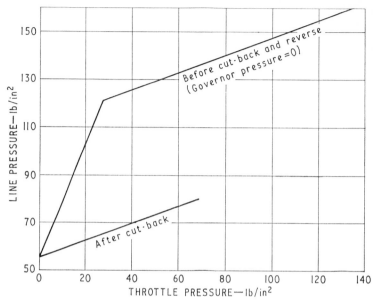

Fig. 13.3. Relationship between line pressure and throttle pressure

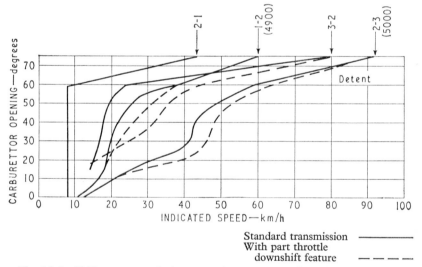

Standard transmission ——————
With part throttle
downshift feature — — — —

Fig. 13.4. Shift pattern relative to carburettor opening and vehicle speed

High-speed engine applications, requiring very high shift speeds up to 7000 rev/min in order to produce a competitive performance, call for special measures to maintain good friction element durability. Increased pressures, friction element groove patterns, in addition to cooling by positive fluid direction and reduced micro-finish of friction element mating metal parts, are but a few possible changes.

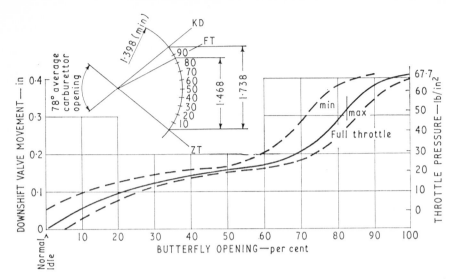

Fig. 13.5. Relationship between carburettor opening, throttle pressure and downshift valve movement with +10 per cent and −5 per cent maladjustment of carburettor linkage

In general, the ideal vehicle for an automatic transmission should have a good power to weight ratio with responsive engine, having a healthy but fairly flat torque curve; an in-line 6 or a V8 proving to be the most satisfactory cylinder arrangements.

Rotary engines, surprisingly, are easily and happily matched to automatic transmissions and, undoubtedly, have a great future as an engine/automatic transmission package, either transaxle or orthodox in-line, whilst any serious consideration of the gas turbine engine for passenger vehicles leaves little option but to specify automatic transmission to (*a*) hold the power turbine, i.e. avoiding a neutral condition, and (*b*) supply sufficient drive-away torque through the medium of the torque converter.

MATCHING A TORQUE CONVERTER TO AN ENGINE

The characteristics of a typical torque converter are shown in Fig. 13.6. For any particular speed ratio (output/input revolutions), the torque absorbed by the impeller member varies as the square of the impeller speed, and since the impeller is directly connected to the engine, it will govern the behaviour of the engine.

The law of *torque* $\propto$ (*speed*)^2 enables us to draw a family of curves (Fig. 13.7) where the torque–speed relation for the impeller, for constant speed ratios, is shown. To determine the combined functioning of the engine and converter, the engine torque/speed characteristics are plotted on the same graph. The intersection of this curve with the family of curves for the converter gives the particular values of torque and speed for this combination. Knowing the speed ratio and the torque ratio at the combination point, the output characteristics can be calculated. Various engine conditions—e.g. full throttle, part throttle, altitude conditions—

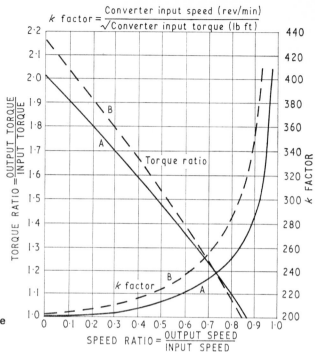

Fig. 13.6. Performance curves of two typical converters

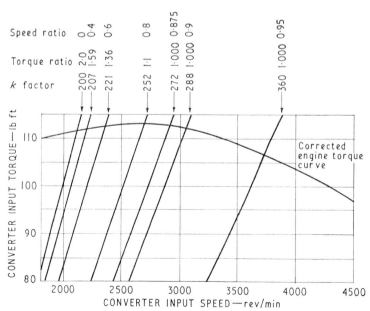

Fig. 13.7. Typical converter performance and engine torque curve plot to obtain engine/converter match characteristics

can be studied using this process, assuming that engine torque/speed characteristics are known.

A correction must be made for the engine torque curve taking into account converter windage losses, transmission front pump losses, under-bonnet breathing conditions, inlet and exhaust manifold set-ups, etc. This correction can be a reduction of 10–25 per cent of the supplied engine curve. Basically, the torque converter must be matched to a vehicle. Different types of vehicles might have the same engine but, depending on the function of the vehicle, the torque converter could need different characteristics.

Some points that must be considered when selecting a converter for a vehicle are:

(1) Stall speed of the engine, i.e. the full throttle engine speed when the turbine speed is made zero.

(2) Vehicle speed at which coupling point occurs in the converter.

(3) Stall/torque ratio requirements of the vehicle.

(4) Number of gear ratios used to supplement the converter.

(5) The engine torque/speed characteristics and the behaviour of the engine at low speeds.

(6) Altitude effects on engine performance.

(7) Engine braking.

The selection of a converter to give the correct stall speed for an engine is important. In Fig. 13.8 the curve A1 is the stall line for the 'A' converter (see

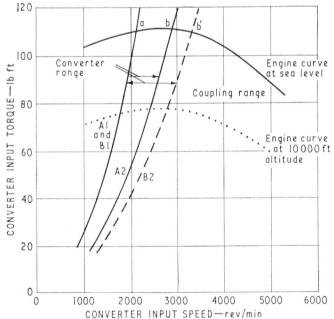

Fig. 13.8. Altitude effect on engine performance and the stall and coupling lines for A and B converters

Fig. 13.6) and the intersection point a with the engine torque curve gives the stall speed for the engine. If the stall K value for this converter is lower or higher than the indicated value, the line A1 will be either to the left or right of the present line and hence will give a lower, or higher, stall speed for this engine. As a general rule, the converter is chosen such that the stall speed for the engine is about one-third of the maximum speed of the engine, although with some current engines which do not behave well in the low-speed range, higher stall speeds are allowed.

Fig. 13.8 also illustrates the altitude effect on the engine torque curve which lowers the stall speed by about 17 per cent, and the torque value at stall by 31 per cent; therefore, it is necessary to consider the high-altitude effects on the vehicle performance in gradients and the cooling performance of the transmission.

'Drive idle' creep and engine 'fussiness' are two hazards one must look out for with too low or too high a stall speed, respectively.

Vehicle speed at which coupling point occurs in the converter depends on the spread of the converter range over the vehicle speed and this depends on the rise of the K factor curve from stall to coupling point. This is illustrated in Fig. 13.8.

Curve A2 is the coupling point line for the 'A' converter and the intersection point b gives the speed at which coupling occurs. Similarly, for the 'B' converter, curve B2 is the coupling line and b gives the corresponding coupling speed; therefore, a converter with a fast rising K curve will spread the torque multiplication period over a greater portion of the vehicle speed range. Hence, a converter with a fast rising curve gives a livelier 'take-off' performance for the vehicle than one with a slow rising curve, but since the converter with the fast rising curve produces more 'slip' and engine speed in the coupling range than that with a slow rising curve, the fuel consumption of the former will be higher than the converter with the latter curve. For passenger cars, this rise of the K factor curve is normally kept around 30 per cent.

BENCH AND FIELD ACCEPTANCE TESTING

Rig and vehicle cycling tests of individual parts, assemblies, and complete transmissions are very much an everyday activity, in order to check the quality of outside and internally manufactured parts and any new developments.

All new installations completed by Borg-Warner are subjected, among other tests, to a standard M.I.R.A. 10 000 mile cycling test, which is equivalent to a life test in that particular vehicle in the hands of a normal user. In conjunction with many of the vehicle manufacturers, tests up to 60 000 miles are not unusual: up to 65 000 full throttle shifts have been logged with engine speeds up to 6000 rev/min. This sort of requirement calls for self-adjusting servos, a recent development which is now available on all Borg-Warner transmissions.

TRANSMISSION MANUFACTURERS' APPROVAL OF FLUIDS AND MATERIALS

Automatic transmission fluids are of extreme importance in the correct functioning of automatic transmissions and are, generally, split into two groups, i.e. Dexron (a GM formulation) and fluids meeting the Ford M2C 33F specification. The latter is favoured by Borg-Warner due, mainly, to its higher static friction characteristics, although we have also seen consistently better gear life from Ford type fluids.

Approval tests are carried out on our own dynamometers on which transmission cycling tests are carried out. It is Borg-Warner's policy to factory fill for life; however, in certain severe applications, such as taxi installations, fluid changes are recommended.

One specific requirement of Borg-Warner, which differs from Ford M2C 33F, is a maximum viscosity of 55 000 cP at −40°C. This requirement is necessary due to the very small engined Model 35 applications where, in extremely low ambient conditions, start and drive-away problems have been experienced.

UNORTHODOX AUTOMATIC TRANSMISSIONS

Over the last three years, Borg-Warner have produced many thousands of transaxle automatic transmissions for in-line and transverse front wheel drive cars, with other similar types at an advanced stage of development for both front and rear engine/transmission packages.

Borg-Warner Hy-Vo chain for the drop drive (Fig. 13.9) is one of the features of these units. The advantages of Hy-Vo chain are many, the major of which are the elimination of the idler gear and its associated bearings, long life, silent operation, and ease of lubrication, coupled with low power loss.

Fig. 13.9

Common fluid supplies for transmission and final drive are favoured from a simplicity point of view, but are rarely satisfactory. Axle lubricants are concerned primarily with lubricity to withstand heavy bearing and gear tooth loadings. Transmission fluid must act as a power transmission medium and as a lubricant at high and low temperatures. It must be compatible with friction elements and a great variety of other materials, in addition to being suitable for use in the hydraulic control system.

Care should be taken to ensure that any heavily loaded ball or roller thrust bearings which, through necessity with transaxle designs, are lubricated by automatic transmission fluid are, in fact, adequately lubricated. Back-to-back lip seals used to separate axle and transmission fluids should, preferably, have an exhaust to atmosphere between the seals.

Special reference to cooling of transaxle transmissions should be made. Owing to the close proximity of the engine's oil, considerable transfer of heat takes place, hence the cooling of any one of the three fluids, i.e. axle, transmission, or engine, can benefit the other two. Certainly a cooler for either engine or transmission oil is recommended where the vehicle is likely to be used for caravan towing.

Where the engine transmission package is sited at the front of the vehicle, considerable cooling benefits can be gained by intelligent ducting of air over the transmission unit. As with orthodox automatic transmissions, oil to water or oil to air coolers can be used satisfactorily.

VOLUME PRODUCTION TECHNIQUES

The complex nature of modern automatic transmissions has, perhaps, more than any other product highlighted the need to eliminate, wherever possible, the human element during manufacture, assembly, and test. To this end, the use of computers in scheduling parts and automated dynamometers, over which every transmission must pass, are now commonplace.

On such items as governors, valve block assemblies, servos, clutch packs, and converters, there are over 450 possible variants currently in production. This is an undesirable situation from a production point of view, but it is necessary to cover the wide range of applications.

Perhaps one of the most significant developments in production techniques and a process already successfully applied in many areas (for example, converter bosses) is friction welding. This process is extremely consistent and will, eventually, be used more extensively in automatic transmission manufacture.

Deep drawn pressings which require little or no machining for clutch cylinders and similar parts are rapidly taking over from existing machined forgings and castings: e.g. sintered parts, fitted as received from the die, and various forms of plastic thrust washers which not only reduce machining and process time and, as a result, cost, but also are actually considerably superior functionally.

The increasing application of transaxle automatic transmissions and the resulting, at least to start with, low volume, will call for more use of NC machines for machining the major castings, although the basic control systems, running gear, and friction elements are likely to be common over a wide range of designs.

Fig. 13.10 shows an example of commonization. The assembly of front and rear clutch and planetary gearset is virtually unchanged over three entirely

Fig. 13.10

different production transmissions, and at least four other prototypes are destined for production over the next two years.

FUTURE TRENDS

Although torque ratios from the converter of up to 2·4:1 are available, the short duration over which this advantage is possible does not compensate for an additional mechanical ratio. Therefore, until the stepped transmission is replaced by some form of infinitely variable design, the trend will be to four speeds or more for better performance, particularly below 2·8 litres and, eventually, for commercial vehicles.

Future requirements indicate a world-wide production capability equal in volume to total vehicle production. This will mean local manufacture of many world-wide common parts; transmissions which are, virtually, sealed units with strategically based overhaul depots throughout the world. The increased use of pressings replacing many cast machined parts will also help reduce price, weight, and overall dimensions.

Economic world-wide usage of manufacturing capacity will be increased. As an example, U.K. manufactured converters are currently being used with U.S.A. manufactured transmissions, both in the U.K. and Japan. U.K. manufactured transmission mechanisms and control systems are assembled into transmissions in Australia and, conversely, some common components are manufactured in the U.S.A. and used in U.K. production.

Amalgamation and commonization, within the major transmission manufacturers and, eventually, between companies currently competing, is a certainty, just as vehicle manufacturers have been forced to merge in order to compete commercially. Dramatic cost reductions will be possible with new production techniques and with increased volumes and commonization of units.

It is certain that it will be within the driveline that one of the greatest single developments in vehicle design will take place over the next 10 years—the general adoption of the automatic transmission.

The MS. of this paper was received at the Institution on 18th December 1969 and accepted for publication on 9th January 1970.

Paper 14. Automatic Gearboxes (Hydrokinetic) for Trucks and Buses

S. F. BURNETT
Director and Chief Engineer, Self-Changing Gears Ltd, Coventry

This paper shows that the hydrokinetic transmission is no newcomer to the field of trucks and buses and that in public service vehicles, in semi-automatic form, it is virtually standard equipment. Economic pressures, increasing traffic densities, etc., will lead to greater use of fully automatic transmissions in buses, and several notable fully automatic hydrokinetic public service vehicle transmissions are reviewed. In the trucking field, economic considerations are also creating a trend to larger and more powerful vehicles which will demand ease and certainty of control, and thus a place for fully automatic transmissions. An examination of the format of commercially successful fully automatic hydrokinetic truck and bus transmissions reveals that transmission designers have made extensive use of epicyclic gearing, and the paper includes an appreciation of the characteristics and advantages of this type of gearing.

INTRODUCTION

It is well known that it is the nature and characteristics of the internal combustion engine which makes necessary a change-speed and torque-multiplying power transmission unit in vehicles which employ the internal combustion engine as prime mover.

The power transmission unit must complement the engine so that their combination results in a power pack that is capable of providing considerable torque, and hence tractive effort, when the vehicle is starting. To meet the varying conditions of normal running, it must make available the developed power of the engine over a wide range of speed and, for manoeuvring and other purposes, a reverse drive.

The almost complete acceptance of the diesel engine as prime mover for commercial vehicles has encouraged engine designers to examine many avenues of development in their search for greater efficiency and increased power. Consequently, engines have emerged that have differing characteristics which demand differing power transmission units so that the total power pack will exhibit the required overall characteristics.

In the general case a naturally aspirated diesel engine has a fairly flat torque curve, quite reasonable levels of torque being produced at low speeds with maximum torque occurring in the middle of the engine speed range. The turbocharged engine is rather different in that maximum torque occurs much nearer to maximum governed speed, the torque falling off more rapidly as compared with the naturally aspirated engine as the speed of the engine falls. The so-called constant horsepower engines are different again in that they develop more torque as the engine speed falls and, consequently, the power output tends to remain constant over a fairly wide range of engine speed. The automotive gas turbine has characteristics similar to the constant horsepower diesel engine but with the very important difference that it produces maximum torque when its power turbine is stalled.

It is against this background of different engines and varying overall vehicle requirements that the automotive engineer must look at transmissions for commercial vehicles.

HISTORICAL

The hydrokinetic transmission is no newcomer to the commercial vehicle world since, in semi-automatic form, it has been almost standard equipment on town buses in the U.K. and elsewhere for many years. During 1908–1910 Dr Fottinger evolved the hydraulic coupling from his earlier invention, the torque converter, but the hydraulic coupling did not undergo any practical development until 1923 when it was exploited as an automatic clutch and torsion damper for shipboard equipments.

The successful application of the hydraulic coupling to motor vehicles was chiefly due to Sinclair, a British engineer, who brilliantly foresaw the possibilities of the unit and the marriage of the hydraulic coupling to Wilson's epicyclic change-speed gearbox. This latter development laid the foundations for many excellent hydrokinetic transmissions, from which the Leyland Motors pneumo-cyclic power shifted hydrokinetic transmission was developed. In semi-automatic form, this transmission is now widely used for public service vehicles.

PUBLIC SERVICE VEHICLES

The demand for fully automatic transmissions in public service vehicles is rapidly increasing. The economic pressures which beset the operating companies are causing them to turn to one-man vehicles and vehicles of increased carrying capacity. In the one-man vehicle the driver is not only required to drive but also to collect fares and operate the entrance and exit doors. In view of these extra duties, it is imperative that the driving of the vehicle should be as easy as possible to reduce driver fatigue to a minimum and thus maintain the highest possible level of safety.

Increasing traffic density is making the driving of public service vehicles more and more arduous, and for this reason alone, excluding the demands of one-man operated vehicles, there is a great need for fully automatic transmissions.

The pneumocyclic transmission has been widely accepted because it meets the public service vehicle operating requirements so adequately. It offers an ease of control which leads to a reduction of driver fatigue with increased safety. It provides a very high level of engine braking and its efficiency is such that satisfactory fuel consumption figures are achieved. The initial cost of this transmission is not prohibitive and, by reason of its construction, it is not difficult to overhaul when this becomes necessary.

Fig. 14.1 is a line diagram of a unit construction four-speed and reverse pneumocyclic gearbox. It comprises an engine-mounted hydraulic coupling connected in series with a compound four-speed and reverse epicyclic running

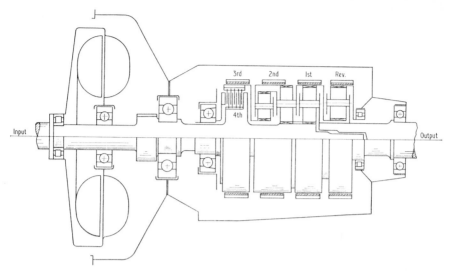

Fig. 14.1. B.L.M.C. four-speed and reverse pneumocyclic transmission

gear. The first, second, and third indirect ratios are obtained when the reaction members of the appropriate epicyclics are arrested by the power operated balanced band type brakes. The direct drive top gear is obtained by the operation of a multiple plate clutch which locks two elements of the compound epicyclic together and thus ensures that the compound epicyclic running gear rotates en bloc.

The power operation of the brakes and direct drive clutch is accomplished either by the use of compressed air from the vehicle's air system or by the use of hydraulic pressure which is generated by in-built transmission pumps. The servo pressure is directed to the brake operating cylinders either by manually operated or electrically operated valves. When electrically operated valves are employed, they may be under the control of a simple selector switch, in which case the transmission is semi-automatic, or under electrical or electronic control which automatically selects the appropriate gear ratio, thus making the transmission fully automatic.

The fully automatic version of the pneumocyclic transmission is an excellent example of a fully automatic hydrokinetic transmission employing a hydraulic coupling. Other manufacturers have favoured the use of torque converters in their fully automatic public service vehicle transmissions, and Fig. 14.2 shows the well-known 2HP/45/2 Busmatic transmission manufactured by Zahnradfabrik of Friedrichshafen, West Germany. This transmission comprises a single-stage two-phase torque converter which embodies a lock-up clutch in series connection with a compound epicyclic running gear and gives an indirect forward and an indirect reverse gear. The arrangement of the running gear is such that when the converter lock-up clutch is operated the power is transmitted directly from the engine flywheel half of the converter casing to the gearbox output shaft.

Hydraulically operated plate clutch brakes are employed to arrest the epicyclic

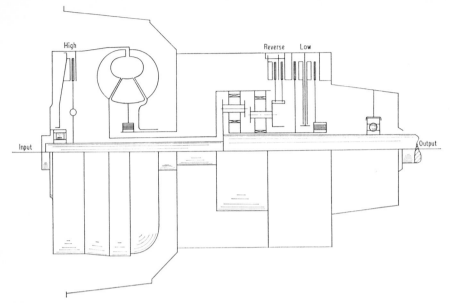

Fig. 14.2. Z.F. 2HP/45/2 Busmatic transmission

running gear reaction members, and to ensure that there is no loss of traction during the change from first gear to second gear a freewheel is used to sustain the first gear reaction during the gear change transition. The hydraulic pressure for gearbox operation is obtained from an inbuilt pump, the servo pressure being directed to the required clutch or clutch brake by means of electrohydraulic valves which are electrically controlled to make the transmission automatic. A kick-down is also provided.

In the first gear mode of operation both the torque converter and the epicyclic reduction are used. When second gear is selected, the drive is direct from input to output, the converter and epicyclic running gear being by-passed.

In common with most heavy duty torque converter transmissions an oil cooler is normally fitted and this can be of either oil to engine cooling water or oil to air type.

Fig. 14.3 illustrates the Voith Engineering Limited type 501 Drivabus differential torque converter transmission. This is a particularly interesting unit in that a differential distributor gear is used between the engine and a single-stage torque converter to give a split drive path.

The differential distributor gear takes the form of a spur differential, the carrier of which can be arrested by a hydraulically operated band brake. The carrier of the differential distributor gear is connected to the torque converter pump wheel, and the output sunwheel of the differential distributor is mounted upon the input shaft of the epicyclic reduction gear set which is located downstream of the torque converter. This final compound epicyclic reduction gear provides a high forward gear range, a low forward gear range, and a reverse gear range.

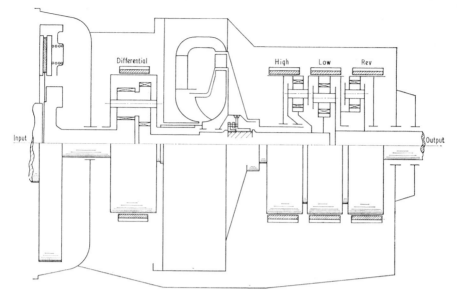

Fig. 14.3. Voith 501 Drivabus transmission

Pneumatically operated band brakes are employed to arrest the reaction members of the final epicyclic reduction gear set; the selection of high range, low range, or reverse is under the control of the driver and is by means of a suitable selector switch.

Located between the torque converter turbine and the final epicyclic reduction gear input shaft is a freewheel which enables torque to be transmitted to the shaft. Automaticity is achieved hydraulically and the mode of operation of the transmission is varied by the application or release of the brake band associated with the differential distributor carrier.

When the vehicle is at rest with, say, the high forward gear range selected, the first motion sunwheel of the differential distributor gear is driven by the engine and the second sunwheel of the differential distributor will be stationary. This condition impresses a rotation upon the differential distributor carrier, and thus upon the torque converter pump wheel, of approximately twice the engine speed. Absorbed engine torque is multiplied hydraulically by the torque converter and conveyed to the final epicyclic reduction gear by the freewheel.

As the vehicle moves off and gains speed, the numerical value of the ratio of engine speed to torque converter pump wheel speed reduces, as does that of the input power transmitted hydraulically through the torque converter, while that part of the input power transmitted mechanically through the differential distributor gear to the final epicyclic reduction gear increases. With this automatic division of power into mechanical and hydraulic paths, high power transmission efficiency is obtained.

When the hydraulic automatic control system senses that the engine is approaching maximum speed, the brake band associated with the carrier of the differential distributor gear is applied and the drive becomes wholly mechanical, the torque converter being by-passed as the turbine freewheel now overruns.

When this transmission is installed with a water-cooled diesel engine the transmission oil is cooled by a water jacket which surrounds the torque converter. When installed with air-cooled engines a separate oil-to-air heat exchanger is fitted.

TRUCK TRANSMISSIONS

Since highway trucks, heavy tractor vehicles, and off-highway vehicles each make their own particular demands on the power pack, the case for automatic transmissions in these vehicles is perhaps best examined by reviewing each category of vehicle separately.

Highway trucks

It is often argued that the advent of motorways in the U.K. and on the Continent has so reduced the frequency of gear shifting that a conventional layshaft transmission is all that is required for the highway truck. Although the highway truck will always make the greatest possible use of motorways, it is inevitable that part of the journey will be on regular roadways and more than likely that its journey will begin and end in a built-up area. It follows that the driver will be subjected to all the problems arising from increased traffic density and, accordingly, an automatic transmission would be welcome, reducing driver fatigue and enhancing safety and efficiency.

The operation of highway trucks is strictly a business undertaking and, as much as the drivers may like the semi-automatic or fully automatic transmissions, the operator must also see some return for the investment which he has made in an improved transmission.

In those cases where direct comparison has been possible, it has emerged that productivity has improved in that more miles per working shift have been accomplished and, equally important, much better industrial relations have been established between the drivers and the operating company. On a strictly financial basis the reduction of down time, the improved productivity, and the much longer life of the service brakes have led to savings which have amortized the premium for the improved transmission.

Compared with current highway trucks grossing at 32 tons with engines of 150–180 hp, i.e. 5–6 hp per ton, vehicles are now emerging which will gross at 40 tons, and there is a modern tendency that 8 hp and preferably 10 hp per ton is necessary to give satisfactory road performance; thus the engine will be in the 320–400 hp bracket. To provide this level of power, the engine is likely to be either a turbocharged diesel or a gas turbine. The turbocharged diesel produces its maximum torque near maximum governed speed, and a well-chosen torque converter will permit an engine having this characteristic to develop its maximum torque and so make available a high level of tractive effort when the vehicle is starting from rest with consequent benefit on its restart capabilities. The use of a torque converter means that there need only be five or six gear steps to give the required range, thus making a transmission format that is entirely suitable for fully automatic operation.

If the gas turbine is chosen as prime mover, the need for a torque converter is debatable as the torque–speed characteristics of the gas turbine are that the torque rises as the speed falls, with maximum torque occurring when the power turbine is stalled. If a stepped transmission is used, economy of gear steps is again possible and automatic control of gear shifting is both possible and desirable.

The constant horsepower diesel engine goes some way to support the view that a simple unsophisticated transmission is all that is needed in a highway truck since this engine is able to make its power available over a wider range of speed than other diesel engines and so reduce the frequency of gear shifting. If this engine is used, it is a provocative thought that perhaps the transmission should so complement the engine that, by being fully automatic, it removes the need for manual gear shifting altogether.

Heavy tractor vehicles

These machines haul the heaviest of trailer-borne payloads and are usually built with engines of 350–400 hp. This means that the power/weight ratio is probably not better than 3 hp per gross ton and gives rise to the need for frequent gear changes. Ease of control and certainty of engagement are essential if efficiency and safety are to be preserved. A fully automatic transmission will adequately satisfy these requirements, but manual override should be provided so that traffic islands, narrow winding streets, and difficult corners can be safely and satisfactorily negotiated.

Off-highway trucks (dumpers)

The off-highway dump truck operates under most difficult and arduous conditions. The terrain is often near impossible and in quarrying or open-cast coal mining, etc., the payload is hauled from the working face up tracks which have severe gradients, difficult bends, and bad surfaces. Driving a heavily loaded vehicle under these conditions is both difficult and dangerous, so much so that ease of control tends to determine the size and weight of machine that one man can handle.

As wages continue to rise, the driver's pay becomes a more significant part of the total cost of production and operators are favouring larger and more powerful machines in an attempt to maintain the labour cost to payload ratio at an economic level. These larger and more powerful machines demand the greatest possible ease of control so that safety is assured and productivity maintained over the working day. On this basis alone there is an almost overwhelming case for a fully automatic transmission but, if the benefits which a torque converter confer on the total driveline are also considered, there can be little doubt that a fully automatic hydrokinetic transmission is a very attractive system for these machines. The appeal of the transmission is enhanced if it is provided with a retarder, and the ability to hold indirect gears is of great value when the vehicle is negotiating low adhesion terrain.

From many points of view there is a compelling case for fully automatic transmissions in trucks, and Fig. 14.4 presents a diagram of the Allison fully automatic truck transmission. A single-stage, three-element torque converter embodying a lock-up clutch is in series connection with a compound epicyclic running gear which is, itself, a series arrangement of two-speed primary splitter and a three-speed and reverse secondary gear set. This running gear provides six forward speeds and a reverse drive, the reaction members of the epicyclic gear sets being arrested by hydraulically operated plate clutch brakes.

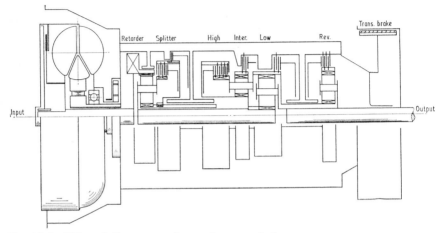

Fig. 14.4. Allison fully automatic truck transmission

The transmission includes a hydraulic retarder or hydrokinetic brake associated with the first motion member of the splitter, such that controlled admission of oil to the working space of the retarder augments engine braking and materially reduces the work of the service brakes.

Automaticity is provided hydraulically and is such that, in the normal driving mode, the torque converter is effective on third gear only, the converter locking when it reaches the coupling phase. During the subsequent gear shifts, the converter unlocks momentarily to ensure the highest possible quality of change.

Manual override is provided so that the lowest gears can be held, and intermediate stations of the driver's selector give limited ranges of automaticity in intermediate gears. The gear-changing speeds are throttle modulated so that the changes occur at higher engine speeds as the power demand is increased. A transmission oil cooler is necessary and, in this regard, care must be taken to ensure that the heat exchanger is capable of dealing with the heat rejection of the in-built hydrokinetic retarder.

THE ADVANTAGES AND CHARACTERISTICS OF EPICYCLIC GEARING

The very extensive use of epicyclic gearing in semi- and fully automatic transmissions is at once apparent when a review is made of those now enjoying commercial exploitation. It is suggested that the high efficiency of power transmission and the constructional advantages which the epicyclic confers are the features which have attracted transmission designers and, accordingly, that a brief assessment of the advantages and characteristics of epicylic is an appropriate supplement to this paper.

The high efficiency of power transmission of the epicyclic is due to the following:

(1) The power transmitted by the dynamic action of the gear teeth is not the total power but the reaction power, which is less than the total power except when the epicyclic is a reverse. Reaction power bears the same relationship to total power as the reaction torque bears to the carrier torque.

(2) The speed of tooth engagement is relatively low.

(3) No external journal loads arise from gear tooth action, since the gear separating forces are balanced and self-contained.

(4) The transmitted tooth load is carried by a multiplicity of gear teeth, resulting in moderate unit loadings.

The contructional advantages of the epicyclic are:

(1) It is constant mesh gearing.

(2) It is a three-element gear set which easily affords a first motion member, an output member, and a reaction member, the control of which gives control of the gear set.

(3) Since hydraulically operated or pneumatically operated band brakes or clutch brakes are widely used to give control of reaction members, and as the operating cylinders of such band brakes or clutch brakes are conveniently associated with the gearcase, the air or oil may be brought into the operating cylinders through static connections.

While the low relative speed of tooth engagement, the absence of external journal loads, and moderate unit loadings contribute to high efficiency, there are other advantages which arise from these characteristics.

The low relative speed of tooth engagement makes a very significant contribution to the attainment of a satisfactory noise level without recourse to unduly high standards of accuracy. The absence of external journal loads relieves the gearcase of the bursting forces which parallel shaft gearing imposes, and makes possible the use of simple lightweight casings. Moderate unit loading and the constant-mesh nature of the epicyclic are the underlying reasons for the long life and durability which is expected of, and usually given by, the automotive epicyclic gear set.

CONCLUSIONS

There is undoubtedly a very strong case for fully automatic transmissions in town buses. Fully automatic operation safeguards the transmission from unintentional abuse, mitigates strongly against bad driving techniques, and so leads to greater passenger comfort.

The ever-increasing traffic density demands the greatest possible ease of control to minimize driver fatigue and so enhance the safety of both the passengers and the vehicle.

The economic pressures which the operating companies are facing, arising from both increased costs and rising wages, are forcing them to turn to one-man buses or to larger and more powerful vehicles having greater carrying capacity.

In the case of the one-man bus, the driver/conductor is concerned with fare collection, entrance and exit door operation, and the safety of his passengers as well as driving, so that total ease of control of the vehicle is imperative and, in this regard, the fully automatic transmission makes a major contribution.

Driving the larger and more powerful machines in dense traffic and over difficult routes requires that the highest level of attention is given to the manipulation of the vehicle and the easement which the fully automatic transmission gives makes for increased efficiency and productivity. In all this, the prime reason for the adoption of automatic transmissions in public service vehicles is one of economics, and similar influences are to be found in the trucking field.

In the search for more economical operation, both over the road and off-highway machines are becoming larger and more powerful, and the ability of a driver to handle these machines safely and efficiently is demanding ease and certainty of control. A fully automatic hydrokinetic transmission accords with this and owing to the benefits it confers on the total driveline—by the almost complete elimination of unintentional driver abuse and by the improved productivity which can be expected from its use—it can make a valuable contribution to the viability of truck operation.

ACKNOWLEDGEMENTS

The author wishes to thank Zahnradfabrik Friedrichshafen A.G. (Friedrichshafen, West Germany), Voith Engineering Ltd (Polmadie, Glasgow), G.M. Power & Industrial (Wellingborough, Northants), and The British Leyland Motor Corporation Ltd (Leyland, Lancs) for the data and drawings which were so willingly supplied and for their permission to make reference to their products.

The MS. of this paper was received at the Institution on 16th January 1970 and accepted for publication on 3rd February 1970.

Paper 15. Automatic Gearboxes (Hydrokinetic), Trans-axle and Light Cars

A. J. ATKINS, CEng, MIMechE

Borg and Beck Company Ltd, Leamington Spa, Warwickshire

This paper outlines the essential requirements for light car transmissions and shows how they differ from those suitable for larger cars. Apart from the obvious size and weight limitations these transmissions must be sufficiently flexible to cope with the usually lower power/weight factors. They must have less power losses and be produced at a cost in proportion to the price of the cars. Comment is made on the intrinsic problems of designing transmissions that are sturdy enough to accept heavy duty and yet are lightweight, efficient, and trouble free while remaining within the price range of the motorist who expects economy with adequate performance.

INTRODUCTION

Since 1945, automatic transmissions for the larger type cars have been fairly well established, and they usually take the form of a two- or three-speed epicyclic running gear behind a hydrokinetic converter. Their introduction in smaller cars has been slower, partly for technical and commercial reasons, the latter being the predominant factor.

The situation is somewhat paradoxical. With the lower power/weight ratios available it is necessary to widen the ratio range—which usually leads to a more sophisticated layout—in order to avoid severe limitations in overall performance. At the same time, costs for these requirements must be carefully controlled, so that they can be kept proportionate to the overall value of the vehicle and thus make it an attractive proposition for the buying public.

With these factors in mind, Automotive Products introduced a four-speed automatic for the F.W.D. Austin Mini in 1965, to be followed by up-rated versions to suit the 1100 and 1300 cm^3 vehicles. Also, more recently, an 'in-line' unit has been introduced to cover the $1\frac{1}{2}$- to $2\frac{1}{2}$-litre range of vehicles, which also include trans-axle versions.

All these transmissions incorporate a hydrokinetic torque converter with a four-speed, spiral bevel running gear which is hydraulically controlled.

Before highlighting some of the special features embodied in their construction, it is considered appropriate to outline a few of the basic requirements and problems involved in light car applications.

CONVERTERS AND GEARS

As a primary coupling between an internal combustion engine and transmission unit, a hydrokinetic torque converter has many advantages, irrespective of engine size. The predominant features include the ability to multiply torque, the inherent smooth engagement, its flexibility throughout the drive range, and an ample heat capacity.

In addition, with the popular three-stage type and relative to its duty, the hydrokinetic torque converter is a reasonably straightforward unit to manufacture; for use in automobiles it is mainly constructed from light steel pressings.

It is not uncommon for critics to adversely comment on its efficiencies, particularly when installed in light cars. The facts are that with the smaller type vehicles, provided there are adequate ratio steps in the transmission, these units are in their coupling range at speeds above 10 mile/h, and efficiencies approach 98 per cent—particularly under normal cruising conditions where engine speeds are comparatively high combined with moderate torque outputs.

An essential difference between large car applications with their higher axle and power/weight ratios is that when quick acceleration is required at intermediate speeds in top (say, overtaking at 50 mile/h) the converter comes into action to augment the accelerating force, in addition to the large reserve of engine power.

With smaller cars and under similar road conditions, the converter usually remains in the coupling range, and for comparable acceleration performance it is necessary to downshift. For this reason, it is desirable to have fairly close ratio steps throughout.

Another factor to be considered is the stall speed. The converter characteristics are usually arranged to provide for a stall speed around 2000 rev/min against the maximum available engine torque, because in practice speeds much in excess of this tend to make the car 'fussy' and noisy at take-away. Unfortunately, with most small car engines, maximum torque occurs higher up the speed range, and if it is off-tune or is taking up from cold with less power available, the converter pulls the engine speed still further down the torque curve.

Another important feature of this type of drive is that the nature of the road surface has an appreciable effect on climbability; that is, on a limiting gradient a pothole or local obstruction may prevent take-away, where by increasing the engagement speed in a manually operated clutch and gearbox, the inertia of the engine can be utilized to assist in overcoming the immediate obstacle. For these reasons it is also necessary to have a sufficiently low first gear ratio to take off successfully from a steep gradient.

In the case of the A.P. spiral bevel running gear the ratios provided are 1, 1·46, 1·84, and 2·68 to 1 in first and reverse, which satisfies the conditions described.

CLUTCHES AND BRAKE BANDS

Many factors must be considered in the choice of using multi-disc clutches or brake bands to control the epicyclic torque reactions or to transmit power. The most desirable features are for consistently smooth engagement and durability combined with a minimal drag and power loss when disengaged.

With multi-disc clutch units the number and type of friction plates is the first consideration. The most widely used facings are made from resinated fibre material which is bonded to a mild steel core plate. Alternative facings are the sintered bronze variety, usually having a lower coefficient of friction and the unit pressures are required to be lower. The main advantage with the sintered bronze type is their resistance to higher temperatures, and unlike the fibre material, a fair proportion of heat is transferred through the facings and core-plates to the driving hub. For this reason, when a clutch is used for heavy duty and frequent power shifting, sintered facings show to advantage.

In all of these applications the clutches are cooled by a supply of oil which is first channelled through the drive shafts and hubs, and then between grooving in the friction facings. Heat is also dissipated through the spacer plates located in the clutch housings, and the width of these and the number of driving teeth have an important function in temperature control (Fig. 15.1).

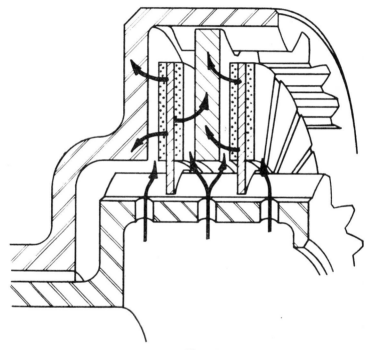

Fig. 15.1. Clutch cooling diagram

In general, it is usually easier to control engagement qualities with multi-disc clutches than with brake bands—particularly when torque reactions are reversed; say, during overrunning engagement conditions. However, careful consideration has to be given to two obvious disadvantages with a multiplicity of friction and spacer plates: they increase the overall length and weight of the transmission, and have a tendency to increase clutch drag, with consequent power loss when disengaged.

Brake bands, however, have fewer parts, take up less space, and heat dissipation and disengaged drag conditions can be more easily controlled.

Other features include the servo effect in fully wrapping applications which can be used to advantage for controlling high reverse reaction torques or, alternatively, when used for smoothing engagement on overrun downshifts. Where the servo characteristics are not desirable, a simple form of linkage system to apply balanced loadings to both ends of the band may be adopted (Fig. 15.2).

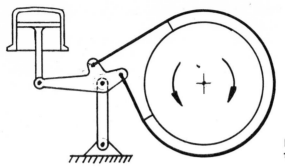

Fig. 15.2. Linkage system to apply balanced loadings

A simple way to minimize drag is to ensure that the bands spring open against fixed stops in the gear casing to provide adequate clearance between the lining and brake drum when in the 'off' position.

One of the disadvantages of the popular single-piece construction is that the torque reaction loadings are transferred to the brake drum supporting shaft, with its consequent deflection according to the location of the bearings and magnitude of loads. A solution to this problem is to use a two-piece band with two reaction points equidistant from the axis and opposite one another, as used on heavy commercial vehicles (Fig. 15.3). However, their complication and expense would be impracticable and unnecessary for light car applications where torque loadings are comparatively moderate.

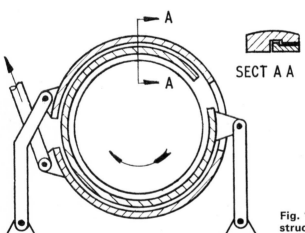

SECT A A

Fig. 15.3. A two-piece construction with two reaction points

HYDRAULICS AND PUMPS

One good reason for controlling the clutches and brake bands hydraulically is that since it is essential to use a pump to feed oil to the converter and clutches for heat dissipation, and to provide for lubrication of the epicyclic gears, its use may be extended to pressurize the clutch and brake band pistons and servos. This, in fact, is the popular arrangement with these types of transmission.

The usual system is for the main pump, which is driven off the input shaft, to supply the clutch pistons or servos at around 100 lb/in². The pressure is controlled by a regulator valve and the surplus flow is channelled through to the other units at lower pressures. It is essential that the pump capacity is sufficient to maintain the desired pressure to the servos at low engine speeds, especially at elevated oil temperatures, by providing for the unavoidable flows through all the leak paths—which include the pump, the spool valves in the valve block, and the respective connections in the oilways. It will be appreciated that at high engine speed, pump outputs become an embarrassment, therefore efficient sealing and reducing the number of connections to a minimum pays dividends in allowing a smaller pump to be used. This, in turn, reduces substantially the overall power losses and working temperatures.

In the A.P. transmissions flow control valves are incorporated which assist in reducing still further the pressures and heat in the pump unit.

GOVERNING

There appears to be a fairly wide variation in the type of governing systems used, with each having advantages and limitations.

To name a few, there are electrical systems, and all hydraulic and mechanical devices. The latter type is used on A.P. transmissions, owing to their consistent performance throughout the temperature range. Also, by substituting various springs which are incorporated in these systems, wide variations in characteristics may be achieved to suit any particular installation. A diagram of the system used in the Mk III transmission is depicted in Fig. 15.4.

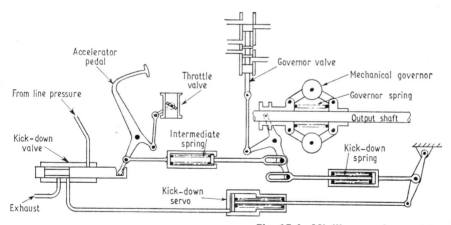

Fig. 15.4. Mk III governing system

AUXILIARY PUMPS

With the advent of quantity produced automatic transmissions which incorporated a hydrokinetic coupling or converter, many were fitted with an auxiliary pump. These pumps, which are usually a gear type and are driven off the output shaft, allow the clutches to be engaged when the engine and main pump are 'dead', thus enabling the vehicle to be tow-started. Unfortunately this facility has many disadvantages apart from cost and complication, and for these and other reasons their fitment has become less popular, especially for light car applications.

One of the problems is the continued loss of power despite the use of the dump valve to isolate the pump from the hydraulic circuit as the main pump takes over. This valve allows the pump to work freely under these conditions. However, as the hydraulic friction through the pump and pipes is far in excess of the pumping horsepower, any reduction in this has a negligible effect and, in addition to the actual power loss, it is absorbed by the sump oil, thus increasing the overall running temperature.

SPACE AVAILABILITY

There are so many variants in trans-axle layouts that space limitations vary widely according to the specific application. They may be used to drive the front or rear wheels, and in some instances part of the vehicle suspension system may be involved. However, it is usually found that it is most desirable, if not essential, for the overall length of the running gear with its associated reaction members to be as short as possible.

In the more orthodox system, i.e. with the transmission mounted behind the engine and driving the rear axle through a propeller shaft, space limitations are more clearly defined, particularly as the body flooring and tunnel are usually designed round a manually operated layshaft gearbox. Fig. 15.5 indicates a few of the associated problems.

It will be appreciated that, to avoid changes to the electric starter mounting and the body flooring, the outside diameter and the overall width of the converter casing is critical. This is where the 'welded up' construction shows to advantage, apart from providing extra rigidity to this unit, as mentioned previously.

Another important consideration—particularly with small cars—is that tunnel space is usually sufficient only to house the running gear, and the hydraulic control system, which includes a valve block and servos, must be mounted below this and the basic floor line. This imposes severe space limitations to avoid

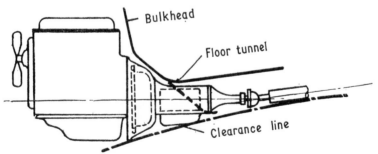

Fig. 15.5. Space criteria, in-line installations

encroaching on the ground clearance, which can be considered on most installations as a line extending from the bottom of the bell housing to a point below the swept diameter of the front propeller shaft universal joint.

GEAR CASING STRESSES

One of the attractive features of epicyclic transmissions is that the torque reactions transmitted to the casing under forward drive conditions are, in each case, relative to the numerical gear reduction minus one, and for this reason torsional stresses are always moderate. The main consideration is to provide adequate longitudinal stiffness in the assembly.

In a 'fore-and-aft' configuration, where the transmission is attached behind the engine as one assembly, it is usual for the mountings to be positioned at each end. A vulnerable point relative to bending stress is therefore at a zone immediately behind the bell housing and adjacent to the sump joint, and any lack of rigidity tends to cause premature failure of the flexible drive plate which couples the crankshaft to the converter.

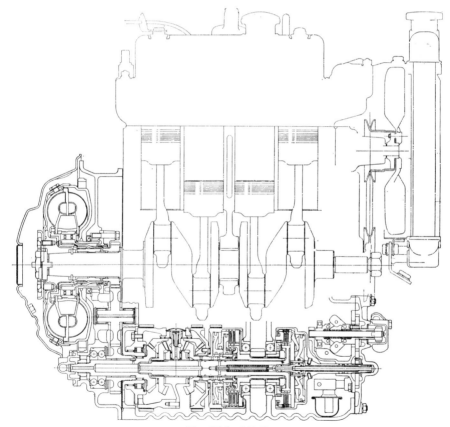

Fig. 15.6. Mk II transmission for B.L.M.C. 1300

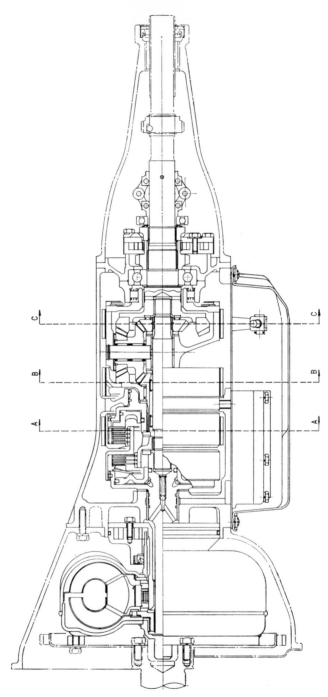

Fig. 15.7. Mk III in-line transmission

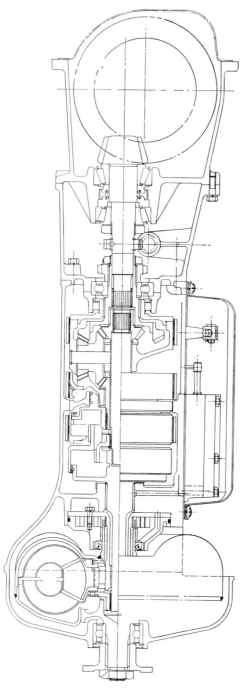

Fig. 15.8. Trans-axle unit, rear drive

THE A.P. SERIES AUTOMATIC TRANSMISSIONS

These transmissions will not be described in detail, and only a few of their more interesting features will be discussed.

A special feature with all of these units is the use of spiral bevel gears in the epicyclic running gear. The attraction of this system is that with only eight gears four well-spaced forward ratios are available, with the reverse corresponding to the low gear reduction. Another point is that the compactness of these assemblies allows for comparatively short mainshafts which, in turn, permits the simplicity of using brake bands for controlling three of the reaction members in each case, without inducing excessive bending stresses on these shafts.

The Mk I transmission was developed especially for the front wheel drive 'Austin Mini', to be subsequently uprated for the B.L.M.C. 1100 and 1300 models and designated the Mk II (see Fig. 15.6).

The basic difference in the Mk II is that apart from increasing the hydraulic line pressure from 80 to 100 lb/in², the multi-disc clutch assembly (which controls third to top gear upshifts) uses three sintered bronze friction plates in place of the two resinated fibre plates that were used on the lower capacity units.

An unusual feature with these transmissions is that a common oil supply is used to serve both the engine and transmission. The system not only allows for an overall compact layout, but eliminates the power loss and expense of a transmission pump as the engine pump is also used for the hydraulic system. This

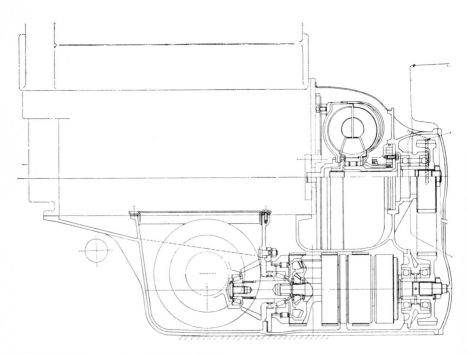

Fig. 15.9. Trans-axle unit, front drive

combined pump has, of course, increased capacity but its power absorption is considerably less than that obtained by the use of two pumps.

In the Mk III in-line transmission (Fig. 15.7) the general layout follows mainly normal practice. However, it will be noticed that part of the valve chest is cast integral with the base of the main gear casing to provide additional stiffness adjacent to the converter housing fixing flange, and this arrangement also affords optimum ground clearance.

Fig. 15.8 shows an example of a trans-axle unit which incorporates the Mk III running gear. A point of interest is the location of the duplex oil seal to isolate the hypoid lubricant from the transmission fluid. It will be noticed that this seal is positioned between the taper roller bearings for supporting the hypoid pinion. This is one of the features which enables the overall length between the converter and axle centre to be at a minimum, and this is essential to avoid encroachment of the seat well. An example of the Mk III transmission incorporated in F.W.D. application can be seen in Fig. 15.9.

ACKNOWLEDGEMENTS

The author wishes to thank the Directors of Automotive Products Co. Ltd for permission to publish this paper, and also to thank his colleagues who have helped in its preparation.

The MS. of this paper was received at the Institution on 15th December 1969 and accepted for publication on 23rd December 1969.

Paper 16. Shunt Hydrostatic Transmissions

J. G. GILES, BSc(Eng), PhD, CEng, FIMechE
Consulting Engineer, Worcester

Typical forms of hydrostatic drives, particularly those with axial piston and vane type equipment, are described. The relative efficiency charts for units used as both pumps and motors are included. Shunt transmissions sharing the power available between hydraulic and mechanical components with a brief mathematical analysis are also included.

INTRODUCTION

Hydrostatic transmissions exhibit the important property of being continuously adjustable over a wide range of transmission ratios, including operation in a reverse direction. These transmissions are of interest to automobile engineers as a possible solution to clutch and gear-change problems and as a means of operating engines more efficiently. Although the penetration of this type of transmission into automobile markets is still small, experience with hydraulic equipment continues to expand in many differing applications. Moreover, automotive transmission design requirements are becoming more difficult to meet with conventional gearboxes without increases in cost and complexity, so that a hydraulic or variable ratio transmission is of growing importance.

The introduction of some mechanical power into the hydraulic drive, in the manner of various 'shunt' transmissions which will reduce the size and, hence, losses of the combined transmission, is of particular interest. Improvements in efficiency have been obtained by this method, and because these shunt versions often include mechanical gearing they appear to be a more suitable compromise solution for production in quantity. This paper is mainly concerned with the performance and efficiency of hydrostatic transmissions and demonstrates how certain 'shunt' versions offer improvements over a part of the operating range by reducing and redistributing the hydraulic losses.

TYPICAL HYDROSTATIC TRANSMISSIONS

There is a considerable variety of design amongst available transmissions and hydraulic equipment, but to obtain a variable ratio transmission it is necessary to employ hydraulic equipment of the variable delivery type. Some reduction in the variety of possible equipment is made by restricting the choice to units whose fluid delivery may be adjusted quickly and easily during operation, but a wide range is still available for selection. Piston-type equipment is usually of the axial arrangement, but radial and in-line designs are also manufactured. Balls may be employed, for instance, as the plungers of piston-type equipment and cylindrical rollers may be used in place of vanes in vane-type hydraulic equipment, so that a seemingly endless number of variations can be collected (1)*.

* *References are given in Appendix 16.1.*

The performance of such equipment shows a correspondingly wide variation, but among the better known equipment the general trends in performance make it possible to separate the various hydraulic losses and to predetermine the performance within a known range of operations (2) (3). As a result it is possible to produce some performance charts which are representative of the actual performance of many different designs.

Hydrostatic pumps and motors are among the most efficient machines, but unfortunately require two conversions of energy to obtain a variable ratio transmission. Mechanical energy is converted into fluid power in the pump, where it is transferred to the hydraulic motor and reconverted to mechanical power—usually at a different torque/speed ratio. The overall efficiency of the conversion is therefore the product of the operating efficiencies of the pump and the hydraulic motor, and some additional losses may be incurred in the flow and control of fluid between the pump and motor units. To obtain an overall efficiency of over 80 per cent for a transmission, it is necessary to maintain efficiencies of over 90 per cent in both units.

TYPICAL PUMPING PERFORMANCE

Considering the efficiency of converting mechanical work into a flow of fluid under pressure from a hydraulic pump, Fig. 16.1 shows some typical output figures for a hydrostatic unit designed to produce a flow of 20 gal/min at 3000 lb/in² when the input shaft is rotated at 2500 rev/min. The design conditions are represented in the figure by the full line rectangle consisting of the two axes—

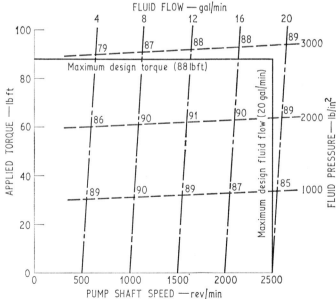

Fig. 16.1. Typical pump performance   Maximum delivery setting.

the lines representing the maximum design torque and the maximum design flow respectively.

Actual test results are more likely to be predicted by the broken lines in Fig. 16.1, which shows that it is necessary to apply an input torque which is slightly higher than the design torque in order to maintain the desired 3000 lb/in² pressure, and also to rotate the pump shaft slightly faster than the design speed in order to obtain the desired rate of fluid flow. The additional input torque is necessary to overcome mechanical friction and/or viscous losses in the pump when the shaft is rotating. Also, some fluid is lost during pumping, this being mainly due to leakage through small working clearances, and some additional shaft rotation is necessary to compensate this leakage or 'slip' loss.

All hydraulic pumps will exhibit these losses, but there will be some variation in the amount of each loss for different designs. From basic theoretical considerations, the conversion of mechanical torque to fluid pressure is given by the following expression:

$$\text{Fluid pressure} = \frac{\text{Applied torque}}{\text{Pump delivery per radian of shaft rotation}}$$

that is,

$$p = \frac{24\pi T}{d} \quad \cdot \quad \cdot \quad \cdot \quad \cdot \quad \cdot \quad \cdot \quad (16.1)$$

where p is the pressure (lb/in²), T the shaft torque (lb ft), and d the pump delivery (in³/rev).

In order to adjust this formula for the known losses which occur in practice, then

$$p = \frac{24\pi C_f(T - T_v)}{d} \quad \cdot \quad \cdot \quad \cdot \quad \cdot \quad \cdot \quad (16.2)$$

where C_f is a frictional loss coefficient and T_v is a viscous drag loss at the input speed, N (lb ft).

Converting this expression into a pump torque efficiency, μ_t:

$$\text{Pump torque efficiency, } \mu_t = C_f \left(1 - \frac{T_v}{T}\right) \quad \cdot \quad \cdot \quad \cdot \quad (16.3)$$

The actual torque needed to obtain a given fluid pressure is indicated by the broken lines in Fig. 16.1 and has been plotted for three levels of pressure.

The basic theoretical expression for fluid flow, Q, is:

$$Q = Nd \quad \cdot \quad \cdot \quad \cdot \quad \cdot \quad \cdot \quad \cdot \quad \cdot \quad (16.4)$$

where Q is the fluid flow (in³/min) and N is the pump speed (rev/min). But, allowing for a fluid leakage loss which increases with pressure:

$$Q = Nd - C_s p$$

where C_s is slip loss (in³/lb in²). Hence, a pump volumetric efficiency, μ_v, can be written:

$$\text{Pump volumetric efficiency, } \mu_v = 100 \left(1 - \frac{C_s p}{Nd}\right) \quad \cdot \quad \cdot \quad (16.5)$$

To obtain a required rate of fluid flow it is necessary to increase the pump speed as seen by the chain-dotted lines which have been plotted on Fig. 16.1 for various rates of fluid flow. By combining equations (16.3) and (16.5) it is possible to write an expression for the pump efficiency, μ_p:

$$\text{Pump efficiency, } \mu_p = 100C_f \left(1 - \frac{C_s p}{Nd}\right)\left(1 - \frac{T_v}{T}\right) \quad . \quad . \quad (16.6)$$

The efficiency of this typical pump has been calculated for the five rates of flow and the three levels of pressure shown on Fig. 16.1. The intersection of two broken lines shows the input speed and input torque needed to obtain the fluid pressure and fluid flow relating to those two lines, and the efficiency has been recorded as a percentage at each intersection on that figure.

When the pump is operated at a reduced delivery rate (as is necessary for use in a variable ratio transmission), then there is a deterioration in all aspects of pump efficiency owing to the fact that T_v and C_s are independent of fluid flow and remain substantially unchanged when the pump's output is reduced. In a typical case, therefore, the total losses are unchanged but the output is reduced and the proportionate losses are therefore higher. Fig. 16.2 shows a similar performance chart plotted for the same pump unit but operating at half the maximum flow setting. It will be noted that the divergence of the broken lines from the design conditions has increased. The efficiencies recorded, as before, at each point of

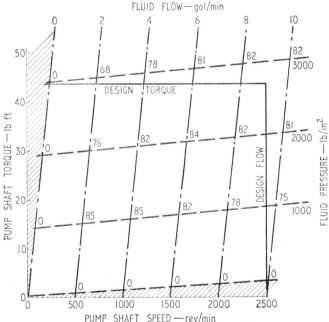

Fig. 16.2. Typical pump performance

Half maximum delivery setting.

intersection are lower than for Fig. 16.1. It will also be noted that by extending the flow and pressure grid to include zero flow and zero pressure conditions, lines of zero output, hence zero efficiency, have been determined.

The shaded portions on Fig. 16.2 show areas close to both axes where there is no output from the pump. Hydraulic power is zero because there is zero flow and zero pressure, but mechanical work is required to rotate the shaft. The shaded areas represent the pump losses which can be approximately determined by running the pump at the zero conditions. Operation of the pump in the shaded areas represents a negative efficiency since the pump is absorbing power and producing no useful work.

Performance of a typical hydraulic motor

Theoretical expressions for the efficiencies of a hydraulic motor are, in fact, identical with those for a pump. Thus, when applying a given flow of fluid at a given pressure to a hydraulic motor the output torque of the motor is reduced by the internal friction and any viscous drag in the mechanism:

$$\text{Motor torque efficiency, } \mu_t = 100C_f \left(1 - \frac{T_v}{T}\right) \quad . \quad . \quad . \quad (16.7)$$

and the leakage of fluid results in 'slip', so that the output speed is reduced by the amount related to the amount of lost fluid:

$$\text{Motor volumetric efficiency, } \mu_v = 100 \left(1 - \frac{C_s p}{Nd}\right) \quad . \quad . \quad (16.8)$$

and by combining these two effects:

$$\text{Motor efficiency, } \mu_m = 100C_f \left(1 - \frac{C_s p}{Nd}\right)\left(1 - \frac{T_v}{T}\right) \quad . \quad . \quad (16.9)$$

The output conditions of a typical hydraulic motor having the same physical dimensions as the previously considered pump are shown in Fig. 16.3.

Mechanical output torque and speed now fall inside the rectangle representing the design conditions, and losses are shown as a shaded area indicating the difference between input conditions. Efficiency percentages are plotted as before at each point of intersection for the same levels of pressure and flow used for Fig. 16.1, and it will be noted that there are similar trends in the values of efficiency, although the motor efficiencies are slightly lower than those for the pump. This difference is due to the fact that the losses are exactly equal, but since measurements are related to shaft torque (T), the mechanical work is higher for the pump, and the mechanical efficiency is thus slightly higher.

As a simple mathematical expression:

$$\text{Pump efficiency} = \frac{1}{1+d} \quad \text{and} \quad \text{Motor efficiency} = \frac{1-d}{1}$$

where d is the internal loss.

Fig. 16.4 shows a similar performance chart for a hydraulic motor which is set to half-maximum fluid delivery condition. A hydraulic motor would be employed

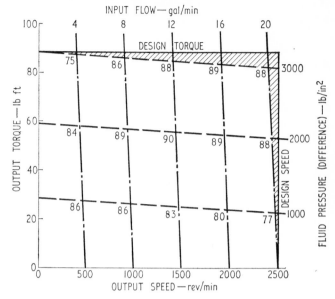

Maximum delivery setting.

Fig. 16.3. Typical fluid motor performance

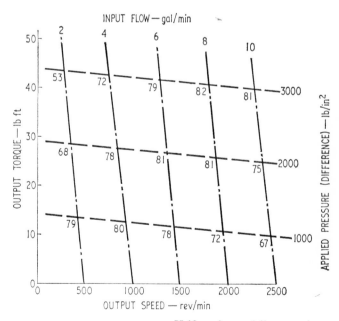

Half maximum delivery setting.

Fig. 16.4. Typical fluid motor performance

in this condition to obtain higher shaft speeds with a reduced fluid flow. The results are similar to those for the pump unit at half delivery. The efficiency falls because the expressions for losses $(C_s p/Nd)$ and (T_v/T) become proportionately larger when the parameters d and T are halved. Also, as before, the motor efficiencies are slightly lower because these efficiencies are evaluated in respect of mechanical work.

Performance of a complete hydraulic transmission

By combining the pump and motor units previously studied it is now possible to construct a variable ratio transmission. Owing to the double conversion of energy, the efficiencies of the transmission are the product of the individual pump and motor efficiencies. In this example the pump and motor are assumed to be identical and the transmission efficiencies are the square of the component efficiencies:

$$\text{Transmission torque efficiency, } \mu_t = C_f{}^2 \left(1 - \frac{T_v}{T}\right)^2 \quad . \quad . \quad (16.10)$$

This equation is illustrated graphically in Fig. 16.5a which compares typical output torques with the ideal (no loss) performance at a 1:1 setting. In a perfect transmission the output torque would equal the input torque, but in the practical example, output torque is moved from the origin by the loss T_v. This loss is illustrated as an intercept drawn for two values of input speed. The slope of the actual output torque has been drawn at 0·95 of the ideal value to allow for the friction factor $C_f{}^2$.

$$\text{Transmission volumetric efficiency, } \mu_v = 100 \left(1 - \frac{C_s p}{Nd}\right)^2 \quad . \quad (16.11)$$

The transmission's slip characteristic or volumetric efficiency is shown in Fig. 16.5b where it is seen that, compared to the ideal output speed, a practical transmission has a 'slip' loss. As a general principle the slip loss shows up as a number of output shaft revolutions below the theoretical figure. Under normal conditions with correct porting, the slip loss is proportional to the pressure developed in the transmission and is independent of speed. Thus, as seen on Fig. 16.5b, the lost revolutions are related to the $(C_s p/Nd)^2$ factor, which again shows up as an intercept from the origin, but the actual output speeds are generally parallel to the ideal output characteristic.

Overall transmission efficiency

By combining the two characteristics, an equation for the overall efficiency of the hydrostatic transmission is obtained:

$$\text{Transmission efficiency, } \mu = 100 C_f{}^2 \left(1 - \frac{T_v}{T}\right)^2 \left(1 - \frac{C_s p}{Nd}\right)^2 \quad . \quad (16.12)$$

It will be noted that there are six factors in the expression for efficiency, and it is necessary to obtain a very high standard in each factor in order to achieve an acceptable level of overall efficiency. The results obtained from Figs 16.1 and

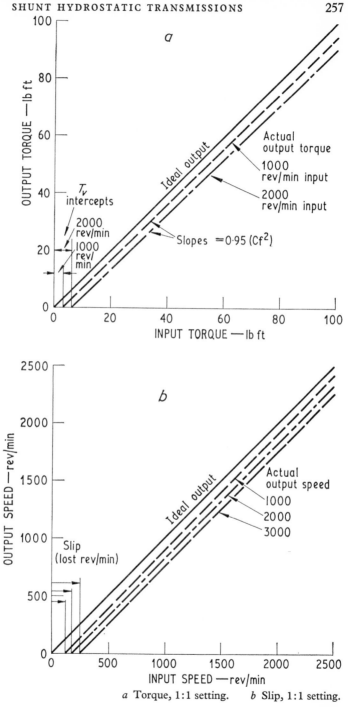

a Torque, 1:1 setting.   *b* Slip, 1:1 setting.

Fig. 16.5. Typical hydrostatic transmission characteristics

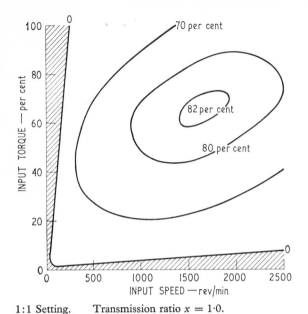

1:1 Setting.   Transmission ratio $x = 1\cdot0$.

**Fig. 16.6. Typical trans-
mission efficiency**

16.3 have been combined to produce Fig. 16.6 which is a chart showing the overall efficiency of the transmission at the 1:1 setting and over the full range of input speeds and torques. The shaded areas close to the axes represent conditions of negative efficiency because no output is available and power is being absorbed by the transmission. However, the efficiency rises quickly and about two-thirds of the area is achieved at over 70 per cent. A useful 'island' at over 80 per cent is available and a peak value of 82 per cent is achieved.

Higher efficiency figures have been quoted for particular transmission designs, but the basic characteristics and distribution are substantially correct. In the estimates made for this figure, no allowances have been made for other losses which inevitably arise in a practical transmission installation, such as

(1) pipe flow losses between the pump and the motor, and
(2) losses in ancillary equipment, e.g.

    (*a*) cooling equipment
    (*b*) control valves and servo-assistance equipment
    (*c*) a priming or boost pump needed to maintain minimum transmission pressure.

Operation of the transmission over a range of ratios requires the pump and/or motor units to be utilized at reduced delivery settings. To obtain a 2:1 torque multiplication with a pump and motor of similar size, it would be necessary to reduce the pump to half its maximum fluid delivery and operate the motor at its

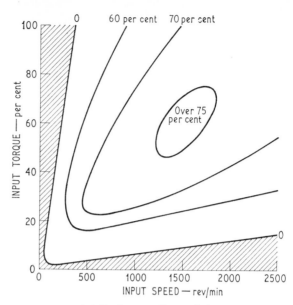

Fig.16.7. Typical transmission efficiency

2:1 Setting.   Transmission ratio $x = 0.5$.
Pump unit at half maximum delivery.

full delivery setting. By combining the results for Figs 16.2 and 16.3 it is possible to obtain another chart, Fig. 16.7, showing the efficiency during operation in such a combination. By including the lower values of efficiency related to the reduced delivery of the pump, the overall efficiencies have consequently dropped and the peak efficiency has fallen to 75 per cent.

For applications where a transmission is required to operate mainly at torque-multiplying conditions, it is more usual to combine a pump with a larger sized hydraulic motor. If a hydraulic motor of twice the fluid capacity of the pump is employed, then the 2:1 torque multiplication condition would be obtained with the pump and motor at maximum delivery and would operate at efficiencies similar to those shown in Fig. 16.6. However, at higher output speeds, or if reduced torque-multiplication was required, this larger motor would need to be adjusted to a reduced delivery setting and it is possible that the combination shown in Fig. 16.8 would be applicable. This shows an efficiency chart for a transmission having a larger motor adjusted to half-maximum delivery in order to obtain a direct drive (1:1 setting). Owing to the predominance of the motor efficiencies there is a slight reduction in these transmission efficiencies when compared to Fig. 16.7.

In view of the large number of contributory factors it is doubtful if any substantial improvement in overall efficiency can be achieved from further development of hydrostatic drives. These drives are already excellent mechanisms and it is difficult to see any significant improvements, particularly if operation over an increasing range of transmission ratios is required.

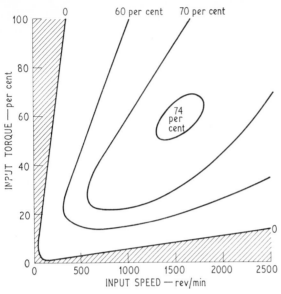

1:1 Setting.　　Transmission ratio $x = 1·0$.

Fig. 16.8. Large motor unit at half maximum delivery

BASIC CHARACTERISTICS OF HYDROSTATIC SHUNT TRANSMISSIONS

A 'shunt' or differential version of a hydrostatic drive provides an alternative means, usually mechanical, for transmitting power by way of a separate path. There are many such arrangements (4) (5) but the object is normally to introduce mechanical power at higher efficiency whilst retaining sufficient hydraulic power to enable the required amount of variation to be achieved. Despite the variety of differential and shunt arrangements, the effect on the hydraulic units is usually to extend their range of torque and speed variation. In particular, many of these shunt arrangements combine the hydraulic units in rotating casings or with gearing so that the hydraulic pump or motor is operated at a zero flow condition.

Thus, for instance, a hydraulic unit may act as a clutch or brake element. For this purpose, the outlet port is blocked so that no fluid flows, but a mechanical torque equal to that applied to the shaft is available as a reaction torque on the casing. If this locked hydraulic unit is permitted to rotate, then power is transmitted at high efficiency by the mechanical components. There are still some losses introduced by the hydraulic components, and although in this 'lock-up' condition the fluid flow and frictional losses are minimized, the normal 'slip' or leakage loss is present. As the transmission moves away from a 'lock-up' point and fluid flows recommence, the normal hydraulic losses are gradually re-introduced, but the benefit of shunt arrangements is to achieve a general low level of hydraulic power so that perhaps only one-third to one-quarter of the input power is transmitted by the fluid path, requiring a small hydraulic drive and bringing a corresponding reduction in losses.

Another limiting condition frequently met in these shunt versions is a different type of zero power condition, which involves rotation of the hydraulic unit at high speed but zero fluid delivery. Thus, although no hydraulic power is being transmitted, the hydraulic components may be absorbing some power from the system and detracting from its efficiency even when the shunt combination may be operating in the purely mechanical mode.

Summarizing the basic characteristics of shunt versions of hydrostatic transmission, therefore, it is possible to state that:

(1) shunt versions introduce mechanical power and reduce the size and power requirement of the hydraulic components in order to reduce transmission losses;

(2) shunt versions extend the range of operating conditions of the hydraulic components; and

(3) shunt versions may introduce hydraulic losses even when operating in the all-mechanical mode.

Casing shunt version

The basic principles of a shunt version of hydrostatic transmission can perhaps best be illustrated by considering a simple example. Fig. 16.9 illustrates a casing shunt version of a hydrostatic transmission intended for motor cycles or other low-powered vehicles. The term 'casing shunt' indicates that it employs an external casing to obtain the mechanical operation and the transmission consists mainly of a rotating casing made up from the outer casings of the pump and motor units. These two casings are bolted on either side of a central port plate which provides communicating ports for fluid flow between pump and motor and for make-up fluid, etc. This rotating casing acts as the output member of the transmission and may be geared or otherwise connected to an output shaft. This casing is supported by bearings on a stationary motor shaft which fits into the motor casing, and is bolted to some stationary member by a flanged portion containing a priming or make-up pump. The internal parts of the hydraulic motor—in this case, rotor and three slippers—are mounted on the stationary shaft. Fluid will flow from the motor when the motor casing is rotated, although in this case the fluid is displaced by rotating the casing about a stationary shaft—the reverse of normal operation.

An input shaft drives the internal parts of the pump unit (motor and slipper in this design) in a conventional way, and in this example an extension shaft is employed to drive the priming pump. Because of the rotation of the pump outer casing, the relative speed of pumping is equal to the difference between the input and output shaft speeds. In this example, a fixed delivery pump is employed and adjustment of the transmission ratio is achieved by altering the fluid delivery from the hydraulic motor unit.

When the hydraulic motor is adjusted to zero delivery, no fluid can flow, even though the casing may be rotating at speed around the motor shaft. Consequently, the pump unit is unable to deliver its fluid and becomes locked, so that the pump casing is taken around with the input shaft. This setting gives a direct drive or 'top gear' condition and, incidentally, illustrates the two zero-flow conditions, one

Complete transmission assembly

Boost pump

Pump unit (fixed delivery)

Port plate

Hydraulic motor (variable delivery)

1 Input shaft. 2 Output shaft.
3 Rotating casing. 4 Boost pump and motor shaft flange.

Fig. 16.9. A low power casing shunt hydromechanical transmission

hydraulic unit operating as a clutch (the pump) and another (the motor) rotating freely at zero flow.

As the motor delivery is increased, a flow of fluid can commence which will cause a reduction in output speed, but the additional torque that is developed in the motor unit is now transmitted to the output shaft, giving the required increase in output torque. At maximum motor delivery, the output speed falls to a speed ratio $x = 1/(1+m)$, where m is the ratio of the fluid displacement per revolution of the motor to that for the pump. At this setting the conditions for the hydraulic units are excellent, both units operating at the maximum delivery and with a comparatively low speed of relative rotation. The proportion of hydraulic power relative to input power is given by

$$\text{Hydraulic power fraction,} f = \frac{m}{1+m} \quad . \quad . \quad . \quad . \quad (16.13)$$

Hence, a fluid power flow fraction of 0·5 occurs at ratios of $x = +0·5$ and $+1·5$ respectively. Zero fluid power flow occurs at $x = 1·0$, giving a 3:1 range of ratios over which the mean hydraulic power is one-quarter of the total input power.

This simple casing shunt example contains all the characteristics of other shunt versions of a hydrostatic drive, and it will be interesting therefore to estimate its operating performance.

Prediction of performance

Using the same graphical method of analysis as employed for the operation of the basic hydrostatic components, it is possible to produce a hypothetical performance grid, Fig. 16.10, for a shunt version of the pump unit. This figure was produced by assuming that the pump shaft was rotated at a fixed speed of 2500 rev/min and that the pump casing was rotated at different speeds (output speeds) as shown on the ordinate of the graph.

Thus, although the slip loss is similar to that shown for the normal pump [equation (16.5)], the torque losses C_f and T_v now apply to the relative speed of the pump, which is the difference between the input and output speeds. Hence the torque efficiency is best at the highest output speed when the relative pumping speed is zero, but this efficiency falls as the output speed falls. Thus Fig. 16.10 shows very high efficiency at a low pressure and at a high casing speed where the relative speed of pump shaft to pump casing is very low. At maximum casing speed, the casing torque is almost the same as the input torque and the overall efficiency consequently corresponds to the volumetric efficiency, and hence leads to the high values of efficiency plotted, as previously, on the points of intersection.

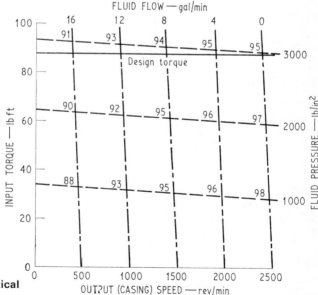

Fig. 16.10. Hypothetical pump characteristic, shunt version

Input speed 2500 rev/min constant.

The effect of this shunt version has been to rearrange the operation so that viscous and frictional losses are virtually removed from the high output speed end of the operating range for the pump unit whose casing also provides extra output torque. The shunt arrangement, however, has a serious effect on the efficiency of the motor unit (Fig. 16.11) which is now working under very difficult operating conditions.

At high output speeds the hydraulic motor is rotating at high relative speed because the motor shaft is held stationary whilst the casing rotates around it. All the frictional (C_f) and viscous (T_v) losses are present whilst the hydraulic motor is delivering zero or very low output power. Thus, at the zero flow condition the motor actually absorbs power from the system, as can be seen from the table below Fig. 16.11. As the motor delivery is increased, its relative rotation falls progressively and some useful power is produced. The efficiency of the motor does not rise above 80 per cent even at the maximum delivery condition (10 gal/min) and the values shown in this table are much lower than the efficiencies given in Fig. 16.3.

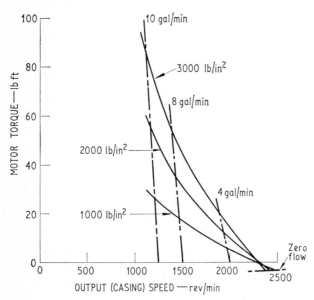

Input speed 2500 rev/min constant.

Typical motor efficiencies

Pressure	Fluid flow, gal/min			
	0	4	8	10
1000	−0·92 hp	79	79	78
2000	−1·15 hp	83	81	82
3000	−1·52 hp	82	80	82

Fig. 16.11. Hypothetical fluid motor performance, shunt version

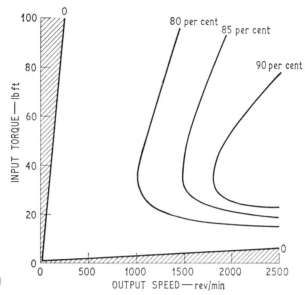

Fig. 16.12. Hypothetical shunt transmission efficiency

Input speed 2500 rev/min constant.

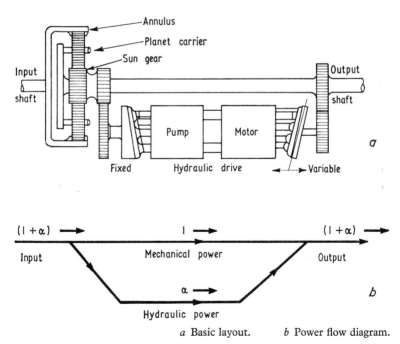

a Basic layout.　　　*b* Power flow diagram.

Fig. 16.13. A geared shunt hydrostatic transmission

The hydraulic efficiency of the combined pump and motor units will mainly be lower in this shunt version than for the normal hydrostatic combination. However, because the proportion of fluid power flowing is so small, the overall efficiency of the shunt version will contain much higher figures than for the hydrostatic transmission. Fig. 16.12 shows that the improved efficiency is maintained not only for a range of input torques but also over a range of ratios. This graph is plotted at a fixed input speed of 2500 rev/min, which is the maximum power condition. At lower input speeds, the relative speed of the motor and pump unit will be reduced so that there is some possibility of further improved efficiency. Therefore, compared to the original combination, the shunt version appears to be very superior in efficiency over this restricted range of operation. The reasons that this shunt version of two hydraulic machines has better efficiency than the more usual combination of the same two machines are as follows:

(1) *Reduced fluid flow*—This is never more than half of the equivalent flow in the 'pure' hydrostatic version and will fall to zero for some operations.

(2) *Reduced friction and viscous drag losses*—The combined relative speeds of operation of the pump and motor are only one-half to two-thirds of the combined speeds in the pure hydrostatic version.

(3) *Reduced slip loss*—The fluid pressure remains constant in the shunt version, whereas it must be increased in the pure hydrostatic version.

(4) *Increased output torque*—The shunt version provides some mechanical torque which is transmitted direct to output.

These advantages do not come without some disadvantages since

(*a*) the rotating casings must be balanced;

(*b*) additional mechanical problems are involved in adjusting the fluid delivery of, and supplying 'make-up' fluid to, the rotating casings;

(*c*) installation and layout are restricted by the necessary combined pump and motor assembly; and

(*d*) operation in the reverse direction involves higher pressures and gives reduced efficiency because the mechanical torque works in opposition.

GEARED SHUNT SYSTEMS

The use of a differential gear in combination with a hydrostatic drive makes it possible to construct other forms of shunt transmission with a 'nul point' or all-mechanical point of operation situated at any desired transmission ratio. This nul point can be selected to increase or decrease the speed of the output shaft, relative to the input shaft, by a suitable choice of gear layout.

A typical gear shunt transmission is shown diagrammatically as Fig. 16.13, where it will be seen that an input shaft connects with the annulus member of an epicyclic gear set. Output drive comes from the planet carrier member so that the gearing provides a speed-reducing mechanism when the sun gear is held stationary. The sun gear is connected to a hydraulic unit—probably of the fixed delivery type—and this fixed pump drives a variable delivery motor connected by gearing to, or concentrically mounted on, the output shaft.

By adjusting the hydraulic motor to zero delivery, the pump unit is unable to rotate and the combination acts as a mechanical reduction gear. The hydraulic

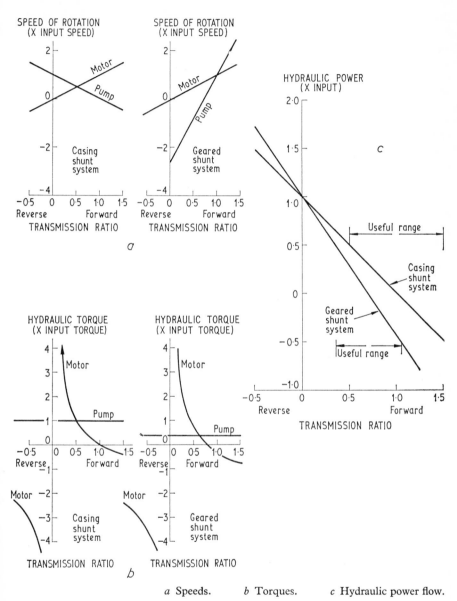

a Speeds.　　*b* Torques.　　*c* Hydraulic power flow.

Fig. 16.14. Operating conditions of hydraulic units when combined in alternative shunt arrangements

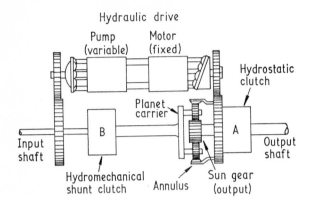

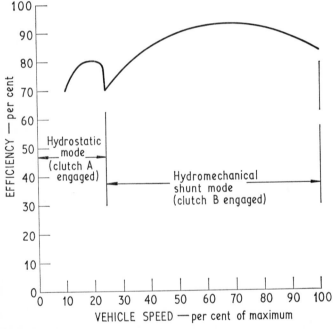

Fig. 16.15. Basic layout and efficiency curve of the SUNDSTRAND dual mode transmission

units—stationary pump, and motor rotating at zero delivery—correspond exactly with the 'lock-up' condition of the previously discussed 'casing shunt' combination. By adjusting the motor unit to some positive or negative delivery setting the pump unit, and hence sun gear, may be rotated with positive or negative sense, giving an increase or decrease in output speed. In such operation the hydraulic drive is transmitting power and provides a range of transmission ratios on each side of the basic reduction ratio.

The conditions of operation of the hydraulic units are also very similar to those for the casing shunt transmission, although the pump speeds are slightly higher. When the transmission is operated at higher ratios, the identities of the pump and motor are interchanged and there is a circulation of power in the output shaft causing an increase in pressure and, hence, losses in the hydraulic drive. It is usual, therefore, to restrict the range of variation above the basic mechanical ratio so that hydraulic power remains a small fraction of the total input power. Again, reverse operation is avoided because the mechanical power works in opposition to the hydraulic power.

Graphs (Fig. 16.14) compose the speeds, torques, and power developed on the hydraulic units in the two types of shunt transmission. It will be noted that in the geared systems the hydraulic power fraction rises more steeply than for the casing shunt system. If the hydraulic power flow is restricted to 50 per cent of the maximum input power, then in either case it is possible to obtain high efficiency and a 3:1 range of variation from these shunt systems without losing the main advantages of the arrangement.

Useful operation is still possible, however, if the amount of variation is extended beyond this 3:1 range, and the SUNDSTRAND dual mode transmission provides an excellent example of a hydrostatic transmission which follows the previous layout of Fig. 16.14, but by the addition of two clutches may be employed in both the pure hydrostatic mode and in a shunt mode using a differential gear. As seen from published performance curves (6) (Fig. 16.15), a comparison of the efficiency curves for the pure hydrostatic and shunt hydrostatic versions is demonstrated, and the shunt version shows a good improvement despite the fact that the hydrostatic components are large enough to transmit the full engine power.

OTHER GEARED SHUNT SYSTEMS

The studies made in this paper indicate that the most efficient combination arises from the use of smaller sized hydraulic components operated over a restricted range. To obtain a wide range of operating transmission ratios additional gearing or gear ratios will be necessary, and one such approach has been seen in the double differential transmission sponsored by N.R.D.C. (Fig. 16.16) which is intended for motor car use. For the wider range of ratios required for commercial vehicles an alternative approach might arise from one of the simpler shunt versions featured in this paper and employed over the suggested 3:1 range of variation but augmented by a further 3:1 gear shift so that a 9:1 overall range of transmission ratios is available. As an interim phase of some such commercial vehicle transmission, it is possible to imagine that an extremely small shunt hydrostatic drive having a small range of variation (less than 2:1) but employed in conjunction with each ratio of a five-speed gearbox (Fig. 16.17) would be

Fig. 16.16. General view of double differential hydromechanical transmission on test installation

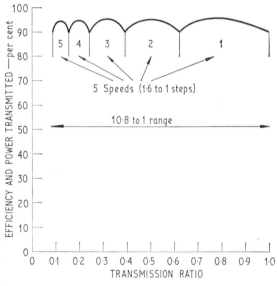

Fig. 16.17. Power transmission characteristics of a shunt hydrostatic drive used in conjunction with a five-speed gearbox

suitable for many transmissions. A combination of this type could be expected to have very high efficiency because of the minimal use of hydraulic power, and would permit full power operation over a 10:1 range of transmission ratios.

DISCUSSION

This paper has featured various versions of hydromechanical shunt transmission arising from the concept of sharing transmitted power between alternative hydraulic and mechanical paths. Improvements in efficiency and reductions in size are achieved although it is never possible to eliminate hydraulic losses completely. The main advantage comes from a redistribution of hydraulic losses so that a small range of speed variation can be obtained at improved efficiency.

The extent of any improvement will depend on the nature of the losses in the hydraulic machines, which must have low frictional and/or viscous losses when rotating at speed with low power flow. Most shunt systems will show a gain as a result of a reduction in the size of the hydraulic components. The paper has illustrated the performance and the losses of hydraulic machines in a graphical manner, but clearly, when the characteristics of performance are known for a range of machines, the effect of various shunt combinations can be calculated. Several workers (7) have proposed means for constructing mathematical models of hydraulic units and these can be extended to embrace the shunt techniques. There seems to be an excellent case for increased study of these shunt systems in conjunction with various types of hydraulic drive whose performance can be correctly synthesized by means of a mathematical model.

CONCLUSIONS

The prospects for improving the efficiency of hydrostatic transmission are enhanced by considering the various shunt systems, although it is not possible to eliminate losses entirely. The size and cost of the hydraulic drive can also be reduced by choosing systems which require a minimum flow of fluid power to obtain the necessary range of variation.

APPENDIX 16.1

REFERENCES
(1) LEZARD, C. V. 'Hydraulic variable speed drives', *Engineer's Digest Survey* 1964 (No. 18, December).
(2) WILSON, W. E. 'Performance criteria for positive displacement pumps and fluid motors', *Trans. Am. Soc. mech. Engrs* 1949 (January).
(3) SCHLOSSER, W. M. J. 'Mathematical model for displacement pumps and motors', *Hydraul. Pwr Transm.* 1961 (April), 252; (May), 324.
(4) GILES, J. G. 'Differential transmissions systems', *Engng Outline* (No. 1/40), 109; reprinted from *Engineering* 1967 **201** and **202**.
(5) GILES, J. G. *Gears and transmissions: Automotive Technology Series* 1969, vol. 4, 169 (Iliffe).
(6) GUEDET, R. H. and LOUIS, J. E. 'Dual mode hydromechanical transmission as applied to gas turbines', A.S.M.E. Paper No. 69-GT-13, 1969 (March).
(7) WILSON, W. E. 'Mathematical models in fluid power engineering', *Hydraul. Pneum. Pwr* 1967 (March), 136.

The MS. of this paper was received at the Institution on 14th October 1969 and accepted for publication on 28th October 1969.

Paper 17. Overdrives

R. L. ABBOTT

Advanced Engineering Manager, G.K.N. Birfield Transmissions Ltd, Erdington, Birmingham 24

Overdrive is defined as gearing which provides a higher ratio than that given by the final drive crown wheel and pinion. The ratio requirements of the modern car are discussed. All types of overdrive gearing are reviewed and the Laycock unit, being the only separate unit now produced in the U.K., is considered in detail. This unit is of particular interest since ratio changes are made under torque. It is, therefore, necessary to consider the changes in rotational energy which result. The paper analyses the factors involved and presents equations relating clutch torque, time, and inertias. Expressions are given for energy transfer to the output shaft and the rate of energy dissipation at the clutch. Some details of the epicyclic gearing and planet bearing loads and life factors are given. Control systems are briefly discussed.

INTRODUCTION

Overdrive is a gear within the gearbox, or an additional gear unit mounted in front of, or behind, the gearbox, which provides a higher gear ratio than is given by the final drive crown wheel and pinion. Overdrive units have been in use for many years, but present-day traffic conditions have introduced a renewed interest. In the U.K. British Leyland have incorporated a step-up gear in the Austin Maxi and in the U.S.A. Borg-Warner have recently put a new overdrive unit into production after dropping the manufacture of overdrives for a number of years. It is of interest to examine the reasons for this trend.

Modern traffic conditions necessitate cars with rapid acceleration and effortless driving and this has tended to produce vehicles which, at high speed, are running beyond the peak of the power curve and at high specific fuel consumption. An additional overdrive gear becomes highly desirable for high-speed cruising on motorways where it not only gives a saving in fuel, but reduces driving fatigue by reducing the engine noise level. It reduces engine wear and mitigates against the oil burning which plagues some vehicles during sustained high-speed motorway cruising.

In the U.S.A. the situation has become somewhat paradoxical. Acceleration is now all-important and power units of over 7 litres, producing more than 400 hp, are not uncommon. With them, vehicles are capable of speeds twice as high as those legally permitted. It would appear sensible, therefore, to use smaller engines, reduce the number of options, and fit a lower axle ratio to obtain the same tractive effort for acceleration and add overdrive for freeway driving.

Notation

E	Total energy dissipated during clutching operation.
E_i	Energy dissipated at clutch due to change in speed of engine.
F	End load on clutch.
G	Ratio overdriven in synchromesh gearbox.

I_c	Inertia of overdrive clutch member and sunwheel.
I_e	Inertia of rotating parts on input side of gearbox.
I_v	Inertia of rotating parts on output side of overdrive, including vehicle polar moment of inertia.
R	Overdrive ratio.
R_i, R_o	Minor and major radii of clutch, respectively.
r	Effective radius of clutch.
r_m	Mean radius of clutch.
T_c, T_e, T_o	Clutch torque, driving and resistive torque, respectively.
T_{im}	Torque on input member.
t	Time.
t_0	Slip period after seating.
$\varXi$	Rate of energy dissipation in clutch.
α	Half included angle of cone clutch.
μ	Coefficient of friction.
ξ	Rate of energy transfer to output shaft.
ω	Angular velocity of output shaft.

SYSTEMS

Obviously there are many overdrive systems, the simplest and cheapest being an additional gear in the gearbox, as exemplified by the Austin Maxi.

Some years ago Daimler changed one of the gear trains in the Wilson box from a reduction gear to a step-up gear turning a four-speed gearbox into a three-speed and overdrive box.

In the U.K., too, we have had the Handa and Murray overdrives, both separate units fitted behind the gearbox. The former had an epicyclic gear set, the reaction member of which was controlled by dog clutches without synchromesh. The Murray unit was a lay shaft box employing helical gears and dog clutches. Both required use of the clutch pedal to obtain 'clean' ratio changes.

All these systems, however, necessitate more effort from the driver. The higher the final drive ratio the less flexible becomes the car, and in the U.K. motorways are already so congested that it is often not possible to remain in overdrive ratio for long periods. It is a decided advantage, therefore, to have a system which does not require disengagement of the engine clutch and with which ratio changes can be made very rapidly. If the kinetic energy resulting from the change in speed of the engine can be used to accelerate the vehicle into overdrive, so much the better. It is perhaps significant that the two systems offering an easy-change facility, the Borg-Warner and Laycock-de-Normanville, have been the ones most widely accepted by the general public in spite of higher costs.

The overdrive unit may be located in front of the gearbox (in which case it has to be designed into the transmission), immediately behind the gearbox (the usual position), or, in the case of I.R.S. vehicles, on the nose of the hypoid unit. The latter position does not affect the speed of the propeller shaft.

BORG-WARNER OVERDRIVE

The Borg-Warner overdrive, the running gear of which is shown in Fig. 17.1, was well known in the U.K. and the U.S.A. for many years and consists basically

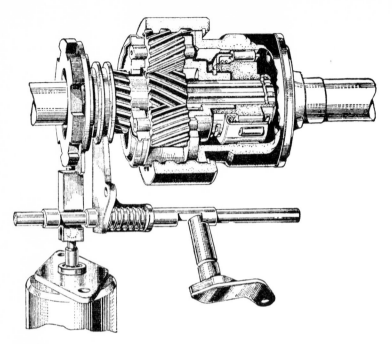

Fig. 17.1. The running gear of the Borg-Warner overdrive

of a simple epicyclic gear set of sun, planets, and annulus and a unidirectional clutch placed between the input and output shafts. The planet carrier is splined to the input shaft; the annulus is the output member. An extension of the sun-wheel, which is the reaction member, is splined to a control plate and both sun-wheel and control plate are free to revolve on the input shaft. Direct forward drive is through the unidirectional clutch; the whole gear train and control plate rotate as one unit. The unit, therefore, freewheels on overrun in direct drive, allowing gear changes to be made in the synchromesh gearbox without using the clutch pedal. The clutch must, of course, be released for starting and stopping. The free wheel may be locked out by use of a driver-operated control which moves the sun gear rearwards to engage lock-up teeth on the planet carrier. The same lock-up is operated automatically for reverse drive by a connection to the reverse selector mechanism in the gearbox. Overdrive is engaged by allowing the vehicle to overrun momentarily. As the input shaft speed reduces relative to the output, the sunwheel turns more slowly, and when the speed of the input shaft is 70 per cent of output speed the sunwheel comes to rest. Any greater difference in speed between input and output shafts would cause the sunwheel to rotate backwards.

When the sunwheel and its control plate come to rest they may be locked to the casing by inserting a solenoid-operated pawl into one of a number of notches in the control plate. The sunwheel thus becomes the reaction member for overdrive ratio. Overdrive may be engaged when the vehicle speed exceeds about 27 mile/h

(43 km/h) by raising the foot from the throttle pedal. A centrifugal governor completes the solenoid circuit to engage the pawl as soon as the sunwheel stops rotating. A blocker ring prevents movement of the pawl until synchronism is achieved.

The return to direct drive may be effected by kicking-down the accelerator pedal. This operates a switch to short circuit the solenoid so that return springs try to withdraw the pawl. However, there is torque reaction on the pawl which prevents its movement, and another electrical contact momentarily cuts the engine ignition to release the pawl. As soon as it is released the ignition circuit is restored and the engine accelerates to give direct drive through the unidirectional clutch. It will be appreciated that whilst in overdrive ratio there is no freewheel condition.

Borg-Warner have recently announced a new overdrive unit, produced in the U.S.A., with an epicyclic gear train giving a ratio of 0·72:1. The unit is designed to be mounted on the nose of the final drive unit and vacuum power is used to move the shift and lock-up actuators. The whole system is electronically controlled and includes an electronic governor, lock-up switch, and floor-mounted kick-down switch.

LAYCOCK OVERDRIVE

The Laycock overdrive uses the de Normanville system which was introduced more than 20 years ago. Fig. 17.2 shows the elements of the system. The gears are epicyclic. The planet carrier is attached to the input shaft, the annulus is attached to the output shaft. Carried on a splined extension of the sunwheel, a double-sided cone clutch engages a stationary brake ring or the outside surface of the annulus.

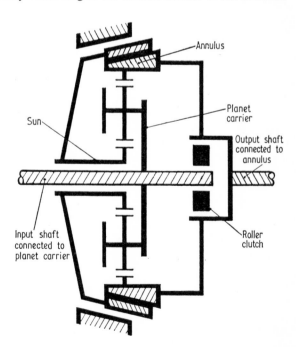

Fig. 17.2. Elements of the Laycock-de-Normanville overdrive unit

A unidirectional clutch connects the input and output shafts. Several types have been produced and the latest, known as Type J, is described below.

In direct drive, driving torque is transmitted through the unidirectional clutch. The cone clutch is held in engagement with the annulus by spring load exerted through a thrust ring and ball bearing. Overrun and reverse drive causes a rearwards thrust of the helical sunwheel which is also used to augment the spring load. Thus the gear train is locked so that overrun and reverse torque can be transmitted. It will be appreciated that the unidirectional clutch would not transmit drive under these conditions.

For planetary ratio the cone clutch is moved forward, by hydraulic pressure, so that it engages the stationary brake ring and brings the sunwheel to rest. The planet wheels are caused to orbit around it and in so doing rotate the annulus and output shaft at a speed greater than that of the carrier and input shaft. The unidirectional clutch overruns.

Hydraulic system

Oil is drawn from the sump through a gauze filter and delivered by way of a pressure filter to the operating pistons, relief valve, and solenoid valve (Fig. 17.3).

Oil passes through the relief valve, which in direct drive maintains a pressure in the system of 25 lbf/in^2 (172 369 N/m^2), to the main drive shaft to lubricate the running gear. A lube relief valve prevents excessive pressure build-up.

Low pressure is maintained in the hydraulic system in order to initiate action when the overdrive ratio is signalled.

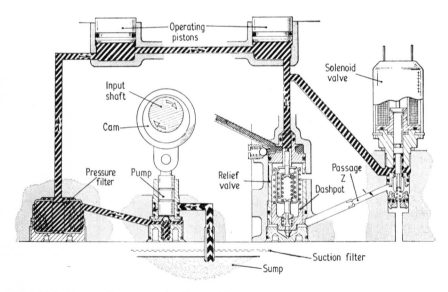

Fig. 17.3. Hydraulic system in direct drive

When the solenoid is energized its valve opens and low-pressure oil is allowed to enter passage Z (Fig. 17.4) which leads to the dashpot. An increase in system pressure results from the out-of-balance between the dashpot piston and relief valve piston areas since the relief valve spring is compressed further as the dashpot piston rises. The arrangement of springs gives the required pattern of pressure changes.

When the solenoid is de-energized its valve is returned by a spring allowing oil to exhaust from the dashpot into passage Z by way of a restricted orifice.

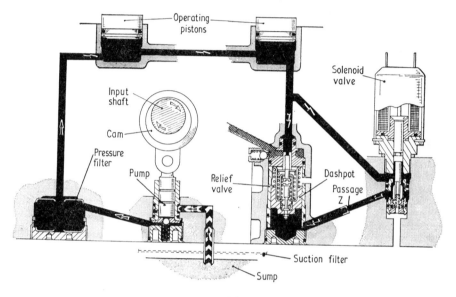

Fig. 17.4. Hydraulic system in overdrive

The relief valve spring is able gradually to relax towards its 'direct drive' position, dropping the system pressure and allowing the cone clutch to leave the brake ring and contact the annulus gently. It will be appreciated that the decaying hydraulic pressure offsets the clutch spring load.

For smooth 'power' disengagements it is desirable to arrange for a pressure pause as the clutch is about to leave the brake ring, so that it drags and slows the rate of acceleration of the engine to give a smoother take-up of the unidirectional clutch. This effect is achieved by a supplementary dashpot spring. The sequence of pressure changes is shown in Figs 17.5 and 17.6.

Gear train

Alternative overdrive ratios of 0·797, 0·778, and 0·748 are available. All gear trains use a common planet carrier. They have, respectively, the following numbers of teeth: 22/29/79, 22/27/77, and 25/24/74. Owing to limitations on the size of the mainshaft and annulus a normal d.p. of 17·51 (1·45 module) is used and a face d.p. of 16·4 (15·5 module). The helix angle is 20° 32' and the normal pressure angle 20°. In order to obtain the optimum section below the teeth of the 20-tooth sunwheel, slightly stub teeth are used with the following proportions:

Addendum	0·051 in (1·295 mm)
Depth	0·117 in (2·972 mm)
Clearance	0·015 in (0.381 mm)

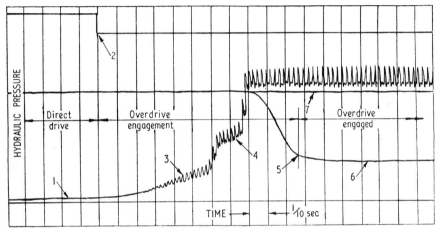

HYDRAULIC PRESSURE CHANGE ON ENGAGEMENT

1 Residual pressure	7 Output speed
2 Initial signal	8 Disengagement signal
3 Dashpot fills	9 Pressure pause which allows smooth synchronism
4 Clutch moves into brake ring	of input and output speeds on power out shift
5 Clutch fully engaged	10 Pressure pause which offsets clutch spring load
6 Input speed	giving smooth overrun shift

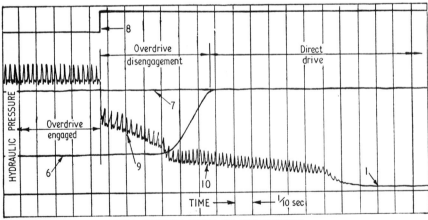

HYDRAULIC PRESSURE CHANGE ON DISENGAGEMENT

Figs 17.5 and 17.6

All gears are made in En 24 steel. Although this is normally a through-hardening steel the sun and planet gears are cyanide hardened to a case depth of 0·005–0·006 in (0·127–0·152 mm). The planets are crown shaved. The annulus is heat treated to 50–55 tonf/in² (772–850 MN/m²) before machining and is not subsequently hardened.

Bearing and tooth loads for an input torque of 300 lbf ft (407 N m) are as follows:

$$\text{Bearing load} = \frac{T \text{ lbf in}}{\text{P.C. radius of planet pin} \times \text{No. of planets}}$$
$$= \frac{300 \times 12}{1 \cdot 525 \times 3}$$
$$= 788 \text{ lbf (3500 N)}$$
$$\text{Tooth load} = 788/2$$
$$= 394 \text{ lbf (1750 N)}$$

The width of the gear is 0·710 in (18 mm), giving a load per inch run of 555 lbf (97 N/mm). Planet bearings can present a problem which is more apparent with an overdrive than with an automatic transmission. At high road speeds the latter is usually in direct drive, when the planets are not turning about their own axes. With an overdrive, however, the planets are not only rotating about their own axes but are orbiting about the centre of the planet carrier and are, therefore, subject to centrifugal loading, often for long periods. It is an advantage to make planet bores as large as possible, consistent with an adequate section below the teeth, as this not only helps to reduce the weight of the gear but permits the use of a pin with minimum deflection. Caged needle bearings are used and, because of uneven distribution of loads due to thrust couples and centrifugal force, two separate bearings are used in each planet. The bearing cages themselves can be a problem since they are subject to centrifugal loading and they should be as light as possible. It will be apparent that these problems are associated with high speeds rather than high loads. Good lubrication is mandatory and the method used is to centrifuge oil from the drilled mainshaft, collecting it in a catcher attached to the planet carrier, from which it is guided into the hollow planet pins and out through a hole placed just in front of the load point of the bearing. The B-10 bearing life is in the order of 6000 h. For purposes of calculation the following conditions are assumed:

5 per cent of life at maximum torque at 4000 rev/min input
65 per cent of life at half torque at 4000 rev/min
15 per cent of life at half torque on overrun at 3000 rev/min
2 per cent of life at 70 per cent of maximum torque at 5000 rev/min
13 per cent of life at 20 per cent of maximum torque at 5000 rev/min

Each source of load is determined and resolved into components parallel and perpendicular to the shaft axis. The bearing reactions due to each component are determined separately. Finally, the radial bearing reactions due to each separate component are combined by vectorial addition into a single load at each bearing condition.

Cone clutches: factors affecting performance

The unit is assessed mainly on the performance of its clutches. Engagement should be smooth and occupy the correct time interval. Incorrect application of the clutch can result in engagements which are unacceptably bumpy or, whilst being smooth in operation, result in failure because the thermal limitations of the clutch are exceeded.

The problem of ratio changing is that of dealing with changes in rotational energy. An understanding of the relationships involved is, therefore, necessary but the subject cannot be dealt with completely within the scope of this paper and only essential expressions are given.

When overdrive is fitted behind the main gearbox, two factors which have a considerable effect on the degree of disturbance experienced during a ratio change in the unit are (a) the size of the overdrive ratio and (b) the ratio in use in the gearbox.

In a power-on upshift the clutch must absorb the kinetic energy lost by the mass of the engine due to the change in speed. In addition, it must absorb a portion of the engine work done during the ratio change.

In a power-on downshift, because of the built-in neutral condition, the engine can speed up to accommodate the change in ratio. During power-off downshifts the clutch must absorb the kinetic energy that results from accelerating the engine against friction and compression at the required rate.

The significant torques during a power-on change into overdrive are plotted in Fig. 17.7. The engine torque can be seen to increase during the engagement because the output shaft torque is assumed to be the same immediately before and after the change in ratio. The two values of engine torque are designated T_{e_1} and T_{e_2}. The clutch torque increases above the value $G(1-R)T_{e_2}$ because of engine-side inertia. It can be shown that the torque on the input member is

$$T_{im} = \frac{GT_e I_c + G^2 I_e(1-R)T_c}{I_c + G^2 I_e(1-R)^2} \quad . \quad . \quad . \quad . \quad (17.1)$$

The value of I_c is very small and an important simplification can be made by considering the limit as I_c approaches zero. Equation (17.1) becomes

$$\lim_{I_c \to 0} T_{im} = \frac{T_c}{1-R} \quad . \quad . \quad . \quad . \quad . \quad (17.2)$$

therefore

$$\lim_{I_c \to 0} T_o = \frac{RT_c}{1-R} \quad . \quad . \quad . \quad . \quad . \quad (17.3)$$

Since the value of output torque is dependent on clutch torque it will rise to a higher value than T_{e_1} and then fall to this value when the change is completed. This change in torque will be apparent to the passenger. Awareness of the change can be reduced by extending the period of engagement, but care must be taken to ensure that the heat resulting from engine torque does not damage the clutch. For a power-off downshift the same considerations apply.

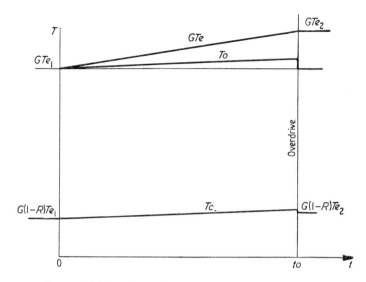

Fig. 17.7. Torques during power-on change into overdrive

Clutch capacity

The capacity of a cone clutch at any instant is given by

$$T_c = \frac{F\mu r}{\sin \alpha} \qquad \cdots \cdots \cdots \quad (17.4)$$

If uniform pressure over the friction area is assumed, the mean radius is given by

$$r_m = \frac{2(R_o^3 - R_i^3)}{3(R_o^2 - R_i^2)} \qquad \cdots \cdots \cdots \quad (17.5)$$

If uniform wear is assumed, the effective radius is given by

$$r = (R_o + R_i)/2 \qquad \cdots \cdots \cdots \quad (17.6)$$

For the type of clutch under consideration there is little difference in the dimensions of R_o and R_i, and the two equations are not significantly different. The assumption of uniform wear gives slightly lower torque capacity, and equation (17.6) is the equation used. During clutch engagement the value of μ varies with rubbing velocity, and the slope of the friction–velocity curve can be taken into account in the analysis. However, for practical purposes it is considered sufficient to assume a mean value for μ. The expressions given below are based on this assumption.

Equations of motion

The slipping time of the clutch, after breaking through the oil film, is given by the equations

$$t_0 = \frac{\omega[G^2 I_e (1-R)^2 + I_c]}{T_c - (1-R)GT_e} \qquad \cdots \cdots \cdots \quad (17.7)$$

and

$$\lim_{I_c \to 0} t_o = \frac{\omega G^2 I_e (1-R)^2}{T_c - (1-R)GT_e} \quad \cdots \cdots \quad (17.8)$$

Energy expressions

The maximum rate of energy dissipation at the clutch occurs at the moment engagement begins. It can be shown that

$$\lim_{I_c \to 0} \mathcal{E} = T_c \left[\frac{\omega - \{T_c - (1-R)GT_e\}t}{(1-R)^2 G^2 I_e} \right] \quad \cdots \cdots \quad (17.9)$$

The total energy dissipated during the clutching operation is given by

$$E = \frac{T_c \omega^2 [(1-R^2)G^2 I_e + I_c]}{2[T_c - (1-R)GT_e]} \quad \cdots \cdots \quad (17.10)$$

and

$$\lim_{I_c \to 0} E = \frac{T_c \omega^2 (1-R)^2 G^2 I_e}{2[T_c - (1-R)GT_e]} \quad \cdots \cdots \quad (17.11)$$

The total amount of energy dissipated as a result of the inertia factor alone— i.e. when there is no driving torque—is independent of clutch torque. It is given by

$$E_i = \frac{\omega^2 (1-R)^2 G^2 T_e}{2} \quad \cdots \cdots \cdots \quad (17.12)$$

It can be shown that the rate of energy transfer to the output shaft, ξ, is given by

$$\xi = \left(\frac{T_{im} - GT_e}{G^2 I_e} \right) \left(G^2 I_e + \frac{I_c}{(1-R)^2} \right) \left[\omega - \frac{(T_{im} - GT_e)t}{G^2 I_e} \right]$$
$$- \left[\frac{T_{im} - GT_e}{(1-R)G^2 I_e} \right] \left[\frac{I_c R \omega}{1-R} - T_c t \right] - T_c \omega \quad . \quad (17.13)$$

and

$$\lim_{I_c \to 0} \xi = \omega \left[\frac{RT_c}{1-R} - GT_e \right] + \frac{T_e [T_c - (1-R)GT_e]}{(1-R)GI_e} \quad \cdots \quad (17.14)$$

This expression is very important since it indicates the amount of disturbance experienced during a ratio change.

Certain simplifying assumptions have been made in the above analysis. Engine output torque, clutch coefficient of friction, and clutch end load have been assumed constant although they will undoubtedly vary during the ratio change. Nevertheless, variations will be so small that they will not seriously affect the results. In arriving at the expression for energy transfer to the output shaft the speed of the shaft is assumed to remain constant. Theoretically this cannot be so since any work done on the shaft, if the tractive effort remains constant, will affect its speed. However, this assumption, whilst simplifying the mathematics, does not materially affect the results.

Control systems

Control systems for the Laycock unit are numerous and vary from a simple circuit incorporating a driver-operated switch, often built into the knob of the

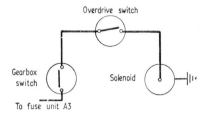

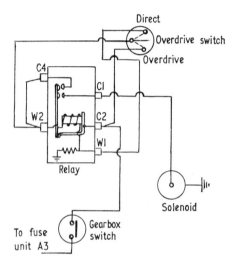

Fig. 17.8. Basic overdrive circuit

Fig. 17.9. Self-cancelling circuit

gear lever, to electronic circuits for switching in or out automatically according to torque and speed.

Because the overdrive unit incorporates a one-way clutch it is necessary to inhibit the use of planetary ratio in reverse gear. Also, since the end load on the overdrive clutch is not intended for use on bottom gear, this gear and often second gear is also inhibited.

It is considered desirable by some vehicle manufacturers to use a self-cancelling overdrive switch so that if planetary ratio is in use when a change is made to a lower gear on which overdrive is inhibited, the control circuit is broken to prevent automatic re-engagement of planetary ratio when the higher gear is re-selected.

When overdrive is used behind an automatic transmission it may be restricted to top gear only by incorporating a pressure switch into the appropriate clutch line of the automatic transmission. Some thought must be given to the effect of a change in ratio on the control system of the automatic transmission since engagement of overdrive at too low a speed could cause hunting.

It is not possible, within the scope of this paper, to describe all control systems, but the two most commonly used circuits are shown in Figs 17.8 and 17.9.

The MS. of this paper was received at the Institution on 29th October 1969 and accepted for publication on 10th November 1969.

Paper 18. Power Take-off Systems for Today's Trucks

R. G. WEBSTER
Director and Chief Designer, Edbro Ltd, Bolton, Lancs.

V. P. RIGBY, C Eng, F I Mech E
Works Director, Edbro Ltd, Bolton, Lancs.

Power take-off systems are necessary for most of today's trucks supplying the power to operate various truck-mounted equipment on tipping gear, garbage packers, fuel tankers, bulk cement tankers, refrigeration trucks, and many more applications. PTOs are gear-driven units that fit to, and obtain their power from, the truck gearbox and transmit the power through a drive shaft to the unit being driven, such as a pump or compressor. Other special PTOs are available which drive off the engine and main driveline. Many types of PTOs are described which cater for a wide range of horsepowers and speeds to suit truck users' needs; they are controlled from the driving cab by direct rods or remotely by flexible cables or air pressure.

Giving the truck user the best and most economical PTO system is dependent upon the PTO transmission and truck manufacturer ensuring that a suitable PTO is available and that the transmission PTO mounting is available to accept the PTO and its drive. More automation on future trucks will make co-operation between these manufacturers increasingly essential, to maintain the continuing expansion of the trucking industry.

INTRODUCTION

Power take-offs (PTOs) are necessary on most of today's trucks. They are used to facilitate material handling and to supply power to all industries using commercial trucks and tractors.

The PTO of 25–30 years ago was only used for tippers and winches. Today, with more mechanization and automation, in addition to tippers, PTOs are now required for compressors, fuelling pumps, garbage packers, refrigeration equipment, blowing bulk cement trucks, tailgate loaders, and, in fact, any accessory that needs a power drive or hydraulic power.

PTOs are gear-driven units that fit to, and obtain their power from, the truck gearbox and transmit the power through a drive shaft to the unit being driven, such as a pump or compressor. Other special PTOs are available which drive off the engine and main driveline.

PTO OPENINGS

The method of PTO drive from the gearbox is usually by means of openings or facings on the sides, top, or bottom of the gearbox, on to which a PTO unit can be fitted to engage with a driver gear wheel in the gearbox, normally located on the layshaft. On early gearboxes the size and shape of the openings were left to the discretion of the individual designer. However, it became obvious that standards should be adopted, and the S.A.E. PTO openings on gearboxes, as shown on Fig. 18.1, covering four- and six-hole facings, came into use.

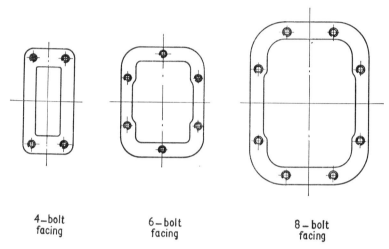

4-bolt
facing

6-bolt
facing

8-bolt
facing

Fig. 18.1. Comparison of four-, six-, and eight-bolt power take-off openings

The four-hole facing was mainly used for tyre pumps, although light tipper pumps also were fitted. In the U.S.A. and U.K. the six-bolt facing became the general standard, for which there is now a wide range of PTOs available. Some Continental gearboxes have six-bolt facings, but the majority are still special. During the last few years an eight-bolt facing has been introduced which has opened a whole new field of design for heavier drives, because gears in the PTO can be made wider.

APPLICATIONS

In the majority of applications the PTO is operated when the truck is stationary. Other PTOs have been made available from the flywheel, the front of the engine crankshaft, and from the split propeller shaft. In the latter, a portion of the driveline of the truck is cut away, and an auxiliary transmission of some type is fitted having PTO facings for the provision of power. This is primarily used when it is necessary to run the accessory continuously, whilst the truck is travelling, in order to avoid difficulties in changing gear. This can occur where drag of the PTO load is transferred to the layshaft of the gearbox.

This does not mean that it is impossible to use the conventional gearbox side-type PTO, but some means of off-loading the PTO is necessary at the time of changing gear.

The conventional PTO installation can also be used when the truck is travelling, e.g. the spreading of road materials, where the truck is being operated constantly in one gear.

It is considered that if the gearbox side-mounted PTO had kept pace with truck development, and had been adequate powerwise, then development of many other alternative methods to secure power would have been unnecessary.

A further type of PTO drive, popular in some Continental trucks, is the rear-mounted layshaft PTO used by Z.F. and Daimler-Benz, where the rear of the layshaft is provided with a splined dog engagement to take a PTO mounted off the rear flange of the gearbox. Whilst this arrangement allows high power transmission and standardization, the PTO output speed is limited to the speed of the layshaft, unless step-up gearing is incorporated. In many cases there is not adequate clearance with the prop shaft, which has led to offset PTOs incorporating the speed-up gears mentioned. Certain U.K. manufacturers have incorporated this feature (e.g. Turners and Eaton, Yale and Towne) on some gearboxes in addition to the side facings.

PTO ADAPTORS

On some gearboxes, even with standard facings, the PTO drive gear is sunk well inside the gearbox casing, due to some design reason. Consequently, a special adaptor gear assembly has first to be fitted to the gearbox before the PTO can be fitted.

Adaptors are also used to change the direction of rotation of the drive shaft, or to speed it up or slow it down. In some cases, only by the use of an adaptor can a PTO be fitted to prevent interference with adjacent chassis components or bulges on the gearbox.

PTO GEARING

The standard S.A.E. facing only partially solves the design and manufacturing problem of the PTO manufacturer. Each gearbox manufacturer has his own ideas on gear design; consequently, an infinite variety of PTOs can emerge through differences between manufacturers of pitch, pressure angle, helix angle, and special corrections. In many gearboxes the PTO driver gear is one of the existing gearbox constant-mesh gears, thus saving fitment of a special PTO gear.

The large variation makes the manufacture of PTOs a very specialized business, and the authors' company carries gear-cutting equipment, tools, hobs, etc., to suit hundreds of combinations of gear tooth forms.

PTO TORQUE AND SPEEDS

The speed of the PTO shaft is determined by the engine rev/min and the gear ratio between the transmission PTO drive gear and driven PTO gears. Whilst much has been done to standardize the PTO with respect to facing sizes and position of the driver gear, the horsepower output is not standard. But if so much is standard, why not the horsepower? The answer to this is, because on practically every transmission, the PTO driver gear runs at a different speed. If the gear in the transmission is small, and its speed low in relation to engine speed, the horsepower output available will be low.

In order to achieve a satisfactory horsepower output from a PTO, a satisfactory PTO speed and torque are required. Since horsepower is a product of torque and rev/min, the higher the torque and the higher the rev/min, the higher will be the horsepower.

Most six-bolt PTO facings are able to provide a torque throughput of 140 lb ft or about 25 hp at 1000 rev/min, but a check has to be made to suit the application with the particular transmission. Some of the eight-bolt facings are now able to transmit full engine torque.

Due to gearbox design, some PTO driver gears are fast running, and in order to transmit high power, large diameter gears are used. For certain applications this may require PTOs with reduction gearing to provide usable PTO drive speeds.

When twin-PTO drives are taken from a gearbox with two facings, it is necessary to ensure that the total power is not overloading the gearbox. This also applies to gearboxes of the Fuller twin-countershaft type, where the layshaft is replaced by twin countershafts. A PTO drive from one of these shafts will be limited to half the torque throughput.

Automatic transmissions also provide some problems. The PTO driver gear is large because it is incorporated on the outer gear of the planetary gear train on the main shaft, as there is no layshaft. A PTO with reduction gears is usually necessary. The PTO speed available will vary in relation to the load imposed by the driven device. Operation is different in that the gearbox selector has to be put in any 'drive' position to stop the PTO driver gear with the truck stopped to permit the PTO to be engaged. After engagement, the gearbox selector is moved to neutral and the power applied. Some available PTOs have clutch engagement by air pressure so that they can be operated whilst the truck is moving, i.e. 'hot shift' type.

CONTROL SYSTEMS

These vary from the simple direct-lever arrangement to remote controls for cab-over-engine trucks and tilt cabs, taking the form of flexible cable units, or air pressure, to shift the PTO in and out of gear. The air-shift is worthy of special mention, because with this shifter the PTO gear must travel its full distance into mesh once the operator moves over the control switch. The danger of leaving the PTO gear partially engaged cannot occur. It is usual to spring load the PTO to the 'out of gear' position so that it is fail safe and will shift out of gear if the air pressure fails. Pressure is taken from the air-brake system with a protection valve to guard against brake failure.

PTO TYPES

Many types of PTOs are available, a selection of which will be discussed.

Side mount, single-speed, one or two gear design

These PTOs meet most power demands. They are manufactured in medium or heavy duty capacities. Medium units are suitable for tipping gears, hoists, tail-lifts, and other intermittently driven equipment rated at around 15–20 hp. Heavy duty units are used for cranes, garbage packer bodies, compressors, and generators rated at about 25 hp.

Side mount, multi-speed PTOs

For special equipment requiring a reverse speed or range of forward speeds
such as:

Two speeds	Forward	No reverse
Two speeds	Forward	One reverse
Two speeds	Forward	Two reverse

Rated capacity about 25 hp for driving winches, cranes, or derricks.

Split shaft PTO

Installed directly in the truck driveline between gearbox and rear axle. A
split-shaft PTO may be operated at any of the speeds of the truck transmission.
Normally designed to transmit full engine power for winches, large generators,
or air compressors. Models for one speed forward, forward and reverse are
available. Units are also available having two or three PTO facings to allow several
PTO-driven accessories to be provided and operated with the truck either
stationary or travelling.

Rear mount PTO

Installed directly on to the rear of the gearbox on layshaft centre line and
operated by dog engagement to layshaft. Only available on certain transmissions,
but PTOs are available in all configurations with ratings up to engine power.

Engine crankshaft drive

This takes the form of a fixed drive from the front end of the engine crankshaft
via a short drive shaft with universal joints at both ends. In some cases a modified
radiator is required to allow the drive shaft to pass through.

Popular available drives allow a power of approximately 30 b.h.p. per 1000
rev/min, and a maximum torque of 160 lb ft.

This drive is suitable for operators who require a continuous drive for chassis-
mounted equipment, such as cement mixers for ready-mixed cement deliveries.

Combination side mount PTO–hydraulic pump units

Pioneered by the authors' company, consisting of a pump directly mounted to
the PTO, eliminating open drive shafts, thus making a more economical installation. These are designed for truck-mounted hydraulic equipment, tippers,
cranes, and garbage packers. Units are available for a wide range of oil flows and
pressures.

CHOOSING A PTO

To select properly a PTO for a specific application, the following questions
must be answered:

(1) How many PTO speeds are required?
(2) What is the rotation?
(3) How much output shaft horsepower and speed are needed to do the job?
(4) Is the gearbox capable of the required power?
(5) Which type of gearbox is to be used?

To assist in answering, the questions will now be discussed.

(1) *How many PTO speeds?*

This depends on the unit being driven, for example:

Single-speed PTOs are used on tippers, tail-lifts, compressors, and pumps. Multi-speed and reversible PTOs are used for winches and other special drive applications.

(2) *What is the rotation?*

This must be arranged to suit whichever PTO can be provided on the particular gearbox and the driven unit.

(3) *How much power and speed?*

This depends on application. Therefore the input horsepower and speed of the unit being driven should be obtained from the manufacturer of the driven unit. Knowing these figures, a check should then be made, and a suitable PTO chosen.

If a PTO can be chosen to meet the horsepower of the unit being driven, at the speed required, then a direct drive can be used, as shown in Fig. 18.2(A).

If, however, the PTO output shaft and driven unit cannot be connected directly, then an indirect drive must be used, as shown in Fig. 18.2(B).

On an indirect drive, if the speed of the PTO output shaft has to be multiplied, i.e. speeded up for the driven unit, then torque at the PTO drive shaft is higher than the unit being driven. If the speed of the PTO output shaft has to be reduced, i.e. geared down, then torque at the PTO drive shaft is less than the unit being driven. This is important, particularly with a speeded-up drive, as it is the torque at the PTO output shaft that matters. It is essential to check this carefully to ensure a correct PTO is chosen, e.g. if it is required to drive a blower at 1000 rev/min and 25 hp, and a PTO can be obtained that will fit to the particular gearbox and provide this horsepower and speed, then a direct drive can be arranged; the torque of PTO output shaft and blower input shaft being equal.

If, however, the blower has to run at 1000 rev/min and only 500 rev/min can be provided by the PTO, due to mechanical considerations, then a speed-up indirect drive is necessary. There is still 25 hp being transmitted, but only at 500 rev/min at the PTO output shaft. This doubles the torque throughput of the PTO from 132 lb ft to 264 lb ft. A PTO has then to be chosen for this torque rating.

(4) *Will the gearbox transmit the power?*

This depends on the particular gearbox. As already pointed out, it is mainly related to the size of the PTO driver gear and its speed. These vary between one gearbox and another.

A guide to determining the amount of horsepower is the 'pitch line velocity' (I)*. This is the speed in ft/min of a point on the pitch line of the PTO driver. Generally, the faster the pitch line velocity, the more horsepower the gearbox can transmit, unless limited by other factors, such as strength of gearbox, gear teeth, bearings, or casing.

* *The reference is given in Appendix 18.1.*

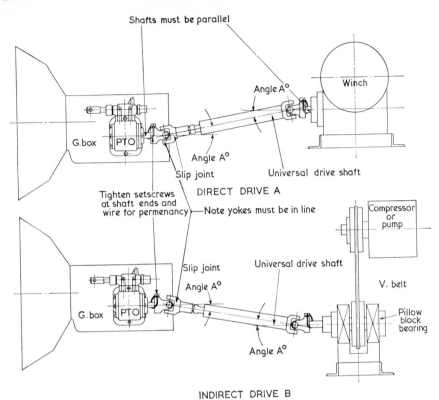

Fig. 18.2. Direct and indirect drive

As a general guide, the pitch line velocity of the gearbox PTO driver gear for light drives on tail-lifts and pumps should not be less than 400 ft/min, which is equivalent to about 15 hp at 1000 engine rev/min; and not less than 650 ft/min for PTOs to transmit 25 hp at 1000 engine rev/min, which is average power on a six-bolt facing.

(5) Which type of gearbox?

The model type must be obtained. Some have more than one PTO facing, and the choice of opening will depend on the application. Reference to a PTO manufacturer's data book will enable a suitable PTO to be chosen to meet the operational needs.

INSTALLATION

The PTO and driven unit must be installed correctly to ensure satisfactory operation. Fig. 18.2 shows examples of typical installations.

It is also essential that PTOs and adaptors are installed with correct face gaskets, to ensure that there is sufficient backlash between the PTO and gearbox driver gears. Backlash must be 0·008–0·012 in with the PTO bolts tightened down to approximately 20 lb ft of torque.

PTOs obtain their lubrication from the gearbox to which they are attached. Filling the gearbox to its normal level with the prescribed lubricant will give adequate lubrication for the PTO. The use of a PTO will slightly increase the oil capacity of the gearbox when the PTO is below the normal oil level.

WHAT IS WANTED FOR TODAY'S PTOs

Greatly improved availability to the customer would result from an increased use of standardization, e.g. by adhering to the S.A.E. standard facings, thus avoiding special PTO castings, as some transmissions still have odd-shaped facings. More standardization on the location of PTO driver gear would reduce the need for special adaptors when the driver gear is deeper in the gearbox than the standard.

All special units which have to be created cost more to the customer and could influence his choice of truck if a suitable PTO cannot be fitted.

Where PTO facings are located on the top of transmissions, problems of proper lubrication of the PTO can arise. Some automatic transmissions provide a tapping-off point on their own pump from which an oil supply can be taken to the PTO bearings.

Bottom PTO facings should be used with caution to avoid contamination fouling PTO parts, as well as ensuring adequate ground clearance.

When a forced oil feed is not available, care should be taken to ensure oil will reach the PTO bearings.

Truck manufacturers should endeavour to ensure adequate space adjacent to the PTO facing so that a PTO can be fitted without having to modify chassis parts or provide special adaptors.

Truck and transmission manufacturers should consider the fitment of both an eight-bolt and a six-bolt facing on heavier units. This is already being done by a few transmission manufacturers and gives considerable scope to the trucker and truck manufacturer to extend the usage of the truck by making it suitable for any special equipment the customer desires.

CONCLUSION

Giving the truck user the best and most economical PTO system is dependent upon the PTO transmission and truck manufacturer ensuring that a suitable PTO is available, the transmission PTO mounting is standard and will provide the power throughput, and the truck has space available to accept the PTO and its drive.

More automation on future trucks will make co-operation between these manufacturers increasingly essential, to maintain the continuing expansion of the trucking industry.

APPENDIX 18.1

REFERENCE

(1) WAGNER, R. W. 'What is expected of today's power take-offs?', S.A.E. Paper 650624, *Int. West Coast Meeting, Vancouver, B.C., Canada* 1965 (16–19 August).

The MS. of this paper was received at the Institution on 17th December 1969 and accepted for publication on 23rd December 1969.

Paper 19. Proportions of Automobile Change Speed Gear Teeth

J. E. WILLN
The Motor Industry Research Association, Lindley, near Nuneaton, Warwickshire

R. J. LOVE
The Motor Industry Research Association, Lindley, near Nuneaton, Warwickshire

Information on the proportions and operating conditions for gear teeth in a range of passenger and commercial vehicle gearboxes is reviewed, and it is explained that such information provides important design data. The operating conditions are considered in terms of sliding velocity, surface contact stress, and root bending stress for the transmission of maximum engine torque. For convenience, methods given by Professor Tuplin have been used for the calculation of tooth stresses, and these have later been combined with a design procedure which may be helpful when considering applications where background experience is limited. The influence of material, production processes, heat treatment, etc., on endurance in terms of root bending fatigue, surface pitting fatigue, and scuffing is discussed, and for this purpose reference is made to past M.I.R.A. research work.

INTRODUCTION

The long-term development of gearbox gears has clearly led to a situation in which many gears are operating reliably at their maximum or near maximum load capacity. Information on service operating conditions therefore constitutes a most important source of design data. In the following, the geometrical proportions loading, etc., of gear teeth in 16 change speed gearbox applications, employed by a number of vehicle manufacturers, are reviewed. The information should prove useful not only in connection with the design of new applications, but also when considering possible increased loadings of existing designs.

In all cases, the gearboxes which have been considered take the form of a mainshaft and layshaft configuration, where gears are referred to as the 'first speed gear pair', 'second speed gear pair', etc. The gears which transmit torque from the engine to the layshaft pinions are called the 'first pair reduction gears'. For the purpose of graphical presentation, gear functions are denoted by symbols, as shown in Table 19.1.

The subject is covered in four sections: the first deals with the geometrical proportions of the tooth forms; the second section reviews a number of past M.I.R.A. reports relating to the improvements which can be obtained in tooth strength by consideration of materials, manufacturing processes, and heat treatment; the third section covers load capacity; and the last section gives an outline of a design procedure incorporating the information reviewed in the earlier sections.

Methods and notation given by Professor W. A. Tuplin [1]* [2] have been used

* References are given in Appendix 19.2.

Table 19.1. Key to graphical presentation

Symbol		Gear function
Passenger vehicles	Commercial vehicles	
○	●	First pair reduction gears
△	▲	First speed gear pairs
□	■	Second speed gear pairs
◁	◀	Third speed gear pairs
◇	◆	Fourth, fifth, and overdrive gear pairs
▽	▼	Reverse gear pairs

for the calculations of tooth stresses, and these are included in Appendix 19.1. There was no very important reason for choosing Tuplin's methods, and it is recognized that individual automobile companies, who differ among themselves, do not in general follow this approach. However, the methods offered by Tuplin are comprehensive, and in this survey they provide a very suitable means for comparing tooth loadings in gears made by various manufacturers. An approach recommended by Tuplin has again been employed in the section on 'Design procedure'.

REVIEW OF DESIGN DIMENSIONS

Centre distance and gear ratio

In practice, selection of centre distance may be influenced by a number of considerations other than the degree of loading, such as bearing design, synchromesh design, inertias, etc. However, Fig. 19.1 indicates that values of centre distance which have been used tend to increase with increasing values of maximum engine torque. Heldt (3) recommends an expression relating these features for passenger vehicle applications, which is given as:

$$C = 0 \cdot 5 \sqrt[3]{T}$$

where C is the centre distance (in) and T is the maximum engine torque (lb ft). In Fig. 19.1 it can be seen that this relationship is in reasonable agreement with most of the passenger vehicle applications that have been considered here. In the case of commercial vehicles, a relationship more appropriate to the data is given by:

$$C = 0 \cdot 72 \sqrt[3]{T}$$

Gear ratios employed in the gearboxes under review are shown in the form of distribution diagrams in Fig. 19.2 for each gear function, indicating the spread of values that have been used in both passenger and commercial vehicle applications.

Number of teeth and tooth pitch

At an early stage in the design calculations it is necessary to select the number of teeth (t) and tooth pitch (p) for the pinion gear which is bound up with the adopted centre distance. As a general rule it is not usual in automotive practice

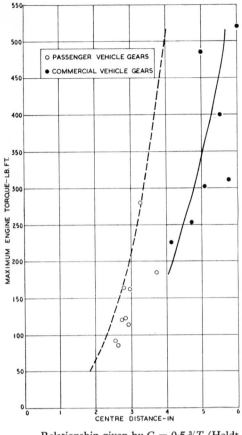

Fig. 19.1. Maximum engine torque plotted against shaft centre distance

- - - - Relationship given by $C = 0.5\sqrt[3]{T}$ (Heldt (3)).
———— Relationship given by $C = 0.72\sqrt[3]{T}$.

to adopt B.S. pitches, although there is a tendency to carry out this procedure in the commercial vehicle field. In Fig. 19.3, which shows values of pinion teeth number (t_1) plotted against reciprocal gear ratio $(1/R_g)$, a straight line relationship, recommended by Tuplin (see Table 1 of reference (1)), gives a reasonable first approximation to the selection for number of pinion teeth from the gear ratio, as follows:

$$t_1 = 15/R_g + 10$$

In selecting tooth pitch it should be strongly emphasized that if there is any practical advantage in adhering to standard pitches, teeth of acceptable proportions can still be generated with this procedure by careful application of correction to the generated profile (described later). For comparison, values of transverse tooth pitch (p_t) and centre distance (C) for the production gears are shown in Fig. 19.4.

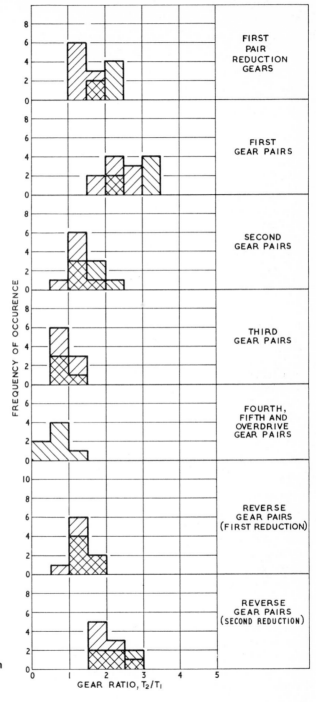

Passenger.

Commercial.

Fig. 19.2. Distribution of gear ratio for each gear function

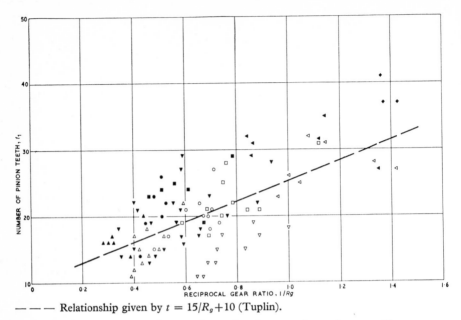

—— —— Relationship given by $t = 15/R_g + 10$ (Tuplin).

Fig. 19.3. Selection of pinion teeth number from reciprocal gear ratio

Face width

To some extent, choice of face width will affect load capacity, and values of face width (f) are generally found to increase with values of transverse tooth pitch (p_t). Tuplin (($\mathbf{1}$), Table 4) suggests that, as a first approximation, face width is given by $2dR_g/(R_g+1)$. However, values of $dR_g/(R_g+1)$ and face width shown in Fig. 19.5 indicate that a more suitable relationship is given by:

$$f = dR_g/2(R_g+1)$$

Helix angle

For the most effective continuity of tooth action between helical gears, one end of each tooth should overlap the end of the next tooth, i.e. the face width should exceed the axial tooth pitch. In other words, tan σ (helix angle) should be greater than p_t/f; values of tan σ and p_t/f have been plotted in Fig. 19.6, and in the majority of cases the condition of tooth overlap has been fulfilled to a varying degree. In general, it can be seen that the helix angles employed in passenger vehicle applications are higher than for commercial vehicle applications.

Correction

In gear tooth generation, a variety of tooth shapes of the same pitch can be obtained from gear blanks of different diameter by cutting to full depth with the same cutter. Any variation from a standard form created in this way is commonly referred to as 'correction'. At the extreme limits, the tooth shape may vary from an 'undercut' form, where there is a deficiency of involute profile and reduced

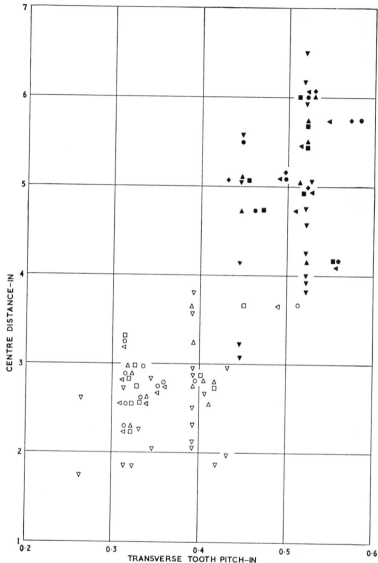

Fig. 19.4. Shaft centre distance plotted against tooth pitch

tooth thickness at the root section, to a 'stub' tooth form, which is pointed with a greatly reduced tip section. In the latter case, the root section is formed by more acceptable proportions from a root bending fatigue point of view. By judicious selection from a range of standard pitches, and hence cutters, and by varying centre distance, it is possible to cut gear teeth for transmitting a specific velocity ratio which will have the required involute profile and the necessary root

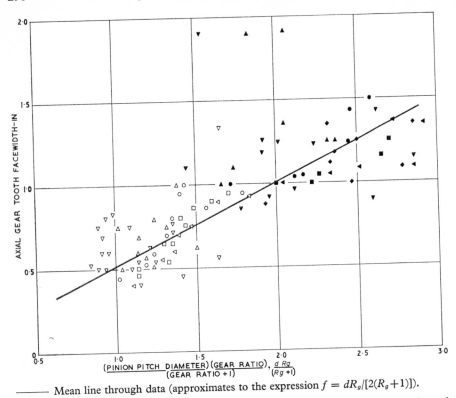

——— Mean line through data (approximates to the expression $f = dR_g/[2(R_g+1)]$).

Fig. 19.5. Selection of face width from empirical factor combining gear ratio and pinion pitch diameter of generation

section to give adequate load capacity in terms of surface pitting and root bending fatigue.

Specification of correction is given in B.S. 436 as a variation of cutting depth from a standard depth and is termed as a K value which can be either positive or negative. Tuplin (1) refers to correction as a diametral adjustment factor V, which is a measure of the so-called addendum for a rack of B.S. proportions. It will be seen from Appendix 19.1 that when the K value is zero, the V value is 2. Values of correction in these terms for the pinion gear teeth under examination are presented in Fig. 19.7. The broken line shown in this diagram indicates the maximum and minimum values of correction recommended by Tuplin, as shown in Appendix 19.1, for both spur and helical gears with a flank angle of 20°. For a helical gear the normal section of the gear tooth approximates in form to the tooth of a spur gear having $t \sec^3 \sigma$ number of teeth (see pp. 63–66 of reference (4)) which is termed the 'equivalent number of teeth' in Fig. 19.7.

Flank angle and pressure angle

It is common practice to use 'pressure angle' to describe the angle which relates the reference diameter, or pitch circle of generation, with the base diameter of the

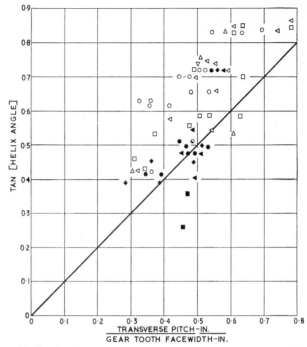

——— Points below this line indicate gears which operate without helical overlap.

Fig. 19.6. Selection of helix angle at the pitch circle of generation for ensuring multiple tooth contact

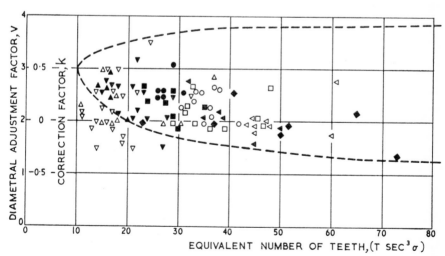

– – – – Maximum and minimum limits recommended by Tuplin for gears cut to British Standard proportions (20° flank angle).

Fig. 19.7. Correction applied to pinion gear teeth

gear. It is considered by Tuplin (1) that 'flank angle' is a more appropriate term in this context, since it is purely a geometrical feature of the gear. The 'pressure angle', on the other hand, is created when the generated gear is meshed with another gear, and is dependent upon the base circles of generation and the centre distance of engagement. When straight tooth gears are meshed at the standard depth of engagement, the pressure angle approximates to the flank angle of the basic rack to which the cutter is conjugate, and in many cases the two angles are equal but there is no essential connection between them.

The 'flank angle' adopted for the British Standard rack and the corresponding rack-shaped cutter is taken as 20°, measured normal to the surface of the cutter. Similarly, most of the gears considered in this survey are found to have a 20° flank angle, although passenger vehicles have some lower values within the range 12°–18°, and some commercial vehicles have higher values within the range 25°–28°.

GEAR MATERIALS AND PRODUCTION PROCESSES

Strength tests

It is usual to assess gear tooth load capacity in terms of the resistance to surface pitting or root bending fatigue. Test rigs which have been employed for investigating these two qualities are described respectively in two M.I.R.A. reports (5) (6).

Material

In one early report (7) three case-hardened steels, En 34, En 39B, and En 320, were considered in terms of bending fatigue. Whilst the En 34 and En 39B gave better results than the En 320, it was to be shown later that no great significance can be placed in these results without detailed consideration being given to the heat treatment which was applied in each case. In two later reports (8) (9) a range of carburizing steels were considered in both bending and pitting fatigue, where similar materials and heat treatments were considered in each case. In the first report (8), where a wider range of heat treatment was examined, the variation of bending strength was about 25 per cent of the average value, which was said to be no greater than the variation that could be expected due to changes in heat treatment on the same material. In the second report (9) the variation of pitting strength was similarly small. The order of merit for the two forms of failure varied, although certain materials were superior in resisting both forms of failure.

Other reports (10) (11) describe tests on two carburizing steels (En 36, En 39A), two through-hardened steels (En 24, En 30A), and a nitrided steel (En 40C), for pitting and bending, respectively. In each case, the case-hardened steels were superior, the nitrided steel giving an intermediate result.

Heat treatment of pack carburized gears

In general, automobile gears are surface hardened in some form, and it has been shown that the degree of resistance to pitting and bending fatigue failure is markedly influenced by the form of heat treatment. In bending fatigue tests (12) and pitting tests (**13**) on En 352 gears, it was shown that treatments giving the same significant feature of case microstructure were generally ranked in the same order of merit for each form of failure. Retained austenite and discontinuous network carbide were found in most of the strongest gears, whereas continuous network carbide was found in some of the weakest gears. Martensitic structures were no better than structures containing discontinuous network or globular carbides. Heat treatment was found to be more significant in bending fatigue than pitting fatigue.

For good overall bending strength it appeared that gears should be 'single' quenched from as high a temperature as is practicable, preferably by direct quenching. Intermediate rather than deep case depths were preferable, 0·020 in being a suitable depth for the 7 d.p. gears examined. The pitting tests indicated that greater case depths (0·035 in on 5 d.p. gears) were desirable. However, thin case depths (0·006–0·008 in) have been used successfully by one manufacturer (see Table 19.2), and this is said to be due to the relatively high core hardness.

Table 19.2. Material specification for the production gears

Type of vehicle	Gear material	Specified material hardness, V.p.n.		Case depth, in
		Surface	Core	
Passenger	S.A.E. 4620	600	—	0·025–0·035
	En 36V	650/700	400	0·020–0·025
	En 18C	780	500/600	0·006–0·008
	En 35A	620/700	260/280	0·025–0·030
	En 361	700	400	0·020
Commercial	En 355	700	555	0·033–0·038
	En 39	600/650	—	0·030–0·040
	En 39	720/780	—	0·030–0·050
	En 355	—	—	0·020–0·025

Gas carburizing

Under similar quenching conditions, gas carburizing gave bending fatigue strengths of the same order as, or in some cases a little less than, pack carburizing (**12**)–(**14**).

Carbo-nitriding and cyaniding

Carbo-nitriding, investigated with En 352 gears (**12**), gave bending results below several of the values obtained with pack carburizing. Hardening by cyaniding gave results similar to those for carbo-nitriding.

Induction hardening

A few bending fatigue experiments were conducted with induction hardened En 9 and En 36 gears (**15**). The ring inductor method was used. The induction hardened En 9 gears had only about one-third of the fatigue strength of conventionally carburized and heat-treated En 36 gears. Also, En 36 gears which had been carburized and then induction hardened with a fast rate of heating gave poor results; a slow rate of heating gave results similar to those for conventionally carburized and heat-treated gears.

The generally poor results obtained with induction hardening appeared to be associated with the inability of the process adopted to produce good tooth root hardness at all positions along the length of the teeth. It is possible that different results would have been obtained with other equipment or techniques.

Tempering

The effect of tempering after carburizing on bending fatigue strength has been examined on a variety of steels (8) (12). In the first investigation (8), involving five steels, tempering produced a loss of strength ranging from 0 to 20 per cent. Further work on an En 352 steel (12) again showed a distinct weakening effect; seven out of the eight gears tested gave a reduction in strength in the range 7–23 per cent, and the reduction was generally greater with an increase in tempering temperature.

Effect of lead

Three reports deal with the effect of lead on both forms of fatigue failure (10) (11) (14). The earlier work on bending fatigue (10) involved the addition of lead in En 24 and En 39A steels, and in both cases there was a reduction in strength of about 30 per cent. However, no significant reduction in resistance to pitting failure was found to occur with either of these steels (11). Later work, on En 353 steel (14), showed reductions in bending fatigue strength ranging between 10 and 20 per cent, depending upon the form of hardening treatment.

Production processes

Two reports (16) (17) show the effect of gear production processes on bending and pitting fatigue strength for En 36 and En 352 respectively. In the second report (17) the results of both investigations have been summarized, indicating that gears formed by hobbing or shaving give reasonably good results for both bending and pitting. Shot-peening after carburizing can considerably improve bending fatigue strength (i.e. about 20 per cent), and increases the resistance to pitting at shorter lives (i.e. 10 per cent at 5×10^6 cycles). It should be noted that the improvement with shot-peening is additional to any improvement which is obtained by shot-blasting (as used for de-scaling). In bending fatigue tests (18), shot-blasting alone improved the strength by 15–20 per cent. The treatment most detrimental to fatigue strength was found to be from wheel grinding after carburizing. Grinding of the roots reduced bending strength by up to 50 per cent (16) and grinding of the tooth surfaces reduced pitting resistance by about 20 per cent (17). Lapping of gear teeth, which gave a considerable improvement in tooth surface finish, gave only a slight increase in resistance to pitting.

The application of phosphating after carburizing reduced pitting strength by about 10 per cent. In bending tests (16), phosphating did not impair the strength of a hobbed gear, and in fact produced some improvement in a gear which had been ground in the roots.

Impact strength

With tests on En 352 gears (12) and En 362 gears (19), case depth had an important influence on impact strength, the strength decreasing markedly with increase in case depth. In general, impact strength increased with increase in quenching temperature. There was no straightforward relationship between impact strength and bending fatigue strength, but a number of gears with good impact strength had good bending fatigue strength; in general, good overall results were obtained with the higher quenching temperatures and relatively small case depths.

In the tests on En 352 (12), the impact strength was improved by tempering. Both carbo-nitriding and cyaniding gave good impact strength. Tests on notched bar specimens, carburized or uncarburized, did not indicate the impact properties of carburized gear teeth.

TOOTH OPERATING CONDITIONS

Relative surface motion

Extreme conditions of load and sliding velocity between gear teeth can give rise to a form of surface failure commonly referred to as 'scuffing'. The relative sliding velocity between contacting gear teeth changes direction at the mesh point and is greatest at the initial and final points of engagement. At the same time, the contact point is found to 'sweep' continuously across the tooth face in one direction throughout the meshing cycle. The two velocities, when combined, give a 'slide/sweep ratio' which, by convention, is said to be positive outside the meshing cylinder and negative inside the meshing cylinder. Large values of slide/sweep ratio are considered to provide unfavourable lubrication conditions. From theoretical considerations (20), the thinnest oil film between gear teeth is found to occur at the initial point of engagement. Experimental evidence, from tests carried out on the I.A.E. $3\frac{1}{4}$-in centres gear test machine, also indicates that lubrication is critical since this is the point from which scuffing is nearly always found to originate.

For comparison, the tooth loads and maximum tip sliding velocities operating between the gears under review for the transmission of maximum engine torque are shown in Fig. 19.8. Results obtained by Manhajm and Mansion (21), giving scuffing conditions for a light naphthenic oil, have been included to illustrate the effect of speed. Fosberry and Mansion (22), in a summary of work, describe fully the effect of lubricating conditions on scuffing load. Variations of sliding velocity, gear materials, surface treatments, and heat treatments are also discussed in some detail. Among the various surface treatments, for example, Fosberry and Mansion (22) have shown the good effect of a ferrous and manganese phosphate treatment,

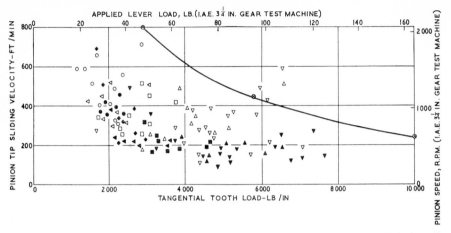

Results of tests on the I.A.E. $3\frac{1}{4}$-in centres machine with a light naphthenic oil (other oils gave less favourable results, see reference (**25**)).

Fig. 19.8. Pinion tooth load–tip sliding velocity conditions at maximum engine torque

which approximately doubled the load-carrying capacity of the test gears. This process is now widely used on automobile final drive gears.

Surface contact stress

Failure by 'pitting' fatigue is associated with the level of surface contact stress in curved surfaces operating in rolling and sliding contact. When pits occur in gear teeth, they usually form adjacent to the mesh point. For the purpose of this survey, maximum surface stresses were derived from the Hertz formulae as defined by Tuplin (**2**) which take into account the elastic modulus of the material, the load per inch of line contact induced by maximum engine torque, and relative radius of curvature at the mesh point.

Since pitting is a fatigue process, life above the endurance limit will be dependent upon the degree of loading, and gears which are used for short periods can be loaded to a higher level than gears used for longer periods. In presenting values of surface contact stress in Fig. 19.9, compensation for gear usage has been made by assembling the data in terms of cycles of stress derived for a distance of 100 000 vehicle miles, employing usage factors given in Table 19.3 which were obtained from Schreier and Mittag (**23**) and *SKF Designers Manual* (**24**). This form of presentation also lends itself to comparison with the fatigue test results discussed under 'Gear materials and production processes', and fatigue curves for two materials which gave good and poor results in terms of pitting failure are included in Fig. 19.9 to indicate the range of laboratory results obtained.

Although discrete values of surface stress and cycles of loading may not be strictly accurate, it is considered that collectively, and with the knowledge that the data have been derived from gears operating in service, sufficient information is built into the presentation of Fig. 19.9 to make it useful for comparing new designs with previous ones.

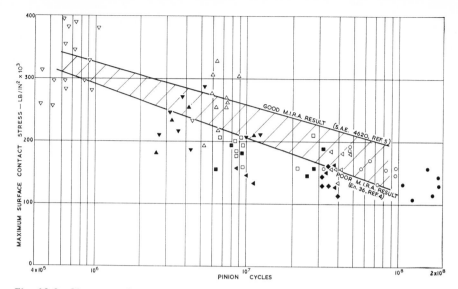

Fig. 19.9. Shows surface contact stress plotted against estimated life cycles for each gear function at maximum engine torque

Table 19.3. Percentage life requirements given by Schreier and Mittag (23) for routes involving flat ground with moderate changes in level

Gear function	Percentage life, L				
	Passenger vehicles		Commercial vehicles		
	3-speed box	4-speed box	4-speed box	5-speed box	6-speed box
First pair reduction gears .	10	18	21·5	22	38
First gear pairs . . .	1	1	0·5*	1	0
Second gear pairs . .	8	2	6·5*	1	1
Third gear pairs . .	—	14	14*	3	2
Fourth gear pairs . .	—	—	—	16	11
Fifth gear pairs . . .	—	—	—	—	24
Reverse gears . . .	0·1†	0·1†	0·5†	1†	1†

* Values given in *SKF Designers Manual GB 515.*
† Values for reverse gears were chosen to suit the data presented in Figs 19.9 and 19.10.

Root bending stress

Calculation of the maximum tensile root bending stress relies upon consideration of the stress concentration which is created by the change in section of the gear in this region. The original 'Lewis formula', discussed by Tuplin (2) and used in past M.I.R.A. reports for comparing fatigue test results, is derived from simple cantilever beam theory and merely gives a nominal value of stress across the root section of the tooth, ignoring any stress concentration at the root fillet. In the

present survey, calculation of tensile root bending stress is carried out, as indicated in Appendix 19.1, using a method similar to that proposed by Tuplin (2)
which is based on results of a photoelastic investigation by Jacobson (25). From
this investigation, stress factors were evolved for a wide range of tooth forms
which Tuplin has adopted for the purpose of deriving allowable tooth loads from
the allowable stresses given in B.S. 436. In order to obtain satisfactory tooth
strength using the allowable stresses given in B.S. 436, Tuplin has increased
Jacobson's stress factors by a value of 1·6 (see p. 6 of reference (2)). It should also
be noted that Tuplin's method derives an allowable load in terms of the load per
inch of face width, tangential to the mesh point, whereas Jacobson in a similar
formula specifies load per inch of face width tangential to the base circle for
calculation of root stress. In the present report, the normal tooth load tangential
to the base circle is used which is assumed to act over the total length of line
contact, i.e. L_c, as shown in Appendix 19.1.

Values of root bending stress obtained for the production gears at maximum
engine torque are shown in Fig. 19.10 plotted in terms of the percentage life for
each gear function given in Table 19.3. It should be noted that because of the
factor of 1·6 introduced by Tuplin, the stresses given in Fig. 19.10 are lower than
the 'actual' stresses (i.e. those predicted by Jacobson) by this factor of 1·6. Also
shown in Fig. 19.10 are two samples of M.I.R.A. fatigue test results (recalculated

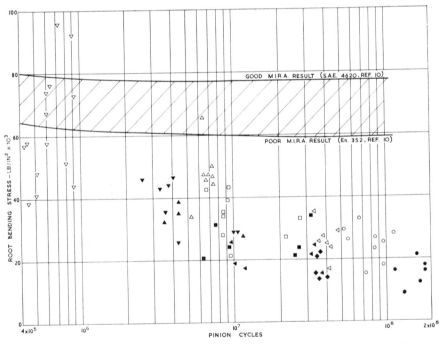

**Fig. 19.10. Shows root bending stress plotted against estimated life cycles for
each gear function at maximum engine torque**

to agree with the Tuplin method) indicating the range over which results have been obtained for various materials, heat treatments, etc.

To enable root bending stress to be compared directly with maximum surface contact stress, corresponding values of stress for all the pinion gears shown in Figs 19.9 and 19.10 are presented in Fig. 19.11. Ranges of stress are also shown for each gear function for both passenger and commercial vehicle applications.

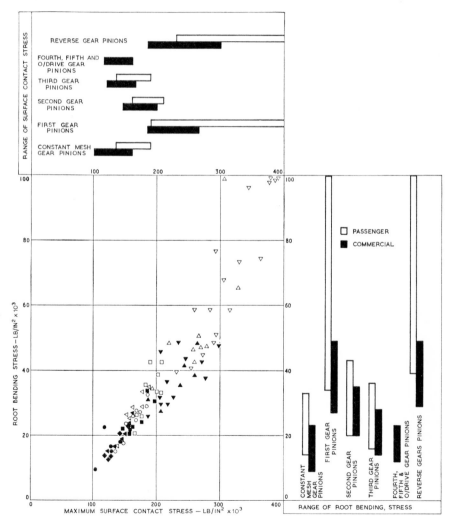

Fig. 19.11. Root bending stress plotted against surface contact stress under conditions of maximum engine torque

Speed effect

The effect of speed on gear loading, created by meshing errors of the teeth, is discussed in some detail by Tuplin in pages 24 and 157 of reference (2). The effect is to produce a varying load in addition to the steady load being transmitted. Tuplin indicates that the critical dynamic loading condition is avoided by choosing numbers of teeth and pitch line velocities which are outside the range given by the expressions:

$$t = 700\,000/dn \quad \text{and} \quad t = 450\,000/dn$$

where t is the number of teeth, d the pitch circle diameter (in), and n the rotational speed.

Graphical representation of these limits has been given in reference (26), which is similar to that reproduced in Fig. 19.12. In this diagram pitch line velocities

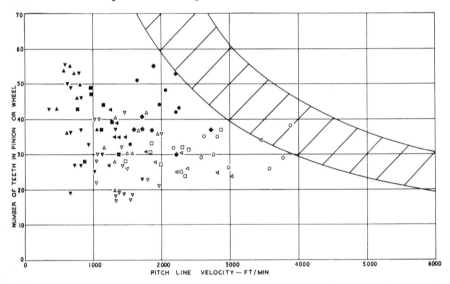

Fig. 19.12. Pitch line velocity of production gears at maximum engine speed in relation to the critical speed zone

at maximum engine speed have also been plotted for all the gears in the present survey which have the larger number of teeth in the meshing pair (usually the wheel or driven gear). In general, most gears operate well clear of the critical region, although many of the first pair reduction gears and overdrive gears were found to come quite close to the lower limit.

Comparison of production designs

It should be emphasized that when comparing the tooth loadings of any existing designs with the data presented in this report, it will be necessary to ensure that the methods of deriving tooth stresses are the same as those given in Appendix 19.1.

DESIGN PROCEDURE

From inquiries made in the automotive industry it would appear that methods of design vary and no basic design procedure has been universally adopted. B.S. 436 is still used to a limited extent, but in passenger vehicle applications, in particular, this is considered by some designers to be too conservative and to result in gears which are uneconomical in size and proportion. In these cases, design procedures are largely based upon past experience where the main criterion of design is root bending strength of the gear teeth. Whilst it is recognized that individual gear designers have established quite adequate design procedures of their own, it was considered that the data gathered in the present survey could be adapted to an alternative procedure based upon that recommended by Tuplin (I) (2). This could be helpful for applications in which experience is limited. The procedure, employing a British Standard tooth form and using the information under review, can be expected to produce gear teeth of comparable proportions to those used in current practice with operating stresses at an acceptable level. Since, by this method, there is no necessity to draw out the tooth proportions, a computer program employing this procedure could be developed for giving manufacturing data for any specific centre distance and gear ratio. A less sophisticated computer program was in fact used for determining the dimensions and operating conditions presented in the preceding sections.

In Fig. 19.13 Tuplin's procedure is presented in a block diagram form with the addition of the empirical information given by comparisons made in the previous sections for gear geometry and load capacity, respectively. A similar presentation of the basic Tuplin procedure also appears in reference (26), which was intended for the design of spur gears and helical gears of more general application. Selection and calculation of various geometric gear features are given as a step-by-step process of 17 stages. Running concurrently with the main procedure are a number of 'check' or 'compare' operations. These are intended to limit the selection of gear dimensions to values that will ensure an efficient design without needless repetition of design calculations. In the latter stages, i.e. 16 and 17, it is recommended that calculations are made for comparison with the existing production gears in terms of sliding velocity and gear tooth stresses derived for conditions of maximum engine torque transmission. Recommendations for choice of gear materials, heat treatment, and production methods have not been made, although a limited amount of information is shown in Table 19.2. However, to obtain an indication of the range of improvements which may be obtained by various means, reference can be made to the section entitled 'Gear materials and production processes'.

APPENDIX 19.1. GEAR LOADING CALCULATIONS

Factors to be calculated

(1) Maximum contact stress (S_{max}), lb/in².
(2) Maximum relative sliding velocity of teeth (V_{st}), ft/mm.
(3) Slide/sweep ratio (R_{ss}).
(4) Maximum tooth bending stress (S_b), lb/in².
(5) Pitch line velocity (V_p), ft/min.
(6) Transverse tangential tooth loading (G_t), lb.

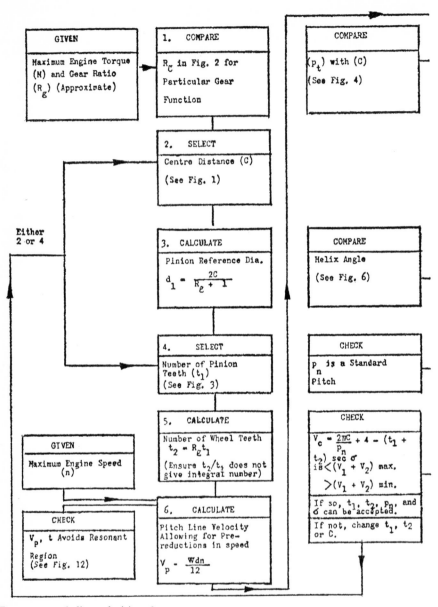

For spur gear helix angle $(\sigma) = 0$.

Fig. 19.13. Suggested procedure for design of automobile gears

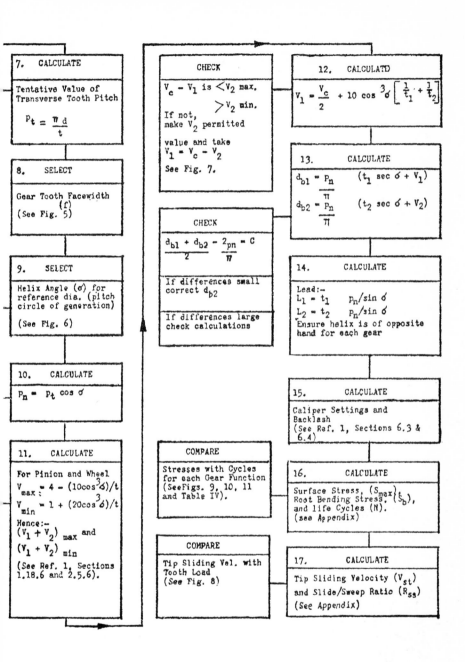

7. **CALCULATE**

Tentative Value of Transverse Tooth Pitch

$$P_t = \frac{\pi \, d}{t}$$

8. **SELECT**

Gear Tooth Facewidth
(f)
(See Fig. 5)

9. **SELECT**

Helix Angle (σ) for reference dia. (pitch circle of generation)

(See Fig. 6)

10. **CALCULATE**

$P_n = P_t \cos \sigma$

11. **CALCULATE**

For Pinion and Wheel
$$V_{max} = 4 - (10\cos^3 \sigma)/t$$
$$V_{min} = 1 + (20\cos^3 \sigma)/t$$
Hence:-
$(V_1 + V_2)_{max}$ and
$(V_1 + V_2)_{min}$
(See Ref. 1, Sections 1.18.6 and 2.5.6).

CHECK

$V_c - V_1$ is $< V_2$ max.
$> V_2$ min.
If not, make V_2 permitted value and take
$V_1 = V_c - V_2$
See Fig. 7.

CHECK

$$\frac{d_{b1} + d_{b2}}{2} - \frac{2_{pn}}{\pi} = C$$

If differences small correct d_{b2}

If differences large check calculations

COMPARE

Stresses with Cycles for each Gear Function (See Figs. 9, 10, 11 and Table IV).

COMPARE

Tip Sliding Vel. with Tooth Load
(See Fig. 8)

12. **CALCULATE**

$$V_1 = \frac{V_c}{2} + 10 \cos^3 \sigma \left[\frac{1}{t_1} + \frac{1}{t_2} \right]$$

13. **CALCULATE**

$$d_{b1} = \frac{P_n}{\pi} \; (t_1 \sec \sigma + V_1)$$
$$d_{b2} = \frac{P_n}{\pi} \; (t_2 \sec \sigma + V_2)$$

14. **CALCULATE**

Lead:-
$L_1 = t_1 \quad P_n/\sin \sigma$
$L_2 = t_2 \quad P_n/\sin \sigma$
Ensure helix is of opposite hand for each gear

15. **CALCULATE**

Caliper Settings and Backlash
(See Ref. 1, Sections 6.3 & 6.4)

16. **CALCULATE**

Surface Stress, (S_{max}), Root Bending Stress, (S_b), and life Cycles (N).
(see Appendix)

17. **CALCULATE**

Tip Sliding Velocity (V_{st}) and Slide/Sweep Ratio (R_{ss})
(See Appendix)

Items (1) and (2) are calculated for two conditions at maximum engine torque and maximum engine speed, respectively.

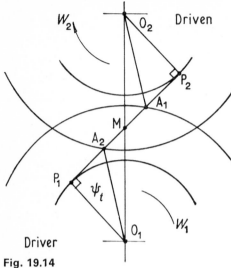

M = mesh point, O_1M are the mesh circle radii $d_m/2$ for pinion and wheel, respectively.

O_1P_1, O_2P_2 are the base circle radii $d_0/2$.

A_1A_2 is the length of path of contact.

O_1A_1, O_2A_2 are the tip circle radii (blank radii) $d_b/2$.

Fig. 19.14

Data

Data required for calculations	Symbol		Identifier for computer	
	Driver	Driven	Driver	Driven
(A) *For each gearbox*				
1. Name				
2. Number of meshing pairs in each gearbox .	n_p	n_p	np	np
3. Input torque to gearbox, condition 1, lb ft .	m_1	m_1	m1	m1
4. Input speed to gearbox (maximum engine torque), rev/min	n_1	n_1	n1	n1
5. Input torque to gearbox, condition 2, lb ft .	m_2	m_2	m2	m2
6. Input speed to gearbox (maximum engine speed), rev/min	n_2	n_2	n2	n2
(B) *For each meshing pair*				
(Gears meshing with more than one other gear appear more than once)				
1. Name				
2. Number of teeth on pre-reduction gears (between — 1st reduction .	r_1	r_2	r1	r2
3. engine input and driver of pair being calculated) — 2nd reduction .	r_3	r_4	r3	r4
4. Face width, in	f_1	f_2	f1	f2
5. Lead, in	L_1	L_2	l1	l2
6. Operating centre distance, in . . .	C	C	C	C
7. Number of teeth	t_1	t_2	t1	t2
8. Transverse flank angle at pitch circle diameter of generation, rad	ψ	ψ	psi	psi
9. Pitch circle diameter of generation (reference diameter), in	d_1	d_2	d1	d2
10. Tip diameter (blank diameter), in . . .	d_{b1}	d_{b2}	db1	db2

Nomenclature

Nomenclature used in calculations	Symbol		Identifier for computer	
	Driver	Driven	Driver	Driven
Mesh diameter, in	d_{m1}	d_{m2}	dm1	dm2
Base circle diameter, in . . .	d_{01}	d_{02}	d01	d02
Transverse pressure angle of engagement (force angle), degrees . . .	ψ_t	ψ_t	psit	psit
Helix angle at base circle radius, degrees	σ_0	σ_0	sig0	sig0
Length of path of contact (Fig. 19.14), in	A_1A_2	A_1A_2	a1a2	a1a2
Transverse tangential tooth load at the mesh point, lb . . .	G_{t1}	G_{t2}	gt1	gt2
Normal tangential tooth load at the mesh point, lb	G_{n1}	G_{n2}	gn1	gn2
Radius of relative curvature . .	R_r	R_r	rr	rr
Length of line contact (average total), in	L_c	L_c	lc	lc
Normal base pitch, in . . .	p_{n0}	p_{n0}	pn0	pn0
Transverse base pitch, in . . .	p_{t0}	p_{t0}	pt0	pt0
Contact stress parameter . . .	S_c	S_c	sc	sc
Maximum surface contact stress at condition 1, lb/in^2	S_{max1}	S_{max1}	smax1	smax1
Maximum surface contact stress at condition 2, lb/in^2	S_{max2}	S_{max2}	smax2	smax2
Gear ratio (number of teeth on driven gear to number of teeth on driver gear)	R_g	R_g	rg	rg
Angular velocity, rad/s . . .	ω_1	ω_2	omeg1	omeg2
Maximum tip sliding velocity (condition 1), ft/min	V_{st11}	V_{st12}	vst11	vst12
Maximum tip sliding velocity (condition 2), ft/min	V_{st21}	V_{st22}	vst21	vst22
Slide/sweep ratio (maximum positive value)	R_{ss12}	R_{ss22}	rss12	rss22
Slide/sweep ratio (maximum negative value)	R_{ss11}	R_{ss21}	rss11	rss21
Transverse tangential load/unit face width at mesh point, lb/in	G_{jt}	G_{jt}	gjt	gjt
Normal pitch at pitch circle radius of generation, in	p_n	p_n	pn	pn
Helix angle at mesh circle radius of engagement, degrees . . .	σ_m	σ_m	sigm	sigm
Helix angle at pitch circle radius of generation, degrees . . .	σ	σ	sig	sig
Maximum diametral adjustment factor .	V_{max1}	V_{max2}	vmax1	vmax2
Minimum diametral adjustment factor .	V_{min1}	V_{min2}	vmin1	vmin2
Tooth strength factor . . .	Y_{n1}	Y_{n2}	yn1	yn2
Diametral adjustment factor (actual) .	V_{act1}	V_{act2}	vact1	vact2
Maximum tensile stress due to tooth bending, lb/in^2	S_{b1}	S_{b2}	sb1	sb2
Pitch line velocity, ft/min . .	v_p	v_p	vp	vp
A_1P_1, P_1M; A_2P_2, P_2M (Fig. 19.14), in	A_1P_1, P_1M	A_2P_2, P_2M	a1p1, p1m	a2p2, p2m
Axial base pitch, in	P_{a0}	P_{a0}	pa0	pa0

Geometric calculations

(1) *Mesh diameter* (d_{m_1})

$$d_{m_1} = 2ct_1/(t_1+t_2), \qquad d_{m_2} = 2ct_2/(t_1+t_2)$$

(2) *Base circle diameter* (d_0)

$$d_{01} = d_1 \cos \psi, \qquad d_{02} = d_2 \cos \psi$$

(see page 12 of reference (**4**)).

(3) *Transverse pressure angle of engagement* (ψ_t)

$$\cos \psi_t = \cos \psi (d_1/d_{m_1})$$

Proof: $d_0 = d \cos \psi$ (see (2) above)

$\qquad\qquad = d_m \cos \psi_t$ (from Fig. 19.14)

therefore $\cos \psi_t = (d/d_m) \cos \psi$

(4) *Base helix angle* (σ_0)

$$\sigma_0 = \tan^{-1} (\pi d_0/L) \quad \text{(page 55 of reference (4))}$$

Note: The helix angle, σ, can be obtained from $\tan^{-1} (\pi d/L)$, where L is the lead and d is the diameter at which the helix angle is required.

(5) *Length of path of contact* (A_1A_2)

Referring to Fig. 19.14:

$$A_1A_2 = A_1M + A_2M \quad \text{(page 44 of reference (2))}$$

where $A_1M = A_1P_1 - P_1M$

$\qquad\qquad A_2M = A_2P_2 - P_2M$

and

$$A_1P_1 = \sqrt{[(A_1O_1)^2 - (O_1P_1)^2]} = \sqrt{[(d_{b_1}/2)^2 - (d_{01}/2)^2]}$$
$$P_1M = \sqrt{[(O_1M)^2 - (O_1P_1)^2]} = \sqrt{[(d_{m_1}/2)^2 - (d_{01}/2)^2]}$$
$$A_2P_2 = \sqrt{[(A_2O_2)^2 - (O_2P_2)^2]} = \sqrt{[(d_{b_2}/2)^2 - (d_{02}/2)^2]}$$
$$P_2M = \sqrt{[(O_2M)^2 - (O_2P_2)^2]} = \sqrt{[(d_{m_2}/2)^2 - (d_{02}/2)^2]}$$

(6) *Tangential load* (G_t)

$$G_{t_1} = \frac{\text{torque}}{\text{radius}} = \frac{24m_1}{d_{m_1}}; \qquad G_{t_2} = \frac{24m_2}{d_{m_1}}$$

where m_1 is the torque at maximum torque (lb ft) and m_2 is the torque at maximum speed (lb ft).

(7) *Tangential load per unit face width* (G_{jt})

$$G_{jt} = G_t/f$$

(8) *Radius of relative curvature at meshing cylinder* (R_r)

$$R_r = \tfrac{1}{2}d_{m_1} \sin \psi_t \sec \sigma_0) \frac{R_g}{1+R_g}$$

where $R_g = t_2/t_1$ (see equation 15.1 of reference (**2**)).

(9) *Normal base pitch* (p_{no})

$$p_{no} = p_{to} \cos \sigma_0 \quad \text{(equation 36.1 of reference (4))}$$

where
$$p_{to} = \frac{\pi d_{01}}{t_1} = \frac{\text{base circle circumference}}{\text{number of teeth}}$$

therefore
$$p_{no} = \frac{\pi d_{01} \cos \sigma_0}{t_1}$$

(10) *Length of line contact* (L_c)

$$L_c = \frac{(A_1 A_2)}{p_{no}} f$$

(see equation 15.3 and Fig. 11.1 of reference (4)). Note that $f = f_1$ or f_2, whichever is less.

Note: In the case of helical gears it is common for several pairs of teeth to be in contact simultaneously, and it can be shown that the total length of line contact will remain constant, providing the face width is an integral multiple of the axial tooth pitch (see page 15 of reference (2)). When this is not the case, the length of contact will fluctuate but this is considered to be unimportant if the face width exceeds the value of axial tooth pitch. For the purpose of comparison in this survey, the total length of line contact is derived assuming the former condition applies, as shown.

For spur gear teeth the length of contact is calculated on the same basis, giving a value equal to a product of the face width and the contact ratio.

Calculation of maximum surface contact stress (S_{max})

Maximum surface contact stress is defined as the maximum stress at any point in the contact zone as derived by the Hertz analysis (2), where the load is assumed to be equally distributed along the total length of line contact (L_c) given above.

(1) *Contact stress parameter* (S_c)

$$S_c = \frac{G_n}{R_r L_c}$$

where $G_n = G_t \sec \sigma_0 \sec \psi_t$, therefore

$$S_c = \frac{G_t \sec \sigma_0 \sec \psi_t}{[R_r(A_1 A_2)f]/p_{no}}$$

$$= \frac{G_t P_{ao} \tan \sigma_0 \sec \psi_t}{R_r(A_1 A_2)f} \quad \text{(since } p_{no} = p_{ao} \sin \sigma_0)$$

$$= \frac{G_t \sec \psi_t \, p_{to}}{R_r(A_1 A_2)f} \quad \text{(since } p_{to} = p_{ao} \tan \sigma_0)$$

$$= \frac{G_t \sec \psi_t \, \pi d_{01}}{R_r(A_1 A_2)f t_1}$$

where f is the minimum value of f_1 or f_2.

Note: $S_c = G_{to}/[(\text{contact ratio}) \ R_r]$, where G_{to} is the transverse load per inch of face width along the path of contact, and the contact ratio is $A_1 A_2/p_{to}$.

(2) *Maximum surface contact stress* (S_{max})

$$S_{max1} = 2250\sqrt{S_{c1}} \quad \text{for steel on steel}$$
$$S_{max2} = 2250\sqrt{S_{c2}} \quad \text{for steel on steel}$$

Calculation of maximum tip sliding velocity (V_{st})

$$V_{st} = \frac{AM}{12}(\omega_1 + \omega_2) \quad (\text{page 44 of reference (2)})$$

where $\omega_1 = 2\pi n$, $\omega_2 = \omega_1/R_g$, and AM is $A_1 M$ or $A_2 M$, whichever is greater (Fig. 19.14).

Calculation of pitch line velocity (V_p)

$$V_p = \frac{n\pi d_m}{12} \ \text{ft/min}$$

Calculation of slide/sweep ratio (R_{ss})

The *sliding velocity* between two surfaces in contact is defined as the velocity of one surface relative to the surface under consideration.

The *sweeping velocity* is defined as the velocity of the contact point or contact line over the surface under consideration.

Driving gear

$$R_{ss11} = \frac{-[1+(t_1/t_2)]}{[(P_1M)/(A_2M)]-1}; \qquad R_{ss12} = \frac{[1+(t_2/t_1)]}{[(P_2M)/(A_2M)]+1}$$

Driven gear

$$R_{ss21} = \frac{-[1+(t_2/t_1)]}{[(P_2M)/(A_1M)]-1}; \qquad R_{ss22} = \frac{[(1+(t_1/t_2)]}{[(P_1M)/(A_1M)]+1}$$

(Reference (4), p. 159, equation A7.2.1 and Fig. A.7.1.)

Note: Notation of Fig. A.7.1 is different to that given in Fig. 19.14.

Calculation of maximum bending stress (S_b)

S_b is defined as the maximum bending tensile stress in the root fillet of a tooth of particular shape, subjected to flank loading (page 22 of reference (2)).

(1) *Normal pitch at pitch radius of generation* (p_n)

$$p_n = \frac{\pi d_1}{t_1} \cos \sigma$$

(cf. proofs for p_n and σ_0) where $\tan \sigma = \pi d_1/L$.

(2) Diametral adjustment factor (V)

The value of V defines the general shape of an involute gear tooth, being large for a pointed tooth and small for teeth which are undercut at the roots (see page 34 of reference (3)).

$$V_{max1} = 4 - \frac{10 \cos^3 \sigma}{t_1} \qquad V_{max2} = 4 - \frac{10 \cos^3 \sigma}{t_2}$$

$$V_{min1} = 1 + \frac{20 \cos^3 \sigma}{t_1} \qquad V_{min2} = 1 + \frac{20 \cos^3 \sigma}{t_2}$$

$$V_{act1} = \frac{\pi d_{b1}}{p_n} - t_1 \sec \sigma \qquad V_{act2} = \frac{\pi d_{b2}}{p_n} - t_2 \sec \sigma$$

(page 14 of reference (2)).

(3) Tooth strength factor (Y)

Y values are non-dimensional quantities relating the maximum fillet tensile stress, tooth loading, and pitch of the gear teeth. The relationship between Y values and V values is given in page 302 of reference (1), which has been determined from photoelastic work carried out on gear teeth.

$$\text{Equivalent number of teeth} = t_1 \sec^3 \sigma_m, \quad t_2 \sec^3 \sigma_m$$

Using chart 4 on page 153 of reference (2), Y_h values are determined as a function of equivalent numbers of teeth and the three V values.

Note: In the case of helical gears a section of a tooth normal to the tooth flank approximates in form to a spur gear having $t \sec^3 \sigma_m$ number of teeth (pages 63–66 of reference (4)).

(4) Maximum bending stress (S_b)

$$S_b = \frac{G_n}{L_c} \cdot \frac{\pi}{p_n} \cdot \frac{1}{Y_h}$$

Correction-relationship between K factors and V values

For a rack of B.S. proportions:

$$\text{Addendum} = \frac{1+K}{\text{(D.P.)}} = \frac{V}{2\text{(D.P.)}}$$

therefore,

$$V = 2(1+K)$$

Calculation of life cycles (N)

Assuming a vehicle milage of 100 000 miles:

$$\text{Gearbox output shaft cycles, } N_c = \frac{2020 \times 10^6 \, R_{aa}}{D_w}$$

where R_{ga} is the rear axle ratio and D_w is the effective diameter of the drive wheels (in).

Employing output shaft cycles (N_c), average cycles for each gear can be derived by consideration of the percentage lives (L) given in Table 19.3 and the gear ratio in each case.

Note: Life cycles for the first pair reduction gears are assumed to be the sum total of pinion life cycles in the other gear functions, i.e. first, second, third, etc.

APPENDIX 19.2

REFERENCES

(1) TUPLIN, W. A. *Gear design* 1961 (The Machinery Publishing Co.).

(2) TUPLIN, W. A. *Gear load capacity* 1961 (Pitman).

(3) HELDT, P. A. *Torque converters or transmissions* 1955, 150 (Chilton Co.).

(4) TUPLIN, W. A. *Involute gear geometry* 1962 (Chatto and Windus).

(5) MANSION, H. D. 'The 5-in centres gear testing machine', *M.I.R.A. Rep. No. 1944/9.*

(6) MANSION, H. D. 'A hydraulic fatigue testing machine for gear teeth', *M.I.R.A. Rep. No. 1949/4.*

(7) FOSBERRY, R. A. C. 'Bending fatigue strength of gear teeth', *M.I.R.A. Rep. No. 1949/7.*

(8) LOVE, R. J. and CAMPBELL, J. G. 'Bending strength of gear teeth: a comparison of some carburizing steels', *M.I.R.A. Rep. No. 1952/5.*

(9) ALLSOPP, H. C., WEARE, A. T. and LOVE, R. J. 'Resistance to pitting of gear teeth: a comparison of nine carburizing steels', *M.I.R.A. Rep. No. 1957/2.*

(10) FOSBERRY, R. A. C. and MANSION, H. D. 'Bending fatigue strength of gear teeth: a comparison of some typical gear steels', *M.I.R.A. Rep. No. 1950/7.*

(11) MANSION, H. D. 'The failure of gears by pitting: a comparison of some typical gear steels', *M.I.R.A. Rep. No. 1951/8.*

(12) LOVE, R. J., ALLSOPP, H. C. and WEARE, A. T. 'The influence of carburizing conditions and heat treatment on the bending fatigue strength and impact strength of gears made from En 352 steel', *M.I.R.A. Rep. No. 1959/7.*

(13) ANDREW, S., HENTON, M. J. and LOVE, R. J. 'Resistance to pitting of gear teeth: a comparison of some carburizing treatments applied to an En 352 steel', *M.I.R.A. Rep. No. 1961/9.*

(14) LOVE, R. J. and ALLSOPP, H. C. 'The effect of lead on the bending fatigue strength of gears made from an 'economy' carburizing steel', *M.I.R.A. Rep. No. 1955/8.*

(15) LOVE, R. J., WHITE, D. and ALLSOPP, H. C. 'Bending fatigue strength of some induction hardened, pack carburized and gas carburized gears', *M.I.R.A. Rep. No. 1954/3.*

(16) LOVE, R. J. 'Bending fatigue strength of carburized gears: a comparison of some production processes', *M.I.R.A. Rep. No. 1953/4.*

(17) ALLSOPP, H. C. and LOVE, R. J. 'Resistance to pitting of gear teeth: a comparison of gear production processes', *M.I.R.A. Rep. No. 1958/4.*

(18) ANDREW, S. 'The effect of shot blasting on the fatigue strength of carburized gears', *Bull. Mot. Ind. Res. Ass.* 1961 (No. 3), 12.

(19) ALLSOPP, H. C. and LOVE, R. J. 'The effect of carburizing conditions and heat treatment on the impact strength of gears made from an En 362 type steel', *M.I.R.A. Rep. No. 1956/6.*

(20) DOWSON, D. and HIGGINSON, G. R. *Elasto-hydrodynamic lubrication* (The Commonwealth and International Library, Pergamon Press).

(21) MANHAJM, J. and MANSION, H. D. 'The effect of temperature and speed and type of oil on gear scuffing', *M.I.R.A. Rep. No. 1947/R/2.*

(22) FOSBERRY, R. A. C. and MANSION, H. D. 'Factors influencing the scuffing of gears: a summary of results of work done on gear scuffing by M.I.R.A. and the I.A.E. Research Department', *M.I.R.A. Rep. No. 1950/8.*

(23) SCHREIER, C. and MITTAG, H.   'Messingen en Kraftfahrzeuggetrieben in Fahrbetrieb', KFZ-Tech. 1959 **9**, 319.

(24) S.K.F. Designers Manual No. GB. 515.

(25) JACOBSON, M. A.   'Bending stresses in spur gear teeth: proposed new design factors based on photo-elastic investigation', Proc. Instn mech. Engrs 1955 **169**, 587.

(26) 'Design of parallel axis spur and helical gears—geometric design', Engng Sci. Data Sheet No. 66001 1966 (Instn Mech. Engrs, London).

The MS. of this paper was received at the Institution on 29th December 1969 and accepted for publication on 5th January 1970.

Paper 20. Cold Forming of Gears

P. F. EGAN
Kelco Automation, Cheltenham, Glos.

G. CONNELL
Kelco Automation, Cheltenham, Glos.

B. JONES
Kelco Automation, Cheltenham, Glos.

It is ever-increasingly important to find and develop new techniques for the manipulation of metal such that the utilization of metal is improved and subsequent machining operations are either substantially reduced or eliminated. When metal rolling as a process is utilized, more often than not substantial advantages such as improvement of physical characteristics and metallurgical properties are apparent. One of the main objectives of this paper is to bring to delegates' attention presently available processes and current developments in the field of cold gear rolling. The paper also outlines the interrelationship of warm and hot rolling to cold rolling, particularly with consideration to the present state of the art where limitations on cold rolling are imposed due to material plasticity and physical geometry considerations. The effects of current rolling processes and proposed development processes represent a radical departure from traditional manufacturing techniques.

INTRODUCTION

It will be readily apparent, after detailed investigations, that rolling gears offer greater advantages than presently available conventional manufacturing methods. Some of these advantages are listed below.

(*a*) A considerable increase in productivity is obtained from roll forming machines when compared to conventional gear producing machines.

(*b*) A considerable increase in both accuracy and consistency of accuracy is achieved. This accuracy is dependent upon the gear rolling dies and is not substantially influenced by machine design or adjustment. Gears produced throughout the life of the rolls are almost identical. Involute form, pitch, surface finish, and other characteristics are consistently held to much better tolerances than would be expected with shaving.

(*c*) Tool cost is considerably less. This is apparent when comparing a life of a set of rolling dies prior to any regrind or rework of approximately 1 500 000 to a shaving cutter parallel when one might expect a maximum of 30 000 gears prior to regrind.

(*d*) Maintenance and floor space requirements are considerably reduced and machine utilization is increased.

(*e*) The capital investment required for the same unit production is substantially reduced.

(*f*) Considerably improved metallurgical and physical strength characteristics of the finished gear are apparent when considering the rolling process. This is in the main due to grain flow characteristics as well as an improvement in surface finish and fillet to involute form blending radius.

(*g*) By virtue of the rolling developments to date the door is open for future developments involving even considerably more savings in material, increased productivity, and general cost reductions.

This paper deals mainly with three specific subjects: pure cold gear rolling applied as an initial development to finish rolling, and full depth rolling applied as a subsequent development; hot rolling of spur type gears; and, finally, the hot and cold gear rolling of crown wheels.

COLD GEAR ROLLING

Gear manufacturing techniques used in the production of precision gears involve either gear forming methods or gear generating methods. Generally speaking, the mass production of gears involves only gear generating techniques. In gear forming methods a cutting tool such as a milling cutter is provided with cutting teeth that can form to the shape of the desired tooth space. The milling cutter teeth are made by a forming method. In gear generating methods, however, the tooth generating tool is formed with a shape which is conjugate to the form of the tooth when the tooth is rolled into contact with it.

A basic gear rack form is used in most gear generating methods. If the tool used is a cutting tool, the cutting action can be accomplished either by reciprocating the rack in the direction of the axis of the gear blank or by rolling the gear blank with respect to the rack. The proper gear tooth profile, which usually is an involute profile form, is produced as successive cuts are taken by the teeth on the rack. However, in other gear generating methods, such as shaping and shaving, a circular cutter form with involute cutting teeth may be used to produce the required action during the generating process. In actual gear manufacturing practice, as in the gear rolling technique, a rack-shaped tool is not used although tools have the same tooth geometry as a basic rack-shaped cutter. An example of this is a gear hobbing tool. In the gear rolling process under discussion provision is made for closing the centre distance between the rotary dies by the use of a hydraulic cylinder system. Both dies are driven by hydraulic motors although this is not mandatory.

As the teeth of the dies engage the gear blank an involute profile is generated on it. The direction of metal flow on one side of the generated gear tooth, which may be the driven side of the involute profile, differs from the direction of flow of the metal on the other side of the tooth, which can be considered to be the coast side. In the latter case metal flows in a radially outward and in a radially inward direction from a location falling on the pitch circle. The metal flow on the driven side, however, originates at the radially outward region and the radially inward region of the gear profile, and then progresses in the direction of the pitch circle location.

Reference to Fig. 20.1*d* will clarify the point. Because this deformation takes

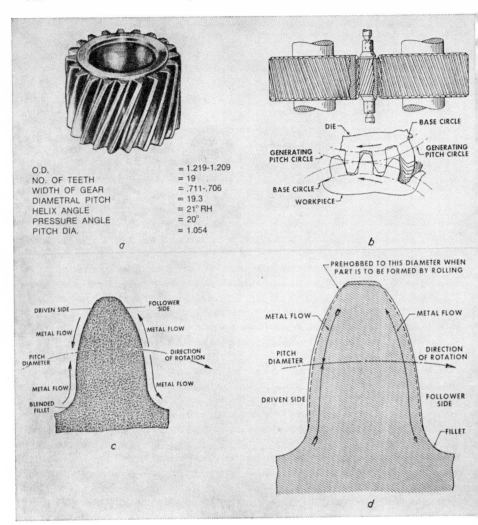

O.D.	= 1.219-1.209
NO. OF TEETH	= 19
WIDTH OF GEAR	= .711-.706
DIAMETRAL PITCH	= 19.3
HELIX ANGLE	= 21° RH
PRESSURE ANGLE	= 20°
PITCH DIA.	= 1.054

Fig. 20.1

place, the gear tooth itself is subject to high compressive stresses, thereby tending to elongate the tooth.

The present state of the art, with implied future development programmes, has been built on a foundation pioneered by the Ford Motor Company, U.S.A., in co-operation with selected machine tool manufacturers. Initially, it was decided to concentrate on the finish rolling of automatic transmission pinions, such as that illustrated in Fig. 20.1a. This involved effectively pre-hobbing a machined blank for subsequent finished rolling operations. Further experience, however, has enabled the rough hobbing operation to be eliminated and replaced by a full depth rolling operation. This, in effect, eliminates both hobbing and shaving with regard to the pinion gear. A further subsequent development is the use of a cold headed blank in place of the previously used machined blank. The main reason the shaving operation was eliminated as a first step was that shaving has traditionally been a most expensive and difficult part of gear production and effectively places serious limitations on the previous hobbing operations required to obtain the end product. Considerable tool life improvements have been achieved by the use of rolling techniques, in addition to better machine utilization and higher and more consistent quality levels.

Shaving operations, as previously envisaged, present certain difficulties in trying to blend the required involute form at the tooth flank with the fillet or root radius. This obviously gives rise to a potential stress raiser and hence possible gear failure. Rolling eliminates these difficulties. It also improves the grain flow characteristics and causes a skin hardening of the cold formed surfaces, in addition to giving an extremely good surface finish. Subsequent to the finish rolling of pre-hobbed blank concept, production machinery has been developed to accept a superficially notched starting blank and then to full depth roll the required form. During initial development considerations it was thought that a final rolling stage as a second operation would be necessary. However, very promising results have been obtained which indicate that the finish rolling operation on a pre-rolled blank will not be necessary.

One of the guide lines in making finish gear rolling a practical production process lies in the design and development of the rolling dies. A considerable amount of expertise is required in establishing the extent of full modification required from the true involute that is necessary to roll form gear teeth in order to produce a true involute on the gear in question to required tolerances. Consideration necessary for the design of the rolls is related to metal flow differences between the driven side of the gear teeth and the coast side, and also to deflections in the gear teeth under rolling pressure. In the main, the rolling dies are the most important part of the rolling process.

It has been found that a vital requirement with regard to machine design is absolute stiffness of the rolling system. In general practice the pre-hobbed blank is left with approximately 0·004 in of metal on the flanks and the outside diameter of the blank is left slightly smaller than the conventional shaving concept.

Quality considerations

As a typical example, considering the pinion gear previously discussed, the involute form is being held well within 0·003 in total and lead crown tolerance is being held well within 0·0005 in total consistently. In addition, the crown is consistently placed centrally.

The lead tolerance is being held within 0·0006 in consistently, and overall dimensions are being held within 0·0008 in. Surface finish is being consistently held between 2 and 5 μin, and an ideal fillet condition is being obtained, obviously enhancing gear durability and tooth strength.

Roll life

A major feature of the cold rolling of gears is that vastly improved tool life is

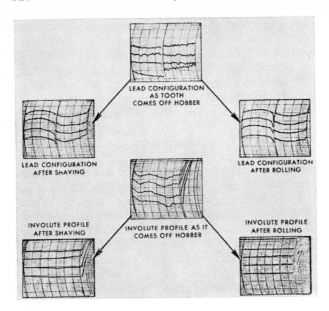

Fig. 20.2

obtained when compared to conventional processes. Roll lives of greater than 1 500 000 gear pinions for the initial set-up, with the possibility of regrinding, are not uncommon. This should be compared to approximately 25 000 pieces per grind for a comparable shaving cutter concept, the total shaving cutter life being in the order of approximately 100 000 pieces.

Fig. 20.2 gives an indication of lead and involute charts after rolling, as distinct from after shaving. During the whole life of the rolling dies there should be no appreciable change of chart characteristics. In other words, pinion gear number 1 should be exactly the same as pinion gear number 1 500 000. Fig. 20.3 illustrates this point. The blended fillet radius and involute form condition is illustrated in Fig. 20.1c.

Cycle times

With regard to the cold rolling of pinion gears, a floor-to-floor time in the order of 5 s per pinion gear (when considering finished rolling) is a feasible and practical proposition based on extensive experience. A cycle time in the order of 7 s is possible and practical for full depth finish rolling of the same pinion from a superficially gashed starting blank.

Further developments have made possible the finish rolling of cluster gears as well as change gears and other similar configurations. In addition, the automatic transmission sunwheel is now being successfully finish rolled as well as full depth rolled. Further considerations later in this paper indicate the future form of development.

Machine tool facility reduction

The Ford Motor Company, U.S.A., is a very good example of how machine

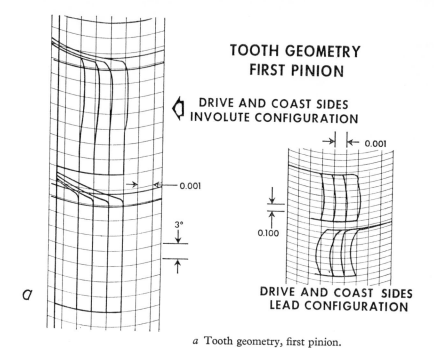

a Tooth geometry, first pinion.

b Tooth geometry, 1 000 000th pinion.

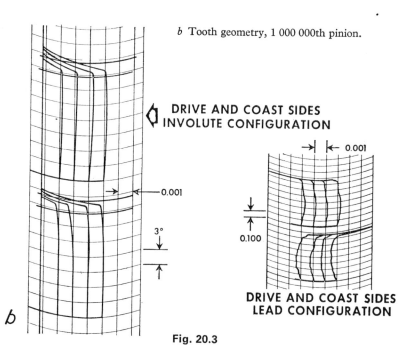

Fig. 20.3

Fig. 20.4. Typical rolling applications

tool facilities can be reduced. After having initially proved the feasibility of eliminating shaving and replacing it with finish rolling, Fords have moved on to the next objective which is to eliminate hobbing in the pinion and sunwheel manufacturing programmes. With regard to the number of machines necessary to obtain the output of planet gears required for 4200 transmissions a day under pre-hobbing finish rolling conditions, the previously required number of machines was reduced from 53 to 44 by replacing 12 shavers with three finish gear rollers.

Subsequent developments have allowed for this number of machines for the same output to be brought down to 23 by cold forming the blanks, gashing them by pot-broaching, and then rough and finish rolling the teeth. Under this method eight spindle automatics and 25 hobbing machines will be replaced, and eventually the blanks can be produced on one cold header and two contour profiling machines. Two machines are required to pot-broach the helical superficial grooves in the preparatory blanks, prior to rough rolling the teeth to shape. After rough rolling excess metal thrown up on the tip of the teeth will be removed by pot-broaching the outside diameter, the same broaching tool being used to chamfer the tooth tip edge on the coast side. Eight machines are presently used for boring and facing the blanks before hobbing, and these will be used for boring and facing the gears after rough rolling.

After further subsequent development work, it is quite possible that the previously required finish rolling operation will not now be necessary, thus eliminating the three finish rolling machines; it is possible that the two contour profiling machines will not be required either. In addition, it is possible that the initial pot-broaching will be replaced by a fast hobbing method to produce the superficial grooves.

Equipment available for cold rolling both full depth and finish

An ever-increasing number of companies are becoming interested in supplying equipment for gear rolling. Equipment is currently available from the U.S.A., Germany, Switzerland, and Japan as well as the U.K. There is available a choice of different systems employing in some cases three rolls, more commonly

Fig. 20.5

Fig. 20.7. Examples of roll formed gears including forged and machined blanks

Fig. 20.8. Front view of heavy-duty gear roll forming machine

Fig. 20.9. Front view of gear roll former showing die position

a Example of rolled steel sprocket.
b Example of hot rolled tractor gear (4 diametral pitch).

Fig. 20.10

two rolls, and even one roll, as a basic machine concept. Some typical rolling applications and equipment are shown in Figs 20.4–20.10. A description of a typical machine known as the 'Kelcoform' is set out below and should be related to the appropriate photographs contained within the text of this paper.

The basic method of operation of the machine is as follows. A set of two circular dies, diametrically opposed, are mounted on stiff spindle assemblies connected to the independent hydraulic cylinder transverse actuators. The rolls are independently driven by separate hydraulic motors mounted directly on to the rolling spindles. In the machine under description the dies are accurately phased together by means of an electronic phasing system, thus eliminating the need for heavy universal spindles and gearboxes with friction brakes, etc.

By this system it is possible to reverse the rolling action rapidly from anti-clockwise to clockwise as part of the rolling cycle just prior to reaching full rolling depth. This has the effect of eliminating possible small surface laps on the coast side and is considered to be highly desirable, particularly when considering full depth rolling. The loading system for the machine depends on the exact gear configuration. When considering the automatic transmission pinions, a simple four-station turret arrangement is preferable, such that loading can take place at a station independent from the rolling position. This obviously achieves the optimum conditions for production. A typical cycle for the cold gear rolling operation is as follows.

Once a gear blank has indexed into the rolling position located on the free rotating arbor, a part pre-rotator engages the blank from the rear of the machine. This action is taking place while the dies are rotating. The pre-blank rotator brings the blank up to a surface speed slightly different to that of the dies. The two hydraulic heads simultaneously actuate inwards, synchronized by means of both a hydraulic and mechanical system, until they engage the gear blank. In the case of finish rolling, the dies continue to full depth and then reverse. An unloading operation takes place and the turret indexes over again to signal the start of a new cycle. In the case of full depth rolling, the dies are brought to within approximately 0·010 in full depth and a roll reversing cycle is then initiated causing the final 0·010 in rolling to take place in an opposite direction. The general forming pattern is illustrated in Fig. 20.1b.

A broad specification for the machine under discussion is listed below.

Specification

Maximum roll force	50 000 lb (22 600 kg)
Maximum roll die diameter	13 in (330 mm)
Minimum roll die diameter	8·625 in (219 mm)
Maximum torque available at dies	300 lb ft (41·5 kg) per die
Roll die speeds	50–300 rev/min
Maximum roll gap (8·625 in dies)	11 in (279 mm)
Minimum roll gap (8·625 in dies)	1 in (25·4 mm)

Maximum roll die width   3 in (76·2 mm)
Maximum rotational phase error   0·001 in (0·025 mm) at 4·25 in
  on roll dies   (108 mm) radius
Machine weight   7 ton (7112 kg)
Floor space   12 ft × 10 ft (3·66 m × 3·05 m)

DEVELOPMENTS IN PROGRESS
Hot gear rolling

Due to limitations with regard to the size of teeth which can be presently cold rolled it is apparent that hot gear rolling may have some merits. It is envisaged that a typical programme of manufacturing as outlined in Fig. 20.11 will actually be common practice for large D.P. gears. Current development programmes allow for the following progressive steps with regard to the element marked 'Finish (as required)' in the figure.

(1) Initially the hot rolled blank will be finish hobbed and shaved.

(2) As a next step the hot rolled blank will be finish hobbed and finish cold rolled.

(3) As a final step the hot rolled blank will be finish cold rolled.

There are many variations on a theme depending, among other factors, on the availability of subsequent process machining. Existing and future manufacturing programmes within the motor industry obviously affect considerations, as do traditions associated with presently accepted manufacturing techniques.

Hot gear rolling process

Two different methods have been developed for rolling gear teeth. The principles of these methods are illustrated in Fig. 20.12.

With the first method shown in Fig. 20.12a, a blank is pushed axially between two toothed wheels which have fixed centres and rotate in opposite directions. The carrier which holds the blank is rigidly geared to the toothed wheel shafts so that a fixed relationship can be maintained with respect to the turning of the three elements. The toothed wheels or rolls have a tapered front lead which facilitates the initial engaging of the blank and provides the good grip required to ensure accurate deformation. When using this first method a long bar can be progressively formed and eventually the gear stick thus produced can be parted off to provide individual gears of the correct thickness. Alternatively, a stack of gear blanks can be effectively bolted together and presented in similar manner to the two fixed centre rolls. After forming, the tie bar is released and the gears separated. This first method is ideally suited for the production of relatively small gears with straight or helical teeth. In practice, only the outside layer of the component blank is heated, to a depth a little greater than the final tooth depth. Induction heating is used to raise the blank temperature to normal forging range which is between 850 and 1000°C, depending upon the material being rolled. The normal limitations of this process give a module up to 4 mm, and up to 200 mm in diameter.

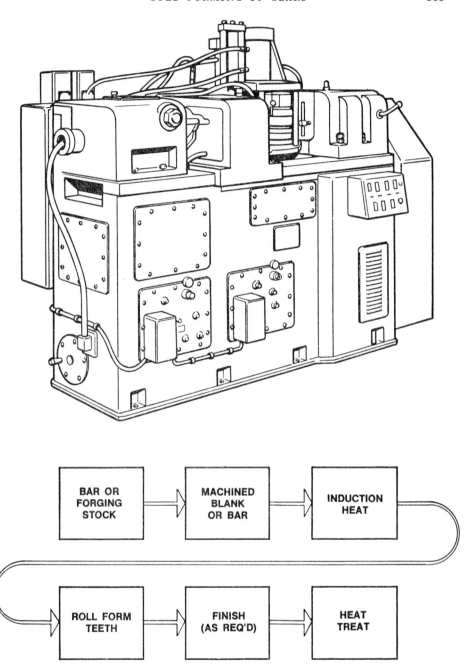

Fig. 20.11. View of spur and helical gear rolling machine and process flow diagram

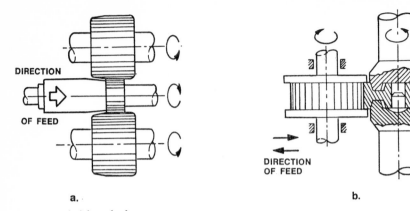

a.   b.

a Axial method.
b Radial method.

Fig. 20.12

The second method is normally used for rolling a single blank component which can either be a machined blank or a forging. The principle of operation involves positioning a blank between rollers which are retracted sideways to a clearance position. The blank is heated and the rollers are fed towards the blank, eventually contacting with it to form the teeth. An alternative method allows for one roller only to be fed in and the work holder may be simultaneously fed towards the other roller. In both methods the metal pushed out by the forming teeth on the roll is forced towards the hollow between two teeth on the roll and eventually forms the tip of the gear tooth. In order to prevent sideways spread of material the rolls in the second method are fitted with side plates as shown in the diagram. Provision can be made for an additional rolling operation to size the outside diameter of the forged blank prior to rolling the gear teeth.

Equipment has been designed and developed in such a way that both methods of operation are incorporated into the same machine. An automatic machine designated Model 30–200 is used for rolling teeth on blanks up to 7·87 in in diameter by 2·36 in facewidth and 1–4 module. The main characteristics of this machine are listed below, together with a similar set of characteristics for a machine designated Model 120–320.

Mill Model 30–200

Maximum diameter of rolled steel stock, mm	200
Maximum width of rolled stock at rolling of gears from separate steel blanks, mm	60
Maximum diameter of rolled steel bar, mm	30
Module of rolled gears	1–4
Production capacity of the mill, pieces/hour	40–100
Power of the main electric motor, kW	36
Weight of mill, ton	10

Mill Model 120–320

Maximum diameter of rolled gear, mm	320
Minimum diameter of rolled gear, mm	120
Module of rolled gears, mm	5–7
Average output, pieces/hour	40
Power of the main electric motor, kW	55
Weight of mill, ton	14

Production rates considerably in excess of those given can be achieved if required by altering the heating and loading sequences.

Gears which are produced by this method are suitable for non-precision applications without any further tooth machining, and their surface finish is better than that of shaved teeth. For precision applications, and particularly when considering larger gears, a finishing operation on a hobbing, shaving and/or finish rolling machine may be necessary, and in this case a material allowance of approximately 0·015 in is left on the tooth flanks. Table 20.1 shows the results of metal saving during the rolling of different gears from stamped blanks when compared with hobbing. It may be noted from this table that the rolling facilitates a metal saving of about 20 per cent of the weight of the blank.

Table 20.1

Gear modules, mm	Number of teeth	Size of gear, mm	Weight of stamped blank for milling, kg	Metal saved by rolling, kg per item
7·0	28	37	12·0	2·68
9·0	24	45	14·7	3·5
6·5	63	70	33·0	5·3
10·5	55	100	125·6	22·0

The formation of gear teeth by rolling changes presently accepted manufacturing processes radically and offers a number of important advantages when compared with a cutting process:

(1) Output rates are considerably higher.

(2) Considerable saving in metal.

(3) Saving in labour.

(4) Strength characteristics are improved and it is often possible to reduce the size of a gear to carry identical loads.

(5) High tool life.

Another application for this process is in the manufacture of sprockets by rolling. These sprockets rolled require no further machining and it was found possible to make a substantial reduction in the thickness of the central part of the disc used as a blank. For example, wheels with a thickness of 11 mm on the toothed part are rolled from a blank 8 mm thick. On a sprocket this represented a saving of 215 ton of metal in the annual production of 250 000 sprockets. Various machine characteristics are shown in Table 20.2.

Table 20.2

Characteristics	Type of mill		
	1	2	3
Maximum pitch of toothed wheels, mm	15·875	25·4	25·4
External diameter of toothed wheels, mm	20–200	140–350	50–300
Weight of mill, tons	4·6	12·5	20·0
Output, items/hour	100–120	80–100	80–100

BEVEL GEAR ROLLING

It was envisaged that it should be sensibily possible to finish cold roll crown wheels both for passenger car applications as well as commercial vehicle applications such as tractors, trucks, etc. In fact, development programmes with regard to the above are well advanced along the following lines. By reference to Figs 20.13 and 20.14 the general pattern of pursuance will be readily apparent without lengthy description. Because of the large volume of metal to be saved by rough hot rolling a forged blank it was decided to start development along these lines. Machinery has been developed which hot rolls crown wheels very successfully. The next step is to take a basically similar machine and finish cold roll the hot rolled blank to achieve a final crown wheel. The development stages to achieve this final result with regard to passenger car applications are broadly as described for hot gear rolling. These, repeated for continuity, are as follows.

(1) Initially the hot rolled blank will be finish cut.

(2) As a next step finish cutting will be eliminated and replaced by cold rolling.

(3) Finally, it is intended to consider a precision formed initial forging or similar starting blank and eliminate all blank preparations.

Bevel gear machinery and process description

The rolling tool performs an operation resulting in successive local deformation of the blank which is heated by high-frequency current. The rolling process effectively replaces the rough machining operation in conventional crown wheel cutting. The bevel gear rolling machine is furnished with a completely automatic cycle which is briefly summarized as follows (see also Fig. 20.14).

(*a*) A blank is loaded either manually or automatically into the chucking position.

(*b*) The cycle of the machine commences and the blank is rotated, hydraulically clamped in position on a driven table. An inductor is fed into position and the blank is heated to rolling temperature.

(*c*) When the blank is raised to the required depth of heating and temperature, heating stops automatically and the inductor is actuated away.

(*d*) The main spindle, which is housed in an inclined slide, is lowered and the rolling tool, which is mounted on a free rotary spindle, gradually engages the blank. The rotation of the upper spindle is caused by a lower synchronizing

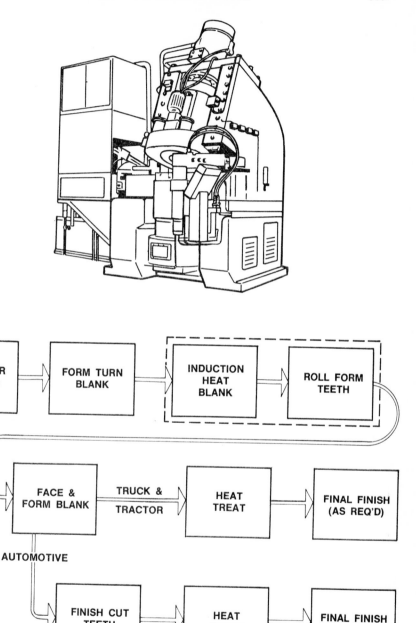

Fig. 20.13. View of bevel gear rolling machine and process flow diagram

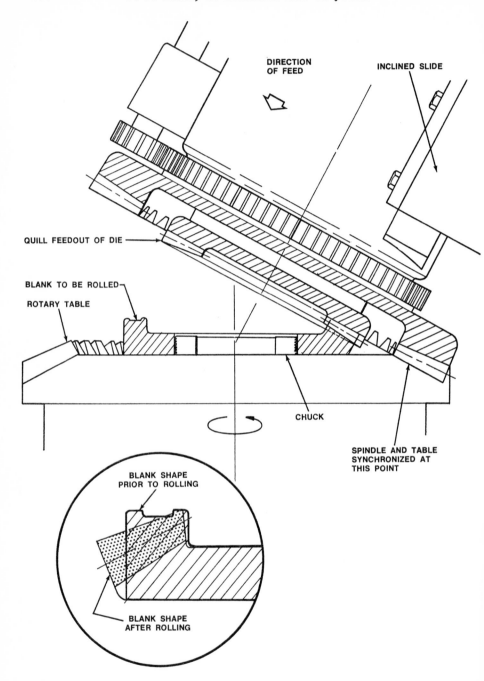

Fig. 20.14. Schematic view of rolling machine spindle and table

gear, mounted on the driver table, engaging with the upper synchronizing gear. This causes the free rotary spindle, and thus the rolling tool, to rotate. When the teeth of the synchronizing bevel gears engage, the tooth rolling tool makes contact with the heated surface of the blank and the tooth rolling process begins. This process continues until the rolling tool, as it moves along the inclined guides of the two cutters, comes to a stop. The tool then ceases to advance and the process is initiated whereby the gear teeth are burnished by the rolling tool and the required form is accurately reproduced. The object of burnishing is to produce teeth of suitably accurate form and required geometry.

(e) After the burnishing operation the top slide retracts and the blank is unloaded automatically by a mechanical arm and transferred on to either a receiving trough or conveyer. During the cycle oxidation of the heated blank surfaces is prevented by shrouding the rolling operation in an atmosphere of protective gas. During the rolling process the rolling tool is automatically lubricated. At the end of the rolling cycle the rolling tools and chuck assembly are cooled each cycle.

Heating of blank during tooth rolling

This is from an electrochemical generator of 60–150 kW with a frequency of 2500 Hz through a reducing transformer and high-frequency inductor directly on the tooth rolling machine. The surface layer of the blank is heated to a temperature of 1100–1150°C while the temperature of the lower layers undergoing deformation must not be below 800°C. The depth of heating is checked macrographically. The blank should be heated to a depth approximately equal to the module below the bottom of the tooth space of the rolled gear.

Tooth rolling tool

This is an assembly consisting of a tooth rolling wheel and inner and outer flanges. The tooth rolling wheel has the form of a gear conjugate with the gear to be rolled.

Cooling and lubrication

The tooth rolling tool and chuck are cooled automatically after the rolled gear has been removed from the chuck. Lubrication of the tool with an aqueous suspension of colloidal graphite is designed to reduce friction during deformation of the metal and to lengthen the life of the tool.

Component condition

It can be considered under the present state of the art that a conventionally forged and machined component is required with normal tolerances. The main difference between the blank required in the rolling process and the blank required for the gear cutting process is that in the case of the former the blank is much lighter because it will be roll formed and all the metal used to produce the tooth form. The inclined face of the forged blank for rolling would be in approximately the pitch line position relative to the back face. During rolling the material from below the pitch line is forced above the pitch line to form the top of the teeth. This in the main is how the material savings are made. The allowance left on the teeth for final machining is approximately 0·015 in.

Location points

Backface and bore. A broad specification for a typical machine is as follows.

Specification

Productivity, components/hour	30
Minimum diameter of rolled gears, mm	200
Maximum diameter of rolled gears, mm	325
Maximum length of rolled tooth, mm	50
Maximum tooth height, mm	20
Maximum diameter of synchronizing bevel gears, mm	620
Limiting cone angle of rolled gears, degrees	62–74
Revolutions of spindle and component, rev/min	40–60
Specifications of electromechanical current converter, kW	50–160
Frequency, Hz	2500
Weight of machine, tons (metric)	20–25

Production rates can be considerably improved by rearranging loading and heating cycles and providing suitable material handling equipment. As a specific example it is envisaged that passenger car crown wheels of approximately 8 in diameter can be rough rolled hot at something in the order of 80 per hour. It is anticipated that the finish rolling operation can be performed at approximately 360 per hour.

The production of crown wheels by this method of rolling obviously has a number of important advantages:

(1) Output rates are higher than conventional cutting machinery.
(2) Considerable saving in metal.
(3) Saving in labour.
(4) Strength and wear characteristics are important.
(5) High tool life.
(6) Less investment in manufacturing facility and saving in floor space.

The MS. of this paper was received at the Institution and accepted for publication on 21st April 1970.

Discussion during Session 2

Papers 11 and 12

Mr Lewis (*Rover Co.*) could well imagine benefits from using a chain drive instead of transfer gears. However, the velocity ratio transmitted by a roller chain might be less constant with consequent greater danger of exciting torsional resonances which could be heard in the car. Had the authors specifically investigated this aspect and, if not, had they encountered any unexplained transmission booms?

He also asked Mr Hoar to comment on the wear problems encountered with HIVO chains.

Mr Hoar replied that, if one took into account all the considerations mentioned in the paper, based mainly on the tensile capacity of the chain, wear was automatically allowed for in the final proportions. Could Mr Davies give some detail about how he had obtained the two graphs showing comparable wear for HIVO and roller chains? One ought to know the speeds and loads and also the relevant sprocket sizes.

Mr Davies (*Renold Ltd*) replied that they had made no detailed study of the effects of torsional vibration. All he could say was that they had replaced gear drives by chains which had been remarkably quiet; but one could well study the implications of the torsionals.

Regarding wear, he had said in the paper that these tests had been carried out under identical conditions. The full torque used was that specified in the Toronado brochure. The wheel sizes were the same for HIVO as for a roller chain. To make their chain run quietly, HIVO had to have eight different wheel sizes and also to face-grind the teeth on the wheel.

Mr Hoar objected that the wear graphs comparing the chains had been obtained only at full torque; a more realistic assessment of wear would take into account the full range of duties at high speed, high load, overdrive, etc.

Mr Jones (*Renold Ltd*) said the oscillograph recording in Paper 12, comparing roller chain and HIVO chain, suggested remarkable differences between polygonal action in the two chains which could well be due to special conditions. With normal running speeds and numbers of teeth (say 20) they had found no such differences.

Strain gauge telemetry as a means of detecting stress variations was only possible at very slow speeds. High-speed ciné photographs (5000 frames/s), however, showed no evidence such as the comparative oscillographs in the paper to suggest polygonal action in roller chain can be detected as greater than that in HYVO chain.

Mr Hoar agreed that the diagram in his paper was strictly based on one condition, as with Mr Davies' wear graph. The figures had been obtained at the Borg-Warner Research Institute, Chicago. He had used 25-tooth sprockets with both roller chain and HIVO, because at that time one could not get below 25 with a HIVO. Now one could get down to 17 teeth, so perhaps they should repeat the experiment.

Mr Avnir (*Ford*) thought it very difficult, without doing real durability testing under actual conditions, to determine which type of chain was better. Cost had a great influence but the roller chain tended to be rather noisier, and probably also more difficult to quieten. He saw scope for refining the involute tooth chain in order to get a quieter drive.

Mr Grandfield (*Automotive Products*) thought economics important, including the production cost of the sprockets. Could the authors give cost comparisons with an equivalent gear train?

Mr Davies (*Renold Ltd*) offered to show Mr Avnir his Wolseley 1800 fitted with a roller chain which had done 32 000 miles.

The 'Toronado' they had converted had a standard roller chain and wheels whereas the HIVO chain needed eight different wheel sizes; and the roller chain ran more quietly. Only a motor manufacturer could supply comparative cost figures.

Mr Davies (*B.M.C.*) said that since he had chosen a Renolds he had not seen anything to justify a change. However, he now had nearly 80 000 B.M.C. trans-axle HIVO-driven transmissions in service without any easily detectable wear, let alone failure.

He confirmed that chains were beneficial in adding some flexibility to the drive line in trans-axle transmissions. Only one of his six new prototypes had no chain drive: and that was the most troublesome of the lot.

Mr Bird (*Shell-Mex*) asked Mr Hoar about the comparative inertias of the two chains. HIVO had apparently only been used with automatic transmissions; what did that do to the synchro cones?

Mr Hoar replied that his first slide had shown the Honda manual box. They had got over the synchromesh problem rather cunningly in that the HIVO transmitted drive from the crankshaft to the flywheel so that its inertia came after the clutch and did not affect the synchro.

Obviously the tensile load in a chain varied inversely with sprocket size and, since HIVO had a better tensile strength than roller chains, it could afford to drop the sprocket size so as to bring total drive inertia down to less than the existing gear sets. HIVO was also considerably more elastic than roller chain. Regarding sprocket selection, General Motors believed in a belt-and-braces policy: they chose to match the sprockets with the chains. At Morse they were satisfied that it did not make a scrap of difference.

A last point on wear: Morse had supplied 900 spare chains to B.M.C. but a few months ago they had had them all returned, because not a single one had been sold. And the model had been going three years!

Regarding chain elasticity Renold have proved that there is no difference between roller and HYVO chain given the same pitch, width and length.

Mr Hamilton-Smith (*Harry Ferguson Research*) reminded Mr Davies that they had been using his roller chains in the late 1950s on prototypes which were still running, 2-litre 100 hp cars with a Ferguson Toronado torque converter, having a stall torque ratio of about 3:1, and the chains were taking the full output down to the centre differential and thence to the front and rear wheels. It had been fitted with a hydraulic chain tensioner. Noise problems were overcome to some degree by staggering the 2-strand chains.

One question for Mr Hoar: HIVO chains were very adjustable, one could vary the pressure angle; would he like to comment on pressure angle in relation to polygonal action?

Mr Hoar replied that the reason for changing the pressure angle from 25° to 30° had been to get below 25 teeth and therefore get smaller sprockets with low inertia on manual transmissions.

Mr Burdess (*Newcastle University*) reported a research project on the dynamics involved in chains and offered details to anyone interested.

Prof. Macmillan complained about the jerk which frequently occurred on engaging a transmission on starting. A low idling stall speed would help to avoid it but to keep it low under cold conditions would make it rise too high under hot conditions. Was it desirable to select neutral when there was likely to be a waiting period in traffic in order to avoid overheating of the transmission? If this was a good idea, it became all the more important to eliminate the jerk.

Mr Hawley referred to dynamometer transmission tests mentioned by Mr Davies: in this kind of test they experienced severe gear pitting and other failures of the automatic gearbox at much below design torques, whereas in service the gearbox transmitted about double this power quite happily. Admittedly the dynamometer test included repeated full-torque changes but the difference between it and actual road service results appeared excessive.

Mr Filderman had been able to overcome the starting jerk by using a small valve which short-circuited the gear-pump at small flow, i.e. in the idling condition. When engine speed increased, the pressure-drop across this valve increased, which closed it.

Mr Davies (*Borg-Warner*) replied that the jerk could be eliminated by accumulators. However, to introduce an accumulator on their existing transmission would permit misuse by rapid engagement, followed by rapid acceleration, which might catch out the clutch and result in failure.

They had studied electronic controls but these still included hydraulics and the control requirements got more and more complicated.

As for the trend towards more than three speeds for cars below 2·8 litres, in Europe larger vehicles were taxed out of existence so that manufacturers stretched their 2·8 litres to perform like a much lower-tuned 4-litre and this had increased the need for more than three ratios on smaller cars. Beyond 4 litres three speeds were sufficient and, certainly, below 1 litre four speeds were a 'must'.

He agreed with Mr Hawley that dynamometer tests were probably twice as severe as normal road use. Such tests had been run at constant ratios for many years before it became obvious that pitting was due to frequent stopping.

Mr Shaw (*Chairman*), referring to the jerk, said it was fundamental to any constant-mesh gear set that, in neutral, with the output shaft at rest, the reaction members associated with the higher gears ran at fixed speed relationships to the input speed. If the rotation of the reaction members at the high-speed end was three times the engine idling speed, there was a fair amount of stored energy in those reaction members. If the gear ratio next to unity was not 1·5 but 1·25, then the situation was much worse, the gear elements were running at many times the input speed. Therefore one of the contributory elements was dissipation of the energy stored in the rotating members of the gear sets responsible for the ratios adjacent to unity.

A very simple way to eliminate the starting jerk was so to arrange the system that there was a momentary rest of the reaction members associated with the gear ratio nearest to unity, before actually applying the band brake or the clutch associated with the starting gear. Obviously, if one limited the rate of application of the starting brake, this helped.

The efficiency of the semi-automatic pneumocyclic transmission was generally very high, in the mid-90s. In support of the torque converter, very careful testing had shown that a transmission such as the Voith Devabus compared well in fuel consumption with the semi-automatic pneumocyclic transmission.

Mr Booth had mentioned the need for a charging pump in the Allison transmission, to ensure the correct functioning of hydraulic couplings. They also had to pump-charge to conduct away a wave of heat engendered during misuse in starting heavier vehicles.

Papers 13, 14 and 15

Mr Thompson showed a very simplified diagram of the electronics of the Leyland transmission with safety features in cases of skid or signal failure, where existing gears were held or, if reverted to top gear, with resetting; and for automatic door opening. The unit had been applied to different prime movers with differing gear ratios from 3 to 5 steps and, with little modification, to a gas-turbine-powered vehicle.

Another development was used for controlling a simple gearbox for manual override, the clutch having a sharp brake to control the inertia for rapid gear changing. The synchronization was electronic and so was the speed-matching system. This, too, was applicable to prime movers like the supercharged diesel with a torque converter or a gas turbine. Although there seemed to be an awful lot of components with an epicyclic gearbox, the system was quite economic compared with other types of fully automatic transmission. It had undergone many thousands of kilometres of testing. To bring the cost down, newer electronic techniques were being used, for instance integral control. This was very cheap to make in quantity and quite adaptable.

Mr Riddle had mentioned £200 for a manual synchromesh box and £700 for one of Mr Burnett's boxes. The cost of electronic control with the associated actuators could be considerably less than £200.

Mr Hollinghurst agreed that the authors had presented an interesting group of papers from the point of view of the lubrication engineer. Mr Burnett could have mentioned that, even with fast, semi-automatic transmission, problems did occur on rear-engine buses where a common oil supply was used for the drive and the transmission.

Mr Davies had mentioned the need for better low-temperature properties in fluids. Did Mr Atkins share this concern for the Automotive Products transmission?

Cold-room studies had been made comparing the cold starting properties of a manual and an automatic transmission with two types of lubricant—a 20W–50 and a 10W–50 engine oil. The automatic transmission had suffered the effect of increased torque converter drag but this could be counteracted to a large degree by reducing the low-temperature viscosity. Whilst synthetics had better high-temperature performance, their low-temperature properties could also have advantages.

Mr Atkins had mentioned bronze clutch plates: did the Mark II transmission show durability with used engine oil as the lubricant? Studies by Mobil had indicated that fuel combustion products in a used engine tended to reduce the life of paper-and-resin friction materials.

Frictional variations between one engine oil and another occurred due to the use of different detergents and this made engine oil harder to calibrate for transmissions than a purpose-designed fluid.

Both Mr Davies and Mr Atkins had commented on the need for special sealing to separate gear oil from the automatic transmission fluid, which was expensive and space consuming. His company was developing products which would serve for both final drive axle and transmission. Since transmission builders specified various fluids they had not tried to go further than good spiral bevel gear protection. The anti-wear and extreme-pressure additives needed for axle protection could reduce life. He showed slides illustrating development work on such fluids. The products had very good oxidation stability and did not need draining for 80 000 miles compared with 40 000 for the fluid then in use; it also had good low-temperature properties and viscosity stability.

Mr Booth (*Conoco Ltd*) asked Mr Burnett for an efficiency comparison between semi- and fully-automatic boxes (with torque converter) for a reasonable amount of hill climbing. The need for an oil-cooler for the torque converter indicated loss of power. Would not the pneumocyclic transmission with electronic control offer the highest overall efficiency?

Mr Brook (*Eaton Axles*) said that with a rear-engined bus, where there was a very short drive, there were two problems. First, modulation of the automatic shift; and second, the fact that where one relied on the output shaft holding the system stationary, any torsional fluctuations coming from the engine were transmitted as hammer-blows to the axle gears.

Mr Lepelletier said that a speaker had mentioned 450 variables making performance prediction difficult. Did he not think that, for transmission signals, the auto-pressure systems would eventually be replaced by some form of remote control, such as the electric control of the new Renault R16? He visualized binary logic, such as used on numerically controlled machine tools; this would provide flexibility in a simpler and easier way than conventional hydraulics. He would also welcome more comment on the trend towards four or more speeds. Had not the time come in Europe for new concepts in transmissions and control systems?

Mr Rawlings (*British Twin Discs*), in a written contribution, agreed on a strong case for hydrodynamic transmissions in town buses. His company had made a three-stage torque converter with a direct-drive clutch, automatically controlled by vehicle speed. The only gears were a forward/reverse set. Starting from rest was by the torque converter, with a torque multiplication factor of around 5. As the speed increased, the tailshaft governor automatically disengaged the converter clutch and engaged the lock-up clutch to give high efficiency in direct drive. The system worked best with engines of a wide speed range on vehicles where weight varied little.

Mr Lewis referred to Mr Davies' mention of a 4-speed gearbox in which it was necessary to lower the 3–4 shift speed so that the shift would occur under normal conditions. This seemed to imply a rather high top gear. An alternative would have been to lower the overall gearing at the expense of fuel consumption. Some manufacturers preferred a high top gear with a 4-speed automatic, which could imply a high utilization of third gear. How did gearboxes stand up under prolonged operation in indirect gears?

Mr Burnett had pointed out that the case of an epicyclic gearbox would be lightened because of the absence of bursting loads; but its beam stiffness was an important factor in controlling driveline vibration.

Mr Davies and Mr Burnett appeared to differ about the need for a hydrodynamic torque converter with an automatic gearbox for a two-shaft gas turbine. A fluid coupling greatly eased gearshift problems since it eliminated resonance between turbine inertia, vehicle inertia and the transmission wind-up stiffness which could be excited by a poor shift. However, it lost some of the low-speed torque so that a torque converter would be preferable. Were there any applications of hydrodynamic couplings or converters on two-shaft gas turbines?

Papers 16, 17 and 18

Mr Hancock (*N.E.L.*) thought Dr Giles' efficiency figures for hydrostatic transmissions not too optimistic: technically such shunt drives had been feasible for a very long time but torque converters had got in first. There was not enough advantage attached to hydrostatics to outweigh the capital now invested in the manufacture of torque converters. Anyway, mechanical efficiency was not everything, what really mattered was vehicle performance.

He then showed slides of vehicles equipped with hydrostatic transmission.

Mr Lewis agreed that part-load transmission efficiency was important on passenger cars since it determined fuel consumptions at cruising speeds. This efficiency was lowered by the conventional automatic transmission's oil pump which absorbed power regardless of load. Infinitely variable drives, on the contrary, made it possible to use low engine speeds at higher throttle opening, giving a substantial improvement in specific fuel consumption. The hydrostatic drive also incurred important torque losses independent of load.

The shunt transmission was ingenious but its advantages were not clear. Two alternatives were mechanical drives, such as the Perbury gear, for which part-load efficiencies remained high over a wide range of speeds and loads; and the variable-frequency electric drive explored by General Motors with which part-load efficiency should actually be higher.

Would Dr Giles comment on the relative efficiencies of simple and shunt hydrostatic transmissions in level cruising conditions for a typical modern car?

Dr Giles, in reply, would not suggest that shunt transmissions were a panacea. Layouts of some vehicles were more suitable for pipework than for mechanical drives but pipes tended to be stiff, even flexible pipes became stiff under pressure. The hydrostatic drive offered better ratio control but hydrokinetic devices had inbuilt characteristics which were not always suitable for the job in hand.

He did not agree with Mr Lewis that the shunt drive was insufficiently efficient to make up engine losses. There was a lot of fuel to be gained by more economic engine operation. He was interested in the Perbury gear and other forms of variable drive but thought electrical ones too expensive.

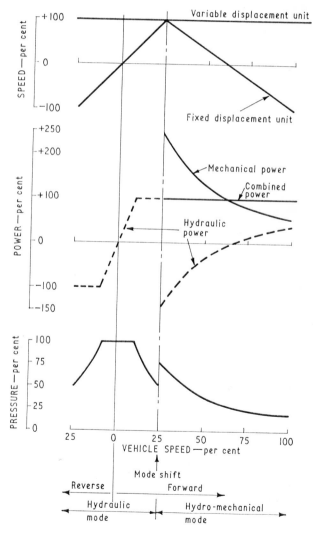

Fig. D1

Dr Looman questioned the shape of the efficiency curve given in Fig. 16.15 in the hydro-mechanical mode and suggested that, rather than smoothly reaching a maximum efficiency at about 75 per cent vehicle speed, there would be a sharp crater in this region, owing to low hydraulic transmission efficiency at low pump displacements.

Mr Booth, in a written contribution, plotted the relative speeds of the fixed and variable displacement hydraulic units against output speed, Fig. D1, and also the resulting proportions of pressure and power. The fixed-displacement unit completely stopped rotating at around 65 per cent output speed when hydraulic power flow was zero, thus acting only as a brake. Leakage was then the principal source of loss. Evidently maximum efficiency occurred when all power transmission was mechanical.

Conversely, the point of minimum efficiency shown in Dr Giles' paper was also valid as it coincided with shifting into the hydro-mechanical mode from the pure hydrostatic mode. The graph showed a very substantial power recirculation with a negative power of $1\cdot5 \times$ input, transmitted hydraulically and requiring a positive power of $2\cdot5 \times$ input to be transmitted mechanically. Both hydraulic units were then rotating at their maximum speed, though not at their maximum pressure.

Dr Giles, replying to Dr Looman, said it was difficult to appreciate the operating conditions in the shunt versions of the hydrostatic drive. In this case the pump unit changed direction, thereby becoming a hydraulic motor. The double differential transmission mentioned in Paper 16, now employed on the Trident aircraft, had two such change points but these presented no insurmountable difficulty.

Papers 19 and 20

Mr Jacobson said it might come as a surprise that the A.A. was interested in both design and manufacture but it was concerned to get fewer gear failures. Mr Egan's enthusiasm was justified. He remembered rolling tail shafts in 9 minutes floor-to-floor time instead of 17 minutes by conventional processes.

The correct design of gears had exercised the minds of engineers for many years. The authors have discarded some of the early work reported since it concerned itself with gearing lubrication problems which had long since been solved. Mass produced gearboxes and associate drive components were now much more accurate and had more than kept pace with increasing power throughput.

Much gear research was carried out under idealized conditions and the designer's efforts could be nullified by poor machining of the gearbox housing or faulty alignment. He showed slides of the results of misalignment which produced rapid pitting fatigue failure. The problem had been solved only by drastically narrowing the face because the elastic deformation of the shaft could not be controlled.

The distortion of gearboxes could be due to insufficient rigidity in the bell housing, incorrect alignment, or periodic outward flexing due to the propeller shaft. The problem could be aggravated by split bearing housings misaligned after re-assembly.

There was no excuse these days for designers failing to incorporate tip and root relief to compensate for the deflection of the teeth and rim sections. We suffered far too many initially noisy gears which the customer was supposed to put up with for the first nine months after purchasing the vehicle.

Photoelastic work had indicated contact stresses much more severe than those calculated on the Hertz formula which assumed that two cylinders were being pressed together. Tip contact for practical purposes was between a knife edge and a cylinder. Tip-easing gave the gears a much better chance of survival under lubrication failure, particularly at high speeds. How close were the tolerances Mr Egan actually achieved in cold rolling?

He disagreed with the authors on the life effect of gear ratios. It was quite safe to design the first and reverse gears on a very much higher permissible stress. He then showed a number of slides illustrating gear design data.

In a further written contribution Mr Jacobson added that in the latest I.Mech.E. Guide on Gear Design, Prof. Tuplin had introduced us to the V-factor for addendum correction. This was somewhat different from the k-factor given in B.S. 436. In fact, if one were to use $V = 2.5$ on the gear and $V = 3.0$ on the pinion, one would achieve about the optimum combination of bending strength, contact loading and lubrication. For example, with a 15-tooth gear with a correction factor of $V = 2.0–3.0$ it was possible to get a bonus in improving slide roll conditions which led to better gear-tooth lubrication and, incidentally, quieter, longer-lasting gears.

Mr Love said that Mr Egan was obviously on a winner. M.I.R.A. had tested splines many years ago and shown that they were three times as strong in fatigue as the corresponding spline, so cold-formed gears can be expected to show a substantial improvement in fatigue strength. He thought they had not fully explored all special treatments for components.

Mr Jacobson was obviously worried because the paper included some old information but facts 20 years ago were still facts today: a lot of people still did not have this information and it might be useful to them.

SESSION 3

Paper 21. Ball and Cylindrical Roller Bearings in Drivelines

T. S. NISBET, C Eng, F I Mech E

Divisional Technical Manager, Ransome, Hofmann, Pollard Ltd, General Bearings Division, P.O. Box 7, Chelmsford, Essex

This paper deals with ball and cylindrical roller bearings in drivelines where, year by year, requirements demand that smaller bearings meet conditions of steadily increasing severity.

Clutch-operating bearings and those for manual gearboxes and overdrives are reviewed. The different requirements for bearings in front-wheel drives and automatic gearboxes are discussed, followed by a consideration of the requirements of propeller shafts, half-shafts and hubs.

INTRODUCTION

This paper is restricted to a consideration of ball and cylindrical roller bearings in driveline applications. There are a large number of variations of these two basic types in common use, and their specialized features have contributed in no small measure to the relatively simple methods of mounting adopted in modern applications.

The single row radial ball bearing

Designed primarily for carrying radial load, single row radial ball bearings of the no-gap type are capable of taking substantial axial load in either direction, with or without radial load. This, combined with the fact that they are less susceptible to the effects of shaft deflection and malalignment than other types of rigid rolling bearings, no doubt explains their widespread use.

Recent developments have been towards the use of larger balls with more closely controlled raceway grooves, resulting in increased load-carrying capacity. This has enabled modern requirements involving the use of ever-smaller bearings for duties of increasing severity to be met, which is essential if the demand for increased power, combined with reduction in weight and cost, is to be met.

Most single row radial ball bearings are now of the no-gap type, the balls being assembled by eccentric displacement of the rings, rather than through filling slots. There is a limited use of gap type or filling slot type bearings which can accommodate a larger number of balls than the no-gap type and therefore have a higher radial load-carrying capacity, but their axial-load capacity is lower.

Apart from the number and size of balls, other important internal features are the radii of the groove raceways and the internal radial clearance in the bearing. The two latter, in conjunction with the ball diameter, determine the angle of contact between the balls and the raceway grooves, and thus influence the amount of axial load that can be carried by the bearing.

The radii of the raceway grooves in relation to ball size are important, as they affect the load-carrying capacity of the bearing, its free running, and its rigidity under load. Most standard ball bearings are made with raceway groove radii in accordance with I.S.O. Recommendation 281 on Dynamic Load Ratings, that is with inner ring groove radii and outer ring groove radii no greater than 52 and 53 per cent of the ball diameter, respectively. Larger groove radii give a reduction in load-carrying capacity, but it cannot always be assumed that appreciably smaller groove radii would give increased capacity, as additional lubrication and extra care in mounting may be necessary.

Single row radial ball bearings are supplied with different amounts of internal radial clearance referred to as '0', '00', '000', and '0000', or Group 2, Normal Group, Group 3, and Group 4, respectively. When selecting the correct grade of fit, however, it is necessary to consider the loss of internal clearance arising from interference fits between the bearing rings and their seatings and, in addition, the effect of any temperature gradient. This is important where radial ball bearings are required to carry axial load, because the contact angle depends upon the residual clearance in the mounted bearing.

The basic bearing and its variations used in driveline applications are illustrated in Figs 21.1a to 21.1f, inclusive.

A few selected applications have been reproduced in Figs 21.13 to 21.22, inclusive, and these comprise Appendix 21.1. These illustrate the use of some of the bearing types discussed and are referred to as they arise in the text.

The basic single row radial ball bearing (Fig. 21.1a) is used for the main positions in all forms of gearboxes (Fig. 21.16), on Carden shafts, in rear hubs,

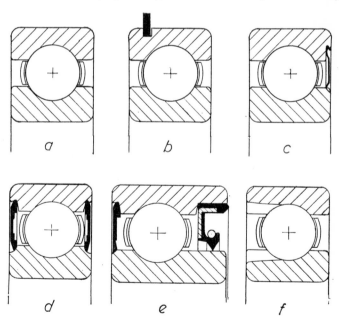

Fig. 21.1. Variations of the single row radial ball bearing

and differential gear carriers (Fig. 21.19), also for clutch operation (Fig. 21.16). In the heavier drives of commercial and cross-country vehicles it is often used for axial loading only in conjunction with cylindrical radial roller bearings (see Figs 21.13 and 21.22).

The single row radial ball bearing with locating snap ring (Fig. 21.1*b*) is widely used at locating positions in all forms of gearboxes (see Fig. 21.14).

The single row radial ball bearing with single dust shield (Fig. 21.1*c*) is commonly used in clutch pilot bearing positions. It is also used in rear-wheel hubs where additional supplementary protection must be provided.

The single row radial ball bearing with two moulded rubber seals (Fig. 21.1*d*) is widely used in rear hubs but, again, additional supplementary protection is required. The bearing is supplied pre-greased by the manufacturers and cannot be relubricated.

The single row radial sealed ball bearing with extended inner and outer rings (Fig. 21.1*e*) has a proprietary garter type seal at one side and a conventional moulded rubber seal at the other side; it is a development of the type shown in Fig. 21.1*d*. There is an increasing interest in this bearing for rear-wheel hubs, as the more efficient proprietary type seal can exclude axle oil as well as retain the bearing grease.

The single row radial ball bearing with filling slots (Fig. 21.1*f*) is occasionally used in gearboxes in heavy-duty, slow-moving equipment, particularly earth-moving vehicles where the loading is predominantly radial.

Miscellaneous radial ball bearings

These include the externally aligning ball bearing and the double row self-aligning ball bearing. The former shown at Fig. 21.2*a* is a development of the basic single row radial ball bearing in Fig. 21.1*a*. The o.d. of the outer ring is ground spherical in form and fitted with an aligning ring of spherical form in its bore. The aligning feature is thus external to the working components of the bearing so that the load-carrying capacity is comparable with that of the equivalent rigid bearing. Owing to friction between the spherical surfaces these bearings are not self-aligning, and the bearing rings have to be squared up with one another when the bearing is being fitted.

The double row self-aligning ball bearing shown in Fig. 21.2*b* is made to the same external dimensions as the single row radial bearing. The bearing is readily able to accommodate malalignment as the outer ring raceway is of spherical form, but this gives little support to the balls so that its load capacity is lower than that of the equivalent single row bearing. In addition, its capacity for carrying axial load is low, due to the small contact angles that can occur between the balls and raceways.

Both types are used in outboard positions where accurate alignment cannot be ensured and at the intermediate support positions on the divided Carden shafts of heavy commercial vehicles (see Fig. 21.18).

Angular contact ball bearings

The single row angular contact ball bearing is similar in construction to the single row radial ball bearing, except that one side of the outer ring (or sometimes

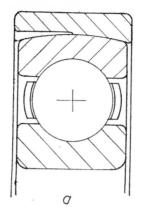

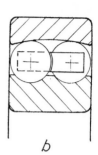

Fig. 21.2. Externally aligning and self-aligning ball bearings

a

b

the inner ring, or both) is cut away. This permits a greater number of balls to be fitted and allows the use of a one-piece cage. The initial contact angle is appreciably larger than in the radial bearing, being normally around 20–35°, and it is obtained by providing the required amount of internal radial clearance.

Where used singly, these bearings can carry axial load in one direction only. If used in pairs adjusted against one another, they can carry combined axial and radial loads in any proportion. Manufacturers can supply these bearings with their rings specially faced during manufacture, so that when clamped together in pairs the correct pre-load or end movement is obtained without any need for adjustment by the user. An example of a pre-loaded pair is shown on the pinion shaft in Fig. 21.19.

Most manufacturers also supply double row angular contact ball bearings, those in common use having two-piece inner rings or two-piece outer rings. These types are supplied either pre-loaded or with end movement, and when selecting the correct adjustment it is necessary to consider the effect of the shaft and housing seating limits.

These angular contact bearings are shown in Figs 21.3a to 21.3c, inclusive.

Single row angular contact ball bearings (Fig. 21.3a), when mounted in pairs, and adjusted against one another, are used for wheel hubs, and for supporting differential gear carriers in rear axles. In the hub application they are mounted back to back to give maximum rigidity, but on differential gear carriers, where the span is greater, they are more usually mounted face to face.

The double row angular contact ball bearing with two-piece outer ring (Fig. 21.3b) is the equivalent of two single row angular contact bearings mounted face to face. When pre-loaded they have a high degree of rigidity and are used in hypoid and spiral bevel pinion shafts for combined radial and axial load. Due to the intersection of the lines of contact between the two rows of balls, this type is rather lacking in lateral stability.

The double row angular contact ball bearing with two-piece inner ring (Fig. 21.3c) is equivalent to two single row angular contact bearings mounted back to back and gives a high degree of lateral rigidity. In addition to its use on hypoid

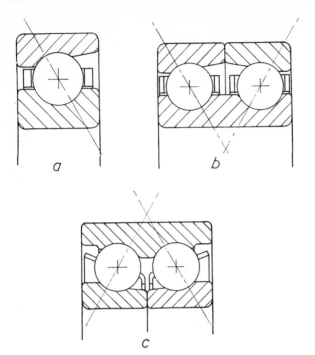

Fig. 21.3. Single and double row angular contact ball bearings

and spiral bevel pinion shafts, it is also used in wheel hubs. These bearings are generally supplied pre-loaded for the pinion shaft applications, but bearings with a controlled amount of initial end movement are preferable for wheel-hub applications. An example of a wheel hub is shown in Fig. 21.17.

Duplex bearings

These are additional types of single row angular contact bearings and are designed to carry axial load in either direction, with or without radial load. The inner and outer rings have two separate and distinct raceways, and it is important that the balls make contact with only one raceway on each ring at any one time. For this reason they are not suitable for radial load alone, and where combined radial and axial load is present the latter must always predominate.

One of the rings is in two pieces so that the only factor limiting the ball complement is the cage. The bearings are generally designed with a nominal contact angle of 30°, but owing to their construction they have appreciably less end movement under a reversing axial load than the equivalent size of single row radial ball bearing.

When intended for axial load only, they should be mounted with a small radial clearance between the o.d. of the outer ring and the bore of the housing to avoid the application of radial loading. Where it is inconvenient to counter-bore the

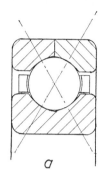
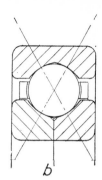

Fig. 21.4. Duplex
bearings

housing to provide this clearance, the bearings can be supplied slightly smaller
on o.d. than standard.

The two types of duplex bearing available are shown in Figs 21.4a and 21.4b.
Both types are used for axial loading on wormshafts and pinion shafts in the final
drives of heavy commercial vehicles, and also in gearboxes where axial loads from
the helical gears may be high. They are generally used in conjunction with
cylindrical roller bearings which carry the radial loading (see Fig. 21.21).

Clutch-operating bearings

These have been classified separately, as they are generally designed specifically
for this duty. Although required to transmit axial load, and therefore operate as
angular contact bearings, their internal radial clearances and therefore contact
angles are more appropriate to those of radial ball bearings. In fact, the basic
radial ball bearing is sometimes used for this duty.

With coil-spring clutches, the bearings are only loaded when the clutch is
disengaged. Thus for most of their lives they are unloaded and not rotating, but
they are subjected to vibration and for this reason the radial internal clearance is
kept small.

With hydrostatic diaphragm clutches, the bearings are subjected to continuous
rotation under light axial load so that there is less need for small radial internal
clearance. However, clutch-operating conditions are not arduous from the loading
point of view so that large contact angles are not necessary. The outer ring raceway groove radius may be larger than in normal radial and angular contact bearings
to assist in accommodating rather more malalignment than might reasonably be
expected of a rigid bearing.

The types of clutch-operating bearings in common use are illustrated in Figs
21.5a to 21.5c inclusive.

The single row radial ball bearing illustrated (Fig. 21.5a) is a narrow series
bearing, but normal light series bearings of this type are also commonly used.
These may be fitted with the conventional two-piece riveted cage and must be
suitably enclosed in a housing (see Fig. 21.16).

The standard type clutch-operating bearing (Fig. 21.5b) was designed in the

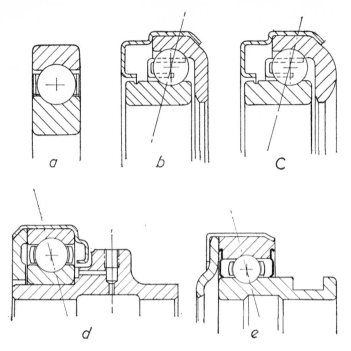

Fig. 21.5. Clutch-operating bearings

first instance for coil-spring clutches and is supplied charged with lubricating grease. The form of the outer ring and the pressed-steel closure are designed to retain the lubricant and exclude foreign matter.

The type shown in Fig. 21.5c was designed for hydrostatic diaphragm clutches. So far as internal construction is concerned, it is very similar to that shown in Fig. 21.5b, but the operating surface on the outer ring is cambered so that it can accommodate the deflection of the diaphragm fingers under load. In future, the cambering might be applied to the diaphragm fingers, in which case the operating surface on the bearing would revert to that shown at Fig. 21.5b. It has been found that the cambered bearing surface tends to wear grooves in the diaphragm fingers.

The type shown in Fig. 21.5d uses a standard open radial ball bearing with separate thrust plate designed to form a closure on one side and retained by a pressed-steel housing, which also forms the closure on the other side. The bearing is shown mounted on its sleeve, and a means of relubrication is indicated.

Fig. 21.5e shows a type which is based on a standard shielded type radial ball bearing with extended inner ring and a separate thrust plate. It may be designed either for coil spring or diaphragm type clutches and, like the types illustrated in Figs 21.5c and 21.5b, is supplied charged with lubricating grease on assembly. The provision of the extended inner ring avoids the need for mounting the bearing on a sliding sleeve, with a consequent saving in space.

INTERNAL GEOMETRY OF SINGLE ROW RADIAL AND ANGULAR CONTACT BALL BEARINGS

Notation

A, A_1 and A_2	The positions of the centre of the inner ring raceway groove curvature.
B	The position of the centre of the outer ring raceway groove curvature.
d	Ball diameter.
Te	Total free end movement.
F_A	The axial load on the bearing.
K_1 and K_2	Deflection contacts for the raceway grooves (average values approximately 0·83).
p	The ball load.
Q	Inner ring raceway groove radius.
R	Outer ring raceway groove radius.
S	Radial internal clearance.
Z	The number of balls.
δ_A	Axial movement under load.
δ_T	Elastic deformation at contact areas between the rings and a ball.
θ	Contact angle (initial).
θ_1	The contact angle under axial load.

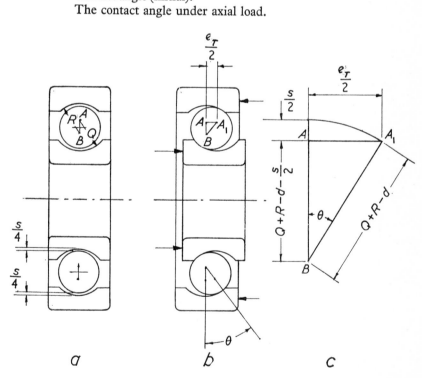

Fig. 21.6. Internal geometry of single row radial and angular contact ball bearings

It is sometimes necessary to know the amount of axial movement that can occur in a radial bearing. Examples are rear-axle drive shaft bearings supporting inboard disc brakes.

The end movement is a function of the ball diameter, the radial internal clearance, and the radii of the two raceway curvatures. The following equations, showing the relationship of these, and the contact angle, can be readily derived from a study of Fig. 21.6c.

$$e_T = 2\sqrt{\left\{(Q+R-d)^2-\left(Q+R-d-\frac{S}{2}\right)^2\right\}} \quad . \quad . \quad . \quad (21.1)$$

or

$$e_T = 2(Q+R-d)\sin\theta \quad . \quad . \quad . \quad . \quad . \quad (21.2)$$

also

$$S = 2\left[Q+R-d-\sqrt{\left\{(Q+R-d)^2-\left(\frac{e_T}{2}\right)^2\right\}}\right] \quad . \quad . \quad (21.3)$$

or

$$S = 2(Q+R-d)(1-\cos\theta) \quad . \quad . \quad . \quad . \quad (21.4)$$

$$\theta = \cos^{-1}\left\{1-\frac{S}{2(Q+R-d)}\right\} \quad . \quad . \quad . \quad . \quad (21.5)$$

When fitted, the radial internal clearance in the bearing will be reduced if the rings are made interference fits on their seatings. This should be allowed for, as the end movement and contact angle in the bearing will also be reduced. As a guide, it may be assumed that for inner rings made interference fits on solid shafts the radial internal clearance of the bearing will be reduced by an amount between 75 and 100 per cent of the interference, depending on the rigidity of the bearing ring. A reasonable allowance for outer rings made an interference fit in substantial bearings would be to reduce the radial internal clearance by 50 per cent of the interference, but particular applications may demand a more detailed study.

Under an applied axial load the contact angle and the end movement in the bearing will increase, but there is no direct procedure for calculating these. From Fig. 21.7b the following equations can be derived:

$$\delta_T = \sqrt{[\{(Q+R-d)\cos\theta\}^2+\{(Q+R-d)\sin\theta+\delta_A\}^2]}-(Q+R-d) \quad . \quad (21.6)$$

and

$$\sin\theta_1 = \frac{(Q+R-d)\sin\theta+\delta_A}{\sqrt{[\{(Q+R-d)\cos\theta\}^2+\{(Q+R-d)\sin\theta+\delta_A\}^2]}} \quad . \quad (21.7)$$

From Hertz theories the following can be derived:

$$\delta_T = \frac{K_1+K_2}{10^5\times d^{1/3}}P^{2/3} \quad . \quad . \quad . \quad . \quad . \quad . \quad (21.8)$$

$$= \frac{K_1+K_2}{10^5\times d^{1/3}}\left(\frac{F_A}{Z\sin\theta_1}\right)^{2/3} \quad . \quad . \quad . \quad . \quad (21.9)$$

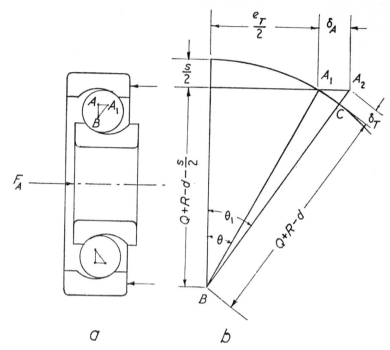

Fig. 21.7. Single row radial and angular contact ball bearings under axial load

These equations can be solved by successive approximation. By assuming values for δ_A calculate the corresponding δ_T from equation (21.6), and $\sin \theta_1$ from equation (21.7). If the value for $\sin \theta_1$ thus obtained is the correct one, then when substituted in equation (21.9) the value obtained for δ_T will be the same as that obtained from equation (21.6). This is a process which lends itself very readily to computerization.

Although the single row radial ball bearing is indicated in Figs 21.6 and 21.7, these equations also apply to angular contact ball bearings and are of use for calculating pre-load between two bearings.

The single row cylindrical roller bearing

This type is available to the same standardized external dimensions as the single row radial and angular contact ball bearings already referred to. It is primarily a radial bearing and has a considerably higher load-carrying capacity than the corresponding size of radial ball bearing, and also a higher degree of radial rigidity.

The standard pattern bearing is made with two fixed lips on one ring for locating the cage and rollers axially. In the United Kingdom the standard pattern has its lips on the inner ring, while on the Continent the preference is for lips on the outer ring. In both cases the opposite ring is a plain annular member without lips. These bearings are shown in Figs 21.8a and 21.8b, respectively, and variations of these basic bearings with other lip arrangements in common use on driveline applications are shown in Figs 21.8c to 21.8f, inclusive.

Again developments have taken place, resulting in the fitting of larger rollers. Special attention has also been given to the blending of the corner radii between the ends of the rollers and the cylindrical surfaces to eliminate stress concentrations and permit maximum use of the load-carrying capacity available. It also enables the bearing to withstand a limited amount of uneven loading, such as would occur as a result of malalignment or shaft deflection.

Owing to the absence of lips on one of the rings, the types shown in Figs 21.8a and 21.8b are unable to locate parts axially. However, where there are lips on both rings the bearing can deal with location duty and is also capable of dealing with axial loading, which may be of quite high magnitude if of an intermittent nature.

The variations shown in Fig. 21.8 will now be discussed.

Those shown in Figs 21.8a and 21.8b are basic standard roller bearings. They are widely used for radial loads in heavy duty gearboxes and on pinion shafts where separate provision is made for carrying the axial loading. They are also used in hubs. The inner and outer rings of these types must be held endways on their seatings (see Figs 21.13 and 21.22).

The type shown in Fig. 21.8c has two fixed lips on each ring and is non-separable. The rollers are assembled by eccentric displacement of the rings, as for ball bearings. Because of this, the number of rollers that can be assembled is

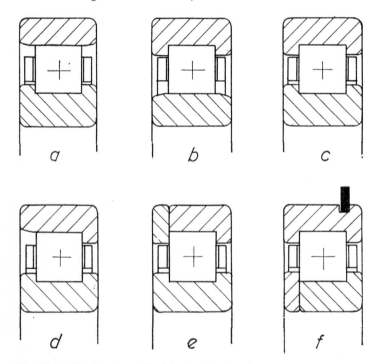

Fig. 21.8. Single row cylindrical roller bearings

less than for the other types shown, and its load capacity is therefore lower. Designed primarily for radial loads, the mounting requirements are similar to those of single row radial ball bearings. It is frequently used in heavy-duty gearboxes and transfer units.

The type with two fixed lips on the inner ring and one on the outer ring is suitable for carrying intermittent load in one direction in addition to radial load (Fig. 21.8d). It is commonly used on layshafts, the main positions in commercial vehicle gearboxes, in idler gears, and in hubs. The outer ring need not be clamped as it is located in one direction by the ends of the rollers, so that a single abutment adjacent to the lip is sufficient (see Figs 21.13, 21.19, 21.20, 21.21, and 21.22).

Figs 21.8e and 21.8f show types which have lips on both rings. They can carry some axial load in either direction in addition to radial load. The presence of the loose lip enables the normal complement of rollers to be fitted, and frequently offers advantages from the point of view of assembly and dismantling of the surrounding components. The type shown in Fig. 21.8e has been successfully used in hub applications in conjunction with those illustrated in Figs 21.8a and 21.8d. Those given in Figs 21.8e and 21.8f are used successfully on the input shafts, layshafts, and mainshafts of commercial vehicle gearboxes for carrying both radial and axial loading from helical gears (see Fig. 21.15).

Special cylindrical roller bearings

A variety of special, wide cylindrical roller bearings is in common use in driveline applications. These are generally used in heavily loaded positions where space is restricted, for example, gearbox spigot positions, in idler gears, and in planet pinions.

Where space is very limited it is common practice to provide hardened raceways direct on the shafts and/or in the bores of the gears, and use the cages and rollers only. In such cases, if it is not possible to obtain the case depth and full hardness normally associated with bearing rings, it may be necessary to apply a factor of safety on the calculated bearing capacities.

Typical examples of a few of these types of bearing are shown in Figs 21.9a to 21.9e, inclusive.

Bearings with multiple rows of caged standard rollers retained in two lipped inner rings (Figs 21.9a and 21.9b) are used on mainshaft spigots and sometimes in heavy duty planet gears (see Figs 21.15 and 21.19).

The bearing shown in Fig. 21.9e is used in a similar way to those shown in Figs 21.9a and 21.9b, but it makes use of a single row of long rollers. For a given overall width of bearing and roller diameter the calculated load capacity is higher with this type owing to the greater length of contact obtained for the rollers.

Special long caged rollers are commonly used in constant mesh spigot positions and in gearbox idler gears (Fig. 21.9d). The cage shown is of special construction without rivets so that it can accommodate a greater number of rollers. The end cap is retained by rolling over the ends of the cage bars.

Fig. 21.9e shows a type designed specifically for use in the idler gears in commercial and heavy-duty gearboxes. Two rows of rollers are well spaced apart in the cage to give a high degree of lateral stability.

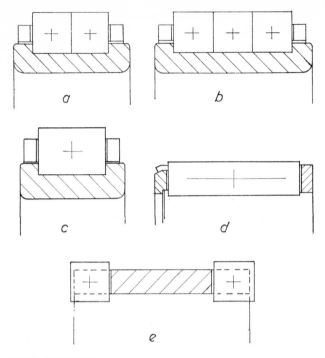

Fig. 21.9. Special cylindrical roller bearings

LOAD RATINGS

For ball and cylindrical roller bearings most bearing manufacturers have now accepted the I.S.O. load/life formulae as a basis for their load ratings. Information on the formulae is published in I.S.O. Recommendation R.281: Roller Bearings, Methods of Evaluating Dynamic Load Ratings. The formulae themselves are of little value to users without full details of the internal construction of the bearings. These details are not normally published, but most bearing manufacturers publish load ratings for their bearings based on the I.S.O. formulae. These can be used to calculate bearing lives for any set of load and speed conditions.

The load rating figure published is generally the C value, which is defined as: 'That constant stationary radial load which a group of apparently identical bearings with stationary outer ring can endure for a rating life of one million revolutions of the inner ring.' This means that where a radial or angular contact ball bearing is required to carry axial or both radial and axial loads, these loads must first be converted to the single equivalent radial load which would give the same life as that which the bearing would attain under the actual conditions of load and speed.

Full information on this procedure is given in I.S.O. Recommendation R.281, and it is also generally contained in individual bearing manufacturers' catalogues.

CALCULATION OF BEARING LOADS

The calculation of the axial loads coming on bearings in such applications as clutch-operating mechanisms is generally straightforward, but when selecting, or checking the suitability of, the bearings of any particular clutch application the maximum load that can arise in that particular design should be considered.

Similar remarks apply to the reaction loads on the ball bearings in the main positions in self-changing gearboxes, automatic transmissions, and overdrive gear units. In addition, the duration of these loads can often be assessed reasonably accurately. Units of this type generally employ epicyclic gears with a series of planet gears evenly spaced around the main axis. Therefore no substantial gear load is imposed on the main bearings, and the only radial loads are those due to the weight of the parts. Generally, these can be ignored, so that only the known axial loads have to be catered for.

In the cases of the planet gear bearings in transmission units, substantial radial loads are usually present. These loads must be calculated, based on the horse-power and speed, or torque, transmitted by the particular gear train.

In conventional change speed gearboxes, transfer boxes, and axle units, etc., calculation of the bearing loads from the gears again presents no difficulties where the horsepower and speed, or torque, transmitted is known. Full information on these calculations is published in catalogues and technical handbooks issued by the bearing manufacturers. The loads should be calculated as accurately as possible, the separating forces on gear teeth as well as the tangential forces being taken into consideration. On helical gears and bevel gears, not only must the axial loads be considered but also the additional radial loading they impose on the bearings due to their lines of action being offset from the shaft axis.

On the layshafts of some heavy-duty commercial vehicle gearboxes three bearing arrangements are used in order to limit shaft deflection. This complicates the load calculations, but an assessment can be made by treating the shaft as two separate spans. The loads thus calculated for the centre bearing will generally be lower than the true figures. If the bearing is found to have a generous amount of capacity in hand, as is often the case, the approximation may suffice.

BASIS OF BEARING LOAD CALCULATION

There are different views on the amount of the available engine torque that should be used when calculating bearing loads in transmission systems. This is because the torque transmitted varies considerably throughout the operating life of any given vehicle. In addition, a vehicle with a high power/weight ratio uses a smaller proportion of the available engine torque for the majority of its life and will make relatively little use of the gear ratios compared with a vehicle having a low power/weight ratio. More research is needed to provide reliable information on these points.

At present, bearing load calculations are usually based on one or more of the following:

(1) A percentage of the maximum engine torque available based empirically on the power/weight ratio of the vehicle.
(2) The maximum torque developed by the engine.
(3) The adhesion torque at the driving wheels.

When using (1) it is usual to assess the lives of the bearings in conjunction with the life requirements for the class of vehicle involved, and the following are often used as a basis:

	miles
	miles
Private cars	50 000
Trucks and light commercial vehicles	100 000
Heavy goods vehicles	200 000
Public service vehicles	200 000
Tractors	30 000
Cross-country vehicles	75 000

With this method it is also necessary to make some assessment of the operating times or proportion of the total milage in the various intermediate ratios. In the absence of reliable data on these subjects there is a variety of ideas, and manufacturers of similar vehicles quote quite different figures.

It is generally agreed that the bearing loads in gear transmission systems should in the first instance be calculated on the maximum torque that can be transmitted, as it is always important to know the maximum load that may come on the bearing. This will in most cases occur at the maximum engine torque condition, but in the lower gear ratios on some vehicles the maximum torque may be limited by wheel adhesion. Where this is the case, the torque should be calculated on the maximum load at the driving wheels. While it is common practice to assume $\mu = 0.8$, it is sometimes necessary to allow for $\mu = 1.0$ or even more on certain vehicles, particularly cross-country types and tractors.

PERMISSIBLE LOADING ON BEARINGS

The maximum permissible load on a bearing may exceed by a substantia margin the I.S.O. static rating (usually denoted by Co in bearing manufacturers' catalogues) where the bearing is rotating, but normally in gear transmission systems the maximum loads imposed should not be greater than $2 \times Co$.

Having obtained the maximum bearing loads by (2) or (3) it is very simple to derive the loads for (1) where all the necessary data are available, and to proceed from there to calculate the composite lives for the bearings, if this method is preferred.

An alternative method is to assess the suitability of the bearings on their maximum loads by calculating the I.S.O. lives for the individual bearings in each gear, ensuring that each of these lives is not less than a certain minimum value. This method is, of course, just as empirical as the previous method, but it has been found to be relatively quick and, when a background of data has been built up, just as reliable.

Values for the I.S.O. lives based on 90 per cent survival are given in the following tables for different classes of vehicle and transmission systems. These figures can be used as a general guide but may require amendment for abnormal conditions of duty.

Table 21.1 deals with conventional systems with a change-speed gearbox incorporating a direct drive for one of the upper ratios, usually fourth.

Most heavy duty commercial vehicles are provided with multi-speed gear transmission systems offering a range of up to ten or more speeds. In many cases,

Table 21.1. Conventional systems

Gear	Private cars		Light commercial vehicles		Public service and heavy goods vehicles	
	Four-speed	Five-speed	Four-speed	Five-speed	Four-speed	Five-speed
1st	25	25	25	25	30	30
2nd	35	45	40	50	250	300
3rd	50	70	80	100	500	600
4th	—	—	—	—	—	—
5th	—	160	—	300	—	750

particularly where used abroad, these vehicles may be required to operate for very long periods at a time in any one of the upper ratios, the driver having selected the ratio most suited to the prevailing road conditions. It is advisable therefore with such multi-speed drives to ensure the bearings have a calculated life of 750 h at maximum engine torque for all such high-range ratios, equivalent to fifth or above.

In automobiles having engines, gearboxes, and final drives built up as units, and situated either at the front or rear of the vehicle, the bearings taking the gear loads are generally loaded in all ratios, including top gear, and due allowance must be made for this additional duty. The conditions for the bearings are similar to those in conventional rear axles, and Table 21.2 gives life figures which have proved satisfactory under these conditions and can be used for both types of application.

Table 21.2. Life figures

Gear	Private cars		Light commercial vehicles		Cross-country vehicles		Public service and heavy goods	
	Four-speed	Five-speed	Four-speed	Five-speed	Four-speed	Five-speed	Four-speed	Five-speed
1st	25	25	25	25	25	25	35	35
2nd	60	60	70	70	70	70	350	350
3rd	90	90	130	130	130	130	650	650
4th	160	160	300	330	250	250	800	800
5th	—	160	—	330	—	250	—	800

Tractors

Bearings in the transmission systems of tractors require consideration rather different from that for other commercial vehicles, as prolonged running is more likely to occur in mid-gear ranges rather than in the top range. For both agricultural and industrial tractor gearbox bearings the minimum I.S.O. life based on maximum torque should not be less than 250 h in the gear which will have maximum use, or less than 35 h in the lowest ratio. The I.S.O. lives for the bearings in the other gears should lie between these values, the actual lives depending on the relative usage expected in service.

For the final drive bearings, which are loaded in all ratios, a similar procedure can be adopted; but for the maximum use gear condition the I.S.O. life should be increased to 300 h and in the lowest ratio to 45 h.

In all forms of transmission systems bearing sizes and types are frequently determined from considerations other than load capacity, and this often results in calculated lives substantially greater than the figures quoted. For the same reasons, other bearings may be heavily loaded only in one or two gears, and it is for these cases that the lives quoted provide guidance.

In the epicyclic gears of automatic transmissions, overdrives, and similar units where more than three planets are employed in each train, it cannot be assumed that the loading will be equally shared. In such cases the following empirical formula is often used:

$$F = \frac{N+3}{2}$$

where N is the total number of planets in the train and F the effective number under load.

PERMISSIBLE MALALIGNMENT

In gear transmission units there is normally little difficulty in obtaining accurate alignment of the components initially, but the effects of deflection under load must be considered. Rigid rolling bearings can withstand appreciable malalignment for short periods, but it is difficult to lay down hard and fast figures. These will depend upon the magnitude of the load on the bearing as well as the duration of the running periods and the degree of reliability expected from the application.

Where bearings are expected to carry substantial loading for appreciable periods it is recommended that the slope of the shaft at the bearing positions should be within 0·012 in/ft for rigid ball bearings and 0·006 in/ft for cylindrical roller bearings.

PRE-LOADING OF ANGULAR CONTACT BALL BEARINGS

Pre-loading is applied to rolling bearings in order to increase their rigidity under the working loads. This is important for hypoid and spiral bevel gears in final drives where deflections must be kept to a minimum to maintain correct meshing of the teeth. Angular contact bearings have an advantage over other types of angular contact bearings in that once correctly adjusted, the pre-load is maintained for long periods, as it is not associated with any plain rubbing surfaces, which tend to bed down rapidly.

The application of pre-load to a pair of angular contact ball bearings is illustrated in Fig. 21.10. The bearing rings have been specially faced during manufacture so that when clamped together during mounting the correct amount of pre-load is applied. Under this condition, when a working axial load is applied

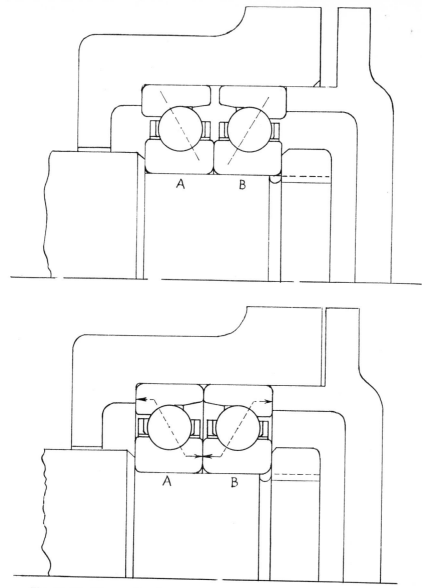

Fig. 21.10. The application of pre-load to two angular contact bearings

along the shaft, assuming from left to right, the row of balls 'A' will move away from load while the row of balls 'B' will move into load. Equilibrium will be reached when the total load on 'B' is greater than on row 'A' by the amount of the externally applied load.

In Fig. 21.11 the curve represents the thrust load/axial deflection relationship

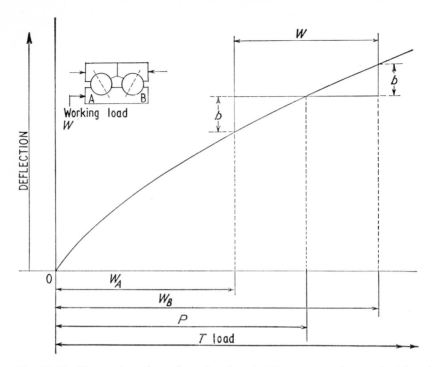

Fig. 21.11. The explanation of pre-loading double row angular contact bearings

for one row of balls. A curve of this nature can be plotted using equations (21.6), (21.7), and (21.9). In the case illustrated, a double row angular contact ball bearing is shown pre-loaded by an axial load of magnitude P. When an external working load W is applied from left to right, the axial deflection on row B is increased by an amount b, whereas the axial deflection on row A is decreased by a similar amount b, giving resultant loads W_B on row B and W_A on row A such that

$$W_B - W_A = W, \quad \text{the working load}$$

It will be appreciated that the externally applied working load W must be greater than the initial pre-load P before the load W_A on row A becomes zero and row B is carrying the full working load. Even under this condition the total end movement under load would be only half what it would have been without the initial pre-load P.

Excessive pre-load must be avoided, as this will reduce the lives of the bearings. A useful guide for final drive bearings is to apply sufficient pre-load to maintain both rows of rolling elements in load when the bearings are subjected to an axial load equivalent to that developed when transmitting full torque in top gear. The resulting deflection characteristics of the pre-loaded bearing may have to be examined in the light of any limitations imposed from the point of view of gear-tooth meshing.

On differential gear carriers pre-loading of AC type bearings may be applied either by means of ring nuts or by the use of shims. The operation must be carefully carried out, as it is easy to overload the bearings. The normal procedure is first to take up the free end movement in the bearing assembly and then apply the pre-load either by a further tightening of the ring nut by a pre-calculated amount, or by inserting additional shims of the required thickness.

CLUTCH-OPERATING BEARINGS

As mentioned, clutch-operating bearing conditions are not usually arduous from the loading aspect. This is partly because the bearing size may be determined by the sleeve component on which it is mounted and partly due to the small proportion of the total running time of the vehicle during which full load occurs. There is a possibility of greater malalignment of clutch-operating bearings compared with other driveline bearings, and this imposes additional duties on the bearing and the lubricant.

The bearing must be as near concentric as possible with the axis of the clutch. Eccentricity can give rise to wear on the operating surfaces with the consequent release of debris which may contaminate the lubricant. It also imposes abnormal radial load on the clutch parts and the bearing. Out of squareness or tilt across the bearing imposes severe duty on the bearing cage, with increased demands on the lubricant. This should be kept within 0·030 in/ft if a reasonable standard of reliability is to be obtained.

Most clutch-operating bearings are pre-lubricated with grease, which may determine the useful life of the bearing, and it must therefore meet the arduous conditions involved. The grease must retain its lubricating properties at high ambient temperatures over a long period of time and operate in bearings with rotating outer rings without undue separation.

On heavy-duty commercial vehicles and tractors, provision is sometimes made for injecting fresh grease at intervals, but this is rarely the case in automobiles. An alternative arrangement used for many years by a well-known British automobile manufacturer is shown in Fig. 21.16, whereby the bearing is lubricated by oil from the gearbox.

DRIVING WHEEL HUB BEARINGS

The operating conditions for the hub bearings in driving wheels depend to a considerable extent upon the type of drive involved. Axle types in general use are semi-floating, three-quarter floating, and fully floating, the bearings for independently sprung driving wheels being dealt with in the same way as those on fully floating axles.

In all cases two conditions have to be considered.

Straight ahead

The load should be calculated on the maximum laden weight at the wheel and also the tangential load at the tyre when transmitting full torque in top gear. The bearings should then be selected to meet the lives specified under the section headed 'Basis of bearing load calculation', allowance being made for the fact that with three-quarter floating and fully floating axles the outer rings of the bearings are rotating.

Cornering

The basis of the load calculation under cornering conditions depends upon the class of vehicle. In all cases the maximum laden weight of the vehicle should be considered, and for private cars it is usual to consider cornering at 0·5g for family saloons and 0·75g for sports cars. For both light and heavy commercial vehicles, cornering at 0·25g is normally assumed to be adequate.

Semi-floating and three-quarter floating axles are usually restricted to private cars and light commercial vehicles. In both types it is normal to use a single radial ball bearing in each hub. When cornering, the bearings are subjected to radial and axial loading, and to a bending moment due to the offset axial load. This bending

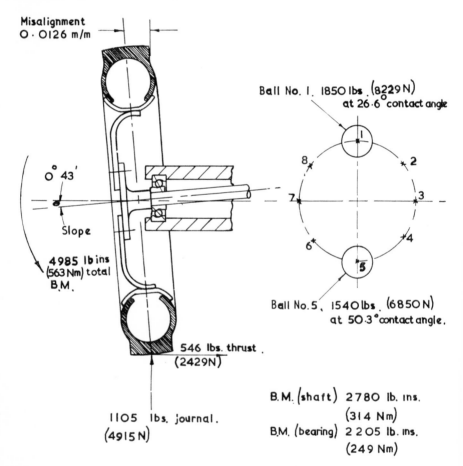

Fig. 21.12. Ball load in rear hub bearings

moment is partly resisted by the half-shaft, but in current designs 50 per cent of this bending moment may come on to the bearing. This can impose heavy stresses, and unless a background of experience is available with similar designs and loading conditions, it is advisable to refer the details to a bearing manufacturer who will, if necessary, calculate the loading and contact angles at individual balls in the bearing.

An example of the conditions that can occur is illustrated in Fig. 21.12, which shows considerable variation between the ball contact angles round the bearing. These range from 26·6° at one side to 50·3° at the opposite side and represent the diagonal path of the balls. Every ball in load, therefore, experiences a change in velocity as it travels round the bearing, and the cage is thus very heavily stressed. It is only because of the relative infrequency and short duration of these conditions that bearings are able to operate, as no bearing could be expected to run continuously under heavy load in what is virtually a fully canted condition. Moulded nylon cages stand up to these conditions particularly well and are preferable to pressed-steel cages where temperature conditions permit their use.

With independently sprung wheels and fully floating axles using two bearings well spaced in each hub, normal methods can be used for calculating the cornering loads. For heavy commercial vehicles it is desirable to ensure that there is a minimum I.S.O. life under these load conditions of 1000 miles. For cars a check should be made to ensure that peak loads do not exceed twice the Co value, unless adequate background experience or test data are available.

On lighter vehicles and cars where one double row angular contact ball bearing might be used in each hub, or two single row angular contact bearings with the span of their effective centres less than the pitch circle diameter of the balls, a complete analysis of the ball loading conditions may be necessary, as for the single row radial bearings on semi- and three-quarter floating axles.

ACKNOWLEDGEMENTS

The author would like to express his thanks to the following companies for their kind permission to reproduce the following: Fig. 21.13, Commercial vehicle gearbox, David Brown Industries; Fig. 21.14, Automobile gearbox, Standard Triumph Engineering; Fig. 21.15, Commercial vehicle gearbox, Albion Motors Ltd; Fig. 21.16, Automobile clutch and gearbox applications, The Rover Co. Ltd; Fig. 21.17, Front hub arrangement, British Motor Corporation Ltd; Fig. 21.18, Propeller shaft centre bearing, Scammell Lorries Ltd; Fig. 21.19, Front axle drive, Scammell Lorries Ltd; Fig. 21.20, Six-speed heavy-duty gearbox, Scammell Lorries Ltd; Fig. 21.21, 'Stalwart' transfer box, Alvis Ltd; Fig. 21.22, Double reduction rear axle, Maudslay Motor Co. Ltd.

APPENDIX 21.1

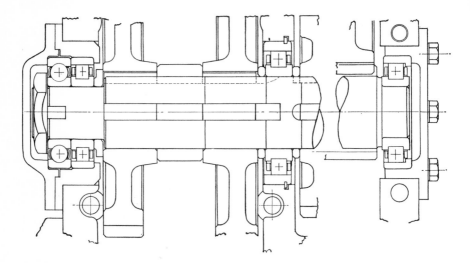

Fig. 21.13. David Brown gearbox. Three-bearing layshaft

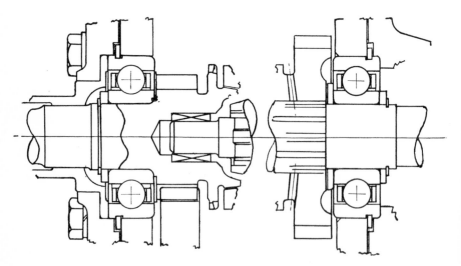

Fig. 21.14. Standard Triumph gearbox. Constant mesh and mainshaft bearings

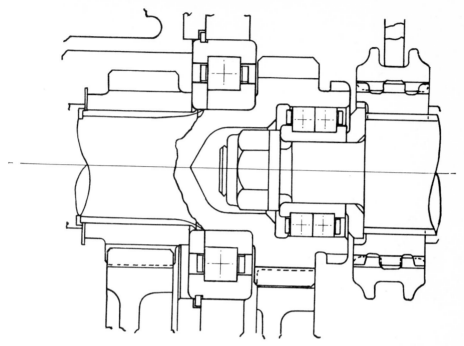

Fig. 21.15. Albion gearbox. Constant mesh pinion and spigot bearings

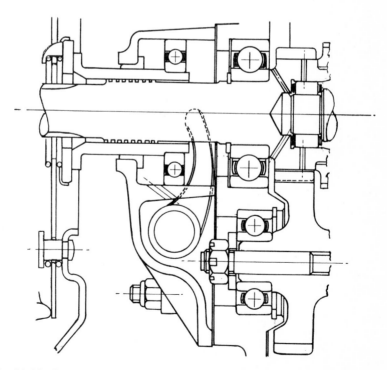

Fig. 21.16. Rover clutch operation. Constant mesh and clutch bearings

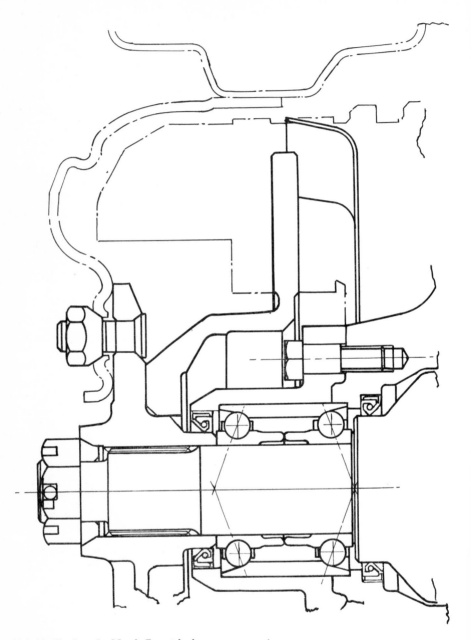

Fig. 21.17. Austin Maxi. Front hub arrangement

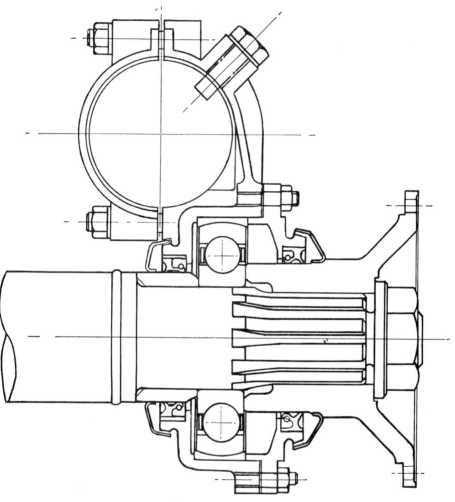

Fig. 21.18. Scammell. Propeller shaft centre bearing

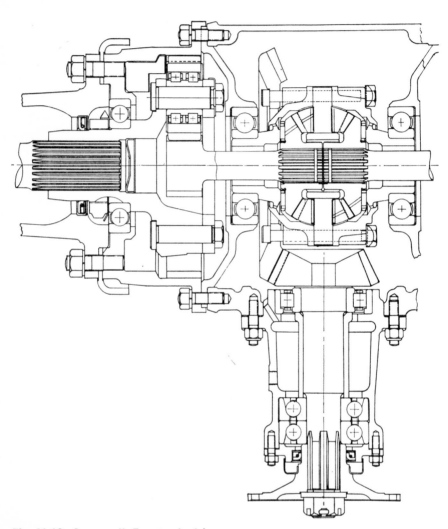

Fig. 21.19. Scammell. Front axle drive

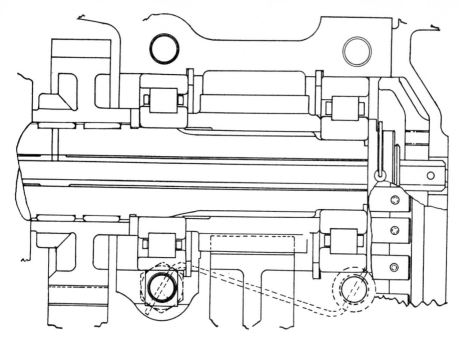

Fig. 21.20. Scammell. Application from six-speed gearbox

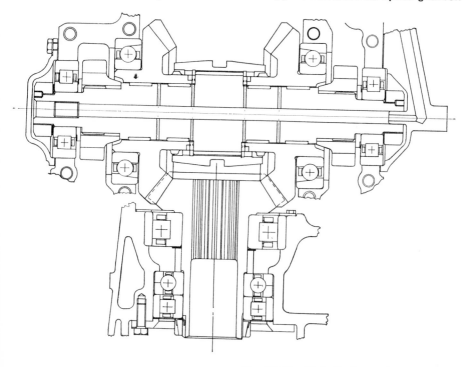

Fig. 21.21. Alvis Stalwart. Transfer box

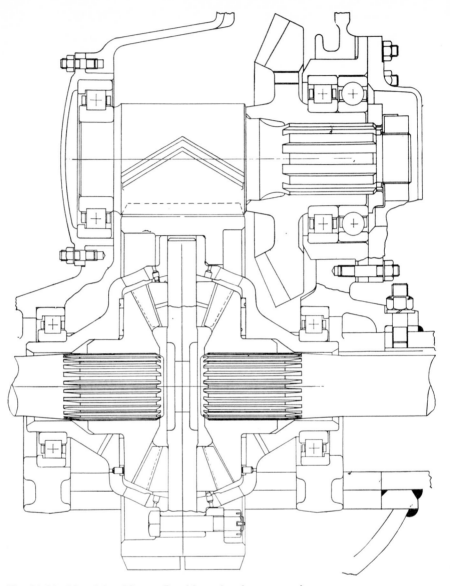

Fig. 21.22. Maudslay Motor. Double reduction rear axle

The MS. of this paper was received at the Institution on 15th October 1969 and accepted for publication on 3rd November 1969.

Paper 22. Tapered Roller Bearings in Automotive Drivelines

T. G. BARNBROOK, CEng, MIMechE
British Timken Division, The Timken Roller Bearing Co.

Important features of taper roller bearings which influence their suitability for use in various driveline applications are reviewed. The meaning of bearing life and capacity is explained and a method of arriving at weighted average loadings is considered. A new type of taper roller bearing, first designed for the rear wheels of fixed axles, is described and comments are made on its use for other automotive applications.

DESIGN AND SPECIAL FEATURES OF THE BEARING

The special features of tapered roller bearings which make them so useful for automotive drivelines are their ability to accept heavy loads (including shock loads) in all directions, their axial and radial rigidity, and their adjustability. Although they have been used for wheels for 70 years, these properties were highlighted through the use of the hypoid gear for axle centres.

Fig. 22.1 shows the cross-section of the bearing, and it will be seen that all the rolling surfaces are parts of cones having a common apex, thus giving a true rolling motion. The different angles of the inner ring and outer ring, known as the cone and cup, ensure that a component of the load is carried through the large end of the roller and the cone rib. This, combined with the geometry of the roller and rib, keeps the rollers in their true position so that the entire length is used for load-carrying purposes and that hydrodynamic lubrication occurs between the roller end and rib, thereby preventing wear. Special techniques of grinding and honing of the rolling surfaces reduce edge loading. A bearing may be designed to suit any purpose by varying the cup, cone, roller angle, and length and diameter of roller.

Adjustability

Unlike most other types of anti-friction bearing, the internal clearance of the bearing is not built in at manufacture, but is adjusted at the fitting stage to the desired clearance or preload. The fit of the cone on the shaft or the cup in the housing, which in other types modifies the internal adjustment, is compensated for by end adjustment of either cup or cone. Normally, this adjustment is by nut for the cone or by shims or spacer for the cup.

Preload or endplay

To obtain the maximum life of a bearing it is best that all the rolling elements are in contact with the tracks of the races under running conditions. This ideal condition does not always exist in driveline applications. Other requirements or

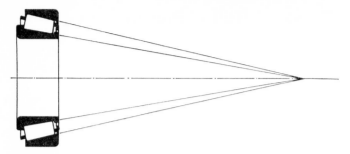

Fig. 22.1. Cross-section of tapered roller bearing showing bearing apex

continually varying loading conditions modify this. Also, because of the temperature variations leading to differential expansion, the bearing setting in the cold condition will be different from the warm running conditions. The heat generated by the gears, bearings, clutch, etc. must travel outwards and be dissipated on the outside of the gearbox or housing which then acts as a radiator. In most cases this is helped by the rapid movement of air over the housings due to the speed of the vehicle. Tapered roller bearings have been running in drivelines for many years and a lot of information has been accumulated which enables us to decide on the correct setting, provided all the facts relating to such things as the material of the housing, the thickness of the housing, and the viscosity and quantity of the oil are correct. A few typical figures for adjustment are:

Gearboxes/trucks 0·001–0·003 in (0·025–0·080 mm) endplay.
Gearboxes/cars 0·001 in (0·025 mm) preload to 0·002 in (0·050 mm) endplay.
Rear axle/pinion 0·002 in (0·050 mm) preload for small cars to 0·001 in (0·025 mm) endplay for large trucks.

It is difficult to give figures for the differential because of the elasticity of the mating parts, and it is best to set initially to a torque figure and then interpret this in terms of stretch of the casing. A typical torque figure for a small car would be 5–15 lb in (0·6–1·7 N m).

Drive wheels 0·001 in (0·025 mm) preload to 0·005 in (0·130 mm) endplay.

If housings are made from aluminium alloy then these figures would be modified. This is referred to later.

BEARING MATERIAL

Opinions differ concerning the right material for tapered roller bearings. Some manufacturers believe that through-hardening ball bearing steel is suitable. We are firmly in favour of high-quality alloy case carburizing steel which is heat treated to give a hard wear-resistant surface on the outside and a tough shock-resistant core. This material has the added advantage that, should a fatigue crack develop in the case, it will not extend beyond the area where the case and core merge. Catastrophic failure is thereby prevented. This steel and its heat treatment are more expensive, but long experience of the bearing in critical applications where durability and safety are essential has proved that the extra cost is worthwhile.

CHOICE OF BEARING

The useful life of a bearing will be decided by wear or a fatigue breakdown of the rolling surfaces. Wear can be caused by the shortage of lubricant or by abrasive particles in the lubricant. If the degree of wear is small the bearing can be readjusted. Usually, if a seal breaks down, allowing lubricant to escape or dirt to enter, it is not discovered until the bearing or other vital parts are irretrievably damaged. Wear of the pinion or differential bearings may be caused by many faults, and these will be dealt with later.

The other reason for bearing renewal is fatigue breakdown and this is the basis of bearing capacity and life calculations. If a number of bearings are tested under the same conditions of load and speed, there will be a wide range in the resultant bearing life, and bearing manufacturers throughout the world have consequently adopted the practice of relating bearing capacity to that life which 90 per cent of the bearings will survive. The criterion of failure with tapered roller bearings is a surface spalling of $0·01$ in^2 (6 mm^2). This is the bearing makers' laboratory assessment and does not mean that the bearing is unfit for further service. Lives which are four or five times greater than the life corresponding to this criterion have been reached in service. Catalogue ratings are given as the load that can be carried at 500 rev/min for 3000 h; that is, 90×10^6 revolutions. These are easily convertible for any other load, speed, and life. The method of calculating the bearing load is given in bearing makers' catalogues and is fairly easy. However, the assessment of the vehicle duties is not so easy; for example, the number of miles a private car is driven per year, the average and peak loading, the area in which the car is driven, and the quality of the driver, can vary over a very wide range. We can use engine power or vehicle tractive effort, or perhaps both, as a guide. For the driving axle we have chosen tractive effort at the wheel related to gross vehicle weight for a certain average speed. This has been checked over many years and we have periodically modified the values in line with service records to obtain a bearing size which is acceptable to the manufacturer and the user for both cost and reliability.

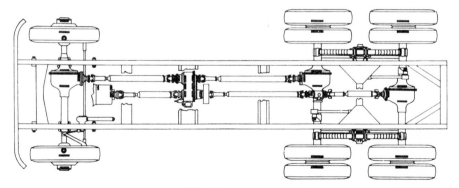

Fig. 22.2. Tapered roller bearings on 6 × 6 truck

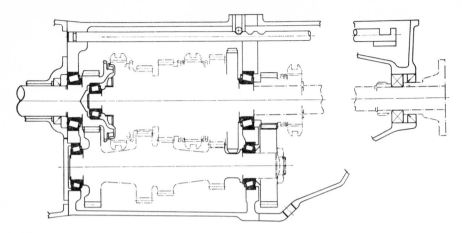

Fig. 22.3. Five-speed gearbox

It is proposed now to give a brief description of the positions in which tapered roller bearings are used in drivelines, and later to deal with the special problems of fits, effect of different housing materials, and the important factor in rear axle centres of wear.

APPLICATIONS

Fig. 22.2 shows the position in which these bearings are used in a 6 × 6 truck. There are 43 tapered roller bearings on the driveline alone.

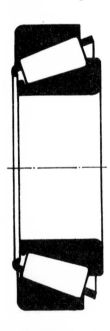

Fig. 22.4. 40° angle bearing

Gearboxes

These can be categorized for passenger cars, trucks, and buses. For passenger cars, tapered roller bearings are used in the five main positions and Fig. 22.3 illustrates this for a five-speed gearbox. These are the input shaft rear, the mainshaft rear, the pocket position between the two, and the layshaft front and rear. The outer race of the pocket bearing is integral with the input shaft rear because of space limitations. Note that although there are three bearings in line on the primary and mainshafts, only one bearing has to be adjusted.

Driving axle centres (cars)

In the days when spiral bevel gears were used in driving axle centres, bearings

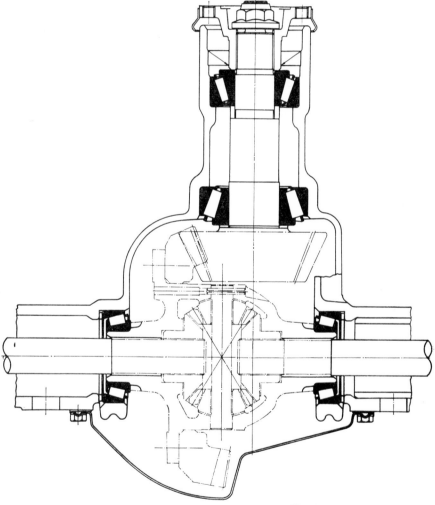

Fig. 22.5. Rear axle centre

could be chosen directly from the catalogue; that is, bearings which were origin-ally designed for other purposes. With the introduction of hypoid gears it was soon clear that with the more exacting requirements of axial and radial rigidity, new bearings would have to be designed. To obtain the required axial rigidity the angle of the cup was steepened, and to retain the radial rigidity the rollers were lengthened considerably and made smaller in diameter to enable more rollers to be included. Some of these differences meant that new methods of manufacture had to be developed. This resulted in the 40° angle bearing which is now universally adopted by all makers of pinion bearings (Fig. 22.4).

Because it is so convenient to use the nut which holds the driving flange to adjust or hold the front pinion bearing, it has been found necessary to hold the flange and bearing rigidly in an axial direction (Fig. 22.5). If this is not done the splines in the driving flange fret severely owing to movement caused by bending and torsion. This can be prevented by using a solid or collapsible spacer between (a) the cone small ends or (b) the front bearing cone and a shoulder on the shaft. If a collapsible spacer is adopted then a semi-automatic method of assembly can be used which collapses the spacer until the required bearing torque is obtained. Owing to the type of construction of the axle centre, differential bearings are very rarely held rigidly in an axial direction, and here again bearing torque can be used as a guide to bearing adjustment.

Rear axle centre (car, box type)

This is a newer type of axle centre with the two tapered roller bearings straddling

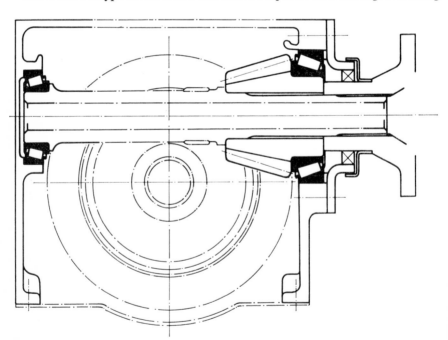

Fig. 22.6. Rear axle centre, car, box type

the pinion (see Fig. 22.6). The pinion mesh is obtained by a spacer between the rear bearing cup and the end wall of the casing. The bearing adjustment is by graduated spacer between the front bearing cup and the pinion shaft endcover, which also acts as a seal carrier.

The differential centre has to be modified to allow the pinion shaft to pass across the crown-wheel. Although not shown in the figure, oilways are built into the axle casing to feed oil to the front pinion bearing.

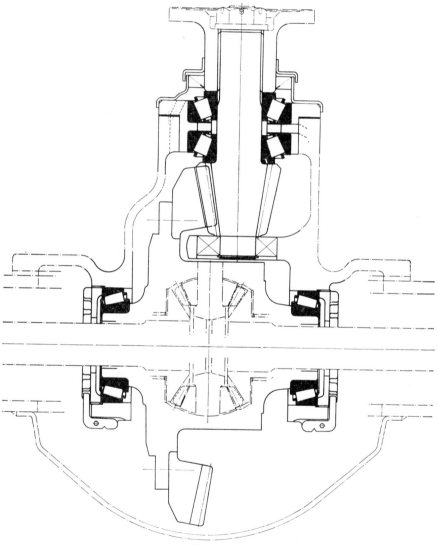

Fig. 22.7. Single reduction axle centre, truck

Single reduction axle centre (trucks)

In truck axle centres (Fig. 22.7) the pinion can be overhung but is more normally straddle mounted; that is, it has an outboard support (usually a cylindrical roller bearing) mounted in a housing which lies between the end of the pinion and the differential centre. Owing to the restrictions of space, this housing can

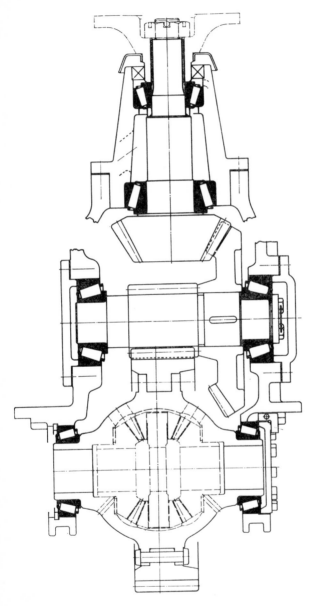

Fig. 22.8. Rear axle
double reduction, truck

very rarely be given enough support. The two tapered roller bearings on the pinion shaft are steep angled and are usually mounted in an adaptor for ease of assembly and adjustment; that is, the correct bearing adjustment can be built in before assembling it into the axle housing and gear mesh can be effected by shims between the bearing carrier flange and the front face of the housing.

Truck rear axle double reduction

In this example (see Fig. 22.8) the driving shaft is mounted about 10 in above the axle centre. This permits the design to be adapted to drive on to a second driving axle by extending the pinion shaft. The first reduction is by the bevel pinion to a crown-wheel on the cross-shaft. Also mounted on the cross-shaft is a spur or helical gear which meshes with a gear mounted on the differential centre, thus giving the second reduction.

Tapered roller bearings are used at the six positions. The pinion bearings are preloaded as in the single reduction axle. The cross-shaft is adjusted by means of shims under the endcover and the differential, which no longer has the tilting forces from the crown-wheel but the lesser thrust force from the helical or spur gear. A slight clearance can be allowed.

To simplify assembly the gears on the cross-shaft are threaded on to it whilst in position on the axle.

Transaxles (cars), front wheel drive

Transaxles, which are a combination of the gearbox and axle centre, are used in either front wheel drive cars or in rear wheel drives when the engine is at the rear. Fig. 22.9 shows a front engined, front wheel drive. The idler gear, which is

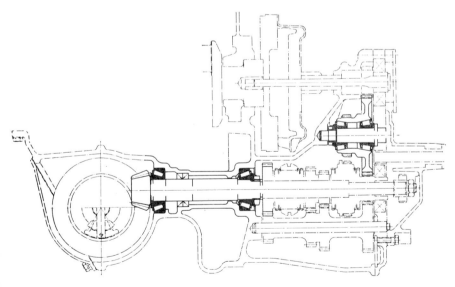

Fig. 22.9. Transaxle front wheel drive, car

mounted on two tapered roller bearing cones, connects the clutch extension to the main gear shafts. As space is limited, the bearing cups are integral with the idler gear. The pinion shaft is an extension of the mainshaft and has two tapered roller bearings.

Transaxles (cars), rear wheel drive

This is the type of transaxle normally used for a rear engined, rear wheel drive car (see Fig. 22.10). The power enters the input shaft at the front end. The pinion shaft is also the gearbox mainshaft. Although the gears on the shaft are in mesh,

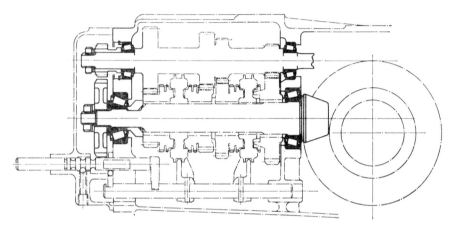

Fig. 22.10. Transaxle rear wheel drive, car

none is directly driven. The tapered roller bearings on the input shaft are adjusted by a graduated spacer between the backface of the rear cup and the snap ring. Unlike the normal pinion mounting, the adjustment of the two tapered roller bearings on the pinion shaft is by a nut behind the reverse gear—no spacer being required.

Front driving axle car, independently sprung wheels

In this application the inner races or cones rotate while the cups are stationary (see Fig. 22.11). The cones can be mounted on the driving shaft or tubular extension of the driving flange, which itself is splined on to the driving shaft. The bearing cones, separated by a solid spacer, are locked endwise by means of the driving shaft nut through the backface of the inner cone on to a shoulder on the driving shaft. Because of disc brakes the bearings are finally adjusted to a small endplay or preload. A feature of this design is that the bearing adjustment is obtained by a method known as 'set-right'. This is based on probability, and only one size of spacer is used. The bearing length and associated parts are held to closer than normal tolerances. In this case the extreme range of adjustment is 0·001 in (0·025 mm) preload to 0·005 in (0·130 mm) endplay. The faces which abut the bearing cones are hardened to inhibit fretting corrosion which would lead to a loss of adjustment and clamping force. Lubrication is by grease.

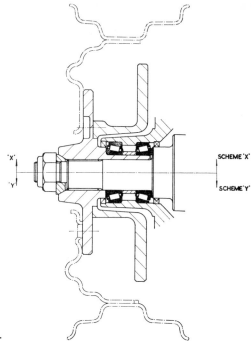

Fig. 22.11. Front driving axle,
independently sprung wheels, car

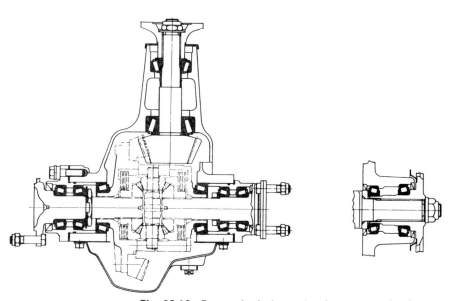

Fig. 22.12. Rear axle, independently sprung wheels, car

Rear axle with independently sprung wheels (car)

In the example shown (Fig. 22.12), there are two universal joints between the axle centre and each wheel. Owing to the design of suspension some of the thrust from the wheel is applied back to the axle centre even in straight-ahead drive. The axle centre is similar to solid axles except for the mounting of the quarter shaft. The differential bearings do not take any of the wheel load and the two outboard bearings mounted on each quarter shaft accept thrust loads from the wheels and loads induced by the disc brakes. The differential bearings are adjusted by shims under the outboard bearing adaptor flange while the outboard bearings are adjusted by a solid spacer between their cones. The two wheel bearings at each side are adjusted by preselected spacers between the end face of the driving sleeve and the inner abutment ring.

Front wheel drive truck

Two tapered roller bearings are mounted on a stationary tube similar to a fully floating rear wheel (see Fig. 22.13). Experience has indicated that the wheel tube should have a hardness of not less than 290 Brinell where the bearings are seated. This will prevent a localized collapse of the tube induced by the shock loads passing through the bearing on to the tube. Steep angle bearings are used on the steering pivot and enclose the constant velocity joint.

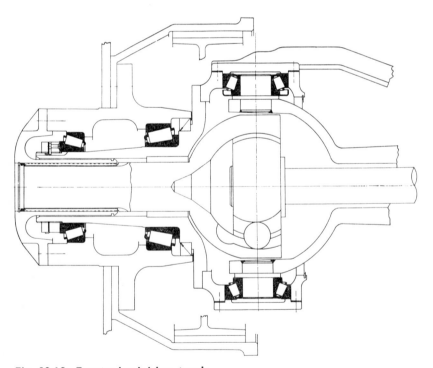

Fig. 22.13. Front wheel drive, truck

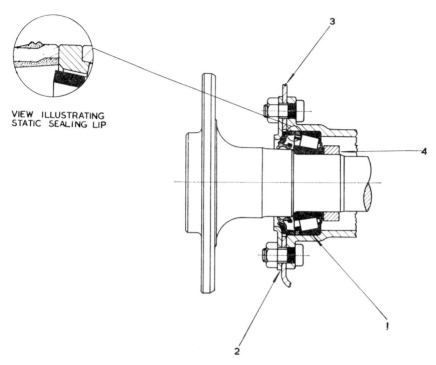

VIEW ILLUSTRATING
STATIC SEALING LIP

Fig. 22.14. Semi-floating rear wheels

Rear wheels (semi-floating)

The older method of using tapered roller bearings is to have a single bearing in each wheel with the cone of the bearing fitted to the drive shaft, having a shrunk-on ring or nut to prevent axial movement with the cup in the stationary housing (see Fig. 22.14). The inner ends of the drive shaft are separated by a pad in the differential centre. This allows each bearing to take thrust from one direction only; the inward thrust, say, from the offside being carried on the nearside bearing, and vice versa. This is a very successful application but has the slight disadvantage that the bearing has to be adjusted by shims under the housing cover at one end. To overcome this a new bearing has recently been developed. It still uses tapered rollers and still has all the advantages of the tapered construction but it differs from the more normal bearing in that the cone thrust rib has been transferred to the cup. The small end of the roller, as well as the large end, is ground accurately and the cone small rib, which normally only serves to prevent the bearing falling apart until it is fitted, now acts as a secondary rib. This is a self-contained bearing capable of taking thrust from both directions. The thrust pad at the centre is no longer required and each bearing can sustain thrust loads in both directions. No adjustment is necessary. These bearings are now in production and the prototypes have run well over 100 000 miles each (160 000 km).

LIGHT ALLOY HOUSINGS

There has been a tendency to use aluminium alloy for rear axle centres, gear-boxes, and transaxle casings. For bearings there are two important differences from the more usual iron and steel. These differences, and how they modify bearing usage, are listed below:

(1) The linear coefficient of expansion for aluminium is more than twice that of iron and steel. For a given rise in temperature the aluminium alloy will expand much more and therefore heavier bearing fits should be used. There is a big difference in using aluminium for cars to that of stationary equipment, and this is the very great cooling effect when the vehicle is travelling. It has the effect of an automatically adjusted fan and lower interference fits than one might at first expect can be used; the faster the vehicle goes, the more heat is generated but at the same time the cooling is more effective. For these conditions we would recommend the average of the fits normally given for steel and aluminium alloy. For the differential the normal fit for steel or malleable iron housings is loose to allow the cup to align itself. Here a tight or transitional fit is preferred.

(2) The elastic modulus of aluminium alloy is a little over one-third that of steel, and this means that for aluminium alloy gearboxes of similar section there is some diaphragming of the end of the boxes and, to a lesser degree, this occurs in the rear axle. Because of this care has to be taken in the method of measuring the preload to ensure that apparent preload is not lost in housing elasticity.

HYPOID GEARS AND LOSS OF ADJUSTMENT

The hypoid rear axle centre has been with us for many years. This type of gear increases the load on the bearing and necessitates the use of an e.p. oil of high viscosity for the gears. The much heavier loads and the need for greater rigidity meant that tapered roller bearings were a necessity, but the use of the special e.p. oil introduced new problems for the bearings. If the pinion bearings can be isolated from the rest of the axle and lubricated with a mineral oil of medium viscosity, no wear would be discovered over many years despite the heavy loads. However, this is impractical and with some oils we must live with a minute loss of adjustment. This can be comparable with the wear of the gears, so that in a well-designed and clean axle with correct oil, no adverse effects are apparent. Over the last 20 years the author has catalogued a number of faults which have in each case caused apparent loss in preload of the pinion bearings; these can be divided into the following four groups:

(1) Wear due to abrasive attack.
(2) Wear due to lubricant flow problems and quality of oil.
(3) Changes due to stress relief, incorrect manufacture and fitting, or bad design.
(4) Incorrect bearings (deflection of bearings or wrong choice of bearing).

Some of the reasons (marked with an asterisk) are dealt with in the paper by Wren entitled 'Laboratory testing of automotive drive axles' (Paper 44 at this conference) and are not detailed in the following list.

Wear due to abrasive attack

(*a*) Abrasive particles. These can be of two types: particles left in the axle casing or wheel tube at assembly. They may be from the sand core of the casting process, from sand or shot blasting before machining, or they may be just dirt. Examples have been known of sand lodging in the U form of a pressed sheet metal endcover.

(*b*) Wear particles from gear or differential parts.

(*c*)* Abrasive from gear-marking compound.

(*d*) Gear hardening. Bad heat treatment of gears can lead to their wear and release of abrasive particles. If the lapping process of the gears has not been under full load, pieces of hardened scale can later be released when under full load.

(*e*)* Running-in compound left in gears.

(*f*)* Abrasiveness of oil. E.p. oils contain additives which can remove bearing material.

(*g*) Sand or similar material, collected around the breather opening, drawn into the axle when it cools. The solution in this case is to extend the breather pipe to a protected part of the vehicle.

(*h*) Products of fretting corrosion. If pinion shaft is not large enough in diameter the faces of mating parts may fret and release abrasive particles.

Wear due to lubricant flow problems and quality of oil

(*a*) Oil passing up the axle tube when turning a long curve starves the axle centre of oil. Baffles can prevent this.

(*b*) Restriction of oil to front bearing. It is important, particularly with the smaller pinion bearings, to design the oil channel between the bearings so that the oil is directed at the gap between the cone and cup. We have seen several cases where the oil has been directed to a spot which is screened and no oil has got through to the bearing.

(*c*) Initial starvation of oil to the front bearing. This occurs if a car is driven too hard before the oil has a chance to get round throughout the axle. A solution to this problem is to smear the rollers of the front bearing lightly with grease. Sometimes motoring of the axle to test gear contacts at low speeds with no oil also causes a smearing of the rib of the bearing.

(*d*) Low oil level. The space in a rear axle is not very great and what appears to be a good level on a drawing board often proves too low in practice. We have seen many cases where the oil level has been raised in fairly new axles.

(*e*) Return of oil from the front of the front pinion bearing restricted. This prevents new oil getting in and makes the entrapped oil hotter.

(*f*) Flinger between front seal and front cone backface too close to cone backface. Oil cannot get through and this causes surging; this leads to overheating.

(*g*)* We have found a large difference between various makes of oils for limited slip differentials as far as their effect on wear is concerned, particularly when high temperatures are involved.

(*h*) Oil return in front of front bearing at too low a position. This should be high enough to allow a well of oil between the two bearings.

(*i*) Poor seals leading to a loss of oil (very rare). Damage of seals occurs at initial fitting and this also leads to a loss of oil.

(*j*) Tilt of pinion excessive, causing starvation of oil at the front position.

(*k*) Wear due to chemical attack following breakdown of the oil caused by excessively high temperatures or the presence of moisture in the axle.

(*l*) Rear axle design used at front of vehicle without modification to the oil collecting and distribution system so that oil is directed away from the front bearing.

Changes due to stress relief, incorrect manufacture and fitting, or bad design

(*a*) Stretching and settling of gear casing.

(*b*) Bad fitting of bearings, spacers, and flange of pinion. If the cups are pressed in carelessly they may create burrs which prevent the cup settling correctly on its backface. Out-of-squareness of nuts, flange faces, and spacer faces. Hardened washer out of parallel and soft washers may permit deformation.

(*c*) Severe out-of-alignment of housings, cup bores, and faces.

(*d*)* Bad gear shapes leading to local loads and wear. Also bad initial positioning of gears.

(*e*) Excessive preload. This may lead to initial smearing of roller ends and rib.

(*f*) Bearings not turned when fitted so that bearing rollers are not in their correct position and apparent preload may be endplay.

(*g*) Ribbing of casing excessive in relation to the thickness of the casing, causing local stressing of the cup.

(*h*) Weakness of design of axle causing excessive distortion leading to wear.

(*i*) Ring gear not stiffened due to cut-away parts of differential carrier.

Incorrect bearings (deflection of bearings or wrong choice of bearing)

(*a*) Defective bearings. Hypoid pinion bearings are very critical parts of the assembly. Over the years techniques of manufacture have been developed to minimize wear in this type of application.

(*b*) Wrong choice of bearing. Not rigid enough for the application. This occasionally occurs when a successful axle is uprated without changing the bearings.

ACKNOWLEDGEMENT

The author wishes to thank the Timken Roller Bearing Company for the information given in this paper and for their permission to use it.

The MS. of this paper was received at the Institution on 29th August 1969 and accepted for publication on 10th November 1969.

Paper 23. Needle Bearings and their Applications in Automotive Industries

W. HOFFMAN
Ina Needle Bearings AG, Nadellager, W. Germany

The author describes briefly the development of needle roller bearings since 1922. Various types of modern bearings are described and illustrated and many of the examples illustrate up-to-date applications in driveline components.

INTRODUCTION

With the development of the motor car into the mass means of transport which it has become today, the anti-friction bearing in its automotive applications gained ever-increasing importance. In particular, the requirements and demands of vehicle and engine builders gave stimuli to anti-friction bearing technology, which resulted in more suitable and improved bearing designs. Nowadays, needle bearings form a considerable proportion of all anti-friction bearings used in automotive engineering.

The accelerated progress of the automotive industries after the war has continuously confronted designers with new and formidable tasks. The trend towards more compact designs, coupled with the rising output from power units, has, in turn, created considerable problems for the anti-friction bearing industry. The overall height of the classical types of anti-friction bearings presented drawbacks. New ways and means had to be found to satisfy the ever-increasing demands made on anti-friction bearings.

Product development in the bearing industry is by necessity slow because every solution recognized as an improvement presupposes the development of economic and suitable means of mass production. The first needle bearings in motor cars became available in the thirties. They were mainly used in secondary applications, where they replaced plain friction bearings. A period of almost 20 years elapsed before the needle bearing gained its rightful spread of applications in motor cars. It mostly replaced plain bearings, which could not be further developed to accommodate increasing outputs and improvements of designs.

In the early design stages the designer faces the choice of incorporating either a plain bearing or an anti-friction bearing, partly because of the low overall height offered by the plain bearing. In order to illustrate that both the plain bearing and the anti-friction bearing have their advantages and disadvantages, a comparison will be made of the two types, elaborating further on the anti-friction bearing and more particularly on the needle bearing, which is a type of anti-friction bearing.

ANTI-FRICTION BEARINGS

In general, the following are the advantages of the anti-friction bearing:

(1) Low friction characteristics. Friction during start-up is no higher than running friction.

(2) The low demands made on maintenance and lubrication. The use of grease as a lubricant is particularly advantageous when considering the ever-increasing periods between services.

(3) The possibility of applying loads from all directions. Generally, it can be said that it is immaterial from which direction load is applied to an anti-friction bearing.

(4) Depending on the design of the anti-friction bearing, the high axial load-carrying capacity. Known types of bearings are capable of taking simultaneously high radial and axial loads.

(5) All anti-friction bearings distinguish themselves by short axial lengths.

(6) Anti-friction bearings are equally suitable for low revolutions.

(7) The high degree of security in performance, provided the correct type of bearing is selected.

Naturally, anti-friction bearings do have some disadvantages, and these are now listed:

(1) In many applications anti-friction bearings are sensitive to shock and impact loads. A phenomenon which we call 'false brinelling' is often encountered in automotive anti-friction bearing applications. However, there are solutions to counter such a contingency and these will be discussed later.

(2) Anti-friction bearings cannot always be operated at their maximum speeds without certain special safeguards.

PLAIN BEARINGS

Against these features, these are the advantages of the plain bearing:

(1) Insensitivity to shock and impact loads.

(2) Plain bearings are particularly suitable for high-speed applications and they are quiet running.

A formidable disadvantage of plain bearings is their very high start-up friction. With all such bearings, very exact controls are necessary when they are being fitted. A plain bearing cannot be loaded from all directions. The direction of the loads is, in most cases, dependent on the positioning of the oil feed.

ROLLING ELEMENTS

The advantages enumerated above have firmly established the anti-friction bearing in automotive applications. It is virtually inconceivable to think of an automotive design without this design and machine element.

Whilst the generally known anti-friction bearing types, such as deep groove ball bearings, self-aligning ball bearings, spherical roller bearings, and cylindrical roller bearings, have been widely used, the needle bearing, because of its design features, was scantily applied and only in quite secondary applications.

The bearing was formed of a ring of loose needle rollers, which were extremely long in relation to their diameter. Pins or shafts, bores in gears, pulleys or levers were used as raceways.

It has been stated frequently that a needle bearing is a rolling plain bearing. The thoughts of the inventor of German Patent No. DRP 393 788 of 28th July 1922 were really directed towards the creation of a plain bearing in which a bearing shell or bush was replaced by a multitude of thin needle rollers, closely crowded together, and in contact with one another. This resulted in a kind of breaking friction sufficiently large for the needle rollers to form, at normal bearing load, a complete unit, rotating freely, as would a bearing bush, around the shaft. This arrangement failed to prove itself, however, and the needle rollers were therefore given clearance between one another and the raceways, so that they were able to roll off as in a roller bearing.

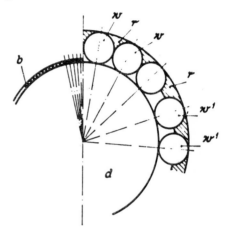

(121) DRP 393 788 28.7. 1922

Fig. 23.1 G. HOFFMANN.

Fig. 23.1 shows the fundamental conception of German Patent DRP 393 788. Owing to failures which occurred with the bearings designed in accordance with DRP 393 788, it was recognized that guidance of the rolling element was of decisive importance. Figs 23.2 and 23.3 show U.S. Patent No. 501 868 of 18th July 1893, and U.S. Patent No. 725 763 of 21st April 1903, from which it can be seen that even then attempts were made to provide a cage for the guidance of the rolling elements.

Fig. 23.2 shows a bearing design in which the rolling element is guided below the pitch line. The American Orange Company is still using this design today.

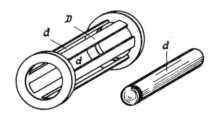

(255) USA 501 868 (22. 3. 1892) 18. 7. 1893

Fig. 23.2. Early needle roller cage J. A. CAMERON.

Fig. 23.3 shows a cage with pitch line guidance of the rolling element, and in addition with retention of the rollers to stop them falling inwards. Today this principle is widely used in the large-scale manufacture of plastic cages. At the time, however, manufacturing techniques and suitable machines were not available to produce high-precision cages, or in fact to produce needle rollers to sufficiently close tolerances.

The application of needle bearings was therefore restricted to the full complement type, at least in Europe, and even then in subordinate applications only. Nowadays, such bearings are more widely used, particularly in universal joints in motor cars. But in this field, too, new developments have been made, and these will be discussed later. A universal joint with needle bearings is shown in Fig. 23.4.

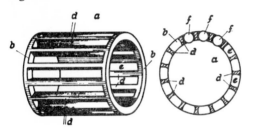

(256) USA 725 763 (1. 10. 1897) 21.4.1903
L. V. W. NOYES.

Fig. 23.3. Early needle roller cage

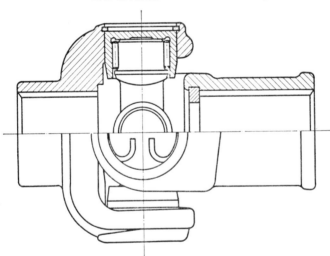

Fig. 23.4. Universal joint with fully crowded needle rollers

In addition, the planetary assemblies of automatic gearboxes and the sprockets of Gemmer-type steering boxes are still, for the most part, using full complement bearings. Fig. 23.5 shows a Gemmer-type steering gear.

Further applications of full complement bearings are restricted to suspension units. Fig. 23.6 shows the knee-action suspension, system Dubonnet, which has

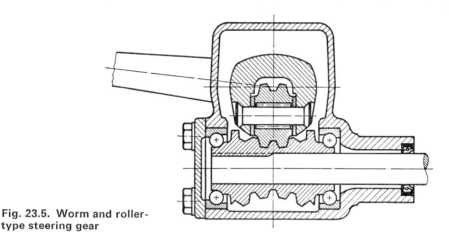

Fig. 23.5. Worm and roller-
type steering gear

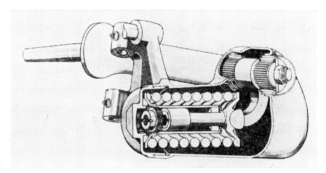

Fig. 23.6. Front
suspension unit used
by Opel and Vauxhall

been used for a long time by Opel. It must be emphasized when mentioning full complement type bearings that their function is largely dependent on the precision of shafts and housings and of the rolling elements themselves.

It is well known that the classical anti-friction bearings, the rolling elements of which can take the shape of balls, cylindrical rollers, barrelled rollers, or tapered rollers, are guided by the form of the raceways. Guidance by clearance may be singled out; this is used in cylindrical roller bearings, where the rolling element is guided axially between the shoulders with as little clearance as possible.

In the case of tapered roller bearings, pre-load is used and the rollers are guided along the shoulders by means of the load forces peculiar to this type of bearing.

All these bearing types use a cage, whose function is not to guide the rolling elements but only to retain them and to prevent them coming into contact with one another.

As already mentioned, the original needle bearing designs used rolling elements which were very long and thin in relation to their diameter and which ran directly on the raceways, without cages. Because of the unfavourable ratio of length to diameter, which in the case of needle rollers is greater than 2, the guidance of the rolling element by means of clearance, as is the case with cylindrical roller bearings, is not possible. These relationships are shown in Fig. 23.7.

The rolling element, in this case the needle roller, can therefore skew, i.e. become misaligned. In this condition the positioning of the needle roller is incorrect and a precise and accurate roll-off is impossible. If there are no means by which the needle roller is given guidance, it will not rotate square to the raceways but will move axially, performing a spiral motion, which in turn will cause misalignment of the raceways. The raceways therefore twist axially, which will result, in certain instances, in locking of the bearing. In addition, the misaligned needles will lift off the convex inner raceway and be in contact at only two points with the concave outer raceway. Three-point contact is the inevitable result, and the effect of the radial load will deflect the misaligned needle roller. In spite of its misalignment, the needle will be in contact along the generatrix of the raceway. There is therefore only apparent line contact; alternating bending stress occurs, which can lead to the fracture of the needle roller.

Because of these conditions, the clearance in the full complement bearing has to be sufficiently large to ensure that the ends of the misaligned needle rollers do not touch the outer raceway when passing through the unloaded zone. The radial clearance which is necessary results in a very small load-carrying zone, and therefore the specific load on individual needle rollers can be very high. In other words, the load-carrying figures arrived at with the iso-equation can never be reached in practice.

Apart from this major disadvantage, full complement bearings have a high friction coefficient, which is caused by the loose needle rollers revolving in contact with one another at twice the circumferential speed. These disadvantages have therefore to be eliminated by more suitable designs, to achieve an anti-friction bearing which functionally corresponds to the cylindrical roller bearing but retains its very low radial height.

Fig. 23.7. Fully crowded needle roller bearing with group cage

NEEDLE CAGES

Early attempts to prevent needle rollers skewing had already been made by using suitable guiding elements. This is illustrated in Fig. 23.7. First, the incorporation of a guide frame was tried. This frame surrounded a group of needle rollers and was carefully guided between the shoulders of the outer race. However, this solution did not give the hoped-for satisfaction because the necessary guidance was still lacking; further, the skewing of the needle rollers was not eliminated. As illustrated in Fig. 23.8 the first self-contained needle cage was drawn and pressed, which retained several needle rollers in one pocket.

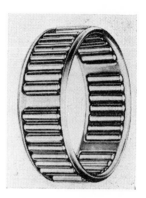

Fig. 23.8. Groups of needle rollers within a single cage

This design did not prove successful either, because the size of each pocket necessitated wider tolerances which could result in a whole needle package skewing. Trunnion-ended needle rollers were used which, when skewing, bored themselves into the side ribs of the cage; this led to bearing failure. Therefore the design was abandoned in 1951.

In view of these results, the only way remaining was to design a cage which would give individual guidance to the needle rollers. The resulting basic modifications thus converted the full complement needle bearing into a full status anti-friction bearing:

(1) The bearing was provided with a cage, in which each individual needle roller was guided within a pocket.

(2) The accuracy of the needle roller, which was 0·01 mm diameter, had been increased to 0·002 mm. Needle rollers were gauged into tolerance groups and each cage contained only one such diameter group.

(3) The needle rollers were retained in the cage so that it could be used as an independent anti-friction bearing unit.

As previously stated, the needle bearing thus became a fully fledged anti-friction bearing.

Fig. 23.9 shows comparison measurements between full complement and cage-guided bearings. These were carried out at the Technical High School at Stuttgart in 1949/50.

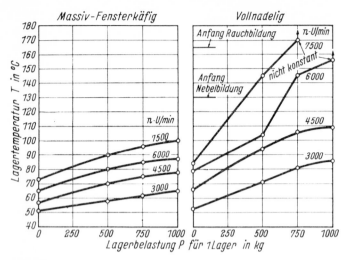

Fig. 23.9. Bearing temperatures relative to shaft speeds and loads for fully crowded needle roller bearings and for needle roller bearings with group cages

It can be seen that with a needle bearing of 40 mm shaft diameter, the maximum speed was approximately 4500 rev/min. This corresponds to an $n.Li$ value of some 160 000 under ideal test conditions. However, in practice the limit of this value was in the region of 100 000.

In contrast, the bearing with a machined window cage shows stable temperature conditions up to $n = 7500$. This corresponds to an $n.Li$ value of approximately 350 000. At the present time, $n.Li$ values up to 400 000 can be achieved in practice without difficulty.

Once the superiority of the cage bearing had been established, complete units of very small radial height were made, using turned and ground raceways. In the

Fig. 23.10. Thrust-type needle roller bearing

main, the outer race together with the needle cage forms a self-contained element into which a cylindrical inner race can be mounted. The inner races are inter-changeable so that, when separately mounted, mix-ups occurring during assembly would not be detrimental to the radial clearances of the bearings. Nowadays, because manufacturing technology has greatly advanced, large quantity appli-cations may utilize, instead of a machined cage, a precision drawn cage or, where temperature conditions allow, a plastic cage.

Fig. 23.10 shows a thrust needle cage. Such cages are precision drawn and their configuration affords particularly good lubricant retention.

APPLICATIONS OF NEEDLE BEARINGS

The following few examples will show some typical applications of needle bearings in modern automotive designs.

Fig. 23.11 shows a six-speed commercial gearbox, of which Messrs Z.F. of Friedrichshafen have manufactured over 100 000 units, and which are mainly to be found in heavy trucks and tractor units with traction output up to 38 tons. The same gearbox is also used in other types of vehicles, such as dumper trucks. All the loose gears are running on double-row needle cages. Needle cages are also used in the intermediary application of the reverse gear. The bearing arrangement of the reverse gear is particularly interesting in this design. The gear is provided with two shoulders, the raceway is plunge-ground, and the needle rollers are only introduced into the cage during assembly of the gear. To engage reverse, the gear wheel together with the needle rollers can be moved axially.

In these heavy gearbox applications the problems of indentations (or false brinelling) are frequently encountered. This occurs particularly in the upper gears and leads quickly to a considerable increase in the noise level and finally to the breakdown of the bearing. It was imperative that these indentations be

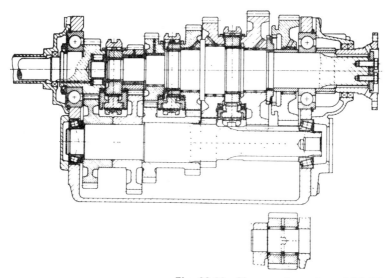

Fig. 23.11. Six-speed gearbox, AK6-80

prevented. This could only be achieved by producing a movement of the cage while the gear is engaged, and while no axial movement occurs between shaft and gear wheel. After innumerable tests and many failures, a needle cage with slanted pockets was used, in which the pocket is no longer diametrical but oblique to the centre of the cage. In this manner advantage may be taken of the tumbling motions of the gear and the cage, caused by the radial clearance of the cage in the bore, to achieve a creeping effect of the bearing assembly by means of the oblique pockets. This solution has succeeded, and the use of slanted pockets has totally eliminated indentations.

It should be noted that when using needle cages in gear wheels no additional lubrication through the mainshaft is used. Lateral lubrication pockets in the gear wheels will provide sufficient lubricant, which is available from the base of the gears.

This cross-section of the gearbox does not show the gear selector rods and linkages, which are provided with shell-type needle bearings. Shell bearings with bore dimensions of 20 and 14 mm are used. Because only a static load occurs, the problem of indentations has again been eliminated by the use of slanted pockets in the needle cage. In this application, the creep effect has been achieved by using slanted pockets and the normal vibrations from the vehicle.

Fig. 23.12 is a section through the probably familiar eight-speed gearbox R60 made by Volvo. Here again, needle cages, in matched pairs, are used in the loose gears. The very high idler revolutions of the intermediary wheel of the reverse gear reached an $n.Li$ value of approximately 450 000.

Fig. 23.13 illustrates another interesting application. This eight-speed gearbox of Messrs Z.F. uses axial and radial needle cages in the loose gears. In this case, the provision of sufficient lubricant occurs through lubrication holes.

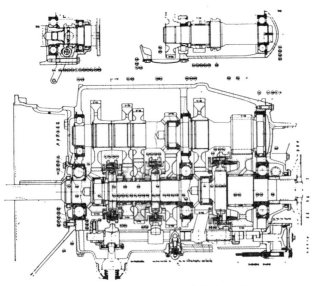

Fig. 23.12. Bearing arrangement of eight-ratio truck gearbox

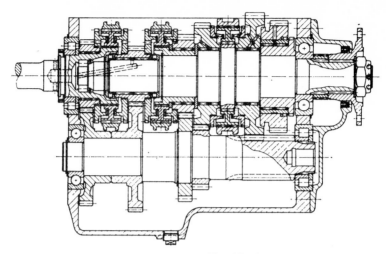

Fig. 23.13. Eight-speed gearbox

Fig. 23.14 shows the final drive of a four-speed synchromesh car gearbox.

The design of the Volkswagen gearbox is familiar to many. In this case, plastic cages made of polyamid 6.6 were used for the first time in the loose gears. These cages can withstand temperatures of up to 120°C because of the glass-fibre reinforcements used. This gearbox uses needle bearings with and without inner races in the drive shafts and the driven shaft respectively. The reverse gear uses two shell-type needle bearings.

A shell-type bearing is also used in the clutch spigot position. Here the misalignment between engine and gearbox can, under certain circumstances, be considerable. It is therefore necessary to crown the shaft to prevent edge loading of the needle rollers. Replacing the previously used plain bearing with a needle bearing resulted in the primary shaft remaining stationary when the clutch was disengaged. The reason for this was the very low friction coefficient of the needle

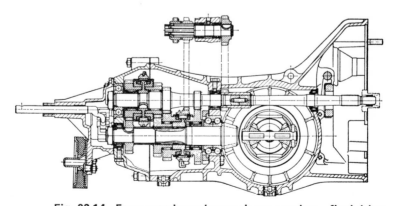

Fig. 23.14. Four-speed synchromesh car gearbox—final drive

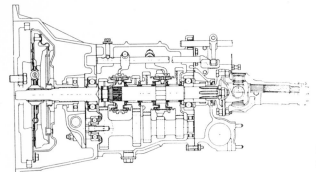

Fig. 23.15. Rover
gearbox

bearing. Needle bearings in this application are greased for life. Experience has shown that this bearing outlives the vehicle itself.

The most interesting development in gearboxes for motor vehicles took place in the U.K., and more particularly with the gearbox of the Rover 2000. Fig. 23.15 shows a cross-section through this gearbox. For the first time, axial support of the loose gears was given by needle thrust bearings in conjunction with very thin thrust washers. As thrust washers are by their nature not 100 per cent flat, the following procedure is used.

The second and third gears are mounted, the synchromesh put in place and, by means of a calibrated axial washer, a slight pre-load is achieved so that the gears run without clearance both when idling or transmitting torque. This brings about a considerable improvement in the running noise level of the gearbox. However, special steps had to be taken to obtain adequate lubrication.

Fig. 23.16 shows the five speed DS 25-1 racing car gearbox by Z.F. This gearbox was to some extent used by Lotus and as far as is known is still used in the Ford GT 40. The bearing application of the loose gear in the second speed proved

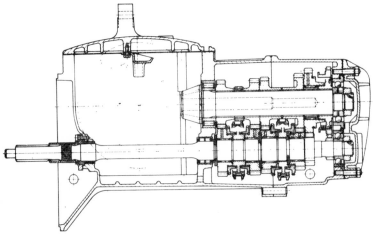

Fig. 23.16. Overhang five-speed gearbox as used for racing and sports cars with inter-axle mounted engines

problematical. Split needle cages had to be used which were subjected to speeds of 14 500 rev/min. After very extensive investigations and tests, the results of which were more or less negative, it was decided to use a silver-plated aluminium cage in this application. The use of aluminium allowed the weight of the two cage halves to be kept as low as possible and the silver plating produced an outstanding improvement in the cage's anti-friction property. This particular gearbox was used by Jim Clark on his Lotus in the World Championship Race at Nürburgring, and a two-speed version of this gearbox was incorporated in the car with which he won the Indianapolis race. This kind of bearing application in racing gearboxes tests anti-friction bearings to their limits because of the prevalent temperature and rev/min conditions.

In an automatic gearbox at present used by Daimler-Benz, apart from radial needle cages, deep drawn shell-type bearings are used to support the planetary gears. It should be noted that in this application the planetary gear bearings are still of the full complement type, and they function perfectly.

Figs 23.17 and 23.18 show hydro-steering mechanisms manufactured by Z.F. and Daimler-Benz, in which performance has been improved by replacing plain bearings with radial and axial needle bearings.

It was mentioned at the beginning of the paper that recent developments have made it possible for thin-walled shell-type bearings, with full complement needle rollers, to be used increasingly in universal joints and steering joints. The specially

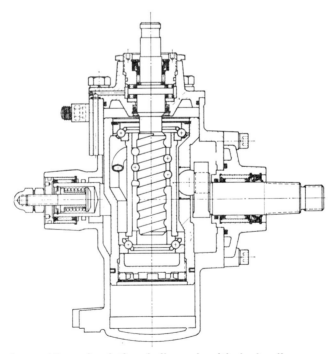

Fig. 23.17. Steering box with recirculating balls and with hydraulic servo assistance

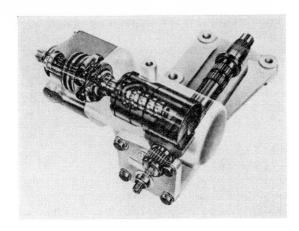

Fig. 23.18. Z.F. recirculating ball hydro-steering unit

developed assembly machines, in conjunction with thin-walled shell bearings, make it possible to eliminate all axial play, which is of considerable advantage. Such universal joints are at present being used by Daimler-Benz and BMW; and, through the B.R.D. Company, Aldridge, by Ford and Vauxhall in the U.K. Special assembly machines had to be developed in order to achieve faultless assemblies.

Fig. 23.19*a* illustrates a bearing with outer race only and Fig. 23.19*b* shows a complete bearing with outer and inner races.

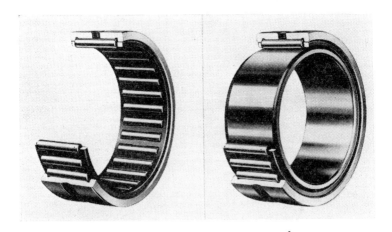

a   *b*

Fig. 23.19. Caged needle roller bearing with outer race and with inner race

OTHER BEARING TYPES

There are, of course, many other bearing types, e.g. the combined bearing capable of taking low axial forces. The bearing shown in Fig. 23.20 (NKIB) is only capable of taking start-up loads.

Fig. 23.20. Combination needle roller and thrust bearing

For higher axial loads, the bearing design illustrated in Fig. 23.21 has been evolved.

Yet another type of bearing with outer race is the precision-drawn type of needle bearing. With this bearing, the optimum has been achieved as far as radial height is concerned, and it does not require any more space than a plain friction-type bearing. Shell bearings are pressed into a housing, and in most cases no further axial location is required. However, when using shell-type bearings, particular care must be taken when manufacturing the housing bores, because each deviation of tolerance will bring about a deformation of the outer race, which generally is only 1 mm thick. Some types of shell bearings with needle cages are widely used, particularly in the automotive industries.

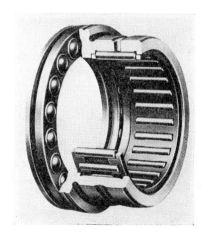

Fig. 23.21. Combination needle roller and thrust bearing

AXIAL NEEDLE THRUST CAGES

Parallel to the evolution of radial cages, the development of axial needle thrust cages with very low axial height took place. It is a fallacy to think that the rolling elements in axial needle cages are tapered. In actual fact, cylindrical rollers are used. The friction loss resulting from the skid of the rollers depends on the ratio of the pitch circle diameter to the length of the rolling elements. On this basis these bearings have been designed for friction values between 0·003 and 0·0045. It can be seen from this that the friction loss is relatively high in comparison with that of the radial needle bearing. This means that special attention must be paid to lubrication, particularly when operating at high revolutions. In spite of the higher friction loss which results from the skidding tendency, this type of bearing is capable of taking high loads at relatively high revolutions.

This bearing type is particularly advantageous in automotive and automatic gearbox applications, as it requires no more axial space than a thrust washer. All that has been said regarding hardness, surface quality, and accuracy of the raceways for radial needle bearings equally applies to the raceways of thrust needle cages.

Fig. 23.22 shows the increase in temperature of a thrust bearing, dependent on speed and load.

It should be mentioned that end-profiled needle rollers are nowadays used as standard, in order to minimize high end loads and to prevent an unnecessary reduction of bearing life.

It has been established that cage-guided needle bearings do not differ in their running behaviour from other types of anti-friction bearings. Life tests have proved that the usual equations used in the anti-friction bearing industry for static and dynamic load capacities equally apply to needle bearings.

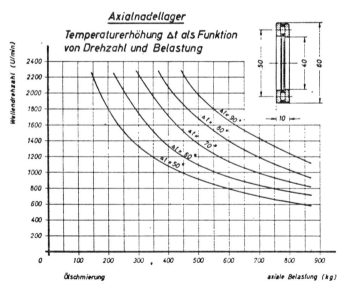

Fig. 23.22. Characteristic temperature chart of a needle-type journal bearing

The dimensions of a needle bearing in automotive applications are not solely determined by the static and dynamic load-carrying capacities. They very frequently have to satisfy, in addition, other design considerations.

For instance, in a gearbox the bearing dimensions are mainly determined by the dimensions of the gears and the shafts. In the final analysis, the correct bearing proportions are usually confirmed by durability tests on the test bench or in a test car. Life calculations are still considered to be the basic formula for determining the load-carrying capacity of anti-friction bearings, though in many instances bearing designs are utilized which have proved themselves in practice in similar applications. There are applications in which it is not the load-carrying capacity of a needle cage but more particularly its rigidity and endurance that are the most important factors. The big-end applications of high-speed internal combustion engines are a good example.

As with other anti-friction bearings, needle bearings require very small quantities of lubricant for reliable operation, because the fractional friction loss caused by the cage during roll-off of the rolling elements is minimal. Over-lubrication produces a sharp rise in friction owing to the churning effect of the lubricant.

With an appropriate choice of grease and a good sealing arrangement, needle bearings can be lubricated for life. This is particularly applicable for suspension bearings and universal joints, where the revolutions of the rolling elements and the consequent churning effect of the lubricant are small. A truly maintenance-free operation depends, however, on the perfect functioning and design of the sealing arrangement and the life of the lubricant.

SUMMARY

There are, of course, many other application possibilities for needle bearings in automotive applications. In particular, the use of water-pump bearings, in which the higher belt tensions have led to the replacement of one of the two ball-bearing rows by needle bearings. Such designs are currently being used by BMW, Munich, and Auto-Union, Ingolstadt. In addition, mention should be made of small two-stroke engines, such as those used in chain saws, snow scooters, etc. Nowadays, they would be inconceivable without the use of needle bearings in con-rods and gudgeon pins.

This paper is intended as a general synopsis of the development of needle bearings, particularly since the war, and information is given, by means of a few examples, concerning the application possibilities of this type of anti-friction bearing.

The MS. of this paper was received at the Institution on 25th August 1969 and accepted for publication on 16th January 1970.

Paper 24. Plain Bearings for Automotive Drivelines

R. D. JAMES, B Sc (Eng) C Eng M I Mech E

The Glacier Metal Co. Ltd, Alperton, Wembley, Middlesex

This paper investigates the common factors which may account for the preference for plain bearings in parts of the driveline. Theoretical and practical performances are compared and discrepancies are detailed and rationalized where possible. The paper continues to show the need for more experimental data from which computed results might be modified to allow for aspects of the environment for which no precise mathematical model yet exists.

INTRODUCTION

For many years plain bearings in one form or another have been employed in various automotive driveline components. The reasons for their usage have been frequently arbitrary and in some cases simply traditional. In some applications plain bearings have been so trouble free that one tends to forget their existence, while in others their unsuitability has become quickly apparent. In recent years our knowledge of the fundamental aspects of plain bearing performance has increased dramatically, and one is now able to predict, with reasonable accuracy, the degree of severity of a given application, and on this basis select from a range of bearing materials the one most likely to perform satisfactorily.

The major factor in the furtherance of our knowledge of plain bearing performance has been the advent of quick and reliable computer techniques using practical solutions of Reynolds' equation for steady and rotating load applications. By such methods it is quite feasible that a bearing designer can sit at a computer and, by changing such input parameters as bearing length, clearance operating viscosity, etc., can arrive at the optimum design literally within minutes rather than hours.

Thus one is in a position to quantify, with reasonable accuracy, the factors influencing plain bearing performance, and equipped with this facility it is possible to examine in detail various driveline applications, both successful and unsuccessful, to see if any common factors emerge to resolve hitherto unexplained discrepancies. The fundamental criterion in the applications considered will be that of minimum oil film thickness. This parameter is used as a yardstick to compare one application with another, but it must be stressed that the values computed are not absolute since the program is, as yet, unable to accommodate such variables as shaft deflection, housing deformation, and pressure–viscosity effects in the oil film.

Nonetheless, the computer technique is a very valuable design aid and does much to obviate the need for purely intuitive judgements as to the suitability, or otherwise, of a bearing design.

The three major areas of application or potential application for plain bearings in automotive drivelines for the purposes of this paper are considered to be (*a*) the gearbox, (*b*) the driveshaft(s), and (*c*) the final drive.

GEARBOXES

Manual gearboxes

Plain bearings are by no means unknown in manual gearboxes and find application in such areas as mainshafts, layshafts, reverse idlers, and tailshafts. Figs 24.1 and 24.2 show respectively typical three-shaft and two-shaft manual gearboxes, with the most common areas of plain bearing application marked.

Plain bearings have much to offer the gearbox designer, particularly in terms of reduced noise level. Unlike rolling element bearings which, by their very nature, generate noise, plain bearings are inherently silent in operation when properly designed, and they can effectively attenuate noise and vibration generated by other components.

In addition to a reduction in gearbox noise level, plain bearings are relatively inexpensive compared with other bearing types since they are most commonly formed from bi-metallic strip on a semi-continuous basis. It would be wrong to give the impression that these advantages are attainable in every case by merely substituting plain bearings of the appropriate dimensions for rolling element bearings. This is clearly not the case, and indeed there are areas where plain bearings will not be able to sustain given combinations of loads and speeds, or where their lubrication requirements cannot be adequately met. Nonetheless,

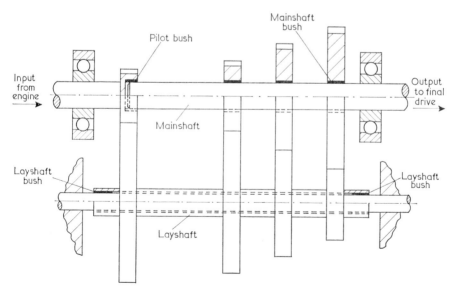

Fig. 24.1. Typical three-shaft gearbox

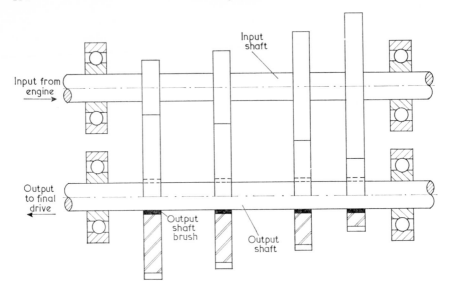

Fig. 24.2. Typical two-shaft gearbox

many areas of successful or potentially successful application of plain bearings in gearboxes do exist, and it is now proposed to examine some of these in detail.

Mainshaft applications

Where plain bearings are used in such applications, two possible configurations are commonly employed. The first uses bushes, usually in steel-backed lead–bronze, which are fitted in the bores of the mainshaft gears and rotate with the gears. When a gear is driving, there is theoretically no relative motion between the bush and the mainshaft, although fretting can occur. When the gear is disengaged, the bush and gear are driven independently of the mainshaft by the mating layshaft gear. Under these conditions the loads on the bush are minimal, but speeds can be high. In both cases the bush experiences a rotating load. The other possible arrangement for mainshaft bushes is to use bushes which are effectively members of the mainshaft. This is effected most commonly by the use of solid bronze bushes which may be keyed to the mainshaft or otherwise mechanically retained.

In such applications, the bushes are present primarily to prevent seizure of the gears to the mainshaft which may otherwise occur when the gear is disengaged and driven by the layshaft, and to prevent fretting damage when the gear is engaged. Opinion is divided as to the necessity of bushes in such applications, and at least one major motor manufacturer uses no bushes in these areas. However, if bushes are to be deleted, then extra care is required in the manufacture of the gears and the mainshaft in terms of hardness, material specification, and component surface finish. There is probably no economic advantage between one system and the other, but the inherent surface properties of the bush material are considered to add significantly to the overall factor of safety and general durability of the assembly.

The most common material specifications used for mainshaft bushes, whether solid or steel-backed, is a lead–bronze containing approximately 80 per cent Cu, 10 per cent Pb, and 10 per cent Sn. This composition may, of course, be varied to suit specific requirements—the lead content being increased to provide improved resistance to seizure and the tin content increased to provide better fretting resistance.

The lubrication requirements of these bushes are quite readily accommodated by provision of such features as helical grooves or indents in the i.d. when the bush rotates with the gear, or by grooves on the o.d. of solid bushes which are fixed to the mainshaft.

Although many gearbox designers recognize the need to provide an oil feed to the bushes, little attention is paid to the equally important problem of getting the oil away again. Provision for exit of the oil is not difficult to incorporate, and when properly designed can add significantly to the bush performance by avoiding stagnant pockets of lubricant which become progressively hotter and, hence, less effective. Plain bearings in such areas of application do not require a pressure-fed lubricant, but do require that the lubricant be circulated.

Layshaft applications

Two basic arrangements are usually adopted: in the first an integral gear/shaft design is used and the shaft runs in bearings fitted to the gearbox casing; in the second, the gear cluster is separate from the shaft which is an interference fit in the gearbox casing, and plain bushes or needle roller bearings are fitted to the i.d. of the gear cluster which rotates about the fixed shaft (see Fig. 24.3).

In either arrangement the choice between rolling element or plain bearings is largely a matter of designer's preference. Both designs incorporate certain desirable features. The predominant problem in such applications is that of edge-loading of the bearings by virtue of the fact that the layshaft deflects significantly under operating loads. This phenomenon produces an arduous operating condition for both types of bearing since the loading may be three or four times higher than that calculated on the assumption that no deflection occurs. The problem is less acute with the integral gear/shaft arrangement which is inherently stiffer in bending. However, in both designs the degree of edge-loading may be

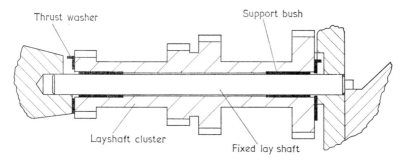

Fig. 24.3. Typical layshaft arrangement

minimized by judicious design of the components involved. For example, if one considers the integral gear/shaft arrangement where the bearings are fitted to the gearbox casing, the structural design of the casing in the area of the bearings may be so arranged that conjugate deflections of the shaft and housing occur and the bearing will thus tend to follow the deflected shape of the shaft more closely.

When plain bearings are used for the layshaft support a particular form of bearing material is often necessary because of the problem of edge-loading and the inherently low values of oil film thickness obtaining in these applications. A material such as a graphite impregnated lead–bronze or possibly a p.t.f.e.–lead-filled bronze is probably the most suitable. This is primarily because the bushes do not operate under hydrodynamic lubrication conditions but rather under boundary lubrication conditions. In such an operating environment the inherently good surface lubricity of the filled bronzes can be of great benefit. A sample design calculation for a typical layshaft bush is given in Table 24.1, and the influence of such parameters as bearing length, operating oil viscosity, and dimensional clearance is demonstrated.

Reverse idler bearings

Fig. 24.4 shows, diagrammatically, a typical reverse idler gear assembly from an automotive gearbox. A cursory examination of the general form of the gear will indicate some of the problems faced by the bearing designer when considering this application. The fundamental problem is one of asymmetrical loading which gives rise to edge-loading of the bearing and hence locally high loads. These loadings, in turn, imply low oil film thicknesses and high oil film pressures. In view of these considerations, the surface properties of the bush material specified must be the best obtainable commensurate with adequate fatigue strength and, naturally, low cost. As with layshaft bushes the most suitable material appears to be some form of filled bronze.

A phenomenon observed particularly with reverse idler bushes (and some

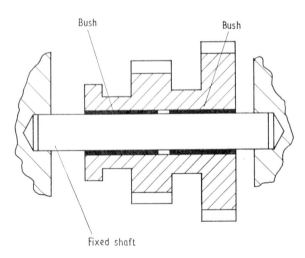

Bush   Bush

Fixed shaft

Fig. 24.4. Typical reverse idler cluster

Table 24.1. Bearing design computations

Application	Speed, rev/min	Load, lbf (kN)	Operating temperature, °C	Bush diameter, in (mm)	Bush length, in (mm)	Diametral clearance, in (mm)	Minimum film thickness, in $\times 10^{-4}$ (mm $\times 10^{-3}$)
Layshaft bush	4000	2365 (10·6)	120	0·75 (19·0)	1·25 (31·7)	0·001 (0·025)	0·5 (1·27)
	4000	2365 (10·6)	120	0·75 (19·0)	1·25 (31·7)	0·002 (0·050)	0·3 (0·76)
	4000	2365 (10·6)	120	0·75 (19·0)	1·56 (39·6)	0·001 (0·025)	0·8 (2·03)
	4000	2365 (10·6)	120	0·75 (19·0)	0·94 (23·9)	0·001 (0·025)	0·2 (0·51)
	4000	2365 (10·6)	150	0·75 (19·0)	1·25 (31·7)	0·001 (0·025)	0·3 (0·76)
Reverse idler bush	1760	1670 (7·46)	120	0·625 (15·9)	1·40 (35·5)	0·001 (0·025)	0·3 (0·76)
	1760	1670 (7·46)	120	0·625 (15·9)	1·40 (35·5)	0·002 (0·050)	0·2 (0·51)
	1760	1670 (7·46)	120	0·625 (15·9)	1·75 (44·4)	0·001 (0·025)	0·6 (1·53)
	1760	1670 (7·46)	120	0·625 (15·9)	1·05 (26·7)	0·001 (0·025)	0·2 (0·51)
	1760	1670 (7·46)	150	0·625 (15·9)	1·40 (35·5)	0·001 (0·025)	0·2 (0·51)
Gearbox extension tube bush	5820	250 (1·12)	120	1·375 (34·9)	1·50 (38·1)	0·001 (0·025)	4·1 (10·4)
	5820	250 (1·12)	120	1·375 (34·9)	1·50 (38·1)	0·002 (0·050)	6·6 (16·8)
	5820	250 (1·12)	120	1·375 (34·9)	1·875 (47·6)	0·001 (0·025)	4·2 (10·7)
	5820	250 (1·12)	120	1·375 (34·9)	1·125 (28·6)	0·001 (0·025)	3·5 (9·00)
	5820	250 (1·12)	150	1·375 (34·9)	1·50 (38·1)	0·001 (0·025)	3·8 (9·70)

Table 24.2. Typical bearing loads and speeds for an input torque of 1000 lbf ft

Condition	Parameter	Bearing identification and type					
		1 Journal	2 Journal	3 Thrust	4 Thrust	5 Journal	6 Journal
1st speed	Load, lbf (N)	970 (4340)	1090 (4880)	635 (2845)	1053 (4720)	0 (0)	0 (0)
	Speed, rev/min	2480	2480	2475	1851	1851	1149
2nd speed	Load, lbf (N)	988 (4430)	1083 (4850)	300 (1345)	1053 (4720)	158 (706)	0 (0)
	Speed, rev/min	2480	2480	975	1338	1338	840
3rd speed	Load, lbf (N)	975 (3740)	596 (2675)	387 (1770)	1202 (5380)	41 (184)	0 (0)
	Speed, rev/min	834	975	261	915	915	0
4th speed	Load, lbf (N)	964 (4310)	525 (2355)	727 (3260)	835 (3730)	0 (0)	0 (0)
	Speed, rev/min	261	261	0	0	0	0
Reverse	Load, lbf (N)	1008 (4510)	725 (3250)	120 (237)	334 (1500)	475 (2130)	905 (4060)
	Speed, rev/min	2480	2480	2475	1851	1851	1149

similar applications such as planet gear bushes in epicyclic gear trains) is the occasional tendency of the bush to move axially out of its housing in service, often with annoying and sometimes serious consequences. At first sight one is tempted to overcome this tendency by such expedients as increasing the interference fit of the bush in its housing or by adopting mechanical means of restraint. None of these palliatives is entirely satisfactory since, in some cases, bushes which required a force of possibly 1–2 tonf (10–20 kN) to insert them in their housings readily overcame the mechanical constraints and moved inexorably outwards in service!

The basic problem would seem to lie with the physical shape of the gears into which the bushes are inserted, and is certainly a function of the loading pattern which is axially asymmetric and which rotates with the gear. This is a problem currently under investigation, but it should be stressed that its mention here does not mean that the problem is universal, although it is undoubtedly disquieting when it occurs.

Gearbox tailshaft bearings

This is an area where plain bearings are almost universally applied. Fig. 24.5 shows a typical tailshaft support bush which is most commonly supplied in steel-backed white metal. The loads on such bushes are normally quite low since the bush performs primarily the function of a steady. Nonetheless, speeds are relatively high (engine revolutions in direct top gear) and when trouble occurs it normally takes the form of wiping and ultimate seizure. This is principally because too little attention is paid to the effective lubrication of such bushes, probably on the assumption that because white metal is such a tolerant material, splash lubrication will suffice. In some cases this is indeed so, but most

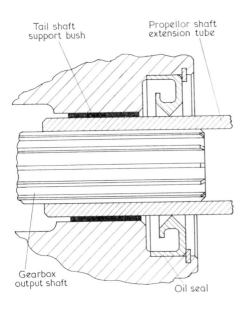

Tail shaft
support bush

Propellor shaft
extension tube

Gearbox
output shaft

Oil seal

Fig. 24.5. Typical tailshaft arrangement

manufacturers now recognize the need to supply a more positive feed of oil to the tailshaft bush by galleries cast into the tailshaft housing and a special groove in the bush bore. The results of a design calculation for a typical tailshaft bush are given in Table 24.1.

Automatic gearboxes

In the U.K. production of passenger vehicles with automatic transmission constituted 8–10 per cent of total production in 1968, and according to all the indications this figure will continue to increase.

The areas of application, actual or potential, for plain bearings in such gearboxes are numerous. Fig. 24.6 shows a section through a typical automatic gearbox, indicating the areas considered feasible for plain bearing applications. An indication of the severity of some of these applications is given in Table 24.2. It will be noticed that, particularly in the case of the bevel gear thrust washers, the conditions are such that the maximum load is imposed as the relative speed of rotation approaches zero. This is a loading condition under which no hydrodynamic film will be generated, but one which may be sustained by a material such as p.t.f.e.-filled bronze with inherently good surface lubricity.

One area of such gearboxes where plain bearings are unlikely to be successful is in the planet wheels of the bevel gear train. In general, the loads tend to be very high and the conditions under which the bush would be required to operate are those that, unfortunately, would induce it to move axially out of its housing.

Referring to Fig. 24.6 we will consider, by way of example, those bearings marked ▼ (an input shaft support bearing and a bevel gear support bearing). The results of the computation involved in assessing the likelihood of successful operation are summarized for both bearings in Table 24.3.

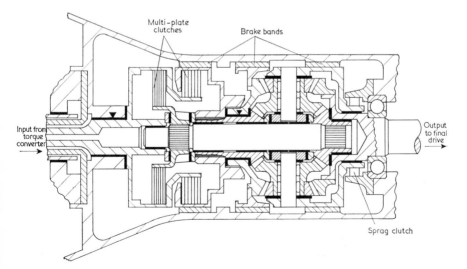

Fig. 24.6. Simplified section through an Automotive Products gearbox

Table 24.3

Parameter			Mainshaft support bearing		Bevel gear support bearing	
Rotational speed	.	.	rev/min	3000		973	
Diameter	.	.	in (mm)	1·25	(32)	1·50	(38)
Length	.	.	in (mm)	1·25	(32)	0·75	(19)
Diametral clearance	.		in (mm)	0·0025	(0·063)	0·0025	(0·063)
Viscosity at 60°C	.	.	cS (m²/s)	170	$(1·7 \times 10^{-4})$	170	$(1·7 \times 10^{-4})$
Oil inlet temperature	.	.	(°C)	100		100	
Radial load	.	.	lbf (kN)	450	(2·0)	704	(3·13)
Eccentricity ratio	.	.	. . .	0·8		0·98	
Oil flow	.	.	gal/min (m³/s)	0·042	$(2·5 \times 10^{-6})$	0·009	$(0·54 \times 10^{-6})$
H.p. loss	.	.	watts	0·03	(22·4)	0·01	(7·5)
Temperature rise	.		degC	4·3		6·7	
Minimum oil film thickness							
Computed	.	.	in (mm)	0·000 25 $(0·64 \times 10^{-3})$		0·000 20 $(0·51 \times 10^{-3})$	
Allowable	.	.	in (mm)	0·000 23 $(0·58 \times 10^{-3})$		0·000 25 $(0·64 \times 10^{-3})$	

If, as stated earlier, the value of minimum oil film thickness is used as the fundamental criterion of performance, then a comparison of the 'computed' with the 'allowable' values indicates very clearly the marked difference between the mainshaft bearing and the bevel gear bearing. However, one must be very careful when interpreting such results since, as mentioned earlier, the computer program used does not consider such factors as shaft deflection. Nonetheless, the method is an advance over the intuitive method used previously and has shown good correlation with practical results.

The term 'allowable film thickness' refers to a value of oil film thickness considered to incorporate a safety factor sufficiently generous to ensure, in theory at least, infinite operating life for the bearings. This concept is employed when considering the performance of bearings for large items of capital plant such as steam turbines, and is thus not really appropriate when considering automotive components designed for finite lives. For automotive purposes, a computed value of film thickness which is greater than, say, half the 'allowable' value is considered to be satisfactory.

In the two specific cases considered, the computed value of oil film thickness for the mainshaft bearing exceeds the 'allowable' value, whereas that computed for the bevel gear bearing is less than one-tenth of the 'allowable' value and it is unlikely that a plain bearing would perform satisfactorily in that position.

DRIVESHAFT APPLICATIONS

In this category it is proposed to consider the substitution of plain bearings for needle rollers in the Hooke's joints used almost universally for propeller shafts and axle shafts. Market surveys have indicated that plain bearings could provide an acceptable alternative in these applications, especially if a material could be used which was reasonably tolerant to the ingress of dirt and moisture. (The seals on the Hooke's joints are at best only partially effective.)

Propeller shaft joints

'Propeller shaft' refers to the shaft transmitting the driving torque from an engine situated remote from the final drive gears, i.e. typically in a front engine/ rear drive configuration. These shafts rotate at the same speed as the gearbox output or third motion shaft, which on the majority of British cars is normally engine speed with top gear engaged. The bearings in the Hooke's joints on these shafts are loaded by the torque produced by the engine and transmitted through the gearbox. Owing to torque multiplication effects in the gearbox, the highest torque applied to the propeller shaft joints occurs when the lowest gear is engaged. The joint adjacent to the gearbox output shaft operates normally under more arduous loading conditions than the joint at the other end of the shaft, which tends to be subject to attenuated transmission shock loads due to the inherent torsional flexibility of the shaft.

The angular movement of propeller shaft joints is caused by relative motion between the gearbox and rear axle, and is generally low because the shafts are relatively long.

Axle shaft joints

Axle shafts are defined in this context as shafts which transmit the driving torque to the road wheels from the final drive assembly. The fact that these shafts come after the final drive gears is significant because a further torque multiplication is involved. This means in practice that the torque on axle shaft joints may be approximately four times greater than that on conventional propeller shaft joints under the same input conditions from the engine. In addition, because they are relatively short compared with propeller shafts, the angular movement of axle shafts is much greater for a given vertical displacement of the driven wheels. Thus the Hooke's joints in axle shafts are, in general, operating under more arduous conditions in terms of loads and deflections than those in conventional propeller shafts.

Axle shafts are usually restricted to those vehicles which employ a front engine and independent rear suspension layout, and those where an engine/gearbox/final drive 'package' is situated at the front or rear of the vehicle. In addition to the normal torque loads discussed above, some axle shafts are subjected to suspension and braking loads since in certain configurations they laterally locate the driven wheels.

Driveshaft bearings

At the present time the Hooke's joints in propeller shafts and axle shafts use needle roller bearings housed in hardened steel cups running against hardened steel spiders. The life of these bearings is predominantly a function of the efficiency of sealing. Fig. 24.7 shows a section through a typical Hooke's joint and the sealing arrangement is clearly visible. Once the seals deteriorate sufficiently the roller bearings are subjected to the ingress of road dirt and moisture, and corrosion or abrasion eventually leads to a breakdown of the bearings in a relatively short time.

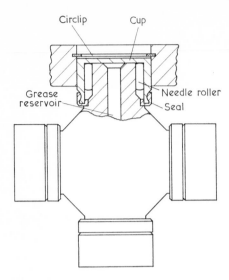

Fig. 24.7. Section through a typical Hooke's joint

Another problem associated with such bearings is their tendency to 'brinell' in service, as shown in Fig. 24.8. This effect produces considerable irregularities in the surfaces against which the needles operate. Once initiated the deterioration is cumulative, and produces irregular movement of the joint with consequent transmission harshness.

In an attempt to produce bearings that would be less sensitive to deficiencies in the sealing arrangement and would not be subject to 'brinelling' effects, the performance of various plain bushes in driveshaft applications is currently being evaluated. Such bushes are normally made from steel strip to which various plastic materials are bonded on a continuous basis. Fig. 24.9 shows a microsection through a typical material (Glacier DX) which comprises a steel backing on to which is sintered an open pore matrix of Cu–Sn. An acetal copolymer is rolled into the matrix so that a surface layer of about 0·010 in (0·25 mm) thick is formed. The surface may be subsequently pin-indented to provide reservoirs for the lubricant used in service.

Bushes formed from such material are inserted into cups similar to those which house the needle rollers, and the joint is then assembled in the normal way. Fig. 24.10 shows such an arrangement diagrammatically. Test results to date have been encouraging and indicate something of the potential of plain bearings for driveshaft applications. Figs 24.11 and 24.12 show components of a modified universal joint which operated for approximately 25 000 miles in the axle shaft of an uprated Hillman 'Imp' vehicle—maximum torque 52 lbf ft (70 N m) at 4300 rev/min, including an arduous 600-mile stop–start test. The photographs show the components to be in good condition, and the maximum change in clearance after operation was found to be only 0·0016 in. No perceptible wear of the joint was found on cursory examination after removal from the vehicle, and it is estimated that the potential life of such joints with plain bearings would be in excess of 40 000 miles.

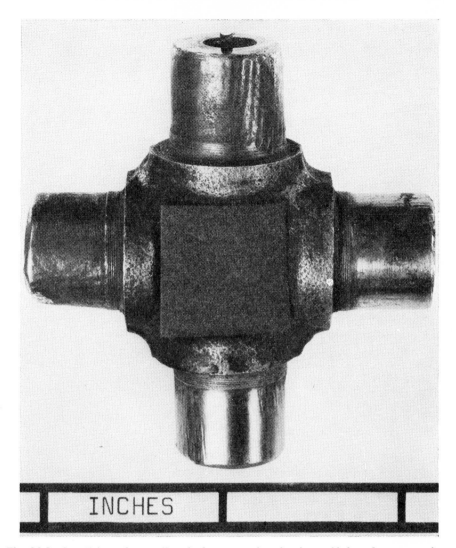

INCHES

Fig. 24.8. Condition of propeller shaft conventional universal joint after approximately 15 000 miles operation

THE FINAL DRIVE

The two fundamental areas of application of plain bearings in the final drive assembly are both in the differential unit. Fig. 24.13 shows a section through a typical automotive differential unit, and the areas of plain bearing application, planet gear, and axle thrust washers are indicated. In both applications the thrust washers are present to carry the separating forces generated between the gears when torque is transmitted. The axle thrust washers are normally in the form of

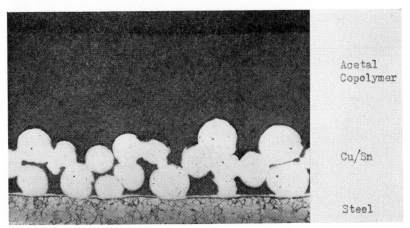

Fig. 24.9. Photomicrograph of section through Glacier DX material (×100 magnification)

an annulus stamped from phosphor-bronze strip with embossed grooves on both thrust faces to ensure optimum lubrication.

The planet-gear thrust washers are again stamped from phosphor-bronze strip, but unlike the sun-gear washers they are part-spherical rather than flat and their surfaces are ball-indented to facilitate retention of the lubricant. The washers for both applications are generally trouble-free in service and, as with many well-established vehicle components, their presence is often taken for granted.

In the more heavily loaded applications—mainly commercial and agricultural

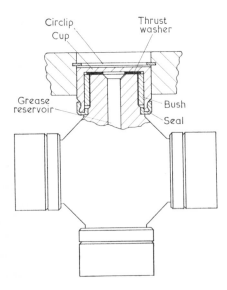

Fig. 24.10. Section through a Hooke's joint modified to accept plain bearings

Fig. 24.11. Glacier DX
driveshaft bush after
25 000 miles in an
uprated Hillman 'Imp'
vehicle

vehicle final drives—plain bushes are normally fitted to the bores of the planet gears (see Fig. 24.13). The material most commonly used is a lead–bronze or, in some cases, a p.t.f.e.-filled lead–bronze.

Unfortunately, these bushes are subject to forces which tend to cause the bushes to move out of their housings in service. In certain cases the expedient of fitting a flanged or 'headed' bush has proved effective. The head is produced by coining a plain cylindrical bush in a suitable die, and locates in a machined register in the planet-gear bore.

CONCLUSIONS

The examples referred to in the paper have been chosen to indicate that the design of plain bearings for driveline components is in a transitional stage. On the one hand, there exist numerous applications where such bearings have been successfully operating for many years, simply because they have been developed by trial and error and have been found to be suitable only after extensive testing. On the other hand, some of the examples quoted serve to indicate that with the advent of quick and reliable computation methods now available, bearing designers are becoming increasingly able to assess objectively the factors influencing bearing performance and the probability of success or failure in a given application.

In addition, many of the components which have in the past been designed by, for want of a better term, 'traditional' means, may well prove to be over-designed and represent areas of potential cost reduction. The need for testing will, of course, remain but the significant difference will be that the test programmes will be directed towards confirming theoretically predicted performance of components rather than testing, at random, various specifications in the hope that one may eventually prove satisfactory.

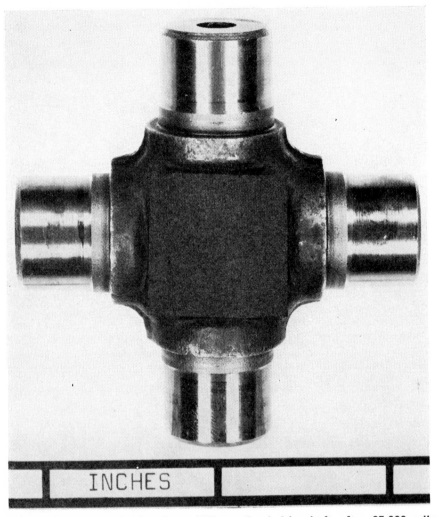

Fig. 24.12. Universal joint from Hillman 'Imp' driveshaft after 25 000 miles operation with Glacier DX bushes

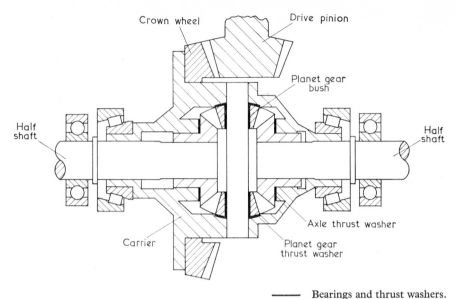

———— Bearings and thrust washers.

Fig. 24.13. Section through a typical differential unit

ACKNOWLEDGEMENTS

The author wishes to express his appreciation to his colleagues in the Research and Development Organization of the Glacier Metal Company Limited and also to transmission designers throughout the British Automotive Industry for their assistance in the preparation of this paper. The author also wishes to thank the directors of the Glacier Metal Company Limited for their permission to publish the paper.

The MS. of this paper was received at the Institution on 2nd December 1969 and accepted for publication on 9th December 1969.

Paper 25. Synchromesh Mechanisms

J. AUSTEN
F. Porsche K.G., Stuttgart-Zuffenhausen, Porschestrasse 42

INTRODUCTION

The continuously increasing density of traffic in the highly civilized countries demands synchronized transmissions to relieve the driver of overwork and so make a contribution to safety on the roads. Practically all passenger cars and most of the trucks today that have manually operated shift transmissions are synchronized.

THE SYNCHROMESH SYSTEM

The synchromesh system in the transmission is used to maintain equivalent revolutions by friction between parts rotating at various speeds during gear changing. Whilst the speed of the secondary side of the transmission (connected through the axle drive and stub axles directly to the rolling road wheels) is dependent on the driving speed, the rotation of the primary side is reduced, after releasing the clutch, from the motor rotation speed to zero.

According to the design of the transmission (Fig. 25.1) and the oil temperature, this coasting takes 3–10 seconds. The gear train never reduces to this zero speed with an incorrectly releasing clutch system, and this is a major disadvantage when changing gear.

Practically, this means decelerating the primary side including the driven plate of the clutch when changing up, e.g. from second to third gear, to reach equivalent revolutions. When changing down, however, the primary side, including the gear trains, bearings, and the driven plate of the clutch, has to be accelerated. The considerable friction of the gear trains, the bearings, and the drag of the oil must be taken over by the synchromechanism during the gear change. The inherent drag of hydraulic pumps and power take-offs (P.T.Os), when fitted, has to be overcome, and this additional force essentially increases the gear shifting forces when changing down.

When changing up, the friction of the parts to be synchronized helps to retard the fast rotating primary side and so assist the synchromesh system. However, when changing down, especially with cold transmission and highly viscous oil, the synchromesh elements have to carry out much more work to attain a speed equivalent to that of the gear train.

The foregoing requirements are easily met, but they become much more complicated when, at the synchronized side of the transmission, P.T.Os are connected to pumps, winches, farming implements, etc. It is essential to realize that P.T.Os are at the secondary side of the transmission or can be released by the clutch during shifting. The Porsche Company have developed comparatively simple methods of calculating the stress of every synchro unit at the preliminary design stage. Resulting from long experience, the size for every item of the synchromesh system in a transmission can be defined. As the friction and the

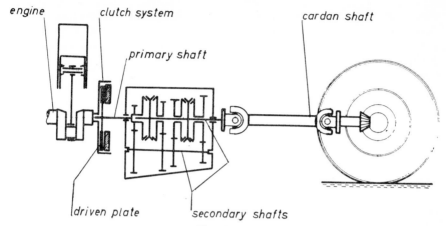

Fig. 25.1. Diagram of a transmission system

drag can only be determined by testing the first of a new transmission type, the calculated values of the stress in the different gears are added, or subtracted, according to the synchro sizes. As stated earlier, the driven plate of the clutch system has to be accelerated or decelerated during gear changing.

The calculation method referred to above assumes a vehicle travelling at a constant speed. This gives, for a given road wheel speed and axle ratio, an accurately determined rotational speed for the secondary shaft of the transmission. As shown in Fig. 25.2, the synchro hub, and therefore the sliding dog, is rigidly connected to the drive shaft. The following example explains in detail the synchro unit operation for a gear change down from a higher to a lower gear.

At engaged third speed the opposite cog-wheel of the second speed also rotates, caused by the gear ratio having lower revolutions than the corresponding

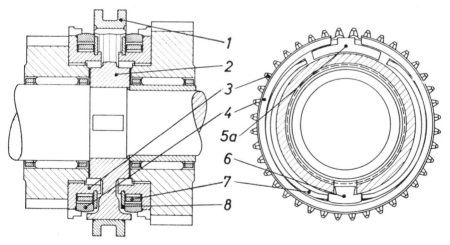

Fig. 25.2. Porsche synchro unit at gear change

cog-wheel of the third speed. As the revolutions of the sliding dog are not changing, the cog-wheel of the second speed has to be accelerated during gear changing by the elements of the synchromesh system until the revolutions are equal. At this condition the driven shaft, carrying all cog-wheels, and the primary side with the driven plate of the clutch are also accelerated.

In order to simplify the calculation, the moments of inertia of all parts influenced by the synchromesh system are reduced to the gear that has to be shifted. With this new complex moment of inertia that the synchromesh system has to overcome, the calculation of the stresses is continued. A further calculation, the difference in revolutions that has to be overcome during the shifting can easily determine the amount of work required to be done by the synchromesh system during shifting. The result of the calculation allows a determination of a standardized size of synchro unit. Fig. 25.3 shows a cross-section through a modern five-speed transmission with synchronized forward speeds.

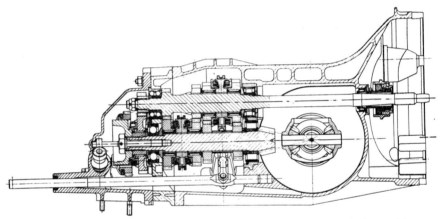

Fig. 25.3. Cross-section through a modern five-speed transmission with synchronized forward speeds

Naturally, one always seeks, for reasons of efficiency, to produce for any transmission one size only of synchro units. On bigger transmissions, however, two or even three different sizes of synchromesh systems can be applied. For testing of the calculated synchro elements in the prototype state relatively simple test benches are used to achieve quickly reproducible endurance values and shifting forces.

Using the calculation basis of a vehicle travelling at constant speed, test benches were built, the main component being a flywheel equivalent to the inertia of the rolling vehicle. These flywheels are driven by electric motors which can be regulated. The flywheel itself is connected over a cardan shaft to the output flange of the test transmission. For normal transmissions, trucks included, an output of the motor of about 10–15 kW is sufficient. The rotating flywheel simulates the rolling vehicle whilst the transmission is pushed over the cardan shaft. Fig. 25.4 shows a test bench for transaxle gearboxes.

Fig. 25.4. Test bench for transaxle gearboxes. Normally four test gearboxes are running simultaneously

The primary side of the transmission with the driven plate of the clutch at a selected gear is put into rotation and, according to the gear change, accelerated or decelerated. This test showed that the second speed has the most critical synchromesh unit. This results from the fact that the stressing of the lower speeds of a transmission is much higher than that at the upper speeds. As there is only occasional shifting down into first speed, the first has the biggest load, but because of the small number of shiftings in the lifetime of a transmission, there is much less danger of wear than in the much more often used second gear. Therefore most tests are made, especially for controlling purposes, with a shifting cycle third–second–third. Compressed air cylinders simulating human hand-forces at the gear lever are controlled by impulse switches and electro-pneumatic valves. This test installation permits automatic endurance tests of 100 000–200 000 gear changes. In the case of disengagement of the synchromesh system or overheating of any component, the test bench can be automatically stopped by acoustical or thermal control systems.

A few years ago 80 000–100 000 gear changes for passenger cars, and 200 000 for trucks, into second speed, were regarded as a normal life usage. Today, normal mass production requires much higher endurance: 200 000 changes for passenger cars and 250 000–300 000 for trucks are achieved today before the wear of the friction surfaces of the synchromesh system is so severe that the synchro teeth of the sliding dog come into contact with the synchro teeth of the cog-wheel before reaching equivalent revolutions.

In the car itself the early disengagement of the synchromesh system is often caused by defective clutching. Tests have shown that synchromesh systems can withstand forced clutch gear changing to a greater extent than a mechanical clutch operated by a foot pedal.

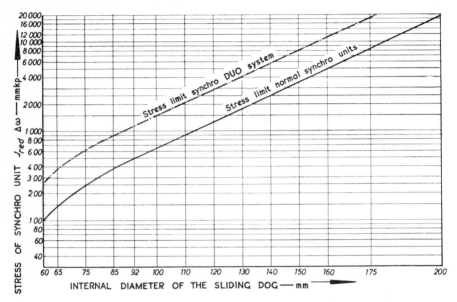

Fig. 25.5. Curve of limit values of the Porsche synchromesh system

The curve shown in Fig. 25.5 was obtained as a result of extensive test transmission applications ranging from small passenger cars to giant trucks. This indicates that nowadays the test procedures have to be arranged within very small limits for their special purpose of application. Tests are often used to determine the production tolerances range and consequently it is often possible to allow wider tolerances and so lower the production costs. It was possible, for example, to widen the limits for the contact surfaces in the Porsche synchromesh system. This enabled the grinding operations to be changed into turning and milling operations which resulted in an appreciable lowering in manufacturing costs. The designer has a wide range of possibilities to consider when engaging in a new transmission project to ensure that the complete synchronized transmission will satisfy all the requirements of shifting forces, 'feel', and endurance.

First, the masses that have to be synchronized should be as small as possible. Take, for example, the driven plates of the clutches that later consume 60–70 per cent of the acceleration/deceleration work. The result of an investigation was that European medium class cars with about 1500 cm³ engine volume have an inertia of the driven plates between 29·1 and 51·0 cm g² (0·002 and 0·0038 lb ft²).

In view of the fact that the moment of inertia in the stress calculation is multiplied by the square of the gear ratio of the gear that has to be synchronized, it is well worthwhile to investigate every means of unloading the driven plate. Furthermore, it should be attempted to design the form of the cog-wheels as advantageous as possible by reducing weight. It is preferable to provide a place for all sliding dogs (or at least one) at the primary side of the transmission, as the inertia of the two wheels with their synchromesh units is not included in the calculation, because they do not belong directly to the parts driven by the driving axle. Further improvements are achieved by an accurate design of the shifting forks, the shifting rods, and the shifting lever. By careful attention to all such details efficiency ratios of 80–90 per cent are possible.

The design of the transmission housing should be considered, especially with highly loaded transmissions, at an early stage in the project development. Special attention should be paid to ensure that the transmission housing is not too close to the rotating cog-wheels, to avoid troublesome oil pumping when cold.

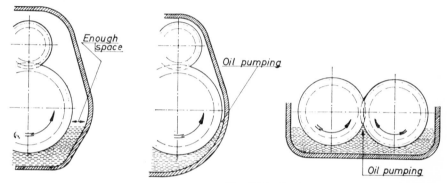

Fig. 25.6. Typical transmission housings

This pumping effect is more severe, as shown in Fig. 25.6, when the axles of the transmission rotating wheels are on the same horizontal level. If another solution of the design is not possible, a change of the direction of rotation should be considered to annul the pumping effect of the teeth; or at least to accomplish the lubrication and oil supply by means of a small pump instead of allowing the wheels to rotate in the oil sump. Quite often there are transmissions that have a very high oil level for safety reasons, e.g. the maintaining of a steady oil temperature. Experiences with highly loaded car transmissions with floating cog-wheels on needle bearings have shown that the oil supply is sufficient when the smallest wheel of the lower axle of the transmission just rotates in the oil sump.

More has been required from lubricating oils within the past years. A few years ago non-additive mineral oils were used in practically all manually operated transmissions, whereas nowadays almost everywhere high-additive transmission oils are preferred. It is even a necessity for the transaxle design, with pinion and crown wheel in the same oil sump, to use the best oils to keep the wear and temperature within limits. This leads to transmission oils with a high percentage of additives that reduce the friction on the loaded flanks of the teeth as much as possible. Oils of this kind are brought on the market and produced in America as well as in Europe by all well-known oil companies in accordance with a specification of the American Ministry of Defense. These oils, according to the specification Mil-L2105 A or Mil-L2105 B, have a high percentage of the additive

Anglamol 99 of the Lubrizol Company and have the quality of extensively reducing the friction.

The friction, however, on the friction surfaces of all synchro systems is severely reduced. This effect leads towards a smoothing of the friction cone of synchro systems, especially when brass or bronze is one of the friction materials. The severely reduced friction on the synchro parts allows an overshifting before equivalent revolutions are reached. This gives the annoying scratching that indicates the breakdown of the synchromesh endurance. Tests have proved that the synchro systems can be made to work satisfactorily by washing out the transmission housing and refilling with normal transmission oil.

As the transmissions, however, are stressed increasingly higher, the future will require that the synchro systems must be insensitive towards the influences of the oils. This is the reason why the Porsche Company has developed a different synchro system that is, by an alteration of the servo parts, thrust block, brake band, and anchor block (see Fig. 25.2), widely insensitive towards all known high-additive transmission oils. The big advantage of the Porsche synchro system is the fact that it not only relies on the friction cone between the sliding dog and the cogwheel, but has an essential support through the three parts mentioned above that have a remarkable influence on shifting forces and endurance by an alteration of the angle of contact and the materials.

The extreme reduction of endurance from 200 000 shiftings down to 8000–15 000 shiftings, using Mil-L2105 B oil, found at the beginning on the test benches, could be increased by the above-mentioned alterations, without increasing shifting forces, up to 200 000 shiftings.

Our experience with transmissions of all different vehicles indicates the need for new solutions that are quite often not considered by car and equipment producers.

The hydraulically operated one-plate clutches widely used in passenger car production often cause trouble. After a certain working time the clutches often fail to release properly without the driver realizing it, so that when changing gear a major or minor torque drag is left over that has to be absorbed by the synchromesh system. This overstressing of the synchro system leads to difficult shifting and a reduced endurance of the synchro units. It should be considered, too, that many drivers get tired of operating a clutch with high pedal forces and fail to release the clutch completely.

As with power brake systems and power steering the operation of the clutch system should be as light as possible to save the synchro system. This need is supported by experience with transmissions with automatic selection built in series where the clutch is operated by an electro-pneumatic control of the shift lever. This clutch is safely released at every gear change by the vacuum of the motor and closed again automatically after the finished gear selection.

As briefly mentioned before, the gear change linkage design should be reviewed, especially for steering-column gear change. Linkages are designed with too much clearance resulting from too wide tolerances in production, so that insufficient shifting forces and 'doughy' shifting occur. As an example, a well-known car built in quantity has had shifting forces and shifting times reduced to almost half by improvements in the linkage of the shifting.

I have avoided complicated formulae, as the synchro systems have so many figures in the calculation that are difficult to determine exactly. Friction is only one of them with a major influence. Tests with large numbers of systems and experience on the road often give the only guides to further improvement and development.

The MS. of this paper was received at the Institution on 15th December 1969 and accepted for publication on 12th January 1970.

Paper 26. Synchromesh Mechanisms: Experience of Heavy Truck Gearboxes

I. ROSEN, S. KRUK, P. O. EKER and H. MELLGREN

Aktiebologat Volvo, Gothenburg, Sweden

The design characteristics of different synchronizers with comparisons of designs, performance, and dependability in operation are discussed. The theory of operation is dealt with in detail. The influence of experience in practice on design from the effects of clash, hard gear changing, wear, clutch and oil drag are included. Suitable materials, machinery processes, and interdependence of dimensions are described. The paper concludes with notes on practical and laboratory tests and future development.

INTRODUCTION

To make driving safe and comfortable, synchronizers have been incorporated in the manual gearboxes of trucks. The synchromesh mechanisms make the gear change independent of the skill of the driver, and increase the average life of the gearbox.

For these reasons the synchromesh type of truck gearbox is being used extensively and rapid progress is being made in the development of better synchronizers.

At Volvo the policy has always been to make the truck as safe to handle and as easy to operate as possible. It is our contention that a driver should have at his command a gearbox which is simple to operate, does not require much thought, has only one gear lever, and reduces pedal effort to a minimum. In other words, he should be in control of a system that is as easy to handle as a private car.

In accordance with this ideal the design staff at Volvo had to face the fact that eventually they would need to design a suitable large synchronized transmission.

At this point it was thought that the synchronizer could be purchased from some other manufacturer, but after testing all the synchronizers available, not one fulfilled the necessary Volvo standard.

We carried out a comparison test of the pros and cons of different types and the items that were acceptable to our specifications, and Volvo now supplies a range of gearboxes for the engines of the largest trucks available, which, as far as we know, are the largest fully-synchronized gearboxes in production.

Notation

A	Proximity dimension.
a_c	Clearance.
$C_1 C_2, B$	Dimensions which prevent blocking.
D	Dimension securing blocking.
E_D	Drag energy.
E_s	Synchronizing energy.

F_{ch}	Engaging sleeve chamfer force.
F_s	Interlock ball force.
F_t	Tangential blocking force.
I_p, I_G, I_n, I_s	Inertia of driven part relative to its axis.
I_R	Reflected rotational inertia.
K_1	Constant, a function of the cone angle, radius, and friction.
K_2	Constant, a function of the chamfer angle, radius, and friction.
N, G, a, b, h	Design parameters.
P	Power.
R	Gear ratio.
R_B	Blocking chamfers pitch radius.
R_c	Mean cone radius.
$r_1 R_s$	Radius.
S_R	Direction of the relative speed.
T_B	Blocking torque.
T_D	Drag torque.
T_R	Reacting torque.
T_s	Synchronizing torque.
t	Time.
t_s	Duration of synchronization.
W	Wear allowance.
Z	$(= C_2 - C_1)$.
z_1, z_2, z_3, z_4	Number of gear teeth.
α_G	Gear acceleration or deceleration.
γ	The angle of the chamfers at the pitch radius.
μ_B	Coefficient of friction between the blocking surfaces.
μ_c	Coefficient of friction between the cones.
μ_{cs}	Static coefficient of friction.
μ_s	Coefficient of friction between the guide sleeves.
ϕ	Cone angle.
ω_1	Angular velocity of gear before the gear change.
ω_2	Angular velocity of gear after the gear change.
$\Delta\omega, \omega$	Relative speeds.

BRIEF DESIGN CHARACTERISTICS OF DIFFERENT SYNCHROMESH MECHANISMS

The following blocking synchronizers are compared:

Type 1: Volvo (Fig. 26.1).

Type 2: Strut (Fig. 26.2).

Type 3: Pin (Fig. 26.3).

The 'Porsche-synchromesh', being a servo brake, is not discussed in this paper.

Theory and operation of the Volvo type synchronizer

The Volvo, strut, and pin are the blocking synchronizers most commonly used by gearbox manufacturers. Generally speaking, these synchronizers have cone

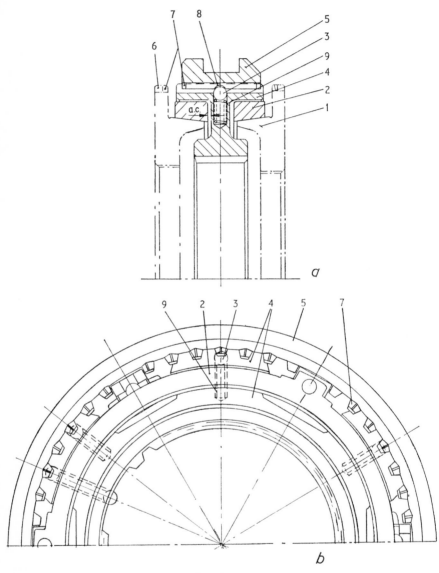

Fig. 26.1. Volvo blocking type synchronizer

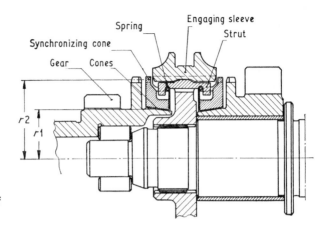

Fig. 26.2. Strut type of blocking synchronizer

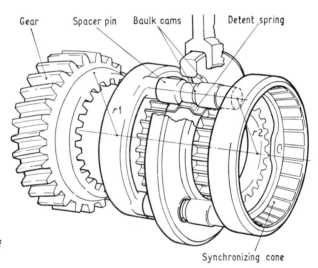

Fig. 26.3. Pin type of blocking synchronizer

surfaces which, during the gear change period, reduce the relative speeds of the synchronized parts and, at the same time, make it impossible to change before the speed difference is reduced to zero.

In order to describe the operation of the type 1 synchronizer (Figs 26.1 and 26.4) the following definitions are used:

(1) *Engaging ring cone (gear cone)*—The friction surface on the gear.
(2) *Synchronizing cone*—A friction element driven by the guide sleeve.
(3) *Interlock balls*—The energizing elements which provide the load on the synchronizing cone through the guide sleeve to move it into the blocking position.
(4) *Guide sleeve*—The axial movable element which limits the turning of the synchronizing cone and pilots the engaging sleeve, the interlock balls, and its springs.

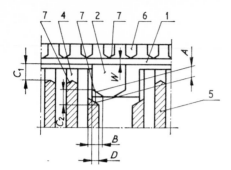

Fig. 26.4. Characteristic synchronizer dimensions

(5) *Engaging sleeve*—The axial movable element which locks up the gear to the shaft through the guide sleeve, and during synchronizing loads the synchronizing cone over the blocking surfaces and the guide sleeves.

(6) *Engaging ring splines*—Splines adjacent to the engaging ring. The engaging ring forms one unit with the gear.

(7) *Chamfers*—Angular surfaces on the periphery of the synchronizing cones on the engaging sleeve splines and on the engaging ring splines.

(8) *Detent*—The annular groove on the inner diameter of the engaging sleeve. The interlock balls nest in this annular groove when the engaging sleeve is in the neutral position.

(9) *Spring*—The energizing springs which force the interlock balls into the detent annulus and cause the guide sleeve to be loaded upon movement of the engaging sleeve.

The characteristic synchronizer dimensions

Proximity dimension—The axial distance between the synchronizing cone and the engaging sleeve chamfers when the synchronizing cone blocker body is against the side of the guide sleeve slot and the interlock ball has just started to ride out of the detent annulus. (Blocking position, *A* in Fig. 26.4.)

Dimension securing blocking (*D*, Fig. 26.4)—The circumferential distance between the end of the engaging sleeve and the synchronizing cone blocking chamfer surfaces when the synchronizing cone is in the blocking position ($D > 0$).

Dimensions which prevent blocking (Fig. 26.4): *Dimension C_1*—The distance between the head surface of the synchronizing cone and the engaging sleeve splines; this must be less than C_2. *Dimension C_2*—The axial distance between the end of the engaging sleeve and synchronizing cone blocking chamfer surfaces. *Dimension B*—The circumferential distance between the beginning of the sleeve and synchronizing cone blocking chamfer surfaces when the synchronizing cone is in the blocking position ($B > 0$).

Wear allowance—The distance between the synchronizing cone head surface and the engaging ring at the moment when the first contact of the cones occurs.

Operation of synchronizer

The operation of the synchronizer may be divided into six periods:

Period 1 (Fig. 26.5). An axial shifting force is applied to the engaging sleeve to

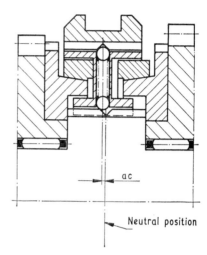

Fig. 26.5. Synchronizer in interlock ball detent position

initiate the gear change. This force makes the engaging sleeve and the guide sleeve move axially out of the neutral position, taking up the clearance *ac*. The guide sleeve now contacts the synchronizing cone.

Period 2 (Fig. 26.6). When the clearance *ac* is zero, the interlock ball, the guide

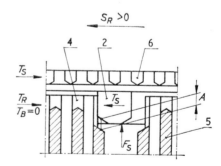

Fig. 26.6. Synchronizer in Period 2 position

sleeve, and the cone surfaces are loaded by the engaging sleeve (force F_s) which will continue the movement when the opposite forces are overcome as a result of energizing springs. The magnitude of the force F_s is a function of the energizing spring load (Fig. 26.7), the contact angle between the ball and detent annulus, the coefficient of friction between these surfaces, and the centrifugal forces.

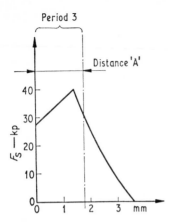

Fig. 26.7. Axial force F_s versus axial travel of engaging sleeve

Period 3 (Fig. 26.7). The shifting force acts on the sleeve. The sleeve moves through the distance A to the contact position between the synchronizing cone and the engaging sleeve of the blocking chamfers, while the interlock balls ride out of the detent groove and carry the synchronizing cone through the guide sleeve with force F_s. During Period 2, the synchronizing cone is already loaded by the force F_s. The action of F_s and oil drag, resulting from the relative speed between the cones, moves the synchronizing cone to the blocking position at which the synchronizing cone blocker body is against the side of the guide sleeve slot. Further, during the loading of the cone surfaces the oil present is removed and the coefficient of friction increases. This period is most important for the dependability of function. It is necessary to build up a determined coefficient of cone friction when the chamfers come into the contact position; this makes sure that the synchronizing torque is higher than the blocking torque.

Period 4 (Fig. 26.8). The chamfers of the engaging sleeve load the chamfers of

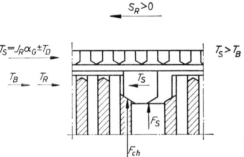

Fig. 26.8. Synchronizer in Period 4 position

the synchronizing cone and the acting forces build up rapidly. The major synchronization now takes place. The synchronizing cone is loaded by the torques T_s, T_B, and T_R:

$$T_s = K_1(F_s + F_{ch}) \quad \text{and} \quad T_s = I_R \alpha_G + T_D \quad . \quad . \quad . \quad (26.1)$$

where T_s is the synchronizing torque, K_1 a constant which is a function of the cone angle, radius, and friction, F_s the interlock ball force acting on the synchronizing cone F_{ch} the engaging sleeve chamfer force acting on the synchronizing cone chamfer, I_R the reflected rotational inertia, α_G the gear acceleration, and T_D the drag torque reflected to the gear;

$$T_B = K_2 F_{ch} \quad . \quad . \quad . \quad . \quad . \quad . \quad (26.2)$$

where T_B is the blocking torque and K_2 is a constant, which is a function of the chamfer angle, radius, and friction;

$$T_R = T_s - T_B \quad . \quad . \quad . \quad . \quad . \quad . \quad (26.3)$$

where T_R is the reacting torque from the guide sleeve on the synchronizing cone. (During synchronizing the reacting torque, T_R, is equal to or greater than zero.)

Period 5 (Fig. 26.9). The synchronization is completed. The relative speed

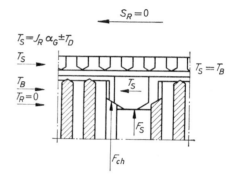

Fig. 26.9. Synchronizer in Period 5 position

between the gear and the synchronizing cone has approached zero and the friction on the cone surface locks the gear to the synchronizing cone. The synchronizing torque, T_s, falls to T_B and $T_R = 0$. The blocking torque is here defined as:

$$T_B = I_R \alpha_G \pm T_D \quad . \quad . \quad . \quad . \quad . \quad . \quad (26.4)$$

If the torque $T_B \pm T_D$ is greater than zero, the synchronizing cone and locked gear (as one unit) move aside to allow the engaging sleeve splines to pass. At the position $C_2 = 0$ (Fig. 26.4) the synchronizing cone is no longer energized by the engaging sleeve chamfers and the guide sleeve. The guide sleeve should stop to energize the synchronizing cone just before the contact position of the chamfers, but this will be given in greater detail later in the paper.

Period 6 (Fig. 26.10). The engaging sleeve moves from position $C_2 = 0$ (Fig.

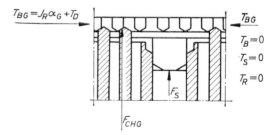

Fig. 26.10. Synchronizer in Period 6 position

26.4) to contact with the engaging ring splines. The engaging ring can take any number of positions and may also block the travel of the engaging sleeve (see Fig. 26.10). A blocking torque, T_{BG}, is built up on the contact angles of the engaging ring splines and the engaging sleeve splines which move the engaging ring (gear) and the synchronizing cone aside; the sleeve then passes through and the lock-up is complete (Fig. 26.11). If the synchronizing cone is still locked to the engaging ring, the torque T_{BG} must release it.

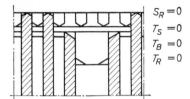

$S_R = 0$
$T_S = 0$
$T_B = 0$
$T_R = 0$

Fig. 26.11. Synchronizer in gear change completed position

Comparison of the strut type and pin type with the Volvo blocking synchronizer

The most important design feature of a blocking synchronizer must be reliability since the advantages gained from synchromesh gearboxes must not be discredited through malfunction. The reliability of the Volvo design has been successful for the following reasons:

(1) The initial blocker is adjusted to the synchronizing position to obtain maximum safety against clash *even* with large friction surfaces.

(2) The blocking function is dependable since the blocking surfaces are separated from the engaging ring splines—some clashes do not destroy the blocking surfaces.

(3) The blocking surfaces are made from case-hardened steel which gives minimum wear.

(4) Precision machined steel cones give low wear at the opposite cone.

(5) Large friction surfaces (on the brass cone) give low wear and allow over-loading for short periods.

(6) The large diameter on the engaging ring splines, which gives large chamfer angle of the splines, results in a shorter design length.

In comparison, the blocking surfaces on the strut type (Fig. 26.2) are combined with the engaging sleeve chamfers, which means that the function may be destroyed by one clash. Moreover, the synchronizing cone blocking surfaces are made of brass, which provides more wear. The pin type (Fig. 26.3) has a small diameter on the engaging ring splines, and therefore requires a greater constructional length for the same working surfaces and stroke length.

MATHEMATICAL BACKGROUND

Calculation of the synchronizer is based on very elementary physical laws dealing with inertia, speed change, coefficient of friction, time, etc. These problems are discussed below.

Reflected inertia

The calculations should be based on reflected inertia, which depends on the position of the gear or other transmission element relative to the calculated gear with which it is in mesh.

The reflected rotational inertia is defined as follows:

$$I_R = I_n R_G^2 \quad . \quad . \quad . \quad . \quad . \quad . \quad . \quad (26.5)$$

where I_R is the reflected inertia of the driven part to the driving part axis, I_n the inertia of the driven part relative to its axis, and R_G the gear ratio, i.e. the ratio of the number of driving gear teeth to the number of driven gear teeth (z_1/z_2).

For the gear train shown in Fig. 26.12, the inertia of the whole gear train reflected to the I_G gear axis is calculated as:

$$I_R = I_G + I_s R_{G2}^2 + I_p R_{G2}^2 R_{G1}^2 = I_G + I_s \left(\frac{z_4}{z_3}\right)^2 + I_p \left(\frac{z_4}{z_3}\right)^2 \left(\frac{z_2}{z_1}\right)^2 \quad . \quad (26.6)$$

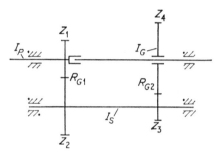

Fig. 26.12. Scheme of gear train for reflected inertia calculation

Synchronizing torque

The axial forces applied to the synchronizing cone develop the friction torque (synchronizing torque), which acts on the synchronized gear (see Fig. 26.13):

$$T_s = \frac{(F_{ch} + F_s)\mu_c R_c}{\sin \phi} \quad . \quad . \quad . \quad . \quad . \quad (26.7)$$

where T_s is the synchronizing torque, F_{ch} the axial force loading the chamfers of the synchronizing cone, F_s the axial force with which the guide sleeve loads the

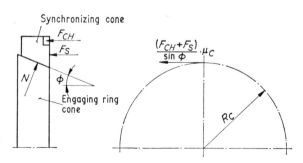

Fig. 26.13. Synchronizing torque force diagram

synchronizing cone, μ_c the coefficient of friction between the cones, R_c the mean cone radius, and ϕ the cone angle.

The synchronizing torque accelerates or decelerates the gear train and the driven plate and may also be expressed as

$$T_s = I_R \alpha_G \pm T_D \quad \ldots \quad \ldots \quad \ldots \quad (26.8)$$

where α_G is the acceleration or deceleration of the gear being synchronized, and T_D is the drag torque.

Time

The duration of the gear change is a basic design value on which the whole operation of the gearbox depends. The duration of the gear change depends mostly on the duration of synchronization, which is a function of synchronizing torque, magnitude of reflected inertia, the relative speed of the gear and the synchronizing cone, and the drag (clutch and oil drag).

The synchronizing duration may be expressed as

$$t_s = \frac{I_R(\omega_2 - \omega_1)}{T_s \pm T_D} \quad \ldots \quad \ldots \quad \ldots \quad (26.9)$$

where t_s is the duration of synchronization, I_R the reflected inertia of the gear train to synchronizer being calculated, ω_1 the angular velocity of gear being synchronized before the gear change, ω_2 the angular velocity of gear being synchronized after the gear change, and T_s is the synchronizing torque.

Blocking torque

The fork and the engaging sleeve axial force, acting through the engaging sleeve blocking chamfers against the synchronizing cone blocking chamfers, F_{ch}, builds the blocking torque. During the synchronization the blocking torque acts in opposition to the synchronizing torque. The blocking torque at the moment of impending motion may be expressed as

$$T_B = R_B F_t = R_B F_{ch} \frac{\sin \gamma - \mu_B \cos \gamma}{\cos \gamma + \mu_B \sin \gamma} \quad \ldots \quad \ldots \quad (26.10)$$

where T_B is the blocking torque, R_B the blocking chamfers pitch radius, F_t the tangential blocking force, γ the angle of the chamfers at the pitch radius (as shown in Fig. 26.14), and μ_B the coefficient of friction between the blocking surfaces.

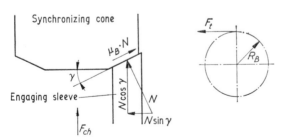

Fig. 26.14. Blocking torque force diagram

The force diagram in Fig. 26.14 shows a relationship between the force acting on the blocking chamfers and helps in the derivation of the tangential blocking force. The axial sleeve force F_{ch}, expressed in terms of N, may be written as

$$F_{ch} = N \cos \gamma + \mu_B N \sin \gamma = N (\cos \gamma + \mu_B \sin \gamma) \quad . \quad . \quad (26.11)$$

The tangential force, in terms of N and the chamfer angle, is

$$F_t = N (\sin \gamma - \mu_B \cos \gamma) \quad . \quad . \quad . \quad . \quad (26.12)$$

From equations (26.11) and (26.12) the tangential force at the pitch radius of blocking chamfer can be calculated:

$$F_t = F_{ch} \frac{\sin \gamma - \mu_B \cos \gamma}{\cos \gamma + \mu_B \sin \gamma} \quad . \quad . \quad . \quad . \quad . \quad (26.13)$$

Cone and chamfer angle relationship

The synchronizing torque and the blocking torque are opposed to each other during synchronization, and to obtain dependable synchronization the synchronizing torque must be greater than the blocking torque. This relationship may be mathematically expressed as

$$\frac{(F_{ch} + F_s)\mu_c R_c}{\sin \phi} > \frac{R_B F_{ch}(\sin \gamma - \mu_B \cos \gamma)}{\cos \gamma + \mu_B \sin \gamma} \quad . \quad . \quad . \quad (26.14)$$

In some designs the force F_s is zero at the instant of indexing of the synchronizing cone chamfers by the engaging sleeve chamfers, and this relationship can then be written as

$$\frac{F_{ch}\mu_c R_c}{\sin \phi} > \frac{R_B F_{ch}(\sin \gamma - \mu_B \cos \gamma)}{\cos \gamma + \mu_B \sin \gamma} \quad . \quad . \quad . \quad . \quad (26.15)$$

and, after some reductions, as

$$\frac{\mu_c R_c}{\sin \phi} > \frac{R_B(\sin \gamma - \mu_B \cos \gamma)}{\cos \gamma + \mu_B \sin \gamma} \quad . \quad . \quad . \quad . \quad (26.16)$$

The blocking torque for a given axial chamfer force, chamfer angle, and blocking chamfer pitch radius is a function of the friction on the blocking chamfer surface.

For friction coefficients, μ_B, between 0 and 0·12 (maximum and minimum) the blocking torque can be calculated. The friction on the blocking chamfer surface, $\mu_B = 0$, determines the proper angles that ensure a blocking condition for synchronization. To calculate the blocking condition at $\mu_B = 0$ the following equation may be used:

$$\frac{\mu_c R_c}{\sin \phi} > R_B \tan \gamma \quad \left(\tan \gamma < \frac{\mu_c R_c}{\sin \phi R_B} \right) . \quad . \quad . \quad (26.17)$$

If μ_c is assumed to be a given value (maximum and minimum), the cone chamfer angle relationship can easily be calculated.

On analysing the equation of the synchronizing torque, it is easy to observe the importance of the cone angle ϕ, which directly influences the effectiveness of acceleration and deceleration of the synchronized parts, and theoretically at $\phi = 0$ the synchronizing torque reaches infinity. In practice, the cone angle is limited by ensuring self-release and preventing seizure of the synchronizing cone. This would interfere with the engaging sleeve spline travel during changing, when the blocking chamfer surfaces of this sleeve have passed the blocking chamfer surfaces of the synchronizing cone. This limit is determined as follows:

$$\mu_{cs} \leqslant \tan \phi \quad . \quad . \quad . \quad . \quad . \quad . \quad (26.18)$$

where μ_{cs} is the static coefficient of friction between the synchronizing cone and the gear cone.

To clarify the relationship between blocking and synchronizing torque, Fig. 26.15 shows torque curves with coefficient of friction values against axial forces F_{ch}.

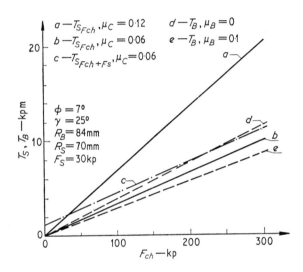

Fig. 26.15. Blocking and synchronizing torque relation versus chamfer force F_{ch}

Kinetic energy

During synchronization there is a change in speed of the gear parts connected with the gear cone, and the kinetic energy dissipated by the synchronizing cone may be expressed as:

$$E_s = \frac{I_R(\omega_2 - \omega_1)^2}{2} \pm E_D \quad . \quad . \quad . \quad . \quad . \quad (26.19)$$

where E_s is the energy dissipated during synchronization at speed change from ω_1 to ω_2 while under the effect of drag torque, and E_D is the energy dissipated during synchronization to overcome drag resistances.

The kinetic energy dissipated during synchronization, expressed as a function of time, can be written as

$$E_s(t) = T_s \left[(\omega_2 - \omega_1)t - \frac{\alpha_G t^2}{2} \right] \quad \text{at } T_s = \text{const. and } T_D = \text{const.} \quad (26.20)$$

where α_G is the acceleration or deceleration of the gear being synchronized and

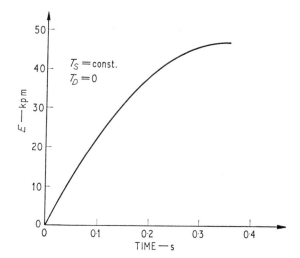

Fig. 26.16. Theoretical dissipation of energy by synchronizing cone during synchronization

t is the time between limits ($t = 0$ and $t = t_s$). Fig. 26.16 shows the kinetic energy dissipated during a certain synchronization at $T_s = $ const. and $T_D = 0$.

Power

The instantaneous power developed during synchronization is calculated as

$$P = T_s \omega \qquad (26.21)$$

where T_s is the synchronizing torque and ω is the relative speed between the synchronizing cone and the engaging ring cone. Expressed as a function of time, equation (26.21) can be written as

$$P = T_s[(\omega_2 - \omega_1) - \alpha_G t] \quad \text{at } \alpha_G = \text{const.} \qquad (26.22)$$

where ω_1 is the angular velocity of the gear before synchronization, ω_2 the angular velocity of the gear after synchronization, and t the moment of synchronization for which the calculation is carried out. Fig. 26.17 shows a diagram of the power developed during a synchronization at $T_s - T_D = $ const.

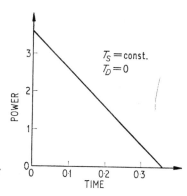

Fig. 26.17. Theoretical development of power during synchronization

DESIGNING A SYNCHRONIZER TO OBTAIN DEPENDABLE SYNCHRONIZATION AND EASY GEAR CHANGING

Dependable synchronization

As mentioned previously, it is necessary to ensure that the synchronizing torque is greater than the blocking torque to establish a blocking condition for synchronization. Mathematical relations do not show any special conditions to be fulfilled. The variable parameters only constitute a dynamic coefficient of friction between the synchronizing cone, the gear cone, and the blocking chamfers. The other parameters (cone angle, chamfer angle, cone and chamfer pitch radius) are constant and depend on the design. An analysis of different synchronizer designs shows that in all cases the synchronizing torque is much greater than blocking torque. Figs 26.15, 26.18, and 26.19 show the condition mentioned above.

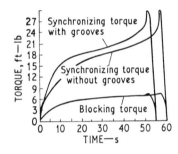

Fig. 26.18. Synchronizing and blocking torque versus time for grooved and ungrooved synchronizing cones

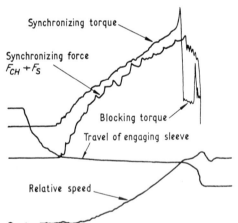

Fig. 26.19. Synchronizing curves versus time

The question arises: 'Why does clash (lack of synchronization) occur in certain designs?'

Clash occurs from a change of coefficient of friction during synchronization. Attempts have been made to explain the alteration of the coefficient of friction by (a) changing the oil temperature, (b) using different kinds of oil, and (c) using different values of relative speeds between the friction surfaces. Although these factors have an influence on the coefficient of friction, they are all controllable.

Tests show that if the speed of shifting was greater than normal, clash could occur even when the synchronizing torque at the end of synchronization was several times greater than the blocking torque. An analysis of the friction curves as a function of time explains the phenomenon of clash. Where there is rapid movement of the sleeve, the development of the coefficient of friction on the surfaces between the synchronizing cone and the gear cone is too slow in comparison with the speed of the sleeve movement. Consequently, the blocking surfaces pass each other, and if the coefficient of friction is not large enough at this moment, clash occurs.

The development of the coefficient of friction on the friction surfaces is shown in Figs 26.20–26.23. The curves in the figures show that the beginning of

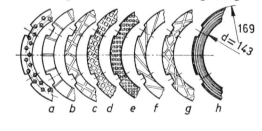

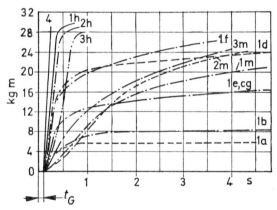

Fig. 26.20. Friction torque versus time for different materials and configurations of friction surfaces

1   Steel, sintered iron.
2   Steel, sintered bronze.
3   Steel, phosphor-bronze.
4   Steel, asbestos (not lubricated).
m   Non-grooved.

synchronization is the most interesting part of the whole process as regards the synchronizer's reliability. It is then that the interlock balls are most effective. They press the synchronizing cone through the guide sleeve against the engaging ring cone. The oil is removed from the friction surfaces and the coefficient of friction builds up to a determined value before the blocking chamfers of the engaging sleeve and synchronizing cone touch each other.

The efficiency of the action of the interlock balls depends on the force with which they press the synchronizing cone and the time of their action—direct on

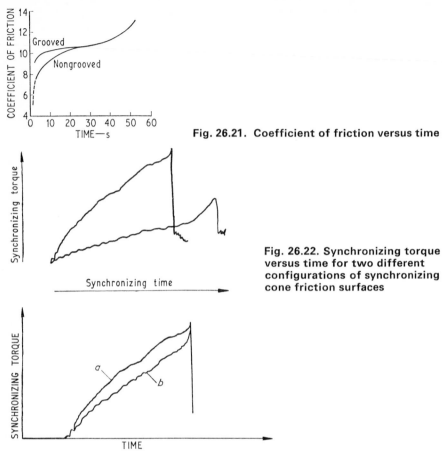

Fig. 26.21. Coefficient of friction versus time

Fig. 26.22. Synchronizing torque versus time for two different configurations of synchronizing cone friction surfaces

a New friction surfaces.
b Friction surfaces after 1000 synchronizations.

Fig. 26.23. Synchronizing torque versus time

distance *A* (see Fig. 26.4). It might be thought that *A* can be reduced to zero and lower if, at the same time, the distance C_2 increases. However, it does not work in this manner, because it is possible that the blocking chamfers of the sleeve may move aside the synchronizing cone (at too low a coefficient of friction on the friction surfaces). When the movement of the synchronizing cone is too great, the action of the interlock balls, which must change the direction of movement, may not be effective enough to prevent the passage of the blocking surfaces.

There are designs in which *A* is almost zero but, at the same time, where the force F_s with which the interlock balls act on the synchronizing cone is relatively large, and because of this (even with the low coefficient of friction at the beginning of the synchronization), the synchronizing torque is greater than the blocking torque. Relation (26.15) explains the function of the force F_s. This type of design is very convenient because the dependability of synchronization may be regulated by the change of the spring forces. On the other hand, the F_s force at work while the blocking surfaces contact makes gear changing difficult. The problem of difficult gear changing will be discussed later.

Easy gear changing

This refers to the condition where only a low level of force is required to change gear. Easy changing influences the time taken to change gear and, consequently, adds to the comfort of driving. Easy changing depends on the duration of synchronization and the resistance of the engaging sleeve movement which, in turn, depends on the oil and clutch drag.

To obtain an easy change gearbox, the design must be such that the synchronizing torque is as large as possible and the blocking torque reaches its maximum value relative to the synchronizing torque. It follows, therefore, that an easy change can be attained more easily if the dependability of synchronization (T_s/T_B) is reduced, and for this reason it is important to control the commencement of synchronization in order to decrease the difference between the synchronizing torque and the blocking torque at the end of the synchronization period.

Let us look more carefully at the torques and forces which act on the synchronizing cone after synchronization, at the moment when the blocking chamfers of the engaging sleeve tend to move the synchronizing cone aside to allow further travel of the sleeve (see Fig. 26.9).

Period 5 (described earlier) explains the phenomena that occur during the first moments after synchronization. The blocking torque, T_B, tries to move the synchronizing cone and the locked gear (one unit) against the resistances from the gear train, the friction forces between the guide sleeve and synchronizing cone, and the resistance of movement:

$$T_B = I_R \alpha_G \pm T_D + F_s \mu_s R_s \quad . \quad . \quad . \quad . \quad (26.23)$$

where μ_s is the coefficient of friction between the guide sleeve and the synchronizing cone, and R_s is the radius of the contact point. As can be seen from equation (26.23), the force F_s after synchronization is not desirable, since it decreases the blocking torque $(F_{ch} = F - F_s)$ and provides added resistance of $F_s \mu_s R_s$ when the synchronizing cone is moved relative to the sleeve.

In Period 6 the force F_{ch} builds up a torque on the engaging ring spline chambers, T_{BG}, which tries to move the gear aside against the resistance of the transmission and the resistance produced on the friction surfaces between the synchronizing cone and the gear cone. Fig. 26.10 and equation (26.24) explain the relationship in this instance:

$$T_{BG} = I_R \alpha_G \pm T_D + \frac{F_s \mu_c R_c}{\sin \phi} \quad . \quad . \quad . \quad . \quad (26.24)$$

From equation (26.24) and the factors mentioned above, F_s should be zero when the blocking surfaces of the engaging sleeve contact the blocking surfaces of the synchronizing cone, or at least should be zero when the sleeve spline chamfers contact the engaging ring spline chamfers, since F_s decreases T_{BG} $(F_{ch} = F - F_s)$ and builds up an *extra* resistance torque which is relatively large: $F_s \mu_s R_c / \sin \phi$.

The relation $\tan \phi > \mu_{cs}$ must also be established.

THE INFLUENCE OF PRACTICAL EXPERIENCE ON THE DESIGN OF THE ELEMENTS OF SYNCHRONIZERS

The design of a synchronizer is theoretically simple, but in practice is not free from problems. As mentioned previously, such problems as dependability of synchronization and easy gear changing can result in clash and high effort during gear changing.

Clash

Analysis of the problem of clash shows that it is influenced by many factors, even with a theoretically correct design of synchronizer.

As mentioned previously, clash occurs when the blocking torque is greater than the synchronizing torque and, as seen from the mathematical relations in a certain design, only the coefficient of friction between the friction surfaces is of decisive importance here. This coefficient depends on: (*a*) friction materials, (*b*) configuration of the friction surfaces, (*c*) lubricant, and (*d*) the relative speed between the friction surfaces.

Friction materials

Different combinations of materials have varying coefficients of friction. The coefficient of friction is constant for a determined test condition. Therefore, the type of material does not influence the changes in coefficient of friction during synchronization.

Configuration of the friction surfaces

The friction surfaces may be analysed from two aspects: shape and finish.

Shape—In practice the friction surfaces are a combination of the smooth surface and the grooved surface in the form of a thread with axial grooves. The grooved surface provides for quicker release of the oil from the friction surfaces and that tends towards an increased coefficient of friction, in spite of the fact that the final coefficient of friction will not be altered.

Tests show that grooves in the form of a thread release the oil from the surfaces most rapidly. The shape of the thread (i.e. the depth and pitch of the thread, and the width of the thread tops) has an influence on the development of the coefficient of friction versus time. The thread may be combined with axial grooves. The shape and number of axial grooves, together with the shape of the thread, must be determined by experiment.

A large oil capacity in a thread may make the presence of axial grooves unnecessary. For example, in the design shown in Fig. 26.24 there is less oil to wipe from

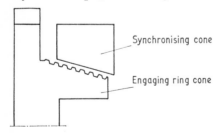

Synchronising cone

Engaging ring cone

Fig. 26.24. Friction surfaces

the friction surface because the centrifugal force removes the oil from the thread and synchronizing cone and, consequently, the oil capacity of the thread increases.

Finish—The finish of the friction surface greatly influences the coefficient of friction. To estimate the surface finish it is not enough merely to check the centre-line average (c.l.a.) value. As two surfaces with the same c.l.a. value may have different wear and coefficients of friction, the surface finish must be specified in both directions; this also applies to the nature of the finish. For example, a harder surface with 'spikes' develops a higher coefficient of friction, but gives greater wear.

Machining of friction surfaces must be carried out under strict control in very rigid machines in order to avoid distortions in the form of vibrations, as these vibrations can result in wavy surfaces.

In one case a wavy surface was obtained with a wave amplitude of 5–10 μm, at which clash occurred. This happened because a surface of this kind provides an increase in the hydraulic effects which, in turn, decrease the coefficient of friction. Figs 26.25–26.27 show, respectively, the roundness diagram of a wavy surface, its contact surface against the engaging ring cone, and development of synchronization when clash occurs.

It is possible to sand-blast parts that have a wavy surface, and thus prevent them being rejected, but when wavy surfaces occur on the gear cone, then it *must* be rejected. Fig. 26.28 shows a roundness diagram of a gear cone with a typical

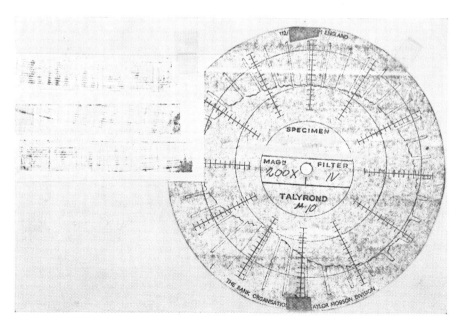

Fig. 26.25. Roundness diagram of synchronizing cone and its contact surface against engaging ring cone

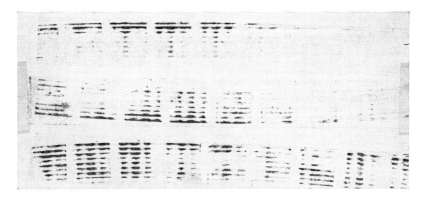

Fig. 26.26. Synchronizing cone contact surface against engaging ring cone

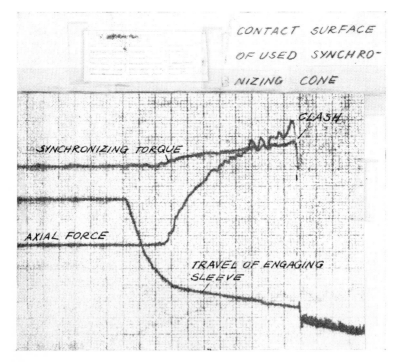

Fig. 26.27. Development of synchronization when clash occurs

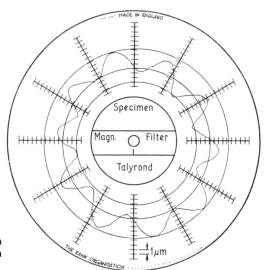

Fig. 26.28. Roundness diagram of engaging ring cone at which clash occurs

wavy surface, being a result of a worn bearing in a grinding machine. When the function of this gear cone was checked in a particular synchronizer, clash occurred.

The finish of the friction surfaces (especially the harder one) should be as near the run-in surface (stabilized finish) as possible. Rough friction surfaces initially make the synchronization more dependable, but when the surfaces become smoother with wear the coefficient of friction decreases and a clash can occur.

A positive co-operation of the friction surfaces was gained when the finish of the gear cone (case-hardened steel with a Rockwell hardness of C60) had a maximum c.l.a. of $0 \cdot 16$ μm. It was manufactured in such a way that there were no 'spikes', the synchronizing surface being made of a copper–zinc alloy.

For the steel–molybdenum combination good results were achieved when the finish of the steel surface had a maximum c.l.a. of $0 \cdot 25$ μm and the molybdenum surface a c.l.a. of $0 \cdot 16$ μm.

Lubricant

The influence of oils and their viscosity on the synchronization is of great importance. A disturbance in the synchronization may occur both at low and high viscosity of the oil owing to the additives and to difficulties in releasing the oil from the friction surfaces.

Figs 26.29 and 26.30 show the change in the viscosity versus temperature and the change in the coefficient of friction for different oils. A high-viscosity oil cannot be wiped from the friction surfaces as quickly as a low-viscosity oil.

In order to prevent clash with a high-viscosity oil, a high value of the force F_s and the distance A in Fig. 26.4 should be used. Of course, decreasing the angle γ can improve the ratio T_s/T_B, but such an improvement increases the effort required during gear changing.

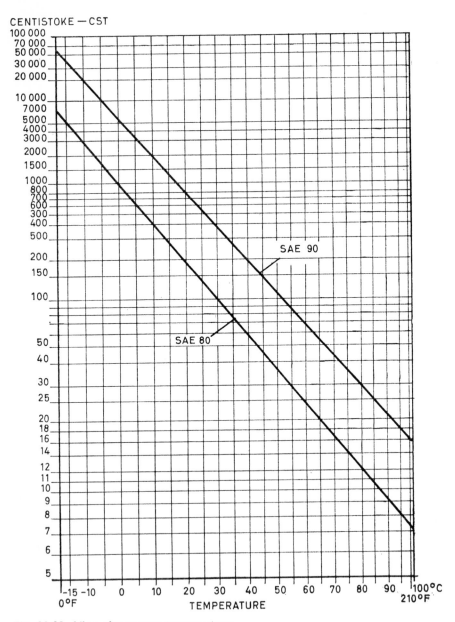

Fig. 26.29. Viscosity versus temperature

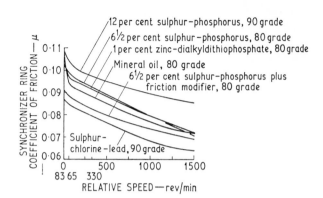

12 per cent sulphur–phosphorus, 90 grade
6½ per cent sulphur–phosphorus, 80 grade
1 per cent zinc–dialkyldithiophosphate, 80 grade
Mineral oil, 80 grade
6½ per cent sulphur–phosphorus plus friction modifier, 80 grade
Sulphur–chloride–lead, 90 grade

SYNCHRONIZER RING
COEFFICIENT OF FRICTION — μ

RELATIVE SPEED — rev/min

Fig. 26.30. Coefficient of friction versus speed for gear lubricant additives

Relative speed

The influence of the relative speeds of the friction surfaces on the coefficient of friction should be considered in the design of a synchronizer. Changing of these speeds has great influence on the hydrodynamic conditions. When the surfaces have, for example, a wavy form, the coefficient of friction decreases at high relative speeds (Fig. 26.31).

Generally, there are no great differences in the relative speeds of the surfaces in common designs of gearboxes, but the modern designs have often a two-range system (Volvo), where the differences in the relative speeds are much greater. For example, for gear changes in a main part of the normal gearbox the relative speeds are about 300 rev/min. In a part of the two-range system, however, the relative speeds increase to 1200 rev/min. Higher relative speeds take place when changing is carried out through several gears (e.g. changing directly from first to third), and this occurs more often in gearboxes with a large number of gears. We must not forget that the influence of relative speeds on the coefficient of friction will be more obvious for a threaded surface with a wide top and large thread pitch.

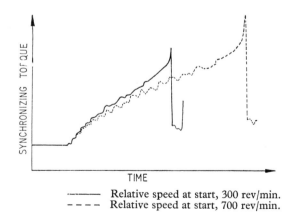

SYNCHRONIZING TORQUE

TIME

Fig. 26.31. Synchronizing torque versus time

———— Relative speed at start, 300 rev/min.
– – – – Relative speed at start, 700 rev/min.

Partial clash

In practice, another form of clash called 'partial clash' may be encountered. In partial clash the engaging sleeve and the engaging ring splines generally have less relative speed when they come into contact than they had at the beginning of the synchronization. The partial clash may be caused by:

(a) excessively low synchronizing torque;

(b) excessively large transmission or clutch drag;

(c) increased blocking torque after destruction of the blocking surfaces;

(d) high oil temperature;

(e) deformation of the synchronizing cone resulting from very large gear-changing force; or

(f) wear of the friction surfaces.

Equation (26.15) shows the influence of the force F_s on the ratio T_s/T_B. If the force F_{ch} is much larger than F_s, the influence of F_s is then very small.

If a design is based on the service function of the force F_s at the normal magnitude of the change forces, and if the driver is compelled to change gear very quickly and use very great force for any particular reason, then the relationship between the blocking torque and the synchronizing torque may be altered to such an extent that clash will occur.

In some designs where the spline chamfers act as the blocking surfaces, any destruction of the chamfer angle can easily occur during any clash and through wear; a change in the chamfer angles means a change in the blocking torque. If clash occurs here it develops as a full clash.

A high temperature of the synchronizing cone and gear cone, or the deformation of the synchronizing cone and wear of the friction surfaces, all have a similar influence on the synchronizer with regard to clash. These factors decrease the wear allowance, W, and as soon as $W = 0$ a clash occurs.

If the oil is at a low temperature, this may increase the oil drag in the transmission. After the completed synchronization, a new difference of the relative speeds occurs, and the engaging sleeve loses its contact with the blocking surfaces of the synchronizing cone and indexes the engaging ring splines. The sensation in this type of clash is much less than in other kinds of clash and depends on the speed of the change. A similar sensation causes clutch drag. The coefficient of friction on the blocking surfaces is almost constant, i.e. it has little influence on the blocking torque.

As a result of the different thermal coefficient of elongation (for most designs), an increase in the temperature causes a decrease in W. During synchronization, heat is emitted which increases the temperature of the elements of the synchronizer, and again causes a decrease in W. The change in W during synchronization can be seen in Fig. 26.32.

Forces acting on the synchronizing cone also enlarge it, i.e. the distance W decreases. Fig. 26.33 shows a change of W versus axial forces acting on the synchronizing cone for a particular design. Wear on the friction surfaces is often the only cause of a decrease in W.

As mentioned above, it is necessary at the design stage to allow for the

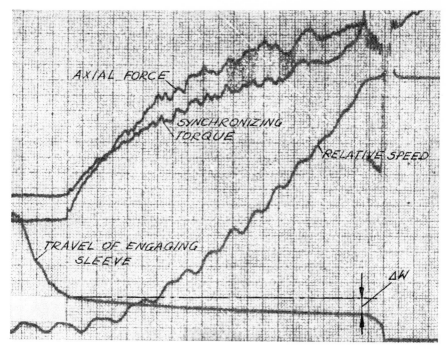

Fig. 26.32. Decrease of distance W during synchronization

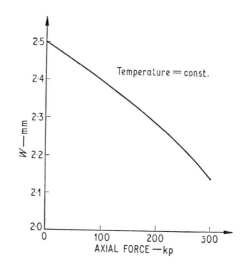

**Fig. 26.33. Dimension W versus axial
force acting on synchronizing cone**

influence of temperature and the gear changing forces. If this is not considered, the life of the synchronizer may be greatly reduced.

When different materials are used it is impossible to reduce the influence of temperature, but the influence of the forces may be reduced by changing the synchronizing cone dimensions. In a particular design the decrease in W, caused by the temperature and the gear change forces, reached 1·0–1·2 mm. In this design the synchronizing cone was made of a copper–zinc alloy.

Difficult gear changing

Difficult gear changing occurs when a larger changing force is necessary than normal. This may depend on design factors or oil and clutch drag.

The influence of design factors

Difficult gear changing depends on the magnitude of the blocking torque relative to all resistances acting against it. The mathematical relations have already been mentioned under the heading 'Easy gear changing'.

From equation (26.23) it follows that F_s should be as small as possible at $A = 0$, and the torque T_B should be as large as possible to counteract the resistance T_D. Experiments carried out by changing A_{max} (Fig. 26.4) in order to decrease F_s at $A = 0$ have shown that the gear changing resistance had decreased.

For a design where the gear changing is made with help of air or oil pressure and the shifting forces are limited, it can happen that by increasing the resistance (oil and clutch drag) the synchronization is completed, but the change is impossible owing to the large force F_s. The force F_s decreases the action of the axial forces acting on the synchronizing cone blocking surface ($F_{ch} = F - F_s$) and builds an extra resistance $F_s \mu_s R_s$.

Another design factor which decreases the effectiveness of the gear changing forces consists of forces blocking the sleeve in the neutral position. These forces reach a maximum value during synchronization, decreasing the efficiency of synchronization (by increasing the time taken) and reducing the gear changing force acting on the sleeve.

Other influences of F_s on difficult or easy gear changing were described previously in 'Easy gear changing'.

In a design where the blocking surfaces are made of copper–zinc alloys, there is a risk that the blocking surfaces will wear, resulting in clash or blocking. In order to avoid blocking, the relationship $G > 0$ must be maintained (see Fig. 26.34), because in other cases the engaging sleeve splines deform the blocking

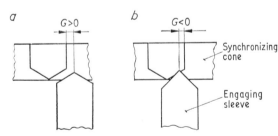

a $G > 0$ *b* $G < 0$

Synchronizing cone

Engaging sleeve

Fig. 26.34. Different positions of engaging sleeve relative to synchronizing cone

surfaces. Such deformation may occur during the first period of use of a synchronizer, especially when there are differences in the chamfer angles of the blocking surfaces (see Fig. 26.34). There are also very severe blocking effects when the chamfers a of the engaging sleeve splines and the gear splines are large. For a ratio of $N/a < 10$ (see Fig. 26.35) blocking often occurs.

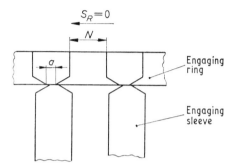

Fig. 26.35. Travel of sleeve stopped

The other design factor which influences the occurrence of blocking is the value $Z = C_2 - C_1$ (see Fig. 26.4). The value of Z should be less than zero if it is desired to use the whole (distance W) lifetime of a synchronizer without blocking sensations before a clash occurs. Vibration in the manufacturing process is another factor which leads to difficult gear changing as the finish of the friction surfaces may be rougher than normal, thus giving a higher coefficient of friction and, according to equation (26.24), a higher resistance to movement ($F_s \mu_{cs} R_c / \sin \phi$). If further μ_{cs} overruns the value $\tan \phi$, seizing occurs. Fig. 26.36 shows the traces of the gear cone finish at which blocking and hard shifting have occurred.

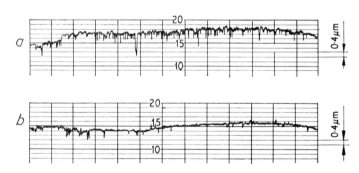

a Finish at which blocking and difficult gear changing occurred.
b Normal finish.

Fig. 26.36. Engaging ring cone finish traces

Oil and clutch drag

The temperature and the oil viscosities influence T_D, which directly causes a high effort during gear changing and longer duration of synchronization. Fig. 26.37 shows the influence of temperature and oil viscosities on oil drag.

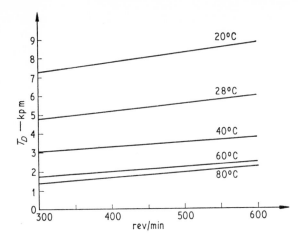

Fig. 26.37. Influence of temperature on oil drag in gearbox, S.A.E. 90

An oil drag transmitted to the synchronized gear directly depends on the ratio between a point of resistance and a synchronized gear (see Figs 26.38 and 26.39), therefore the clutch drag mostly influences the force required to change the low gears. Modern gearboxes are often of a two-range design which permits reduction of the gear ratios in the main part of the boxes. In the Volvo R50 and R60 gearboxes the gear ratio of first, second, third, and fourth gears in the main part (truck gearboxes) of the box is almost four times less than the total gear ratio.

Wear

Unfortunately, where there is friction there is also wear and in the case of

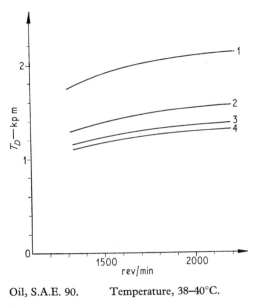

Oil, S.A.E. 90.   Temperature, 38–40°C.

Fig. 26.38. Reflected drag torque of gear train to synchronizer of (1) first and fifth gear, (2) second and sixth gear, (3) third and seventh gear, and (4) fourth and eighth gear versus input rotation

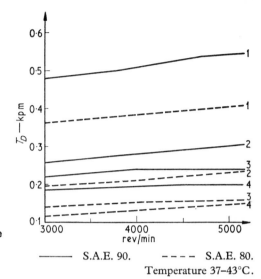

Fig. 26.39. Reflected drag torque of gear train to synchronizer of first gear, second gear, third gear, and fourth gear

——— S.A.E. 90.   – – – – S.A.E. 80.

Temperature 37–43°C.

synchronizers this influences the decrease of W. The life of synchronizer elements depends on many factors, such as:

(a) material,
(b) quality of the friction surfaces,
(c) size of the friction surfaces,
(d) oil and clutch drag, and
(e) design.

Material

The materials of the synchronizer elements have a determining influence on their dimensions. The following combinations of materials are in common use for the friction surfaces: copper alloys against case-hardened steel; molybdenum against case-hardened steel; and aluminium alloys against case-hardened steel.

The copper alloy works very well if the heat loading is under control. In heavy truck gearboxes heat loading of the synchronizers is generally quite high, especially when gear changing is made through several gears (e.g. driving on a slope, or driving without load). Calculations for a determined design have shown that by changing from third to first gear five times more energy will be used during synchronization than when changing from second to first gear.

Further, the life of the synchronizing cone, which during gear changing from second to first was nearly infinity, decreased to 10 000–15 000 when changing from third to first gear. This marked decrease of the synchronizing cone life is a result of the decrease in the mechanical features with increasing temperature (see Fig. 26.40).

Table 26.1 shows the chemical composition of various copper alloys used for friction surfaces. Aluminium alloys are seldom used in friction surfaces. The unpopularity of aluminium alloys, despite their slightly higher coefficient of

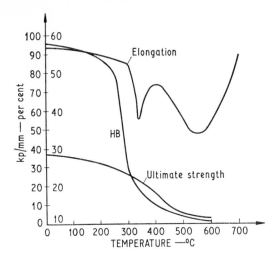

Fig. 26.40. Mechanical properties of copper–zinc alloy versus temperature

Table 26.1. Chemical composition of synchronizing cone materials

Material	Die-cast brass alloy, per cent	Hot-pressed brass alloy, per cent	Die-cast bronze, per cent	Die-cast aluminium-bronze, per cent
Cu	57–60	56–60	87	Remainder
Si	0·9–1·3	0·4–1·0		0·25*
Pb	0·3*	0·3–1·0	11	0·05*
Sn	0·25*	0·2–0·8	11	0·1*
Mn	1·25–2·0	1·0–2·0		1*
Al	0·7–1·1	0·7–1·5		8·5–10·5
Fe	0·25–0·75	0·5–1·2		1·5–3·5
Mg	0·01*			0·05*
Zn	Remainder	Remainder		0·5*
Ni			1	1*

* Maximum value.

friction than copper alloys, is the result of their decreasing *mechanical properties* with increase in temperature, low melting points, and low heat capacities.

The chemical composition of an aluminium alloy used in design of a synchronizer is as follows: 8·17% Si, 3·1% Cu, 0·08% Mn, 0·24% Mg, 0·31% Zn, 1·26% Fe, and the balance aluminium.

Sprayed molybdenum combined with steel is used by some manufacturers at the present time. This material, in which the Rockwell hardness of the surface particles is C57, has shown phenomenal resistance to wear. The characteristic chiefly responsible for its unusual resistance to scuffing is its high melting point of about 2600°C (4750°F). These attributes, plus high thermal conductivity and dimensional stability, account for the superior performance of molybdenum-sprayed synchronizing cones. Another outstanding feature of the flame-sprayed ring is its ability to handle airborne abrasives. The abrasive particles embed themselves below the surface of the porous molybdenum, which not only resists abrasion, but helps to reduce this type of wear in the entire area of the cone gear (or synchronized ring).

Experience with the steel–molybdenum combination for especially heavy work conditions has given a life that is almost eightfold that for steel–copper alloy combinations. A great advantage of the steel–molybdenum combination lies in its coefficient of friction, which is in the same range as steel–copper alloy combinations. This permits full exchangeability of materials with the same design parameters.

Quality of the friction surfaces

As mentioned earlier, not only the finish of the surface but also the shapes and the direction of the roughness influence the wear. The finish of the harder friction surface should be as smooth as possible.

If 'spikes' are observed in the finish traces by the manufacturers, one can be sure that high wear will occur in the delivered parts. The spikes contact the opposite surface first and develop a very high specific pressure and very high thermal load, which tend to fuse the metals together.

Size of the friction surfaces

The specific pressure of friction surfaces clearly influences the resistance to wear. Through proper selection of the ratio a/b and dimension a (Fig. 26.41) with

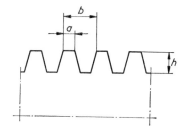

Fig. 26.41. Configuration of friction surface

dependable synchronization, a maximum for the working friction surface is obtained. For a certain design, the initial development was $a = 0.3$ mm, $b = 0.9$ mm, and $h_{min} = 0.35$ mm, but at the end this reached $a = 1.1$ mm, $b = 1.7$ mm, and $h_{min} = 0.5$ mm. This provided a working surface that was twice as large, and the increased surface reduced the temperature on the friction surfaces and negated the mechanical properties of the material.

Another factor which may influence the rate of wear of the friction surfaces is the manner of loading the synchronizing cone. If a synchronizing cone is loaded at three or four points, a deformation of the cone may occur. Consequently, the friction surfaces contact each other only at certain points, and this causes high thermal overloading at these points, resulting in rapid wear. A synchronizing cone which has severe wear in certain areas is shown in Fig. 26.42, which also includes its roundness diagram.

Wear, as described above, may also occur when extremely high oil drag and clutch drag load the synchronizing cone, since the increase in the temperature of the friction surfaces makes them more susceptible to deformation.

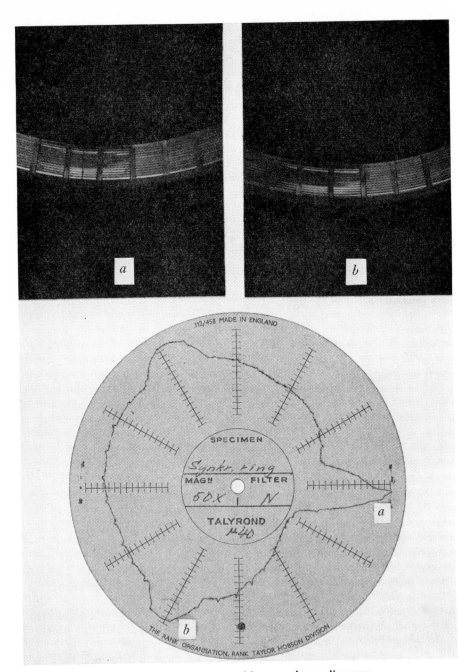

Fig. 26.42. Worn synchronizing cone and its roundness diagram

Local wear is also caused by a badly shaped synchronizing cone. The non-circular shape may also develop drag in the gearbox, an extremely high rate of wear of the opposite friction surface in the form of circular slits, and even clashing as a result of the oil wedge formed at places where contact between friction surfaces no longer exists.

Oil drag and clutch drag

Heavy oil drag and clutch drag shorten the life of synchronizers. The influence of these resistances is most marked on low gears because of the ratio between the point of resistance and the synchronized gear (see Figs 26.38 and 26.39). For instance, the life of the friction surfaces for a certain design is twice as long on third and fourth gears as it is on first and second, and several times more for the friction surfaces of the range part owing to the lack of clutch drag.

Design factors

Freedom of gear selection is a factor that some designers may forget. If the life of any friction surface is calculated for one-step gear changing, the life of this design will be shortened if gears are changed directly, say, from first to third.

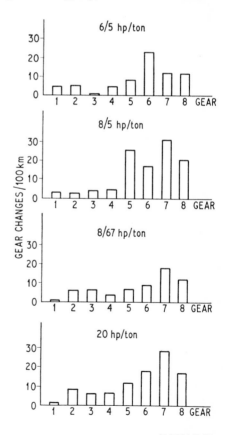

Fig. 26.43. Statistical distribution of gear change frequency on each synchronizer

Gearboxes of heavy trucks have usually several gears and are designed for a heavy load. If a truck is unloaded the driver does not need to pass through all gears to arrive at an optimal gear—he can change through several gears at once. Also, during very adverse road conditions (e.g. travelling on a slope with a heavy load), he must occasionally change down through two stages or more. Such 'jumps' cause a manifold increase in the thermal load on the friction surfaces because the energy used to synchronize increases with the second power of the relative speed of the synchronized part. In the case of materials with limited resistance to high temperature, it is easy with this type of changing to exceed the permissible thermal load, and this leads to rapid wear (Fig. 26.40).

LABORATORY AND PRACTICAL ROAD TESTS

Experiments made with synchronizers may be divided into two categories:

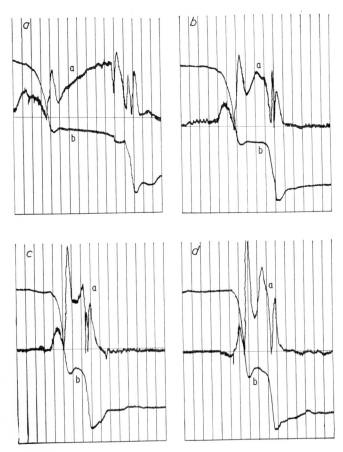

a   Gear changing force.
b   Axial travel of engaging sleeve.

Fig. 26.44. Gear changing force versus time

experiments carried out in laboratories and experiments carried out in gearboxes built into trucks (field research).

The first type of experiment takes place mainly at an early stage of the design work on particular components of the synchronizer, then later with prototypes of synchronizers on test benches and in gearboxes. As far as possible these tests should be based on practical experiments and measurements. It is important that the number of gear changes on each synchronizer should be known (see Fig. 26.43).

Another factor which influences the synchronizer is the gear change system. The gear change force versus time varies for different gear systems (hand or air operation, Figs 26.44 and 26.45). Further, the habit of by-passing one or two gears when changing reduces the life of the synchronizer to a great extent (Fig. 26.46).

The synchronizing cone is one of the most important parts of the synchronizer. It must be properly dimensioned and the fatigue strength should be tested after manufacture. It is recommended that these tests should be carried out during synchronization in order to determine the effect of the thermal loads. Apart from strength, such dimensions as design size, angle of cone, and angle of blocking chamfers can also be determined. The control of the deformation of the synchronizing cone under gear change force load and thermal load is then carried out. These tests can be made on the test equipment shown in Fig. 26.47 with different gear change forces, relative speeds, $\Delta\omega$, and inertia, I_R.

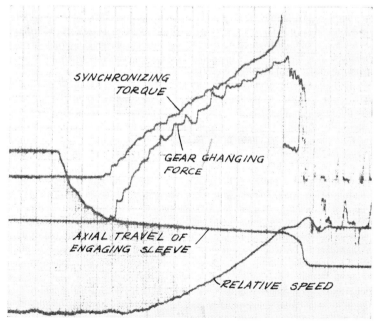

Fig. 26.45. Gear changing force versus time for air operation

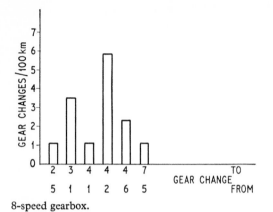

Fig. 26.46. Statistical distribution of gear change frequency through several gears for certain test driving

8-speed gearbox.

Description of the test bench (Fig. 26.47)

The changeable inertia is accelerated and decelerated by the synchronizer from the rotation speed $n = 0$ to the rotation speed of an electric motor to which a flywheel is coupled so that a constant motor speed can be maintained.

Gear changing of the synchronizer is by means of a linkage mechanism powered and regulated by air. This can also be done by other methods.

Development of the axial forces acting on the synchronizing cone and synchronizing torque is measured with the aid of wire strain gauges and is registered on a paper tape. From the trace of the torque acting on the synchronizing cone during the whole gear changing period, the blocking torque developed on the blocking chamfers can easily be determined. Registration of the sleeve travel and changing of the relative speeds versus time is also made at this stage. The lubrication is regulated by adjusting the oil level in the synchronizer box.

In this test, checks are also made of different forms of wiping slots, dimension A, blocking force F_s, types of oil, oil temperatures, influence of relative speeds, and the whole synchronization process. Figs 26.27, 26.32, and 26.45 show the measuring possibilities of this test system.

Influence of the oil drag and clutch drag on the wear of the friction surfaces may be tested by control of the wear of the synchronizing and gear cones which accelerate the synchronized parts.

Another type of bench test consists of endurance-testing the synchronizer in the gearbox, as shown in Fig. 26.48.

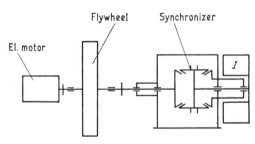

Fig. 26.47. Bench for tests of synchronizers

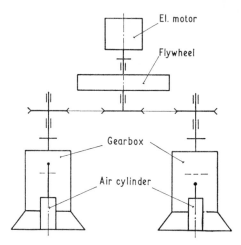

Fig. 26.48. Bench for gearbox tests of synchronizers

Description of the bench test in Fig. 26.48

Two gearboxes coupled with a flywheel and an electric motor are changed at the same time in opposite gears. The gear change mechanism is operated and regulated automatically by air pressure. However, the synchronizers and the whole gear change mechanism can also be tested by hand.

The second kind of test consists of practical tests of the whole design and is made in trucks under driving conditions, where oil drag, clutch drag, various roads and loads, and all other factors which truck design may have to contend with are encountered. These factors influence the life of the synchronizers and supplement the laboratory tests.

The practical tests are very important as they indicate the success or failure of a new design.

DEVELOPMENT

The development of truck transport leads to the manufacture of vehicles with ever-increasing load capacity. A large load capacity requires more powerful engines with a new type of gearbox. The new gearboxes are characterized by larger input torques and an increase in the number of gears.

The larger input torques mean more liberally dimensioned gear parts which must be synchronized. On the other hand, there is an increased demand for short-duration gear changes.

From the equation of movement,

$$T_s - T_D = I_R \frac{\Delta\omega}{t_s} \; ; \qquad t_s = \frac{I_R \Delta\omega}{T_s - T_D} \quad . \quad . \quad . \quad (26.25)$$

it follows that the duration of synchronization may be shortened by increasing the synchronizing torque T_s. For a certain synchronizer this may be attained by:

(a) a better mechanical efficiency in the gear change system;
(b) a larger ratio between the gear lever and the gear fork;

(c) a servo system which amplifies the gear change forces;
(d) the use of multiple cones, as in the Smith design; or
(e) the use of multi-disc synchronizers.

Another opportunity is provided by a change in design, such as transferring the synchronizer from the output shaft to the input shaft or mainshaft. This displacement influences the reduction of the value $I_R \Delta\omega$.

Both the above solutions lead to a reduction in the synchronizing time by using almost the same energy. This increases the power of synchronization and the thermal load of the synchronizer.

The proper thermal loads can be attained by

(a) increasing the friction surfaces;
(b) the use of multiple cones;
(c) the use of multi-disc synchronizers;
(d) the use of a new material, e.g. steel–molybdenum;
(e) a governed system of gear change (blocking a change through several steps);
(f) limitation of maximum gear changing forces; and
(g) better cooling of the friction surfaces.

As a result of the above, the use of multi-disc synchronizers is quite possible in order to resolve the problem of thermal loads during a quick gear change. From multi-disc synchronizers the road to power-shift is but a short step, and this leads to automatic transmissions. In addition, it is possible that the synchromesh of the heavy truck gearboxes will be based on ideas other than the synchronizer. Even now a system based on the method of changing in an unsynchronized gearbox may be encountered, where the work of the driver is done automatically.

This design is not very common today, probably owing to competition from the synchronized gearboxes, but it is possible that, in a gearbox with an input torque of over 150 kp m, the system will be more widely accepted.

APPENDIX 26.1

BIBLIOGRAPHY

(1) SOCIN, R. J. and WALTERS, L. K. 'Manual transmission synchronizers', S.A.E. 680 008.
(2) NIEMANN, G. *Maschinenelemente* 1965.
(3) 'BMC gearbox synchronizers', *Auto. Engr* 1964 (May).
(4) 'A completely new synchromesh', Publication No. 51 893 (Smiths Motor Accessory Division).

The MS. of this paper was received at the Institution on 2nd December 1969 and accepted for publication on 17th December 1969.

Paper 27. Strength of Transmission Shafting

J. E. RUSSELL, MA
British Steel Corporation, Moorgate, Rotherham

The design theory for transmission shafting, both in the elastic and plastic states, is reviewed, with consideration of the effects of splines, fillets, and similar stress-raisers. Data are presented on the actual strengths of such shafts for various steels under static and fatigue loading, and the nature of the fatigue phenomenon briefly discussed. Some typical shafting failures are described, and the appropriate lessons drawn.

INTRODUCTION

The stresses in drive-shafting, whether for automobile or other types of machines, arise very largely from torsional loading. In the majority of instances the design of the shaft and its housings is intended to reduce bending stresses to as low a level as possible, except in those cases where the shaft is deliberately designed to carry a bending in addition to a twisting load. It is unfortunate, therefore, that the greatest accumulation of strength and fatigue data on material apply to bending or direct loading. This means that torsional strengths are estimated by various empirical factors applied to the bending or direct loading data. In the most recent collection of strength data on standard engineering steels (**1**)† the torsional information is trivial in comparison with the rest, specific pieces of information representing less than 2 per cent of the total mechanical property data. This paper will therefore deal mainly with torsion and the estimation of the properties of materials in this loading mode, for design purposes; but some brief remarks on combined torsion and bending are included.

STRESSES

The stresses in plain shafts in pure torsion, and in the elastic region of the material, are well documented in most textbooks on the strength of materials. The relevant formulae are summarized below.

Notation

d Diameter of parallel length of a bar.
G Modulus of rigidity.
L Parallel length of a bar.
M Torque or twisting moment applied to the bar.
γ Shear strain induced in the surface by torque M.
θ Angle of twist *in degrees* of one end with respect to the other, caused by torque M.
τ Shear stress induced in the surface by torque M.

† *References are given in Appendix 27.1.*

For steel, G has a value when determined on small specimens in the laboratory of about $11\cdot5 \times 10^6$ lb/in^2, but on shafts and torsion bars a figure of $10\cdot8 \times 10^6$ lb/in^2 appears to give a better fit to actual torque–twist data, and this value is used. The equivalent metric figure is 7600 kg/mm^2, or 74 600 MN/m^2.

$$\gamma = \frac{\pi}{360}\frac{d\theta}{L} = 0\cdot0087\frac{d\theta}{L}, \quad \text{or} \quad \theta = 115\frac{\gamma L}{d} \qquad \ldots \text{(27.1)}$$

$$\tau = \frac{16M}{\pi d^3} = 5\cdot09\frac{M}{d^3} \qquad \ldots \ldots \text{(27.2)}$$

	lb in	kg mm	S.I. units

$$\frac{M}{\theta} = \frac{G\pi^2 d^4}{5760L} = \quad 1\cdot852\times10^4\frac{d^4}{L} \quad = \quad 13\cdot032\frac{d^4}{L} \quad = \frac{13\cdot032\times10^9 d^4}{L}$$
$$\ldots \text{(27.3)}$$

$$\tau = \frac{G\pi d}{360L}\theta = \quad 9\cdot42\times10^4\frac{d\theta}{L} \quad = \quad 66\cdot29\frac{d\theta}{L} \quad = \quad \text{do.}$$
$$\ldots \text{(27.4)}$$

$$d = \frac{16M}{\pi\tau}^{1/3} = \quad 1\cdot72\left(\frac{M}{\tau}\right)^{1/3} \quad = \quad \text{do.} \quad = \quad \text{do.}$$
$$\ldots \text{(27.5)}$$

$$d = \left[\frac{5760LM}{\pi^2 G\theta}\right]^{1/4} = 8\cdot57\times10^{-2}\left(\frac{LM}{\theta}\right)^{1/4} = 5\cdot263\times10^{-1}\left(\frac{LM}{\theta}\right)^{1/4} = \frac{2\cdot96(LM)^{1/4}}{\theta}$$
$$\ldots \text{(27.6)}$$

$$L = \frac{G\theta}{180}\left(\frac{2\pi^2 M}{\tau^4}\right)^{1/3} = 1\cdot622\times10^5\left(\frac{M}{\tau^4}\right)^{1/3}\theta = \quad 114\cdot1\left(\frac{M}{\tau^4}\right)^{1/3}\theta \quad = \quad \text{do.}$$
$$\ldots \text{(27.7)}$$

Equations (27.5)–(27.7) are useful in certain cases where the spring-like properties of the shaft are being considered (also in torsion bar spring design).

However, actual shafts contain a number of stress-raising features, such as grooves, or fillets between one diameter and another, end-fittings (usually splines), and less frequently oil-holes or keyways.

The stress concentration effects of fillets and grooves have been thoroughly investigated, and have been well summarized in the data sheets published by the Royal Aeronautical Society (2). Figs 27.1 and 27.2 show the stress concentration factors (K_t) for fillets and grooves in torsion, taken from these data sheets, but replotted in a rather more convenient form.

The R.A.E. data sheets are based on the work of Petersen, Lee and Ades, and Rushton and represent a best average of these data, mainly derived from photo-elasticity investigations. For torsion of fillets, the R.A.E. curves are adequately fitted by the equation:

$$K = 1+\left[0\cdot30+\frac{0\cdot16h}{D}\right]\ln\left[1+\frac{0\cdot306h}{r}\tan\left(0\cdot5-\frac{h}{D}\right)\pi\right] \quad \text{where } h = \frac{D-d}{2}$$

which, with appropriate substitutions, is equivalent to the form:

$$K = 1+\left[0\cdot38-\frac{0\cdot08d}{D}\right]\ln\left[1+\frac{0\cdot153(D/d-1)}{r/d}\tan\frac{\pi d}{2D}\right]$$

from which Fig. 27.1 has been plotted.

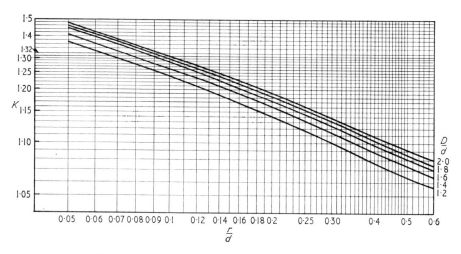

Fig. 27.1. Stress concentration factors, circular fillets in torsion

However, it is often necessary to calculate the amount of twist that may take place in a fillet or groove when the shaft is under load. If the radius of the fillet is small, so that there is a relatively sharp transition between the two diameters, the twist over the fillet is usually also small and can be neglected. Nevertheless, for a relatively smooth transition, over a fair distance, the twist may be appreciable. Two cases which often occur follow.

Straight-line transition

This occurs between one (larger) diameter d_1 and another d_2 over a length L. The result may be expressed in two forms: either as an equivalent constant diameter d' over the length L, or as an equivalent length L' at diameter d_1 or d_2, viz.:

$$d' = \left[\frac{3d_1{}^3d_2{}^3}{d_1{}^2+d_1d_2+d_2{}^2}\right]^{1/4}$$

or L' at the smaller diameter

$$d_2 = \frac{L(d_1{}^2+d_1d_2+d_2{}^2)d_2}{3d_1{}^3}$$

Either of these expressions can be used in any of the previous equations in place of d or L for the calculation of θ for given torque.

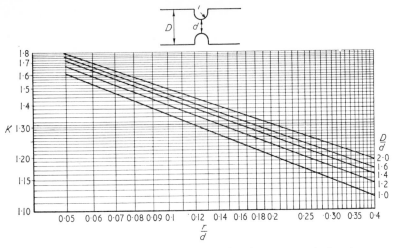

Fig. 27.2. Stress concentration factors, circular grooves in torsion

Circular-profile fillet or groove

An accurate calculation leads to a very complicated result, but a good approximation is obtained by treating the profile of the fillet or groove as a catenary with a radius of curvature at the bottom equal to the fillet or groove radius. For a fillet of radius r running from a *smaller* diameter d over a distance along the shaft of x, the equivalent length x' at diameter d (i.e. which gives the same twist for equal torque) is:

$$x' = \frac{\tanh kx}{k} - \frac{\tanh^3 kx}{3k} = \phi(y)x \qquad \text{(see below)}$$

where $k = \sqrt{\{2/(dr)\}}$, and $\tanh kx$ denotes the hyperbolic tangent of kx.

Alternatively, the equivalent diameter d' for the *same* length x is:

$$d' = \left[\frac{x}{x'}\right]^{1/4} d$$

Note that

$$\frac{x'}{x} = \frac{\tanh kx}{kx} - \frac{\tanh^3 kx}{3kx} = \frac{\tanh y}{y} - \frac{\tanh^3 y}{3y} = \phi(y)$$

where $y = kx$. A graph of $\phi(y)$ is given in Fig. 27.3.

A groove should be regarded as two fillets, and the equivalent twist obtained as the sum of the twists arising from each fillet.

Shafts containing holes

Shafts frequently contain holes, usually for lubricating purposes, and again the stresses round such holes have been experimentally investigated and summarized in the R.A.E. data sheets (2). Fig. 27.4 shows the results, expressed as a ratio

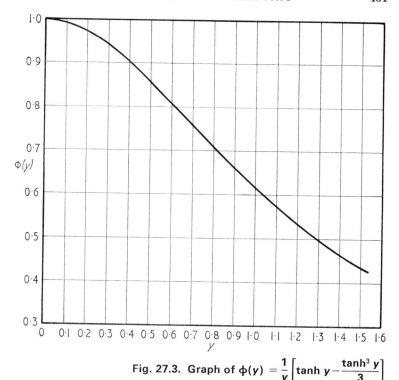

Fig. 27.3. Graph of $\phi(y) = \dfrac{1}{y}\left[\tanh y - \dfrac{\tanh^3 y}{3}\right]$

of the maximum *shear* stress round the hole to the nominal shear stress in the shaft, although the original curves give the ratio of the maximum direct stress at the hole to the nominal shear stress (i.e. $K_t = 4$ at $d/D_0 = 0$). However, the former seems a better mode of expression, as actual fatigue tests on shafts with and without holes show shear strength reduction factors of the order of 2.

The results shown in Fig. 27.4 refer to holes with a sharp corner at the surface of the shaft. In practice, the edge of the hole is usually chamfered off, or machined to a smooth radius; this may alleviate the stress concentration to some extent. Unfortunately, little study appears to have been made of the stress round chamfered oil-holes, but a limited amount of data on fatigue limits on shafts containing such holes suggests that where the radius of the chamfer is about a quarter of the oil-hole diameter, which in turn is small in comparison with the shaft diameter, the theoretical stress concentration is reduced by up to 30 per cent. An assumption of a 20 per cent reduction, for design purposes under such conditions, would appear to be reasonable.

It is occasionally necessary for the oil-holes to be drilled obliquely to the bar instead of perpendicular to the axis; for crankshafts this is always true. However, Field (3) has shown that if the angle between the axis of the hole and the perpendicular direction is less than about 25°, the fatigue strength in torsion is about the same as that of the shaft if the hole were perpendicular to the axis. However, as the angle increases further, the fatigue strength falls off rapidly. For the material

in these tests (a 3·3% Ni–Cr–Mo–V steel, to the now obsolete D.T.D. 331 specification, heat treated to 82 ton/in² u.t.s., and which appears to have been almost
fully notch-sensitive) the fatigue strength in torsion with a 45° inclined hole was
only about 80 per cent of the strength with a perpendicular hole, and only about
61 per cent with a 60° inclined hole.

FATIGUE PROPERTIES AND TENSILE STRENGTH

To estimate the hypothetical fatigue properties of a steel at the drawing-board
stage, it is necessary to have some relation between these properties and the tensile
and/or yield strength parameters which are usually used for specifying the steel.

It is generally assumed that the 'fatigue ratio', i.e. the ratio of the alternating
bend fatigue limit to the tensile strength, is about a half, and for many purposes
this may be near enough. However, there is a fair spread of the yield ratio,
considering all steels from the very softest to the ultra-high tensile ones, as will
be seen from Fig. 27.5 due to Forrest (4). The yield strength of the steel has no
significant influence on the fatigue properties.

In view of these results, it is recommended that for design purposes it should
be assumed that if u = ultimate tensile strength, in tons/in²:

$$\text{Direct stress, alternating fatigue limit} = 0\cdot36u \qquad (u \leqslant 56)$$
$$= 0\cdot5u-8 \qquad (56 < u \leqslant 96)$$
$$= 40 \qquad (u > 96)$$

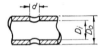

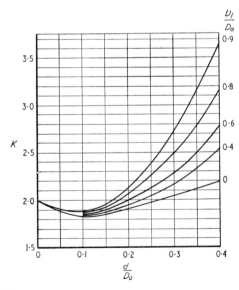

Fig. 27.4. Stress concentration
factors for holes in shafts in torsion

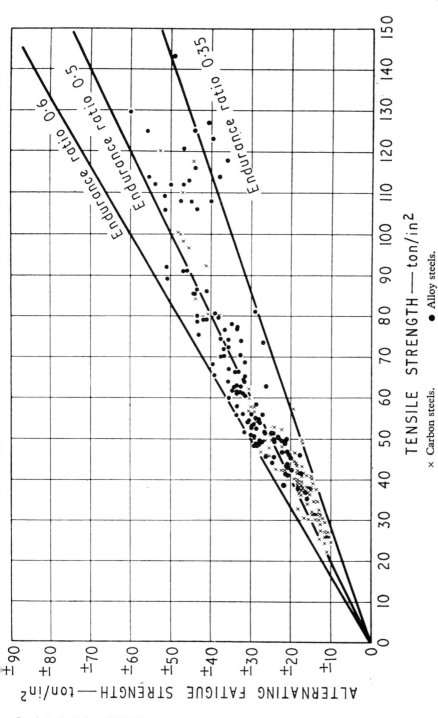

Fig. 27.5. Relation between rotating bending fatigue strength and tensile strength of wrought steels, based on fatigue limit or failure in 10^7 to 10^8 cycles. All results are based on specimens tested in the longitudinal direction (after Forrest (4))

It will be noted that this postulates a maximum fatigue limit of 40 ton/in². Higher values can be obtained from particularly clean steels such as are produced by vacuum-arc remelting, or from shafts that have been case-hardened (by nitriding, carburizing, or induction-hardening). It is difficult to give general data for these special cases, and the above rules should be used for a normal commercial quality of material. However, the fatigue strength of a case-hardened shaft with no stress-raisers of any sort, and on which failure would commence *below* the case, is given roughly by multiplying the fatigue strength of the uncased material by $d/(d-2c)$, where d is the shaft diameter and c is the case-depth.

There is also a considerable reduction of fatigue properties as the size increases, but the above formulae may be taken as applying to shafts of diameters up to about 5 in.

The torsional fatigue properties can be obtained from those for direct stress by application of the shear-energy principle, discussed under 'Bending' below. In effect, this amounts to multiplying the direct stress values by 0·59, the answer being given in shear stress. It should be noted that this only applies to ductile materials such as steels.

NOTCH SENSITIVITY

Actual fatigue limits of materials determined on notched bars as compared with unnotched ones do not generally show all the reduction of fatigue limit that one would anticipate simply by dividing the unnotched-bar fatigue limit by the stress-concentration factor, and the term 'notch-sensitivity' is defined as follows:

$$\text{Notch-sensitivity,} \ \eta = \frac{K_f - 1}{K_t - 1}$$

where K_f is the ratio of the unnotched to notched fatigue limits ('strength-reduction factor').

This parameter is tending to die out in metallurgical circles, as η is not, unfortunately, a constant for the material but tends to vary both with K_t and with the metallurgical condition; however, it is still a useful engineering concept. The available data on bending tests on a large number of steels were analysed by Kuhn and Hardrath (5), who were able to produce an approximate expression for the notch-sensitivity in terms of tensile strength and the notch-radius which is of considerable use for design purposes. Their results were given graphically, but they can be summarized adequately by the formula:

$$\eta = \frac{1}{1 + [2 \cdot 16(175 - u)^4 \times 10^{-10}]/\sqrt{r}}$$

where u is the tensile strength in tons per square inch and r is the notch-radius (inches), whether fillet or groove.

A similar evaluation for torsion tests is unfortunately not available, as the amount of torsion fatigue data on notched specimens is too small. However, Little (6) suggests that η for torsion can be taken as 0·9 times that of bending, and this seems reasonable.

The above results apply only to steels of reasonable ductility for their tensile strength. Cast iron has an extremely low notch-sensitivity; the usual explanation for this is that the presence of the graphite flakes in the material acts as so many stress-raisers, and the presence of one more (the mechanical notch) has only a negligible effect.

SPLINES

Despite the widespread use of splines for joining shafts to each other, or to appropriate housings, there is remarkably little published information on the stresses associated with them. This is probably due to the fact that whatever the nominal stresses, the actual performance of a shaft with a splined end often depends more on the housing details, such as accuracy and tightness of fit, or whether the end of the housing has sharp corners or has the corners relieved in some way.

It is general practice to consider a splined bar as equivalent to a smooth un-splined bar of diameter equal to the root diameter of the splines, and in many cases this is probably adequate. Considering the safety factors that may be allowed between the calculated stresses and those imposed in service, the safety margin is still reasonable, despite the complicating factor that there are obviously con-siderable bending stresses on the splines around the housing end.

Burke and Fisher (7) performed fatigue tests on shafts with two types of splines, one a straight-sided spline with 10 teeth on the shaft, and the other a 32/64-in pitch involute splined shaft. The S–N curves (zero to maximum torque loading) with torques plotted against cycles to failure were naturally quite different, but if they were replotted showing *stresses* calculated as though the splined shaft were in fact an unsplined shaft of diameter equal to the *mean* of the root and outer diameter of the splines, the two S–N curves coincided. Unfortunately, the authors are very vague about the materials of these shafts, although they were obviously case-hardened, presumably by induction, to a hardness of 60 R_c (about 730 Vickers) on the surface. Nevertheless, *for this material* and this type of loading (pulsating), and based on the above 'mean diameter' mode of calculation, the authors give an 'allowable stress' curve which runs slightly below the test data, and this appears to be reasonable.

However, fatigue results on case-hardened materials (whether induction-hardened, carburized, or nitriding) have little relevance to the properties of through-hardened steels. Indeed, it is dangerous to attempt to generalize from results on one mode of case-hardening to another. Nevertheless, it is evident from Burke and Fisher's results that their nominal allowable stresses, based on the mean diameter formula, represent a strength reduction factor of about 1·7–1·8, as compared with the expected unsplined shaft results, at 10^6 cycles. Bearing in mind the fact of the fatigue properties of case-hardened components being generally better than those of direct hardened steels, because of the compressive stresses usually associated with the case, we suggest that 2·0 would represent a reasonable strength-reduction factor for design purposes, always basing on a diameter equal to the mean of the outer and root diameters of the splines. The actual geometry of the splines is relatively unimportant, provided, of course, that they are properly made (especially in respect of giving the proper radius at the bottoms of the splines) and the faces of the splines (both in the shaft and housing) are accurately machined so that the load is taken uniformly on all the splines.

Of course, where splines are cut directly into a cylindrical shaft, with no increase of outer diameter, the stress in the shaft is much less than in the splines, and failure, if it occurs, will always be in the splines. On parts such as torsion bars, where the stress in the parallel part is designed to run up to the highest possible levels, a 'swell' at the heads is inevitable. On such bars it is normal practice to make the root-diameter of the splines at least 20 per cent greater than the shaft-diameter. The use of any of the standard B.S. coarse splines will, using the mean diameter formula, give nominal stresses less than the shaft stress divided by 2·0 and thus satisfy the above formula. The length of the head must, of course, be sufficient to prevent the splines *shearing* off under maximum torque.

STRENGTHENING EFFECT OF SPLINES

It would appear reasonable to suppose that a shaft with splines is 'stronger' than an unsplined shaft of diameter equal to the previous root-diameter. Indeed, shafts are sometimes made where the splines are cut into a head of diameter greater than the shaft-diameter (which indeed is the general practice in Britain), but with root-diameter less than the shaft-diameter, on the assumption that the splines will raise the strength of the head portion above the strength of the shaft. However, this assumption should be made with caution, as it is certainly not always true.

For example, consider a splined shaft of, say, 440/450 Brinell (such as a silico-manganese torsion bar). The permissible stress on the mean diameter of the splines would be about 45 000 lb/in², whereas the permissible stress on the root-diameter *without* splines would be about 90 000 lb/in² (see Fig. 27.6). The splined

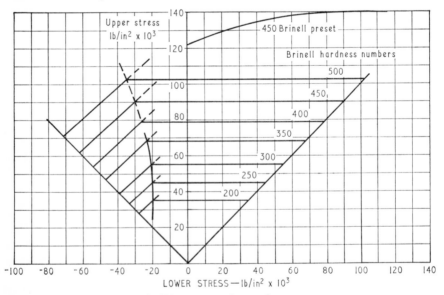

Fig. 27.6. Maximum permissible stresses in torsion

shaft would be the stronger (i.e. could take the greater torque at full load) if

$$\frac{d_m{}^3 \times 45\,000}{5\cdot09} > \frac{d_r{}^3 \times 90\,000}{5\cdot09}$$

where d_r is the root spline diameter and d_m the mean diameter $(d_r + d_o)/2$, where d_o is the outer spline diameter), i.e. if $d_m > 1\cdot26d_r$ or if $d_o > 1\cdot52d_r$. This may well be the case, but not necessarily so—certainly not for B.S. splines.

If the main shaft diameter is d, then the head is stronger than the shaft if

$$d_m > 1\cdot26d \quad \text{or} \quad d_r + d_o > 2\cdot52d$$

which is even less likely to be true if the shaft is undercut and $d_o < d$.

PLASTIC TWISTING OF SHAFTS

It is a well-known practice in the manufacture of torsion bars for suspension-spring purposes to 'pre-set' the bar by giving it an initial permanent twist in the direction in which it will be used in service. This produces a residual stress system which acts in a direction opposite to the service stresses, and thereby partly cancels them out and considerably raises the load-carrying capacity of the bar. It is not usual to pre-set transmission shafts in a similar way, but they may well undergo a permanent twist through overloading in service. By analogy with the torsion bar example, this is not necessarily a bad thing and the shaft may well continue to give good service.

It should be noted, however, that after a total twist equivalent to a surface shear strain of about 0·025 rad the torsional stress–strain curve tends to flatten out quickly and run to failure. Indeed, on torsion bars it is usual to adopt this angle for pre-twisting (leaving a permanent twist of about 0·006 rad in a silico-manganese bar of about 450 Brinell), because any further twist gives no worth-while improvement in load-carrying capacity and may, in fact, damage the bar. Therefore shafts should not be allowed to twist beyond this angle.

BENDING

The effects of bend superimposed on torsion are occasionally encountered in automobile shafting, though not to a very great extent. Nevertheless, some comment on the conditions may be useful.

The possibility of plastic failure under slowly increasing loading and a complex stress system is generally not difficult to assess by the use of the strain-energy principle, which holds true for most ductile materials. This states that plastic flow will occur at any point such that the strain-energy per unit volume at that point exceeds a critical value. In other words, if σ_1, σ_2, and σ_3 are the three principal stresses, and σ_y is the yield point in a tensile test, plastic flow sets in when

$$(\sigma_1 - \sigma_2)^2 + (\sigma_2 - \sigma_3)^2 + (\sigma_3 - \sigma_1)^2 \quad \text{exceeds} \quad 2\sigma_y{}^2$$

However, under dynamic loading, more complicated situations arise. For example, the bend load may be constant while the torsion load is alternating, or vice versa; or both may be varying but not necessarily in phase, and so on.

Gough and Pollard (8) demonstrated that under conditions of combined alternating bend and torsion, both stresses being in phase (i.e. both reaching their maxima together), the bend and torsion fatigue limit components satisfied the same strain-energy principle as above.

Consequently, as regards *fatigue limits* (as distinct from low-life stresses), the alternating fatigue limit in torsion (measured as shear stress) is about 0·59 times that in bend (measured as direct stress). The theoretical value of this factor derived from the above strain–energy equation is $1/\sqrt{3}$ or 0·577, but actual values tend to run slightly higher, and 0·59 is a reliable figure for most purposes. It must be emphasized that this only holds for *ductile* materials. For brittle materials, such as cast iron, the maximum shear stress principle more nearly represents actual fatigue limits, and this ratio then becomes 0·5.

If σ and τ (direct stress and shear stress, respectively) represent the maximum values of bending and torsional surface stresses (combined) on a shaft when running at its fatigue limit, and if σ_f and τ_f are the bending and torsional fatigue limits determined separately (i.e. $\pm\sigma_f$ is the rotary–bend fatigue limit, with no torsion, and $\pm\tau_f$ is the alternating torsion fatigue limit, with no bend), then the shear-energy criterion can be shown to lead to the relation, confirmed by Gough and Pollard's experimental results:

$$\frac{\sigma^2}{\sigma_f{}^2} + \frac{\tau^2}{\tau_f{}^2} = 1$$

If the variation is just anti-phase, i.e. the bending is zero when the torsion is a maximum, and vice versa, then the safest assumption is that the bending and torsion fatigue limits apply independently of each other, and the shaft will fail when either one or the other fatigue limit is exceeded. In practice, the performance will probably be better than this, as the working in one direction will tend to strengthen the material in the other direction. Equally, in the general system where the bend system is unrelated to the torsional one, it is again the safest policy to assume that each acts independently of the other.

When stress-raisers such as fillets or grooves are present on the shaft subject to such combined stressing, then obviously these features determine the overall strength of the shaft. The simplest way of dealing with this situation is to work out the fatigue limits of the material in bend and torsion on the basis of the notch-sensitivity formula and the stress concentration factors, and then apply the appropriate one of the above procedures described above. This is quite reasonable where only small amounts of bend are involved.

A more sophisticated procedure has been described by Little (**6**); but in the author's view it tends to give rather optimistic results through choosing too high values of fatigue ratios.

PERMISSIBLE STRESSES

In order to use the various formulae and stress concentration factors described above, it is necessary to have some idea of the basic maximum permissible stress. Unfortunately, there are not sufficient data on different materials to make the distinctions between them that should be made, but attempting to summarize it in one diagram, Fig. 27.6 is presented. This shows suggested maximum torsional stresses for materials of different hardness value, referring only to heat-treated low-alloy steels, and excluding carbon, high-alloy, and stainless, etc.

There are a number of different conventions for presenting fatigue data, such as the R–M (Range–Mean) curves, Smith curves (upper and lower stress plotted against mean stress), and so on, but the one shown is the most convenient, in the author's opinion, viz. a direct plot of upper stress against lower stress. For all the steels, loaded from zero upwards, always in one direction, the limitation on the stress is usually the elastic limit of the material (unless some permanent set is given, or occurs accidentally). Indeed, only points to the left of the curve AB are determined by the fatigue strength of the material, although where the condition at stress-raisers is being considered, the lines to the left of AB may be produced a little to the right, as shown. The complex stresses at a stress-raiser tend to stave off the onset of plastic flow to a slightly higher stress level. For comparison, a curve is included for material of 450 Brinell (silico-manganese) used for torsion bars and pre-twisted in the service direction. Here fatigue is the limiting condition well into the right-hand side of the diagram, and the large increase in load-carrying capacity is evident.

The fatigue parts of the diagram are based on lives of the order of 300 000. For infinite life the stresses should be reduced by about 10–15 per cent. They should not be taken as applying to shafts larger than about 4 in in diameter.

For dealing with stress-raisers under conditions of non-zero mean stress, the well-known Gunn (9) construction should be used.

FATIGUE AND FATIGUE FAILURES

The vast majority of failures of transmission shafts subject to reversal of loading occur through fatigue, and it is because of this that the stress-raising effects discussed in the previous part of this paper are so important. Whereas under relatively slowly loaded or quasi-static conditions the failure of a ductile material is usually preceded by a large amount of plastic flow and distortion, and the effect of small stress-raisers is swamped in the general plastic condition, this does not occur under dynamic loading, especially if the loads are nearly reversing. Plastic flow in one direction cannot take place, failures are initiated at the small stress-raisers, and the cracks propagate through the shaft at a speed dependent on the type of loading and the material itself.

The various factors leading to failure of shafts, gears, and other components have been exhaustively reviewed by Wulpi (10), and it is not proposed to give a similar review here. However, the situation as regards shafting will now be briefly summarized.

Fatigue failure may be recognized by 'beach markings' on the face of the fracture, emanating from a single point, at which the crack has started. Fig. 27.7 shows a typical example. In some instances, after the fracture has occurred, the machinery has continued to run for a short time before stopping, causing the fractured faces to be banged against each other, thus damaging the appearance of the original fracture. However, such hammering of the faces can usually be recognized, and there is generally sufficient of the original fracture left to indicate the cause of failure. In other instances the face of the crack (usually when it has propagated very rapidly) appears very smooth with no obvious beach lines, but examination under a quite low magnification (often merely a hand-lens) will show them up.

Fig. 27.7. Typical transverse fatigue crack, showing well-developed 'beach markings'

As might be expected, cracks tend to run through the regions of greatest stress, and they tend, moreover, to run perpendicular to the direction of the greatest principal stress at any one position. However, this general rule may need some care in interpretation in particular cases. When a crack has formed and run for a short distance, the stress-pattern in the component will not be quite the same as in the original uncracked state, so that the crack will continue to run but in a direction that might not be initially anticipated. Moreover, any internal stresses in the component before going into service may influence the direction of cracking. For example, in a heavily scragged leaf-spring (which contains initial compressions on the 'tension' side) failure may start at, or below, the surface by a crack perpendicular to the surface. The crack may then turn and proceed parallel to the surface for some distance before turning again and continuing through the leaf. The initial stress component of the service stress is partially relieved by the presence of the crack, thus causing the service stress to revert to something like the stress-system in an unscragged leaf.

Often there is not one but many origins of the crack, or initial failure may have started at one position (or series of positions), and the cracks then initiate another quite independent crack or series of cracks. Perhaps the best example is that of the torsional failure of a splined part of a shaft, which has a 'star' appearance on the face (Fig. 27.8). In such failures the cracks almost invariably start at the corners of the splines, run radially into the shaft (Fig. 27.9), and cause the shaft

Fig. 27.8. 'Star' fatigue failure of a splined shaft

Fig. 27.9. Section of shaft near the fracture, showing fatigue cracks running radially from the corners of the splines

Fig. 27.10. Oblique view of 'star' fatigue failure of a splined shaft, showing axial bulge

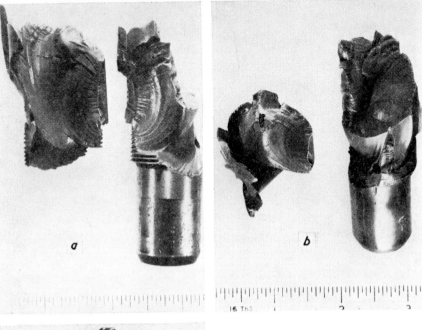

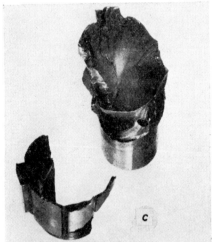

Fig. 27.11. Three views of a splined shaft in which there has been 'peeling' from the surface. The origin of the first crack can be seen in *c*

to be split longitudinally into a bundle of 'bars' joined near the centre. These bars then become subject to bending, as well as torsion, and new fatigue cracks commence to run across the bars at the position of largest bending moment, usually at the position where the splines enter the housing, causing the final break to occur there. A curious feature of such fractures is that they do not go on to break straight across (perpendicular to the axis). The course of the fracture turns out of the perpendicular plane, the final fracture often having an elevation (or depression) in the region of the axis (Fig. 27.10). The cause of this is obscure, but it may be connected with the following observation. In badly fitting splined shafts, or where the housing is bearing on only a relatively small length of the splines, the cracks may again originate at the corners of the splines. Because of the 'strengthening' effect of the unloaded parts of the splines, the cracks are prevented from running radially inwards and take up a direction more nearly circumferential. The result is a more-or-less hollow cylindrical piece that appears to peel off the shaft by a series of fatigue cracks. They in turn generate a series of cracks running through the axis, which cause the final failure (Fig. 27.11a, b, and c).

Without doubt, the general subject of fracture-configuration obtained from the failure of components of complex design has been very badly neglected, and a systematic study would be worth while.

ACKNOWLEDGEMENT

The author wishes to thank Dr F. H. Saniter, Director of Research, British Steel Corporation, Midland Group, for permission to publish this paper.

APPENDIX 27.1

REFERENCES

(1) WOOLMAN, J. and MOTTRAM, R. A. *The mechanical and physical properties of the British Standard En steels* 1966–69, 3 vols. (Pergamon Press).
(2) ROYAL AERONAUTICAL SOCIETY Engineering Data Sheets.
(3) FIELD, J. E. 'The effect of obliquely drilled holes on torsional fatigue strength', *N.E.L. Rept No. 226* (National Engineering Laboratory, East Kilbride, Glasgow).
(4) FORREST, P. G. *Fatigue of metals* 1962 (Pergamon Press).
(5) KUHN, P. and HARDRATH, H. F. 'An engineering method for estimating notch size effect in fatigue tests on steel', *NACA Tech. Note 2805* 1952.
(6) LITTLE, R. E. 'Parts that bend and twist', *Machine Design* 1968 (7th November), 174.
(7) BURKE, P. E. and FISHER, W. 'Design and analysis procedures for shafts and splines', *Automotive Engng Congress*, 1968, S.A.E. Paper 680024.
(8) GOUGH, H. J. and POLLARD, H. V. 'The strength of metals under combined alternating stresses', *Proc. Instn mech. Engrs* 1935, **131**, 3.
(9) GUNN, K. 'Effect of yielding on the fatigue properties of test pieces containing stress-concentrations', *Aeronaut. Q.* 1955 **6**, 277; see also FORREST, reference (4), p. 163.
(10) WULPI, D. J. 'How components fail', *Metal Prog.* 1965 (October) to 1966 (September). Now collected into a single pamphlet (Metal Progress).

The MS. of this paper was received at the Institution on 27th October 1969 and accepted for publication on 10th November 1969.

494

Paper 28. Computer Programs for Calculation of Automotive Driveline Bearing Applications

S. ANDRÉASON
Manager of Laboratory, AB Svenska Kullagerfabriken, SKF Gothenburg Division, Sweden

This paper describes two different computer programs for the calculation of rolling bearing applications in an automotive driveline. The first program gives the effect of bearing preload or internal clearance on bearing deflections and nominal lives in bearing applications with taper roller bearings. As an example, the paper deals with a front hub bearing arrangement with two taper roller bearings used in a front wheel driven car, and also with a pinion of a final drive unit and a gearbox mainshaft incorporating two taper and one cylindrical roller bearing. The second program is used to determine the influence of misalignment and shaft deflection on the load and life of a deep groove ball bearing. To illustrate this effect the layshaft of an automotive gearbox is studied.

INTRODUCTION

In order to be able to select the most suitable rolling bearings and to obtain maximum reliability of the bearing applications in motor vehicles, it is important to evaluate as accurately as possible the magnitude of the bearing loads. Owing to the variable running conditions, these calculations are very complicated and would be extremely time-consuming unless high-speed digital computers were available. This paper describes two computer programs which are specially adapted for the calculation of automotive driveline bearing applications. Since many independent variables are involved in this problem it is difficult to give results that have a general applicability. Instead some examples are dealt with to show how the programs should be used.

The first program permits the calculation of loads, lives, and deflections of taper roller bearings that are given a specific preload or internal clearance, and it applies to two common bearing arrangements. In one case only two taper roller bearings are used; in the other a cylindrical roller bearing is also included, serving as a support bearing. Since the bearing applications are statically indeterminate and their elastic deformations must also be considered, complex and highly non-linear systems of equations are obtained. The program which solves these equations forms a part of program systems for the calculation of hub, pinion, and gearbox bearing applications.

Owing to misalignments and elastic shaft deflections a deep groove ball bearing is often subjected to the action of both force and moment load components. When moments exist the bearing may be heavily stressed with a subsequent reduction in bearing life. The effect of this phenomenon can be taken into account by use of the second program, which computes bearing forces and moments on a shaft mounted in two deep groove ball bearings. As an example, the layshaft of an automotive gearbox is dealt with.

Notation

a	Distance.
b	Bearing distance.
C	Dynamic load capacity of bearing.
c	Distance; non-dimensional constant.
D_w	Ball diameter.
d	Shaft diameter.
d_m	Pitch diameter of bearing.
E	Young's modulus of elasticity.
E'	'Equivalent' modulus of elasticity $[=E/(1-\nu^2)]$.
F	Bearing load.
F_0	Bearing preload.
H	Radial bearing load component.
I	Moment of inertia.
J_r, J_a	Integrals.
K	External force; gear tooth load.
k	'Spring constant' of housing seating.
L	Nominal bearing life.
l	Bearing distance.
l_a	Roller length.
M	Bearing moment.
P	Equivalent bearing load.
p	Exponent.
Q	Rolling element load.
R	Tyre radius.
r	Gear radius.
r_e, r_i	Groove radii of outer and inner ring, respectively.
r_p, r_q	Radii to profile centres of inner and outer rings, respectively.
T_0	Engine torque.
t	Exponent.
V	Radial bearing load component.
x, y, z	Cartesian co-ordinates.
X, Y	Radial and axial factors of bearing.
Z	Number of rolling elements in bearing.
α	Contact angle of bearing.
γ	Tilting angle of bearing inner ring relative to outer ring.
Δ	Total axial bearing displacement caused by preloading.
Δ_a	Axial displacement of pinion caused by external loads.
Δ_r	Radial clearance of bearing.
δ	Elastic contact deformation; displacement of bearing inner ring relative to outer ring.
ϵ	Load parameter of bearing.
ν	Poisson's ratio.
ξ	Non-dimensional constant.
ψ	Angular co-ordinate.

Subscripts

0	Initial.
1, 2, ...	Bearing 1, 2, ..., respectively.
a, n, p, r	In the axial, normal, peripheral, and radial direction, respectively.
x, y, z	In the x, y, and z direction, respectively.
m	Mean.
max	Maximum.

TAPER ROLLER BEARING APPLICATIONS

Theory

For an application having two taper roller bearings the radial bearing loads are obtained directly from the equations of equilibrium when the external forces are known. The axial bearing loads, however, are not calculated so easily since, in this respect, the only information obtainable from the equilibrium equations is the difference between them. Thus the system is statically indeterminate in the axial direction, and in order to compute the bearing loads correctly the elastic deformations of the system must be taken into account. It is, however, clear that they are strongly influenced by the magnitude of the bearing preload or clearance.

In order to select the proper preload or clearance it is therefore necessary to analyse the effect of different amounts of preload or clearance (*a*) on the distribution of axial loads on the two taper roller bearings as well as (*b*) on nominal bearing lives, (*c*) on the elastic deformations, and (*d*) on the internal load distribution of the bearings. Using a digital computer this information can be obtained quite easily by solving numerically the non-linear system of equations derived in Appendices 28.1 and 28.2. The computer program developed for this purpose can be used to analyse various automotive driveline bearing applications and, as an example, results of a computation of a hub bearing arrangement are given later in the paper.

For pinions in heavy commercial vehicles, use is often made of two preloaded taper roller bearings and a cylindrical roller bearing. To ensure proper gear meshing under as many different operating conditions as possible, the choice of preload should be a compromise between long nominal bearing lives, which demand a small preload, and high axial rigidity. Compared to the bearing application discussed above, the arrangement having three bearings is more difficult to calculate as it is statically indeterminate in both axial and radial directions. Assuming the shaft to be rigid, but considering the effects of elastic contact deformations in the bearings and radial deformations of the housing seatings, it is necessary to solve the non-linear and highly complex system of equations derived in Appendix 28.3 to be able to obtain the magnitudes of the bearing loads and deflections for a given value of the preload. The computer program mentioned above can also be used in this case and, as examples, the results are shown of an analysis of pinions in a final drive unit and in a gearbox.

Front hub bearing application

In a certain car with front wheel drive the front hub bearings are two similar taper roller bearings, 1 and 2, as shown in Fig. 28.1, which also illustrates the

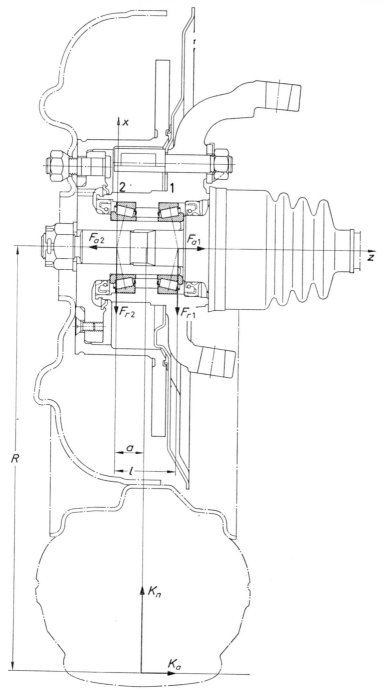

$a = 21$ mm (0·827 in), $l = 44$ mm (1·73 in), $R = 305$ mm (12·0 in).
Bearing data: $l_a = 13$ mm (0·512 in), $Z = 21$, $\alpha = 12.5°$.

Fig. 28.1. Front hub bearing arrangement

positive directions of the forces acting on the wheel, i.e. the tyre/road surface contact forces, K_n and K_a, and the radial and axial bearing loads, F_r and F_a. When mounting, hub bearings should normally be given a certain axial clearance, generally in the range 0·05–0·15 mm (0·002–0·006 in). Here, using results obtained from the computer program referred to above, the consequences of having a bearing clearance beyond this interval will be shown.

It is assumed that the following values apply to the wheel shown in Fig. 28.1: $K_n = 4000, 5000$, and 3000 N (900, 1125, and 675 lbf), respectively, when driving straight ahead, when cornering as outside wheel, and when cornering as inside wheel. The corresponding friction force values are: $K_a = 200$ (because of toe-in), 1250, and −750 N (45, 281, and −168 lbf), respectively. The computer is now used to calculate the bearing loads, etc., under these operating conditions for different values of the axial bearing clearance. Results of one calculation of this kind are shown in Table 28.1. Assuming 90 per cent of the milage to be straight,

Table 28.1. Results of calculation of the hub bearing arrangement shown in Fig. 28.1

$\Delta = -0·10$ mm (−0·0039 in) (clearance); friction hub load $K_a = 1250$ N (281 lbf), normal hub load $K_n = 5000$ N (1125 lbf).

Item		Bearing	
		1	2
Radial load F_r. . . .	N (lbf)	11050 (2480)	−6050 (−1360)
Axial load F_a . . .	N (lbf)	2670 (600)	3920 (881)
Maximum roller load Q_{max} .	N (lbf)	3130 (704)	1480 (333)
Radial displacement δ_r .	mm (in)	0·057 (0·0022)	0·005 (0·0002)
Axial displacement δ_a . .	mm (in)	−0·142 (−0·0056)	0·042 (0·0017)
Maximum contact deformation δ_{max} .	mm (in)	0·025 (0·0010)	0·014 (0·0006)
Load parameter ϵ		0·223	1·43

with the remainder equally divided between left- and right-hand curves, the mean nominal bearing lives are given by the equation

$$\frac{1}{L_m} = \frac{0·90}{L_{straight}} + \frac{0·05}{L_{outside}} + \frac{0·05}{L_{inside}}$$

Fig. 28.2 illustrates the mean bearing lives as a function of the axial bearing clearance. It should be noted that a negative Δ value represents a bearing clearance, and that a positive value indicates that the bearings are preloaded. It will be seen that the magnitudes of the bearing lives are not influenced by a given clearance but that they decrease rapidly when the bearings are preloaded. Thus, from the point of view of fatigue strength it is important that these bearings are not preloaded when mounted, but are given a certain clearance. However, Fig. 28.2 also shows the absolute maximum roller loads in the bearings as a function of the clearance, and it can be seen that the magnitudes of these loads increase with an increase in clearance and that they have minimum values when the bearings are lightly preloaded. This is due to the fact that the number of rollers that are actually loaded decreases with an increase in clearance, and it is thus

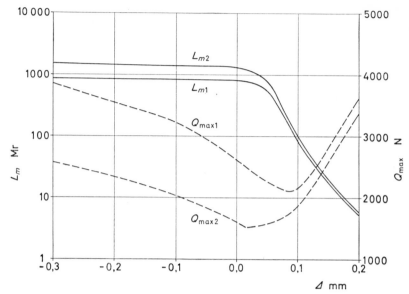

Fig. 28.2. Mean bearing lives and maximum roller loads as function of bearing clearance ($\Delta < 0$) and preload ($\Delta > 0$) for the hub bearings shown in Fig. 28.1

concluded that excessive clearances should be avoided to ensure that the bearings are not too heavily stressed.

Pinion bearings

A pinion equipped with two taper bearings and one cylindrical bearing, and used for the final drive unit of a heavy commercial vehicle, is shown in Fig. 28.3. In order to select the proper preload, the bearing loads and pinion displacements are calculated for different amounts of preloading, using the computer program referred to above. Numerical results of two such computations are given in Table 28.2. In the first instance the housing seatings are considered to be rigid; in the other the radial deflections of the housing seatings are taken into account and it is seen that they have some influence on the magnitudes of the bearing loads. Finally, the nominal bearing lives are determined and the axial displacement Δ_a of the shaft caused by the external forces is obtained from the equation

$$\Delta_a = \delta_{a1} - \delta_{a01} \quad (= \delta_{a02} - \delta_{a2})$$

Assuming the housing seatings to be rigid, the results of these calculations are shown graphically in Fig. 28.4 and it will be seen that a preload of 6000–8000 N (1350–1800 lbf) should be preferred in order to obtain as high an axial rigidity as possible without the bearing lives being considerably reduced.

Automotive gearbox bearings

The computer program developed to analyse taper roller bearing applications may also be used as part of a general program for calculating bearing loads

Table 28.2. Results of calculation of the pinion bearing arrangement shown in Fig. 28.3

Preload $F_0 = 6000$ N (1350 lbf); $\Delta = 0.0482$ mm (0.001 90 in); $\delta_{a01} = 0.0116$ mm (0.000 46 in), $\delta_{a02} = 0.0366$ mm (0.001 44 in). Case (a): $k_1 = k_2 = k_3 = 0$; Case (b): $k_1 = 10^{-7}$ mm/N (0.175×10^{-7} in/lbf), $k_2 = 10^{-6}$ mm/N (0.175×10^{-6} in/lbf), $k_3 = 10^{-5}$ mm/N (0.175×10^{-5} in/lbf).

Item		Bearings: Case (a)			Bearings: Case (b)		
		1	2	3	1	2	3
Radial load component F_x	N	2110	7950	−6060	240	8860	−5100
	(lbf)	(474)	(1790)	(−1360)	(54)	(1990)	(−1150)
Radial load component F_y	N	6120	2090	7790	8960	700	6340
	(lbf)	(1380)	(470)	(1750)	(2010)	(157)	(1430)
Radial load F_r	N	6480	8210	9870	8960	8890	8140
	(lbf)	(1460)	(1850)	(2220)	(2010)	(2000)	(1830)
Axial load F_a	N	23 160	3160	0	23 360	3360	0
	(lbf)	(5210)	(710)	0	(5250)	(755)	0
Maximum roller load Q_{max}	N	3850	2050	2520	4250	2230	2080
	(lbf)	(866)	(461)	(568)	(955)	(501)	(468)
Radial displacement component δ_x	mm	0·0015	0·0080	−0·0049	0·0002	0·0100	−0·0093
	(in)	(0·000 06)	(0·000 31)	(−0·000 19)	(0·000 01)	(0·000 39)	(−0·000 37)
Radial displacement component δ_y	mm	0·0042	0·0021	0·0062	0·0063	0·0008	0·0115
	(in)	(0·000 17)	(0·000 08)	(0·000 24)	(0·000 25)	(0·000 03)	(0·000 45)
Total radial displacement δ_r**	mm	0·0045	0·0083	0·0079	0·0063	0·0100	0·0148
	(in)	(0·000 18)	(0·000 33)	(0·000 31)	(0·000 25)	(0·000 39)	(0·000 58)
Radial displacement δ_r	mm	0·0045	0·0083	0·0079	0·0062	0·0091	0·0067
	(in)	(0·000 18)	(0·000 33)	(0·000 31)	(0·000 24)	(0·000 36)	(0·000 26)
Axial displacement δ_a	mm	0·0317	0·0165	0	0·0317	0·0165	0
	(in)	(0·001 25)	(0·000 65)	0	(0·001 25)	(0·000 65)	0
Maximum contact deformation δ_{max}	mm	0·0197	0·0123	0·0079	0·0212	0·0131	0·0067
	(in)	(0·000 77)	(0·000 48)	(0·000 31)	(0·000 83)	(0·000 52)	(0·000 26)
Load parameter ϵ		2·55	0·766	0·5	1·98	0·740	0·5

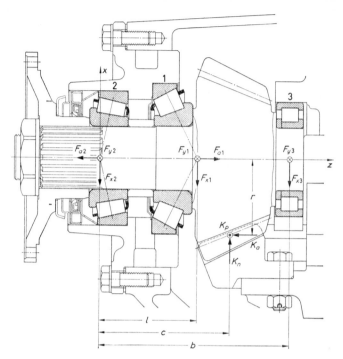

$b = 192$ mm (7·56 in), $c = 131$ mm (5·16 in), $l = 98$ mm (3·86 in), $r = 74$ mm (2·91 in); $K_a = 20\ 000$ N (4500 lbf), $K_n = 4000$ N (900 lbf), $K_p = 16\ 000$ N (3600 lbf). Bearing data: $l_{a1} = l_{a2} = 28$ mm (1·10 in), $l_{a3} = 20$ mm (0·787 in), $Z_1 = Z_2 = Z_3 = 16$, $\alpha_1 = 30°$, $\alpha_2 = 15°$, $\alpha_3 = 0$; $\Delta_{r3} = 0$.

Fig. 28.3. Pinion bearing arrangement

and deflections in manually operated gearboxes of different types. Fig. 28.5 thus shows a gearbox for a front wheel driven car which is advantageously analysed in this way. First, for given gear data and engine torque T_0, the gear tooth load components are computed and shown in Table 28.3. Next, for a given preload F_0 on the taper roller bearings, the bearing loads are calculated for different gear positions, see Table 28.4, and finally equivalent bearing loads, mean bearing loads and nominal bearing lives and bearing deflections are computed. By repeating this procedure for different combinations of bearings, it is possible to make an optimum bearing selection and also to choose an adequate magnitude of preloading for the taper roller bearings.

DEEP GROOVE BALL BEARING APPLICATIONS

Theory

Deep groove ball bearings are normally used to carry radial and/or axial forces, and the magnitude and direction of these are easily obtained from the equations of equilibrium. Further, it is common practice to introduce the assumption that the bearing rings remain parallel when displaced in relation to each

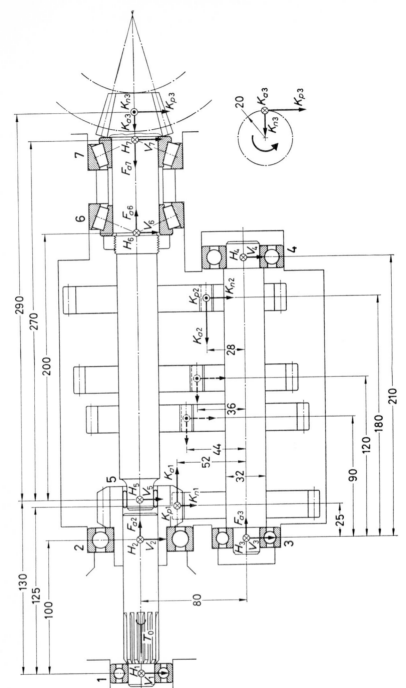

Fig. 28.5. Gearbox with load diagram

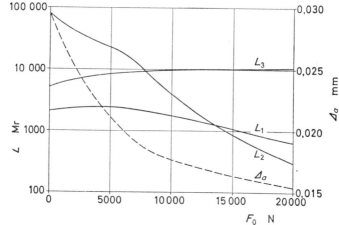

Fig. 28.4. Bearing lives and axial pinion displacement as function of preloading for the pinion shown in Fig. 28.3

other owing to the elastic deformations in the contacts between balls and rings. However, eccentricity and/or misalignment caused by inaccurate manufacture of shaft and housing seatings, as well as elastic shaft deflections, produce tilting of the bearing inner rings in relation to the outer rings and, consequently, the bearings are subjected to the action of bending moments. This condition influences the internal load distribution in the bearings—i.e. the magnitude and direction of the contact forces—and thus the nominal bearing lives are also affected (see Appendix 28.4).

To allow for these phenomena and to consider the effect of bearing clearance, it is necessary to solve the system of non-linear equations in Appendix 28.5. The system includes equations of equilibrium, equations relating bearing deflections to bearing force and moment components, and equations from which the deflections of the shaft are calculated for given external forces and bearing loads. Assuming the shaft diameter to be constant the solution of this system is obtained

Table 28.3. Gear tooth load components of gearbox shown in Fig. 28.5

Engine torque $T_0 = 120$ N m (89 lbf ft).

Gear tooth load		Gear			
		1	2	3	4
K_{a1} .	. N (lbf)	2540 (571)	2540 (571)	2540 (571)	0
K_{n1} .	. N (lbf)	2100 (471)	2100 (471)	2100 (471)	0
K_{p1} .	. N (lbf)	4290 (964)	4290 (964)	4290 (964)	0
K_{a2} .	. N (lbf)	4720 (1060)	3670 (825)	3000 (675)	0
K_{n2} .	. N (lbf)	3900 (877)	3030 (681)	2480 (558)	0
K_{p2} .	. N (lbf)	7960 (1790)	6190 (1390)	5070 (1140)	0
K_{a3} .	. N (lbf)	22700 (5100)	14940 (3360)	10000 (2250)	6580 (1480)
K_{n3} .	. N (lbf)	5130 (1150)	3380 (760)	2260 (508)	1490 (335)
K_{p3} .	. N (lbf)	20690 (4650)	13620 (3060)	9120 (2050)	6000 (1350)

Table 28.4. Bearing loads of gearbox shown in Fig. 28.5

Preload $F_0 = 3000$ N (675 lbf). Bearing data: $l_{a5} = 12$ mm (0·472 in), $l_{a6} = l_{a7} = 18$ mm (0·709 in); $Z_5 = 18$, $Z_6 = Z_7 = 16$; $\alpha_5 = 0$, $\alpha_6 = \alpha_7 = 20°$; $F_{a1} = F_{a5} = 0$.

Bearing load			Gear			
			1	2	3	4
F_{r1} .	.	. N (lbf)	657 (164)	591 (133)	587 (132)	246 (55)
F_{r2} .	.	. N (lbf)	5550 (1250)	5370 (1210)	5340 (1200)	1060 (238)
F_{a2} .	.	. N (lbf)	2540 (571)	2540 (571)	2540 (571)	0
F_{r3} .	.	. N (lbf)	3570 (802)	3340 (750)	3380 (759)	0
F_{a3} .	.	. N (lbf)	2180 (490)	1130 (254)	462 (103)	0
F_{r4} .	.	. N (lbf)	7260 (1630)	3620 (813)	2120 (477)	0
F_{r5} .	.	. N (lbf)	3250 (731)	4150 (933)	4200 (944)	820 (184)
F_{r6} .	.	. N (lbf)	0	523 (118)	1390 (312)	1230 (277)
F_{a6} .	.	. N (lbf)	0	206 (46)	635 (143)	581 (131)
F_{r7} .	.	. N (lbf)	19160 (4310)	12640 (2840)	7850 (1765)	5630 (1266)
F_{a7} .	.	. N (lbf)	17990 (4040)	11480 (2580)	7640 (1720)	7160 (1610)

by use of a computer program specially developed for the purpose. Thus the bearing forces and moments, and subsequently the equivalent bearing loads and the nominal bearing lives, are obtained together with the deflection components.

Layshaft of an automotive gearbox

As an example of how to use the computer program, a study is made of the layshaft of the automotive gearbox shown in Fig. 28.5. Values for the gear tooth load components have already been given in Table 28.3, while the bearing loads, as obtained by means of a conventional method of calculation—i.e. neglecting the influence of bearing moments, misalignments, and shaft deflections—are shown in Table 28.4. For the second gear results of a computation for given values of the initial misalignment angles are illustrated in Table 28.5, and Fig. 28.6 shows graphically the effect of bearing clearances upon the equivalent bearing loads for two different combinations of initial misalignment angles. It will be seen that the shaft deflections and the bearing misalignments have a certain influence on the equivalent bearing loads and thus on the nominal bearing lives.

CONCLUSIONS

Specially developed programs executed on a high-speed digital computer are very suitable for providing relevant information to be used as a basis for the selection of correct rolling bearings for different automotive bearing applications. In addition, these computer programs can be used for an accurate analysis of the influence of factors that are difficult to consider by conventional means, for instance, bearing preload and clearance, bearing misalignments and elastic deflections of shafts, and bearing seatings.

APPENDIX 28.1. LOAD DISTRIBUTION IN A ROLLER BEARING HAVING CONSTANT CONTACT ANGLE

Assuming that the inner ring of a single row roller bearing with the constant contact angle α and with zero clearance will be displaced a distance δ_r in the radial direction and δ_a in the axial direction (see Fig. 28.7), the magnitude of the maximum elastic contact deformation is obtained from the following equation (**I**)*:

$$\delta_{max} = \delta_r \cos \alpha + \delta_a \sin \alpha = 2\epsilon\delta_r \cos \alpha. \quad . \quad . \quad . \quad (28.1a)$$

Table 28.5. Results of calculation of layshaft of gearbox (second gear) shown in Fig. 28.5

Initial misalignment angles $\gamma_{x03} = 0.24°$, $\gamma_{y03} = 0.18°$, $\gamma_{x04} = -0.24°$, $\gamma_{y04} = -0.18°$.
Bearing data: $d_{m3} = 36$ mm (1·42 in), $d_{m4} = 44$ mm (1·73 in); $D_{w3} = 10$ mm (0·394 in)
$D_{w4} = 11$ mm (0·433 in); $Z_3 = Z_4 = 7$; $\varDelta_{r3} = \varDelta_{r4} = 0.010$ mm (0·000 39 in).

Item		Bearing	
		3	4
Radial load component F_x . . N (lbf)		3160 (710)	1970 (443)
Radial load component F_y . . N (lbf)		1160 (260)	−3070 (−690)
Radial load F_r . . . . N (lbf)		3370 (758)	3640 (818)
Axial load F_a . . . . N (lbf)		−1130 (−254)	0
Moment component M_x . . N mm (lbf ft)		11200 (8·3)	−19400 (−14·3)
Moment component M_y . . N mm (lbf ft)		21100 (15·6)	−18200 (−13·4)
Radial displacement component δ_x mm (in)		0·016 (0·0006)	0·024 (0·0009)
Radial displacement component δ_y mm (in)		0·024 (0·0009)	−0·034 (−0·0013)
Axial displacement component δ_z mm (in)		−0·041 (−0·0016)	−0·073 (−0·0029)
Tilting angle γ_x . . . degrees		0·300 (0·0118)	−0·289 (−0·0114)
Tilting angle γ_y . . . degrees		0·274 (0·0108)	−0·246 (−0·0097)
Maximum ball load Q_{max} . . N (lbf)		2160 (486)	3220 (724)
Equivalent load P . . . N (lbf)		3690 (829)	4880 (1100)

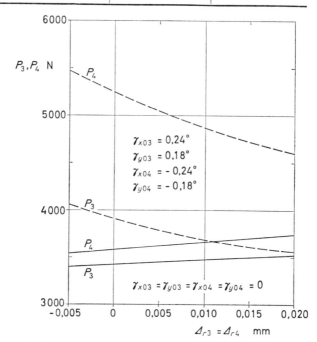

Fig. 28.6. Equivalent loads for the layshaft bearings of the gearbox shown in Fig. 28.5 (second gear) as function of bearing clearances

* *References are given in Appendix 28.6.*

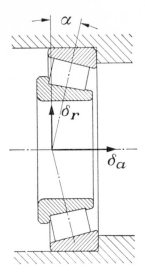

Fig. 28.7. Taper roller bearing with contact angle α and radial and axial displacements δ_r and δ_a

where ϵ is the load parameter

$$\epsilon = \frac{1}{2}\left(1 + \frac{\delta_a \tan \alpha}{\delta_r}\right) \quad \ldots \quad \text{(28.2)}$$

For a cylindrical roller bearing having the radial clearance Δ_r, the value $\epsilon = 0.5$ is used and the maximum elastic contact deformation is expressed:

$$\delta_{max} = \delta_r - \Delta_r/2 \quad \ldots \quad \text{(28.1b)}$$

With sufficient accuracy the maximum rolling element load, Q_{max}, is then derived from the equation

$$Q_{max} = cE'l_a^2(\delta_{max}/l_a)^t \quad \ldots \quad \text{(28.3)}$$

where l_a is the effective roller length, E' is the equivalent modulus of elasticity $[E' = E/(1-\nu^2) = 230\,000 \text{ N/mm}^2 \ (33 \times 10^6 \text{ lbf/in}^2)$ for steel bearings], and c is a non-dimensional constant equal to 0·34 for a taper roller bearing and 0·16 for a cylindrical roller bearing. The value of the exponent t can be taken as 1·33 for a taper roller and 1·11 for a cylindrical roller bearing.

Finally, the radial and axial bearing loads are given by

$$F_r = ZQ_{max} \cos \alpha J_r(\epsilon, t) \quad \ldots \quad \text{(28.4)}$$
$$F_a = ZQ_{max} \sin \alpha J_a(\epsilon, t) \quad \ldots \quad \text{(28.5)}$$

where

$$J_r(\epsilon, t) = \frac{1}{\pi}\int_0^{\psi_0}\left(1 - \frac{1-\cos\psi}{2\epsilon}\right)^t \cos\psi\,d\psi$$

$$J_a(\epsilon, t) = \frac{1}{\pi}\int_0^{\psi_0}\left(1 - \frac{1-\cos\psi}{2\epsilon}\right)^t d\psi$$

and

$$\psi_0 = \begin{cases} \arccos(1-2\epsilon), & 0 \leqslant \epsilon \leqslant 1 \\ \pi, & \epsilon > 1 \end{cases}$$

APPENDIX 28.2. BEARING APPLICATION WITH TWO TAPER ROLLER BEARINGS

A bearing application incorporating two taper roller bearings, 1 and 2, is shown in Fig. 28.8, which also illustrates the positive directions of the forces acting on the shaft. The radial components of the bearing loads are obtained directly from the equations of equilibrium:

$$F_{x1} = \sum (K_{xi}z_i - K_{zi}x_i)/l$$
$$F_{y1} = \sum (K_{yi}z_i - K_{zi}y_i)/l$$
$$F_{x2} = \sum K_{xi} - F_{x1}$$
$$F_{y2} = \sum K_{yi} - F_{y1}$$

where all external force components have to be included in the summations. The resultant radial bearing loads are then obtained from

$$F_r = \sqrt{(F_x^2 + F_y^2)} \quad \dots \dots \quad (28.6)$$

Equilibrium in the axial direction gives

$$F_{a2} - F_{a1} = \sum K_{zi} \quad \dots \dots \quad (28.7)$$

Assuming that all elastic deformations occur in the bearings, and because of the bearing preload (F_0) the inner rings of the bearings are displaced axially through the distances δ_{a01} and δ_{a02} respectively, the relationship between preload F_0 and initial axial displacement is

$$\delta_{a0} = \frac{l_a}{\sin \alpha} \left(\frac{F_0}{cE'l_a^2 Z \sin \alpha} \right)^{1/t}$$

which is applicable to both bearings. The total axial bearing displacement is

$$\Delta = \delta_{a01} + \delta_{a02}$$

It is understood that an initial bearing clearance corresponds to a negative Δ value, and in this case the concept of preload is of no importance.

When the bearings are subjected to the action of external forces the total axial bearing displacement remains unchanged. Thus

$$\delta_{a1} + \delta_{a2} = \Delta. \quad \dots \dots \quad (28.8)$$

By applying equations (28.1)–(28.5) to each of the two bearings, and using equations (28.6) and (28.7), a system of equations is obtained from which values of

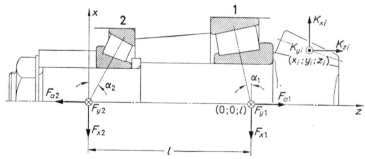

Fig. 28.8. Load diagram for bearing application with two taper roller bearings

F_a, Q_{max}, δ_{max}, δ_r, δ_a, and ϵ for each bearing can be solved by numerical methods —for instance, the Newton–Raphson method. The equivalent bearing loads and the nominal bearing lives are then given by the equations

$$P = XF_r + YF_a \quad \text{and} \quad L = \left(\frac{C}{P}\right)^p$$

where the value $p = 10/3$ should be used.

APPENDIX 28.3. BEARING APPLICATION WITH TWO TAPER ROLLER BEARINGS AND ONE CYLINDRICAL ROLLER BEARING

Fig. 28.9 shows a bearing application incorporating two taper roller bearings, 1 and 2, mounted back-to-back with the preload F_0, and also a cylindrical roller bearing, 3, which carries no axial load and the load parameter of which equals 0·5.
The equations of equilibrium are expressed as:

$$F_{x1} + F_{x2} + F_{x3} = \sum K_{xi} \quad . \quad . \quad . \quad . \quad . \quad . \quad (28.9)$$
$$F_{y1} + F_{y2} + F_{y3} = \sum K_{yi} \quad . \quad . \quad . \quad . \quad . \quad . \quad (28.10)$$
$$F_{x1}l + F_{x3}b = \sum (K_{xi}z_i - K_{zi}x_i) \quad . \quad . \quad . \quad . \quad (28.11)$$
$$F_{y1}l + F_{y3}b = \sum (K_{yi}z_i - K_{zi}y_i) \quad . \quad . \quad . \quad . \quad (28.12)$$

and equations (28.6), (28.7), and (28.8) in Appendix 28.2 also apply in this instance. However, equation (28.8) is valid only when the magnitude of the external axial force is not such as to unload one of the taper roller bearings. Assuming the radial deflection δ_r^* of the housing seating to be proportional to the radial load, i.e. $\delta_r^* = kF_r$ (k being the constant of proportionality), the total radial displacement δ_r^{**} of the inner ring is expressed as

$$\delta_r^{**} = \delta_r + kF_r \quad . \quad . \quad . \quad . \quad . \quad . \quad (28.13)$$

where δ_r is the radial displacement of the inner ring relative to the outer ring (see Fig. 28.10). As a consequence of the assumption that all elastic deformations occur in the bearings and in the bearing seatings, the centre-line of the shaft will

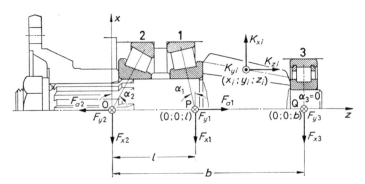

Fig. 28.9. Load diagram for bearing application with two taper and one cylindrical roller bearing

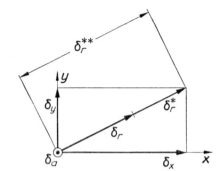

Fig. 28.10. Diagram showing displacement components when the radial deflection of the bearing housing is taken into account

remain straight when the external forces are applied. Thus the following equations are obtained:

$$\frac{\delta_{x2}-\delta_{x1}}{\delta_{x2}-\delta_{x3}}=\frac{l}{b} \quad \ldots \ldots \ldots \quad (28.14)$$

$$\frac{\delta_{y2}-\delta_{y1}}{\delta_{y2}-\delta_{y3}}=\frac{l}{b} \quad \ldots \ldots \ldots \quad (28.15)$$

The resultant radial bearing deflection is (see Fig. 28.10):

$$\delta_r{}^{**} = \sqrt{(\delta_x{}^2+\delta_y{}^2)} \quad \ldots \ldots \ldots \quad (28.16)$$

Finally, the following equation must be satisfied:

$$\frac{\delta_x}{\delta_y}=\frac{F_x}{F_y} \quad \ldots \ldots \ldots \quad (28.17)$$

with the supplementary condition that the two quantities δ_x and F_x, as well as δ_y and F_y, should have the same sign.

By applying equations (28.1)–(28.5) on the two taper roller bearings, equations (28.1), (28.3), and (28.4) on the cylindrical roller bearing, equations (28.6), (28.13), (28.16), and (28.17) on all three bearings, and by using equations (28.7)–(28.12) and equations (28.14) and (28.15), a system of equations is obtained from which all unknown quantities involved can be solved by numerical methods.

APPENDIX 28.4. LOAD DISTRIBUTION IN A DEEP GROOVE BALL BEARING

In a deep groove ball bearing (see Fig. 28.11) the inner ring is displaced through the distances δ_x, δ_y, and δ_z and tilted through the angles γ_x and γ_y relative to the outer ring (see Fig. 28.12). Then, for the angular co-ordinate ψ (see Fig. 28.13), the local contact angle, α, is given by the following equation (2):

$$\tan \alpha = \frac{\delta_z+r_p(\gamma_x \sin \psi-\gamma_y \cos \psi)}{\delta_x \cos \psi+\delta_y \sin \psi+a} \quad \ldots \ldots \quad (28.18)$$

where

$$a = r_p-r_q; \quad r_p =\frac{d_m}{2}-\frac{D_w}{2}-\frac{\Delta_r}{4}+r_i \quad \text{and} \quad r_q =\frac{d_m}{2}+\frac{D_w}{2}+\frac{\Delta_r}{4}-r_e$$

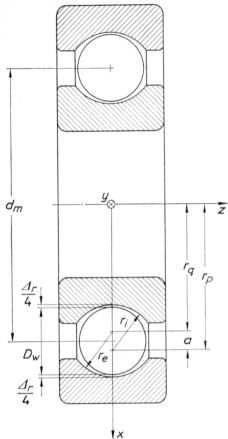

Fig. 28.11. Deep groove ball bearing with characteristic geometrical dimensions

The total elastic contact deformation amounts to

$$\delta = \frac{\delta_x \cos \psi + \delta_y \sin \psi + a}{\cos \alpha} - a - \frac{\Delta_r}{2} \quad . \quad . \quad . \quad (28.19)$$

and the magnitude of the corresponding contact load is

$$Q = \begin{cases} E' \xi D_w{}^2 (\delta/D_w)^{3/2}, & \delta > 0 \\ 0, & \delta \leqslant 0 \end{cases} \quad . \quad . \quad . \quad (28.20)$$

where $E' = E/(1-\nu^2)$ and ξ is a non-dimensional constant, the value of which depends on r_i/D_w and r_e/D_w; for instance, $\xi = 0.480$ for $r_i/D_w = r_e/D_w = 0.5175$. The resultant bearing load and moment components are then obtained from the following equations:

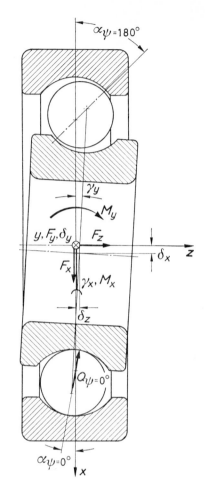

Fig. 28.12. Deep groove ball bearing with load and displacement components

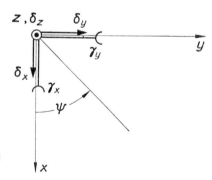

Fig. 28.13. Diagram showing displacement components and angular co-ordinate ψ

$$F_x = \frac{Z}{2\pi} \int_{-\pi}^{\pi} Q \cos \alpha \cos \psi \, d\psi \ . \quad . \quad . \quad . \quad (28.21)$$

$$F_y = \frac{Z}{2\pi} \int_{-\pi}^{\pi} Q \cos \alpha \sin \psi \, d\psi \ . \quad . \quad . \quad . \quad (28.22)$$

$$F_z = \frac{Z}{2\pi} \int_{-\pi}^{\pi} Q \sin \alpha \, d\psi \quad . \quad . \quad . \quad . \quad . \quad (28.23)$$

$$M_x = \frac{Zr_q}{2\pi} \int_{-\pi}^{\pi} Q \sin \alpha \sin \psi \, d\psi \quad . \quad . \quad . \quad (28.24)$$

$$M_y = \frac{Zr_q}{-2\pi} \int_{-\pi}^{\pi} Q \sin \alpha \cos \psi \, d\psi \quad . \quad . \quad . \quad (28.25)$$

Thus, using equations (28.18)–(28.20), it might be said that equations (28.21)–(28.25) express the relationship between load and deflection of a deep groove ball bearing.

The equivalent bearing load is computed from the equation

$$P = \frac{ZJ_r}{J_1} \left[\frac{1}{2\pi} \int_{-\pi}^{\pi} Q^p(\psi) \, d\psi \right]^{1/p} \quad . \quad . \quad . \quad . \quad (28.26)$$

(where $J_1 = 0.5625$, $J_r = 0.2288$, and $p = 3$), and finally the nominal bearing life is obtained from the life formula

$$L = (C/P)^p$$

APPENDIX 28.5. BEARING LOAD COMPONENTS OF A SHAFT WITH TWO DEEP GROOVE BALL BEARINGS

A shaft with constant diameter d and bearing distance l is mounted in two deep groove ball bearings, 3 and 4, and subjected to the action of external forces (see Fig. 28.14). Bearing load components consist of forces and moments. The equations of equilibrium are expressed as:

$$F_{x3} + F_{x4} = \sum K_{xi} \cdot \quad . \quad . \quad . \quad . \quad . \quad (28.27)$$

$$F_{y3} + F_{y4} = \sum K_{yi} \cdot \quad . \quad . \quad . \quad . \quad . \quad (28.28)$$

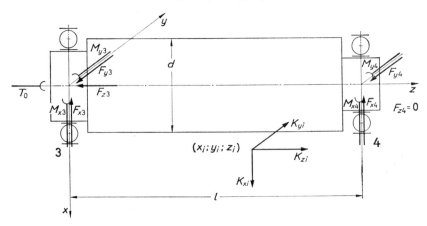

Fig. 28.14. Load diagram of shaft with two deep groove ball bearings

$$M_{x3}+M_{x4}-F_{y4}l = \sum (K_{zi}y_i-K_{yi}z_i) . \quad . \quad . \quad . \quad (28.29)$$

$$M_{y3}+M_{y4}+F_{x4}l = \sum (K_{xi}z_i-K_{zi}x_i) . \quad . \quad . \quad . \quad (28.30)$$

Bearing 4 is assumed to carry no axial load, i.e.

$$F_{z4} = 0 \quad . \quad . \quad . \quad . \quad . \quad . \quad . \quad (28.31)$$

thus

$$F_{z3} = \sum K_{zi} \quad . \quad . \quad . \quad . \quad . \quad . \quad . \quad (28.32)$$

Bearing 3 is assumed to be given the initial misalignments γ_{x03} and γ_{y03}. Owing to the deflection of the shaft there will be additional tilting of the inner ring in relation to the outer ring, which amounts to γ_{x13} and γ_{y13} respectively. Thus the total tilting angles for bearing 3 are (Fig. 28.15):

$$\gamma_{x3} = \gamma_{x03}+\gamma_{x13} \quad . \quad . \quad . \quad . \quad . \quad (28.33)$$

$$\gamma_{y3} = \gamma_{y03}+\gamma_{y13} \quad . \quad . \quad . \quad . \quad . \quad (28.34)$$

Similarly for bearing 4:

$$\gamma_{x4} = \gamma_{x04}+\gamma_{x14} \quad . \quad . \quad . \quad . \quad . \quad (28.35)$$

$$\gamma_{y4} = \gamma_{y04}+\gamma_{y14} \quad . \quad . \quad . \quad . \quad . \quad (28.36)$$

From the basic theory of elasticity the following equations are derived:

$$\gamma_{x13} = -\frac{\delta_{y4}-\delta_{y3}}{l}-\frac{M_{x3}l}{2EI}-\frac{F_{y3}l^2}{6EI}+\frac{1}{6EIl}\sum [K_{yi}(l-z_i)^3+3K_{zi}y_i(l-z_i)^2] \quad . \quad (28.37)$$

$$\gamma_{y13} = \frac{\delta_{x4}-\delta_{x3}}{l}-\frac{M_{y3}l}{2EI}+\frac{F_{x3}l^2}{6EI}-\frac{1}{6EIl}\sum [K_{xi}(l-z_i)^3+3K_{zi}x_i(l-z_i)^2] \quad . \quad (28.38)$$

$$\gamma_{x14} = -\frac{\delta_{y4}-\delta_{y3}}{l}-\frac{M_{x4}l}{2EI}+\frac{F_{y4}l^2}{6EI}-\frac{1}{6EIl}\sum (K_{yi}z_i^3-3K_{zi}y_iz_i^2) \quad . \quad . \quad . \quad (28.39)$$

$$\gamma_{y14} = \frac{\delta_{x4}-\delta_{x3}}{l}-\frac{M_{y4}l}{2EI}-\frac{F_{x4}l^2}{6EI}+\frac{1}{6EIl}\sum (K_{xi}z_i^3-3K_{zi}x_iz_i^2) \quad . \quad . \quad . \quad (28.40)$$

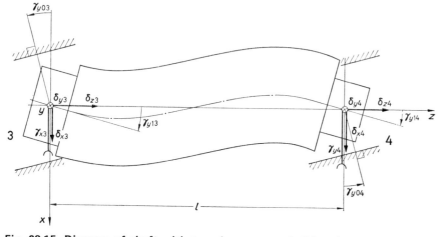

Fig. 28.15. Diagram of shaft with two deep groove ball bearings showing misalignment angles and displacement components

where $I = \pi d^4/64$.

By applying equations (28.21)–(28.25) to each of the two bearings, and using equations (28.27)–(28.40), a system of equations is obtained from which all bearing loads and displacement components can be solved by numerical methods.

APPENDIX 28.6

REFERENCES

(1) LUNDBERG, G. and PALMGREN, A. 'Dynamic capacity of rolling bearings', *Acta polytech.*, *Mech. Engng Series* 1947 **1** (No. 3).

(2) ANDRÉASON, S. 'Theoretische Grundlagen für die Berechnung von mit Kräften und Momenten belasteten Rillenkugellagern' ('Theoretical bases for the calculation of deep groove ball bearings carrying forces and moments'), *Konstruktion* 1969 **21** (No. 3), 105.

APPENDIX 28.7. FRONT HUB BEARING APPLICATION

Since the discussion of this paper at the Conference on Driveline Engineering the equivalent loads and the mean nominal lives of the hub bearings shown in Fig. 28.1 have been recalculated and consequently the standard equation $P = XF_r + YF_a$ should be replaced by the more accurate equation (28.26), at least when the load parameter of the taper roller bearing, ϵ, is less than 0·5.

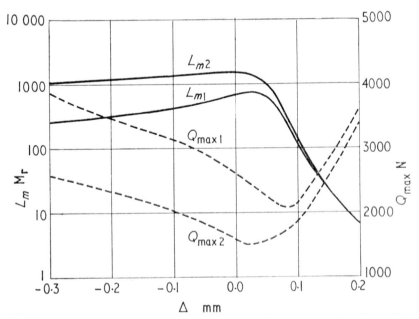

Fig. 28.16. Mean bearing lives and maximum roller loads as function of bearing clearance ($\Delta < 0$) and preload ($\Delta > 0$) for the hub bearings shown in Fig. 28.1 when using equation (28.26) to calculate equivalent bearing loads

Hence, with $J_1 = 0\cdot6495$, $J_r = 0\cdot2453$ and $p = 10/3$, equation (28.26) gives values of the equivalent bearing loads P which, using the life formula $L = (C/P)^p$, will give the mean bearing lives as functions of the axial bearing clearance as shown in Fig. 28.16. It is seen that maximum bearing lives are obtained for zero axial clearance approximately.

The MS. of this paper was received at the Institution on 3rd September 1969 and accepted for publication on 13th November 1969, and the MS. of Appendix 28.7 was received at the Institution on 29th September 1970.

Paper 29. Propeller Shafts and Universal Joints—Characteristics and Methods of Selection

J. W. MACIELINSKI, MSc, CEng, FIMechE

Manager, Special Investigations, G.K.N. Birfield Transmissions Ltd, Erdington, Birmingham.

In this paper, both Hooke's joint and the modern ball type constant velocity unit are considered. Methods by which the specific capacity and life endurance of a joint may be estimated are described. A method of calculation to select a suitable joint for automotive purposes is discussed.

INTRODUCTION

Every vehicle driveline, whether it connects the output from the gearbox to the rear axle or the differential to the rear wheels or to the front wheels, must be capable of performing certain functions. It must be able

(*a*) to transmit efficiently varying torques put in by the power unit;

(*b*) to rotate over a very large speed range;

(*c*) to operate through a wide range of angles; and

(*d*) to accommodate, in the majority of cases, variations in length due to movement of components to which it is attached.

To perform these functions five degrees of freedom must be introduced to the driveline, with two degrees of freedom at the universal joints placed at either end of the driveline.

HOOKE'S JOINT AND COMPROMISE SOLUTIONS

Various methods of meeting these demands are known, the oldest being the Hooke's (or Cardan) type of joint which has served the mechanical engineer well for a considerable period. However, with the increased demand for higher speeds and torques, and a more sophisticated approach to designs by the modern automobile industry, the inherent shortcomings of the Hooke's joint, in respect of non-uniform transfer of motion when operating at an angle, have forced engineers to look for another solution that would transfer the motion uniformly at any required angular position of the joint. The concept of the constant velocity joint has been evolved, and after the usual initial struggle with the more conservatively minded designers it has finally become universally accepted. Several successful solutions of this joint are now available.

Between these two basically different concepts of the universal joint there are various compromise solutions which aim at either reducing sliding friction or increasing the flexibility of the driveline, or both. Two-armed pot joints (basically non-constant velocity), three-armed pot joints (basically constant velocity), and various rubber joints can be classified as compromise solutions (see Figs 29.1–29.3).

The transfer of torque from one shaft to another by Hooke's joints is generally achieved through four needle roller bearings, each of which is located at the end of one of the arms of the journal cross which forms the connection between the input and output yokes. The working conditions of needle bearings in Hooke's joints are similar to those of normal support needle bearings as both must withstand loading forces directed perpendicularly to the bearing surface. The peg of the joint, however, oscillates in the race once per revolution of the shaft. This means that, in the Hooke's joint needle bearing, each point on the surface of the race is subjected at least twice, depending upon the joint angle, to the loading force in one revolution of the joint, whereas in the normally used needle bearing it happens only once.

The schematic exploded view of a Hooke's joint (Fig. 29.4) shows the direction of the forces acting on the journal bearings when the joint is operating at an angle α.

The input torque (T_1) on the drive shaft (1) causes a reaction torque (T_2) on the output shaft (2) which appears in the form of a couple (F_2) acting on the yokes at the distance s (which is the actual span of the journal cross). Therefore, $T_2 = F_2 \times s$. The reaction F'_2 of the force F_2 on the cross member is equal and opposite in direction to the force F_2, and the torque which reacts on the journal is $F'_2 \times s$ and lies in the plane of the journal. Since, due to its supports, the journal cross can transfer only forces in its own plane, the perpendicular arm of the cross will react to the torque T_2 with torque $Q \times s$, where Q also lies in the plane of the cross member. On the other hand, the input shaft (1), which transmits torque T_1, also creates a couple F_1 on the yokes. Therefore $T_1 = F_1 \times s$. Reaction forces F'_1 lying normal to the plane of the input yokes act on the cross member at an angle α to the force Q. To balance the difference on the planes of acting and reacting forces a third pair of forces R'_1, which act in the plane of the yoke, is created causing a secondary moment $R'_1 \times s$ which, together with the couple $F'_1 \times s$, results in the couple $Q \times s$. Obviously a reaction to this secondary couple R_1 will show acting on the yoke in the perpendicular plane. This couple does not transfer the driving torque but causes bending on the yokes and the shafts, creating loading forces on the shaft support bearings.

Further consideration of the secondary forces shows that their magnitude and direction alter with the momentary position of the cross member, oscillating between maximum and zero. This is shown clearly in the lower part of Fig. 29.4 where the same system of forces is shown at the same angularity when the joint is turned through 90°. Generally, the magnitude of this secondary couple depends on the shaft angle and it increases rapidly with the increase in angle. At $\phi = 0$ (Fig. 29.4a) only the input shaft (1) is subject to secondary forces, and at $\phi = 90°$ (Fig. 29.4b) only the output shaft (2). In intermediate positions the secondary couples act on both shafts; their magnitude has the characteristics of a sine or cosine wave with one complete oscillation per revolution, and the force on a rotating yoke changes direction with rotation. Thus, as both magnitude and direction of secondary forces change during rotation, it results in a complex excitation of the system (**1**)* (**2**).

---

* *References are given in Appendix 29.1.*

a Flange type Hooke's joint.
b Bendix–Weiss constant velocity joint.
c Birfield constant velocity joint.   **Fig. 29.1**

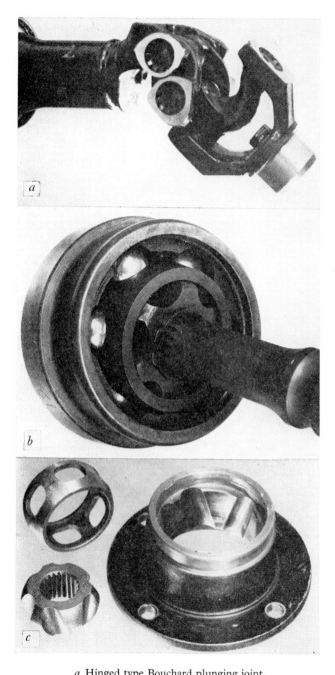

a Hinged type Bouchard plunging joint.
b Offset spheres G.K.N. plunging joint.

Fig. 29.2

c Exploded view of Lohr–Bromkamp plunging joint.

a Two-armed pot joint.
b Three-armed pot joint.
c 'Moulton' type flexible joint, part sectioned.
d 'Layrub' shaft with flexible joints.

Fig. 29.3

The equations for the secondary couple can be defined as follows:
at $\phi = 0°$,

$$T_{b1} = R'_1 s = Qs \sin \alpha = T_2 \sin \alpha = F'_1 s \frac{\sin \alpha}{\cos \alpha} = T_1 \tan \alpha$$

at $\phi = 90°$,

$$T_{b2} = R'_2 s = Qs \sin \alpha = T_1 \sin \alpha = F'_2 s \frac{\sin \alpha}{\cos \alpha} = T_2 \tan \alpha$$

and the input and output torques are:
at $\phi = 0°$,

$$T_1 = F'_1 s$$

$$T_2 = F'_2 s = \frac{F'_1 s}{\cos \alpha} = \frac{T_1}{\cos \alpha} = T_{2 \, max}$$

at $\phi = 90°$,

$$F'_1 s = Qs$$

$$T'_2 = F'_2 s = Qs \cos \alpha = T_1 \cos \alpha = T_{2 \, min}$$

The consideration of these formulae allows calculation of the output torque and secondary couple fluctuations during one rotation of the joint. Therefore, the ratio of non-uniform torque transfer is:

$$U = \frac{T_{2 \, max} - T_{2 \, min}}{T_1} = \frac{1}{\cos \alpha} - \cos \alpha = \frac{\sin^2 \alpha}{\cos \alpha} = \tan \alpha \sin \alpha$$

which is identical with the ratio of non-uniform angular velocity.

Having thus established the actual variation of torques transferred through the joint, let us consider the approach to the selection of joint sizes suitable for given conditions.

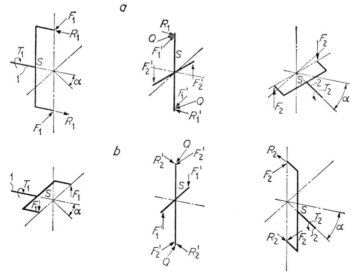

Fig. 29.4. Schematic exploded view of a Hooke's joint

SELECTION OF JOINT SIZES

Since we are dealing basically with a needle roller bearing transferring the load directed at it radially, it is generally accepted that the Hertzian theory for needle rollers applies to this case. According to the theory, the criterion of bearing loads is the load Q_s that a bearing can carry for 10^6 revolutions of the inner race before failure occurs (3) (4).

For all calculations related to the life of needle bearings in Hooke's type joints, use is made of the expression

$$Q_s = 49Z^{2/3}dl \text{ newtons}$$

where d is the diameter (mm), l the needle length (mm), and Z the number of rollers; or

$$Q_s = 7100Z^{2/3}dl \text{ lb}$$

where d and l are in inches. The value of Q_s thus found is then used for calculating the life.

According to Palmgren (3) any average bearing life expressed in millions of revolutions is:

$$L_N = \left(\frac{Q_s}{Q}\right)^3 = \frac{60N_iH}{10^6}$$

in which N_i is the number of revolutions per minute of the inner ring, H the life in hours, L_N the life in millions of revolutions, and Q the actual journal load. For 1 000 000 revolutions the specific life, H_s, in hours would be:

$$H_s = \frac{10^6}{60N_i}$$

In the normal needle bearing each needle is subjected to one loading cycle per revolution of the inner race. In a Hooke's joint, where the bearing oscillates once per revolution, each point on a bearing race is subject to load twice in each revolution. Therefore, the specific load, calculated from the formula above, will refer to a life of 500 000 shaft revolutions instead of 1 000 000. Life, in hours, is therefore calculated as:

$$H_s = \frac{5 \times 10^5}{60 \times N_i}$$

when

$$L_N = \left(\frac{Q_s}{Q}\right)^3 = \frac{60N_iH}{5 \times 10^5}$$

Solving this equation for H, and introducing the formula for specific loading Q_s, we find that

$$H_s = \frac{7100^3Z^2d^3l^3 \times 5 \times 10^5}{60Q^3N_i} = \frac{2 \cdot 98 \times 10^{15}Z^2d^3l^3}{Q^3N_i}$$

or, in metric dimensions:

$$H = \frac{51 \times 10^6Z^2d^3l^3}{Q^3N_i}$$

The oscillation of the journal peg is obviously of importance for establishing the life parameter. In contrast to the normal roller bearing, the rollers in the Hooke's joint are forced to move forwards and backwards along the arc equal to $2 \times 2\alpha$ in each revolution, where α is the shaft angle. At large angles of the shaft, the load may therefore act on the peg through several rollers in turn. In relation to the shaft speed, due to oscillating movement, the needle revolves at a mean speed n_r depending on the peg/needle diameter ratio, angularity of the shaft, and its speed n:

$$n_r = \frac{D}{d} n \sin \alpha$$

(where D is the peg diameter and d is the needle diameter), at the same time changing its position relative to the plane in which the load is acting. This has an effect on the endurance of the bearing due to variation of angular velocity of the needles. The larger the shaft angle, the greater are these stress variations. To allow for this effect it is usual to accept an empirical corrective angular factor introduced in the calculation of bearing capacity:

$$C = \sqrt[3]{\frac{\sin \alpha}{\sin 3°}} \times \frac{1}{\cos \alpha}$$

by which the torque accepted for calculations must be multiplied.

As we then know the specific load per bearing or specific torque we can calculate, by a direct comparison, the life of the joint for any given load or torque. Generally, if T_1, n_1 and T_2, n_2 are torques and speeds in different conditions, the lives in hours (H_1 and H_2) are given by:

$$H_1 = \frac{K}{T_1{}^3 n_1} \quad \text{and} \quad H_2 = \frac{K}{T_2{}^3 n_2}$$

where K is a constant for a particular joint.

We can then write

$$\frac{H_1}{H_2} = \frac{T_2{}^3 n_2}{T_1{}^3 n_1}$$

and when there is no change in speed of joint:

$$\frac{H_1}{H_2} = \left(\frac{T_2}{T_1}\right)^3$$

Table 29.1 gives the calculated specific loads and torques for Hooke's type joints as currently manufactured by my company. When the specific load or torque is known one can establish the capacity rating most suitable for selection of the joint for the application. In Hooke's joints the basic rating is the load or torque which gives 5000 h bearing life at 100 shaft rev/min. The angle at this stage can be neglected since for basic rating conditions it is assumed that the joint works at an angle of 3° or less.

As

$$\left(\frac{Q_s}{Q}\right)^3 = \frac{60NH}{5 \times 10^5}$$

Table 29.1. Specific loads and torques

Series	Number of rollers, Z	Nominal diameter of roller, in	Effective roller length, in	Specific load, Q_s lbf (N)		Specific torque, T_s, lbf in (N m)	
1140	34	0·062 5	0·375	1 745	(7 762)	3 894	(440)
1300	25	0·093 75	0·371	2 112	(9 395)	5 812	(657)
1310	25	0·093 75	0·449	2 555	(11 365)	7 670	(867)
1350	27	0·093 75	0·618	3 700	(16 458)	12 487	(1 411)
1410	34	0·078 125	0·605	3 526	(15 684)	13 878	(1 568)
1510	38	0·093 75	0·618	4 658	(20 720)	19 791	(2 236)
1600	35	0·125	0·618	5 865	(26 089)	29 330	(3 314)
1700	36	0·125	0·868	8 420	(37 454)	48 684	(5 501)
1800	45	0·125	0·868	9 021	(40 127)	56 679	(6 404)
1900	42	0·157 5	1·113	15 035	(66 879)	125 346	(14 163)
2000	61	0·137 8	1·325	20 095	(89 387)	167 672	(18 946)
2020	43	0·187 5	1·487	24 294	(108 065)	203 462	(22 990)

the rating load is

$$Q = Q_s \sqrt[3]{\frac{5 \times 10^5}{60 \times 100 \times 5000}} = \frac{Q_s}{3 \cdot 915}$$

and the corresponding torque is

$$T_r = Q \times s$$

In a similar manner, the loading or torque for any other condition of joint working can be found, and life of the joint in these conditions can also be calculated.

In the journal bearings only half of the rollers are loaded at any one time, the roller in the plane of load being stressed highest. Furthermore, as the journal peg oscillates the rollers move forwards and backwards at a rate determined by the proportions of peg diameter to roller diameter when slip is disregarded.

According to investigations carried out by Stribeck [4], the load (lbf) on the most highly stressed roller should be accepted as:

$$P_a = \frac{5Q}{Z} = \frac{5T}{Z \times s} \qquad \cdot \quad \cdot \quad \cdot \quad \cdot \quad \cdot \quad (29.1)$$

According to Hertz [4] the mean pressure (tonf/in²) on the contact area between roller and peg would be:

$$P_{mean} = 1 \cdot 607 \sqrt{\frac{P_a}{l \times d \times \sigma}} \qquad \cdot \quad \cdot \quad \cdot \quad \cdot \quad (29.2)$$

in which

$$\sigma \text{ (coefficient of conformity)} = \frac{2D_i}{D_i + d} \qquad \cdot \quad \cdot \quad \cdot \quad (29.3)$$

and where D_i is the peg diameter (in), d the roller diameter (in), l the effective roller length (in), and P_a the bearing load (lbf).

The stress in the centre of the pressure area represents the maximum pressure and is given by:

$$P_{max} = \frac{4}{\pi} P_{mean} = 1\cdot273 P_{mean}$$

Substituting in the above, from equations (29.1)–(29.3) we find

$$P_{mean} = 2\cdot540 \sqrt{\frac{T(D_i+d)}{Zsld D_i}} \text{ tonf/in}^2$$

When making calculations it is more expedient to use the mean pressure over the whole contact area instead of a maximum pressure over a central point in the contact pressure area.

Tables 29.2 and 29.3 give the data for the range of joints manufactured by my company, and the corresponding pressures in the contact area for different loading conditions. The specific torque is the factor of the specific bearing load (Q_s) and the journal span, and the specific bearing load is the load ensuring the life of the joint for 10^6 revolutions of the inner race.

If a series of joints were to be designed in which all dimensions were in constant proportion between sizes of joints, then the contact mean pressures would be the same for all the joints at the indicated torque rating.

Table 29.2. Torques applicable to Hooke's joints of Hardy-Spicer manufacture

Torque values are given in lbf in (N m).

Series	Specific torque	Application (continuous) torque	Short duration torque	Safe static torque	Ultimate torque
1140	3 894 (440)	994 (112)	5 050 (571)	10 000 (1 130)	16 000 (1 808)
1300	5 812 (657)	1 484 (168)	6 800 (768)	13 000 (1 469)	21 000 (2 373)
1310	7 670 (867)	1 959 (221)	8 800 (994)	17 160 (1 939)	27 400 (3 096)
1350	12 487 (1 411)	3 189 (360)	14 200 (1 605)	24 480 (2 766)	39 200 (4 429)
1410	13 878 (1 568)	3 545 (400)	18 100 (2 045)	30 000 (3 390)	48 000 (5 424)
1510	19 791 (2 236)	5 055 (571)	27 600 (3 119)	44 400 (5 017)	71 000 (8 023)
1600	29 330 (3 314)	7 492 (847)	35 800 (4 045)	61 200 (6 915)	98 000 (11 074)
1700	48 684 (5 501)	12 435 (1 405)	57 500 (6 497)	97 200 (10 983)	155 000 (17 514)
1800	56 679 (6 401)	14 477 (1 636)	81 800 (9 243)	140 400 (15 864)	224 000 (25 311)
1900	125 346 (14 163)	32 017 (3 618)	148 000 (16 723)	254 000 (28 701)	406 000 (45 876)
2000	167 672 (18 946)	42 828 (4 839)	231 000 (26 102)	396 000 (44 746)	633 000 (71 526)
2020	203 462 (22 990)	51 970 (5 872)	244 000 (27 571)	420 000 (47 458)	672 000 (75 933)

Table 29.3. Mean pressures in roller contact areas in the torque conditions presented in Table 29.2

Pressures are given in tonf/in^2 (N/mm^2).

Series	At specific torque		At application torque		At short duration torque		At safe static torque	
1140	124·7	(1926)	63·0	(973)	142·0	(2193)	199·8	(3086)
1300	133·8	(2066)	67·6	(1044)	144·4	(2230)	201·1	(3106)
1310	133·8	(2066)	67·6	(1044)	143·3	(2213)	199·9	(3087)
1350	131·3	(2028)	66·3	(1024)	139·8	(2159)	182·7	(2822)
1410	124·8	(1927)	63·0	(973)	142·6	(2202)	188·5	(2911)
1510	121·9	(1883)	61·6	(951)	143·9	(2222)	182·5	(2818)
1600	123·9	(1914)	62·6	(967)	136·9	(2114)	179·0	(2765)
1700	123·5	(1907)	62·4	(964)	134·2	(2073)	174·5	(2695)
1800	113·2	(1748)	57·2	(883)	135·9	(2099)	178·1	(2751)
1900	119·2	(1841)	60·2	(930)	129·6	(2002)	169·7	(2621)
2000	110·8	(1711)	56·0	(865)	130·0	(2008)	170·2	(2629)
2020	118·7	(1833)	60·0	(927)	130·0	(2008)	170·8	(2638)

However, in the series of joints discussed in Table 29.3 such geometrical proportions do not exist for the basic dimensions. It follows that the mean pressures in the contact areas cannot be exactly the same. Whereas the specific load depends only on the dimensions of the roller bearings, the specific torque also introduces the varying dimensions of the span, and in calculating the pressures on the contact area the proportion of peg to roller diameters plays an important role. A graph showing the influence of D/d ratio on the pressure on contact area is shown in Fig. 29.5. Because of this, the larger joints show generally lower contact pressures than the smaller joints.

The contact area mean pressures in the needle bearing at the application torque (A.T.) have been accepted for the condition when the joint revolves at 100 rev/min,

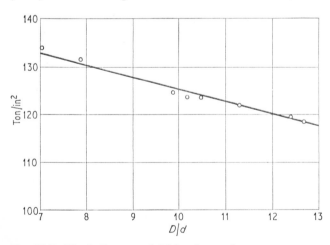

Fig. 29.5. The influence of D/d ratio on the pressure-on-contact area

with an angularity of 3° or less to provide for nominal life. This condition, although giving a general guide to the joint's working possibilities, is not very practical from the actual application point of view, where we have often to deal with much higher speeds and larger angles. Another set of torque figures has to be used and manufacturers of Hooke's type shafts have established certain practical conditions which are claimed to indicate the possibility of application.

Short-duration torque (S.D.T.) represents the maximum torque that may be applied for short periods of time, such as during starting or normal low gear operation of vehicles. Safe static torque (S.S.T.), also known as effective shock load, is the load arising from a torque applied suddenly and of very short duration. Its magnitude obviously depends on the resilience of the driveline. Finally, ultimate torque (U.T.) is the torque that can be expected to bring about mechanical failure of one or more components in the joint.

The selection of the joint will have to rely on a comparison of the actual working conditions for which the joint is to be selected, with the S.D.T., S.S.T., and U.T. at selected speeds and angles, as described above.

Effects of pressure

The pressures in the contact areas under ultimate torque conditions may sometimes be of interest, as in these conditions (by definition) not only the journal bearing but any part of the universal joint may fail. They vary between 250 and 220 tonf/in², according to the joint size.

It is important, however, to add that when the joint is called upon to transmit the load statically—i.e. with no rotation taking place—excessive loads will cause permanent deformation at the contact zone, which will impair the fitness of the needle bearings for subsequent rotation under lighter loads. A higher maximum force, Q_{max}, can more readily be accepted when the joint is rotating than when it is at rest. This force is usually accepted as $Q_{max} = 1 \cdot 3 Q_s$, therefore the maximum contact area mean pressures in static conditions should be correspondingly lower than in dynamic conditions.

Dynamic carrying capacity

It is obvious that the dynamic carrying capacity of needle bearings, Q_s, being larger than the static capacity Q_{max}, is determined by different factors bearing little relation to each other. In the scope of this paper, however, this must be left with reference to the work of Hertz, Stribeck, Palmgren (3), and others who have confirmed this point. Sufficient to say that the hardness of the material plays a much more important part in static than in dynamic loads.

Rotary motion

The Hooke's type joint connecting two intersecting shafts does not transmit the rotary motion of the input shaft uniformly to the output, and to overcome this it is usual to connect these shafts with a system of two joints connected by an intermediate element which may be a double yoke, a centring device, or a short intermediate shaft or tube. The assembly is built so that the opposite yokes of the two joints are always in the same plane and the angles of both joints are equal.

Although this system offers the advantage of uniform velocity of the output with that of the input, the intermediate element rotates with a cyclic non-uniform angular velocity, the magnitude of which is influenced primarily by the angle of the shafts in question.

The growth in dimensions necessary to transmit higher torques results in larger moments of inertia of all rotating parts and larger stresses due to angular accelerations and decelerations in components connecting the joints. Also, the differences between input and output angles have similar effects, causing vibrations with a frequency of twice the speed of the shaft and of amplitudes proportional to the inertias of the components. This leads to shortening of the theoretically calculated life of the joint. It was mainly to overcome this unwelcome property of Hooke's joints that constant velocity joints were introduced.

CONSTANT VELOCITY JOINTS

Most constant velocity or homokinetic joints transmit the torque from input to output by driving and driven elements mounted concentrically to each other on the ends of the opposite input and output shafts. These elements have tracks—generally circular in section to accommodate the ball—which are curved mostly in the plane perpendicular to the shaft axis, with each pair of tracks carrying a torque-transmitting ball. The essential feature to ensure constant velocity between input and output shafts is that the torque-transmitting balls are steered or guided in such a manner that they always lie in the plane bisecting the angle between the driving and driven axes. This is achieved by suitable design of the joint. Assuming now that the track centre-lines are on the same plane as the related shaft axes (see Fig. 29.6), and assuming that they are symmetrically arranged, it follows that the angular velocity of the output is equal to that of the input, regardless of the actual shape of the track centre-lines.

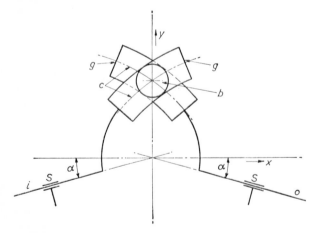

b	Ball.	s	Swivel joint.
c	Track-centre line.	x	Reference axis.
g	Guiding tracks.	y	Axis of symmetry.
i	Input shaft.	α	Bisecting angle.
o	Output shaft.		

Fig. 29.6

The track centre-line, which is the line traversed by the centre of the ball, is formed as an arc with a radius struck from a centre which may, but need not, be on the centre of the joint.

This radius can be either equal to or a multiple of the distance between the ball centres and the joint centre, or it may be infinity (Fig. 29.7).

In the first instance we deal with arcuate tracks, in the last with straight tracks. Also, the track centre-lines may be parallel to each other or may cross each other at some preferred angle. Finally, the centre of the track radius may be at the centre of the joint or offset from it. Combinations of some of these properties are used on various types of joint that are now available.

Apart from these considerations, these particular types of constant velocity joint can also be classified by the way in which the torque is transferred by the balls, whether the balls are in pure compression or are subject to shear (Fig. 29.8). The first was the original Weiss joint (1925), the second the original Rzeppa (1928). An example of the Rzeppa type, but with the balls under compression, is the Birfield joint, which was originally developed about 1944. By introducing angular contact of the balls in the tracks, this joint achieved theoretical compression conditions for the balls.

In considering the working of a ball-type constant velocity joint, the contact between the balls and the track is most important. Some of the more modern designs of the joint rely on point contact by the introduction of a measure of conformity between ball and track. It follows that considerations similar to those applicable to the investigations of Hertz apply also in this instance (4).

However, when the joint is revolving under load, the motion of the ball in its track is far from steady. This movement has been investigated by Phillips (5) who, with the aid of a model of the joint, studied the sliding action of the ball when in motion between the tracks. His findings confirmed that a ball working in a track is subject partly to rolling and partly to sliding action. Moreover, the sliding motion of the ball can be considered in two directions: axially along the tracks, and peripherally in the direction of joint revolution.

Of greater interest is the discovery that, although in Rzeppa-type joints with spherical tracks the peripheral component of the slide velocity never changes direction, in the straight track joint it changes direction four times per complete revolution. The axial component of the slide velocity, however, changes in magnitude and velocity in either type. Also, the total sliding velocity of the balls in

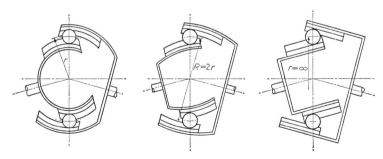

Fig. 29.7

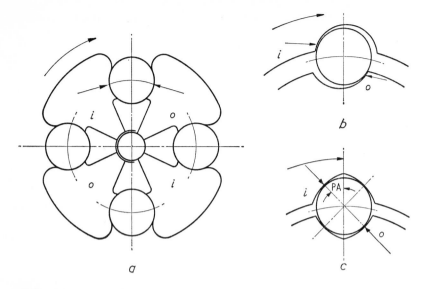

a Balls under compression.
b Ball under shear.
c Ball under compression.

PA Pressure angle.

i input.   *o* output.   **Fig. 29.8**

straight (cylindrical) tracks is not much greater than in joints with arcuate (spherical) tracks.

To assess constant velocity joint nominal capacity, this phenomenon is not taken into consideration since calculations are based primarily on static conditions. Sliding of the ball, however, influences the life endurance of the joint and must be taken into account when the dynamic capacity of the joint is being considered. The dynamic capacity of the joint is based on the fatigue life under repeated stress reversals and not, as in static conditions, on permanent deformation under load.

Before we consider the fatigue effects on the endurance of the joints, it is appropriate to mention that the driveline as a whole forms a definite static and dynamic system which can transmit vibrations appearing at various points in and outside the driveline.

The basic torsional loading of such a system is due to the torque developed by the engine and the reactions to this torque due to resistance to vehicle motion. Since we are dealing with the characteristics of a dynamic system, the torque in the driveline will depend not only on the magnitude of external loading, but also on dynamic parameters such as inertia and stiffness in various elements of the drive system. These additional dynamic loadings cause an increase of stresses in the system over those statically calculated. Therefore, a knowledge of the true stresses in the drive elements is absolutely essential for correct selection of the size of the universal joints and the driveline.

Loading

There are two different forms of loading which ought to be contemplated: a momentary loading caused by sudden application of driving torque against stationary components, and fatigue loading caused by continuous variation of torque and speed when the parts are in motion. The calculations of each of these conditions are independent of each other, although one often finds in practice that correct calculations for fatigue conditions prove entirely adequate for strength of the components when under momentary loading.

Momentary loadings are caused (1) by a change in the condition of a vehicle from rest to motion, (2) during braking of the vehicle, or (3) while the vehicle is in motion, when vibration of the driving system is created due to resonance with the vibration of the engine, rear axle, or any other part connected with the drive-line.

Various experiments conducted on this subject, mainly in East Germany and the U.S.S.R., indicate that, from the stress point of view, the highest loading occurs on starting the vehicle. It is, therefore, the general practice among joint manufacturers to calculate the permissible stresses on the joints based on maximum calculated torque from this vehicle condition and to accept a torque magnifying factor of 1·2 to 1·8, depending on the type of vehicle in question. Therefore, the first selection of a joint is usually conducted on static strength considerations, with a suitable correction for momentary loadings. Only after the acceptance of a basic size of joint can the further calculations to establish its endurance be carried out.

Torque

The torque which can be transmitted by a joint depends on several interrelated factors:

(*a*) the number of balls (n), which is normally four or six, but on larger size joints eight or more balls may have to be employed;

(*b*) the size of the balls, defined by their diameter (d);

(*c*) the conformity factor (ψ) of the track, which is a relationship between the radii of curvature of the track at the point of contact in planes perpendicular to, and parallel to, the direction of rolling and the radius of the ball;

(*d*) the pitch circle radius of the balls (R);

(*e*) the pressure angle (Δ), which is the angle between the joint radius through the ball centre and the ball radius through the track contact point;

(*f*) the load per ball (P_a); and

(*g*) the permissible pressure on the contact area, under normal load, which may be termed static ball/track capacity (P_{mean}).

These factors are all connected by formulae derived from the Hertzian theory of contact between loaded curved surfaces. As an example we shall adapt them to the construction of Birfield/Rzeppa joints (see Fig. 29.3).

Let the maximum pressure in the contact area be P_{max} (tonf/in²). Then

$$P_{\mathrm{max}} = 1 \cdot 5 P_{\mathrm{mean}} = \frac{23600}{2240 \mu \nu} \{P_a (\textstyle\sum \rho)^2\}^{1/3} \qquad . \quad . \quad . \quad (29.4)$$

where μ and ν are Hertzian coefficients of shape of the bodies under load, and

$$\sum \rho = 1/r_{11} + 1/r_{12} + 1/r_{21} + 1/r_{22}$$

in which $r_{11}, r_{12}, r_{21},$ and r_{22} are the respective radii of torque transferring bodies in the direction of rolling and in the plane 90° to the direction of rolling, where prefix 1 refers to the ball and prefix 2 to the track.

It is more convenient to express $\sum \rho$ in terms of conformity ψ. The relation between $\sum \rho$ and ψ varies with the type of track and its shape; for example, for straight tracks it becomes

$$\sum \rho = \frac{2(2\psi - 1)}{\psi d} \qquad \qquad \cdots \qquad (29.5)$$

which is comparatively simple since some of the operating radii are infinite. However, when one deals with arcuate tracks the formulae become much more complicated.

Substituting equation (29.5) in equation (29.4), and rearranging,

$$P_{max}^3 = \left(\frac{23600}{2240}\right)^3 \frac{1}{(\mu\nu)^3} P_a \frac{4(2\psi - 1)^2}{\psi^2 d^2} \qquad \cdots \qquad (29.6)$$

or

$$P_a = K P_{max}^3$$

where

$$K = \left(\frac{2240}{23600}\right)^3 (\mu\nu)^3 \frac{\psi^2 d^2}{4(2\psi - 1)^2}$$

The torque transmitted by the joint is

$$T = P_a n R \sin \Delta = K_1 P_{max}^3$$

where $K_1 = KnR \sin \Delta$. Therefore the pressure in the contact area increases as the cube root of the torque.

We are then faced with the question: 'What is the permissible value of compressive stress in the contact area?' If this is known it will define the torque capacity ratings in static conditions. For Birfield joints this has been established by some very extensive and lengthy experiments, and for ultimate conditions of torque the maximum compressive stress is accepted as $P_{max} = 242$ tonf/in^2.

The term 'ultimate' means the load at which, or past which, complete failure may occur at any point in the joint, although this stress refers to the track conditions only. Therefore, for normal working conditions much lower stresses in the contact areas must be employed. For continuous application torques $P_{max} = 139$ tonf/in^2, and for short-duration torques $P_{max} = 207$ tonf/in^2 are accepted.

For these static stresses the capacities of a range of joints, as manufactured by my company, have been established and are given in Table 29.4.

Whereas the static capacity of the joints is based on the load to cause permanent deformation of the track in a given time, the dynamic capacity is based on fatigue life under repeated stress reversals and will determine the joint endurance.

Track fatigue, which determines the life of the joint, can generally be expected to develop first in the highest stressed contact areas between ball and track. Since the loads calculated at even the highest torques are always well within the

Table 29.4. Torque ratings for Birfield joints

Joint size	Application torque, lbf in (N m) $P_{max} =$ 139 tonf/in^2 (2147 N/mm^2)		Short-duration torque, lbf in (N m) $P_{max} =$ 207 tonf/in^2 (3197 N/mm^2)		Safe static torque, lbf in (N m) $P_{max} =$ 226 tonf/in^2 (3490 N/mm^2)		Ultimate torque, lbf in (N m) $P_{max} =$ 242 tonf/in^2 (3737 N/mm^2)	
75	1 580	(178)	5 233	(591)	6 807	(769)	8 356	(944)
87	2 508	(283)	8 308	(939)	10 807	(1 221)	13 266	(1 499)
100	3 744	(423)	12 400	(1 401)	16 130	(1 822)	19 800	(2 237)
113	5 331	(602)	17 685	(1 998)	22 969	(2 595)	28 195	(3 186)
125	7 312	(826)	24 217	(2 736)	31 502	(3 559)	38 669	(4 369)
150	12 636	(1 428)	41 850	(4 728)	54 439	(6 151)	66 825	(7 550)
175	20 064	(2 267)	66 452	(7 508)	86 441	(9 766)	101 611	(11 480)
200	29 952	(3 384)	99 200	(11 208)	129 040	(14 580)	158 400	(17 897)
225	42 648	(4 819)	141 248	(15 959)	183 737	(20 760)	225 542	(25 483)
250	58 500	(6 610)	193 750	(21 891)	252 031	(28 476)	309 375	(34 955)

theoretical capacity of the ball, it follows that the first signs of fatigue failure should be encountered on the tracks, assuming of course that the geometry of the tested joint (i.e. the manufacture) is correct.

Fatigue failure

Track failure can take various forms, such as permanent indentation of the tracks at the point of contact, pitting, flaking, or smearing. Only in rare cases can the life be limited by wear on other mating surfaces unless the joint is subjected to excessive axial loadings during its life. As wear depends on many factors—material of the component, hardness and case depth, method and quality of surface treatment, type of lubricant used, angularity, running temperatures, and so on—it is practically unpredictable. When the cumulative tolerances determining the joint clearances pass the extreme design limits, one can rule that the joint is really at the end of its life. This can be simply checked by measuring the axial float between the inner and outer members of the joint. Each type of joint behaves differently in this respect, and, as an example, tabulation of maximum permissible axial float for the Birfield joint is given in Table 29.5. These figures are based upon extreme tolerance limits, although it is known that in good working conditions the joints can still be used at figures greater than those quoted.

Table 29.5. Maximum permissible axial float

Values are given in inches (millimetres).

Joint size								
75	87	100	113	125	150	175	200	225
0·024 (0·61)	0·026 (0·66)	0·026 (0·66)	0·026 (0·66)	0·029 (0·71)	0·032 (0·81)	0·034 (0·86)	0·036 (0·92)	0·036 (0·92)

When abrasion becomes a limiting factor in the life of a joint—as in the case of a joint running at moderate speeds, low torques, and small angles—it is impossible to predict its life and the assessment of joint life must be based on pure fatigue considerations, which are more tangible.

LIFE OF JOINT

When the endurance life of the joint is investigated by testing, the results are very scattered, but if the number of joints tested is large enough to enable a dispersion curve to be produced, it generally indicates that the longest joint life rarely exceeds four times the average life, and that about 90 per cent of the joints have a longer life than one-fifth of the mean life (Fig. 29.9). In this respect a definite relationship between angular contact bearings and constant velocity joints is established. From the calculated relationship, according to Palmgren (3), the material stress which 90 per cent of the bearings can endure is only about 16·5 per cent smaller than that stress which gives a life in excess of the average. Experiments conducted on the joints seem to support this statement.

As already stated, the approach to estimating the life of the joint when fatigue of the working surfaces acting under load, rather than mechanical wear, determines its life, must take into account the loads transferred through torque-loaded elements and the number of stress cycles. Loads are always proportional to torques and stress cycles to the revolutions per unit time.

Since ball/track contact is, in practice, invariably a combination of sliding and rolling, it is difficult to apply a simple theory on which to base life calculations. There are three alternative approaches:

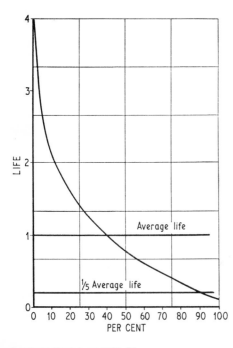

Fig. 29.9. Life dispersion according to Palmgren (3)

(*a*) Pure rolling conditions can be accepted, in which case the theory of angular contact bearings can be directly applied.

(*b*) The ball/track contact conditions can be assumed similar to conditions at the contact points of a pair of mating gears.

(*c*) The approach at (*b*) can be modified by applying correction suitable for a constant velocity joint.

For a joint running at constant speed, all the above methods give a relationship between torque and life of the form $L \propto 1/T^3$, and this relationship is accepted. For condition (*a*) the life at constant load depends on the number of stress cycles. Thus the relation of life to speed, taking into account that each point of the track is stressed twice per revolution, can be expressed as $L \propto 1/2N$, where $2N$ is the number of stress cycles per minute and N is the number of joint revolutions per minute.

The gear theory (*b*) gives dual relationship between life and speed (see B.S. 436). For speeds below 1000 rev/min

$$L \propto \sqrt{(1/N)}$$

and for speeds above 1000 rev/min.

$$L \propto 1/N$$

The constant velocity joint theory (*c*) is based on a similar relationship to (*b*), but for speeds below 1000 rev/min a corrected formula derived from extensive experimentation has been accepted for life:

$$L \propto 1/N^{0.577}$$

For speeds above 1000 rev/min the formula at (*b*), where $L \propto 1/N$, remains unaltered.

Also, for the constant velocity joint an angular factor has been introduced, the value of which is empirical, derived from experiments, and can be expressed by the formula:

$$\text{Angular factor } A = (1-\sin \alpha) \cos^2 \alpha$$

where α = joint angle; and the relationship between life and angle has been found to be

$$L \propto A^3$$

The nomogram, Fig. 29.10, gives the calculated angular factors for various joint angles.

Combining the torque, speed, and angle relationship to the life, we can now state that for speeds below 1000 rev/min:

$$L \propto A^3/T^3N^{0.577}$$

and for speeds over 1000 rev/min,

$$L \propto A^3/T^3N$$

For Birfield joints on the basis of theoretical considerations supported by extensive rig tests, the following formulae for joint life are being used:

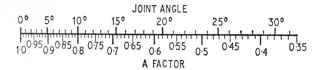

Fig. 29.10. Calculated angular factors for various joint angles

for $N < 1000$ rev/min,

$$L = \frac{21400 T_{100}{}^3 A_x{}^3}{T_x{}^3 N_x{}^{0.577}}$$

and for $N \geqslant 1000$ rev/min,

$$L = \frac{396580 T_{100}{}^3 A_x{}^3}{T_x{}^3 N_x}$$

where T_{100} is the joint application torque (see Table 29.4), T_x the actual working torque (lbf in), A_x the angular factor for actual working angle, and N_x the joint working speed (rev/min).

To make use of these life formulae the value of T_{100} (the application torque) given in Table 29.4 is accepted for calculations. It was originally found that this torque corresponded to a criterion of surface stresses between ball and track

$$S_c = \frac{P_a}{d^2} = 1200 \text{ lbf/in}^2$$

and in these conditions the rated life corresponds to 1500 h at 100 rev/min and an angle of 3°.

Since the change of life formulae occurs at 1000 rev/min this is the obvious speed at which to rate the joint. Therefore, the equivalent life (hours) for rated torque should be:

$$1500 \left(\frac{100}{1000}\right)^{0.577} = 400$$

It is now possible to calculate any life of the joint for any other conditions of the application—i.e. for T_x (torque), N_x (speed), and A_x (angle)—by direct comparison with the rated torque conditions. Thus:

for $N_x < 1000$ rev/min,

$$\frac{L_x}{400} = \frac{T_{100}{}^3 A_x{}^3}{T_x{}^3 \times 0.94^3} \cdot \left(\frac{1000}{N_x}\right)^{0.577}$$

and for $N_x \geqslant 1000$ rev/min,

$$\frac{L_x}{400} = \frac{T_{100}{}^3 A_x{}^3}{T_x{}^3 \times 0 \cdot 94^3} \cdot \frac{1000}{N_x}$$

In this way it is possible to assess mathematically the life of the joint under any steady loading, speed, and angle conditions.

Unfortunately it is very seldom that such conditions occur. In applications in which the joints are mostly employed (i.e. in motor vehicles) we encounter continuous variations of torque passing through the transmission line, greatly varying speeds of the driving shafts, and continuous variation of angles due to road conditions and to varying loads on the driving wheels due to acceleration and deceleration of the vehicle when in motion. In other words, the variation in working conditions is great in magnitude and duration, and some more accurate method must be applied to find the total life of the joint in such circumstances.

Tractive effort

To calculate the endurance of joints we must obviously start from the transmission torque conditions that are developed by the engine through various speed ratios, and also from the capability of the vehicle to transmit the available torque through the wheels.

If the maximum engine torque is T_E, the torques available at the main driving shaft will be:

$$
\begin{aligned}
\text{in first gear} \qquad & T_1 = i_1 T_E \\
\text{in second gear} \qquad & T_2 = i_2 T_E \\
\text{in third gear} \qquad & T_3 = i_3 T_E \\
& \vdots
\end{aligned}
$$

where $i_1, i_2, i_3, \ldots$ are the respective ratios in the gearbox.

When the final drive through halfshafts is considered, the corresponding torque in each line will be:

$$T_n = \frac{T_E i_n i_f}{2}$$

where i_n is the respective gearbox ratio and i_f the final drive ratio.

On the other hand, the torque T_W obtainable in the shaft from the road conditions can be found from the following:

for the mainshaft drive,

$$T_W = W_a R_r \mu \frac{1}{i_a}$$

and for the halfshaft drive,

$$T_W = \frac{W_a R_r \mu}{2}$$

where W_a is the weight over driving axle, R_r the wheel rolling radius, μ the coefficient of adhesion, and i_a the total reduction ratio.

The coefficient of adhesion, μ, accepted for passenger vehicles is $0\cdot6-0\cdot8$, whereas for heavy vehicles it may reach $0\cdot9-1\cdot0$ in exceptional circumstances, e.g. for cross-country vehicles, earthmovers, etc.

Tractive effort available at the driving wheels should be corrected by the magnitude of dynamic weight transfer due to acceleration or deceleration of the vehicle when in motion, calculated from

$$\varDelta W_d = \frac{H}{l}\cdot\frac{T}{R_r}-fW_d$$

where H is the height of centre of gravity, l the wheelbase, f the coefficient of rolling resistance, and W_d the vehicle weight. Therefore, the final tractive effort at the driving wheels must be taken as follows:

for main driveline,

$$T_W = (W_a+\varDelta W_d)R_r\mu\,\frac{1}{i_a}$$

or for halfshaft drive,

$$T_W = \frac{(W_a+\varDelta W_d)R_r\mu}{2}$$

Only the smaller torque calculated from these two—i.e. the maximum engine torque or tractive effort—should be accepted in calculations. The wheels cannot transfer to the ground a torque greater than their limit of adhesion, nor can the engine exceed its maximum torque whatever the tractive effort at the wheels.

Joint speeds

To establish various conditions of joint speeds at various gear ratios, one should first assume a value for the mean vehicle speed V_m throughout its life. According to Jaskiewicz (**6**), this should be:

For passenger vehicles of small engine capacity	25–30 mile/h
For passenger vehicles of medium/large engine capacity	35–50 mile/h
For heavy goods vehicles	20–25 mile/h
For buses	25–30 mile/h

When the mean speed of the vehicle has been assumed, the mean speed of the drive shaft can now be found by calculation. The mean wheel revolutions can be calculated from

$$N_W = 168(V_m/R_r) \text{ rev/min}$$

where V_m is in miles per hour and R_r is in inches. The mean speed of the main drive shaft is

$$N_m = N_W i_f$$

To find the mean speeds of the joint at various gear ratios of i_1, i_2, i_3, etc. it is first necessary to establish the percentage of life spent by the vehicle in each of the gears throughout its total life. The average times in each of the gears expressed as a percentage of total vehicle (joint) life depend in the first instance on the road conditions under which the vehicle is going to work. Schreier and Mittag (7) have, in their investigations, divided the route types into categories (see Table 29.6). For various road conditions they investigated the average time in each gear for different types of vehicles, and their results are presented in Table 29.7.

Table 29.6. Route types

Test road indication	Route and characteristics	Difference of road levels, m
I	Flat ground with moderate changes in level	280
II	Hilly country	400
III	Mountainous country	500
IV	High mountains	940
V	City travelling	—

Therefore, for further calculations, when the ground conditions for the vehicle are known, the average percentages of the times in Table 29.7 can be applied. However, for a vehicle whose duties cannot be foreseen, which includes most of the newly designed passenger cars, the best solution would be to calculate endurance life on the basis of the average of all the times for various road characteristics, e.g. for passenger cars with a four-speed gearbox a time average usage of gears could be taken as

1·5 per cent in first gear	(0·015 of total time)
6·0 per cent in second gear	(0·06 of total time)
37·0 per cent in third gear	(0·37 of total time)
55·5 per cent in fourth gear	(0·555 of total time)

Having accepted the average speed of the vehicle (V_m) throughout its life, the total distance in miles (S) travelled by the vehicle in its life (L) hours will be

$$S = LV_m$$

The total distance travelled must be the sum of proportions of times spent by the vehicle in each of its gears—i.e. $\epsilon_1 L, \epsilon_2 L, \epsilon_3 L, \ldots, \epsilon_n L$ (hours)—multiplied by the corresponding mean velocities of the vehicle in each gear. Therefore, the total distance travelled can be calculated:

$$S = V_m L = \frac{N_e R_r}{168} \cdot \frac{1}{i_f} \left(\frac{\epsilon_1 L}{i_1} + \frac{\epsilon_2 L}{i_2} + \ldots + \frac{\epsilon_n L}{i_n} \right)$$

from which engine speed N_e can be found:

$$N_e = \frac{168 V_m}{R_r} i_f \frac{1}{\sum (\epsilon_n / i_n)}$$

If N_e is the average engine speed in revolutions per minute, the average shaft speeds in each gear can be calculated:

$$N_1 = N_e / i_1; \quad N_2 = N_e / i_2; \quad N_3 = N_e / i_3; \quad \text{etc.}$$

Thus the joint speeds for establishing the joint life at each gear ratio are found.

Table 29.7. Time spent in each gear as percentage of total running time

Type of vehicle and number of gear ratios	Type of test road (as Table 29.6)	Percentage of time spent in each gear					
		1	2	3	4	5	6
Heavy vehicle without trailer; six-speed gearbox	I	0	1	2	11	24	62
	II	1	1	8	20	40	30
	III	1	1	5	22	43	28
	IV	1	1	23	16	31	28
	V	1	1	6	25	46	21
Heavy vehicle as above, but with trailer	I	1	1	4	12	29	53
	II	1	10	18	25	28	18
	III	1	6	30	28	24	11
	IV	1	23	18	18	28	12
	V	1	2	10	30	45	12
Medium vehicle without trailer; five-speed gearbox	I	1	1	3	16	79	—
	II	1	3	23	36	37	—
	III	1	5	27	40	27	—
	IV	1	19	19	25	36	—
	V	2	4	20	42	32	—
Medium vehicle as above but with trailer	I	1	3	12	25	59	—
	II	3	23	23	29	22	—
	III	3	30	28	30	9	—
	IV	7	28	23	21	21	—
	V	1	8	28	46	17	—
Passenger car; four-speed gearbox	I	1	2	14	83	—	—
	II	1	7	39	53	—	—
	III	1	6	48	45	—	—
	IV*	—	—	—	—	—	—
	V	3	9	47	41	—	—
Passenger car; three-speed gearbox	I	1	8	91	—	—	—
	II	2	29	69	—	—	—
	III	2	38	60	—	—	—
	IV*	—	—	—	—	—	—
	V	6	40	54	—	—	—

* Not investigated.

ENGINE TORQUE

Seldom during its life will the vehicle utilize its full engine torque. Generally it works at much lower torque values, particularly in the lower gear ratio range. Therefore, to arrive at realistic torques corresponding to the average speeds calculated above, a torque utilization factor should be introduced by which the maximum torques calculated for each gear must be corrected. For example, Jaskiewicz (6) suggested the following for passenger vehicles with a four-speed gearbox:

> fourth gear: 90 per cent maximum engine torque, η_4
> third gear: 80 per cent maximum engine torque, η_3
> second gear: 70 per cent maximum engine torque, η_2
> first gear: 60 per cent maximum engine torque, η_1

The maximum engine torque, T_E, having previously been calculated, the average torque in each gear can be accepted as follows:

in the mainshaft,

$$T_N = T_E i_n \eta_n$$

or in the final drive,

$$T_N = \frac{T_E i_n i_f \eta_n}{2}$$

Thus the speeds and torques are found for each gear from which the life of the joint in each separate condition can be calculated using the theory as derived above, where the basic torque is selected from the tabulations of joint ratings, i.e. at $N = 1000$ rev/min:

$$\alpha = 3° \quad \text{and} \quad L = 400 \text{ h}$$

The actual joint working angles are derived from design considerations of the investigated vehicle. Therefore, we can finally tabulate the results in the form shown in Table 29.8.

Table 29.8

Gear ratio	Torque at the joint	Corresponding joint speed	Angles factor	Calculated life in each gear
1	T_1	N_1	A_1	L_1
2	T_2	N_2	A_2	L_2
3	T_3	N_3	A_3	L_3
4	T_4	N_4	A_4	L_4

The sum of the fractions of life used in each gear must equal unity:

$$\frac{\epsilon_1 L}{L_1} + \frac{\epsilon_2 L}{L_2} + \frac{\epsilon_3 L}{L_3} + \cdots = \sum \frac{\epsilon_n L}{L_n} = 1$$

From this the true life of the joints can now be determined, and by multiplying $L \times V_m$ the expected total milage of the vehicle can be found.

SUMMARY

When discussing this method, one can see that it relies on acceptance of several factors, some based on experimental findings and others simply assumed. However, it appears that with the construction still 'on the board', this is probably the best available approach to the problem, and although the accepted variable factors may sometimes be changed in accordance with the duties envisaged for a particular vehicle, the basic line of approach should remain unaltered.

The method of estimating joint endurance life from the considerations of torque and speed conditions calculated from the known vehicle data should be employed at the earlier stages of transmission design. However, there may be occasions when adaptation of the joint for an existing vehicle is required, and in such cases the estimate of joint life endurance can also be achieved, perhaps more accurately, by finding the actual energy consumed by the vehicle in a given time and distance. Here a valuable indication is the actual average fuel consumption, f_m, in miles per gallon over the total distance travelled by the vehicle.

Accepting that the fuel consumption of an average small car petrol engine is K (the value varies between 0·45 and 0·65 lb/b.h.p. h) and knowing the average speed of the vehicle V_m over the distance S, then taking the weight of 1 gal of petrol to be approximately 8 lb the average horsepower used by the vehicle can be calculated:

$$\text{b.h.p.} = \frac{V_m}{f_m} \cdot \frac{8}{K}$$

If the vehicle mean speeds in corresponding gears are V_1, V_2, V_3, and the percentage of the time T spent in the particular gear is accepted in accordance with Table 29.7 above, we can write:

$$V_m = \frac{V_1 T_1 + V_2 T_2 + V_3 T_3 + \cdots}{T_1 + T_2 + T_3 + \cdots}$$

where

$$T_1 = \epsilon_1 \sum T; \quad T_2 = \epsilon_2 \sum T; \quad \cdots; \quad T_n = \epsilon_n \sum T$$

and finally

$$V_m = \epsilon_1 V_1 + \epsilon_2 V_2 + \epsilon_3 V_3 + \cdots$$

Accepting now that the average engine speed is constant over the whole range of speed, we can state that

$$V_1 = V_4 \frac{i_4}{i_1}; \quad V_2 = V_4 \frac{i_4}{i_2}; \quad \text{etc.}$$

from which the mean speed is

$$V_4 = \frac{V_m}{i_4 \sum (\epsilon_n / i_n)}$$

and all the average vehicle speeds in consecutive gears can now be established in similar manner. From the calculated average speeds of the vehicle in each gear, the speed of the propeller shaft can now be calculated:

$$N_n = 168 \frac{V_n}{R_r} \cdot \frac{i_f}{i_n}$$

and the actual torques transferred through the joints in average conditions in each gear can be determined:

$$T_n = 63\,000 \frac{\text{b.h.p.}}{N_n} \text{ lbf in}$$

Thus a set of conditions can be found which depict average torques and speeds, and supplemented by joint angles from the design, they enable joint life to be assessed in exactly the same manner as in calculations from the vehicle technical data.

CONCLUSION

Both methods of life calculations for joints have been used by Hardy-Spicer Limited for a considerable time and the results obtained from rig and road tests generally agree with the calculated figures. However, it must be stated that since these methods necessarily rely on several assumptions which, although confirmed by tests, may in practice differ from the actual use of the vehicle, they cannot be accepted without reservation. Nevertheless, they enable the designer to work within certain logical limits which he may, if necessary, correct from his own experience, and they allow the joints to be accepted for given applications with reasonable certainty.

ACKNOWLEDGEMENT

The author wishes to thank the management of G.K.N. Birfield Transmissions Limited for permission to use some of the data from their products.

APPENDIX 29.1

REFERENCES

(1) BURKHALTER, R. and MAZZIOTTI, P. J. 'The low-silhouette driveline', S.A.E. Paper 691, 1956 (January).
(2) MAZZIOTTI, P. J. 'Dynamic characteristics of truck driveline systems'.
(3) PALMGREN, A. 'Ball and roller bearing engineering', SKF Industries Inc., Philadelphia.
(4) ALLEN, R. K. Rolling bearings 1960 (reprint) (Pitman, London).
(5) PHILLIPS, J. R. and WINTER, H. 'Über die Frage des Gleitens in Kugelgleichgelenken' ('The question of sliding in ball type universal joints'), VDI Z 1968 110 (6), 228.
(6) JASKIEWICZ, ZB. Mechaniczne Napedy Samochodow (The mechanical automobile drives) 1966, vol. I; 1968, vol. IV (Warsaw).
(7) SCHREIER, G. and MITTAG, H. 'Messungen an Kraftfahrzeugbetrieben im Fahrbetrieb' ('The measurement of vehicle drive during vehicle motion'), KFZ-Tech. 1959 (No. 8).

The MS. of this paper was received at the Institution on 15th October 1969 and accepted for publication on 18th November 1969.

Discussion during Session 3

Papers 21 to 24

Mr Andréason (*S.K.F.*) said that in Mr Nisbet's paper there were two constants used in the formulae which should be equipped with units. Second, would the author comment on the influence of a radial load on the load distribution within an angular contact ball-bearing? Also, Mr Nisbet had said that double-row bearings should be used with a certain amount of clearance. His work had shown both theoretically and experimentally that, used as hub-bearings, they should in fact be slightly loaded.

He then showed on a slide the internationally accepted formula for predicting the fatigue life of a bearing with 90 per cent probability. According to this theory the failure criterion was the first sign of fatigue visible on either the races or on the rolling elements. In the formula the only factors determining the life were the bearing load and the load capacity. In fact there were several others.

He then showed an equation now under discussion in America which introduced a reliability factor that made it possible to calculate the life with any probability; a factor for operating conditions, e.g. lubrication; and a material factor.

In Mr Nisbet's paper there was a calculation of the bore load due to misalignment in a hub bearing: could the author explain this method of calculation in more detail? Also, in cornering, the direction of loading the hub-bearing was displaced due to the tyre deformation; he would like some comment on this from the manufacturers of tyres.

Could Mr Barnbrook explain his claim that, for maximum life in a taper-roller bearing, all the rollers must be in contact with the tracks. Finally, what was the load-carrying capacity of taper unit bearings in the two axial directions?

Mr Haigh (*D. A. Stuart Oil Co.*) said that, not only would bearings lubricated with a straight mineral oil suffer no wear but some 5 per cent of sulphurous additives, in the axle, would actually increase the length of time in which bearing preload was maintained. This was extremely important, for if you could maintain high-powered gears in the position in which they were designed to run, they had a much better chance of remaining quiet.

Mr Atkins said he had been brought up to use an abutment washer and a nice meaty lock-nut to bolt the bearing race against the shaft. In these days of value-analysis they had to make do with circlips. Did Mr Nisbet consider them adequate? Would Mr Barnbrook comment on how to avoid problems of expansion between the casing and the gears when taper bearings were used on each side of the layshaft?

Finally, Mr James had shown a diagram of an automatic transmission but on what had he based his torque capacity figures? Had it been tested under special conditions of very light loading?

Mr Beavis (*Lubrizol*) said the standard method of checking production assembly of preloaded bearings was to measure the frictional torque. This was not always representative of radial and axial loads on the bearings, due to tolerance variations in manufacture. The resulting variation in loads must affect the heat input to the complete axle assembly, and especially the lubricant.

Their tests on pinion bearings, with a straight mineral oil and bearing preloads at the upper limit recommended by the manufacturers, had shown cases of roller seizure. This might indicate the advantage of EP additives in the lubricant to overcome the high contact/stress problems at the roller end. Bearing life was often taken up to the onset of fatigue on the track. Taper-bearings had to be relied on to locate the pinion and ring gear so that end wear and the resultant loss of preload must be as important as fatigue failure.

The abrasiveness of certain EP oils, as referred to in Mr Barnbrook's paper, was perhaps due to abrasive debris, rather than the nature of the lubricant itself. Certainly EP additives modified the material to prevent scuffing but this was hardly abrasive action. Would Mr Barnbrook comment in more detail on the wear effects of different limited-slip oils, in particular the friction-modified materials, and their effects on wear?

Mr Milton (S.K.F.) referred to the cylindrical roller bearings shown in Fig. 21.8, Paper 21. He did not agree with Mr Nisbet's suggestion that the choice between Design A or Design B was a matter of national feelings. Design A was a cheaper bearing to make because it was easier to cut the flanges into the inner ring whereas B had them in the outer ring. A more important consideration was suitability for a particular application. It was often more convenient to keep rollers, cage and outer ring as one unit to be assembled into the housing where it could be packed with grease.

Furthermore, with Design B an induction heating coil with a bore slightly larger than the track could be used to expand large bearings for shrink-fitting. The lubricant in a bearing was centrifuged outwards to where the sliding friction occurred between the roller ends and flanges in the outer ring, so that Design B had the best lubrication. Mr Milton also hoped more information would be forthcoming on the axial load capacity of cylindrical bearings.

His organization used a considerable amount of through-hardening steel for bearings, but also carburizing steel. Both left residual compression after heat treatment so that crack propagation could be avoided.

Finally, did Mr Barnbrook recommend his failure-criterion of an affected area of 6 mm for very large, as well as smaller, taper bearings?

Mr Horty (Ford Motor Co.) said they attributed seizure problems on plain bearings to the grinding process. If grinding was done at right angles to the direction of rotation, minute feathers were formed and the bearing was being rubbed up the wrong way! They had also found that about 75 per cent of bearing push-out was against the direction of the grinding tracks. Could Mr James comment on this and also on the use of roto-finish which some bearing manufacturers objected to?

Mr Milward (G.K.N.) said Mr Hoffmann had mentioned that thin-walled bearings in Hookes' joints gave a larger pin diameter on the cross-bend. They had found this impossible for propeller shafts because they had to maintain adequate stock round the outside of the yoke to sustain the pressures required to retain the bearings. There was therefore no gain in capacity but the inner shaft was justified by giving a better balance.

Mr Shaw said that, on the Rover gearbox with needle bearings, Mr Hoffmann had rather exaggerated the lubrication problem on the thrust bearings. They had had initial problems but solved them by stealing Mr Haigh's idea of slots in the gears which carried the oil through. But they would never design another gearbox without a simple oil pump in it. As for bushes coming out, this could only be prevented by peening, riveting or staking. Perhaps a good adhesive of the modern types may do the trick?

Mr Nisbet, replying to Mr Andréason, agreed the formula allowed for the axial load only; this was deliberate, so as to indicate preload on a paired unit in relation to the axial interference fit. He also agreed that hub bearings should be preloaded. He had been referring to the state in which they were generally supplied. To allow for fitting, a certain loss of clearance had to be accepted so that one finished up with a preloaded pair. This had to be looked at in individual cases, depending on the seating limits proposed.

Mr Barnbrook said the ideal condition for long life was a slight radial preload. He agreed with Mr Andréason about life (they would alter some of their formulae to take account of factors such as viscosity of the oil) and also the criterion of failure. A ball-bearing made point contact so that every ball hit a spall each time and here the criterion of failure must be spalling. But rollers tended to bridge a spall.

His criterion for failure of 0.01 in^2 affected area covered by automotive sizes. The thrust capacity of a taper unit bearing in the right direction was approximately three times that in the other direction.

Mr Nisbet said that in the paper they had used the I.S.O. load/life formula for life factors. He had not allowed for improvements in material or components so as to maintain a common basis, going back for some years. For the majority of automobile applications a 90 per cent survival basis was sufficient. The use of vacuum de-gassed steels certainly cut down the rogue 10 per cent to give greater reliability.

As for calculation of ball-loads on hub-bearings, there was a rapid graphical solution but now the full analysis could be put on a computer program so that the solution was straightforward.

They preferred the circlips to be backed up by a thick washer. The main thrust in the bearing referred to was taken on a solid shoulder so that the circlip was only a safeguard; also against reverse thrusts. He agreed with Mr Atkins about clamping the race; one had to rely on the grip on the inner ring on the shaft in the first instance and only if that failed should the circlip come into play.

He did not want to make too much of the national aspects of roller bearings, but in Britain the standard type had a plain outer ring and a two-lipped inner. Continental manufacturers seemed to prefer the plain inner ring and it would be desirable to concentrate on one pattern only. He thought the plain inner was the winner because it also facilitated assembly. In automobile work he did not think there was much difference in speed capacities but for really high speeds the two lips on the outer race gave an advantage. They did tend, however, to trap sludge.

Mr James replied to Mr Horty that the effect of grinding 'feathers' was well known. Particles of free graphite could get detached from the surface of cast iron crankshafts, leaving sharp edges which subsequently 'machined away' the bearing material. He was interested in the effect of the direction of grinding on bush push-out and would like to see any results. He would expect improved performance after roto-finishing, since the grinding feathers would tend to be knocked off.

Unfortunately, both tables in his paper contained errors, specifically Table 24.2. The input torque was not 1000 lb ft but 100 lb ft. He had used Automotive Products' figures in the computation of the oil-film thickness.

Mr Hoffmann replied to Mr Milward that the minimum amount of material between the top of the yoke and the bore should be about 5–6 mm.

Mr Barnbrook agreed with Mr Haigh about the loss of preload in pinions, but one must not confuse preload with frictional torque. It was convenient to use frictional torque but this soon reduced to as little as a third of the original, which did not mean a loss of preload. To get the right preload in the gearbox they checked all bearings for deflection, frictional torque etc., but one could discover more in five minutes on an actual test than from all the computer programs used for this purpose. In practice they used as much preload as possible without getting too hot.

Mr Love, commenting on Paper 27, was disappointed to find no reference to the influences on shaft strength of various surface treatments. Special treatments often produced changes of strength much greater than changes of detailed shape. Form rolling of splines, for instance, could improve the fatigue strength by 150 per cent (1). There was surprisingly little information on strength in view of the detailed studies available for some time (1) (2). These also show that the type of fracture often observed in spline shafts (e.g. Figs 27.8 to 27.10) was not simply due to fatigue. It was usually the result of two-stage loading, involving one or two cycles of high loading causing plastic flow, followed by some 5000 or so of much lower load. This type of fracture did not occur in hard (e.g. induction hardened) shafts.

Mr Barnbrook said that Mr Bevis too might have confused frictional torque with loss of preload. One did not just make a taper roller and then put something round it, there was much more to designing bearings; some pressure on the rib was needed but not too much. After a short time of warming up there was hydrodynamic lubrication and one could ignore the rib as a source of heat.

He agreed that straight mineral oils might lead to scuffing if too much preload were present. Abrasiveness of EP oils had, perhaps, been an unfortunate word to use with oil experts present, but he had tested all fuels for so-called abrasiveness for one could get deep scars with these oils. Of course all the debris from the gears went through the bearings. There were some limited-slip differential oils that wore out bearings very quickly, others caused no wear at all.

His firm used case-hardening material because it gave a tough core and very little distortion in hardening, one could quench very accurately leaving a minimum of grinding stock and thus avoid grinding burns or cracks. Also, a crack at the outside or at the point of maximum shear could only carry on to the junction of the case and the cone so that catastrophic failures were avoided. The case is always slightly in compression whereas with through-hardening steels there was a residual tension.

REFERENCES

(1) ANDREW, S. and HENTON, A. J. 'The effect of material, heat transfer, surface treatment, and production method, on the strength of splined shafts', M.I.R.A. Report No. 1963/6, December 1962.

(2) ALLSOPP, H. C., LOVE, R. J., and ANDREW, S. 'Torsional strength of splined shafts and similar coupling members', M.I.R.A. Report No. 1959/3, January 1959.

Papers 25 to 29

Mr Nisbet (*Ransome Hoffmann Pollard*) said the equations in Appendix 28.4 of Paper 28 could no doubt be applied to a single radial ball bearing when used in the rear hub of a floating rear axle. However, as the bearing carried a substantial bending moment, it was important to know at least the maximum bore load and the range of contact angles. This data would have been equally useful in assessing fatigue life under more normal running conditions.

Did Mr Andréason's work cover a single taper roller bearing in a rear hub of a semi-floating axle and, if so, how did he arrive at the proportion of bending moment taken by the bearing?

Mr Burdess (*Newcastle University*) reported studies, made jointly with Professor Maunder (*Newcastle University*), on the speed variations in a Hooke's joint transmission.

The variations of speed in a Hooke's joint transmission depend not only on the joint's kinematics but also on the general dynamics of the system, including driving and load torques. In the following analysis it is assumed that all components are rigid and that the speed fluctuations are small compared with the mean speed.

The transmission shown in Fig. D2 consists of two shafts S_1 and S_2 of moments of inertia I_1 and I_2 respectively connected at angle α by a Hooke's joint,

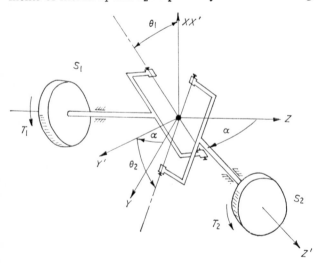

Fig. D2. The transmission

and rotating through angles θ_1 and θ_2 from a common position in which the input yoke of the joint is perpendicular to the plane of the shaft axes. Torques T_1 and T_2 are applied to S_1 and S_2 in the positive sense of the rotations and are assumed to be linear functions of speed, i.e.

$$\left.\begin{array}{l} T_1 = a_1+b_1\theta_1 \\ T_2 = -(a_2+b_2\theta_2) \end{array}\right\} \quad \cdots \cdots \cdots \quad (1)$$

where a_1, a_2 and b_2 are normally positive, b_1 is normally negative, and the effects of viscous friction in the shaft bearings can be included in the coefficients b.

From the well-known kinematic relations

$$\tan \theta_2 = \cos \alpha \tan \theta_1 . \quad \cdots \cdots \cdots \quad (2)$$

$$\dot\theta_2 = (\dot\theta_1 \cos \alpha)/(1-\sin^2 \alpha \sin^2 \theta_1)$$

and Lagrange's equation

$$\frac{\mathrm{d}}{\mathrm{d}t}\left(\frac{\partial T}{\partial \dot\theta_1}\right) - \frac{\partial T}{\partial \theta_1} = Q_1 \quad \cdots \cdots \cdots \quad (3)$$

where the kinetic energy T is

$$T = \tfrac{1}{2}[I_1+(I_2 \cos^2 \alpha)/(1-\sin^2 \alpha \sin^2 \theta_1)^2]\dot\theta_1{}^2 \quad \cdots \cdots \quad (4)$$

and the generalized force Q_1 can be shown to be

$$Q_1 = [a_1-a_2 \cos \alpha/(1-\sin^2 \alpha \sin^2 \theta_1)]+[b_1-b_2 \cos^2 \alpha/(1-\sin^2 \alpha \sin^2 \theta_1)^2]\dot\theta_1$$
$$\cdots \cdots \quad (5)$$

the governing equation of motion for θ_1 can be derived as

$$[I_1+I_2(1-\epsilon)/(1-\epsilon \sin^2 \theta_1)^2]\ddot\theta_1+I_2\epsilon(1-\epsilon) \sin 2\theta_1 \dot\theta_1{}^2/(1-\epsilon \sin^2 \theta_1)^3$$
$$= [a_1-a_2(1-\epsilon)^{1/2}/(1-\epsilon \sin^2 \theta_1)]+[b_1-b_2(1-\epsilon)/(1-\epsilon \sin^2 \theta_1)^2]\dot\theta_1 \quad (6)$$

where $\epsilon = \sin^2 \alpha$.

Although this equation cannot be solved exactly, an approximate result may be obtained by a method of small perturbations. If $\epsilon = 0$ (collinear shafts), the equation reduces to the simple form

$$(I_1+I_2)\ddot\theta_1 = (a_1-a_2)+(b_1-b_2)\dot\theta_1 \quad \cdots \cdots \quad (7)$$

If $b_1 = b_2 = 0$, a steady-state solution can only result if $a_1 = a_2$ in which case the steady speed is arbitrary. If either b_1 or b_2 is not zero, the steady speed is given by

$$\dot\theta_1 = \frac{a_1-a_2}{b_2-b_1} = \omega . \quad \cdots \cdots \cdots \quad (8)$$

In the general case when $\epsilon \neq 0$, we assume

$$\theta_1 = \Omega t + \sum_{r=1}^{\infty} \epsilon^r x_r . \quad \cdots \cdots \cdots \quad (9)$$

where $\Omega \approx \omega$ and x_r are periodic functions of time. If equation (9) is substituted into equation (6) and coefficients of like powers of ϵ equated, we obtain after some algebraic manipulation

$$\Omega = \omega$$

$$x_1 = \frac{\mu}{8(1+\lambda)}\sqrt{\frac{\left(1+\dfrac{\beta_1+\beta_2}{\mu}\right)^2+\left(\dfrac{2\lambda}{\mu}\right)^2}{1+\dfrac{(\beta_1-\beta_2)^2}{4(1+\lambda)^2}}}\,\sin\,(2\omega t+\phi)\ . \quad . \quad (10)$$

where $\mu = a_1/I_1\omega^2$, $\lambda = I_2/I_1$, $\beta_i = b_i/I_1\omega$ and

$$\phi = -\tan^{-1}\left[\frac{\mu(1+\lambda)+\beta_1(1+2\lambda)+\beta_2}{(\mu+\beta_2-\beta_1)\left(\dfrac{\beta_2-\beta_1}{2}\right)+2\lambda(1+\lambda)}\right]$$

The corresponding result for θ_1, correct to first-order terms in ϵ, is

$$\theta_1 \doteq \omega t+\frac{\epsilon\mu}{8(1+\lambda)}\sqrt{\frac{\left(1+\dfrac{\beta_1+\beta_2}{\mu}\right)^2+\left(\dfrac{2\lambda}{\mu}\right)^2}{1+\dfrac{(\beta_1-\beta_2)^2}{4(1+\lambda)^2}}}\,\sin\,(2\omega t+\phi)\ . \quad (11)$$

The amplitude of the cyclic speed variation in S_1 may thus be expressed in terms of the mean speed ω as

$$\psi = (\dot\theta_{\max}-\omega)/\omega$$

$$\doteq \frac{\epsilon\mu}{4(1+\lambda)}\sqrt{\frac{\left(1+\dfrac{\beta_1+\beta_2}{\mu}\right)^2+\left(\dfrac{2\lambda}{\mu}\right)^2}{1+\dfrac{(\beta_1-\beta_2)^2}{4(1+\lambda)^2}}}\quad . \quad . \quad . \quad . \quad (12)$$

This result will be elaborated in a later paper, but some interesting trends are shown in the attached diagrams, calculated in each case for $b_1 = b_2 = 0$, i.e. for the condition in which the transmitted torque is substantially independent of speed. The factor ψ may then be interpreted directly as a measure of the amplitude of speed variation per cycle if the mean speed (which is arbitrary in this condition) is assumed to remain constant as the other parameters are varied.

Fig. D3 shows a general increase in ψ for all values of inertia ratio λ as the torque parameter μ increases, the increase being most marked for low λ, i.e. small values of load inertia. Fig. D4, drawn for a fixed inertia ratio $\lambda = 3$ and joint angles varying from 5° to 20°, again shows a general increase in ψ as μ increases, the increase being small at small shaft angles but large at higher angles. Finally, Fig. D5 shows how ψ varies at a fixed joint angle $\alpha = 15°$ with variations in inertia ratio λ, drawn for convenience on a logarithmic scale: in this case, ψ may increase or decrease with λ depending on the torque parameter μ, but in all cases as λ becomes large (high load inertia) the fluctuation tends to a limit $\epsilon/2$, which corresponds to a condition in which S_2 turns at constant speed.

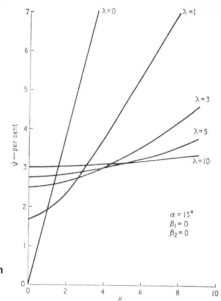

Fig. D3. Variation of speed fluctuation factor ψ with load parameter μ for constant inertia ratio λ

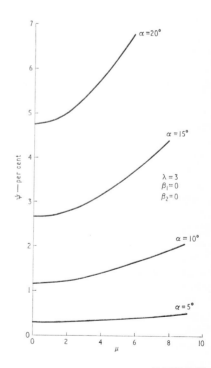

Fig. D4. Variation of speed fluctuation factor ψ with load parameter μ for constant joint angle α

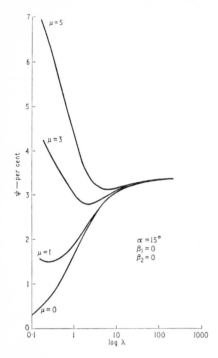

Fig. D5. Variation of speed fluctuation factor ψ with inertia ratio λ for constant load parameter μ.

The results show that the absolute speed variation at each end of a Hooke's joint transmission, as opposed to the simple kinematic speed ratio between the two ends, is a complex function of the torque characteristics and the general dynamics of the system. Although they cannot be eliminated, the fluctuations can be reduced by suitable choice of design parameters.

Prof. Macmillan (*M.I.R.A.*) said that during last year they had heard of an American constant velocity joint based on an entirely new principle, a six-piece mechanism. What did Mr Macielinski think of its possibilities? The great advantage appeared to be the absence of balls and, therefore, of slip and yet it was a true constant velocity joint. He also thought there must be something wrong with the diagram in Fig. 29.8 because in both A and B the forces on the balls were not in static equilibrium.

Mr Jacobson (*A.A.*) said that in the Automobile Association's experience one of the main bugbears of constant velocity joints was insufficient protection against dirt, grit and moisture. Instead they were charged with lubricant which, when it got soaked with salt-laden moisture, quickly wore out the joint.

Had Mr Macielinski any comments on how to achieve better dynamic balance in universal joints to avoid resonance which wore out the tail shaft seals? and on the amount of resilience desirable in a split universal joint?

Mr Macielinski, in reply, considered Mr Burdess' contribution very valuable to the theory of the joint. In the first instance it would help not the designer but the noise and vibration engineer. He knew of the very ingenious six-piece mechanism mentioned by Prof. Macmillan but the acceleration of the linkage might cause vibration. The bearings of such a linkage were very heavily loaded, requiring special design. At present only plain bearings were used. Admittedly this joint maintained the constant velocity even at right angles. It might be more useful for instruments where rotary motion could be transferred accurately without any backlash at very high angles but at a very low speed.

In reply to Mr Jacobson, of course there were many methods of protecting a joint, for instance by a metal cowling. That would be expensive and take much more space. Therefore they had decided to use rubber seals. Ten years ago these had been less adequate but the present seals used in constant velocity joints of British manufacture would last at least 100 000 miles.

The balance of propeller shafts was a very difficult problem. His firm did not balance them statically, only dynamically at speeds up to 4000 rev/min, to limits of 22 g cm. Resilience of the propeller shaft was nearly the same, whether it was in one or two pieces. Resilience was really dictated by the motor car and depended on what was attached to the shaft. If one wanted to increase it one could use a 'sandwich' of two concentric tubes with rubber bonded in between.

Mr Foot (*Hoffmann*) said that, with misalignment, there was a deflection of the shaft due to the deflections on the bearing and this caused a stress concentration at one end of each roller. Gross loading shifted the point of the resultant maximum load on a roller and this increased the effective centre distance. Had Mr Andréason taken this into account when calculating the maximum roller load? To what extent did this compensate for the clearance factor?

Also, he would have thought that the minimum clearance would depend on the maximum contact stress at the lower edge, rather than maximum roller load. His organization used a computer program to assess the bore load and maximum contact angles on front hub bearings of the double roll type. Provided the bearings satisfied the straight-ahead conditions and the ball-contact under cornering was satisfactory, they did not introduce any factor to allow for cornering.

Dr Looman reported work on computer programs for gearbox design. First the geometrical layout was determined and then anticipated stresses calculated. The programs were arranged to calculate many things simultaneously which ensured optimum computer utilization. This parallel calculating, however, had the disadvantage that one always had to calculate the complete package. They were now trying to break down the programs into components so that the designer could carry on a dialogue with the computer at each stage.

Mr Andréason replied to Mr Foot that the influence of misalignment was not included in his paper. He thought it of minor importance in taper bearings because the stress levels were low. In ball bearings it had to be taken into account and the theory involved would be published shortly. He did not agree that the effect of cornering was small: his diagram showed clearly that it was dangerous to the life of a bearing.

In answer to Mr Nisbet, the internal load-distribution on a taper bearing subjected to moments could be obtained from the equations in his paper but, if one wished to calculate individual bore loads, one had to know the position of the bore in relation to the load line. Using integrals instead, one eliminated this influence and the error introduced was not greater than 1 or 2 per cent.

Mr Wren (*British Timken*) referred to Mr Andréason's Fig. 28.2, showing the dependence of wheel bearing life on bearing adjustment, through a very wide range, from about 0·008 in preload to about 0·013 in end play. As preload approached zero, bearing life rose to something like 109×10^6 revolutions but beyond this it appeared to remain constant. This he could not understand because on the same graph the maximum roller loads increased by some 50–70 per cent in the wide range of end play.

During their deflection tests they had found that the thrust pad wore away by 0·010 to 0·020 in, so that he hated to think what happened subsequently on the road.

Mr Andréason later agreed with Mr Wren that the equation for Fig. 28.2 was only a generally accepted approximation to bearing life but a more accurate equation was (28.26) in his paper.

Made and Printed in Great Britain by William Clowes and Sons, Ltd.,
London, Beccles and Colchester